15th Edition

UNDERSTANDING COMPUTERS:
TODAY AND TOMORROW

INTRODUCTORY

DEBORAH MORLEY

CHARLES S. PARKER

CENGAGE
Learning

Australia • Brazil • Japan • Korea • Mexico • Singapore • Spain • United Kingdom • United States

CENGAGE
Learning®

Understanding Computers: Today and Tomorrow, 15th Edition
Deborah Morley and Charles S. Parker

Vice President, General Manager: Dawn Gerrain

Product Director: Kathleen McMahon

Product Team Manager: Donna Gridley

Director, Development: Marah Bellegarde

Product Development Manager: Leigh Hefferon

Senior Content Developer:
  Michelle Ruelos Cannistraci

Developmental Editor: Pam Conrad

Product Assistant: Melissa Stehler

Marketing Manager: Gretchen Swann, Kristie Clark

Production Director: Patty Stephan

Content Project Manager: Jennifer Feltri-George

Manufacturing Planner: Fola Orekoya

Rights Acquisition Specialist: Christine Myaskovsky

Production Service: Integra Software Services Pvt. Ltd.

Cover Designer: GEX Publishing Services

Cover Image: ©Olivier Le Moal/Shutterstock

For product information and technology assistance, contact us at
Cengage Learning Customer & Sales Support, 1-800-354-9706
For permission to use material from this text or product, submit all requests online at **www.cengage.com/permissions.**
Further permissions questions can be e-mailed to
permissionrequest@cengage.com

Library of Congress Control Number: 2013952741

ISBN-13: 978-1-285-76730-7

Cengage Learning
200 First Stamford Place, 4th Floor
Stamford, CT 06902
USA

Cengage Learning is a leading provider of customized learning solutions with office locations around the globe, including Singapore, the United Kingdom, Australia, Mexico, Brazil, and Japan. Locate your local office at:
www.cengage.com/global

Cengage Learning products are represented in Canada by Nelson Education, Ltd.

To learn more about Cengage Learning, visit **www.cengage.com**

Purchase any of our products at your local college store or at our preferred online store **www.cengagebrain.com**

Notice to the Reader
Publisher does not warrant or guarantee any of the products described herein or perform any independent analysis in connection with any of the product information contained herein. Publisher does not assume, and expressly disclaims, any obligation to obtain and include information other than that provided to it by the manufacturer. The reader is expressly warned to consider and adopt all safety precautions that might be indicated by the activities described herein and to avoid all potential hazards. By following the instructions contained herein, the reader willingly assumes all risks in connection with such instructions. The publisher makes no representations or warranties of any kind, including but not limited to, the warranties of fitness for particular purpose or merchantability, nor are any such representations implied with respect to the material set forth herein, and the publisher takes no responsibility with respect to such material. The publisher shall not be liable for any special, consequential, or exemplary damages resulting, in whole or part, from the readers' use of, or reliance upon, this material.

Printed in the United States of America
1 2 3 4 5 6 7 19 18 17 16 15 14

PREFACE

In today's technology-oriented society, computers and technology impact virtually everyone's life. *Understanding Computers: Today and Tomorrow, 15ᵗʰ Edition* is designed to ensure that students are current and informed in order to thrive in our technology-oriented, global society. With this new edition, students not only learn about relevant cutting-edge technology trends, but they also gain a better understanding of technology in general and the important issues surrounding technology today. This information gives students the knowledge they need to succeed in today's world.

This nontechnical, introductory text explains in straightforward terms the importance of learning about computers and other computing devices, the various types of devices and their components, the principles by which computers work, the practical applications of computers and related technologies, the ways in which the world is being changed by these technologies, and the associated risks and other potential implications of computers and related technologies. The goal of this text is to provide readers with a solid knowledge of computing fundamentals, an understanding of the impact of our technology-oriented society, and a framework for using this knowledge effectively in their lives.

KEY FEATURES

Just like its previous editions, the Introductory version of *Understanding Computers: Today and Tomorrow, 15ᵗʰ Edition* (which contains the first nine chapters of the sixteen-chapter Comprehensive version) provides current and comprehensive coverage of important topics. Flexible organization and an engaging presentation, combined with a variety of learning tools associated with each chapter, help students master the important computing concepts they will encounter in school, on the job, and in their personal lives.

Currency and Accuracy

The state-of-the-art content of this book reflects the latest technologies, trends, and classroom needs. To reflect the importance of mobile computing today, the entire text has an increased emphasis on smartphones, media tablets, mobile apps, and the issues that surround them, such as mobile security. All topics and figures have been updated for currency and, to ensure the content is as accurate and up to date as possible, numerous **Industry Expert Reviewers** provided feedback and suggestions for improvements to the content in their areas of expertise. Throughout the writing and production stages, enhancements were continually made to ensure that the final product is as current and accurate as possible.

Comprehensiveness and Depth

Accommodating a wide range of teaching styles, *Understanding Computers: Today and Tomorrow, 15ᵗʰ Edition* provides comprehensive coverage of traditional topics while also covering relevant, up-to-the-minute new technologies and important societal issues. This edition has an increased emphasis on mobile computing, cloud applications, and social media and includes the following new topics:

> New hardware developments, including smartphones, media tablets, smart watches, Google Glass, hybrid notebook-tablet computers, tiny PCs like the Raspberry Pi

and Chromecast, GPUs, immersion cooling systems, tablet and smartphone docks, personal 3D printers, projector phones, perceptual computing, gesture input, touch mice, tablet storage devices, DNA storage, Internet monitors, and 4K (Ultra HD) Blu-ray Discs.

➤ New software developments and issues, including Windows 8, iOS 7 and other new mobile operating systems, Office 2013/365, the Google Play store, sending documents to the cloud, and the impact of cloud computing.

➤ New mobile and Web applications, including Bring Your Own Device (BYOD), mobile ticketing, mobile data caps, group messaging, geofencing, NFC, Google Now, social media integration, and cloud printing.

➤ New networking technologies, including new and emerging Wi-Fi standards, the Internet of Things (IoT), Bluetooth Smart, software defined networking (SDN), and new Wi-Fi-enabled products such as smart thermostats, scales, and Wi-Fi locks.

➤ New security risks, including BYOD security issues, social media hacks, and scareware, ransomware, and chargeware.

➤ New security precautions, including digital tattoos and other emerging biometric systems, Intel Identity Protection Technology (IPT), and soft and hard tokens for OTPs/two-factor authentication.

Readability

We remember more about a subject if it is made interesting and exciting, as well as presented in a straightforward manner. This book is written in a conversational, down-to-earth style—one designed to be accurate without being intimidating. Concepts are explained clearly and simply, without the use of overly technical terminology. More complex concepts are explained in an understandable manner and with realistic examples from everyday life.

Chapter Learning Tools

1. **Outline**, **Learning Objectives**, **and Overview**: For each chapter, an **Outline** of the major topics covered, a list of student **Learning Objectives**, and a **Chapter Overview** help instructors put the subject matter of the chapter in perspective and let students know what they will be reading about.

2. **Boldfaced Key Terms and Running Glossary**: Important terms appear in boldface type as they are introduced in the chapter. These terms are defined at the bottom of the page on which they appear and in the end-of-text glossary.

3. **Chapter Boxes**: In each chapter, a **Trend** box provides students with a look at current and upcoming technology trends; an **Inside the Industry** box provides insight into some of the practices and issues related to the computer industry; a **How It Works** box explains in detail how a technology or product works; and a **Technology and You** box takes a look at how computers and technology are used in everyday life.

4. **Ask the Expert Boxes**: In each chapter, three **Ask the Expert** boxes feature a question about a computing concept, a trend, or how computers are used on the job or otherwise in the real world along with the response from an expert. Experts for this edition include a former Navy pilot, a guitarist

from a rock band, a professional animator, and executives from notable companies like McDonald's, Microsoft, ARM, Lenovo, Logitech, SanDisk, Kingston, Seagate, The Linux Foundation, Sony Animations, D-Link, and Symantec.

5. **Marginal Tips and Caution Elements**: **Tip** marginal elements feature time-saving tips or ways to avoid a common problem or terminology mistake, or present students with interesting additional information related to the chapter content. **Caution** elements warn of a possible problem students should avoid.

6. **Illustrations and Photographs**: Instructive, current, full-color illustrations and photographs are used to illustrate important concepts. Figures and screenshots show the latest hardware and software and are annotated to convey important information.

7. **Summary and Key Terms**: The end-of-chapter material includes a concise, section-by-section **Summary** of the main points in the chapter. The chapter's Learning Objectives appear in the margin next to the relevant section of the summary so that students are better able to relate the Learning Objectives to the chapter material. Every boldfaced key term in the chapter also appears in boldface type in the summary.

8. **Review Activities**: End-of-chapter **Review Activities** allow students to test themselves on what they have just read. A matching exercise of selected **Key Terms** helps students test their retention of the chapter material. A **Self-Quiz** (with the answers listed at the end of the book) consists of ten true-false and completion questions. Five additional easily graded matching and short-answer **Exercises** are included for instructors who would like to assign graded homework. Two short **Discussion Questions** for each chapter provide a springboard to jump-start classroom discussions.

9. **Projects**: End-of-chapter **Projects** require students to extend their knowledge by doing research and activities beyond merely reading the book. Organized into six types of projects (**Hot Topics**, **Short Answer/ Research**, **Hands On**, **Ethics in Action**, **Presentation/ Demonstration**, and the new **Balancing Act** project that states a current issue and students pick and defend a side on that issue), the projects feature explicit instructions so that students can work through them without additional directions from instructors. A special marginal icon denotes projects that require Internet access.

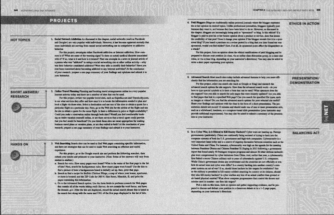

References and Resources Guide

A **References and Resources Guide** at the end of the book brings together in one convenient location a collection of computer-related references and resources, including a **Computer History Timeline**, a **Guide to Buying a PC**, **A Look at Numbering Systems** feature, and a **Coding Charts** feature.

NEW and Updated Expert Insight Features

In the exciting **Expert Insight** feature located at the end of each module, industry experts provide students with personal insights on topics presented in the book, including their

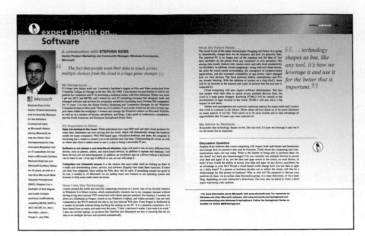

personal experiences with technology, key points to remember, and advice for students. The experts, professionals from **D-Link**, **Logitech**, **Microsoft**, and **McAfee** for the Introductory version of this text, provide a unique perspective on the module content and how the topics discussed in the module impact their lives and their industry, what it means for the future, and more!

Student and Instructor Support Materials

Understanding Computers: Today and Tomorrow, 15th Edition is available with a complete package of support materials for instructors and students. Included in the package are **CourseMate**, the **Instructor Companion Site**, and, if access to SAM has been purchased, **SAM Computer Concepts** material is available. The student and instructor resources for the Introductory version are the same as those for the Comprehensive version. To access support materials, please refer to the supplements for the Comprehensive version of *Understanding Computers: Today and Tomorrow, 15th Edition*.

CourseMate

The *Understanding Computers, 15th Edition* includes **CourseMate**, which helps you make the grade. CourseMate includes:

> **Key Term Matching** and **Flashcards**—allow students to test their knowledge of selected chapter key terms.

> **Interactive Quiz**—allows students to test their retention of chapter concepts.

> **Global Technology Watch**—provides additional reading on the latest technology topics.

> **Beat the Clock**—allows students to test how ready they are for upcoming exams.

> **Crossword Puzzles**—incorporate the key terms from each chapter into an online interactive crossword puzzle.

> **Online Videos**—include several videos per chapter related to the topics in that chapter, as well as practical "How To" information related to chapter topics.

> **Further Exploration**—includes links to additional information about content covered in each chapter.

> **Interactive eBook**—includes highlighting, note taking, and search capabilities.

> **Engagement Tracker**—monitors student engagement in the course.

> **Additional Resources**—include additional resources that can be viewed or printed, such as **Expert Insights**; an **Online Study Guide**, **Online Summary**, and **Online Glossary** for each chapter; a **Guide to Buying a PC** and a **Computer History Timeline**; and more information about **Numbering Systems** and **Coding Charts**.

(Go to **cengagebrain.com** to access these resources.)

Instructor Companion Site

Everything you need for your course in one place! This collection of book-specific lecture and class tools is available online via **www.cengage.com/login**. Access and download PowerPoint presentations, images, Instructor's Manual, videos, and more.

Electronic Instructor's Manual

The **Instructor's Manual** is written to provide instructors with practical suggestions for enhancing classroom presentations. The Instructor's Manual provides: **Lecture Notes, Teacher Tips, Quick Quizzes, Classroom Activities, Discussion Questions, Key Terms,** a **Chapter Quiz,** and more!

Cengage Learning Testing Powered by Cognero

Cengage Learning Testing Powered by Cognero is a flexible, online system that allows you to:

> ➤ Author, edit, and manage test bank content from multiple Cengage Learning solutions
> ➤ Create multiple test versions in an instant
> ➤ Deliver tests from your LMS, your classroom, or wherever you want

PowerPoint Presentations

This book has **Microsoft PowerPoint presentations** available for each chapter. These are included as a teaching aid for classroom presentation, to make available to students on a network for chapter review, or to be printed for classroom distribution. Instructors can customize these presentations to cover any additional topics they introduce to the class. **Figure Files** for all figures in the textbook are also available online.

SAM: Skills Assessment Manager

SAM 2013 is designed to help bring students from the classroom to the real world. It allows students to train and test on important computer skills in an active, hands-on environment. SAM's easy-to-use system includes powerful interactive exams, training, and projects on the most commonly used Microsoft Office applications. SAM simulates the Office 2013 application environment, allowing students to demonstrate their knowledge and think through the skills by performing real-world tasks such as bolding text or setting up slide transitions. Add in live-in-the-application projects and students are on their way to truly learning and applying skills to business-centric documents.

Designed to be used with the New Perspectives Series, SAM includes handy page references, so students can print helpful study guides that match the New Perspectives Series textbooks used in class. For instructors, SAM also includes robust scheduling and reporting features.

ACKNOWLEDGMENTS

We would like to extend a special thank you to all of the industry professionals who provided their expertise for the **Expert Insight** features:

Introduction Module: Daniel Kelley, Vice President, Marketing, D-Link Systems, Inc.
Hardware Module: Ali Moayer, Senior Director of Engineering, Logitech
Software Module: Stephen Rose, Senior Product Marketing and Community Manager, Windows Commercial, Microsoft
Networks and the Internet Module: Greg Hampton, Vice President, Product Management, McAfee
Business on the Web Module: Jim Griffith, Dean of eBay Education, eBay
Systems Module: Stuart Feldman, Past President of ACM and Vice President, Engineering, Google
Computers and Society Module: Frank Molsberry, Sr. Principal Engineer and Security Technologist, Dell Inc.

In addition, we are very grateful to the numerous Industry Expert Reviewers that perform technical reviews and provide helpful suggestions each edition to ensure this book is as accurate and current as possible. We would also like to thank the Educational Reviewers who have helped to define and improve the quality of this text over the years. In particular, we would like to thank the following individuals:

Industry Expert Reviewers

Julie Anne Mossler, Director of Communications, Groupon; Alan Tringham, Senior Marketing Communications Manager, ARM; The Wi-Fi Alliance; Mike Hall, Corporate Communications, Seagate Technology; Kevin Curtis, CTO, InPhase Technologies; Sriram K. Peruvemba, Vice President, Marketing, E Ink Corporation; Jim Sherhart, Senior Director of Marketing, Data Robotics; Jack Dollard, Marketing, Mitek Systems; Joe Melfi, Director of Product Marketing for Cloud Solutions, D-Link Systems; Dave Gelvin, President, Tranzeo Wireless USA; Kevin Raineri, Director, Sales and Marketing, Innovative Card Technologies; Bill Shribman, Executive Producer, WGBH Interactive; Mike Markham, Vice President of Sales, Cadre Technologies; Renee Cassata, Marketing Manager, iDashboards; Russell T. Cross, Vice President of AAC Products, Prentke Romich Company; Dr. Kimberly Young, Director, The Center for Internet Addiction Recovery; Jason Taylor, Worldwide Director of Corporate Communications, MobiTV; Nicole Rodrigues, Public Relations Manager, MobiTV; Stephen Yeo, Worldwide Strategic Marketing Director, IGEL Technology; Bob Hirschfeld, Public Information Officer, Lawrence Livermore National Lab; Bryan Crum, Vice President of Communication, Omnilert, LLC; David Bondurant, MRAM Product Manager, Freescale Semiconductor, Inc.; Rick McGowan, Vice President & Senior Software Engineer, Unicode, Inc.; Margaret Lewis, Director of Commercial Solutions, AMD; Mark Tekunoff, Senior Technology Manager, Kingston Technology; Billy Rudock, Customer Service Staff Engineer, Seagate Technology; James M. DePuydt, Ph.D., Technology Director, Imation Corporation; Dan Bloom, Sr. PR Manager, SanDisk; Kevin Curtis, CTO, InPhase Technologies; Gail Levy, Director of Marketing, TabletKiosk; Novell Marketing; John McCreesh, Marketing Project Lead, OpenOffice.org; Jackson Dunlap, ESP Systems; Laura Abram, Director of Corporate Marketing, Dust Networks; Kevin Schader, Communications Director, ZigBee Alliance; Mauro Dresti, Linksys Product Marketing Manager; Lianne Caetano, Executive Director, WirelessHD, LLC; Brad Booth; Howard Frazier; Bob Grow; Michael McCormack; George Cravens, Technical Marketing, D-Link Systems; Christiaan Stoudt, Founder, HomeNetworkHelp.Info; Douglas M. Winneg, President, Software Secure, Inc.; Frank Archambeault, Director of Network Services, Dartmouth College; Adam Goldstein, IT Security Engineer, Dartmouth College; Ellen Young, Manager of Consulting Services, Dartmouth College; Becky Waring, Executive Editor, JiWire.com; Ellen Craw, General Manager, Ilium Software; Michael Behr, Senior Architect, TIBCO; Joe McGlynn, Director of Product Management, CodeGear; John Nash, Vice President of Marketing, Visible Systems; Josh Shaul, Director of Technology Strategy, Application Security, Inc.; Jodi Florence, Marketing Director, IDology, Inc.; Dr. Maressa Hecht Orzack, Director, Computer Addiction Services; Janice K. Mahon, Vice President of Technology Commercialization, Universal Display Corporation; Dr. Nhon Quach, Next Generation Processor Architect, AMD; Jos van Haaren, Department Head Storage Physics, Philips Research Laboratories; Terry O'Kelly, Technical Communications Manager, Memorex; Randy Culpepper, Texas Instruments RFID Systems; Aaron Newman, CTO and Co-Founder, Application Security Inc.; Alan Charlesworth, Staff Engineer, Sun Microsystems; Khaled A. Elamrawi, Senior Marketing Engineer, Intel Corporation; Timothy D. O'Brien, Senior Systems Engineer, Fujitsu Software; John Paulson, Manager, Product Communications, Seagate Technology; Omid Rahmat, Editor in Chief, Tom's Hardware Guide; Jeremy Bates, Multimedia Developer, R & L Multimedia Developers; Charles Hayes, Product Marketing Manager, SimpleTech, Inc.; Rick McGowan, Vice President & Senior Software Engineer, Unicode, Inc.; Russell Reynolds, Chief Operating Officer & Web Designer, R & L Multimedia Developers; Rob Stephens, Director, Technology Strategies, SAS; Dave Stow, Database Specialist, OSE Systems, Inc.

Educational Reviewers

Marc Forestiere, Fresno City College; Beverly Amer, Northern Arizona University; James Ambroise Jr., Southern University, Louisiana; Virginia Anderson, University of North Dakota; Robert Andree, Indiana University Northwest; Linda Armbruster, Rancho Santiago College; Michael Atherton, Mankato State University; Gary E. Baker, Marshalltown Community College; Richard Batt, Saint Louis Community College at Meremec; Luverne Bierle, Iowa Central Community College; Fariba Bolandhemat, Santa Monica College; Jerry Booher, Scottsdale Community College; Frederick W. Bounds, Georgia Perimeter College; James Bradley, University of Calgary; Curtis Bring, Moorhead State University; Brenda K. Britt, Fayetteville Technical Community College; Cathy Brotherton, Riverside Community College; Chris Brown, Bemidji State University; Janice Burke, South Suburban College; James Buxton, Tidewater Community College, Virginia; Gena Casas, Florida Community College, Jacksonville; Thomas Case, Georgia Southern University; John E. Castek, University of Wisconsin-La Crosse; Mario E. Cecchetti, Westmoreland County Community College; Jack W. Chandler, San Joaquin Delta College; Alan Charlesworth, Staff Engineer, Sun Microsystems; Jerry M. Chin, Southwest Missouri State University;

Edward W. Christensen, Monmouth University; Carl Clavadetscher, California State Polytechnic University; Vernon Clodfelter, Rowan Technical College, North Carolina; Joann C. Cook, College of DuPage; Laura Cooper, College of the Mainland, Texas; Cynthia Corritore, University of Nebraska at Omaha; Sandra Cunningham, Ranger College; Marvin Daugherty, Indiana Vocational Technical College; Donald L. Davis, University of Mississippi; Garrace De Groot, University of Wyoming; Jackie Dennis, Prairie State College; Donald Dershem, Mountain View College; John DiElsi, Marcy College, New York; Mark Dishaw, Boston University; Eugene T. Dolan, University of the District of Columbia; Bennie Allen Dooley, Pasadena City College; Robert H. Dependahl Jr.; Santa Barbara City College; William Dorin, Indiana University Northwest; Mike Doroshow, Eastfield College; Jackie O. Duncan, Hopkinsville Community College; John Dunn, Palo Alto College; John W. Durham, Fort Hays State University; Hyun B. Eom, Middle Tennessee State University; Michael Feiler, Merritt College; Terry Felke, WR Harper College; J. Patrick Fenton, West Valley Community College; James H. Finger, University of South Carolina at Columbia; William C. Fink, Lewis and Clark Community College, Illinois; Ronald W. Fordonski, College of Du Page; Connie Morris Fox, West Virginia Institute of Technology; Paula S. Funkhouser, Truckee Meadows Community College; Janos T. Fustos, Metropolitan State; Gene Garza, University of Montevallo; Timothy Gottleber, North Lake College; Dwight Graham, Prairie State College; Wade Graves, Grayson County College; Kay H. Gray, Jacksonville State University; David W. Green, Nashville State Technical Institute, Tennessee; George P. Grill, University of North Carolina, Greensboro; John Groh, San Joaquin Delta College; Rosemary C. Gross, Creighton University; Dennis Guster, Saint Louis Community College at Meremec; Joe Hagarty, Raritan Valley Community College; Donald Hall, Manatee Community College; Jim Hanson, Austin Community College; Sallyann Z. Hanson, Mercer County Community College; L. D. Harber, Volunteer State Community College, Tennessee; Hank Hartman, Iowa State University; Richard Hatch, San Diego State University; Mary Lou Hawkins, Del Mar College; Ricci L. Heishman, Northern Virginia Community College; William Hightower, Elon College, North Carolina; Sharon A. Hill, Prince George's Community College, Maryland; Alyse Hollingsworth, Brevard College; Fred C. Homeyer, Angelo State University; Stanley P. Honacki, Moraine Valley Community College; L. Wayne Horn, Pensacola Junior College; J. William Howorth, Seneca College, Ontario, Canada; Mark W. Huber, East Carolina University; Peter L. Irwin, Richland College, Texas; John Jasma, Palo Alto College; Elizabeth Swoope Johnson, Louisiana State University; Jim Johnson, Valencia Community College; Mary T. Johnson, Mt. San Antonio College; Susan M. Jones, Southwest State University; Amardeep K. Kahlon, Austin Community College; Robert T. Keim, Arizona State University; Mary Louise Kelly, Palm Beach Community College; William R. Kenney, San Diego Mesa College; Richard Kerns, East Carolina University, North Carolina; Glenn Kersnick, Sinclair Community College, Ohio; Richard Kiger, Dallas Baptist University; Gordon C. Kimbell, Everett Community College, Washington; Robert Kirklin, Los Angeles Harbor Community College; Judith A. Knapp, Indiana University Northwest; Mary Veronica Kolesar, Utah State University; James G. Kriz, Cuyahoga Community College, Ohio; Joan Krone, Denison University; Fran Kubicek, Kalamazoo Valley Community College; Rose M. Laird, Northern Virginia Community College; Robert Landrum, Jones Junior College; Shelly Langman, Bellevue Community College; James F. LaSalle, The University of Arizona; Chang-Yang Lin, Eastern Kentucky University; Linda J. Lindaman, Black Hawk College; Alden Lorents, Northern Arizona University; Paul M. Lou, Diablo Valley College; Deborah R. Ludford, Glendale Community College; Kent Lundin, Brigham Young University-Idaho; Barbara J. Maccarone, North Shore Community College; Wayne Madison, Clemson University, South Carolina; Donna L. Madsen, Kirkwood Community College; Randy Marak, Hill College; Gary Marks, Austin Community College, Texas; Kathryn A. Marold, Ph.D., Metropolitan State College of Denver; Cesar Marron, University of Wyoming; Ed Martin, Kingsborough Community College; Vickie McCullough, Palomar College; James W. McGuffee, Austin Community College; James McMahon, Community College of Rhode Island; William A. McMillan, Madonna University; Don B. Medley, California State Polytechnic University; John Melrose, University of Wisconsin—Eau Claire; Dixie Mercer, Kirkwood Community College; Mary Meredith, University of Southwestern Louisiana; Marilyn Meyer, Fresno City College; Carolyn H. Monroe, Baylor University; William J. Moon, Palm Beach Community College; Marilyn Moore, Purdue University; Marty Murray, Portland Community College; Don Nielsen, Golden West College; George Novotny, Ferris State University; Richard Okezie, Mesa Community College; Joseph D. Oldham, University of Kentucky; Dennis J. Olsen, Pikes Peak Community College; Bob Palank, Florissant Community College; James Payne, Kellogg Community College; Lisa B. Perez, San Joaquin Delta College; Savitha Pinnepalli, Louisiana State University; Delores Pusins, Hillsborough CC; Mike Rabaut, Hillsborough CC; Robert Ralph, Fayetteville Technical Institute, North Carolina; Herbert F. Rebhun, University of Houston-Downtown; Nicholas John Robak, Saint Joseph's University; Arthur E. Rowland, Shasta College; Kenneth R. Ruhrup, St. Petersburg Junior College; John F. Sanford, Philadelphia College of Textiles and Science; Kammy Sanghera, George Mason University; Carol A. Schwab, Webster University; Larry Schwartzman, Trident Technical College; Benito R. Serenil, South Seattle Community College; Allanagh Sewell, Southeastern Louisiana University; Tom Seymour, Minot State University; John J. Shuler, San Antonio College, Texas; Gayla Jo Slauson, Mesa State College; Harold Smith, Brigham Young University; Willard A. Smith, Tennessee State University; David Spaisman, Katherine Gibbs; Elizabeth Spooner, Holmes Community College; Timothy M. Stanford, City University; Alfred C. St. Onge, Springfield

Technical Community College, Massachusetts; Michael L. Stratford, Charles County Community College, Maryland; Karen Studniarz, Kishwaukee College; Sandra Swanson, Lewis & Clark Community College; Tim Sylvester, Glendale Community College; Semih Tahaoglu, Southeastern Louisiana University; Jane J. Thompson, Solano Community College; Sue Traynor, Clarion University of Pennsylvania; William H. Trueheart, New Hampshire College; James D. Van Tassel, Mission College; James R. Walters, Pikes Peak Community College; Joyce V. Walton, Seneca College, Ontario, Canada; Diane B. Walz, University of Texas at San Antonio; Joseph Waters, Santa Rosa Junior College, California; Liang Chee Wee, University of Arizona; Merrill Wells, Red Rocks Community College; Fred J. Wilke, Saint Louis Community College; Charles M. Williams, Georgia State University; Roseanne Witkowski, Orange County Community College; David Womack, University of Texas, San Antonio; George Woodbury, College of the Sequoias; Nan Woodsome, Araphoe Community College; James D. Woolever, Cerritos College; Patricia Joann Wykoff, Western Michigan University; A. James Wynne, Virginia Commonwealth University; Robert D. Yearout, University of North Carolina at Asheville; Israel Yost, University of New Hampshire; and Vic Zamora, Mt. San Antonio College.

We would also like to thank the people on the Cengage team—their professionalism, attention to detail, and enormous enthusiasm make working with them a pleasure. In particular, we'd like to thank Donna Gridley, Michelle Ruelos Cannistraci, Jennifer Feltri-George, Christine Myaskovsky, and Pam Conrad for all their ideas, support, and tireless efforts during the design, writing, rewriting, and production of this book. We would also like to thank Marissa Falco for the interior design and GEX Publishing Services for the cover design. We want to thank Sreejith Govindan and Integra for all their help managing the production of the book. Thanks also to Kathleen McMahon.

We are also very appreciative of the numerous individuals and organizations that were kind enough to supply information and photographs for this text and the many organizations, as well as Daniel Davis of Tinkernut.com, that generously allowed us to use their content for the Online Videos, which can be found on CourseMate.

We sincerely hope you find this book interesting, informative, and enjoyable to read.

Deborah Morley
Charles S. Parker

BRIEF CONTENTS

CONTENTS

INSIDE THE INDUSTRY Open Source
Software 215
TECHNOLOGY AND YOU Mobile
Ticketing 218
TREND Airline Apps 220
HOW IT WORKS Gesture Input with
Microsoft Office 226

**Expert Insight
on Software 252**

INSIDE THE INDUSTRY Wireless
Power 258
TREND Stadium Wireless Networks 266
TECHNOLOGY AND YOU Wi-Fi SD
Cards 282
HOW IT WORKS Smart Homes 287

UNDERSTANDING COMPUTERS:
TODAY AND TOMORROW

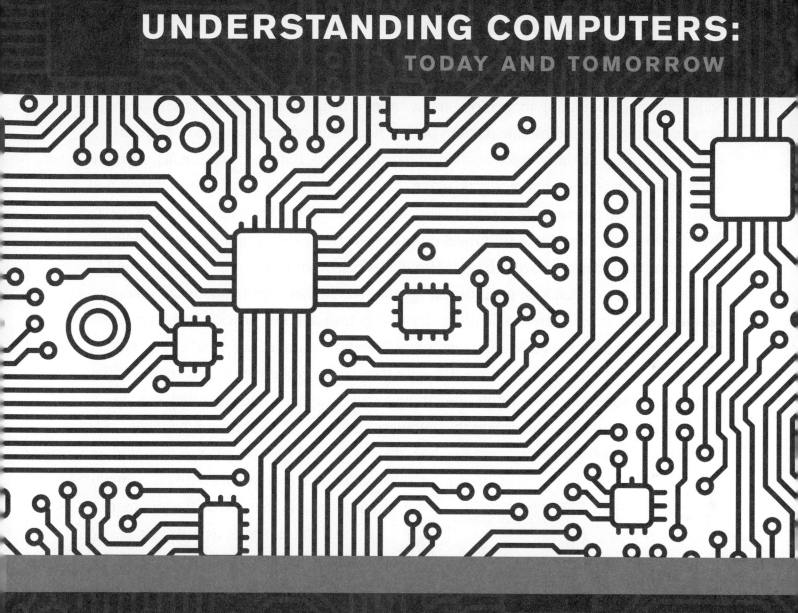

⏻ module

Introduction

Today, computers are virtually everywhere in our society. People encounter and use computers and computing technology many times during the average day. Individuals use personal computers and mobile devices both at home and while on the go to perform a variety of important daily tasks, such as to pay bills, shop, manage investments, communicate with others, research products, make travel arrangements, check current news and weather, look up phone numbers, and view maps of locations. They also use these devices for a growing number of entertainment purposes, such as playing games, downloading and listening to music, viewing friends' Facebook pages, and watching TV shows and movies. Businesses, schools, government agencies, and other organizations use computers and related technologies to facilitate day-to-day transactions, provide better services to customers, communicate with others, retrieve and disseminate information, and assist managers in making good decisions. Because they are so embedded in our society today, it is essential for everyone to know something about computers and what they can do.

This module introduces you to computers and some of their uses. Chapter 1 helps you to understand what computers are, how they work, and how people use them today. Chapter 1 also provides an overview of common computer terms and concepts that you will encounter throughout this text, as well as gives you a brief look at how to use a computer to perform basic tasks and to access resources on the Internet and the World Wide Web.

in this module

*"Software . . .
allows us to
utilize the
hardware of the
machine itself
in ways that
are seemingly
unending."*

For more comments from
Guest Expert **Daniel Kelley**
of D-Link Systems, see the
**Expert Insight on . . .
Personal Computers**
feature at the end of the
module.

chapter 1

Introduction to the World of Computers

After completing this chapter, you will be able to do the following:

1. Explain why it is essential to learn about computers today and discuss several ways computers are integrated into our business and personal lives.

2. Define a computer and describe its primary operations.

3. List some important milestones in computer evolution.

4. Identify the major parts of a personal computer, including input, processing, output, storage, and communications hardware.

5. Define software and understand how it is used to instruct the computer what to do.

6. List the six basic types of computers, giving at least one example of each type of computer and stating what that computer might be used for.

7. Explain what a network, the Internet, and the World Wide Web are, as well as how computers, people, and Web pages are identified on the Internet.

8. Describe how to access a Web page and navigate through a Web site.

9. Discuss the societal impact of computers, including some benefits and risks related to their prominence in our society.

OVERVIEW

Computers and other forms of technology impact our daily lives in a multitude of ways. We encounter computers in stores, restaurants, and other retail establishments. We use computers and the Internet regularly to obtain information, experience online entertainment, buy products and services, and communicate with others. Many of us carry a mobile phone or other mobile device with us at all times so we can remain in touch with others on a continual basis and can access Internet information as we need it. We also use these devices to pay for purchases, play online games with others, watch TV and movies, and much, much more.

Businesses also use computers extensively, such as to maintain employee and customer records, manage inventories, maintain online stores and other Web sites, process sales, control robots and other machines in factories, and provide business executives with the up-to-date information they need to make decisions. The government uses computers to support our nation's defense systems, for space exploration, for storing and organizing vital information about citizens, for law enforcement and military purposes, and other important tasks. In short, computers and computing technology are used in an endless number of ways.

Understanding Computers: Today and Tomorrow is a guide to computers and related technology and how they are being used in the world today. It will provide you with a comprehensive introduction to computer concepts and terminology and give you a solid foundation for any future courses you may take that are related to computers or their use in the world today. It will also provide you with the basic knowledge you need to understand and use computers in school, on the job, and in your personal life, as well as give you an overview of the various societal issues related to technology, such as security and privacy issues, ethical considerations, and environmental concerns.

Chapter 1 is designed to help you understand what computers are, how they work, and how people use them. It introduces the important terms and concepts that you will encounter throughout this text and in discussions about computers with others, as well as includes an overview of the history of computers. It also takes a brief look at how to use a computer to perform basic tasks and to access resources on the Internet and the World Wide Web in order to provide you with the knowledge, skills, and tools you need to complete the projects and online activities that accompany this textbook. The chapter closes with an overview of the societal impact of computers. ∎

> **TIP**
>
> Most of the computer concepts introduced in this chapter are discussed in more detail in subsequent chapters of this text.

COMPUTERS IN YOUR LIFE

Computers today are used in virtually every aspect of most individuals' lives—at home, at school, at work, and while on the go. The next few sections provide an overview of the importance of computers and some of the most common computer-related activities that individuals may encounter every day.

Why Learn About Computers?

Fifty years ago, computers were used primarily by researchers and scientists. Today, computers are an integral part of our lives. Experts call this trend *pervasive computing*, in which few aspects of daily life remain untouched by computers and computing technology. With pervasive computing—also referred to as *ubiquitous computing*—computers are found virtually everywhere and computing technology is integrated into an ever-increasing number of devices to give those devices additional functionality, such as enabling them to communicate with other devices on an ongoing basis. Because of the prominence of computers in our society, it is important to understand what a computer is, a little about how a computer works, and the implications of living in a computer-oriented society.

Prior to about 1980, computers were large and expensive, and few people had access to them. Most computers used in organizations were equipped to do little more than carry out high-volume processing tasks, such as issuing bills and keeping track of inventories. The average person did not need to know how to use a computer for his or her job, and it was uncommon to have a computer at home. Furthermore, the use of computers generally required a lot of technical knowledge and the use of the *Internet* was reserved primarily for researchers and educational institutions. Because there were few good reasons or opportunities for learning how to use computers, the average person was unfamiliar with them.

Beginning in the early 1980s, things began to change. *Microcomputers*—inexpensive *personal computers* that you will read about later in this chapter—were invented and computer use increased dramatically. The creation of the *World Wide Web* (*WWW*) in the late 1980s and the graphical *Web browser* in the early 1990s started the trend of individuals buying and using computers for personal use. Today, *portable computers* and *mobile phones* have brought personal computing to a whole new level—nearly 90% of all U.S. households have a computer or mobile phone, and most individuals use some type of computer on the job. Whether you become a teacher, attorney, doctor, engineer, restaurant manager, salesperson, professional athlete, musician, executive, or skilled tradesperson, you will likely use a computer to obtain and evaluate information, to facilitate necessary on-the-job tasks, and to communicate with others. Today's computers are very useful tools for these purposes; they are also taking on new roles in our society, such as delivering entertainment on demand. In fact, computers and the traditional communications and entertainment devices that we use every day—such as telephones, televisions, gaming devices, and home entertainment systems—are *converging* into single units with multiple capabilities. For instance, you can check your *e-mail* (electronic messages), watch videos, and view other Internet content on your living room TV; you can make telephone calls via your personal computer; and you can view Internet content and watch TV on your *smartphone* or other *mobile device* (see Figure 1-1). As a result of this *convergence* trend, the computer is no longer an isolated productivity tool; instead, it is an integral part of our daily lives.

FIGURE 1-1
Convergence.
Many devices today include computing or Internet capabilities.

Courtesy Netflix

TELEVISIONS
Can be used to access Web pages, e-mail, streaming movies, and other Internet content, in addition to viewing TV content.

Used with permission from Microsoft Corporation

SMARTPHONES
Can be used to access Internet content, play music and games, take photos, watch TV shows, and more, in addition to making phone calls.

Just as you can learn to drive a car without knowing much about car engines, you can learn to use a computer without understanding the technical details of how a computer works. However, a little knowledge gives you a big advantage. Knowing something about cars can help you make wise purchasing decisions and save money on repairs. Likewise, knowing something about computers can help you buy the right one for your needs, get the most efficient use out of it, be able to properly *upgrade* it as your needs change, and have a much higher level of comfort and confidence along the way. Therefore, basic **computer literacy**—knowing about and understanding computers and their uses—is an essential skill today for everyone.

>**Computer literacy.** The knowledge and understanding of basic computer fundamentals.

Computers in the Home

Home computing has increased dramatically over the last few years as computers and Internet access have become less expensive and as a vast array of online consumer activities have become available. Use of the Internet at home to look up information, exchange e-mail, shop, watch TV and videos, download music and movies, research products, pay bills and manage bank accounts, check news and weather, store and organize *digital photos*, play games, make vacation plans, and so forth is now the norm for many individuals (see Figure 1-2). Many individuals also use a computer at home for work-related tasks, such as to review work-related documents or check work e-mail from home.

As the Internet, wireless technology, and devices such as computers, televisions, mobile phones, *digital video recorders* (*DVRs*), and *gaming consoles* continue to converge, the computer is also becoming a central part of home entertainment. *Wireless networking* allows the use of computers in virtually any location and both online and offline content to be sent wirelessly from one device to another. Both voice and video telephone calls can be made over your Internet connection, and your TV can display Internet content.

Computing technologies also make it possible to have *smart appliances*—traditional appliances (such as refrigerators, thermostats, or ovens) with some type of built-in computer or communications technology that allows them to be controlled by the user via a smartphone or the Internet, to access and display Internet information, or to perform other computer-related functions. *Smart homes*—homes in which household tasks (such as watering the lawn, turning the air conditioning on or off, making coffee, monitoring the security of the home and grounds, and managing home entertainment content) are controlled by a main computer in the home or by the homeowner remotely via a smartphone—have arrived, and they are expected to be the norm in less than a decade. Some believe that one primary focus of smart appliances and smart homes will be energy conservation—for instance, the ability to perform tasks (such as running the dishwasher and watering the lawn) during nonpeak energy periods and to potentially transfer waste heat from one appliance (such as an oven) to another appliance (such as a dishwasher) as needed.

Computers in Education

Today's youth can definitely be called the *computing generation*. From *handheld gaming devices* to mobile phones to computers at school and home, most children and teens today have been exposed to computers and related technology all their lives. Although the amount of computer use varies from school to school and from grade level to grade level, most students today have access to computers at school—and some schools have completely integrated computers into the curriculum, such as by adopting *e-book* (electronic) textbooks that run on school-owned portable computers, or allowing students to bring in devices to use in class (referred to as *BYOD* or *Bring Your Own Device*). Many schools (particularly college campuses) today also have *wireless hotspots* that allow students to connect their personal computers or mobile devices wirelessly to the Internet from anywhere on campus. Today, students at all levels are typically required to use a computer to some extent as part of their normal coursework—such as for preparing papers, practicing skills, doing Internet research, accessing Internet content (for instance, class *Web pages* or their campus *YouTube* channel), or delivering presentations—and some colleges require a computer for enrollment.

Computers are also used to facilitate *distance learning*—an alternative to traditional classroom learning in which students participate, typically at their own pace, from their current location (via their computers and Internet connections) instead of physically going to class. Consequently, distance learning gives students greater flexibility to schedule class time around

REFERENCE
Retrieving information, obtaining news, viewing recipes, shopping online, and exchanging e-mail are popular home computer activities.

PRODUCTIVITY
Home computers are frequently used for editing and managing digital photos and home videos, creating and editing work-related documents, paying bills, and other productivity tasks.

ENTERTAINMENT
Home computers and gaming consoles are becoming a central hub for entertainment, such as the delivery of photos, videos, music, games, TV shows, instant messages, and social networking updates.

FIGURE 1-2
Computer use at home.

COMPUTER LABS AND CLASSROOMS
Many schools today have computers and Internet access available in the classroom and/or a computer lab for student use.

CAMPUS WIRELESS HOTSPOTS
Many students can access the Internet from anywhere on campus to do research, check e-mail, and more, via a campus hotspot.

DISTANCE LEARNING
With distance learning, students—such as these U.S. Army soldiers—can take classes from home or wherever they happen to be at the moment.

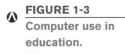

FIGURE 1-3
Computer use in education.

their personal, family, and work commitments, as well as allows individuals located in very rural areas or stationed at military posts overseas to take courses when they are not able to attend classes physically. Some examples of computer use in education are shown in Figure 1-3.

Computers on the Job

Although computers have been used on the job for years, their role is continually evolving. Computers were originally used as research tools for computer experts and scientists and then as productivity tools for office workers. Today, computers are used by all types of employees in all types of businesses—including corporate executives, retail store clerks, traveling sales professionals, artists and musicians, engineers, police officers, insurance adjusters, delivery workers, doctors and nurses, auto mechanics and repair personnel, and professional athletes. In essence, the computer has become a universal tool for on-the-job decision making, productivity, and communications (see Figure 1-4). Computers are also used extensively for access control at many businesses and organizations, such as *authentication systems* that allow only authorized individuals to enter an office building, punch in or out of work, or access the company network via an access card or a fingerprint or hand scan, as shown in Figure 1-4 and discussed in detail in Chapter 9. In addition to jobs that require the use of computers by employees, many new jobs have been created simply because computers exist, such as jobs in electronics manufacturing, online retailing, Internet applications, and technology-related computer support.

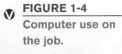

FIGURE 1-4
Computer use on the job.

DECISION MAKING
Many individuals today use a computer to help them make on-the-job decisions.

PRODUCTIVITY
Many individuals today use a computer to perform on-the-job tasks efficiently and accurately.

OFF-SITE COMMUNICATIONS
Many individuals use portable computers or mobile devices to record data, access data, or communicate with others when they are out of the office.

AUTHENTICATION
Many individuals are required to use authentication systems to punch in and out of work, access facilities, or log on to company computers.

TECHNOLOGY AND YOU

Restaurant iPad Ordering Systems

You may have used your iPad or other device to place a pickup order at your local eatery; you may also have had a server use an iPad to take your order at a restaurant. Nice innovations, but guess what's next? Placing your order yourself at a restaurant using an iPad.

This new trend of using iPads and *e-menus* to have customers place their orders in restaurants is growing rapidly. In addition to enabling customers to place their orders at their convenience without waiting for a server, it also allows the restaurant to provide more resources to customers (such as photographs of menu items, pairing suggestions for appetizers and drinks, and so forth). The overall goal is to allow customers to control their dining experience from the time they are seated until they choose to pay the check. And, yes, they pay via the iPad as well (see the credit card reader at the top right of the iPad shown in the accompanying photo).

iPad ordering systems work especially well for restaurants that offer customized menu items. For example, Stacked, one of the first large-scale adopters of restaurant iPad ordering systems, offers typical American food (such as pizza, burgers, and salads) at its Southern California restaurants but everything on the menu is customizable—customers choose from a wide variety of ingredients, toppings, and sauces. The iPad systems enable customers to build their selections, adding or removing ingredients, until they are satisfied with the order (the price adjusts as they change their selections). This allows customers to build their orders at a comfortable pace without having to remember them until a server arrives, or having to make that many decisions with a server waiting.

More than 7,000 e-menu-enabled iPads are also arriving at airport restaurants in three airports in North America. They will be used not only for placing orders but also for providing travelers with free access to Facebook, Twitter, e-mail, games, news, and flight updates while they wait (for security purposes, all personal information is wiped from the device as soon as the home button is pressed).

The two biggest risks for restaurants introducing iPad ordering systems is customer acceptance (most offer assistance from servers if the customer desires to help alleviate any customer concerns about using the devices) and technology issues. To avoid network or Internet outage issues, some restaurants are implementing redundant systems, such as multiple routers that can be used if the main router goes down or a 4G Internet connection that the system can use to access the Internet via a cellular connection if the main Internet source goes down.

Courtesy of Square, Inc.

Computers are also used extensively by military personnel for communications and navigational purposes, as well as to control missiles and other weapons, identify terrorists and other potential enemies, and perform other necessary national security tasks. To update their computer skills, many employees in all lines of work periodically take computer training classes or enroll in computer certification programs.

Computers on the Go

In addition to using computers in the home, at school, and on the job, most people encounter and use all types of computers in other aspects of day-to-day life. For example, it is common for consumers to use *consumer kiosks* (small self-service computer-based stations that provide information or other services to the public, including those used for ATM transactions, bridal registries, ticketing systems, and more), *point-of-sale (POS) systems* (such as those found at most retail stores to check customers out—see the Technology and You box for a look at how you may soon be using iPads to order at restaurants), and *self-checkout systems* (which allow retail store customers to scan their purchases and pay

PORTABLE DEVICES
Many people today carry a portable computer or smartphone with them at all times or when they travel in order to remain in touch with others and to access Internet resources.

CONSUMER KIOSKS
Electronic kiosks are widely available to view conference or gift registry information, print photographs, order products or services, and more.

MOBILE PAYMENT SYSTEMS
Allow individuals to pay for purchases using a smartphone or other device.

CONSUMER AUTHENTICATION SYSTEMS
Allow only authorized members, such as theme park annual pass holders as shown here, access to facilities.

FIGURE 1-5
Computer use while on the go.

for them without a salesclerk) while in retail stores and other public locations. Individuals may also need to use a computer-based consumer authentication system to gain access to a local health club, theme park, or other membership-based facility (see Figure 1-5).

In addition, many individuals carry a *portable computer* or *mobile device* with them on a regular basis to remain electronically in touch with others and to access information (such as stock quotes, driving directions, airline flight updates, movie times, news headlines, and more) as needed while on the go. These portable devices are also commonly used to watch TV, download and listen to music, access *Facebook* pages and other *social networking sites*, and perform other mobile entertainment options. Smartphones can also be used to pay for products and services (refer again to Figure 1-5), as well as remotely deposit checks, transfer money to others, pay bills electronicially, and perform other *mobile banking* applications. *GPS* (*global positioning system*) capabilities are frequently built into smartphones, cars, and other devices to provide individuals with driving directions and other navigational aids while traveling or hiking.

WHAT IS A COMPUTER AND WHAT DOES IT DO?

A **computer** can be defined as a programmable, electronic device that accepts data, performs operations on that data, presents the results, and stores the data or results as needed. The fact that a computer is *programmable* means that a computer will do whatever the instructions—called the *program*—tell it to do. The programs used with a computer determine the tasks the computer is able to perform.

The four operations described in this definition are more technically referred to as *input*, *processing*, *output*, and *storage*. These four primary operations of a computer can be defined as follows:

> **Input**—entering data into the computer.

> **Processing**—performing operations on the data.

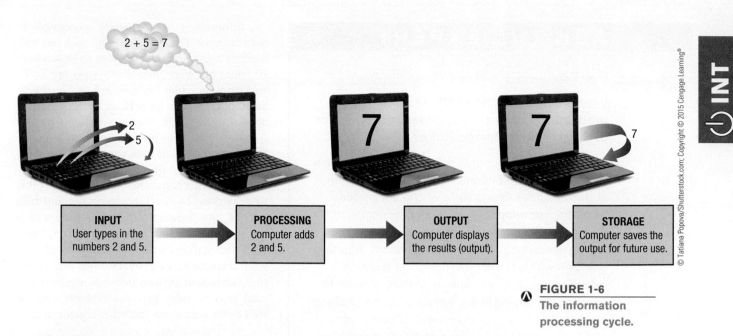

2 + 5 = 7

| **INPUT** User types in the numbers 2 and 5. | **PROCESSING** Computer adds 2 and 5. | **OUTPUT** Computer displays the results (output). | **STORAGE** Computer saves the output for future use. |

FIGURE 1-6
The information processing cycle.

➤ **Output**—presenting the results.

➤ **Storage**—saving data, programs, or output for future use.

For example, assume that you have a computer that has been programmed to add two numbers. As shown in Figure 1-6, input occurs when data (in this example, the numbers 2 and 5) is entered into the computer, processing takes place when the computer program adds those two numbers, and output happens when the sum of 7 is displayed on the computer screen. The storage operation occurs any time the data, a change to a program, or the output is saved for future use.

For an additional example, look at a supermarket *barcode reader* to see how it fits this definition of a computer. First, the grocery item being purchased is passed over the barcode reader—input. Next, the description and price of the item are looked up—processing. Then, the item description and price are displayed on the cash register and printed on the receipt—output. Finally, the inventory, ordering, and sales records are updated—storage.

This progression of input, processing, output, and storage is sometimes referred to as the *IPOS cycle* or the *information processing cycle*. In addition to these four primary computer operations, today's computers almost always perform **communications** functions, such as sending or retrieving data via the Internet, accessing information located in a shared company database, or exchanging data or e-mail messages with others. Therefore, communications—technically an input or output operation, depending on which direction the information is going—is often considered the fifth primary computer operation.

Data vs. Information

As just discussed, a user inputs **data** into a computer, and then the computer processes it. Almost any kind of fact or set of facts can become computer data, such as the words in a letter to a friend, the numbers in a monthly budget, the images in a photograph, the notes in a song, or the facts stored in an employee record. When data is processed into a meaningful form, it becomes **information**.

>**Output.** The process of presenting the results of processing; can also refer to the results themselves. >**Storage.** The operation of saving data, programs, or output for future use. >**Communications.** The transmission of data from one device to another. >**Data.** Raw, unorganized facts. >**Information.** Data that has been processed into a meaningful form.

ASK THE EXPERT

Rob Bredow, CTO, Sony Pictures Imageworks

What position might a college student graduating with a computer degree qualify for at Sony Pictures Imageworks?

We employ a number of talented engineers (typically computer science or computer engineering majors) at Sony Pictures Imageworks whose specialties range from developing completely new computer graphics techniques to focusing on our high performance networking and disk configurations. A recent graduate with experience in computer graphics rendering might, for example, help write shaders to simulate the lighting in the surface of a new challenging material like skin or cloth used for both animated and live-action films. We recently hired an engineer who first joined us as an intern and, because of her enthusiastic attitude and technical abilities, is now on the front lines of our Linux support team deploying new hardware and supporting artists working on our films. In summary, a great attitude—along with strong computer, math, and engineering skills—are qualities we love to see in our technology teams at Sony Pictures Imageworks.

Information is frequently generated to answer some type of question, such as how many of a restaurant's employees work less than 20 hours per week, how many seats are available on a particular flight from Los Angeles to San Francisco, or what is Hank Aaron's lifetime home run total. Of course, you don't need a computer system to process data into information; for example, anyone can go through time cards or employee files and make a list of people who work a certain number of hours. If this work is done by hand, however, it could take a lot of time, especially for a company with a large number of employees. Computers, however, can perform such tasks almost instantly, with accurate results. *Information processing* (the conversion of data into information) is a vital activity today for all computer users, as well as for businesses and other organizations.

Computers Then and Now

The basic ideas of computing and calculating are very old, going back thousands of years. However, the computer in the form in which it is recognized today is a fairly recent invention. In fact, personal computers have only been around since the late 1970s. The history of computers is often referred to in terms of *generations*, with each new generation characterized by a major technological development. The next sections summarize some early calculating devices and the different computer generations.

Precomputers and Early Computers (before approximately 1946)

Based on archeological finds, such as notched bones, knotted twine, and hieroglyphics, experts have concluded that ancient civilizations had the ability to count and compute. The *abacus* is considered by many to be the earliest recorded calculating device; it was used primarily as an aid for basic arithmetic calculations. Other early computing devices include the *slide rule*, the *mechanical calculator*, and Dr. Herman Hollerith's *Punch Card Tabulating Machine and Sorter*. This latter device (see Figure 1-7) was the first electromechanical machine that could read *punch cards*—special cards with holes punched in them to represent data. Hollerith's machine was used to process the 1890 U.S. Census data and it was able to complete the task in two and one half years, instead of the decade it usually took to process the data manually. Consequently, this is considered to be the first successful case of an information processing system replacing a paper-and-pen-based system. Hollerith's company eventually became *International Business Machines* (*IBM*).

First-Generation Computers (approximately 1946–1957)

The first computers were enormous, often taking up entire rooms. They were powered by thousands of *vacuum tubes*—glass tubes that look similar to large light bulbs—which needed replacing constantly, required a great deal of electricity, and generated a lot of heat. *First-generation computers* could solve only one problem at a time because they needed to be physically rewired with cables to be reprogrammed (see Figure 1-7), which typically took several days (sometimes even weeks) to complete and several more days to check before the computer could be used. Usually paper punch cards and paper tape were used for input, and output was printed on paper.

Two of the most significant examples of first-generation computers were *ENIAC* and *UNIVAC*. ENIAC, shown in Figure 1-7, was the world's first large-scale, general-purpose computer. Although it was not completed until 1946, ENIAC was developed during World War II to compute artillery-firing tables for the U.S. Army. Instead of the 40 hours required for a person to compute the optimal settings for a single weapon under a single set of conditions using manual calculations, ENIAC could complete the same calculations in less than two minutes. UNIVAC, released in 1951, was initially built for the U.S. Census Bureau and was used to analyze votes in the 1952 U.S. presidential election. Interestingly, its correct prediction of an Eisenhower victory only 45 minutes after the polls closed was not publicly aired because the results were not trusted. However, UNIVAC became the first computer to be mass produced for general commercial use.

Second-Generation Computers (approximately 1958–1963)

The second generation of computers began when the *transistor*—a small device made of *semiconductor* material that acts like a switch to open or close *electronic circuits*—started to replace the vacuum tube. Transistors allowed *second-generation computers* to be smaller, less expensive, more powerful, more energy-efficient, and more reliable than first-generation computers. Typically, programs and data were input on punch cards and *magnetic tape*, output was on punch cards and paper printouts, and magnetic tape (see Figure 1-7) was used for storage. *Hard drives* and *programming languages* (such as *FORTRAN* and *COBOL*) were developed and implemented during this generation.

PRECOMPUTERS AND EARLY COMPUTERS
Dr. Herman Hollerith's Punch Card Tabulating Machine and Sorter is an example of an early computing device. It was used to process the 1890 U.S. Census data.

FIRST-GENERATION COMPUTERS
First-generation computers, such as ENIAC shown here, were large and bulky, used vacuum tubes, and had to be physically wired and reset to run programs.

SECOND-GENERATION COMPUTERS
Second-generation computers, such as the IBM 1401 mainframe shown here, used transistors instead of vacuum tubes so they were smaller, faster, and more reliable than first-generation computers.

THIRD-GENERATION COMPUTERS
Third-generation computers used integrated circuits, which allowed the introduction of smaller computers such as the IBM System/360 mainframe shown here.

FOURTH-GENERATION COMPUTERS
Fourth-generation computers, such as the original IBM PC shown here, are based on microprocessors. Most of today's computers fall into this category.

FIFTH-GENERATION COMPUTERS
Some aspects of fifth-generation computers, such as the natural language input and artificial intelligence used by the IBM Watson computer shown competing on *Jeopardy!* here, already exist.

Third-Generation Computers (approximately 1964–1970)

The replacement of the transistor with *integrated circuits* (*ICs*) marked the beginning of the third generation of computers. Integrated circuits incorporate many transistors and electronic circuits on a single tiny silicon *chip*, allowing *third-generation computers* to be even smaller and more reliable than computers in the earlier computer generations. Instead of punch cards and paper printouts, *keyboards* and *monitors* were introduced for input and output; hard drives were typically used for storage. An example of a widely used third-generation computer is shown in Figure 1-7.

FIGURE 1-7
A brief look at computer generations.

Fourth-Generation Computers (approximately 1971–present)

A technological breakthrough in the early 1970s made it possible to place an increasing number of transistors on a single chip. This led to the invention of the *microprocessor* in 1971, which ushered in the fourth generation of computers. In essence, a microprocessor contains the core processing capabilities of an entire computer on one single chip. The original *IBM PC* (see Figure 1-7) and *Apple Macintosh* computers, and most of today's traditional computers, fall into this category. *Fourth-generation computers* typically use a keyboard and *mouse* for input, a monitor and *printer* for output, and *hard drives, flash memory media,* and *optical discs* for storage. This generation also witnessed the development of *computer networks, wireless technologies,* and the Internet.

Fifth-Generation Computers (now and the future)

Fifth-generation computers are most commonly defined as those that are based on *artificial intelligence*, allowing them to think, reason, and learn (see one example in Figure 1-7). Some aspects of fifth-generation computers—such as voice and touch input and *speech recognition*—are being used today. In the future, fifth-generation computers are expected to be constructed differently than they are today, such as in the form of *optical computers* that process data using light instead of electrons, tiny computers that utilize *nanotechnology*, or as entire general-purpose computers built into desks, home appliances, and other everyday devices.

Ⅴ **FIGURE 1-8**
Common hardware listed by operation.

Hardware

The physical parts of a computer (the parts you can touch and discussed next) are called **hardware**. The instructions or programs used with a computer—called *software*—are discussed shortly. Hardware components can be *internal* (located inside the main box or *system unit* of the computer) or *external* (located outside the system unit and connected to the system unit via a wired or wireless connection). There are hardware devices associated with each of the five computer operations previously discussed (input, processing, output, storage, and communications), as summarized in Figure 1-8 and illustrated in Figure 1-9.

INPUT	PROCESSING
Keyboard	CPU
Mouse	**OUTPUT**
Microphone	Monitor/display screen
Scanner	Printer
Digital camera	Speakers
Digital pen/stylus	Headphones/headsets
Touch pad/touch screen	Data projector
Gaming controller	**STORAGE**
Fingerprint reader	Hard drive
COMMUNICATIONS	CD/DVD/Blu-ray disc
Modem	CD/DVD/Blu-ray drive
Network adapter	Flash memory card
Router	Flash memory card reader
	USB flash drive

Input Devices

An *input device* is any piece of equipment that is used to input data into the computer. The input devices shown in Figure 1-9 are a *keyboard, mouse,* and *microphone*. Other common input devices include *scanners, digital cameras, digital pens* and *styluses, touch pads* and *touch screens, fingerprint readers,* and *gaming controllers*. Input devices are discussed in more detail in Chapter 4.

Processing Devices

The main *processing device* for a computer is the *central processing unit (CPU)*. The CPU is located inside the system unit and performs the calculations and comparisons needed for processing;

>**Hardware.** The physical parts of a computer system, such as the keyboard, monitor, printer, and so forth.

FLASH MEMORY CARD READER
Reads and writes flash memory cards.

DVD DRIVE
Reads and writes CD and DVD discs.

HARD DRIVE
Located inside the system unit; stores programs and most data.

SYSTEM UNIT
Case that contains the CPU, memory, power supply, storage devices, and all other internal hardware.

MONITOR
Lets you see your work as you go; the primary output device.

PRINTER
Produces printed copies of computer output.

MICROPHONE
Captures spoken input.

SPEAKERS
Produce audio output.

USB PORTS
Connect external devices that use the USB interface.

ROUTER
Connects devices so they can share an Internet connection and data.

MODEM
Connects the computer to the Internet.

KEYBOARD
Used to type instructions into the computer; a primary input device.

CD AND DVD DISCS
Used to deliver programs and store large multimedia files.

MOUSE
Used to make on-screen selections; a primary input device.

FLASH MEMORY CARDS
Used to store digital photos, music files, and other content.

USB FLASH DRIVE
Used to store documents, digital photos, music files, and other content to be moved from one PC to another.

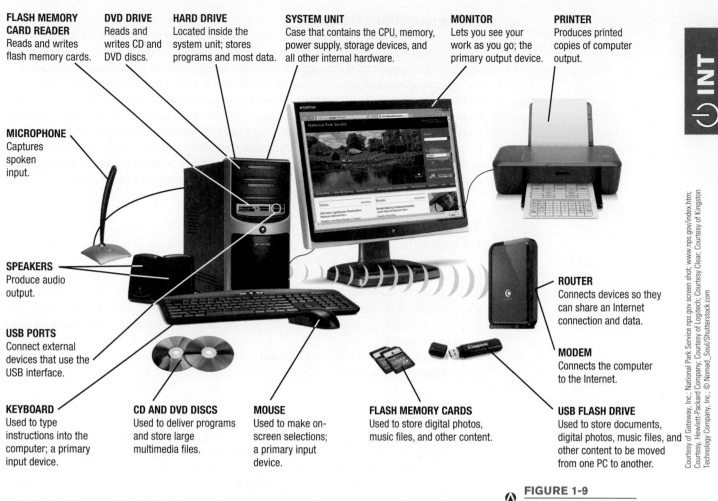

FIGURE 1-9
Typical computer hardware.

it also controls the computer's operations. For these reasons, the CPU is often considered the "brain" of the computer. Also involved in processing are various types of *memory* that are located inside the system unit and used to store data and instructions while the CPU is working with them, as well as additional processors such as the *graphics processing unit (GPU)*. The CPU, GPU, memory, and processing are discussed in detail in Chapter 2.

Output Devices

An *output device* accepts processed data from the computer and presents the results to the user, most of the time on the display screen (*monitor*), on paper (via a *printer*), or through a *speaker*. Other common output devices include *headphones* and *headsets* (used to deliver audio output to a single user) and *data projectors* (used to project computer images onto a projection screen). Output devices are covered in more detail in Chapter 4.

Storage Devices

Storage devices (such as *DVD drives* and *flash memory card readers*) are used to store data on or access data from *storage media* (such as *DVD discs* and *flash memory cards*). Some storage hardware (such as a *hard drive* or a *USB flash drive*) includes both a storage device and storage medium in a single piece of hardware. Storage devices are used to save data, program settings, or output for future use; they can be installed inside the computer, attached to the computer as an external device, or accessed remotely through a network or wireless connection. Storage is discussed in more detail in Chapter 3.

Communications Devices

Communications devices allow users to communicate electronically with others and to access remote information via the Internet or a home, school, or company computer network. Communications hardware includes *modems* (used to connect a computer to the Internet), *network adapters* (used to connect a computer to a computer network), and *routers* (used to create a small network so a variety of devices can share an Internet connection and data). A variety of modems and network adapters are available because there are different types of Internet and network connections—a modem used to connect to the Internet via a wireless connection and that also contains a built-in wireless router is shown in Figure 1-9. Communications hardware and computer networks are discussed in more detail in Chapter 7; connecting to the Internet is covered in Chapter 8.

Software

The term **software** refers to the programs or instructions used to tell the computer hardware what to do. Software is traditionally purchased on a CD or DVD or is downloaded from the Internet; in either case, the software typically needs to be *installed* on a computer before it can be used. Software can also be run directly from the Internet (via Web pages) without being installed on your computer; this is referred to as *cloud software, Web-based software, Software as a Service (SaaS)*, and *cloud computing* and is discussed in more detail in Chapter 6.

Computers use two basic types of software: *system software* and *application software*. The differences between these types of software are discussed next.

System Software

The programs that allow a computer to operate are collectively referred to as *system software*. The main system software is the **operating system**, which starts up the computer and controls its operation. Common operating system tasks include setting up new hardware, allowing users to run other software, and allowing users to manage the documents stored on their computers. Without an operating system, a computer cannot function. Common *desktop operating systems* designed for personal computers are *Windows, Mac OS*, and *Linux*; these and other operating systems (such as *Android, iOS,* and other *mobile operating systems* used with mobile phones and other mobile devices) are discussed in detail in Chapter 5.

To use a computer, first turn on the power to the computer by pressing the power button, and then the computer will begin to **boot**. During the *boot process*, part of the computer's operating system is loaded into memory, the computer does a quick diagnostic of itself, and then it launches any programs—such as security software—designated to run each time the computer starts up. You may need to supply a password to *log on* to your computer or a computer network to finish the boot process.

Once a computer has booted, it is ready to be used and waits for input from the user. Most software today uses a variety of graphical objects (such as *icons, buttons,* and *tiles*) that are selected with the mouse (or with a finger or stylus for a computer that supports touch or pen input) to tell the computer what to do. For instance, the **Windows desktop** (the basic workspace for computers running the Windows operating system; that is, the place where documents, folders, programs, and other objects are displayed when they are being used), along with some common graphical objects used in Windows and many other software programs, is shown in Figure 1-10.

>**Software.** The instructions, also called computer programs, that are used to tell a computer what it should do. >**Operating system.** The main component of system software that enables a computer to operate, manage its activities and the resources under its control, run application programs, and interface with the user. >**Boot.** To start up a computer. >**Windows desktop.** The background work area displayed on the screen for computers running Microsoft Windows.

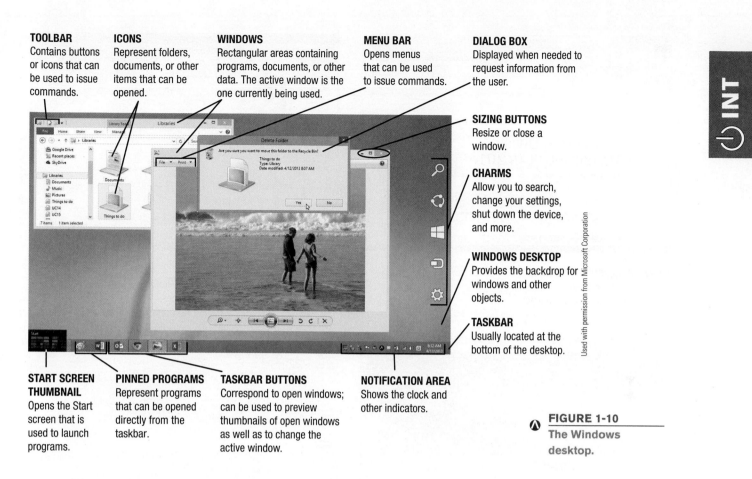

TOOLBAR
Contains buttons or icons that can be used to issue commands.

ICONS
Represent folders, documents, or other items that can be opened.

WINDOWS
Rectangular areas containing programs, documents, or other data. The active window is the one currently being used.

MENU BAR
Opens menus that can be used to issue commands.

DIALOG BOX
Displayed when needed to request information from the user.

SIZING BUTTONS
Resize or close a window.

CHARMS
Allow you to search, change your settings, shut down the device, and more.

WINDOWS DESKTOP
Provides the backdrop for windows and other objects.

TASKBAR
Usually located at the bottom of the desktop.

Used with permission from Microsoft Corporation

START SCREEN THUMBNAIL
Opens the Start screen that is used to launch programs.

PINNED PROGRAMS
Represent programs that can be opened directly from the taskbar.

TASKBAR BUTTONS
Correspond to open windows; can be used to preview thumbnails of open windows as well as to change the active window.

NOTIFICATION AREA
Shows the clock and other indicators.

FIGURE 1-10
The Windows desktop.

Application Software

Application software (see Figure 1-11) consists of programs designed to allow people to perform specific tasks using a computer, such as creating letters, preparing budgets, managing inventory and customer databases, playing games, watching videos, listening to music, scheduling appointments, editing digital photographs, designing homes, viewing Web pages, burning DVDs, and exchanging e-mail. Application software is launched via the operating system, such as by using the *Windows Start screen* for Windows 8 computers (or the *Windows Start menu* for older versions of Windows), and is discussed in greater detail in Chapter 6.

There are also application programs that help users write their own programs in a form the computer can understand using a *programming language* like *BASIC*, *Visual Basic*, *COBOL*, *C++*, *Java*, or *Python*. Some languages are traditional programming languages for developing applications; others are designed for use with Web pages or multimedia programming. *Markup* and *scripting* languages (such as *HTML*, *XHTML*, and *JavaScript*) used to create Web pages are covered in Chapter 10; traditional programming languages are discussed in detail in Chapter 13.

Computer Users and Professionals

In addition to hardware, software, data, and *procedures* (the predetermined steps to be carried out in particular situations), a computer system includes people. *Computer users*, or *end users*, are the people who use computers to perform tasks or obtain information.

TIP

Application software programs are also referred to as *apps*.

> **Application software.** Programs that enable users to perform specific tasks on a computer, such as writing letters or playing games; also called *apps*.

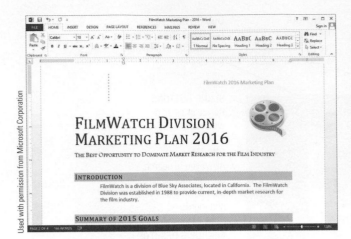

WORD PROCESSING PROGRAMS
Allow users to create written documents,
such as reports, letters, and memos.

MULTIMEDIA PROGRAMS
Allow users to play music or videos and transfer content to
and from CDs, DVDs, and portable devices.

WEB BROWSERS
Allow users to view Web pages and
other information located on the Internet.

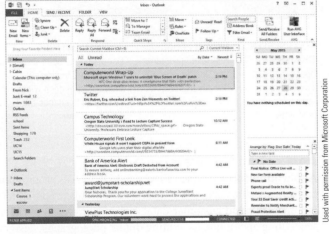

E-MAIL PROGRAMS
Allow users to compose, send, receive, and manage electronic
messages; some also include calendars, to-do lists, and
other features.

FIGURE 1-11
Examples of
application
software.

Anyone who uses a computer is a computer user, including an accountant electronically preparing a client's taxes, an office worker using a word processing program to create a letter, a supervisor using a computer to check and see whether or not manufacturing workers have met the day's quotas, a parent e-mailing his or her child's teacher, a college student researching a topic online, a doctor updating a patient's electronic medical record, a child playing a computer game, and a person shopping online.

Programmers, on the other hand, are computer professionals who write the programs that computers use. Other *computer professionals* include *systems analysts* (who design computer systems to be used within their companies as discussed in Chapter 12), *computer operations personnel* (who are responsible for the day-to-day computer operations at a company, such as maintaining systems or troubleshooting user-related problems), and *security specialists* (who are responsible for securing the company computers and networks against *hackers* and other intruders who are discussed in more detail in Chapter 9). Computer professionals are discussed in more detail in Chapter 12.

COMPUTERS TO FIT EVERY NEED

The types of computers available today vary from the tiny computers embedded in consumer products, to the mobile devices that do a limited number of computing tasks, to the powerful and versatile *desktop* and *portable computers* found in homes and businesses, to the superpowerful computers used to control the country's defense systems. Computers are generally classified in one of six categories, based on size, capability, and price.

> - *Embedded computers*—tiny computers embedded into products to perform specific functions or tasks for that product.

> - *Mobile devices*—mobile phones, small tablets, and other small personal devices that contain built-in computing or Internet capabilities.

> - *Personal computers*—fully functioning portable or desktop computers that are designed to be used by a single individual at a time.

> - *Servers*—computers that host data and programs available to a small group of users.

> - *Mainframe computers*—powerful computers used to host a large amount of data and programs available to a wide group of users.

> - *Supercomputers*—extremely powerful computers used for complex computations and processing.

In practice, classifying a computer into one of these six categories is not always easy or straightforward. For example, some high-end personal computers today are as powerful as servers, and some personal computers today are the size of a mobile phone or smaller (see the Trend box). In addition, new trends impact the categories. For example, small tablet devices (often called *mobile tablets*, *media tablets*, or just *tablets*) are typically considered mobile devices because they are only slightly larger than a mobile phone, are typically used primarily for viewing Web content and displaying *multimedia* content instead of general-purpose computing, and usually run a mobile operating system. However, larger, more powerful tablet computers running a desktop operating system are typically considered personal computers. So even though the distinction between some of the categories (particularly mobile devices and personal computers) is blurring, these six categories are commonly used today to refer to groups of computers designed for similar purposes.

Embedded Computers

An **embedded computer** is a tiny computer embedded into a product designed to perform specific tasks or functions for that product. For example, computers are often embedded into household appliances (such as dishwashers, microwaves, ovens, coffeemakers, and so forth), as well as into other everyday objects (such as thermostats, answering machines, treadmills, sewing machines, DVD players, and televisions), to help those appliances and objects perform their designated tasks. Typically, cars also use many embedded computers to assist with diagnostics, to notify the user of important conditions (such as an underinflated tire or an oil filter that needs changing), to control the use of the airbag and other safety devices (such as cameras that alert a driver that a vehicle is in his or her blind spot—see Figure 1-12—or

FIGURE 1-12
Embedded computers. This car's embedded computers control numerous features, such as notifying the driver when a car enters his or her blind spot.

A camera located under the mirror detects moving vehicles in the driver's blind spot.

A light indicates that a moving vehicle is in the driver's blind spot.

Courtesy Volvo Cars of North America

>**Embedded computer.** A tiny computer embedded in a product and designed to perform specific tasks or functions for that product.

TREND

Tiny PCs

Computers have shrunk again. Forget tiny notebooks or even media tablets if you want portability—today's newest tiny PCs are the size of a USB flash drive.

Some of these new computers actually do look just like a USB flash drive; others are just a small circuit board, sometimes enclosed in a case. Whatever their appearance, the idea is similar—you connect them to a display device and an input device (if needed) and you are good to go.

These emerging tiny PCs are designed to connect in different ways and have different capabilities. For example, Google's *Chromecast* (shown in the accompanying photo) plugs directly into an HDTV using its built-in HMDI connector. After connecting Chromecast, you can stream online content (such as videos, movies, and music) via Wi-Fi from your smartphone, tablet, or laptop to that HDTV. The *Raspberry Pi* tiny PC can connect to an HDTV via HDMI, as well as to a standard TV via RCA jacks. Instead of being used in conjunction with another device like Chromecast, however, the Raspberry Pi is a stand-alone computer that can be used with USB input devices (such as a keyboard and mouse) and connects to the Internet via an Ethernet port. Another tiny stand-alone PC is the *Cstick Cotton Candy*. This device, the size of a USB flash drive, can connect to another computer or an HDTV via its built-in HDMI and USB ports, to peripheral devices via USB or Bluetooth, and to the Internet via Wi-Fi.

The flexibility of these devices and the apps that can be used with them vary from device to device, based on the operating system used (most use a version of Linux or Android, though Chromecast uses Chrome) and the amount of storage available (devices with a USB port typically support USB flash drives or hard drives for additional storage if needed). But for turning a TV at any location into your own personal computer, gaming device, or video player, tiny PCs are definitely the way to go.

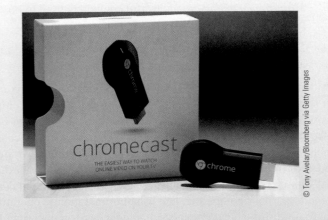

© Tony Avelar/Bloomberg via Getty Images

auto braking systems that engage when a front collision is imminent, as discussed in the Chapter 5 Technology and You box), to facilitate the car's navigational or entertainment systems, and to help the driver perform tasks. Embedded computers are designed for specific tasks and specific products and so cannot be used as general-purpose computers.

Mobile Devices

A **mobile device** is loosely defined as a very small (typically pocket-sized) device that has built-in computing or Internet capability. Mobile phones are the most common type of mobile device and can typically be used to make telephone calls, send *text messages* (short text-based messages), view Web pages, take digital photos, play games, download and play music, watch TV shows, and access calendars and other personal productivity features. Mobile phones that include computing and Internet capabilities (such as the one in Figure 1-13) are called **smartphones** (less capable mobile phones are sometimes referred to as *feature phones*). Handheld gaming devices (such as the *Nintendo 3DS*), *portable digital media players* (such as the *iPod Touch*), *smart watches*, and other personal devices that include Internet capabilities can also be referred to as mobile devices. As previously mentioned, **media tablets** (such as the

---

>**Mobile device.** A very small device that has built-in computing or Internet capability. >**Smartphone.** A mobile device based on a mobile phone that includes Internet capabilities and can run mobile apps. >**Media tablet.** A mobile device, usually larger than a smartphone, that is typically used to access the Internet and display multimedia content.

one shown in Figure 1-13) designed for Web browsing, playing movies and other multimedia content, gaming, and similar activities are also typically considered mobile devices. Mobile devices are almost always powered by a rechargeable battery system and typically include wireless connectivity to enable the device to connect to a wireless hotspot or to a *cellular provider* for Internet access.

Today's mobile devices typically have small screens and some, but not all, have keyboards. Because of this, mobile devices are most appropriate for individuals wanting continual access to e-mail, brief checks of Web content (such as doing a quick Web search, checking movie times or weather forecasts, looking up driving directions, or getting updates from Web sites like Facebook), and music collections rather than for those individuals wanting general Web browsing and computing capabilities. This is beginning to change, however, as mobile devices continue to grow in capabilities, as wireless communications continue to become faster, and as mobile input options (such as voice and touch input, and mobile keyboards) continue to improve. For instance, many mobile devices can perform Internet searches and other tasks via voice commands, some can be used to pay for purchases while you are on the go, many can view virtually any Web content, and some can view and edit documents stored in a common format, such as *Microsoft Office* documents. For a look at how tech clothing can be used to organize your mobile devices while you are on the go, see the Inside the Industry box.

SMARTPHONES   **MEDIA TABLETS**

Courtesy HTC / Courtesy Amazon

FIGURE 1-13
Mobile devices.

Personal Computers (PCs)

A **personal computer** (**PC**) or **microcomputer** is a small computer designed to be used by one person at a time. Personal computers are widely used by individuals and businesses today and are available in a variety of shapes and sizes, as discussed next.

> **TIP**
>
> For tips on buying a personal computer, see the "Guide to Buying a PC" in the References and Resources Guide located at the end of this book.

CAUTION CAUTION CAUTION CAUTION CAUTION CAUTION CAUT

Because many mobile devices and personal computers today are continually connected to the Internet, securing those devices against *computer viruses* and *hackers*—as introduced later in this chapter and discussed in detail in Chapter 9—is essential for both individuals and businesses.

FIGURE 1-14
Desktop computers.

Desktop Computers

Conventional personal computers that are designed to fit on or next to a desk (see Figure 1-14) are often referred to as **desktop computers**. Desktop computers can use a *tower case* (designed to sit vertically, typically on the floor), a *desktop case* (designed to be placed horizontally on a desk's surface), or an *all-in-one case* (designed to incorporate the monitor and system unit into a single piece of hardware).

TOWER COMPUTERS   **ALL-IN-ONE COMPUTERS**

Courtesy Dell Inc.; Courtesy Lenovo

> **Personal computer (PC).** A type of computer based on a microprocessor and designed to be used by one person at a time; also called a **microcomputer**. > **Desktop computer.** A personal computer designed to fit on or next to a desk.

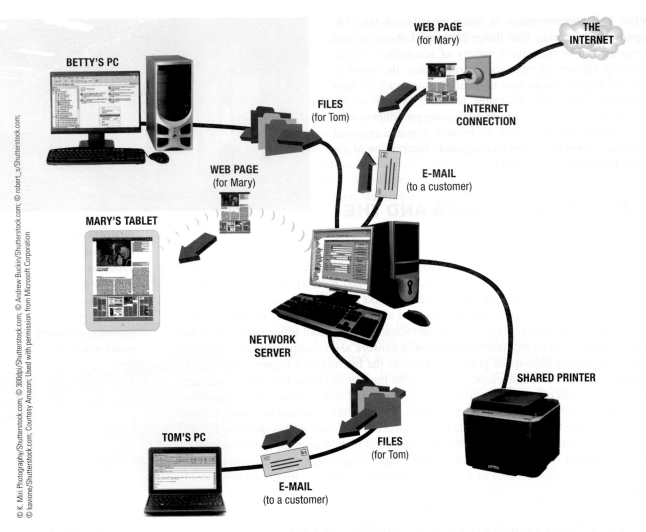

© K. Miri Photography/Shutterstock.com; © 300dpi/Shutterstock.com; © Andrew Buckin/Shutterstock.com; © robert_s/Shutterstock.com; © kavione/Shutterstock.com; Courtesy Amazon; Used with permission from Microsoft Corporation

FIGURE 1-20
Example of a
computer network.

and accessing content located on *Web pages*. While the term *Internet* refers to the physical structure of that network, the **World Wide Web** (**WWW**) refers to one resource—a collection of documents called **Web pages**—available through the Internet. A group of Web pages belonging to one individual or company is called a **Web site**. Web pages are stored on computers (called **Web servers**) that are continually connected to the Internet; they can be accessed at any time by anyone with a computer (or other Web-enabled device) and an Internet connection. A wide variety of information is available via Web pages, such as company and product information, government forms and publications, maps, telephone directories, news, weather, sports results, airline schedules, and much, much more. You can also use Web pages to shop, bank, trade stock, and perform other types of online financial transactions; access *social media* like *Facebook* and *Google+* social networking sites and *blogs*; and listen to music, play games, watch television shows, and perform other entertainment-oriented activities (see Figure 1-21). Web pages are viewed using a **Web browser**, such as *Internet Explorer (IE)*, *Chrome*, *Safari*, *Opera*, or *Firefox*.

✓ TIP

Although some people use the terms *Internet* and *Web* interchangeably, technically the Web—the collection of Web pages available over the Internet—is only one resource available via the Internet.

>**World Wide Web (WWW).** The collection of Web pages available through the Internet. >**Web page.** A document, typically containing hyperlinks to other documents, located on a Web server and available through the World Wide Web. >**Web site.** A collection of related Web pages usually belonging to an organization or individual. >**Web server.** A computer that is continually connected to the Internet and hosts Web pages that are accessible through the Internet. >**Web browser.** A program used to view Web pages.

LOOKING UP INFORMATION

ACCESSING SOCIAL NETWORKS

WATCHING VIDEOS, TV SHOWS, AND MOVIES

FIGURE 1-21
Some common Web activities.

Accessing a Network or the Internet

To access a local computer network (such as a home network, a school or company network, or a public wireless hotspot), you need to use a network adapter (either built into your computer or attached to it) to connect your computer to the network. With some computer networks you need to supply logon information (such as a *username* and a password) to *log on* to a network. Once you are connected to the network, you can access network resources, including the network's Internet connection. If you are connecting to the Internet without going through a computer network, your computer needs to use a modem to connect to the communications media (such as a telephone line, cable connection, or wireless signal) used by your ISP to deliver Internet content. Network adapters and modems are discussed in more detail in Chapter 7.

Most Internet connections today are *direct* (or *always-on*) *connections*, which means the computer or other device being used to access the Internet is continually connected to the ISP's computer. With a direct connection, you only need to open your Web browser to begin using the Internet. With a *dial-up connection*, however, you must start the program that instructs your computer to dial and connect to the ISP's server via a telephone line, and then open a Web browser, each time you want to access the Internet.

To request a Web page or other resource located on the Internet, its **Internet address**—a unique numeric or text-based address—is used. The most common types of Internet addresses are *IP addresses* and *domain names* (to identify computers), *URLs* (to identify Web pages), and *e-mail addresses* (to identify people).

>**Internet address.** An address that identifies a computer, person, or Web page on the Internet, such as an IP address, domain name, or e-mail address.

IP Addresses and Domain Names

IP addresses and their corresponding **domain names** are used to identify computers available through the Internet. IP (short for *Internet Protocol*) addresses are numeric, such as *207.46.197.32*, and are commonly used by computers to refer to other computers. A computer that hosts information available through the Internet (such as a Web server hosting Web pages) usually has a unique text-based domain name (such as *microsoft. com*) that corresponds to that computer's IP address in order to make it easier for people to request Web pages located on that computer. IP addresses and domain names are unique; that is, there cannot be two computers on the Internet using the exact same IP address or exact same domain name. To ensure this, specific IP addresses are allocated to each network (such as a company network or an ISP) to be used with the computers on that network, and there is a worldwide registration system for domain name registration. When a domain name is registered, the IP address of the computer that will be hosting the Web site associated with that domain name is also registered; the Web site can be accessed using either its domain name or corresponding IP address. When a Web site is requested using its domain name, the corresponding IP address is looked up using one of the Internet's *domain name system* (*DNS*) *servers* and then the appropriate Web page is displayed. While today's IP addresses (called *IPv4*) have 4 parts separated by periods, the newer *IPv6* addresses have 6 parts separated by colons in order to have significantly more unique addresses. The transition from IPv4 to IPv6 is necessary because of the vast number of devices connecting to the Internet today.

Domain names typically reflect the name of the individual or organization associated with that Web site and the different parts of a domain name are separated by a period. The far right part of the domain name (which begins with the rightmost period) is called the *top-level domain* (*TLD*) and traditionally identifies the type of organization or its location (such as *.com* for businesses, *.edu* for educational institutions, *.jp* for Web sites located in Japan, or *.fr* for Web sites located in France). The part of the domain name that precedes the TLD is called the *second-level domain name* and typically reflects the name of a company or an organization, a product, or an individual. There were seven original TLDs used in the United States; additional TLDs and numerous two-letter *country code TLDs* have since been created (see some examples in Figure 1-22) and more are in the works. More than 250 million domain names are registered worldwide.

ORIGINAL TLDS	INTENDED USE
.com	Commercial businesses
.edu	Educational institutions
.gov	Government organizations
.int	International treaty organizations
.mil	Military organizations
.net	Network providers and ISPs
.org	Noncommercial organizations

NEWER TLDS	INTENDED USE
.aero	Aviation industry
.biz	Businesses
.fr	French businesses
.info	Resource sites
.jobs	Employment sites
.mobi	Sites optimized for mobile devices
.name	Individuals
.pro	Licensed professionals
.uk	United Kingdom businesses

FIGURE 1-22
Sample top-level domains (TLDs).

TIP

Only the legitimate holder of a trademarked name (such as Microsoft) can use that trademarked name as a domain name (such as microsoft.com); trademarks are discussed in detail in Chapter 16.

Uniform Resource Locators (URLs)

Similar to the way an IP address or domain name uniquely identifies a computer on the Internet, a **Uniform Resource Locator** (**URL**) uniquely identifies a specific Web page (including the *protocol* or standard being used to display the Web page, the Web server hosting the Web page, the name of any folders on the Web server in which the Web page file is stored, and the Web page's filename, if needed).

>**IP address.** A numeric Internet address used to uniquely identify a computer on the Internet. >**Domain name.** A text-based Internet address used to uniquely identify a computer on the Internet. >**Uniform Resource Locator (URL).** An Internet address (usually beginning with http://) that uniquely identifies a Web page.

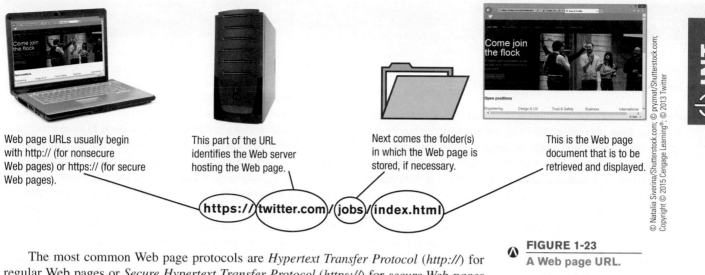

Web page URLs usually begin with http:// (for nonsecure Web pages) or https:// (for secure Web pages).

This part of the URL identifies the Web server hosting the Web page.

Next comes the folder(s) in which the Web page is stored, if necessary.

This is the Web page document that is to be retrieved and displayed.

https:// twitter.com / jobs / index.html

FIGURE 1-23
A Web page URL.

The most common Web page protocols are *Hypertext Transfer Protocol* (*http://*) for regular Web pages or *Secure Hypertext Transfer Protocol* (*https://*) for *secure Web pages* that can safely be used to transmit sensitive information, such as credit card numbers. *File Transfer Protocol* (*ftp://*) is sometimes used to upload and download files. The *file extension* used in the Web page filename indicates the type of Web page that will be displayed (such as *.html* and *.htm* for standard Web pages created using *Hypertext Markup Language*, as discussed in Chapter 10). For example, looking at the URL for the Web page shown in Figure 1-23 from right to left, we can see that the Web page is called *index.html*, is stored in a folder called *jobs* on the Web server associated with the *twitter.com* domain, and is a secure Web page because the *https://* protocol is being used.

E-Mail Addresses

To contact people using the Internet, you often use their **e-mail addresses**. An e-mail address consists of a **username** (an identifying name), followed by the @ symbol, followed by the domain name for the computer that will be handling that person's e-mail (called a *mail server*). For example,

jsmith@cengage.com
maria_s@cengage.com
sam.peterson@cengage.com

are the e-mail addresses assigned respectively to jsmith (John Smith), maria_s (Maria Sanchez), and sam.peterson (Sam Peterson), three hypothetical employees at Cengage Learning, the publisher of this textbook. Usernames are typically a combination of the person's first and last names and sometimes include periods, underscores, and numbers, but cannot include blank spaces. To ensure a unique e-mail address for everyone in the world, usernames must be unique within each domain name. So, even though there could be a *jsmith* at Cengage Learning using the e-mail address *jsmith@cengage.com* and a *jsmith* at Stanford University using the e-mail address *jsmith@stanford.edu*, the two e-mail addresses are unique. It is up to each organization with a registered domain name to ensure that one—and only one—exact same username is assigned to its domain. Using e-mail addresses to send e-mail messages is discussed later in this chapter; other forms of online communications—such as text messaging and chat—are covered in Chapter 8. For a look at how online communications are being used to help keep college students safe, see the How It Works box.

> **E-mail address.** An Internet address consisting of a username and computer domain name that uniquely identifies a person on the Internet.
> **Username.** A name that uniquely identifies a user on a specific computer network.

HOW IT WORKS

Campus Emergency Notification Systems

Recent emergencies, such as school shootings and dangerous weather, have increased attention on ways organizations can quickly and effectively notify a large number of individuals. Following the Virginia Tech tragedy in 2007, which involved a shooting rampage lasting about two hours and killing more than 30 individuals, the *Higher Education Opportunity Act* was signed into law. The law provides grants and other assistance to colleges and universities to create an emergency communications system that can be used to contact students when a significant emergency or dangerous situation emerges. In response, colleges across the United States are implementing emergency notification systems to notify students, faculty, staff, and campus visitors of an emergency, severe weather condition, campus closure, or other critical event.

Because nearly all college students in the United States today have mobile phones, sending emergency alerts via text message is a natural option. To be able to send a text message to an entire campus typically requires the use of a company that specializes in this type of mass communications. One such company is *Omnilert*, which has systems installed in more than 800 colleges and universities around the country. With the Omnilert campus notification system—called *e2Campus*—the contact information of the students, faculty, and staff to be notified is entered into the system and then the individuals can be divided into groups, depending on the types of messages each individual should receive. Individuals can also opt in to alerts via text message. When an alert needs to be sent, an administrator sends the message (via a mobile phone or computer) and it is distributed to the appropriate individuals (see the accompanying illustration). In addition to text messages, alerts can also be sent simultaneously and automatically via virtually any voice or text communications medium, such as voice messages, e-mail messages, RSS feeds, instant messages, Twitter feeds, Facebook pages, school Web pages, personal portal pages, desktop pop-up alerts, TTY/TDD devices, digital signage systems (such as signs located inside dorms and the student union), indoor and outdoor campus public address (PA) systems, information hotlines, and more.

To facilitate campus emergency notification systems, some colleges now require all undergraduate students to have a mobile phone. Some campuses also implement other useful mobile services, such as tracking campus shuttle buses, participating in class polls, accessing class assignments and grades, and texting tips about suspicious activities or crimes to campus security. An additional safety feature available at some schools is the ability to use the phones to activate an alert whenever a student feels unsafe on campus; these alerts automatically send the student's physical location (determined via the phone's GPS coordinates) to the campus police so the student can be located quickly.

Courtesy of Omnilert LLC

Pronouncing Internet Addresses

Because Internet addresses are frequently given verbally, it is important to know how to pronounce them. A few guidelines are listed next, and Figure 1-24 shows some examples of Internet addresses and their proper pronunciations.

➤ If a portion of the address forms a recognizable word or name, it is spoken; otherwise, it is spelled out.

➤ The @ sign is pronounced *at*.

➤ The period (.) is pronounced *dot*.

➤ The forward slash (/) is pronounced *slash*.

TYPE OF ADDRESS	SAMPLE ADDRESS	PRONUNCIATION
Domain name	berkeley.edu	berkeley dot e d u
URL	microsoft.com/windows/ie/default.asp	microsoft dot com slash windows slash i e slash default dot a s p
E-mail address	president@whitehouse.gov	president at white house dot gov

Surfing the Web

Once you have an Internet connection, you are ready to begin *surfing the Web*—that is, using a Web browser to view Web pages. The first page that your Web browser displays when it is opened is your browser's starting page or *home page*. Often this is the home page for the Web site belonging to your browser, school, or ISP. However, you can use your browser's customization options to change the current home page to any page that you plan to visit regularly. From your browser's home page, you can move to any Web page you desire, as discussed next.

Using URLs and Hyperlinks

To navigate to a new Web page for which you know the URL, type that URL in the browser's *Address bar* (shown in Figure 1-25) and press Enter. Once that page is displayed, you can use the *hyperlinks*—graphics or text linked to other Web pages—located on that page to display other Web pages. In addition to Web pages, hyperlinks can also be linked to other types of files, such as to enable Web visitors to view or download images, listen to or download music files, view video clips, or download software programs.

The most commonly used Web browsers include Internet Explorer (shown in Figure 1-25), Chrome (shown in Figure 1-26), Safari, and Firefox. Most browsers today include *tabbed browsing* (which allows you to have multiple Web pages open at the same time and to drag a tab to move that window), the ability to search for Web pages using the Address bar, and tools for *bookmarking* and revisiting Web pages, as discussed shortly. Browsers today also typically include security features to help notify you of possible threats as you browse the Web, *download managers* to help you manage your downloaded files, and *crash recovery* features, such as the ability to open the last set of Web pages that

FIGURE 1-24
Pronouncing Internet addresses.

TIP

The *home page* for a Web site is the starting page of that particular site; the *home page* for your browser is the Web page designated as the first page you see each time the browser is opened.

FIGURE 1-25
Surfing the Web with Internet Explorer. URLs, hyperlinks, and favorites can be used to display Web pages.

BACK AND FORWARD BUTTONS Move between Web pages that have been recently viewed.

ADDRESS BAR Type a URL in the Address bar and press Enter to display the corresponding Web page.

HYPERLINKS Point to a hyperlink to see the corresponding URL on the status bar; click the hyperlink to display that page.

STATUS BAR Displays URLs as well as includes zoom options and security indicators.

TABS Click the rightmost tab to open a new tab.

FAVORITES LIST Click a page name to display that Web page.

HOME, FAVORITES, AND TOOLS BUTTONS Display your home page, Favorites list, and Tools menu, respectively.

Courtesy NASA

were open before you accidentally closed your browser or before the browser or computer *crashed* (stopped working). In any browser, you can use the Back button to return to a previous page and the Home button to display your browser's home page. To print the current Web page, click the Tools button in Internet Explorer and select *Print* from the displayed menu.

Using Favorites and the History List

All Web browsers have a feature (usually called *Favorites* or *Bookmarks* and accessed via a Favorites or Bookmarks menu, button, or bar) that you can use to save Web page URLs. Once a Web page is saved as a favorite or a bookmark, you can redisplay that page without typing its URL—you simply select its link from the Favorites or Bookmarks list (refer again to Figure 1-25). You can also use this feature to save a group of tabbed Web pages to open the entire group again at a later time. Web browsers also maintain a *History list*, which is a record of all Web pages visited during the period of time specified in the browser settings; you can revisit a Web page located on the History list by displaying the History list and selecting that page.

Most Web browsers today allow you to delete, move into folders, and otherwise organize your favorites/bookmarks, as well as to search your favorites/bookmarks or History list to help you find pages more easily. In Windows 8, you can also *pin* (lock) a Web page to keep it handy—drag the site's icon on the left of the Address bar to pin a site to the Windows taskbar; use the Tools menu to add the site to your Start screen.

Because many individuals use multiple devices (such as a personal computer and a smartphone) to surf the Web today, it is becoming more common to want to *sync* your browser settings (such as bookmarks, history, passwords, and so forth) across all of your devices. Most browsers today have synching capabilities; typically an online account (such as your Google account for Chrome or your SkyDrive account for Internet Explorer) is used to securely sync the devices.

Searching the Web

People typically turn to the Web to find specific types of information. There are a number of special Web pages, called *search sites*, available to help you locate what you are looking for on the Internet. One of the most popular search sites—*Google*—is shown in Figure 1-26. To conduct a search, you typically type one or more *keywords* into the search box on a search site, and a list of links to Web pages matching your search criteria is displayed. There are also numerous *reference sites* available on the Web to look up addresses, phone numbers, ZIP codes, maps, and other information. To find a reference site, type the information you are looking for (such as "ZIP code lookup" or "topographical maps") in a search site's search box to see links to sites containing that information. Searching the Web is discussed in more detail in Chapter 8.

E-Mail

Electronic mail (more commonly called **e-mail**) is the process of exchanging electronic messages between computers

FIGURE 1-26
The Google search site displayed in the Chrome browser.

OTHER SEARCHES
Use these options to search for images, maps, videos, news, video, products for sale, and more, as well as access your Gmail, Google Drive, or Google Calendar.

Google Chrome screenshot © Google Inc.

KEYWORD SEARCHES
Because the Search option is selected, type keywords here and press Enter to see a list of Web pages matching your search criteria.

> **Electronic mail (e-mail).** Electronic messages sent from one user to another over the Internet or other network.

over a network—usually the Internet. E-mail is one of the most widely used Internet applications—Americans alone send billions of e-mail messages daily and use of *mobile e-mail* (e-mail sent via a mobile device) is growing at an astounding rate. You can send an e-mail message from any Internet-enabled device (such as a personal computer or mobile device) to anyone who has an Internet e-mail address. As illustrated in Figure 1-27, e-mail messages travel from the sender's device to his or her ISP's *mail server*, and then through the Internet to the mail server being used by the recipient's ISP. When the recipient's computer retrieves new e-mail (typically on a regular basis as long as the computer is powered up, connected to the Internet, and the e-mail program is open), it is displayed on the computer he or she is using. In addition to text, e-mail messages can include attached files, such as documents, photos, and videos.

E-mail can be sent and received via an *e-mail program*, such as *Microsoft Outlook* or *Mac OS X Mail*, installed on the computer being used (sometimes referred to as *conventional e-mail*) or via a Web page belonging to a Web mail provider such as *Gmail* or *Outlook.com* (typically called *Web mail*). Using an installed e-mail program is convenient for individuals who use e-mail often and want to have copies of sent and received e-mail messages stored on their computer. To use an installed e-mail program, however, it must first be set up with the user's name, e-mail address, incoming mail server, and outgoing mail server information. Web mail does not require this setup and a user's e-mail can be accessed from any device with an Internet connection by just displaying the appropriate Web mail page and logging on. Consequently, Web-based e-mail is more flexible than conventional e-mail because it can be accessed easily from any computer or other device with an Internet connection. However, Web mail is typically slower than conventional e-mail and messages can only be viewed when the user is online and logged on to his or her Web mail account, unless an e-mail program is used to download the e-mail messages to a computer.

Web-based e-mail is typically free and virtually all ISPs used with personal computers include e-mail service in their monthly fee. Mobile e-mail may require a fee, depending on the data plan being used. Other types of mobile communications, such as text messages and multimedia messages that typically use the *Short Message Service (SMS)* and *Multimedia Message Service (MMS)* protocols, respectively, may also incur a fee. Messaging and other types of online communications that can be used in addition to e-mail are discussed in Chapter 8.

FIGURE 1-27
How e-mail works.

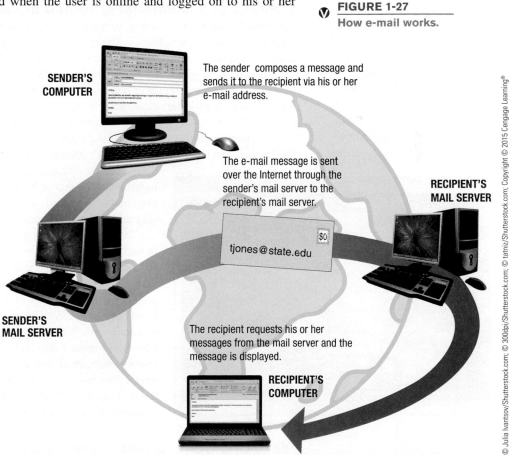

SENDER'S COMPUTER

The sender composes a message and sends it to the recipient via his or her e-mail address.

The e-mail message is sent over the Internet through the sender's mail server to the recipient's mail server.

RECIPIENT'S MAIL SERVER

tjones@state.edu $0

SENDER'S MAIL SERVER

The recipient requests his or her messages from the mail server and the message is displayed.

RECIPIENT'S COMPUTER

COMPUTERS AND SOCIETY

The vast improvements in technology over the past decade have had a distinct impact on daily life, both at home and at work. Computers have become indispensable tools in our personal and professional lives, and related technological advancements have changed the way our everyday items—cars, microwaves, coffeepots, toys, exercise bikes, telephones, televisions, and more—look and function. As computers and everyday devices become smarter, they tend to do their intended jobs faster, better, and more reliably than before, as well as take on additional capabilities. In addition to affecting individuals, computerization and technological advances have changed society as a whole. Without computers, banks would be overwhelmed by the job of tracking all the transactions they process, moon exploration and the space shuttle would still belong to science fiction, and some scientific advances—such as DNA analysis and gene mapping—would be nonexistent. In addition, we as individuals are getting accustomed to the increased automation of everyday activities, such as shopping and banking, and we depend on having fast and easy access to information via the Internet and rapid communications via e-mail and messaging. In addition, many of us would not think about making a major purchase without first researching it online. In fact, it is surprising how fast the Internet and its resources have become an integral part of our society. But despite all its benefits, *cyberspace* has some risks. Some of the most important societal implications related to computers and the Internet are introduced next; many of these issues are covered in more detail in later chapters of this text.

Benefits of a Computer-Oriented Society

The benefits of having such a computer-oriented society are numerous, as touched on throughout this chapter. The capability to virtually design, build, and test new buildings, cars, and airplanes before the actual construction begins helps professionals create safer end products. Technological advances in medicine allow for earlier diagnosis and more effective treatment of diseases than ever before. The benefit of beginning medical students performing virtual surgery using a computer instead of performing actual surgery on a patient is obvious. The ability to shop, pay bills, research products, participate in online courses, and look up vast amounts of information 24 hours a day, 7 days a week, 365 days a year via the Internet is a huge convenience. In addition, a computer-oriented society generates new opportunities. For example, technologies—such as *speech recognition software* and Braille input and output devices—enable physically- or visually-challenged individuals to perform necessary job tasks and to communicate with others more easily.

In general, technology has also made a huge number of tasks in our lives go much faster. Instead of experiencing a long delay for a credit check, an applicant can get approved for a purchase, loan, or credit card almost immediately. Documents and photographs can be e-mailed or faxed in mere moments, instead of taking at least a day to be mailed physically. We can watch many of our favorite TVs shows online (such as the *Survivor* episode shown in Figure 1-28) and access up-to-the-minute news at our convenience. And we can download information, programs, music files, movies, and more on demand when we want or need them, instead of having to order them and then wait for delivery or physically go to a store to purchase the desired items.

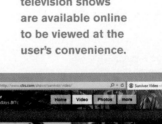

FIGURE 1-28
Episodes of many television shows are available online to be viewed at the user's convenience.

CBS Broadcasting Inc.

Risks of a Computer-Oriented Society

Although there are a great number of benefits from having a computer-oriented society and a *networked economy*, there are risks as well. A variety of problems have emerged from our extensive computer use, ranging from stress and health concerns, to the proliferation of *spam* (unsolicited e-mails) and *malware* (harmful programs that can be installed on our computers without our knowledge), to security and privacy issues, to legal and ethical dilemmas. Many of the security and privacy concerns stem from the fact that so much of our personal business takes place online—or at least ends up as data in a computer database somewhere—and the potential for misuse of this data is enormous. Another concern is the repercussions of collecting such vast amounts of information electronically. Some people worry about creating a "Big Brother" situation, in which the government or another organization is watching everything that we do. Although the accumulation and distribution of information is a necessary factor of our networked economy, it is one area of great concern to many individuals. And some Internet behavior, such as downloading music or movies from an unauthorized source or viewing pornography on an office computer, can get you arrested or fired.

Security Issues

One of the most common online security risks today is your computer becoming infected with a malware program, such as a *computer virus*—a malicious software program designed to change the way a computer operates. Malware often causes damage to the infected computer, such as erasing data or bogging down the computer so it does not function well. It can also be used to try to locate sensitive data on your computer (such as Web site passwords or credit card numbers) and send that data to the malware creator or to take control of your computer to use as part of a *botnet* (a network of computers used without their owners' knowledge) for criminal activities. Malware is typically installed by downloading a program that secretly contains malware or by clicking a link on a Web page or in an e-mail message that then installs malware. In addition to computers, malware and other security threats are increasingly being directed toward smartphones and other mobile devices. To help protect your computer or mobile device, never open an e-mail attachment from someone you do not know or that has an executable *file extension* (the last three letters in the filename preceded by a period), such as *.exe*, *.com*, or *.vbs*, without checking with the sender first to make sure the attachment is legitimate. You should also be careful about what files you download from the Internet. In addition, it is crucial to install *security software* on your computer and mobile devices and to set up the program to monitor your devices on a continual basis (see Figure 1-29). If a virus or other type of malware attempts to install itself on your computer or mobile device (such as through an e-mail message attachment or a Web link), the security program will block it. If malware does find its way onto your computer or mobile device, the security program will detect it during a regular scan, notify you, and attempt to remove it.

Another ongoing security problem is *identity theft*—in which someone else uses your identity, typically to purchase goods or services. Identity theft can stem from personal information discovered from offline means—like discarded papers or stolen mail—or from information found online, stolen from an online database, or obtained via a malware program. *Phishing*—in which identity thieves send fraudulent e-mails to people masquerading as legitimate businesses to obtain Social Security numbers or other information needed for identity theft—is also a major security issue today. Common security concerns and precautions, such as protecting your computer from malware and protecting yourself against identity theft and phishing schemes, are discussed in detail in Chapter 9.

Privacy Issues

Some individuals view the potential risk to personal privacy as one of the most important issues regarding our networked society. As more and more data about our everyday activities is collected and stored on devices accessible via the Internet, our privacy is at risk because the potential for privacy violations increases. Today, data is collected about practically anything we buy online or offline, although offline purchases may not be associated with our identity unless we use a credit card or a membership or loyalty card. At issue is not that data is collected—with virtually all organizations using computers for recordkeeping, that is unavoidable—but rather how the collected data is used and how secure it is. Data collected by businesses may be used only by that company or, depending on the businesses' *privacy*

FIGURE 1-29
Security software.
Security software is crucial for protecting your computer and mobile devices from malware and other threats.

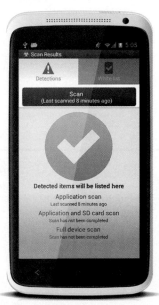

Courtesy Bullguard

policy, may be shared with others. Data shared with others often results in spam, which is considered by many to be a violation of personal privacy. Privacy concerns and precautions are discussed in detail in Chapter 15.

CAUTION CAUTION CAUTION CAUTION CAUTION CAUTION CAUT

Using your primary e-mail address when shopping online or signing up for a sweepstake or other online activity will undoubtedly result in spam being sent to that e-mail address. Use a *throw-away e-mail address* (a free e-mail address from Gmail or another free e-mail provider that you can change easily) for these activities instead to help protect your privacy and cut back on the amount of spam delivered to your regular e-mail account.

Differences in Online Communications

There is no doubt that e-mail and other online communications methods have helped speed up both personal and business communications and have made them more efficient (such as avoiding the telephone tag problem). As you spend more and more time communicating online, you will probably notice some differences between online communications methods (such as e-mail and social networking updates) and traditional communications methods (such as telephone calls and written letters). In general, online communications tend to be much less formal and, in fact, many people compose and send e-mail messages quickly, without taking the time to reread the message content or check the spelling or grammar. However, you need to be careful not to be so casual—particularly in business—that your communications appear unprofessional or become too personal with people you do not know.

To help in that regard, a special etiquette—referred to as *netiquette*—has evolved to guide online behavior. A good rule of thumb is always to be polite and considerate of others and to refrain from offensive remarks. This holds true whether you are asking a question via a company's e-mail address, posting a message on someone's Facebook page, or messaging a friend. With business communications, you should also be very careful with your grammar and spelling to avoid embarrassing yourself. Some specific guidelines for proper online behavior are listed in Figure 1-30.

Another trend in online communications is the use of abbreviations and *emoticons*. Abbreviations or *acronyms*, such as BTW for "by the way," are commonly used to save time in all types of communications today. They are being used with increased frequency in text messaging and e-mail exchanged via mobile phones to speed up the text entry process. Emoticons are illustrations of faces showing smiles, frowns, and other expressions that are created with keyboard symbols—such as the popular :-) smile emoticon—and allow people to add an emotional tone to written online communications. Without these symbols, it is sometimes difficult to tell if the person who sent the online communication is serious or joking because you cannot see the individual's face or hear his or her tone of voice.

FIGURE 1-30

Netiquette. Use these netiquette guidelines and common sense when communicating online.

RULE	EXPLANATION
Use descriptive subject lines	Use short, descriptive subject lines for e-mail messages and online posts. For example, "Question regarding MP3 downloads" is much better than a vague title, such as "Question."
Don't shout	SHOUTING REFERS TO TYPING YOUR ENTIRE E-MAIL MESSAGE OR ONLINE POST USING CAPITAL LETTERS. Use capital letters only when it is grammatically correct to do so or for emphasizing a few words.
Watch what you say	Things that you say or write online can be interpreted as being sexist, racist, or in just general bad taste. Also check spelling and grammar—typos look unprofessional and nobody likes wading through poorly written materials.
Don't spam your contacts	Don't hit *Reply All* to an e-mail when a simple *Reply* will do. The same goes for forwarding e-mail chain letters, *retweeting* every joke you run across, or sending every funny YouTube video you find—to everyone you know.
Be cautious	Don't give out personal information—such as your real name, telephone number, or credit card information—to people you meet online.
Think before you send or post	Once you send an e-mail or text message or post something online, you lose control of it. Don't include content (such as compromising photos of yourself) that you would not want shared with others, and don't tag people in photos that are unflattering to them. In addition, don't e-mail or post anything if emotions are running high—wait until you calm down.

While most people would agree that using abbreviations and emoticons with personal communications is fine, they are not usually viewed as appropriate for formal business communications.

The Anonymity Factor

By their very nature, online communications lend themselves to *anonymity*. Because recipients usually do not hear senders' voices or see their handwriting, it is difficult to know for sure who the sender is. Particularly on *forums* (online discussions in which users post messages and respond to other posts), in *virtual worlds* (online worlds that users can explore), and other online activities where individuals use made-up names instead of real names, there is an anonymous feel to being online.

Being anonymous gives many individuals a sense of freedom, which makes them feel able to say or do anything online. This sense of true freedom of speech can be beneficial. For example, a reserved individual who might never complain about a poor product or service in person may feel comfortable lodging a complaint by e-mail. In online discussions, many people feel they can be completely honest about what they think and can introduce new ideas and points of view without inhibition. Anonymous e-mail is also a safe way for an employee to blow the whistle on a questionable business practice, or for an individual to tip off police to a crime or potential terrorist attack.

But, like all good things, online anonymity can be abused. Using the Internet as their shield, some people use rude comments, ridicule, profanity, and even slander to attack people, places, and things they do not like or agree with. Others may use multiple online identities (such as multiple usernames on a message board) to give the appearance of increased support for their points of view. Still others may use multiple identities to try to manipulate stock prices (by posting false information about a company to drive the price down, for instance), to get buyers to trust an online auction seller (by posting fictitious positive feedback about themselves), or to commit other illegal or unethical acts.

It is possible to hide your true identity while browsing or sending e-mail by removing personal information from your browser and e-mail program or by using privacy software that acts as a middleman between you and Web sites and hides your identity, as discussed in more detail in Chapter 15. But, in fact, even when personal information is removed, ISPs and the government may still be able to trace communications back to a particular computer when a crime has occurred, so it is difficult—perhaps impossible—to be completely anonymous online.

Information Integrity

The Web contains a vast amount of information on a wide variety of topics. While much of the information is factual, other information may be misleading, biased, or just plain wrong. As more and more people turn to the Web for information, it is crucial that they take the time to determine if the information they obtain and pass on to others is accurate. There have been numerous cases of information intended as a joke being restated on a Web site as fact, statements being quoted out of context (which changed the meaning from the original intent), and hoaxes circulated via e-mail. Consequently, use common sense when evaluating what you read online, and double-check information before passing it on to others.

One way to evaluate online content is by its source. If you obtain information from a news source that you trust, you should feel confident that the accuracy of its online information is close to that of its offline counterpart. For information about a particular product, go to the originating company. For government information, government Web sites are your best source for fact checking. There are also independent Web sites (such as the *Snopes* Web site shown in Figure 1-31) that report on the validity of current online rumors and stories.

FIGURE 1-31

Snopes.com. This Web site can be used to check out online rumors.

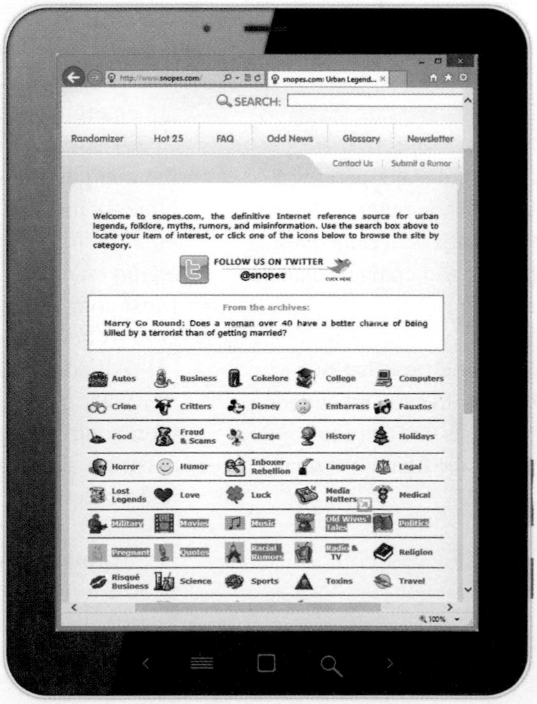

© robert_s/Shutterstock.com; Courtesy www.snopes.com

SUMMARY

COMPUTERS IN YOUR LIFE

Computers appear almost everywhere in today's world, and most people need to use a computer or a computerized device frequently on the job, at home, at school, or while on the go. **Computer literacy**, which is being familiar with basic computer concepts, helps individuals feel comfortable using computers and is a necessary skill for everyone today.

Computers abound in today's homes, schools, workplaces, and other locations. Most students and employees need to use a computer for productivity, research, or other important tasks. Individuals often use computers at home and/or carry portable computers or mobile devices with them to remain in touch with others or to use Internet resources on a continual basis. Individuals also frequently encounter computers while on the go, such as *consumer kiosks* and *point-of-sale (POS) systems*.

WHAT IS A COMPUTER AND WHAT DOES IT DO?

A **computer** is a *programmable* electronic device that accepts **input**; performs **processing** operations; **outputs** the results; and provides **storage** for data, programs, or output when needed. Most computers today also have **communications** capabilities. This progression of input, processing, output, and storage is sometimes called the *information processing cycle*.

Data is the raw, unorganized facts that are input into the computer to be processed. Data that the computer has processed into a useful form is called **information**. Data can exist in many forms, representing *text*, *graphics*, *audio*, and *video*.

One of the first calculating devices was the *abacus*. Early computing devices that predate today's computers include the *slide rule*, the *mechanical calculator*, and Dr. Herman Hollerith's *Punch Card Tabulating Machine and Sorter*. First-generation computers, such as *ENIAC* and *UNIVAC*, were powered by *vacuum tubes*; second-generation computers used *transistors*; and *third-generation computers* were possible because of the invention of the *integrated circuit (IC)*. Today's *fourth-generation computers* use *microprocessors* and are frequently connected to the *Internet* and other *networks*. *Fifth-generation computers* are emerging and are, at the present time, based on *artificial intelligence*.

A computer is made up of **hardware** (the actual physical equipment that makes up the computer system) and **software** (the computer's programs). Common hardware components include the *keyboard* and *mouse* (*input devices*), the *CPU* (a *processing device*), *monitors/display screens* and *printers* (*output devices*), and *storage devices* and *storage media* (such as *CDs*, *DVD drives, hard drives, USB flash drives*, and *flash memory cards*). Most computers today also include a *modem*, *network adapter*, or other type of *communications device* to allow users to connect to the Internet or other network.

All computers need *system software*, namely an **operating system** (usually *Windows*, *Mac OS*, or *Linux*), to function. The operating system assists with the **boot** process, and then controls the operation of the computer, such as to allow users to run other types of software and to manage their files. Most software programs today use a variety of graphical objects that are selected to tell the computer what to do. The basic workspace for Windows' users is the **Windows desktop**.

Application software (also called *apps*) consists of programs designed to allow people to perform specific tasks or applications, such as word processing, Web browsing, photo touch-up, and so on. Software programs are written using a *programming language*. Programs are written by *programmers*; *computer users* are the people who use computers to perform tasks or obtain information.

COMPUTERS TO FIT EVERY NEED

Embedded computers are built into products (such as cars and household appliances) to give them added functionality. **Mobile devices** are small devices (such as *mobile phones* and **media tablets**) with computing or Internet capabilities; an Internet-enabled mobile phone is called a **smartphone**.

Small computers used by individuals at home or work are called **personal computers (PCs)** or **microcomputers**. Most personal computers today are either **desktop computers** or **portable computers** (**notebook computers**, **laptop computers**, **tablet computers**, **hybrid notebook-tablet computers,** and **netbooks**) and typically conform to either the *PC-compatible* or *Mac* standard. **Thin clients** are designed solely to access a network; **Internet appliances** are ordinary devices that can be used to access the Internet.

Medium-sized computers, or **servers**, are used in many businesses to host data and programs to be accessed via the company network. A growing trend is **virtualization**, such as creating separate virtual environments on a single server that act as separate servers or delivering each users' desktop to his or her device. The powerful computers used by most large businesses and organizations to perform the information processing necessary for day-to-day operations are called **mainframe computers**. The very largest, most powerful computers, which typically run one application at a time, are **supercomputers**.

COMPUTER NETWORKS AND THE INTERNET

Computer networks are used to connect individual computers and related devices so that users can share hardware, software, and data as well as communicate with one another. The **Internet** is a worldwide collection of networks. Typically, individual users connect to the Internet by connecting to computers belonging to an **Internet service provider (ISP)**—a company that provides Internet access, usually for a fee. One resource available through the Internet is the **World Wide Web** (**WWW**)—an enormous collection of **Web pages** located on **Web servers**. The starting page for a **Web site** (a related group of Web pages) is called the *home page* for that site. Web pages are viewed with a **Web browser**, are connected with *hyperlinks*, and can be used for many helpful activities.

To access a computer network, you need some type of *modem* or *network adapter*. To access the Internet, an Internet service provider (ISP) is also used. **Internet addresses** are used to identify resources on the Internet and include numerical **IP addresses** and text-based **domain names** (used to identify computers), **Uniform Resource Locators** or **URLs** (used to identify Web pages), and **e-mail addresses** (a combination of a **username** and domain name that is used to send an individual e-mail messages).

Web pages are displayed by clicking hyperlinks or by typing appropriate URLs in the browser's *Address bar. Favorites/Bookmarks* and the *History list* can be used to redisplay a previously visited Web page and *search sites* can be used to locate Web pages matching specified criteria. **Electronic mail (e-mail)** is used to send electronic messages over the Internet.

COMPUTERS AND SOCIETY

Computers and devices based on related technology have become indispensable tools for modern life, making ordinary tasks easier and quicker than ever before and helping make today's worker more productive than ever before. In addition to the benefits, however, there are many risks and societal implications related to our heavy use of the Internet and the vast amount of information available through the Internet. Issues include privacy and security risks and concerns (such as *malware*, *identity theft*, *phishing*, and *spam*), the differences in online and offline communications, the anonymity factor, and the amount of unreliable information that can be found on the Internet.

Chapter Objective 6:
List the six basic types of computers, giving at least one example of each type of computer and stating what that computer might be used for.

Chapter Objective 7:
Explain what a network, the Internet, and the World Wide Web are, as well as how computers, people, and Web pages are identified on the Internet.

Chapter Objective 8:
Describe how to access a Web page and navigate through a Web site.

Chapter Objective 9:
Discuss the societal impact of computers, including some benefits and risks related to their prominence in our society.

REVIEW ACTIVITIES

KEY TERM MATCHING

a. computer

b. hardware

c. Internet

d. processing

e. software

f. storage

g. supercomputer

h. tablet computer

i. Uniform Resource Locator (URL)

j. Web site

Instructions: Match each key term on the left with the definition on the right that best describes it.

1. _____ A collection of related Web pages usually belonging to an organization or individual.

2. _____ An Internet address, usually beginning with http://, that uniquely identifies a Web page.

3. _____ A programmable, electronic device that accepts data input, performs processing operations on that data, and outputs and stores the results.

4. _____ A portable computer about the size of a notebook that is designed to be used with a digital pen.

5. _____ Performing operations on data that has been input into a computer to convert that input to output.

6. _____ The operation of saving data, programs, or output for future use.

7. _____ The fastest, most expensive, and most powerful type of computer.

8. _____ The instructions, also called computer programs, that are used to tell a computer what it should do.

9. _____ The largest and most well-known computer network, linking millions of computers all over the world.

10. _____ The physical parts of a computer system, such as the keyboard, monitor, printer, and so forth.

SELF-QUIZ

Instructions: Circle **T** if the statement is true, **F** if the statement is false, or write the best answer in the space provided. **Answers for the self-quiz are located in the References and Resources Guide at the end of the book.**

1. **T F** A mouse is one common input device.

2. **T F** Software includes all the physical equipment in a computer system.

3. **T F** A computer can run without an operating system if it has good application software.

4. **T F** One of the most common types of home computers is the server.

5. **T F** An example of a domain name is *microsoft.com*.

6. _____ is the operation in which data is entered into the computer.

7. A(n) _____ computer is a portable computer designed to function as both a notebook and a tablet PC.

8. _____ is frequently used with servers today to create several separate environments on a single server that function as separate servers.

9. Electronic messages sent over the Internet that can be retrieved by the recipient at his or her convenience are called _____.

10. Write the number of the term that best matches each of the following descriptions in the blank to the left of its description.

a. _____ Allows access to resources located on the Internet.

b. _____ Supervises the running of all other programs on the computer.

c. _____ Enables users to perform specific tasks on a computer.

d. _____ Allows the creation of application programs.

1. Application software
2. Operating system
3. Programming language
4. Web browser

INT

EXERCISES

1. For the following list of computer hardware devices, indicate the principal function of each device by writing the appropriate letter—I (input device), O (output device), S (storage device), P (processing device), or C (communications device)—in the space provided.

a. CPU _____

b. Monitor _____

c. Mouse _____

d. Keyboard _____

e. Hard drive _____

f. Modem _____

g. Speakers _____

h. DVD drive _____

i. Microphone _____

2. Supply the missing words to complete the following statements.

a. The Internet is an example of a(n) _____, a collection of computers and other devices connected together to share resources and communicate with each other.

b. The starting page for a Web site is called the site's _____.

c. For the e-mail address *jsmith@cengage.com*, *jsmith* is the _____ and *cengage.com* is the _____ name.

d. The e-mail address pronounced *bill gee at microsoft dot com* is written _____.

3. What are three differences between a desktop computer and a portable computer?

4. List two reasons why a business may choose to network its employees' computers.

5. If a computer manufacturer called Apex created a home page for the Web, what would its URL likely be? Also, supply an appropriate e-mail address for yourself, assuming that you are employed by that company.

DISCUSSION QUESTIONS

1. There is usually a positive side and a negative side to each new technological improvement. Select a technology you use every day and consider its benefits and risks. What benefits does the technology provide? Are there any risks involved and, if so, how can they be minimized? If you chose not to use this technology because of the possible risks associated with it, how would your life be affected? Who should determine if the benefits of a new technology outweigh the potential risks? Consumers? The government?

2. The ubiquitous nature of mobile phones today brings tremendous convenience to our lives, but will misuse of new improvements to this technology result in the loss of that convenience? For instance, camera phones are now banned in many fitness centers, park restrooms, and other similar facilities because some people have used them inappropriately to take compromising photos, and mobile phones are banned in many classrooms because of the disruption of constant text messaging and the use of the phone by dishonest students to cheat on exams. Do you think these reactions to mobile phone misuse are justified? Is there another way to ensure the appropriate use of mobile phones without banning their use for all individuals? Should there be more stringent consequences for those who use technology for illegal or unethical purposes?

PROJECTS

HOT TOPICS

1. **Mobile TV** As discussed in this chapter, TV is one of the newest entertainment options available for smartphones. From live TV to video clips and movies, mobile TV is taking off.

     For this project, investigate the mobile TV options available today. Find at least two services and compare features, such as cost, compatibility, channels, and programming. Do your selected services offer live TV, video-on-demand, or both? If you have a smartphone, are any of the services available through your mobile provider? Are there currently Web sites where mobile users can view episodes of TV shows for free, like personal computer users can? What is the current status of the push by the *Open Mobile Video Coalition* to have a free mobile TV standard across the United States? Have you ever watched TV on a smartphone? If so, how do you rate your experience and would you do it again? If not, would you want to watch TV on a smartphone? Do you think mobile TV is the wave of the future? Why or why not? At the conclusion of your research, prepare a one-page summary of your findings and opinions and submit it to your instructor.

SHORT ANSWER/ RESEARCH

2. **Buying a New PC** New personal computers are widely available directly from manufacturers, as well as in retail, computer, electronic, and warehouse stores. Some stores carry only standard configurations as set up by the manufacturers; others allow you to customize a system.

     For this project, assume that you are in the market for a new personal computer. Give some thought to the type of computer (such as desktop, notebook, or tablet computer) that best fits your lifestyle and the tasks you wish to perform (such as the application programs you wish to use, how many programs you wish to use at one time, and how fast you desire the response time to be). Make a list of your hardware and software requirements (refer to the "Guide to Buying a PC" in the References and Resources Guide at the end of this book, if needed), being as specific as possible. By researching newspaper ads, manufacturer Web sites, and/or systems for sale at local stores, find three systems that meet your minimum requirements. Prepare a one-page comparison chart, listing each requirement and how each system meets or exceeds it. Also include any additional features each system has, and information regarding the brand, price, delivery time, shipping, sales tax, and warranty for each system. On your comparison sheet, mark the system that you would prefer to buy and write one paragraph explaining why. Turn in your comparison sheet and summary to your instructor, stapled to copies of the printed ads, specifications printed from Web sites, or other written documentation that you collected during this project.

HANDS ON

3. **The Internet** The Internet and World Wide Web are handy tools that can help you research topics covered in this textbook, complete many of the projects, and perform the online activities available via the textbook's Web site that are designed to enhance your learning and help you prepare for exams on the content covered in this textbook.

     For this project, find an Internet-enabled computer on your campus, at home, or at your public library and perform the following tasks, then submit your results and printout to your instructor. (Note: Some of the answers will vary from student to student.)

   a. Open a browser and the Google search site. Enter the search terms *define: Internet* to search for definitions of that term. Click on one result to display the definition. Use your browser's *Print* option to print the page.

   b. Click your browser's *Back* button to return to the Google home page. Use your browser's Bookmark or Favorites feature to bookmark the page. Close your browser.

   c. Reopen your browser and use its Bookmark or Favorites feature to redisplay the Google home page.

   d. Google yourself to see if you can find any information online. On your printout from part a, indicate how many hits were returned for this search and if any on the first page of hits really contained information about yourself.

4. **Gossip Sites** A recent trend on college campuses today is the use of campus gossip sites, where students can post campus-related news, rumors, and basic gossip. These sites were originally set up to promote free speech and to allow participants to publish comments anonymously without repercussions from school administrators, professors, and other officials. However, they are now being used to post vicious comments about others. What do you think of campus gossip sites? Is it ethical to post a rumor about another individual on these sites? How would you feel if you read a posting about yourself on a gossip site? School administrators cannot regulate the content because the sites are not sponsored or run by the college, and federal law prohibits Web hosts from being liable for the content posted by its users. Is this ethical? What if a posting leads to a criminal act, such as a rape, murder, or suicide? Who, if anyone, should be held responsible?

   For this project, form an opinion about the ethical ramifications of gossip Web sites and be prepared to discuss your position (in class, via an online class discussion group, in a class chat room, or via a class blog, depending on your instructor's directions). You may also be asked to write a short paper expressing your opinion.

ETHICS IN ACTION

5. **Online Education** The amount of distance learning available through the Internet and World Wide Web has exploded in the last couple of years. A few years ago, it was possible to take an occasional course online—now, an entire college degree can be earned online.

   For this project, look into the online education options available at your school and two other colleges or universities. Compare and contrast the programs in general, including whether or not the institution is accredited, the types of courses available online, whether or not an entire certificate or degree can be earned online, and the required fees. Next, select one online course and research it more closely. Find out how the course works in an online format—including whether or not any face-to-face class time is required, whether assignments and exams are submitted online, which software programs are required, and other course requirements—and determine if you would be interested in taking that course. Share your findings with the class in the form of a short presentation. The presentation should not exceed 10 minutes and should make use of one or more presentation aids, such as a whiteboard, handouts, or a computer-based slide presentation (your instructor may provide additional requirements). You may also be asked to submit a summary of the presentation to your instructor.

PRESENTATION/ DEMONSTRATION

6. **Should Social Media Activity Cost You a Job?** When you apply for a new job, there's a good chance that the company will take a look at your social media activity, such as your Facebook page, blog activity, and even Craigslist listings. In fact, many companies now require job applicants to pass a social media background check before offering them a job. Companies are trying to protect themselves by looking for such things as racist remarks and illegal activities, as well as get a feel for whether or not an individual would be a good fit for the company. But should individuals have to risk losing a job if they post a photo of themselves in a racy Halloween costume or make an offhand comment that an employer may misinterpret? What if a company denies you a job based on inaccurate information or information they wouldn't be allowed to ask in a job interview, such as information relating to your age, race, gender, religion, and so forth? And what if someone else posts and tags a questionable photo of you— should a potential employer be able to use that or other third-party information to make a decision about your future? To be safe, should job applicants have to abstain from social media activity in order to protect themselves, even though such sites are typically viewed as places to casually interact with others on personal free time? Or is everything a potential employer finds online fair game?

   Pick a side on this issue, form an opinion and gather supporting evidence, and be prepared to discuss and defend your position in a classroom debate or in a 1–2 page paper, depending on your instructor's directions.

BALANCING ACT

expert insight on...

Personal Computers

Courtesy of D-Link Systems

![D-Link Building Networks for People]

Daniel Kelley is the Vice President of Marketing for D-Link Systems, Inc. and is responsible for connectivity solutions tailored for home and business users. He has more than 15 years of professional marketing experience and holds a Bachelor of Arts degree in communications. As a result of Daniel's leadership and thriving marketing programs, many of the programs initiated in North America, including the implementation of numerous social media campaigns hosted on D-Link's social media platforms, have been adopted worldwide.

A conversation with DANIEL KELLEY
Vice President, Marketing, D-Link Systems, Inc.

> *"Putting a full-fledged computer with virtually unlimited potential into one's pocket has changed how we interact with information and with others in ways we're still discovering."*

My Background . . .

As the Vice President of Marketing for D-Link Systems, Inc., I am responsible for the overall marketing and branding of the company and its products. My focus is on creating demand and loyalty from customers through a range of disciplines including advertising, sponsorships, press relations, social media, and channel marketing. Although I hold a degree in communications, which helped launch my career in marketing, I attribute most of my skills to real-world marketing experience and constantly challenging myself to learn and stay on top of the latest marketing tactics, platforms, and trends.

It's Important to Know . . .

The evolution from the first massively-sized computers to today's small devices, such as the iPhone, has created a major shift in the industry. Once the average consumer could get a powerful PC in his or her home, it started what we now view as the natural integration of technology in our daily lives. Putting a full-fledged computer with virtually unlimited potential into one's pocket has changed how we interact with information and with others in ways we're still discovering.

Software is the interactive way a customer sees and uses a device, such as a PC, tablet, or phone. Software—in the form of applications (or apps)—allows us to utilize the hardware of the machine itself in ways that are seemingly unending.

Social media's influence will continue to grow and impact how we communicate. The noticeable shift from customers trusting impersonal third-party reviews of products and services to those of friends, family members, and others via social media sites is changing the way businesses market themselves and communicate with customers. We've also seen a rapid adoption of short video platforms such as Vine and Instagram, which is a key indicator that individuals are looking to capture and share more video for not only entertainment but also for everyday interactions.

How I Use this Technology . . .

Growing up, I always had an interest in all things creative and spent much of my time drawing, painting, and doing other creative projects. I carried this interest through my education, learning design graphics, animation, video, and Web development programs. The knowledge of these programs and my eye for design helps me provide direction on creative projects and allows me to dive in and give more specific examples or direction as needed. Today, I also use a laptop, tablet, and my smartphone every day to work and communicate with others from home, the office, and while traveling. My most used app is Catch, which helps me create and keep track of notes and ideas across all of my devices.

What the Future Holds . . .

One of the trends I personally find the most interesting is the rapid evolution of wearable technology. With the introduction of Google Glass and wellness-focused products such as FitBit, I see a very rapid adoption of new solutions designed to integrate technology with our clothing and accessories, which will lead to an entirely new way of interacting with information in our daily lives. We've become empowered in ways never dreamed of just decades ago, with endless information and new communication vehicles at our fingertips, and we've seen a rapid and dramatic shift from face-to-face conversations and phone calls to texting, e-mail, and social media as preferred ways to communicate. This shift will continue to accelerate, with video calls and video messages becoming a primary communication medium. However, we have to be careful we don't become more isolated and detached from others in public social situations so we can continue to interact positively with each other in the future.

> *"As we put more of ourselves out there in the cloud, we make ourselves more vulnerable."*

Another concern for the future is privacy. As we put more of ourselves out there in the cloud, we make ourselves more vulnerable. With any new technology or service, there are going to be those looking to exploit it and cause harm to others for personal gain and we've seen how private information doesn't necessarily remain private. This should encourage individuals to protect themselves as much as possible, such as using strong online passwords and just using common sense when determining what to share online.

I'm hoping that one of the biggest impacts of technology in the future is in the medical field or solving big problems like world hunger. Technology advancements, such as the use of 3D printers to create live tissue that can be used for replacing lost body parts, can have a very positive impact on our health and wellness. This same 3D printing technology has the potential to create a large food supply (utilizing protein "ink" from meal worms, for instance) for third-world countries where food is desperately needed. As much as technology advances our entertainment and social interaction, I am more interested to see how it can actually improve how we take care of those in need.

My Advice to Students . . .

Jump in with both feet. Take things apart, build things, and constantly learn new things through education and resources such as the Internet and books. We are living in a truly remarkable time where opportunities abound in the tech field, and those who apply themselves and commit to learning, trying, and doing will have an upper hand for building a career or leading the next wave of where tech can take us.

Discussion Question

Daniel Kelley views wearable technology as one of the most interesting trends evolving today. Think about the tasks you use your mobile phone and personal computer for today. Could they be performed using a wearable mobile device, such as Google Glass or perhaps a wearable smartphone? If not, what changes would need to be made in the future in order to perform these tasks using a wearable device? Is the wearable mobile device the computer of the future? Be prepared to discuss your position (in class, via an online class discussion group, in a class chat room, or via a class blog, depending on your instructor's directions). You may also be asked to write a short paper expressing your opinion.

> **For more information about D-Link, visit the official Web site at dlink.com. D-Link also communicates through social sites (facebook.com/dlink and twitter.com/dlink), and has a resource center located at resource.dlink.com.**

Hardware

When most people think of computers, images of hardware usually fill their minds. Hardware includes the system unit, keyboard, mouse, monitor, and all the other interesting pieces of equipment that make up a computer system. This module explores the rich variety of computer hardware available today. But, as you already know, hardware needs instructions from software in order to function. Hardware without software is like a car without a driver or a canvas and paintbrush without an artist. Software is discussed in detail in the next module.

This module divides coverage of hardware into three parts. Chapter 2 describes the hardware located inside the system unit, which is the main box of the computer and where most of the work of a computer is performed. Chapter 3 discusses the different types of devices that can be used for storage. Chapter 4 covers the wide variety of hardware that can be used for input and output.

"Hardware will continue to shrink in size while increasing in capabilities."

For more comments from Guest Expert **Ali Moayer** of Logitech, see the **Expert Insight on . . . Hardware** feature at the end of the module.

chapter 2

The System Unit: Processing and Memory

After completing this chapter, you will be able to do the following:

1. Understand how data and programs are represented to a computer and be able to identify a few of the coding systems used to accomplish this.

2. Explain the functions of the hardware components commonly found inside the system unit, such as the CPU, GPU, memory, buses, and expansion cards.

3. Describe how peripheral devices or other hardware can be added to a computer.

4. Understand how a computer's CPU and memory components process program instructions and data.

5. Name and evaluate several strategies that can be used today for speeding up the operations of a computer.

6. List some processing technologies that may be used in future computers.

OVERVIEW

The system unit of a computer is sometimes thought of as a mysterious "black box" and often the user does not have much understanding of what happens inside it. In this chapter, we demystify the system unit by looking inside the box and closely examining the functions of the parts. Consequently, the chapter gives you a feel for what the CPU, memory, and other devices commonly found inside the system unit do and how they work together to perform the tasks that the user requests.

To start, we discuss how a computer represents data and program instructions. Specifically, we talk about the codes that computers use to translate data back and forth from the symbols that computers can manipulate to the symbols that people are accustomed to using. These topics lead to a discussion of how the CPU and memory are arranged with other components inside the system unit and the characteristics of those components. Next, we discuss how a CPU performs processing tasks. Finally, we look at strategies that can be used today to speed up a computer, plus some strategies that may be used to create faster and better computers in the future.

Many of you will apply this chapter's content to conventional personal computers—such as desktop and portable computers. However, it is important to realize that the principles and procedures discussed in this chapter apply to other types of computers as well, such as those embedded in toys, consumer devices, household appliances, cars, and other devices, and those used with mobile devices, servers, mainframes, and supercomputers. ■

DATA AND PROGRAM REPRESENTATION

In order to be understood by a computer, data and software programs need to be represented appropriately. Consequently, *coding systems* are used to represent data and programs in a manner that can be understood by the computer. These concepts are discussed in the next few sections.

Digital Data Representation

Virtually all computers today—such as the embedded computers, mobile devices, personal computers, servers, mainframes, and supercomputers discussed in Chapter 1—are *digital computers*. Most digital computers are *binary computers*, which can understand only two states, usually thought of as *off* and *on* and represented by the digits 0 and 1. Consequently, all data processed by a binary computer must be in binary form (0s and 1s). The 0s and 1s used to represent data can be represented in a variety of ways, such as with an open or closed circuit, the absence or presence of electronic current, two different types of magnetic alignment on a storage medium, and so on (see Figure 2-1).

Regardless of their physical representations, these 0s and 1s are commonly referred to as *bits*, a computing term derived

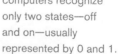
FIGURE 2-1

Ways of representing 0 and 1. Binary computers recognize only two states—off and on—usually represented by 0 and 1.

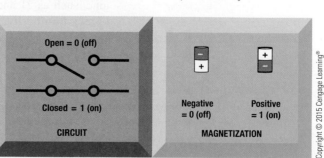

Open = 0 (off)

Closed = 1 (on)

CIRCUIT

Negative = 0 (off)

Positive = 1 (on)

MAGNETIZATION

from the phrase *binary digits*. A **bit** is the smallest unit of data that a binary computer can recognize. Therefore, the input you enter via a keyboard, the software program you use to play your music collection, the term paper stored on your USB flash drive, and the digital photos located on your mobile phone are all just groups of bits. Representing data in a form that can be understood by a digital computer is called *digital data representation*.

Because most computers can only understand data and instructions in binary form, binary can be thought of as the computer's *natural language*. People, of course, do not speak in binary. For example, you are not likely to go up to a friend and say,

$$0100100001001001$$

which translates into the word "HI" using one binary coding system. People communicate with one another in their natural languages, such as English, Chinese, Spanish, and French. For example, this book is written in English, which uses a 26-character alphabet. In addition, most countries use a numbering system with 10 possible symbols—0 through 9. As already mentioned, however, binary computers understand only 0s and 1s. For us to interact with a computer, a translation process from our natural language to 0s and 1s and then back again to our natural language is required. When we enter data into a computer system, the computer translates the natural-language symbols we input into binary 0s and 1s. After processing the data, the computer translates and outputs the resulting information in a form that we can understand.

A bit by itself typically represents only a fraction of a piece of data. Consequently, large numbers of bits are needed to represent a written document, computer program, digital photo, music file, or virtually any other type of data. Eight bits grouped together are collectively referred to as a **byte**. It is important to be familiar with this concept because *byte* terminology is frequently used in a variety of computer contexts, such as to indicate the size of a document or digital photo, the amount of memory a computer has, or the amount of room left on a storage medium. Because these quantities often involve thousands or millions of bytes, prefixes are commonly used in conjunction with the term *byte* to represent larger amounts of data (see Figure 2-2). For instance, a **kilobyte (KB)** is equal to 1,024 bytes, but is usually thought of as approximately 1,000 bytes; a **megabyte (MB)** is about 1 million bytes; a **gigabyte (GB)** is about 1 billion bytes; a **terabyte (TB)** is about 1 trillion bytes; a **petabyte (PB)** is about 1,000 terabytes (2^{50} bytes); an **exabyte (EB)** is about 1,000 petabytes (2^{60} bytes); a **zettabyte (ZB)** is about 1,000 exabytes (2^{70} bytes); and a **yottabyte (YB)** is about 1,000 zettabytes (2^{80} bytes). Using these definitions, 5 KB is about 5,000 bytes, 10 MB is about 10 million bytes, and 2 TB is about 2 trillion bytes.

Computers represent programs and data through a variety of binary-based coding systems. The coding system used depends primarily on the type of data that needs to be represented; the most common coding systems are discussed in the next few sections.

Representing Numerical Data: The Binary Numbering System

A *numbering system* is a way of representing numbers. The numbering system we commonly use is called the **decimal numbering system** because it uses 10 symbols—the digits 0, 1, 2, 3, 4, 5, 6, 7, 8, and 9—to represent all possible numbers. Numbers greater than nine, such as 21 and 683, are represented using combinations of these 10 symbols. The **binary numbering system** uses only two symbols—the digits 0 and 1—to represent all

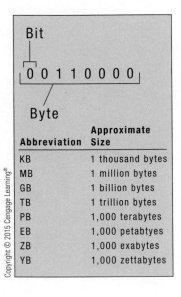

FIGURE 2-2

Bits and bytes.
Document size, storage capacity, and memory capacity are all measured in bytes.

Bit

0 0 1 1 0 0 0 0

Byte

Abbreviation	Approximate Size
KB	1 thousand bytes
MB	1 million bytes
GB	1 billion bytes
TB	1 trillion bytes
PB	1,000 terabytes
EB	1,000 petabtyes
ZB	1,000 exabytes
YB	1,000 zettabytes

Copyright © 2015 Cengage Learning®

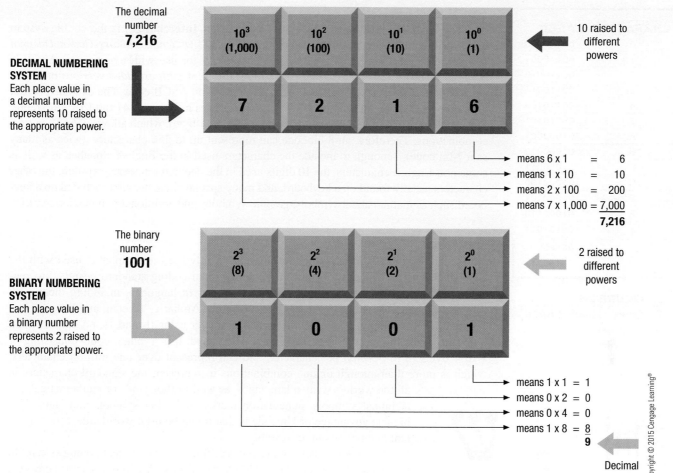

DECIMAL NUMBERING SYSTEM
Each place value in a decimal number represents 10 raised to the appropriate power.

The decimal number **7,216**

10^3 (1,000)	10^2 (100)	10^1 (10)	10^0 (1)
7	2	1	6

10 raised to different powers

means 6 x 1   =   6
means 1 x 10   =   10
means 2 x 100   =   200
means 7 x 1,000 = 7,000
7,216

BINARY NUMBERING SYSTEM
Each place value in a binary number represents 2 raised to the appropriate power.

The binary number **1001**

2^3 (8)	2^2 (4)	2^1 (2)	2^0 (1)
1	0	0	1

2 raised to different powers

means 1 x 1 = 1
means 0 x 2 = 0
means 0 x 4 = 0
means 1 x 8 = 8
9

Decimal equivalent

Copyright © 2015 Cengage Learning®

FIGURE 2-3
Examples of using the decimal and binary numbering systems.

TIP

For more information about and examples of converting between numbering systems, see the "A Look at Numbering Systems" section in the References and Resources Guide at the end of this book.

possible numbers. Consequently, binary computers use the binary numbering system to represent numbers and to perform math computations.

In both numbering systems, the position of each digit determines the power, or exponent, to which the *base number* (10 for decimal or 2 for binary) is raised. In the decimal numbering system, going from right to left, the first position or column (the ones column) represents 10^0 or 1; the second column (the tens column) represents 10^1 or 10; the third column (the hundreds column) represents 10^2 or 100; and so forth. Therefore, as Figure 2-3 shows, the decimal number 7,216 is understood as $7 \times 10^3 + 2 \times 10^2 + 1 \times 10^1 + 6 \times 10^0$ or $7,000 + 200 + 10 + 6$ or 7,216. In binary, the concept is the same but the columns have different place values. For example, the far-right column is the ones column (for 2^0), the second column is the twos column (2^1), the third column is the fours column (2^2), and so on. Therefore, although 1001 represents "one thousand one" in decimal notation, 1001 represents "nine" ($1 \times 2^3 + 0 \times 2^2 + 0 \times 2^1 + 1 \times 2^0$ or $8 + 0 + 0 + 1$ or 9) in the binary numbering system, as illustrated in the bottom half of Figure 2-3.

Coding Systems for Text-Based Data

While numeric data is represented by the binary numbering system, text-based data is represented by binary coding systems specifically developed for text-based data—namely, *ASCII*, *EBCDIC*, and *Unicode*. These codes are used to represent all characters that can appear in text data—such as numbers, letters, and special characters and symbols like the dollar sign, comma, percent symbol, and mathematical symbols.

CHARACTER	ASCII
0	00110000
1	00110001
2	00110010
3	00110011
4	00110100
5	00110101
A	01000001
B	01000010
C	01000011
D	01000100
E	01000101
F	01000110
+	00101011
!	00100001
#	00100011

FIGURE 2-4
Some extended ASCII code examples.

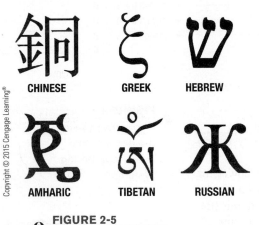

CHINESE   GREEK   HEBREW

AMHARIC   TIBETAN   RUSSIAN

FIGURE 2-5
Unicode. Many characters, such as these, can be represented by Unicode but not by ASCII or EBCDIC.

ASCII and EBCDIC
ASCII (American Standard Code for Information Interchange) is the coding system traditionally used with personal computers. *EBCDIC (Extended Binary-Coded Decimal Interchange Code)* was developed by IBM, primarily for use with mainframes. ASCII is a 7-digit (7-bit) code, although there are several different 8-bit *extended versions* of ASCII that contain additional symbols not included in the 7-bit ASCII code. The extended ASCII character sets (see some examples of 8-bit ASCII codes in Figure 2-4) and EBCDIC represent each character as a unique combination of 8 bits (1 byte), which allows 256 (2^8) unique combinations. Therefore, an 8-bit code can represent up to 256 characters (twice as many as a 7-bit code)—enough to include the characters used in the English alphabet, as well as some non-English characters, the 10 digits used in the decimal numbering system, the other characters usually found on a keyboard, and many special characters not included on a keyboard such as mathematical symbols, graphic symbols, and additional punctuation marks.

Unicode
Unlike ASCII and EBCDIC, which are limited to only the Latin alphabet used with the English language, **Unicode** is a universal international coding standard designed to represent text-based data written in any ancient or modern language, including those with different alphabets, such as Chinese, Greek, Hebrew, Amharic, Tibetan, and Russian (see Figure 2-5). Unicode uniquely identifies each character using 0s and 1s, no matter which language, program, or computer platform is being used. It is a longer code, consisting of 1 to 4 bytes (8 to 32 bits) per character, and can represent over one million characters, which is more than enough unique combinations to represent the standard characters in all the world's written languages, as well as thousands of mathematical and technical symbols, punctuation marks, and other symbols and signs. The biggest advantage of Unicode is that it can be used worldwide with consistent and unambiguous results.

Unicode is quickly replacing ASCII as the primary text-coding system. In fact, Unicode includes the ASCII character set so ASCII data can be converted easily to Unicode when needed. Unicode is used by most Web browsers and is widely used for Web pages and Web applications (Google data, for instance, is stored exclusively in Unicode). Most recent software programs, including the latest versions of Microsoft Windows, Mac OS, and Microsoft Office, also use Unicode, as do modern programming languages, such as Java and Python. Unicode is updated regularly to add new characters and new languages not originally encoded—the most recent version is *Unicode 6.2*.

Coding Systems for Other Types of Data
So far, our discussion of data coding schemes has focused on numeric and text-based data, which consists of alphanumeric characters and special symbols, such as the comma and dollar sign. Multimedia data, such as graphics, audio, and video data, must also be represented in binary form in order to be used with a computer, as discussed next.

Graphics Data
Graphics data consists of still images, such as photographs or drawings. One of the most common methods for storing graphics data is in the form of a *bitmap image*—an image made up of a grid of small dots, called *pixels* (short for *picture elements*), that

are colored appropriately to represent an image. The color to be displayed at each pixel is represented by some combination of 0s and 1s, and the number of bits required to store the color for each pixel ranges from 1 to 24 bits. For example, each pixel in a *monochrome graphic* can be only one of two possible colors (such as black or white). These monochrome images require only one bit of storage space per pixel (for instance, the bit would contain a 1 when representing a pixel that should display as white, and the bit would contain a 0 for a pixel that should display as black). Images with more than two colors can use 4, 8, or 24 bits to store the color data for each pixel—this allows for 16 (2^4), 256 (2^8), or 16,777,216 (2^{24}) colors respectively, as shown in Figure 2-6.

The number of bits used per pixel depends on the type of image being stored; for instance, the *JPEG* images taken by most digital cameras today use 24-bit *true color images*. While this can result in large file sizes, images can typically be *compressed* when needed, such as to reduce the amount of storage space required to store that image or to send a lower-resolution version of an image via e-mail.

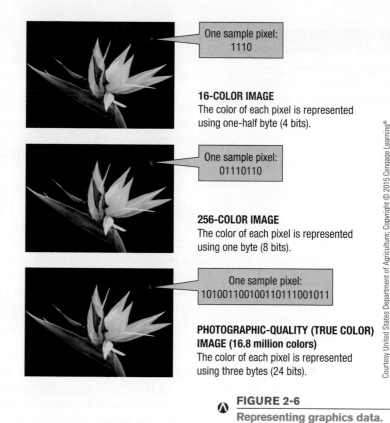

One sample pixel:
1110

16-COLOR IMAGE
The color of each pixel is represented using one-half byte (4 bits).

One sample pixel:
01110110

256-COLOR IMAGE
The color of each pixel is represented using one byte (8 bits).

One sample pixel:
101001100100110111001011

PHOTOGRAPHIC-QUALITY (TRUE COLOR) IMAGE (16.8 million colors)
The color of each pixel is represented using three bytes (24 bits).

Courtesy United States Department of Agriculture; Copyright © 2015 Cengage Learning®

FIGURE 2-6
Representing graphics data.
With bitmapped images, the color of each pixel is represented by bits; the more bits used, the better the image quality.

Audio Data

Like graphics data, *audio data*—such as a song or the sound of someone speaking—must be in digital form in order to be stored on a storage medium or processed by a computer. To convert analog sound to digital sound, several thousand *samples*—digital representations of the sound at particular moments—are taken every second. When the samples are played back in the proper order, they re-create the sound of the voice or music. For example, audio CDs record sound using 2-byte samples, which are sampled at a rate of 44,100 times per second. When these samples are played back at a rate of 44,100 samples per second, they sound like continuous voice or music. With so many samples, however, sound files take up a great deal of storage space—about 32 MB for a 3-minute stereo song (44,100 times × 2 bytes × 180 seconds × 2 channels).

Because of its large size, audio data is usually compressed to reduce its file size when it is transmitted over the Internet or stored on an iPod or other portable digital media player. For example, files that are *MP3-encoded*—that is, compressed with the *MP3 compression algorithm* developed by the *Motion Pictures Expert Group* (*MPEG*)—are about 10 times smaller than their uncompressed digital versions, so they download 10 times faster and take up one-tenth of the storage space. The actual storage size required depends on the *bit rate*—the number of bits to be transferred per second when the file is played—used when the file is initially created; audio files using the common bit rate of 128 *Kbps* (thousands of bits per second) are about one-tenth the size of the original CD-quality recording.

TIP

For more examples of ASCII, EBCDIC, and Unicode, see the "Coding Charts" section in the References and Resources Guide at the end of this book.

ASK THE EXPERT

Courtesy Unicode Inc.

Mark Davis, President, The Unicode Consortium

What should the average computer user know about Unicode?

Whenever you read or write anything on a computer, you're using Unicode. Whenever you search on Google, Yahoo!, MSN, Wikipedia, or other Web sites, you're using Unicode. It's the way that text in all the world's languages can be stored and processed on computers.

Video Data

Video data—such as home movies, feature films, video clips, and television shows—is displayed using a collection of frames; each frame contains a still image. When the frames are projected one after the other (typically at a rate of 24 *frames per second* (*fps*) for film-based video and 30 or 60 fps for video taken with digital video cameras), the illusion of movement is created. With so many frames, the amount of data involved in showing a two-hour feature film can be substantial. Fortunately, like audio data, video data can be compressed to reduce it to a manageable size. For example, a two-hour movie can be compressed to fit on a single DVD disc; it can be compressed even further to be delivered over the Web.

Representing Software Programs: Machine Language

Just as numbers, text, and multimedia data must be represented by 0s and 1s, software programs must also be represented by 0s and 1s. Before a computer can execute any program instruction, such as requesting input from the user, moving a file from one storage device to another, or opening a new window on the screen, it must convert the instruction into a binary code known as **machine language**. An example of a typical machine language instruction is as follows:

01011000011100000000000100000010

A machine language instruction might look like a meaningless string of 0s and 1s, but it actually represents specific operations and storage locations. The 32-bit instruction shown here, for instance, moves data between two specific memory locations on one type of computer system. Early computers required programs to be written in machine language, but today's computers allow programs to be written in a programming language, which is then translated by the computer into machine language in order to be understood by the computer. Programming languages and *language translators* are discussed in detail in Chapter 13.

INSIDE THE SYSTEM UNIT

The **system unit** is the main case of a computer or mobile device. It houses the processing hardware for that device, as well as a few other components, such as storage devices, the power supply, and cooling fans. The system unit for a desktop computer often looks like a rectangular box, as in Figure 2-7. The system units for all-in-one computers, notebooks, tablets, and mobile devices are much smaller and are usually combined with the device's display screen to form a single piece of hardware. However, these system units typically have components that are similar to those found in desktop computers. As shown in Figure 2-7, a system unit contains one or more *processors*, several types of *memory*, interfaces to connect external *peripheral devices* (such as printers), and other components all interconnected through sets of wires called *buses* on the *motherboard*. These components are discussed in detail in the next few sections.

The Motherboard

A *circuit board* is a thin board containing *computer chips* and other electronic components. Computer chips are very small pieces of silicon or other semiconducting material that contain *integrated circuits* (*ICs*), which are collections of electronic circuits containing

---

>**Machine language.** A binary-based language for representing computer programs that the computer can execute directly. >**System unit.** The main box of a computer that houses the CPU, motherboard, memory, and other devices.

CPU
Performs the calculations and does the comparisons needed for processing, as well as controls the other parts of the computer system.

POWER SUPPLY
Converts standard electrical power into a form the computer can use.

FAN
Cools the CPU.

HARD DRIVE
Stores data and programs; the principal storage device for most computers.

EXPANSION CARD
Connects peripheral devices or adds new capabilities to a computer.

EXPANSION SLOTS
Connect expansion cards to the motherboard to add additional capabilities.

MOTHERBOARD
Connects all components of the computer system; the computer's main circuit board.

MEMORY (RAM) MODULES
Store data temporarily while you are working with it.

MEMORY SLOTS
Connect memory modules to the motherboard.

DRIVE BAYS
Hold storage devices, such as the DVD and hard drives shown here.

DVD DRIVE
Accesses data stored on CDs or DVDs.

FLASH MEMORY CARD READER
Accesses data stored on flash memory cards.

USB PORTS
Connect USB devices to the computer.

microscopic pathways along which electrical current can travel, and *transistors*, which are switches controlling the flow of electrons along the pathways. The main circuit board inside the system unit is called the **motherboard**.

As shown in Figure 2-7, the motherboard has a variety of chips, boards, and connectors attached to it. All devices used with a computer need to be connected via a wired or wireless connection to the motherboard. Typically, *external devices* (such as monitors, keyboards, mice, and printers) connect to the motherboard by plugging into a *port*—a special connector exposed through the exterior of the system unit case. The port is either built directly into the motherboard or created via an *expansion card* inserted into an *expansion slot* on the motherboard. Wireless external devices typically use a *transceiver* that plugs into a port on the computer to transmit data between the wireless device and the motherboard or they use wireless networking technology (such as *Bluetooth*) built into the motherboard. Ports and system expansion are discussed in more detail later in this chapter; wireless networking is covered in Chapter 7.

FIGURE 2-7
Inside a typical system unit. The system unit houses the CPU, memory, and other important pieces of hardware.

The Power Supply and Drive Bays

Most personal computers plug into a standard electrical outlet. The *power supply* inside a desktop computer connects to the motherboard to deliver electricity to the computer. Portable computers almost always contain a *rechargeable battery pack* to power the computer when it is not connected to a power outlet, as well as an external power supply adapter that connects the computer to a power outlet to recharge the battery when needed. Some mobile devices are also charged via a power outlet; others are recharged by connecting them to a computer. One issue with newer portable computers and mobile devices is the growing use of built-in

> **Motherboard.** The main circuit board of a computer, located inside the system unit, to which all computer system components connect.

batteries. Although these batteries allow the devices to be lighter and are supposed to last for the typical life of the device, they are more difficult and expensive to replace if they fail. In fact, consumers often decide to just discard a device when its built-in battery fails, resulting in an increase in *electronic trash* (*e-trash*). The ramifications of the growing amount of e-trash, such as discarded mobile phones and other electronics, that is being generated worldwide is discussed in Chapter 16.

Most conventional computers (such as desktop computers) also contain *drive bays* (rectangular metal racks) inside the system unit into which storage devices (a *hard drive*, *DVD drive*, and *flash memory card reader*, for instance) can be inserted and secured. Storage devices inside the system unit are connected via a cable to the motherboard, as well as to the internal power supply if the device requires it. Storage devices with removable media that need to be inserted into and removed from the drive (such as a DVD drive) are accessible through the front of the system unit (refer again to Figure 2-7). Storage devices that are not used in conjunction with removable storage media (such as an internal hard drive) are not visible outside the system unit. Many desktop computers come with empty drive bays so users can add additional storage devices as needed.

Processors

Computers and mobile devices today contain one or more **processors** (such as *CPUs* and *GPUs*), which consist of a variety of circuitry and components that are packaged together and connected directly to the motherboard. The primary processor is the **central processing unit (CPU)**—also called the **microprocessor** when talking about personal computers—which does the vast majority of the processing for a computer. CPUs are typically designed for a specific type of computer, such as for desktop computers, servers, portable computers (like notebook and tablet computers), or mobile devices (like media tablets and mobile phones). Most personal computers and servers today use Intel or Advanced Micro Devices (AMD) CPUs; media tablets and mobile phones often use processors manufactured by other companies (such as ARM) instead. In fact, many mobile processors (such as the *Snapdragon* from Qualcomm, the *Tegra 4* from NVIDIA, the *Exynos* from Samsung, and the *A6X* from Apple) are based on ARM processors, such as the ARM *Cortex-A9*. Some examples of common processors, along with some of their characteristics that are defined and discussed shortly, are shown in Figure 2-8.

Most CPUs today are **multi-core CPUs**; that is, CPUs that contain the processing components or *cores* of multiple independent processors on a single CPU. For example, **dual-core CPUs** contain two cores and **quad-core CPUs** contain four cores. Up until just a few years ago, most CPUs designed for desktop computers had only a single core; as a result, a common way to increase the amount of processing performed by the CPU was to increase the speed of the CPU. However, heat constraints are making it progressively more difficult to continue to increase CPU speed, so CPU manufacturers today are focusing on multi-core CPUs to increase the amount of processing that a CPU can do in a given time period.

Multi-core CPUs allow computers to work simultaneously on more than one task at a time, such as burning a DVD while surfing the Web, as well as to work faster within a single application if the software is designed to take advantage of multiple cores. Another benefit of multi-core CPUs is that they typically experience fewer heat problems than *single-core CPUs* because each core typically runs slower than a single-core CPU, although the total processing power of the multi-core CPU is greater. In addition to heat reduction, one goal of CPU manufacturers today is creating CPUs that are as energy-efficient as possible in order to reduce power consumption and increase battery life. For example, one new Intel CPU contains a special part, called the *Power Control Unit*, which is designed to turn individual

---

>**Processor.** A chip (such as the CPU or GPU) that performs processing functions. >**Central processing unit (CPU).** The chip located on the motherboard of a computer that performs most of the processing for a computer. >**Microprocessor.** A central processing unit (CPU) for a personal computer. >**Multi-core CPU.** A CPU that contains the processing components or core of more than one processor in a single CPU. >**Dual-core CPU.** A CPU that contains two separate processing cores. >**Quad-core CPU.** A CPU that contains four separate processing cores.

Four cores

Shared Level 3
cache memory

DESKTOP PROCESSORS

MOBILE PROCESSORS

TYPE OF CPU	NAME	NUMBER OF CORES	CLOCK SPEED	TOTAL CACHE MEMORY
SERVER	Intel Xeon (E7 family)	6–10	1.73–2.66 GHz	18–30 MB
	AMD Opteron (6300 series)	4–16	1.8–3.5 GHz	20–32 MB
DESKTOP	Intel Core i7 (3rd gen)	4–6	2.5–3.6 GHz	8–12 MB
	AMD FX	4–8	3.1–4.2 GHz	8–16 MB
MOBILE (NOTEBOOKS)	Intel Core i7 Mobile (3rd gen)	2–4	1.06–3.0 GHz	4–8 MB
	AMD Athlon II Neo	1–2	1.3–1.7 GHz	1–2 MB
MOBILE (MOBILE DEVICES)	ARM Cortex-A9	1–4	800 MHz–2 GHz	up to 2 MB
	ARM Cortex-A15	1–4+	1–2 GHz	up to 4 MB
	NVIDIA Tegra 4*	4	1.9 GHz	2 MB

*Based on ARM Cortex-A15

FIGURE 2-8
CPU examples and characteristics.

parts of the processor off when they are not needed to save power and then wake them up again as soon as they are needed. In addition, CPU manufacturers are increasingly using materials that are not toxic when disposed of in order to reduce e-trash, as discussed in detail in Chapter 16. Most CPUs today also support virtualization and other recent technologies.

CPUs used in desktop computers typically have 4 cores; server processors may have 10 cores or more. Portable computers can use one of the CPUs that desktop computers use (which is more common with notebooks designed as *desktop replacements* than with lightweight traveling notebooks or tablets) or a *mobile processor*. Mobile processors typically run a little slower than comparable desktop CPUs, but they are often multi-core and they run cooler and consume less power to allow devices to run longer on battery power without a recharge.

Another processor located inside the system unit is the **graphics processing unit (GPU)**, which takes care of the processing needed to display images (including still images, animations, and video)—and particularly 3D images—on the screen. (For a look at how GPUs were used to create the new *Transformers: The Ride 3D* at Universal Studios, see the How It Works box.) While GPUs (one example is shown in Figure 2-9) can be located on the motherboard or on a *video graphics card* (as discussed later in this chapter), a growing trend is to integrate both the CPU and GPU into the CPU package. For instance, both Intel Core i7 and Qualcomm Snapdragon processors have integrated GPUs; AMD calls their integrated processors *APUs* or *accelerated processing units*. Mobile processors tend to integrate other capabilities into the processor package as well, such as support for multimedia capture and playback, GPS capabilities, and connectivity (cellular, Wi-Fi, USB, and/or Bluetooth capabilities, for instance). A processor that contains all the necessary capabilities for a single device is sometimes referred to as a *system-on-a-chip (SoC)*.

In addition to computers and mobile devices, processors are incorporated into a variety of products today, such as TVs, smart meters, cars, gaming consoles, exercise machines, electric toothbrushes, and ATM machines, as well as other

FIGURE 2-9
A GPU.

>**Graphics processing unit (GPU).** The chip that does the processing needed to display images on the screen; can be located on the motherboard, inside the CPU, or on a video graphics board.

HOW IT WORKS

GPUs and *Transformers: The Ride 3D* at Universal Studios

At the Universal Studios Hollywood theme park, passengers can take a ride through a Transformers battlescape, thanks to the new *Transformers: The Ride 3D* ride. A motion platform, a 2,000 foot-long track, 14 huge screens (some of which curve around the audience), and 34 projectors fitted with custom 3D lenses are used to create the realistic experience, which is helped by motion that is synchronized with the action and a 14-channel audio system built into the ride vehicle. But the star of the show is the ride's impressive photorealistic 3D images.

The *Transformers: The Ride 3D* imagery uses *4K resolution*, which is four times greater than the typical movie. The images took two years to create at Industrial Light and Magic (ILM) and were more difficult to create than initially expected due to their 3D nature, the 4K resolution, and the fact that the images had to be associated with the proper perspective for each of the screens. According to Chick Russell, show producer at Universal Studios, "We were using every single server and computer that ILM had. This was the most complex project ILM ever worked on."

One key, according to Jeff White, the visual effects supervisor at ILM, was being able to see the 3D animations play back in real time as they were being developed (see the accompanying photo)—for that, they relied on the speed of NVIDIA's Quadro GPUs. Considering every robot in the ride is over a million polygons, a lot of rendering power is needed to pull that off and the GPUs delivered.

Total cost: $40 million. Result: The most technically advanced ride that Universal Studios has ever produced.

Courtesy NVIDIA

computing hardware such as printers, digital cameras, and modems. The CPUs for these devices are typically different from the ones used in personal computers and determine the processing capabilities of the device. For example, the next-generation *Xbox One* gaming console uses an AMD CPU instead of the IBM CPU used by the Xbox 360—because of this, Xbox 360 game discs are not compatible with the new system.

Processing Speed

One measurement of the *processing speed* of a CPU is the *CPU clock speed*, which is typically rated in *megahertz (MHz)* or *gigahertz (GHz)*. A CPU with a higher CPU clock speed means that more instructions can be processed per second than the same CPU with a lower CPU clock speed. For instance, a Core i7 processor running at 3.2 GHz would be faster than a Core i7 processor running at 2.66 GHz if all other components remain the same. CPUs for the earliest personal computers ran at less than 5 MHz; today's fastest CPUs designed for PCs have a clock speed of more than 4 GHz. Although CPU clock speed is an important factor in computer performance, other factors (such as the number of cores, the amount of *memory*, the speed of external storage devices, the GPU being used, and the *bus width* and *bus speed*) greatly affect the overall processing speed of the computer. As a result, computers today are typically classified less by CPU clock speed and more by the computer's overall processing speed or performance.

One measurement of overall processing speed is the maximum number of instructions the CPU can process per second—such as *megaflops*, *gigaflops*, and *teraflops* (millions, billions, and trillions of floating point operations per second, respectively). It is also common for experts associated with computer journals, technical Web sites, and other organizations to test the performance of CPUs. These tests—called *benchmark tests*—typically run the same series of programs on several computer systems that are identical except for one component (such as the CPU) and measure how long each task takes in order to determine the overall relative performance of the component being tested. Because the large number of factors affecting computer performance today makes it increasingly difficult for consumers to evaluate the performance of CPUs and computers, benchmark tests are becoming an extremely important resource for computer shoppers.

Word Size

A computer word is the amount of data (typically measured in bits or bytes) that a CPU can manipulate at one time. While CPUs just a few years ago used 32-bit words (referred to as *32-bit processors*), most CPUs today are *64-bit processors* (that is, they can simultaneously process 64 bits, or 8 bytes, at one time). Usually, a larger word size allows for faster processing and the use of more RAM, provided the software being used is written to take advantage of 64-bit processing. For instance, a computer with a 64-bit processor running the 64-bit version of the Windows operating system can use more RAM and has a higher performance than the same computer running the regular 32-bit version of Windows. However, much of today's software is still 32-bit software.

Cache Memory

Cache memory is a special group of very fast memory circuitry located on or close to the CPU. Cache memory is used to speed up processing by storing the data and instructions that may be needed next by the CPU in handy locations. In theory, it works the same way you might work at your desk; that is, with the file folders or documents you need most often placed within an arm's length and with other useful materials placed farther away but still within easy reach. The computer works in a similar manner. Although it can access items (data, instructions, and programs, for instance) in RAM relatively quickly, it can work much faster if it places the most urgently needed items into areas—cache memory—that allow even faster access. When cache memory is full and the CPU calls for additional data or a new instruction, the system overwrites as much data in cache memory as needed to make room for the new data or instruction. This allows the data and instructions that are most likely still needed to remain in cache memory.

Cache memory today is usually *internal cache* (built right into the CPU chip). In the past, some cache memory was *external cache* (located close to, but not inside, the CPU), but that is less common today. Cache memory level numbers indicate the order in which

>**Cache memory.** A group of fast memory circuitry located on or near the CPU to help speed up processing.

the various levels of cache are accessed by the CPU when it requires new data or instructions. *Level 1 (L1) cache* (which is the fastest type of cache but typically holds less data than other levels of cache) is checked first, followed by *Level 2 (L2) cache*, followed by *Level 3 (L3) cache* if it exists. If the data or instructions are not found in cache memory, the computer looks for them in RAM, which is slower than cache memory. If the data or instructions cannot be found in RAM, then they are retrieved from the hard drive—an even slower operation. Typically, more cache memory results in faster processing. Most multi-core CPUs today have some cache memory (such as a L1 and L2 cache) dedicated to each core; they may also use a larger shared cache memory (such as L3 cache) that can be accessed by any core as needed.

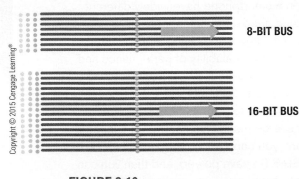

8-BIT BUS

16-BIT BUS

Copyright © 2015 Cengage Learning®

FIGURE 2-10
Bus width. A wider bus can transfer more data at one time than a narrower bus.

Bus Width, Bus Speed, and Bandwidth

A *bus* is an electronic path over which data can travel. There are buses inside the CPU, as well as on the motherboard. You can picture a bus as a highway with several lanes; each wire in the bus acts as a separate lane, transmitting one bit at a time. The number of bits being transmitted at one time is dependent on the *bus width*—the number of wires in the bus over which data can travel. Just as a wider highway allows more cars to travel at one time, a wider bus allows more data to be transferred at one time (see Figure 2-10). The *bus speed* is also a very important factor because the bus width and bus speed together determine the bus's **bandwidth**—that is, the amount of data that can be transferred via the bus in a given time period; the amount of data actually transferred under real-life conditions is called **throughput**.

Memory

Memory refers to chip-based storage. When the term *memory* is used alone, it refers to chip-based storage (typically *random access memory* or *RAM*, discussed next) that is located inside the system unit and used by the computer to store data on a short-term, temporary basis. In contrast, the term *storage* refers to the amount of long-term storage available to a computer—usually in the form of the computer's internal hard drive or removable storage media (such as CDs, DVDs, flash memory cards, and USB flash drives, all discussed in the next chapter), but it can also be in the form of chip-based *internal storage*—especially in mobile devices.

In addition to RAM, computer users should be familiar with four other types of computer memory. Two of these—*cache memory* and *registers*—are **volatile** like RAM, which means that their content is erased when power to the memory ceases; the other two—*read-only memory (ROM)* and *flash memory*—are **nonvolatile**. Cache memory has already been discussed; the other four types of memory are explained next.

Random Access Memory (RAM)

RAM (random access memory), also called *main memory* or *system memory*, is used to store the essential parts of the operating system while the computer is running, as well as the programs and data that the computer is currently using. When someone uses the term *memory* in reference to computers, he or she is usually referring to RAM. Because RAM is volatile, its content is lost when the computer is shut off. Data in RAM is also deleted

> **Bandwidth.** The amount of data that can be theoretically transferred through a communications medium in a given period of time.
> **Throughput.** The amount of data that is actually transferred through a communications medium under real-life conditions. > **Memory.** Chip-based storage. > **Volatile.** A characteristic of memory or storage in which data is not retained when the power to the computer is turned off.
> **Nonvolatile.** A characteristic of memory or storage in which data is retained even when the power to the computer is turned off.
> **RAM (random access memory).** Chips connected to the motherboard that provide a temporary location for the computer to hold data and program instructions while they are needed.

when it is no longer needed, such as when the program using that data is closed. If you want to retrieve a document later, you need to save the document on a storage medium before closing it, as discussed in more detail in Chapter 3. After the document is saved to a storage medium, it can be retrieved from the storage medium when it is needed, even though the document is erased from RAM when the document or the program being used to create that document is closed.

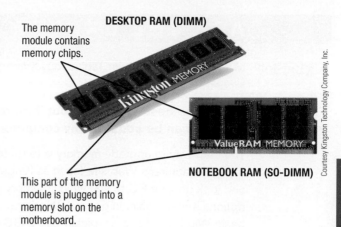

DESKTOP RAM (DIMM)

The memory module contains memory chips.

This part of the memory module is plugged into a memory slot on the motherboard.

NOTEBOOK RAM (SO-DIMM)

Courtesy Kingston Technology Company, Inc.

Like the CPU, RAM consists of electronic circuits etched onto chips. While smartphones and other mobile devices typically use *embedded memory chips*, the memory chips for servers and personal computers are typically arranged onto circuit boards called *memory modules* (see Figure 2-11), which, in turn, are plugged into the motherboard. Most desktop and server memory modules today are *dual in-line memory modules* or *DIMMs*. Notebook computers typically use a smaller type of memory module referred to as a *small outline DIMM* or *SO-DIMM*, though smaller devices may use the even smaller *Mini-DIMMs* or *Micro-DIMMs* instead. Most personal computers sold today have slots for two to four memory modules and at least one slot will be filled. For example, in the motherboard shown in Figure 2-7, there are two memory modules already installed and room to add an additional two modules, if needed. If you want to add more RAM to a computer and no empty slots are available, you must replace at least one of the existing memory modules with a higher capacity module in order to increase the amount of RAM in that computer.

FIGURE 2-11
RAM memory modules.

RAM capacity is measured in bytes. The amount of RAM that can be installed in a computer system depends on both the CPU in that computer and the operating system being used. For instance, while computers using 64-bit CPUs today can utilize a virtually unlimited amount of RAM (older 32-bit CPUs can use up to only 4 GB of RAM), a 64-bit operating system is needed in order to use more than 4 GB of RAM. In addition, different versions of a 64-bit operating system may support different amounts of RAM; for instance, the 64-bit versions of Windows 8 can use up to 4, 128, or 512 GB of RAM, depending on the edition of Windows 8 being used. Consequently, when you are considering adding more RAM to a computer, it is important to determine that your computer can support it. More RAM allows more applications to run at one time and the computer to respond more quickly when a user switches from task to task. Most personal computers sold for home use today have 2 to 8 GB of RAM.

TIP

With devices that use embedded memory chips instead of memory modules, you typically cannot expand or replace the RAM.

In addition to knowing the type of memory module and the amount of memory your computer can support, it is also important to select the proper type and speed of RAM when adding new memory. Most personal computers today use *SDRAM* (*synchronous dynamic RAM*). SDRAM is commonly available in *DDR* (*double-data rate*), *DDR2*, and *DDR3* versions. DDR memory sends data twice as often as ordinary SDRAM to increase throughput, DDR2 transmits twice as much data in the same time period as DDR, and DDR3 is about twice as fast as DDR2. Each type of SDRAM is typically available in a variety of speeds (measured in MHz)—for optimal performance, you should use the type and speed of RAM your computer was designed to use.

TIP

You can connect a portable storage device (such as a USB flash drive) and use it as additional memory if your computer supports the *Windows ReadyBoost* feature available in recent versions of Windows.

To further improve memory performance, memory today typically uses a *dual-channel memory architecture*, which has two paths that go to and from memory and so it can transfer twice as much data at one time as *single-channel memory architecture* of the same speed. *Tri-channel* (three paths) and *quad-channel* (four paths) *memory architecture* are also beginning to be used for higher performance. In order to take advantage of the improved performance of using multiple paths, multi-channel RAM typically needs to be installed in matched sets, such as two 2 GB dual-channel memory modules instead of a single 4 GB dual-channel memory module. As the number of cores used with CPUs grows,

ASK THE EXPERT

Kingston

Mark Tekunoff, Senior Technology Manager, Kingston Technology

What's the best way to find out if more memory can be added to my computer?

The best way to upgrade memory is to go to a memory manufacturer's Web site (such as Kingston.com) and look up your PC to see which memory upgrade options are available. In general, Windows Vista and basic Windows 7 users typically use 2 GB to 4 GB of memory. For 32-bit Windows 7 users, we recommend 3 GB to 4 GB of RAM; advanced users with 64-bit Windows 7 see advantages by using 4 GB to 8 GB of RAM. Windows 8 users should install a minimum of 4 GB. Power users who create or manipulate content such as large photos, stitching panoramic images, or processing video content will benefit from using 8 GB to 16 GB of system memory.

RAM performance is becoming increasingly important to ensure that data can be delivered to the CPU fast enough to match its processing capabilities.

While RAM as we know it today is volatile, *nonvolatile RAM* (*NVRAM*) retains its data when the power to the device is off. There are several types of nonvolatile RAM becoming available or under development. For instance, *magnetic RAM* (commonly referred to as *MRAM*) uses *magnetic polarization* rather than an electrical charge to store data, *memristor-based RAM* uses *memristors* (short for *memory resistors*) that change their resistance in response to current flowing through them, *NRAM* uses *carbon nanotubes* (discussed later in this chapter), and *PRAM* (*phase change random access memory*) has a special coating that changes its physical state when heat is applied (similar to the rewritable CDs and DVDs discussed in Chapter 3).

The most common applications for nonvolatile RAM today include storing critical data for enterprise systems as they operate to guard against data loss and saving the data necessary to help industrial automation and robotics systems recover quickly from a power loss. Other emerging applications include "instant-on" computers and mobile devices that can be turned on and off like an electric light, without any loss of data. Another advantage of nonvolatile RAM is that it doesn't require power to retain data so, when used in mobile devices, it consumes less power which can extend battery life. It is expected that, in the future, a form of nonvolatile RAM will replace volatile RAM, flash memory chips, and possibly even hard drives in computers. As capacities increase (Crossbar recently announced the development of a 1 TB NVRAM chip), that day may be getting closer.

Regardless of the type of RAM used, the CPU must be able to find data and programs located in memory when they are needed. To accomplish this, each location in memory has an address. Whenever a block of data, instruction, program, or result of a calculation is stored in memory, it is usually stored in one or more consecutive addresses, depending on its size (each address typically holds only one byte). The computer system sets up and maintains directory tables that keep track of where data is stored in memory in order to facilitate the retrieval of that data. When the computer has finished using a program or set of data, it frees up that memory space to hold other programs and data. Therefore, the content of each memory location constantly changes. This process can be roughly compared with the handling of the mailboxes in your local post office: the number on each P.O. box (memory location) remains the same, but the mail (data) stored inside changes as patrons remove their mail and as new mail arrives (see Figure 2-12).

FIGURE 2-12

Memory addressing.

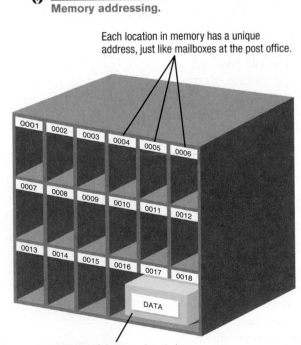

Each location in memory has a unique address, just like mailboxes at the post office.

Programs and blocks of data are almost always too big to fit in a single address. A directory keeps track of the first address used to store each program and data block, as well as the number of addresses each block spans.

Registers

A **register** is high-speed memory built into the CPU. Registers are used by the CPU to store data and intermediary results temporarily during processing. Registers are the fastest type of memory used by the CPU, even faster than Level 1 cache. Generally, more registers and larger registers result in increased CPU performance. Most CPUs contain multiple registers; registers are discussed in more detail later in this chapter.

Read-Only Memory (ROM)

ROM (read-only memory) consists of nonvolatile chips that permanently store data or programs. Like RAM, these chips are attached to the motherboard inside the system unit, and the data or programs are retrieved by the computer when they are needed. An important difference, however, is that you can neither write over the data or programs in ROM chips (which is the reason ROM chips are called *read-only*) nor erase their content when you shut off the computer's power. Traditionally, ROM was used to store the permanent instructions used by a computer (referred to as *firmware*). However, ROM is increasingly being replaced with *flash memory*, as discussed next, for any data that may need to be updated during the life of the computer.

Flash Memory

Flash memory consists of nonvolatile memory chips that can be used for storage by the computer or the user. Flash memory chips have begun to replace ROM for storing system information, such as a computer's *BIOS (basic input/output system)* or *Unified Extensible Firmware Interface (UEFI)* in Windows 8 computers—the sequence of instructions the computer follows during the boot process. For instance, one of the computer's first activities when you turn on the power is to perform a *power-on self-test* or *POST*. The POST takes an inventory of system components, checks each component to see if it is functioning properly, and initializes system settings, which produces the beeps you may hear as your computer boots. Traditionally, these instructions have been stored in ROM. By storing this information in flash memory instead of ROM, however, the boot sequence can be updated as needed. Similarly, firmware for personal computers and other devices (such as mobile phones and networking hardware) are now typically stored in flash memory that is embedded in the device so the firmware can be updated over the life of the product.

Flash memory chips are also built into many types of devices (such as media tablets, handheld gaming devices, mobile phones, digital cameras, and portable digital media players) for user storage, as well as built into storage media and devices (such as flash memory cards and USB flash drives). Flash memory media and devices used for storage purposes are discussed in more detail in Chapter 3.

Fans, Heat Sinks, and Other Cooling Components

One by-product of packing an increasing amount of technology into a smaller system unit is heat, an ongoing problem for CPU and computer manufacturers. Because heat can damage components and cooler chips can run faster, virtually all computers today employ *fans*, *heat sinks* (small components typically made out of aluminum with fins that help to dissipate heat), or other methods to cool the CPU and system unit. For instance, desktop computers today typically include several fans (such as a fan on the power supply that can be seen on the back of the computer, a fan on the video graphics board, and a fan and a heat

> **TIP**
>
> Product descriptions for media tablets and other devices that use built-in flash memory for storage sometimes refer to that storage as *memory*—it's important for shoppers to realize that this quantity refers to storage, not RAM.

>**Register.** High-speed memory built into the CPU that temporarily stores data during processing. >**ROM (read-only memory).** Nonvolatile chips located on the motherboard into which data or programs have been permanently stored. >**Flash memory.** Nonvolatile memory chips that can be used for storage by the computer or user; can be built into a computer or a storage medium.

Courtesy Green Revolution Cooling

SERVERS
Often use liquid cooling systems; an immersion cooling system is shown here.

Fans

Liquid cooling system

Courtesy of ABS Computer Technologies Inc.

DESKTOP COMPUTERS
Can use fans, heat sinks, and liquid cooling systems to cool the inside of the computer.

Built-in fan is powered by a USB cable that connects to the notebook.

Courtesy Belkin International, Inc.

NOTEBOOK COMPUTERS
Typically have at least one internal fan; notebook cooling stands can be used to cool the underside of the computer.

FIGURE 2-13
Computer cooling methods.

TIP

To more easily fit into the shrinking notebook and tablet PC form factors, fans the size and thickness of a credit card are in development and expected to become available before 2015.

sink on top of the CPU), while notebook computers typically include at least one fan. Mobile device cases today aren't designed for fans and so their cooling system typically relies on using mobile CPUs that run cooler than desktop CPUs and on adapting the speed and power of the device's components to cool the device as needed. However, as the speed and capabilities of mobile devices continue to increase, additional cooling methods may become necessary and are currently under development.

For servers and desktop computers that require a greater degree of cooling than fans can provide, *liquid cooling systems* can be used. Conventional liquid cooling systems consist of liquid (often a water solution) filled tubes that draw heat away from processors and other critical components. While significantly more expensive than fans and requiring more room inside the system unit, these systems can cool specific components to a greater degree than fans, can significantly reduce air-conditioning costs in server rooms, and are quieter. As shown in Figure 2-13, some desktop computers use a combination of fans and water cooling systems. An emerging possibility for cooling the servers in large data centers—such as the ones used to provide cloud services—is *immersion cooling* where the hardware is actually submerged into units filled with a liquid cooling solution (refer again to Figure 2-13). To cool the underside of a notebook computer—one of the problem areas—a *notebook cooling stand* (such as the one shown in Figure 2-13) can be used.

Because heat is an ongoing problem with computers, new cooling technologies are continually being developed. One emerging possibility is a cooling system—such as a liquid cooling system or an *ion pump cooling system*, which continuously cools the air with no moving parts—built directly into the CPU design.

Expansion Slots, Expansion Cards, and ExpressCard Modules

Expansion slots are locations on the motherboard into which **expansion cards** (also called *interface cards*) can be inserted to connect those cards to the motherboard. Expansion cards are used to give desktop (and to a limited extent, notebook) computers additional

---

>**Expansion slot.** A location on the motherboard into which expansion cards are inserted. >**Expansion card.** A circuit board that can be inserted into an expansion slot location on a computer's motherboard to add additional functionality or to connect a peripheral device to that computer.

capabilities, such as to connect the computer to a network, to add a TV tuner to allow television shows to be watched and recorded on the computer, to add a hard drive to the computer, or to connect a monitor to the computer. Today, some basic capabilities (such as the necessary connectors for speakers and monitors) are often integrated directly into the motherboard instead of requiring the use of an expansion card. However, an expansion card can be added and used when needed. For instance, a *video graphics card* can be added to a computer to add additional capabilities not allowed by the computer's *integrated graphics* feature. Most new desktop computers come with a few empty expansion slots on the motherboard so that new expansion cards can be added when new capabilities are needed. There are several different types of expansion cards, such as *PCI* and *PCIe*—each corresponds to a specific type of expansion slot, as discussed in the next section, and they are not interchangeable.

It is much less common to add an expansion card to a notebook or other portable computer because most capabilities (such as graphics and networking capabilities) are integrated directly into the motherboard or CPU or are added during manufacturing using an interface designed specifically for smaller devices, such as *Mini-PCIe* or *Mobile PCIe* (*M-PCIe*). When additional functionality or an external port is needed, an external adapter compatible with that portable computer is typically used, as discussed next.

Traditionally, *PC Cards* and then *ExpressCard modules* were inserted into the appropriate slot on a notebook computer to add additional functionality without having to work inside the system unit. While some notebooks designed for business use still include an ExpressCard slot today, most adapters (such as network adapters) are available in USB versions and so can be used with any desktop or portable computer that has an available USB port. Expansion for mobile devices is usually much more limited than with portable and desktop computers and is often restricted to devices that can plug into a USB port or flash memory card slot. Ports are discussed in more detail shortly.

Figure 2-14 shows an expansion card, an ExpressCard module, and a USB adapter. Regardless of their form, expansion devices designed to connect external devices (such as a monitor or piece of networking hardware) have a port accessible to connect that device; those that do not need to connect to additional hardware (such as a hard drive card or wireless networking card) do not have an exposed port.

FIGURE 2-14
Types of expansion.

The port on this network interface card is accessible through the exterior of the system unit's case.   This part of the card plugs into an empty PCIe slot on the motherboard.

There is no external port because this is a wireless networking card.   This end of the card is inserted into an ExpressCard slot.

This end of the adapter is inserted into an empty USB port.   There is no external port because this is a wireless networking adapter.

PCIe
EXPANSION CARDS
(for desktop computers)

EXPRESSCARD
MODULES
(for portable computers)

USB ADAPTERS
(for any device with an available USB port)

Courtesy D-Link Systems, Inc.;
Courtesy NETGEAR

Buses

As already discussed, a **bus** in a computer is an electronic path over which data travels. There are buses located within the CPU to move data between CPU components; there are also a variety of buses etched onto the motherboard to tie the CPU to memory and to peripheral devices (one possible *bus architecture* for a desktop computer is shown in Figure 2-15). The buses that connect peripheral (typically input and output) devices to the motherboard are often called **expansion buses**. Expansion buses connect directly to ports

FIGURE 2-15

Buses and expansion slots.

Buses transport bits and bytes from one component to another, including the CPU, RAM, and peripheral devices.

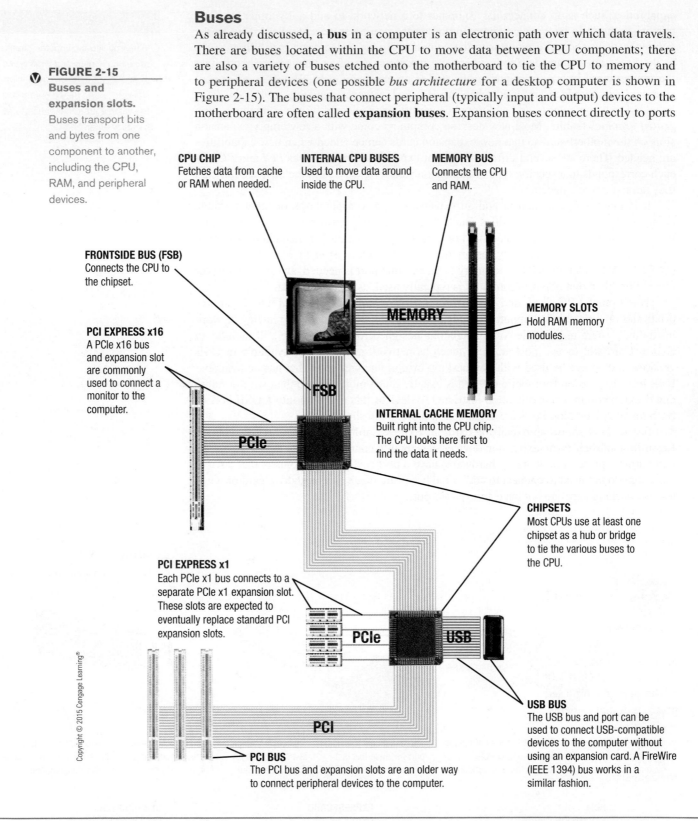

CPU CHIP
Fetches data from cache or RAM when needed.

INTERNAL CPU BUSES
Used to move data around inside the CPU.

MEMORY BUS
Connects the CPU and RAM.

FRONTSIDE BUS (FSB)
Connects the CPU to the chipset.

MEMORY SLOTS
Hold RAM memory modules.

PCI EXPRESS x16
A PCIe x16 bus and expansion slot are commonly used to connect a monitor to the computer.

INTERNAL CACHE MEMORY
Built right into the CPU chip. The CPU looks here first to find the data it needs.

CHIPSETS
Most CPUs use at least one chipset as a hub or bridge to tie the various buses to the CPU.

PCI EXPRESS x1
Each PCIe x1 bus connects to a separate PCIe x1 expansion slot. These slots are expected to eventually replace standard PCI expansion slots.

USB BUS
The USB bus and port can be used to connect USB-compatible devices to the computer without using an expansion card. A FireWire (IEEE 1394) bus works in a similar fashion.

PCI BUS
The PCI bus and expansion slots are an older way to connect peripheral devices to the computer.

>**Bus.** An electronic path on the motherboard or within the CPU or other computer component along which data is transferred. >**Expansion bus.** A bus on the motherboard used to connect peripheral devices.

on the system unit case or to expansion slots on the motherboard (some of the most common expansion buses and expansion slots are illustrated in Figure 2-15). It is important to realize that expansion slots are not interchangeable—that is, each type of expansion slot is designed for a specific type of expansion card, such as *PCI* or *PCI Express (PCIe)*. The specific buses shown in Figure 2-15 are discussed next; other common buses not shown in Figure 2-15 include those used to connect a hard drive (as discussed in Chapter 3) and those used for networking connections (discussed in Chapter 7). Portable computers and mobile devices have at least some of the buses discussed next, but typically not as many.

Memory Bus

One relatively recent change in the bus architecture used with most personal computers today is connecting the CPU directly to RAM, as shown in Figure 2-15. This change allows for increased performance; the bus used to connect the CPU to RAM is typically called the **memory bus**.

Frontside Bus (FSB)

The **frontside bus** (**FSB**) connects the CPU to the *chipset*—a set of chips that connects the various buses together and connects the CPU to the rest of the bus architecture. Because of the importance of the FSB connection, CPU manufacturers typically use special high-speed technologies; for instance, Intel uses its *QuickPath Interconnect* (*QPI*) technology and AMD uses its *HyperTransport Technology*.

PCI and PCI Express (PCIe) Bus

The *PCI (Peripheral Component Interconnect)* *bus* has been one of the most common types of expansion buses in past years. In new computers, however, the PCI bus has essentially been replaced with the **PCI Express (PCIe) bus**. The PCIe bus is available in several different widths. The 16-bit version of PCIe (referred to as *PCIe x16*) is commonly used with video graphics cards to connect a monitor to a computer; expansion cards for other peripherals often connect via the 1-bit PCIe bus (referred to as *PCIe x1*). PCIe is extremely fast—the current version (*PCIe 3.0*) of the 1-bit PCIe bus, at 16 *Gbps* (billions of bits per second), is approximately 16 times faster than the standard PCI bus; PCIe x16 is significantly faster at 256 Gbps. The upcoming *PCIe 4.0* standard essentially doubles the speed of each PCIe bus.

USB Bus

One of the more versatile bus architectures is the **Universal Serial Bus (USB)**. The USB standard allows 127 different devices to connect to a computer via a single USB port on the computer's system unit. At 12 *Mbps* (millions of bits per second), the original *USB 1.0* standard is slow. However, the newer *USB 2.0* standard supports data transfer rates of 480 Mbps and the newest 4.8 Gbps *USB 3.0* standard (also called *SuperSpeed USB*) is about 10 times as fast as USB 2.0. The convenience and universal support of USB have made it one of the most widely used standards for connecting peripherals (such as keyboards, mice, printers, digital cameras, and storage devices) today.

FireWire Bus

FireWire (also known as *IEEE 1394*) is a high-speed bus standard developed by Apple for connecting devices—particularly multimedia devices like digital video cameras—to

TIP

While technically the term *chipset* can refer to any set of chips, it most commonly refers to the chips (traditionally a set of two but often a single chip today) that connect the various buses to each other and to the CPU.

TIP

The wireless *Bluetooth* standard is increasingly being used to connect peripheral devices to a computer to reduce the dependence on USB ports; Bluetooth and wireless networking are discussed in detail in Chapter 7.

>**Memory bus.** The connection between the CPU and RAM. >**Frontside bus (FSB).** The bus that connects the CPU to the chipset that connects to the rest of the bus architecture. >**PCI Express (PCIe) bus.** One of the buses most commonly used to connect peripheral devices. >**Universal Serial Bus (USB).** A universal bus used to connect up to 127 peripheral devices to a computer without requiring the use of additional expansion cards. >**FireWire.** A high-speed bus standard sometimes used to connect digital video cameras and other multimedia hardware to a computer.

a computer. Like USB, FireWire can connect multiple external devices via a single port. FireWire is relatively fast—the original FireWire standard supports data transfer rates of up to 320 Mbps, the newer FireWire standard (called *FireWire 800*) supports data transfer rates up to 800 Mbps, and the emerging *FireWire 3200* standard is expected to support 3.2 Gbps transfer rates.

Ports and Connectors

As already mentioned, **ports** are the connectors located on the exterior of the system unit that are used to connect external hardware devices. Each port is attached to the appropriate bus on the motherboard so that when a device is plugged into a port, the device can communicate with the CPU and other computer components. Several of the original ports used with desktop computers—such as the *parallel ports* traditionally used to connect printers, as well as the *keyboard* and *mouse ports* traditionally used to connect keyboards and mice—are now considered *legacy ports* and so are not typically included on newer computers. Typical ports for a desktop computer and the connectors used with those ports are shown in Figure 2-16; these and additional ports you might find on your computer are discussed next.

➤ *Monitor ports* are used to connect a monitor to a computer. Traditionally, monitors connect via a *VGA connector* or *Digital Video Interface (DVI)* connector. *High-definition monitors* usually connect via an *HDMI (High-Definition Multimedia Interface)*; mobile devices typically use a *Mini-HDMI port* or the even smaller *Micro-HDMI port* instead. Additional options for connecting monitors, such as *Display Port* and wireless options, are discussed in Chapter 4.

FIGURE 2-16

Typical ports for desktop computers and examples of connectors.

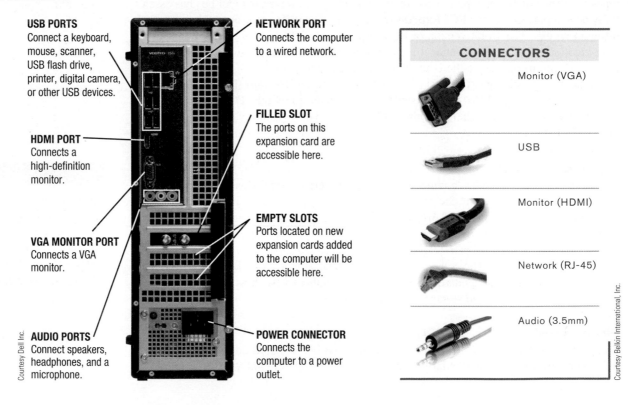

USB PORTS
Connect a keyboard, mouse, scanner, USB flash drive, printer, digital camera, or other USB devices.

HDMI PORT
Connects a high-definition monitor.

VGA MONITOR PORT
Connects a VGA monitor.

AUDIO PORTS
Connect speakers, headphones, and a microphone.

NETWORK PORT
Connects the computer to a wired network.

FILLED SLOT
The ports on this expansion card are accessible here.

EMPTY SLOTS
Ports located on new expansion cards added to the computer will be accessible here.

POWER CONNECTOR
Connects the computer to a power outlet.

CONNECTORS

Monitor (VGA)

USB

Monitor (HDMI)

Network (RJ-45)

Audio (3.5mm)

Courtesy Dell Inc.

Courtesy Belkin International, Inc.

>**Port.** A connector on the exterior of a computer to which a device may be attached.

➤ *Network ports* are used to connect a computer to a computer network via a networking cable—typically a cable using an *RJ-45 connector*, which looks similar to a telephone connector (refer again to Figure 2-16) but is larger. Networks and networking hardware are discussed in detail in Chapter 7.

➤ *USB ports* are used to connect USB devices (such as keyboards, mice, printers, hard drives, and digital cameras) to a computer via a USB connector. Multiple USB devices can connect to a single USB port via a *USB hub*, such as the one shown in Figure 2-17. Smaller *mini-USB ports* or the even smaller *micro-USB ports* are often included on mobile devices instead of a full-sized USB port.

Courtesy Belkin International, Inc.

FIGURE 2-17
USB hubs. A USB hub is used to connect multiple USB devices to a single USB port.

➤ *FireWire (IEEE 1394) ports* are used to connect FireWire devices to the computer via a FireWire connector. Similar to a USB hub, a *FireWire hub* can be used to connect multiple devices to a single port. FireWire connections are most often used with digital video cameras and other multimedia peripherals.

➤ *IrDA (Infrared Data Association) ports* and *Bluetooth ports* are used to receive wireless transmissions from devices; because the transmissions are wireless, these ports do not use a plug. IrDA ports are commonly used to "beam" data from a portable computer or mobile device to a computer. Bluetooth ports are most often used with wireless keyboards, mice, and headsets. Wireless data transmission is discussed in more detail in Chapter 7.

➤ *Flash memory card slots* are used to connect flash memory cards or other hardware using a flash memory card interface. As discussed shortly, some hardware for portable computers is designed to connect using these slots.

➤ *Audio ports* are used to connect speakers, headphones, or a microphone to the computer.

➤ *eSATA (external SATA) ports* are used to connect external SATA devices (most commonly, an external hard drive). External hard drives that connect via eSATA are much faster than external hard drives that connect via a USB or FireWire connection. Hard drives are discussed in detail in Chapter 3.

➤ *Thunderbolt ports* (available primarily on Apple devices at the present time) are used to connect peripheral devices (such as storage devices and monitors) via Thunderbolt cables. At 10 Gbps, Thunderbolt is extremely fast and up to six devices can be daisy-chained together to connect them via a single Thunderbolt port.

Most computers today support the *Plug and Play* standard, which means the computer automatically configures new devices as soon as they are installed and the computer is powered up. If you want to add a new device to your computer and there is an available port for the device you want to add, then you just need to plug it in. If the appropriate port is not available, you need to either install the appropriate expansion card to create the necessary port or use a USB or FireWire version of the device, if you have one of those two ports available on your computer. USB and FireWire devices are *hot-swappable*, meaning they can be plugged into their respective ports while the computer is powered up. Hot-swappable devices—along with some removable storage media, such as flash memory cards—are recognized by the computer as soon as they are connected to it and can be used right away. Other devices are recognized by the computer when the computer is first powered up after the device has been added.

TIP

Mobile phones, media tablets, and other devices that may be used in conjunction with a mobile phone network will also have a *Subscriber Identity Module (SIM) card slot* to hold the appropriate *SIM card*.

TIP

HDMI and Thunderbolt cables can be used to transmit both audio and video data; Thunderbolt cables can transfer power as well.

TREND

Tablet Docks

Notebook computer docking stations for use in the home or office have been available for several years. These docking stations make it easier for users to connect their portable computers to hardware (such as a second monitor, a wired printer, or a wired network connection) that stays behind at the home or office. In response to the unprecedented popularity of mobile devices today, new docking options are becoming available. For example, *tablet docks* are emerging to help tablet users with productivity in addition to mobility.

Some tablet docks are designed primarily as a stand to hold the device for easier, hands-free viewing. But, increasingly, tablet docks are including a keyboard for easier data entry; these types of docks typically include a special *docking port* to connect the tablet to the dock. Tablet docks can also have additional functionality, including ports to connect peripheral devices (such as a mouse or an additional monitor) to the tablet. Some tablet docks include a second battery to extend the battery life of the device; others incorporate battery-charging capabilities into the dock so the device can be recharged while it is docked. Some tablets—such as the

detachable hybrid notebook-tablet computers discussed in Chapter 1 and the media tablet shown in the accompanying photo—are sold as a package with both the tablet and dock included for flexibility. Stand-alone docks are also available for iPads and other tablets that do not come with a dock.

Up next: Docks for your mobile phone.

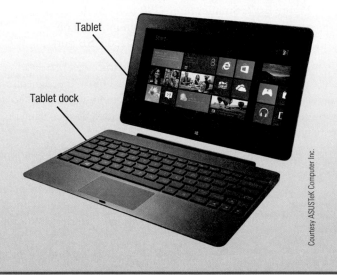

Tablet

Tablet dock

Courtesy ASUSTeK Computer Inc.

Portable computers have ports similar to desktop computers (see Figure 2-18), but they often have fewer of them. Smartphones and other mobile devices have a more limited amount of expandability (for a look at an emerging trend for media tablets—*tablet docks*—see the Trend box). However, mobile devices commonly have a USB port, HDMI port, and/or a flash memory card slot (an adapter must be used in conjunction with the special *Lightning port* on Apple mobile devices to provide a USB port to connect compatible USB devices). The most common type of flash memory cards used with mobile devices today

◈ FIGURE 2-18
Typical ports for
portable computers.

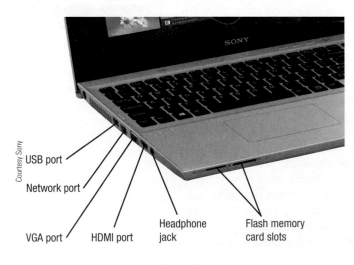

Courtesy Sony

USB port
Network port
VGA port
HDMI port
Headphone jack
Flash memory card slots

NOTEBOOK COMPUTERS

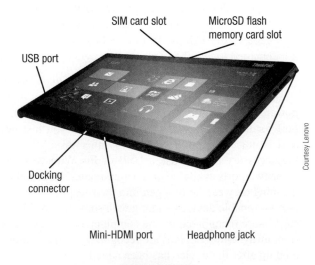

SIM card slot
MicroSD flash memory card slot
USB port
Docking connector
Mini-HDMI port
Headphone jack

Courtesy Lenovo

MOBILE DEVICES

use the *Secure Digital (SD)* format. Regular SD slots can be used with both SD flash memory cards and with peripheral devices adhering to the *Secure Digital Input/Output (SDIO) standard. MiniSD* and *microSD slots* can be used with the smaller *miniSD* and *microSD cards*, as discussed in more detail in Chapter 3.

HOW THE CPU WORKS

As already discussed, a CPU consists of a variety of circuitry and components packaged together. The key element of the processor is the *transistor*—a device made of semiconductor material that controls the flow of electrons inside a chip. Today's CPUs contain hundreds of millions of transistors, and the number doubles approximately every 18 months. This phenomenon is known as *Moore's Law* and is explained in the Inside the Industry box. The primary components of a typical CPU are discussed next.

Typical CPU Components

To begin to understand how a CPU works, you need to know how the CPU is organized and what components it includes. This information will help you understand how electronic impulses move from one part of the CPU to another to process data. The architecture and components included in a CPU (referred to as *microarchitecture*) vary from processor to processor. A simplified example of the principal components that might be included in a single core of a typical CPU is shown in Figure 2-19 and discussed next. There are also additional components that are typically located inside the CPU, but not within each core. For instance, there are buses to connect the CPU cores to each other (typically via QuickPath Interconnect (QPI) or HyperTransport Technology connections), buses to connect each core to the CPU's *memory controller* (which controls the communication between the CPU cores and RAM), and buses to connect each core to any cache memory that is shared between the cores. If the CPU contains a graphics processing unit (GPU), as in the most recent CPU designs from Intel and AMD, that would be located inside the CPU package as well.

FIGURE 2-19
Inside a CPU core.

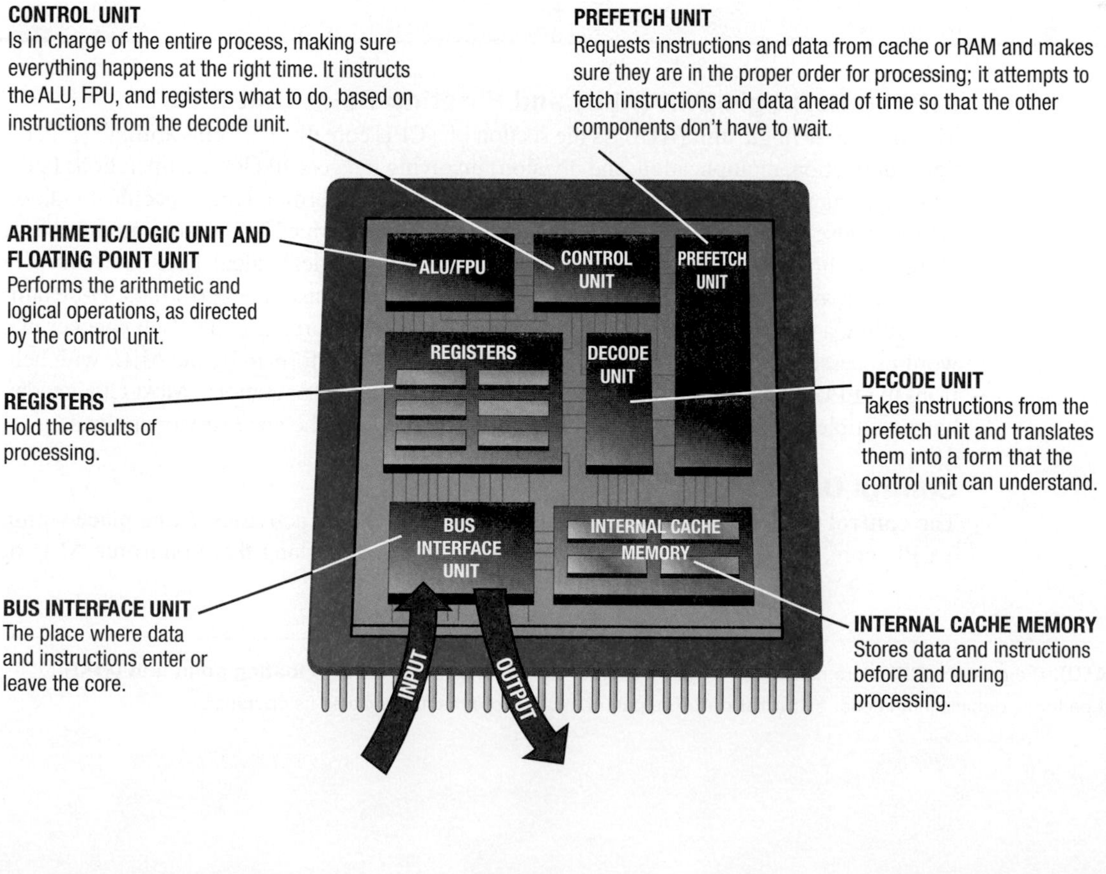

CONTROL UNIT
Is in charge of the entire process, making sure everything happens at the right time. It instructs the ALU, FPU, and registers what to do, based on instructions from the decode unit.

PREFETCH UNIT
Requests instructions and data from cache or RAM and makes sure they are in the proper order for processing; it attempts to fetch instructions and data ahead of time so that the other components don't have to wait.

ARITHMETIC/LOGIC UNIT AND FLOATING POINT UNIT
Performs the arithmetic and logical operations, as directed by the control unit.

REGISTERS
Hold the results of processing.

BUS INTERFACE UNIT
The place where data and instructions enter or leave the core.

DECODE UNIT
Takes instructions from the prefetch unit and translates them into a form that the control unit can understand.

INTERNAL CACHE MEMORY
Stores data and instructions before and during processing.

ALU/FPU • CONTROL UNIT • PREFETCH UNIT • REGISTERS • DECODE UNIT • BUS INTERFACE UNIT • INTERNAL CACHE MEMORY • INPUT • OUTPUT

Copyright © 2015 Cengage Learning®

INSIDE THE INDUSTRY

Moore's Law

In 1965, Gordon Moore, the co-founder of Intel and shown in the accompanying photograph, observed that the number of transistors per square inch on chips had doubled every two years since the integrated circuit was invented. He then made a now-famous prediction—that this doubling trend would continue for at least 10 more years. Here we are, close to 50 years later, and transistor density still doubles about every 18 months. Due to technological breakthroughs, *Moore's Law* has been maintained for far longer than the original prediction and most experts, including Moore himself, expect the doubling trend to continue for at least another decade. In fact, Intel states that the mission of its technology development team is to continue to break barriers to Moore's Law.

Interestingly, other computer components also follow Moore's Law. For example, storage capacity doubles approximately every 20 months, and chip speed doubles about every 24 months. Consequently, the term *Moore's Law* has been expanded and is now used to describe the amount of time it takes components to double in capacity or speed. Many experts predict that, eventually, a physical limit to the number of transistors that can be crammed onto a chip will end Moore's Law for current CPU technology. But new technology is being developed all the time and so the end of Moore's Law is not yet in sight.

Courtesy Intel Corporation

Gordon Moore (1970).

Arithmetic/Logic Unit (ALU) and Floating Point Unit (FPU)

The **arithmetic/logic unit** (**ALU**) is the section of a CPU core that performs arithmetic (addition, subtraction, multiplication, and division) involving integers and logical operations (such as comparing two pieces of data to see if they are equal or determining if a specific condition is true or false). Arithmetic requiring decimals is usually performed by the **floating point unit** (**FPU**). Arithmetic operations are performed when mathematical calculations are requested by the user, as well as when many other common computing tasks are performed. For example, editing a digital photograph in an image editing program, running the spell checker in a word processing program, and burning a music CD are all performed by the ALU, with help from the FPU when needed, using only arithmetic and logical operations. Most CPUs today have multiple ALUs and FPUs that work together to perform the necessary operations.

Control Unit

The **control unit** coordinates and controls the operations and activities taking place within a CPU core, such as retrieving data and instructions and passing them on to the ALU or

---

>**Arithmetic/logic unit (ALU).** The part of a CPU core that performs logical operations and integer arithmetic. >**Floating point unit (FPU).** The part of a CPU core that performs decimal arithmetic. >**Control unit.** The part of a CPU core that coordinates its operations.

FPU for execution. In other words, it directs the flow of electronic traffic within the core, much like a traffic cop controls the flow of vehicles on a roadway. Essentially, the control unit tells the ALU and FPU what to do and makes sure that everything happens at the right time in order for the appropriate processing to take place.

Prefetch Unit

The **prefetch unit** orders data and instructions from cache or RAM based on the current task. The prefetch unit tries to predict what data and instructions will be needed and retrieves them ahead of time in order to help avoid delays in processing.

Decode Unit

The **decode unit** takes the instructions fetched by the prefetch unit and translates them into a form that can be understood by the control unit, ALU, and FPU. The decoded instructions go to the control unit for processing.

Registers and Internal Cache Memory

As mentioned earlier, registers and cache memory are both types of memory used by the CPU. Registers are groups of high-speed memory located within the CPU that are used during processing. The ALU and FPU use registers to store data, intermediary calculations, and the results of processing temporarily. CPU registers are also used for other purposes, such as to hold status information, program counters, or memory addresses. Internal cache memory (such as the Level 1 and Level 2 cache typically built into each core of a CPU and the Level 3 cache that is often shared by all cores of the CPU) is used to store instructions and data for the CPU in order to avoid retrieving them from RAM or the hard drive.

Bus Interface Unit

The **bus interface unit** allows the core to communicate with other CPU components, such as the memory controller and other cores. As previously mentioned, the memory controller controls the flow of instructions and data going between the CPU cores and RAM.

The System Clock and the Machine Cycle

As mentioned at the beginning of this chapter, every instruction that you issue to a computer—by either typing a command or clicking something with the mouse—is converted into machine language. In turn, each machine language instruction in a CPU's *instruction set* (the collection of basic machine language commands that the CPU can understand) is broken down into several smaller, machine-level instructions called *microcode*. Microcode instructions, such as moving a single piece of data from one part of the computer system to another or adding the numbers located in two specific registers, are built into the CPU and are the basic instructions used by the CPU.

In order to synchronize all of a computer's operations, a **system clock**—a small quartz crystal located on the motherboard—is used. The system clock sends out a signal on a regular basis to all other computer components, similar to a musician's metronome or a person's heartbeat. Each signal is referred to as a *cycle*. The number of cycles per second is measured in *hertz (Hz)*. One megahertz (MHz) is equal to one million ticks of the system clock.

>**Prefetch unit.** The part of a CPU core that attempts to retrieve data and instructions before they are needed for processing in order to avoid delays. >**Decode unit.** The part of a CPU core that translates instructions into a form that can be processed by the ALU and FPU. >**Bus interface unit.** The part of a CPU core that allows it to communicate with other CPU components. >**System clock.** The timing mechanism within the computer system that synchronizes the computer's operations.

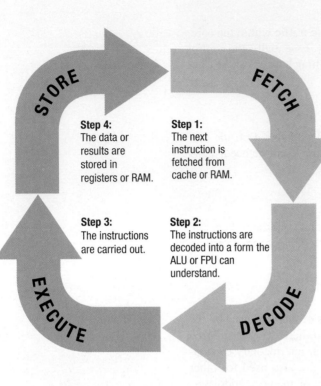

STORE

Step 4:
The data or
results are
stored in
registers or RAM.

FETCH

Step 1:
The next
instruction is
fetched from
cache or RAM.

Step 3:
The instructions
are carried out.

Step 2:
The instructions are
decoded into a form the
ALU or FPU can
understand.

EXECUTE

DECODE

FIGURE 2-20
A machine cycle.
A machine cycle is
typically accomplished
in four steps.

Many personal computers today have system clocks that run at 200 MHz, and all devices (such as CPUs) that are synchronized with these system clocks run at either the system clock speed or at a multiple of or a fraction of the system clock speed. For example, a CPU with a *CPU clock speed* of 2 GHz uses a multiplier of 10, meaning that the CPU clock essentially "ticks" 10 times during each system clock tick. During each CPU clock tick, the CPU can execute one or more pieces of microcode. Virtually all CPUs today can process more than one piece of microcode at one time—a characteristic known as *superscalar*, which is the ability to process multiple *instructions per cycle* (*IPC*). A CPU with a higher CPU clock speed processes more instructions per second than the same CPU with a lower CPU clock speed.

Whenever the CPU processes a single piece of microcode, it is referred to as a **machine cycle**. Each machine cycle consists of the four general operations illustrated in Figure 2-20 and discussed next.

1. *Fetch*—the program instruction is fetched.
2. *Decode*—the instructions are decoded so the control unit, ALU, and FPU can understand them.
3. *Execute*—the instructions are carried out.
4. *Store*—the original data or the result from the ALU or FPU execution is stored in the CPU's registers.

Because each machine cycle processes only a single microcode instruction, many seemingly simple commands (such as multiplying two numbers) might require more than one machine cycle, and a computer might need to go through thousands, millions, or even billions of machine cycles to complete a user command or program instruction. For instance, a CPU processing the command 2 + 3 would typically require at least four machine cycles, such as to:

1. Fetch the number 2 from RAM, decode it, and store it in register X.
2. Fetch the number 3 from RAM, decode it, and store it in a register Y.
3. Fetch and decode the addition instruction, then add the two numbers (currently stored in registers X and Y) and store the sum in register Z.
4. Fetch and decode the instruction to display the sum, and then output the sum (currently stored in register Z) to RAM.

MAKING COMPUTERS FASTER AND BETTER NOW AND IN THE FUTURE

Over the years, computer designers have developed a number of strategies to achieve faster, more powerful, and more reliable computing performance. Researchers are also constantly working on ways to improve the performance of computers of the future. There are several ways computer users can speed up their existing computers today, and a

> **Machine cycle.** The series of operations involved in the execution of a single machine-level instruction.

number of technologies are being developed by manufacturers to improve computers both today and in the future.

Improving the Performance of Your System Today

Several strategies you can use to try to improve the performance of your current computer are discussed next.

Add More Memory

With today's graphic-intensive interfaces and applications, much more memory is required than was necessary even a couple of years ago. If your computer is just a few years old, slows down significantly when you have multiple programs open, and has less than 4 GB of RAM installed, you should consider adding more memory to your system. To accomplish this, first check to see if there is room inside your computer for any additional memory modules (either by looking inside the computer or by using a scanning utility like the one shown in Figure 2-21 that is available on some memory manufacturers' Web sites). You can then determine (either by the scan information or by checking with your computer's manufacturer) the maximum amount of memory that can be added to your computer and what type and speed of RAM your computer requires. If you do not have enough empty memory slots in your computer, you will need to remove some of the old memory modules and replace them with newer, higher capacity ones in order to add more memory to your system. Remember that some memory modules must be added in sets (such as pairs or triplets) for optimal performance.

Details the quantity and type of RAM that is currently installed.

Lists options for memory expansion.

FIGURE 2-21
Online memory scanners can help you determine what memory can be added to your computer.

CAUTION CAUTION CAUTION CAUTION CAUTION CAUTION CAUT

Never open the case of your computer when it is powered up or plugged into an electrical outlet. To avoid damaging your computer with the static electricity stored in your body, consider wearing an *antistatic wristband*.

TIP

If your computer is running slowly and you have many programs and windows open, close a few to see if your performance improves; if not, try rebooting your PC to reset the system files.

Perform System Maintenance

As you work and use your hard drive to store and retrieve data, and as you install and uninstall programs, most computers tend to become less efficient. One reason for this is because as large documents are stored, retrieved, and then stored again, they often become *fragmented*—that is, not stored in contiguous (adjacent) storage areas. Because the different pieces of the document are physically located in different places, it may take longer for the computer to retrieve or store them. Another reason a computer might become inefficient is that when programs are uninstalled, pieces of the program are sometimes left behind or references to these programs are left in operating system files, such as the *Windows registry*. In addition, as a hard drive begins to get full, it takes longer to locate the data stored on the hard drive. All of these factors can result in a system performing more slowly than it should.

To avoid some of these problems, regular system maintenance should be performed. Some system maintenance tips every computer user should be aware of are:

➤ Uninstall any programs that you no longer want on your computer in order to free up space on your hard drive. Be sure to use the proper removal process, such as the *Uninstall or change a program* option in the Windows Control Panel or an *Uninstall* option for that program located on the Start menu or Start screen. Windows users

FIGURE 2-22
Windows Disk Cleanup. Running the Disk Cleanup program can help free up room on your hard drive.

> **TIP**
>
> Windows users should also reboot their computers at least once per week to clear out memory, stop programs that might be running unnoticed in the background, and otherwise increase performance.

> **TIP**
>
> Using an external USB or FireWire hard drive to store your data makes it very fast and easy to move your data to a different computer, when needed. It also protects your data from being lost if the main hard drive on your computer stops working or if you need to restore your computer's main hard drive back to its original state.

can also periodically use a *registry cleaner* (a number of free registry cleaners are available online) to clean the Windows registry by removing references to nonexistent programs.

> Remove any unnecessary programs from the startup list so they don't run every time the PC boots. Windows 8 users can use the Startup tab on the Task Manager (users of older versions of Windows can run the *msconfig* command using the search box at the bottom of the Start menu) to view and change the programs that run automatically, as discussed in more detail in Chapter 5.

> If you have large files (such as digital photos or videos) stored on your computer that you do not need on a regular basis but want to keep, consider moving them to a DVD disc or an external hard drive and then deleting them from your hard drive to free up space. Make sure the files open on the storage medium before deleting the files from your hard drive, and consider copying important files to two different storage media. Backing up files, deleting files, and types of storage media are discussed in more detail in later chapters.

> Delete the temporary files (such as installation files, Web browsing history, and files in the Recycle Bin) stored by your computer and Web browser to free up room on your hard drive. You can delete these files manually, if desired, but the *Windows Disk Cleanup* program shown in Figure 2-22 can locate and delete these temporary files for you.

> *Error-check* and *defragment* your hard drive periodically to make it work more efficiently. Windows users can right-click a hard drive icon in File Explorer or Windows Explorer, select *Properties*, and then select the *Check* or *Check now* option on the Tools tab to check that hard drive for errors, or select *Optimize* or *Defragment now* to defragment that hard drive. Many computers are set up to defragment hard drives automatically on a regular basis.

> Scan for *computer viruses* and *spyware* continually. A computer that suddenly slows down might be the result of a computer virus, spyware program, or other threat. As discussed in Chapter 9, security software can help detect and correct these problems.

> Clean out the dust from inside the system unit of desktop computers once or twice a year using a can of compressed air or a small vacuum cleaner designed for this purpose. Although the dust may not slow down your system by itself, it can slow down the fans that cool your computer as well as cause the components inside your computer to run hotter than they should, which can cause problems with your computer such as overheating, burned out components, and periodic shutting down without warning. Notebook users should also clean their fans when needed and check the bottom of their computers to see if there is a removable dust filter—if there is one, it should be cleaned periodically.

Buy a Larger or Second Hard Drive

As already mentioned, hard drives become less efficient as they fill up. If your hard drive is almost full and you do not have any data or programs that you can remove, consider buying and installing a second hard drive. The new hard drive can be an internal hard drive if you have an empty drive bay inside your computer. It can also be an external hard drive that connects via an available (typically USB) port. Hard drives are discussed in detail in Chapter 3.

Upgrade Your Internet Connection

If your system seems slow primarily when you are using the Internet, the culprit might be your Internet connection. If you are using a *conventional dial-up connection* (the relatively slow Internet access available via your telephone line), consider upgrading to a faster type of connection. Switching to *cable, satellite, DSL, fixed wireless,* or another type of *broadband Internet service* is more expensive than dial-up, but it is significantly faster. The differences between these and other types of Internet connections are described in Chapters 7 and 8.

Upgrade Your Video Graphics Card

If you are using a desktop computer and programs, documents, and other items seem slug-gish as they are displayed on your monitor, you can check to see if a video upgrade might help. First, determine if your computer has the graphics processing unit integrated into the motherboard, into the CPU, or on a separate video graphics card. If it uses graphics integrated into the motherboard, then installing a separate video card containing adequate video memory may speed up your system because it will free up the RAM currently being used for video memory. You may also want to buy and install a new video card if your video graphics card isn't adequate and you are a gamer, computer artist, graphical engi-neer, or otherwise use 3D-graphic-intensive applications. Users of notebooks that have *switchable graphics* capabilities can select integrated graphics when they are working on battery power to save power, and then switch to using the video graphics card when extra performance is needed or when the computer is plugged in.

> **TIP** ✓
>
> While it is sometimes possible to upgrade the video graphics card in a notebook computer, it is much more difficult to upgrade a notebook computer than it is to upgrade a desktop computer.

Strategies for Making Faster and Better Computers

Researchers and manufacturers are using several strategies today to continue to build faster and better personal computers. Some relate to technology in general (such as the *virtual-ization* trend discussed in Chapter 1); others are techniques used specifically to speed up the CPU. Some of these strategies are described in the next few sections.

Improved Architecture

Computer manufacturers are continually working to improve the basic architecture of comput-ers, such as to make them faster, cooler, quieter, more energy efficient, and more reliable. For example, new designs for motherboards and CPUs are always under development, and com-puter components are continually being built smaller, so more power and capabilities can be contained in the same size package. In fact, today's CPUs—which are formed using a process called *lithography* that imprints patterns on semiconductor materials—typically contain tran-sistors that are 32 or 22 *nanometers* (*nm*) in size (1 nanometer is a billionth of a meter), though 14 nm chips are expected to be available by 2014, and transistors as small as a single atom have been created in lab settings. As lithography techniques continue to improve, transistors will likely continue to shrink, allowing more transistors to fit on the same-sized CPU. Creating components smaller than 100 nm fits the definition of *nanotechnology*, which is discussed in more detail shortly.

Other improvements include developing faster memory and faster bus speeds to help speed up processing and to help reduce or eliminate bottlenecks and creating CPUs with an increasing number of cores and integrated GPUs. CPUs are also increasingly including additional technology to meet new needs, such as support for virtualization and increased 3D graphics processing. Improvements to CPU instruction set designs are made as needed to expand the instruction set design for new applications—particularly the growing use of multimedia applications, such as editing digital movies and photos and burning music CDs.

Improved Materials

Traditionally, CPU chips used aluminum circuitry etched onto a silicon chip. As the number of aluminum circuits that can be packed onto a silicon chip without heat dam-age or interference approached its limit, chipmakers began to look for alternate materials.

Copper was one of the next choices because it is a far better electrical conductor, and it can produce chips containing more circuitry at a lower price. As transistors have continued to shrink (which results in an increased leakage of current), CPU manufacturers have looked to new materials that reduce current leakage to allow more reliable high-speed operation. For instance, Intel switched to a new material called *high-k* for some of the silicon components in its CPUs.

A possibility for an entirely new material is the *graphene chip*, which uses *graphene*—flat sheets of carbon, such as those used to create *carbon nanotubes* (which are discussed shortly)—instead of silicon. However, instead of rolling up graphene, which is the process used when making carbon nanotubes, the graphene for chips is cut into strips. According to Georgia Tech physics professor Walter de Heer, one of the leading researchers in this area, silicon can't keep up with the current growth in chip technology and graphene may be the answer. Because electrons move through graphene with almost no resistance, they generate little heat; graphene also allows any heat that is generated to dissipate quickly. As a result, graphene-based chips can operate at much higher speeds than silicon and require less power. For example, during the initial tests of the first graphene CPU to be developed, it ran a tablet for 3 months before requiring a battery recharge.

For integrating computer components into clothing and other flexible materials (such as to create clothing, backpacks, and other objects that can control your electronic devices or display content on demand), as well as for creating flexible devices (such as the flexible smartphone screens that are expected to be available soon), *flexible electronic components* (see Figure 2-23) are needed and are currently being developed by a number of companies. In addition to the ability to be bent without damaging the circuitry, flexible circuits will be thinner, lighter, generate little heat, and consume significantly less energy than conventional processors. And, if the circuitry is made from plastic (which some researchers believe is a viable alternative to silicon), it means that future CPUs could be printed on plastic sheets and be much faster than, but cost about the same as, today's silicon chips.

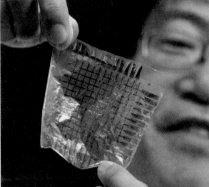

FIGURE 2-23
Flexible electronics.

Pipelining

In older, single-core computer systems, the CPU had to finish processing one instruction completely before starting another. Today's computers, however, can process multiple instructions at one time. One way to accomplish this within each core is through **pipelining**. With pipelining, a new instruction begins executing as soon as the previous one reaches the next stage of the pipeline. Figure 2-24 illustrates this process with a 4-stage pipeline. Notice that while the pipelined CPU is executing one instruction, it is simultaneously fetching and getting the next instruction ready for execution. Without a pipeline, the ALU and FPU would be idle while an instruction is being fetched and decoded.

Pipelines for CPUs today usually have between 4 and 20 stages, and the machine cycle is broken down in as many parts as needed to match the number of stages used. For example, with a 10-stage pipeline, the 4 steps of the machine cycle would be broken down into a total of 10 steps so that all stages of the pipeline can be used at one time. Pipelining increases the number of machine cycles completed per second, which increases the number of instructions performed per second, which improves performance.

Multiprocessing and Parallel Processing

The use of more than one processor or processing core in a computer (such as using multiple CPUs in a server, mainframe, or supercomputer, or using a multi-core CPU in a personal computer) is common today. When two or more processors or processing cores are located within a single computer, techniques that perform operations simultaneously—such

> **Pipelining.** The capability of a CPU or CPU core to begin processing a new instruction as soon as the previous instruction completes the first stage of the machine cycle.

Stages

Fetch Instruction 1	Decode Instruction 1	Execute Instruction 1	Store Result Instruction 1	Fetch Instruction 2	Decode Instruction 2	Execute Instruction 2

WITHOUT PIPELINING
Without pipelining, an instruction finishes an entire machine cycle before another instruction is started.

Stages

Fetch Instruction 1	Fetch Instruction 2	Fetch Instruction 3	Fetch Instruction 4	Fetch Instruction 5	Fetch Instruction 6	Fetch Instruction 7
	Decode Instruction 1	Decode Instruction 2	Decode Instruction 3	Decode Instruction 4	Decode Instruction 5	Decode Instruction 6
		Execute Instruction 1	Execute Instruction 2	Execute Instruction 3	Execute Instruction 4	Execute Instruction 5
			Store Result Instruction 1	Store Result Instruction 2	Store Result Instruction 3	Store Result Instruction 4

WITH PIPELINING
With pipelining, a new instruction is started when the preceding instruction moves to the next stage of the pipeline.

Copyright © 2015 Cengage Learning®

FIGURE 2-24

Pipelining. Pipelining streamlines the machine cycle by executing different stages of multiple instructions at the same time so that the different parts of the CPU are idle less often.

as **multiprocessing** (where each processor or core typically works on a different job) and **parallel processing** (where multiple processors or cores work together to make one single job finish sooner)—are possible.

The use of multiprocessing and parallel processing can increase astronomically the number of calculations performed in any given time period. For example, the Titan supercomputer (shown in Figure 1-19 in Chapter 1) uses approximately 299,008 processing cores and operates at more than 17 petaflops; that is, it is able to process more than 17 quadrillion operations per second. To increase efficiency in multiprocessing systems, CPUs specifically designed to work with a particular number of processors (such as two or eight) can be used. These CPUs include technology (such as direct links between the processors) to improve communications and increase efficiency.

A concept related to multiprocessing is *multithreading*—the ability of a CPU (or software) to execute multiple streams of instructions (called *threads*) within a single program at the same time. For instance, many Intel CPUs are capable of running 2 threads per core, so a 4-core CPU could simultaneously execute 8 threads, providing the software being used supported it. Because this technique (called *Hyper-Threading Technology* by Intel) utilizes processing power in the chip that would otherwise go unused, it lets the chip operate more efficiently, resulting in faster processing.

Future Trends

Some of the strategies discussed in the prior sections are currently being used, but some ideas are further from being implemented on a wide-scale basis. Selected trends we will likely see more of in the near future are discussed next.

Nanotechnology

Although there are varying definitions, most agree that **nanotechnology** involves creating computer components, machines, and other structures that are less than 100 nanometers in size. As already discussed, today's CPUs contain components that fit the definition of

> **Multiprocessing.** The capability to use multiple processors or multiple processing cores in a single computer, usually to process multiple jobs at one time faster than could be performed with a single processor. > **Parallel processing.** A processing technique that uses multiple processors or multiple processing cores simultaneously, usually to process a single job as fast as possible. > **Nanotechnology.** The science of creating tiny computers and components by working at the individual atomic and molecular levels.

TECHNOLOGY AND YOU

"Magic" Glass

A smartphone with a non-glare, self-cleaning screen? That could be the wave of the future based on a recent development by MIT researchers. By creating nano-sized conical patterns on the surface of the glass using coating and etching techniques, the researchers were able to eliminate its reflective properties, resulting in glass that resists fogging and glare (see the accompanying illustration) and is even self-cleaning.

In addition to making it easier to use mobile devices outdoors, the technology has a host of other possible applications, such as being used for eyeglasses, televisions, car windshields, and even windows in buildings. It could also be applied to solar panels, which can lose as much as 40% of their efficiency within three months due to dust and dirt accumulating on their surfaces. But, for most people, it will likely be the possibility of a tablet or smartphone with glass that eliminates reflections and cleans itself of fingerprints that gets the most attention.

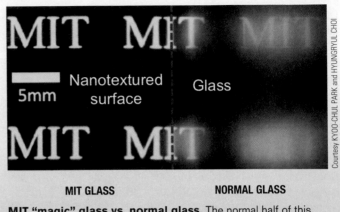

Courtesy KYOO-CHUL PARK and HYUNGRYUL CHOI

MIT GLASS   **NORMAL GLASS**

MIT "magic" glass vs. normal glass. The normal half of this piece of glass (right) can fog up and produce glare; the MIT glass half (left) remains clear.

nanotechnology. However, some experts believe that, eventually, current technology will reach its limits. At that point, transistors and other computer components may need to be built at the atomic and molecular level; that is, starting with single atoms or molecules to construct the components. Prototypes of computer products built in this fashion include the *single atom transistor*, which is a single switch that can be turned on and off like a transistor but is made from a single organic molecule, and tiny nickel-based *nanodots* that would, theoretically, allow about 5 TB of data to be stored on a hard drive roughly the size of a postage stamp. In other nanotechnology developments, prototypes of tiny *nanogenerators* have been developed that can be squeezed currently to generate power, but are expected to eventually be able to power mobile devices with low-frequency vibrations, such as a heartbeat or a simple body movement like walking. For a look at a recent nanotechnology development that may lead to new and improved glass on your future mobile phone, see the Technology and You box.

One nanotechnology development that is already being used in a variety of products available today is **carbon nanotubes (CNTs)**, which are tiny, hollow tubes made up of carbon atoms. The wall of a single-walled carbon nanotube is only one carbon atom thick and the tube diameter is approximately 10,000 times smaller than a human hair. Carbon nanotubes have great potential for future computing products because they can conduct electricity better than copper, are 100 times stronger than steel at one-sixth the weight, conduct heat better than diamonds, and can transmit electronic impulses faster than silicon. One recent development is *carbon nanotube* fibers that look and act like thread but conduct heat and electricity like a metal wire (see Figure 2-25). According to the researchers, these

> **Carbon nanotubes (CNTs).** Tiny, hollow tubes made of carbon atoms.

fibers are expected to eventually be used in new products for the aerospace, automotive, medical, and smart-clothing markets.

CNT products currently on the market include lithium ion batteries, and several nanotube-based computing products—like nanotube-based display screens and memory—are currently under development. In addition, IBM researchers are experimenting with a combination of DNA molecules and carbon nanotubes to make smaller, more powerful, and more energy-efficient computer chips. Because carbon nanotubes can transmit electricity and are transparent, they are also being used for product development in the areas of TVs, solar cells, light bulbs, and other similar noncomputing applications. In addition, because of their strength and lightness for their size, carbon nanotubes are being integrated into products that benefit from those characteristics, such as automobile panels, airplanes, tennis rackets, and racing bikes. In fact, the Army recently initiated a two-year program to develop carbon nanotube products to replace conventional copper-based wires and cables in aircraft. Carbon nanotubes are also beginning to be combined with other materials, such as plastic, to increase the durability of materials used to produce other consumer items, such as surfboards.

Two other recent developments are *nanofilters* that can remove contaminants from water sources and *nanosensors* that can detect cancer-causing toxins or cancer drugs inside single living cells. Possible future applications of nanotechnology include disposing of e-trash by rearranging dangerous components at the atomic level into inert substances, *nanosponges* that can enter the bloodstream and soak up toxins, improved military uniforms that protect against bullets and germ warfare, and computers and sensors that are small enough to be woven into the fibers of clothing or embedded into paint and other materials. Some of the devices generated by nanotechnology research may contain or be constructed out of organic material.

FIGURE 2-25
Carbon nanotubes.
This light bulb is powered and held in place by two carbon nanotube fibers.

FIGURE 2-26
Quantum computers.
This vial of liquid contains a 7-qubit computer.

Quantum Computing

The idea of **quantum computing** emerged in the 1970s, but it has received renewed interest lately. Quantum computing applies the principles of quantum physics and quantum mechanics to computers, going beyond traditional physics to work at the subatomic level. Quantum computers differ from conventional computers in that they utilize atoms or nuclei working together as *quantum bits* or *qubits*. Qubits function simultaneously as both the computer's processor and memory, and each qubit can represent more than just the two states (one and zero) available to today's electronic bits; a qubit can even represent many states at one time. Quantum computers can perform computations on many numbers at one time, making them, theoretically, exponentially faster than conventional computers. Physically, quantum computers in the future might consist of a thimbleful of liquid whose atoms are used to perform calculations as instructed by an external device.

While quantum computers are still in the pioneering stage, working quantum computers do exist. For instance, in 2001 the researchers at IBM's Almaden Research Center created a 7-qubit quantum computer (see Figure 2-26) composed of the nuclei of seven atoms that can interact with each other and be programmed by radio frequency pulses. This quantum computer successfully factored the number 15—not a complicated computation for a conventional computer, but the fact that a quantum computer was able to understand the problem and compute the correct answer is viewed as a highly significant event in the area of quantum computer research.

One of the obstacles to creating a fully functional quantum computer has been the inability of qubits to hold information for long periods of time. Recently, UCLA

> **Quantum computing.** A technology that applies the principles of quantum physics and quantum mechanics to computers to direct atoms or nuclei to work together as quantum bits (qubits), which function simultaneously as the computer's processor and memory.

scientists developed a new technique for cooling molecules, which may be applied to future quantum computers in order to bring the molecules to the state at which they can be manipulated to store and transmit data. In addition, scientists in Australia have created a silicon quantum bit using a single atom—this development is viewed as a big step forward in the development of silicon-based quantum computers. These breakthroughs are viewed as significant steps toward the ability to create more sophisticated working quantum computers in the future.

Quantum computing is not well suited for general computing tasks but is ideal for, and expected to be widely used in, highly data-intensive applications, such as *encryption* (discussed in Chapter 9) and code breaking.

Optical Computing and Silicon Photonics

Optical chips, which use light waves to transmit data, are also currently in development. A possibility for the future is the **optical computer**—a computer that uses light, such as from laser beams or infrared beams, to perform digital computations. Because light beams do not interfere with each other, optical computers can be much smaller and faster than electronic computers. For instance, according to one NASA senior research scientist, an optical computer could solve a problem in one hour that would take an electronic computer 11 years to solve. While some researchers are working on developing an all-optical computer, others believe that a mix of optical and electronic components—or an *opto-electronic computer*—may be the best bet for the future. Opto-electronic technology is already being used to improve long-distance fiber-optic communications. Initial opto-electronic computer applications are expected to be applied to the area of speeding up communications between computers and other devices, as well as between computer components. In fact, IBM recently created chips that have both optical and electrical functions combined on a single silicon chip and that use standard semiconductor processes—a feat that was thought to be impossible until recently. One additional benefit of opto-electronic chips is reduced power consumption. While increased bandwidth (such as between servers, between CPU cores, or between the CPU and memory) increases power consumption using electrical connections, the impact is much less with opto-electronic chips because they move data with light instead of electricity.

The process of sending optical information among computers and other electronic devices using standard silicon manufacturing techniques—essentially converging *photonics* (the control and manipulation of light) and electronics—is referred to as *silicon photonics*. This technology is viewed as one possible low-cost solution to future data-intensive computing applications, such as *telemedicine* and the processing required by cloud data centers. For example, Intel and Facebook recently announced a collaboration to define the next generation of technologies to be used to power the world's larger data centers, and the technologies include silicon photonics architecture. In addition to the potential use for transferring large amounts of data very quickly between computers, silicon photonics technology is also expected to be used to transfer data quickly between components within a computer—such as between the cores of a CPU as the number of cores and necessary connections increase. According to Patrick Gelsinger, when he was a senior vice president at Intel, "Today, optics is a niche technology. Tomorrow, it's the mainstream of every chip that we build."

One development in this area by Intel Labs researchers in 2010 (see Figure 2-27) is the creation of a silicon-based optical data connection with integrated lasers (called a 50 Gbps *Silicon Photonics Link*). This device uses

FIGURE 2-27
A 50 Gbps Silicon Photonics Link.

Courtesy Intel Corporation

> **Optical computer.** A computer that uses light, such as from laser beams or infrared beams, to perform digital computations.

a silicon transmitter and receiver; the transmitter contains four lasers to send data (at 50 Gbps) over a single optical fiber. In 2013, Intel demonstrated the technology moving data at 100 Gbps.

Tera-Scale Computing

As demand by consumers and businesses for online software, services, and media-rich experiences continues to increase, some experts predict that **tera-scale computing**—the ability of a computer to process one trillion floating point operations per second (teraflops)—will eventually be more common. While supercomputers currently reach teraflop and petaflop speeds, much of today's tera-scale research is focusing on creating multi-core processors with tens to hundreds of cores used in conjunction with multithreaded hardware and software to achieve teraflop performance. The research also includes working on developing higher-speed communications between computers, such as between Web servers and high-performance mobile devices or computers, to help facilitate high-performance cloud computing.

Intel, one of the leaders in tera-scale research, has created a *Single-Chip Cloud Computer* (*SCC*) that contains 48 cores on a single silicon CPU chip and resembles a cloud of computers integrated into silicon. It incorporates technologies intended to scale multi-core processors to 100 cores and more. Intel has also developed a 20-megabyte SRAM memory chip that is attached directly to the processor in order to speed up communication between processors and memory. This design allows thousands of interconnections, which enable data to travel at more than one *terabyte per second* (*TBps*) between memory and the processor cores. It is expected that this speed will be needed to handle the terabytes of data used by applications in the near future. In fact, *exascale computers* that perform 1 million trillion calculations per second and may have as many as 100 million CPU cores are expected to appear by 2018.

3D Chips

Three-dimensional (*3D*) *chips* are another technique for packing an increasing number of components onto small chips. With 3D chips, the transistors are layered, which cuts down on the surface area required. Typically, 3D chips are created by layering individual silicon wafers on top of one another, using cameras to align the wafers properly. However, researchers at the University of Southampton, UK, have developed wafers that contain matching sets of pegs and holes, similar to the way LEGO bricks fit together. In preliminary tests, the researchers lined up the edges of two chips by hand and pressed them together—images taken with an electron microscope show that the two chips aligned roughly five times better than with the camera-based technique. While still in the research stage, the researchers believe that this new design could aid the development of 3D chips and other 3D electronic components.

3D chips are now being used with memory, flash memory, and CPUs. For example, recent Intel CPUs (such as 3rd generation Core processors) include a 3D transistor called *Tri-Gate* (see the illustration in Figure 2-28). Tri-Gate transistors provide increased performance and low voltage, making them ideal for use in small devices, such as mobile devices. In addition, Samsung recently announced the release of the world's first mass-produced 3D flash memory chip. By using a special etching technology to drill down through the chip layers to connect them electronically, Samsung plans to eventually produce chips with 24 layers.

FIGURE 2-28
3D chips. In this 3D transistor, the electrical current (represented by the yellow dots) flows on three sides of a vertical fin.

Courtesy Intel Corporation

> **Tera-scale computing.** The ability of a computer to process data at teraflop speeds.

SUMMARY

DATA AND PROGRAM REPRESENTATION

Most *digital computers* work in a two-state, or *binary*, fashion. It is convenient to think of these binary states in terms of 0s and 1s. Computer people refer to these 0s and 1s as bits. Converting data to these 0s and 1s is called *digital data representation.*

While most individuals use the **decimal number system** to represent numbers and perform numeric computations, computers use the **binary numbering system**. Text-based data can be represented with one of several fixed-length binary codes (such as **ASCII** (**American Standard Code for Information Interchange**) or **Unicode**) that represent single characters of data—a numeric digit, alphabetic character, or special symbol—as strings of **bits**. Each string of eight bits is called a **byte**. Use of Unicode is growing because it can represent text in all written languages, including those that use alphabets different from English, such as Chinese, Greek, and Russian.

The storage capacity of computers is often expressed using prefixes in conjunction with the term *byte* to convey the approximate quantity being represented, such as using **kilobyte** (**KB**), about one thousand bytes; **megabyte** (**MB**), about one million bytes; **gigabyte** (**GB**), about one billion bytes; or **terabyte** (**TB**), about one trillion bytes. Other possibilities are **petabyte** (**PB**), about 1,000 terabytes; **exabyte** (**EB**), about 1,000 petabytes; **zettabyte** (**ZB**), about 1,000 exabytes; and **yottabyte** (**YB**), about 1,000 zettabytes.

The binary system can represent not only text but also graphics, audio, and video data. **Machine language** is the binary-based code through which computers represent program instructions. A program must be translated into machine language before the computer can execute it.

INSIDE THE SYSTEM UNIT

Personal computers typically contain a variety of hardware components located inside the **system unit**. For instance, *chips* are mounted onto *circuit boards*, and those boards are positioned in slots on the **motherboard**—the main circuit board for a computer. Every computer (and most mobile devices) has one or more **processors**, such as a **central processing unit** (**CPU**)—also called a **microprocessor** when referring to personal computers—and a **graphics processing unit** (**GPU**), that perform the processing for the computer. CPU chips differ in many respects, such as what types of computer the CPU is designed for, *clock speed*, and *word size*. They can also be **multi-core CPUs**, such as the **dual-core** (two cores) and **quad-core** (four cores) **CPUs** now available. Another difference is the amount of **cache memory**—memory located on or very close to the CPU chip to help speed up processing. Other important differences are the general architecture of the CPU and the bus speed and width being used. The overall *processing speed* of the computer determines its performance. One of the most consistent measurements of overall performance is a *benchmark test.*

Memory refers to chip-based storage. The main memory for a personal computer is **RAM** (**random access memory**). Traditional RAM is **volatile** and used to hold programs and data temporarily while they are needed; **nonvolatile** RAM is under development. RAM is available in different types and speeds, and is measured in bytes. **ROM** (**read-only memory**) is a type of nonvolatile memory that stores nonerasable programs. **Flash memory** is a type of nonvolatile memory that can be used for storage by the computer or the user. Flash memory chips can be found in many personal computers and mobile devices; flash memory chips are also integrated into storage media and devices. **Registers** are memory built into the CPU chip to hold data before or during processing. *Fans*, *heat sinks*, and other techniques are used to compensate for the heat that CPUs and other components generate.

Desktop computers contain internal **expansion slots**, into which users can insert **expansion cards** to give the computer added functionality. Expansion of portable computers and mobile devices is more limited and typically obtained via external ports.

A computer **bus** is an electronic path along which bits are transmitted. The **memory bus** moves data between the CPU and RAM. The **frontside bus** (**FSB**) connects the CPU to the *chipset*, which connects the CPU and memory to the rest of the *bus architecture*. Common **expansion buses** include the *PCI* and **PCI Express** (**PCIe**) **buses**, **Universal Serial Bus** (**USB**), and **FireWire**. The performance of a bus can be measured by the bus's **bandwidth** or **throughput**; that is, the amount of data that can (theoretically and under real-life conditions, respectively) be transferred via the bus in a given time period.

System units typically have external **ports** that are used to connect peripheral devices to the computer. Notebook, tablet, and netbook computers may have fewer ports than desktop computers. Mobile device users often add new capabilities via USB ports or *Secure Digital* (*SD*) *cards* or other types of flash memory cards.

Chapter Objective 3:
Describe how peripheral devices or other hardware can be added to a computer.

HOW THE CPU WORKS

CPUs today include at least one **arithmetic/logic unit** (**ALU**), which performs integer arithmetic and logical operations on data, and most include at least one **floating point unit** (**FPU**), which performs decimal arithmetic. The **control unit** directs the flow of electronic traffic between memory and the ALU/FPU and also between the CPU and input and output devices. Registers—high-speed temporary holding places within the CPU that hold program instructions and data immediately before and during processing—are used to enhance the computer's performance. The **prefetch unit** requests data and instructions before or as they are needed, the **decode unit** decodes the instructions input into the CPU, internal cache stores frequently used instructions and data, and the **bus interface unit** allows the various parts of the CPU to communicate with each other.

The CPU processes instructions in a sequence called a **machine cycle**, consisting of four basic steps. Each machine language instruction is broken down into several smaller instructions called *microcode*, and each piece of microcode corresponds to an operation (such as adding two numbers located in the CPU's registers) that can be performed inside the CPU. The computer system has a built-in **system clock** that synchronizes all of the computer's activities.

Chapter Objective 4:
Understand how a computer's CPU and memory components process program instructions and data.

MAKING COMPUTERS FASTER AND BETTER NOW AND IN THE FUTURE

There are several possible remedies for a computer that is performing too slowly, including adding more memory, performing system maintenance to clean up the computer's hard drive, buying a larger or additional hard drive, and upgrading the computer's Internet connection or video card, depending on the primary role of the computer and where the processing bottleneck appears to be. To make computers work faster overall, computer designers have developed a number of strategies over the years, and researchers are continually working on new strategies. Some of the strategies already being implemented include improved architecture, **pipelining**, **multiprocessing**, **parallel processing**, and the use of new or improved materials.

One possibility for future computers is **nanotechnology** research, which focuses on building computer components at the individual atomic and molecular levels. Some computer and consumer products (such as NRAM, solar cells, tennis rackets, and bikes) using **carbon nanotubes** or **CNTs** (tiny hollow tubes made of carbon atoms) are currently on the market. **Quantum computing** and **optical computers** are other possibilities being researched, along with *silicon photonics*, **tera-scale computing**, and *three-dimensional (3D) chips*.

Chapter Objective 5:
Name and evaluate several strategies that can be used today for speeding up the operations of a computer.

Chapter Objective 6:
List some processing technologies that may be used in future computers.

REVIEW ACTIVITIES

KEY TERM MATCHING

a. ASCII

b. binary numbering system

c. byte

d. central processing unit (CPU)

e. control unit

f. motherboard

g. nanotechnology

h. parallel processing

i. RAM (random access memory)

j. Universal Serial Bus (USB)

Instructions: Match each key term on the left with the definition on the right that best describes it.

1. _____ A processing technique that uses multiple processors or processing cores simultaneously, usually to process a single job as fast as possible.

2. _____ A fixed-length, binary coding system used to represent text-based data for computer processing on many types of computers.

3. _____ A group of 8 bits.

4. _____ A universal bus used to connect up to 127 peripheral devices to a computer without requiring the use of additional expansion cards.

5. _____ Chips connected to the motherboard that provide a temporary location for the computer to hold data and program instructions while they are needed.

6. _____ The chip located on the motherboard of a computer that performs most of the processing for a computer.

7. _____ The main circuit board of a computer, located inside the system unit, to which all computer system components connect.

8. _____ The numbering system that represents all numbers using just two symbols (0 and 1).

9. _____ The part of the CPU that coordinates its operations.

10. _____ The science of creating tiny computers and components by working at the individual atomic and molecular levels.

SELF-QUIZ

Instructions: Circle **T** if the statement is true, **F** if the statement is false, or write the best answer in the space provided. **Answers for the self-quiz are located in the References and Resources Guide at the end of the book.**

1. **T F** A storage medium that can hold 256 GB can hold about 256 billion characters.

2. **T F** The amount of data that can be transferred over a bus in a given time period determines the bus's volatility.

3. **T F** Cache memory is typically built into a CPU.

4. **T F** A bus is a pathway, such as on the motherboard or inside the CPU, along which bits can be transferred.

5. **T F** Computers that process data with light are referred to as quantum computers.

6. The ability of a computer to process data at teraflop speeds is referred to as _____.

7. A CPU with four separate processing cores is referred to as a(n) _____ CPU.

8. A(n) _____ is a connector on the exterior of a computer into which a peripheral device may be plugged.

9. Multi-core CPUs allow _____, in which the CPU is able to work on multiple jobs at one time.

10. Number the following terms from 1 to 9 to indicate their size from smallest to largest.

a. _____ Petabyte   d. _____ Yottabyte   g. _____ Zettabyte

b. _____ Kilobyte   e. _____ Exabyte   h. _____ Terabyte

c. _____ Gigabyte   f. _____ Byte   i. _____ Megabyte

EXERCISES

HW

1. What do each of the following acronyms stand for?

a. KB _____   c. GPU _____   e. PCIe _____

b. RAM _____   d. USB _____   f. CPU _____

2. Using the ASCII code chart in this chapter or in the References and Resources Guide at the end of the book, decode the following word. What does it say?

01000011   01000001   01000110   01000101

_____   _____   _____   _____

3. Supply the missing words to complete the following statements.

a. The smallest piece of data (a 0 or 1) that can be represented by a computer is called a(n) _____.

b. _____ is an international coding system for text-based data using any written language.

c. L1 is a type of _____.

d. The part of the CPU that performs logical operations and integer arithmetic is the _____.

4. Assume you have a USB mouse, USB keyboard, and USB printer to connect to a computer, but you have only two USB ports. Explain one solution to this problem that does not involve buying a new mouse, keyboard, or printer.

5. If your computer seems sluggish, list two things you could do to try to speed it up without resorting to purchasing an entirely new system.

DISCUSSION QUESTIONS

1. As discussed in the chapter, one push by computer manufacturers is making computers run as efficiently as possible to save battery power and electricity. What do you think is the motivation behind this trend? Is it social responsibility or a response to consumer demands? Should the energy consumption of electronic devices be regulated and controlled by the government or another organization? Why or why not? How responsible should consumers be for energy conservation in relation to electronic use? In your opinion, what, if anything, should all computer users do to practice *green computing*?

2. In addition to being used with computers and consumer products, there are also processors and other components designed to be implanted inside the human body, such as the *VeriChip* (discussed in Project 4), implantable wafers containing medication and a processor that delivers the medication at the appropriate time and dosage, *camera pills* that are swallowed to transmit images of an individual's digestive system to a receiving unit, and pacemakers designed to regulate an individual's heart rate. One step further is *brain-to-computer interfacing (BCI)*, which involves implanting electrodes directly into the human brain to restore lost functionality or to facilitate the communications ability of severely disabled individuals, such as by enabling them to control a mouse using only their thoughts. What do you think about these implantable chip applications? Are the benefits worth the risk of something going wrong with the chips implanted inside your body? Are there any privacy risks? Would you consider using an implanted device? Why or why not?

PROJECTS

HOT TOPICS

1. **Tablet Docks** As mentioned in the Trend box, there are an increasing number of docks available for tablet devices. Similar to docks designed for notebook computers, tablet docks can help make your work environment more comfortable and productive. They can also make it easier to move from one work environment to another (such as from your desk at the office to your home office).

   For this project, select two tablet docks and compare them. Do they come with or are they made to work with a specific tablet? What functionality does the dock add? Are there advantages of one dock over the other? If yes, what are they? If you had a tablet device, would you want to use either of these docks? Why or why not? At the conclusion of your research, prepare a one-page summary of your findings and opinions and submit it to your instructor.

SHORT ANSWER/ RESEARCH

2. **Adding Memory** Adding additional RAM to a computer is one of the most common computer upgrades. Before purchasing additional memory, however, it is important to make sure that the memory about to be purchased is compatible with the computer.

   For this project, select a computer (such as your own computer, a school computer, or a computer at a local store) and then determine (by looking at the computer or asking an appropriate individual—such as a lab aide in the school computer lab or a salesperson at the local store) the following: manufacturer and model number, CPU, current amount of memory, total memory slots, operating system, and the number of available memory slots. (If you look inside the computer, be sure to unplug the power cord first and do not touch any components inside the system unit.) Once you have the necessary information, call a local store or use your information and a memory supplier's Web site to determine the appropriate type of memory needed for your selected computer. What choices do you have in terms of capacity and configuration? Can you add just one memory module, or do you have to add memory in pairs? Can you keep the old memory modules, or do they have to be removed? At the conclusion of your research, prepare a one-page summary of your findings and recommendations and submit it to your instructor.

HANDS ON

3. **Intel Museum Tour** Intel Corporation has a great deal of interesting information about processors on its Web site, including details about its processors, chipsets, motherboards, wireless products, and other components Intel manufactures, as well as information about the various types of devices that you can buy that use Intel technology. In addition, an interesting collection of exhibits related to the history of processors and how processing technology works is available through its online museum.

   For this project, go to the Intel Museum at **www.intel.com/museum/index.htm** (if this URL no longer works, go to the Intel home page at www.intel.com and search for "Intel Museum"). Once you are at the Intel Museum home page, visit the online exhibits to locate an exhibit or documents related to processors or memory, such as *From Sand to Circuits*, *Making Silicon Chips*, or *Moore's Law*, and then tour the exhibit or read through the available information, making a note of at least three interesting facts you didn't know before. At the conclusion of this task, prepare a short summary listing the tour you took and the interesting facts you recorded and submit it to your instructor.

4. **People Chips** The *VeriChip* is a tiny chip that was designed to be implanted under a person's skin, such as on the forearm. VeriChips were designed to be used primarily for identification purposes—the unique number contained in a VeriChip can be read by a proprietary scanner and can be used in conjunction with a database, such as to provide hospital emergency room personnel with health information about an unconscious patient. However, implanted chips can also be used to control access to secure areas and for electronic payment purposes. What do you think of implanted devices, such as the VeriChip, being used for access control (such as for government buildings or highly secure facilities), for expediting passage through security check points (such as at airports), or for making electronic payments (such as at a grocery store)? Would you be willing to be "chipped" if it made some tasks (such as unlocking your home or car) easier or some types of transactions (such as ATM withdrawals) more secure? Is it ethical for a government to require its citizens to be chipped, similar to a national ID card? Is it ethical for a business to request or require that its employees be chipped for security purposes?

For this project, form an opinion about the ethical use and ramifications of human-implantable chips and be prepared to discuss your position (in class, via an online class discussion group, in a class chat room, or via a class blog, depending on your instructor's directions). You may also be asked to write a short paper expressing your opinion.

5. **Binary Conversions** As discussed in the chapter, all numbers processed by the CPU must be represented in a binary format. Binary (base 2) represents all numbers using 2 digits, decimal uses 10 digits, and hexadecimal uses 16 digits.

For this project, research how to convert a three-digit decimal number to both binary and hexadecimal and back again, without the use of a calculator (see the "A Look at Numbering Systems" feature located in the References and Resources Guide at the end of this book). Next, determine how to represent the decimal number 10 in base 3 (the numbering system that uses only the digits 0, 1, and 2). Share your findings with the class in the form of a short presentation, including a demonstration of the conversions between binary and hexadecimal and the representation of the decimal number 10 in base 3. The presentation should not exceed 10 minutes and should make use of one or more presentation aids such as a whiteboard, handouts, or a computer-based slide presentation (your instructor may provide additional requirements). You may also be asked to submit a summary of the presentation to your instructor.

6. **Should Computers Run Vital Systems Like the Stock Market?** In 2013, the stock market tumbled in response to a tweet from the Associated Press that President Obama had been injured by explosions at the White House. One problem? It never happened. Another problem? The computers that analyze natural language to allow high-speed trading saw the words "explosion," "Obama," and "White House" and caused the reaction. Today, computers run a number of vital systems and are viewed by many as the safer alternative to avoid human error. But the AP Twitter account was hacked by humans to cause the Wall Street incident—what is to prevent hackers from using the nation's computerized systems to do harm? What types of safeguards are needed to continue to use computers to run vital systems? Or should there always be a human ultimately in charge? What if cyberterrorists gain control over the country's financial or defense systems? What about the computer that run water purification and other health-related systems? Could computerized systems be endangering our lives instead of helping them?

Pick a side on this issue, form an opinion and gather supporting evidence, and be prepared to discuss and defend your position in a classroom debate or in a 1–2 page paper, depending on your instructor's directions.

chapter 3

Storage

After completing this chapter, you will be able to do the following:

1. Name several general characteristics of storage systems.

2. Describe the two most common types of hard drives and what they are used for today.

3. Discuss the various types of optical discs available today and how they differ from each other.

4. Identify some flash memory storage devices and media and explain how they are used today.

5. List at least three other types of storage systems.

6. Summarize the storage alternatives for a typical personal computer.

OVERVIEW

In Chapter 2, we discussed the role of RAM, the computer's main memory. RAM temporarily holds program instructions, data, and output while they are needed by the computer. For instance, when you first create a letter or other word processing document on your computer, both the word processing program and the document are temporarily stored in RAM. But when the word processing program is closed, the computer no longer needs to work with the program or the document, and so they are both erased from RAM. Consequently, anything (such as your word processing document) that needs to be preserved for future use needs to be stored on a more permanent medium. Storage systems fill this role.

We begin this chapter with a look at the characteristics common among all storage systems. Then, we discuss the primary storage for most personal computers—the hard drive. From there, we turn our attention to optical discs, including how they work and the various types of optical discs available today. Next, we discuss flash memory storage systems, followed by a look at a few other types of storage systems, including network and cloud storage, smart cards, holographic storage, and the storage systems used with large computer systems. The chapter concludes with a discussion about evaluating the storage alternatives for a typical personal computer. ■

STORAGE SYSTEMS CHARACTERISTICS

All *storage systems* have specific characteristics, such as having both a *storage medium* and a *storage device*, how portable and volatile the system is, how data is accessed and represented, the type of storage technology used, and so on. These characteristics are discussed in the next few sections.

Storage Media and Storage Devices

There are two parts to any storage system: the **storage medium** and the **storage device**. A storage medium is the hardware where data is actually stored (for example, a *DVD* or a *flash memory card*); a storage medium is inserted into its corresponding storage device (such as a *DVD drive* or a *flash memory card reader*) in order to be read from or written to. Often the storage device and storage medium are two separate pieces of hardware (that is, the storage medium is *removable*), although with some systems—such as a *hard drive* or most *USB flash drives*—the two parts are permanently sealed together to form one piece of hardware.

Storage devices can be *internal* (located inside the system unit), *external* (plugged into an external port on the system unit), or *remote* (located on another computer, such as a network server or Web server). Internal devices have the advantage of requiring no additional

---

>**Storage medium.** The part of a storage system, such as a DVD disc, where data is stored. >**Storage device.** A piece of hardware, such as a DVD drive, into which a storage medium is inserted to be read from or written to.

The letter C is usually assigned to the first hard drive.

CD/DVD drives are usually assigned letters after the hard drives, such as D in this example.

© AS-kom/Shutterstock.com

Any storage devices attached to the computer via USB ports are typically assigned next, such as E for this USB flash drive.

Other letters, beginning with F in this example, are used for any other storage devices attached to the computer, such as via this built-in flash memory card reader.

FIGURE 3-1

Storage device identifiers. To keep track of storage devices in an unambiguous way, the computer system assigns letters of the alphabet or names to each of them.

desk space and are usually faster than their external counterparts. External devices, however, can be easily transported from one location to another (such as to share data with others, to transfer data between a work computer and a home computer, or to take digital photos to a photo store). They can also be removed from the computer and stored in a secure area (such as for backup purposes or to protect sensitive data). Remote devices are accessed over a network. Some remote storage devices, such as those accessed via the Internet, have the additional advantage of being accessible from any computer with an Internet connection.

Regardless of how storage devices are connected to a computer, letters of the alphabet and/or names are typically assigned to each storage device so that the user can identify each device easily when it needs to be used (see Figure 3-1). Some drive letters, such as the letter C typically used with the primary hard drive, are usually consistent from computer to computer and do not change even if more storage devices are added to the computer. The rest of the drive letters on a computer may change as new devices are added either permanently (such as when an additional hard drive is installed inside the computer) or temporarily (such as when a USB flash drive, digital camera, external hard drive, or portable digital media player is connected to the computer). When a new storage device is detected, the computer just assigns and reassigns drive letters, as needed.

Volatility

As discussed in Chapter 2, conventional RAM is volatile so programs and documents held in RAM are erased when they are no longer needed by the computer or when the power to the computer is turned off. Storage media, however, are nonvolatile, so the data remains on the media even when the power to the computer or storage device is off. Consequently, storage media are used for anything that needs to be saved for future use.

Random vs. Sequential Access

When the computer receives an instruction that requires data located on a storage medium, it must go to the designated location on the appropriate storage medium and retrieve the requested data. This procedure is referred to as *access*. Two basic access methods are available: *random* and *sequential*.

Random access, also called *direct access*, means that data can be retrieved directly from any location on the storage medium, in any order. A random access device works in a manner similar to a CD or DVD player used to play music or movies; that is, it can jump directly to a particular location on the medium when data located at that location is needed. Virtually all storage devices used with computers today for day-to-day storage—including hard drives, CD/DVD drives, and USB flash drives—are random access devices.

Media that allow random access are sometimes referred to as *addressable* media. This means that the storage system can locate each piece of stored data at a unique *address*, which is determined by the computer system. With *sequential access*, however, the data can only be retrieved in the order in which it is physically stored on the medium. One type of storage device that is sometimes used with computers for backup purposes and that uses sequential access is a *magnetic tape drive*. Computer tapes work like audiocassette tapes or videotapes—to get to a specific location on the tape, you must play or fast forward through all of the tape that comes before the location you want to access.

Logical vs. Physical Representation

Anything (such as a program, letter, digital photograph, or song) stored on a storage medium is referred to as a **file**. Data files are also often called *documents*. When a document that was just created (such as a memo or letter in a word processing program) is saved, it is stored as a new file on the storage medium designated by the user. During the storage process, the user is required to give the file a name, called a **filename**; that filename is used to retrieve the file when it is needed at a later time.

To keep files organized, related documents are often stored in **folders** (also called *directories*) located on the storage medium. For example, one folder might contain memos to business associates while another might hold a set of budgets (see Figure 3-2). To organize files further, you can create *subfolders* (*subdirectories*) within a folder. For instance, you might create a subfolder within the *Budgets* subfolder for each fiscal year. In Figure 3-2, both *Budgets* and *Memos* are subfolders inside the *My Documents* folder; the *Budgets* subfolder contains two additional subfolders (*Current year* and *Next year*).

Although both the user and the computer use drive letters, folder names, and file-names to save and retrieve documents, they perceive them differently. The user typically views how data is stored (what has been discussed so far in this section and what appears in the *File Explorer file management program* screen shown in Figure 3-2) using *logical file representation*. That is, individuals view a document stored as one complete unit in a particular folder on a particular drive. Computers, however, use *physical file representation*; that is, they access a particular document stored on a storage medium using its physical location or locations. For example, the *ABC Industries Proposal Memo* file shown in Figure 3-2 is *logically* located in the *Memos* folders in the *My Documents* and *Debbie* folders on the hard drive C, but the content of this file could be *physically* stored in many different pieces scattered across that hard drive. When this occurs, the computer keeps track of the various physical locations used to store that file, as well as the logical representations (filename, folder names, and drive letter) used to identify that file, in order to retrieve the entire file when needed. Fortunately, users do not have to be concerned with how files are physically stored on a storage medium because the computer keeps track of that information and uses it to retrieve files whenever they are requested.

FIGURE 3-2

Organizing data.
Folders are used to organize related items on a storage medium.

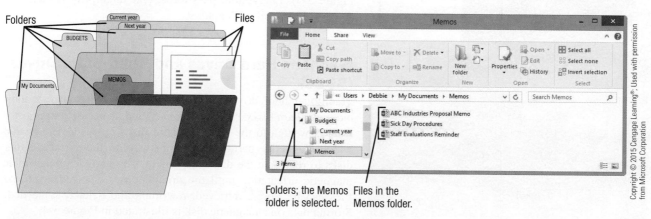

Folders

Files

Folders; the Memos folder is selected.   Files in the Memos folder.

Copyright © 2015 Cengage Learning®. Used with permission from Microsoft Corporation

---

>**File.** Something stored on a storage medium, such as a program, a document, or an image. >**Filename.** A name given to a file by the user; it is used to retrieve the file at a later time. >**Folder.** A named place on a storage medium into which the user can place files in order to keep the files stored on that medium organized.

Type of Storage Technology Used

Data is stored *magnetically* or *optically* on many types of storage media. With magnetic storage systems, such as conventional hard drives, data is stored magnetically on the storage medium, which means the data (0s and 1s) is represented using different magnetic alignments. The storage device can change the magnetic alignment when needed, so data can be written to the medium, deleted from the medium, or rewritten to the medium. Optical storage media (such as CDs and DVDs) store data optically using laser beams. On some optical media, the laser burns permanent marks to represent 0s and 1s into the surface of the medium so the data cannot be erased or rewritten. With *rewritable* optical media, the laser changes the reflectivity of the medium to represent 0s and 1s but it does not permanently alter the disc surface so the reflectivity of the medium can be changed back again as needed. Consequently, the data stored on a rewritable optical disc can be changed.

Some storage systems use a combination of magnetic and optical technology. Others use a different technology altogether, such as *flash memory storage systems* that represent data using *electrons* (electrons are either trapped or not trapped inside *flash memory cells* to represent 0s and 1s). Some of the most widely used storage systems are discussed next.

HARD DRIVES

With the exception of computers designed to use only network storage devices (such as thin clients and some Internet appliances), virtually all personal computers come with a **hard drive** that is used to store most programs and data. *Internal hard drives* (those located inside the system unit) are not designed to be removed, unless they need to be repaired or replaced. *External hard drives* typically connect to a computer via an external port (such as a USB, Thunderbolt, or FireWire port) or a wireless connection and are frequently used for additional storage (such as for digital photos, videos, and other large multimedia files—particularly for users of media tablets and other devices with limited internal storage, as discussed in the How It Works box), to move files between computers, and for backup purposes. Hard drives are also incorporated into other consumer products, such as mobile phones, portable digital media players, digital video recorders (DVRs), gaming consoles, digital camcorders, and more, although some mobile devices today use only flash memory chips for internal storage.

For security purposes, both internal and external hard drives today are available with built-in *encryption* that automatically encrypts (essentially scrambles) all data stored on the hard drive and limits access to the hard drive to only authorized users, typically via a *password* or fingerprint scan (see Figure 3-3). Encryption, passwords, and fingerprint readers are discussed in detail in Chapter 9.

FIGURE 3-3

Encrypted hard drives. The data stored on this external hard drive is accessed via a fingerprint scanner.

Courtesy Apricorn

Magnetic Hard Drives and Solid-State Drives (SSDs)

Traditional hard drives are *magnetic hard drives* that contain *magnetic hard disks, read/write heads,* and an *access mechanism.* Data is written to the magnetic hard disks by read/write heads, which magnetize particles a certain way on the surface of the disks to represent the data's 0s and 1s. The particles retain their magnetic orientation until the orientation is changed again, so files can be stored, retrieved, rewritten, and deleted as needed. Storing data on a magnetic disk is illustrated in Figure 3-4.

>**Hard drive.** The primary storage system for most computers; used to store most programs and data used with a computer.

A newer type of hard drive is the *solid-state drive* (*SSD*) that uses flash memory technology instead of magnetic technology to store data. While magnetic hard drives are currently less expensive and are available in larger capacities than SSDs (though 1 TB SSDs are now available), the use of SSDs is growing rapidly—especially with portable computers (like notebook and netbook computers) and mobile devices. This is because the flash memory technology that SSDs are based on allows for faster operation (one study showed a ninefold increase in performance over conventional magnetic hard drives), reduced power consumption (SSDs use at least 50% less power than magnetic hard drives use), and increased shock-resistance because they have no moving parts. Flash memory technology is discussed in more detail later in this chapter.

Magnetic Hard Drives

A **magnetic hard drive** (the traditional type of hard drive) contains one or more metal *hard disks* or *platters* that are coated with a magnetizable substance. These hard disks are permanently sealed inside the hard drive case, along with the *read/write heads* used to store (*write*) and retrieve (*read*) data and an *access mechanism* used to move the read/write heads in and out over the surface of the hard disks (see Figure 3-5). Hard drives designed for desktop computers (sometimes referred to as *desktop hard drives*) typically use 2.5-inch or 3.5-inch hard disks and notebook hard drives typically use 2.5-inch hard disks. Portable digital media players, mobile phones, and other mobile devices that include a magnetic hard drive typically use tiny 1.5-inch or smaller hard drives instead. Regardless of the size, one hard drive usually contains a stack of several hard disks; if so, there is a read/write head for each hard disk surface (top and bottom), as illustrated in Figure 3-5, and these heads move in and out over the disk surfaces simultaneously.

Disk surface

The read/write head inscribes data by aligning each of the magnetic particles in one of two ways.

Particles aligned one way represent 0s; the other way represent 1s.

FIGURE 3-4
Storing data on magnetic disks.

FIGURE 3-5
Magnetic hard drives.

READ/WRITE HEADS
There is a read/write head for each hard disk surface, and they move in and out over the disks together.

HARD DISKS
There are usually several hard disk surfaces on which to store data. Most hard drives store data on both sides of each disk.

ACCESS MECHANISM
The access mechanism moves the read/write heads in and out together between the hard disk surfaces to access required data.

2.5-INCH HARD DRIVE LOCATED INSIDE A NOTEBOOK COMPUTER

MOUNTING SHAFT
The mounting shaft spins the hard disks at a speed of several thousand revolutions per minute while the computer is turned on.

SEALED DRIVE
The hard disks and the drive mechanism are hermetically sealed inside a case to keep them free from contamination.

INSIDE A 3.5-INCH HARD DRIVE

Copyright © 2015 Cengage Learning®

Courtesy of Hitachi Global Storage Technologies; Courtesy Western Digital

>**Magnetic hard drive.** A hard drive consisting of one or more metal magnetic disks permanently sealed, along with an access mechanism and read/write heads, inside its drive.

HOW IT WORKS

More Storage for Your Tablet

For many users, the internal storage capacity (typically less than 64 GB) of a media tablet just doesn't cut it. While minimizing the built-in flash memory of these devices is necessary to keep the cost and size down, many users want more. While some users connect their device to a desktop or notebook computer to transfer content (movies, music, photos, and more) to and from their mobile devices, there is another, easier option—going wireless.

A number of new storage products are emerging that connect directly to your devices (including tablets, smartphones, and computers) via Wi-Fi so you don't have to worry about cables or how to connect to a device that doesn't have a USB port. Sizes and configurations vary widely—from the 32 GB Kingston SSD *Wi-Drive* to the 1TB Seagate *Wireless Plus* magnetic hard drive (shown in the accompanying photograph) that can hold up to 500 high-definition movies. These hard drives typically have built-in Wi-Fi capabilities and data can be transferred in both directions (such as to stream a movie from the hard drive to your tablet or smart TV, or to transfer photos or videos taken with your phone to the hard drive). Unlike cloud storage, these hard drives can be used in locations (such as while traveling in a car or an airplane) where you don't have Internet access and, because these hard drives are accessed locally, you can play back full HD video without any buffering or stuttering. The Wireless Plus even allows up to eight devices to access the hard drive at one time and it has a 10-hour battery life, which makes it even more useful while you are on the go.

To use one of these wireless hard drives with your mobile device, you need to download the appropriate media app from your app store (such as the *App Store* for iPad and iPhone users or *Google Play* for Andriod users) and launch it. You should then have quick and easy wireless access to the hard drive. You can also connect these hard drives to your computer, if you wish, via Wi-Fi.

While carrying an extra device with you may be inconvenient at times, until 1 TB mobile devices come along, it works.

Courtesy of Seagate Technology LLC

The surface of a hard disk is organized into **tracks** (concentric rings) and pie-shaped groups of **sectors** (small pieces of a track), as shown in Figure 3-6. On most computer systems, the smallest amount of disk space on a hard drive that can be used to store a file is a **cluster**—one or more adjacent sectors. The computer numbers the tracks, sectors, and clusters so it can keep track of where data is stored. The computer uses a *file system* to record where each file is physically stored on the hard drive and what filename the user has assigned to it. When the user requests a document (always by filename), the computer uses its file system to retrieve it. Because a cluster is the smallest area on a hard drive that a computer can access, everything stored on a hard drive always takes up at least one cluster of storage space.

In addition to tracks, sectors, and clusters, hard drives are also organized into **cylinders** (refer again to Figure 3-6). A cylinder is the collection of one specific track located on each hard disk surface. In other words, it is the area on all of the hard disks inside a hard drive that can be accessed without moving the read/write access mechanism, once it has been moved to the proper position. For example, the hard drive shown

---

>**Track.** A concentric path on a disk where data is recorded. >**Sector.** A small piece of a track. >**Cluster.** One or more sectors; the smallest addressable area of a disk. >**Cylinder.** The collection of tracks located in the same location on a set of hard disk surfaces.

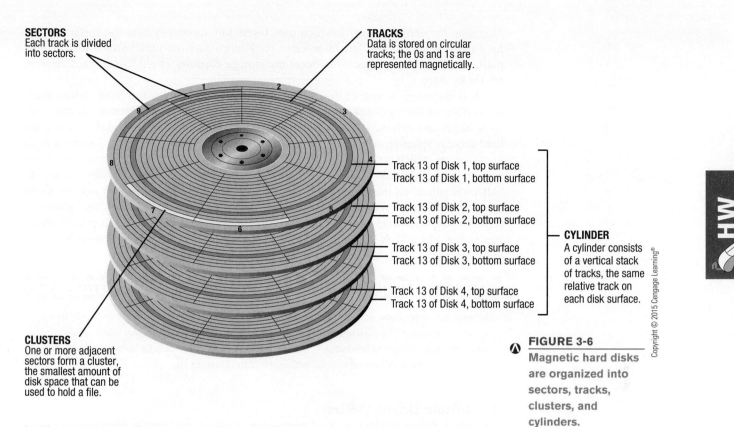

SECTORS
Each track is divided into sectors.

TRACKS
Data is stored on circular tracks; the 0s and 1s are represented magnetically.

Track 13 of Disk 1, top surface
Track 13 of Disk 1, bottom surface

Track 13 of Disk 2, top surface
Track 13 of Disk 2, bottom surface

Track 13 of Disk 3, top surface
Track 13 of Disk 3, bottom surface

Track 13 of Disk 4, top surface
Track 13 of Disk 4, bottom surface

CYLINDER
A cylinder consists of a vertical stack of tracks, the same relative track on each disk surface.

CLUSTERS
One or more adjacent sectors form a cluster, the smallest amount of disk space that can be used to hold a file.

FIGURE 3-6
Magnetic hard disks are organized into sectors, tracks, clusters, and cylinders.

in Figure 3-6 contains four hard disks, which means there are eight possible recording surfaces (using both sides of each hard disk). Consequently, a cylinder for that hard drive would consist of eight tracks, such as track 13 on all eight surfaces. Because all of the read/write heads move together, all of the tracks in a cylinder are accessible at the same time.

Traditionally, the magnetic particles on a hard disk have been aligned horizontally, parallel to the hard disk's surface (referred to as *longitudinal magnetic recording*). To increase capacity and reliability, most new hard drives today use *perpendicular magnetic recording* (*PMR*), in which the bits are placed upright (as in Figure 3-4) to allow them to be closer together than is possible with a horizontal layout. For instance, PMR currently allows a recording density up to 1 *terabit per square inch* (*Tb/inch²*), which results in internal hard drives with capacities up to about 4 TB of storage for a 3.5-inch hard drive, 1 TB for a 2.5-inch hard drive, and 100 GB for a 1-inch hard drive.

To allow for higher capacities, new hard drive technologies are under development. For instance, hard drives filled with helium gas (to reduce friction) and hard drives using *shingled magnetic recording (SMR)*, which squeezes more data onto disks by overlapping the data tracks on them like the shingles on a roof, are both expected to become available sometime in 2014 and offer increased capacities. Another option in the future is *Heat-Assisted*

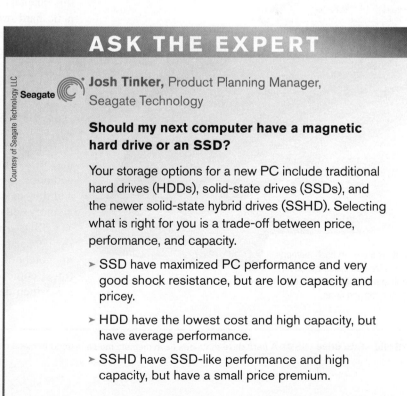

ASK THE EXPERT

Josh Tinker, Product Planning Manager, Seagate Technology

Should my next computer have a magnetic hard drive or an SSD?

Your storage options for a new PC include traditional hard drives (HDDs), solid-state drives (SSDs), and the newer solid-state hybrid drives (SSHD). Selecting what is right for you is a trade-off between price, performance, and capacity.

➤ SSD have maximized PC performance and very good shock resistance, but are low capacity and pricey.

➤ HDD have the lowest cost and high capacity, but have average performance.

➤ SSHD have SSD-like performance and high capacity, but have a small price premium.

Magnetic Recording (HAMR), which uses lasers to temporarily heat the surface of the hard disks when storing data in order to pack more data onto the surface than is normally possible—it is expected to boost the storage capacity of a 3.5-inch hard drive to 60 TB by 2016.

It is important to realize that a magnetic hard drive's read/write heads never touch the surface of the hard disks at any time, even during reading and writing. If the read/write heads do touch the surface (for example, if a desktop computer is bumped while the hard drive is spinning or if a foreign object gets onto the surface of a hard disk), a *head crash* occurs, which typically does permanent damage to the hard drive. Because the read/write heads are located extremely close to the surface of the hard disks (less than one-half millionth of an inch above the surface), the presence of a foreign object the width of a human hair or even a smoke particle on the surface of a hard disk is like placing a huge boulder on a road and then trying to drive over it with your car. When hard drives containing critical data become damaged, *data recovery firms* may be able to help out, as discussed in the Inside the Industry box.

CAUTION   CAUTION   CAUTION   CAUTION   CAUTION   CAUTION   CAUT

Because you never know when a head crash or other hard drive failure will occur—there may be no warning whatsoever—be sure to *back up* the data on your hard drive on a regular basis. Backing up data—that is, creating a second copy of important files—is critical not only for businesses but also for individuals and is discussed in detail in Chapter 5 and Chapter 15.

Solid-State Drives (SSDs)

Solid-state drives (SSDs) are hard drives that use flash memory technology instead of spinning hard disk platters and magnetic technology (see Figure 3-7); consequently, SSDs have no moving parts and data is stored as electrical charges on the flash memory media located within the SSD. These characteristics mean that SSDs (along with the other types of flash memory storage systems discussed later in this chapter) are not subject to mechanical failures like magnetic hard drives, and are, therefore, more resistant to shock and vibration. They also consume less power, generate less heat, make no noise, and are much faster than magnetic hard drives. Consequently, SSDs are an especially attractive option for portable computers and mobile devices. Although previously too expensive for all but specialty applications, prices of SSDs (also sometimes called *flash memory hard drives*) have fallen significantly over the past few years (although they are still significantly more expensive per GB than conventional magnetic hard drives) and they are becoming the norm for netbooks, mobile devices, and other very portable devices. In addition to cost, another disadvantage of SSDs is that flash memory cells can wear out with repeated use.

SSDs are most often 2.5-inch drives so they can easily be used instead of conventional magnetic hard drives in notebooks, netbooks, and other personal computers (most come with a bracket so the drive can also be used in a 3.5-inch drive bay of a desktop computer). There are also

⊙ FIGURE 3-7
Solid-state drives (SSDs).

Courtesy Transcend Information USA

Data is stored in flash memory chips located inside the drive; unlike magnetic drives, there are no moving parts.

>**Solid-state drive (SSD).** A hard drive that uses flash memory media instead of metal magnetic hard disks.

INSIDE THE INDUSTRY

Data Recovery Experts

It happens far more often than most people imagine. A home computer crashes and all the family's digital photos are lost, a tablet computer is dropped and the files are no longer accessible, a mobile phone falls into a pool and no longer works, or a business is flooded and the computers storing the business's critical files are damaged. If the data on a damaged device is backed up, then it is fairly easy and inexpensive to restore it onto a new hard drive or device. If the data is not backed up, however, it is time to seek help from a data recovery expert.

Professional data recovery firms, such as DriveSavers in California, specialize in recovering critical data from damaged storage devices (see the accompanying photos). Engineers open the damaged device (in a *Class 100 clean room* to minimize contamination and maximize data recovery) and then make an image of the data located on that device, bit by bit, onto a target drive. The target drive is then used to reconstruct the data; if the file directory is not recovered, engineers try to match the jumbled data to file types in order to reconstruct the original files. Once the data recovery process is complete, the customer receives the data on a new hard drive. To ensure data is safe and remains confidential, DriveSavers has numerous security certifications; in fact, it is used by government agencies to recover critical data.

Professional data recovery firms are also used when hard drives and other storage media simply stop working. In fact, DriveSavers estimates that 75% of its business is due to malfunctioning devices. With the vast amounts of digital data (such as photos, music, home videos, personal documents, and school papers) that the average person stores today, data recovery firms are increasingly being used by individuals to recover personal data, in addition to being used by businesses to recover critical company data.

Data loss can happen to any business or individual, even to the rich and famous. A few celebrity clients of DriveSavers include Bruce Willis, Conan O'Brien, Harrison Ford, Sean Connery, and Bill Oakely, the executive producer of *The Simpsons*, whose computer crashed taking scripts for 12 episodes of the show with it. In some cases, data loss is a result of a natural disaster or an unusual circumstance; for instance an iMac computer that contained the only digital pictures of a survivor's family was destroyed by the recent Japanese tsunami; a laptop was trapped for two days beneath a sunken cruise ship in the Amazon River; and a server went down at a Fortune 500 company, which caused them to lose all its financial data and stockholder information. In all of these cases, DriveSavers was able to recover all of the lost data.

Data recovery firms stress the importance of backing up data to avoid data loss. According to Scott Gaidano, president of DriveSavers, "The first thing we tell people is back up, back up, back up. It's amazing how many people don't back up." It is also important to make sure the backup procedure is working. For instance, the Fortune 500 company mentioned previously performed regular backups and kept the backup media in a fire-resistant safe, but the backup system failed after its server crashed because all the backup media were blank.

Because potentially losing all the data on a storage medium can be so stressful and traumatic, DriveSavers has its own data-crisis counselor, a former suicide hotline worker. Fortunately for its clients, DriveSavers has an extremely high recovery rate. While the services of data recovery experts are not cheap, when the data on a damaged device is critical data, using a data recovery expert is your best chance for getting your data back.

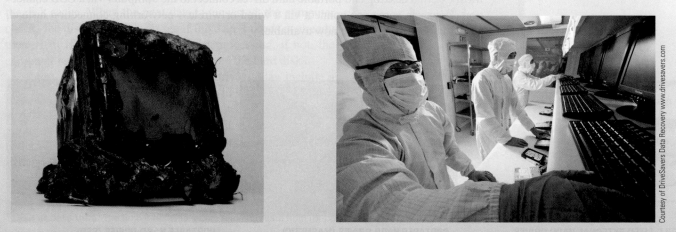

Courtesy of DriveSavers Data Recovery www.drivesavers.com

Data recovery. The data on this destroyed computer (left) was recovered by data recovery experts in a clean room (right).

memory to reduce the number of times the hard disks in a hybrid hard drive need to be read, hybrid hard drives can also use the flash memory to temporarily store (cache) data to be written to the hard disks, which can further extend the battery life of portable computers and mobile devices. The additional flash memory in a hybrid hard drive can also allow encryption or other security measures to be built into the drive.

Hard Drive Partitioning and File Systems

Partitioning a hard drive enables you to divide the physical capacity of a single hard drive logically into separate areas, called *partitions* or *volumes*. Partitions function as independent hard drives and are sometimes referred to as *logical drives* because each partition is labeled and treated separately (such as C drive and D drive) when viewed in a file management program such as File Explorer or Windows Explorer for Windows computers, but they are still physically one hard drive. One or more partitions are created when a hard drive is first *formatted* (prepared for data storage). For instance, many new personal computers come with two partitions: a C drive partition ready to use for programs and data and a D drive partition set up as a *recovery partition*. A recovery partition (see Figure 3-10) contains the data necessary to restore a hard drive back to its state at the time the computer was purchased and is designed to be used only if the computer malfunctions.

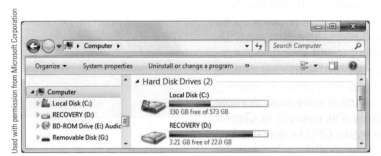

Used with permission from Microsoft Corporation

FIGURE 3-10

Hard drive partitions. New personal computers today often come with the primary hard drive divided into two partitions.

In the past, operating systems could only use hard drives up to 512 MB, so hard drives larger than that limit had to use multiple partitions. While today's operating systems can use much larger hard drives and, therefore, do not require the use of multiple partitions, partitioning a large hard drive can make it function more efficiently. This is because operating systems typically use a larger cluster size with a larger hard drive. Because even tiny files have to use up one entire cluster of storage space, disk space is often wasted when a large cluster size is used. When a hard drive is partitioned, each logical drive can use a smaller cluster size because each logical drive is smaller than the original hard drive.

Users can create additional partitions on a hard drive if desired, but they should be careful when partitioning a hard drive because deleting a partition erases all data contained on that partition. One reason advanced users may partition a primary hard drive is to be able to use two different operating systems on the same hard drive—such as Windows and Linux (these and other operating systems are discussed in detail in Chapter 5). With a *dual-boot system* such as this, the user specifies the operating system to be run each time the computer boots. Another reason for partitioning a hard drive is to create the appearance of having separate hard drives for file management, multiple users, or other purposes. For instance, some users choose to partition a new second or external hard drive into multiple logical drives to organize their data before storing data on that hard drive. Storing data files on a separate physical hard drive or logical partition makes it easier for the user to locate data files. It also enables users to back up all data files simply by backing up the entire hard drive or partition containing the data.

The partition size, cluster size (on magnetic hard drives), maximum drive size, and maximum file size that can be used with a hard drive are determined by the *file system* being used. For instance, Windows users have three file system options to choose from: the original *FAT* file system (not commonly used with hard drives today, though it is used with some removable storage devices like USB flash drives), the newer *FAT32* file system, and the newest *NTFS* file system. The recommended file system for computers running current versions of Windows is NTFS because it supports much larger hard drives and files than either FAT or FAT32 and it includes better security and error-recovery capabilities. Computers with older versions of Windows have to use FAT32, which has a maximum partition size of 32 GB and a maximum file size of 4 GB.

Hard Drive Interface Standards

Hard drives connect, or interface, with a computer using one of several different standards. The most common internal *hard drive interface standard* for desktop computers today is *serial ATA (SATA)*. The SATA standard was designed to replace the older, slower *parallel ATA (PATA)* standard, which is also referred to as *Fast ATA* and *EIDE (Enhanced Integrated Drive Electronics)*. SATA is faster (up to 6 Gbps for *SATA III* devices) than PATA and uses thinner cables, which means SATA hard drives take up less room inside the system unit. External hard drives most often connect to the computer via a USB, Thunderbolt, or FireWire port, though an *eSATA (external SATA)* interface can be used to connect to the computer via an eSATA port if faster speeds are desired.

The most common hard drive interfaces used with servers are *serial attached SCSI (SAS)*, which is a newer version of the SCSI interface, and *Fibre Channel*, which is a reliable, flexible, and very fast standard geared for long-distance, high-bandwidth applications. For network storage, new standards, such as *Internet SCSI (iSCSI)* and *Fibre Channel over Ethernet (FCoE)*, have evolved that communicate over the Internet or another network using the *TCP/IP* networking standard. Networks and networking standards are discussed in Chapter 7.

> **TIP**
>
> You can transfer the data from the hard drive of an old or broken computer if the hard drive is still functioning—just use an appropriate transfer cable (such as SATA to USB) to connect the drive to a USB port on your new computer.

OPTICAL DISCS AND DRIVES

Data on **optical discs** (such as *CDs* and *DVDs*) is stored and read *optically*; that is, using laser beams. General characteristics of optical discs are discussed next, followed by a look at the various types of optical discs available today.

Optical Disc Characteristics

Optical discs are thin circular discs made out of *polycarbonate substrate*—essentially a type of very strong plastic—that are topped with layers of other materials and coatings used to store data and protect the disc. Data can be stored on one or both sides of an optical disc, depending on the disc design, and some types of discs use multiple recording layers on each side of the disc to increase capacity. An optical disc contains a single spiral track (instead of multiple tracks like magnetic disks), and the track is divided into sectors to keep data organized. As shown in Figure 3-11, this track (sometimes referred to as a *groove* in order to avoid confusion with the

FIGURE 3-11
How recorded optical discs work.

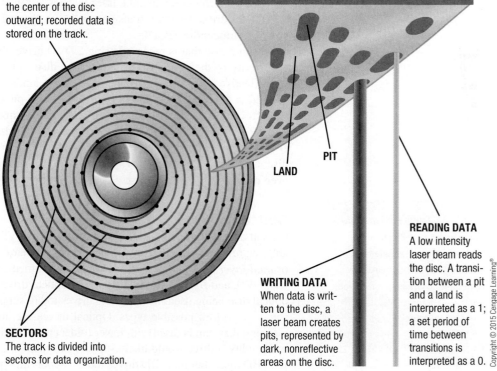

TRACK
A single track spirals from the center of the disc outward; recorded data is stored on the track.

SECTORS
The track is divided into sectors for data organization.

LAND

PIT

WRITING DATA
When data is written to the disc, a laser beam creates pits, represented by dark, nonreflective areas on the disc.

READING DATA
A low intensity laser beam reads the disc. A transition between a pit and a land is interpreted as a 1; a set period of time between transitions is interpreted as a 0.

Copyright © 2015 Cengage Learning®

> **Optical disc.** A type of storage medium read from and written to using a laser beam.

term *tracks* used to refer to songs on an audio CD) begins at the center of the disc and spirals out to the edge of the disc.

Advantages of optical discs include large capacity for their size (as discussed shortly) and durability (they are more durable than magnetic media and don't degrade with use like some magnetic media do). However, the discs should be handled carefully and stored in their cases when they are not in use in order to protect the recorded surfaces of the discs from scratches, fingerprints, and other marks that can interfere with the usability of the discs. Optical discs are the standard today for software delivery; they are also commonly used for backup purposes, and for storing and/or transporting music, photo, video, and other large files.

Representing Data on an Optical Disc

Data is written to an optical disc in one of two ways. With *read-only optical discs* like movie, music, and software CDs and DVDs, the surface of the disc is molded or stamped appropriately to represent the data. With *recordable* or *rewritable optical discs* that can be written to using an *optical drive* such as a *DVD drive*, as discussed shortly, the reflectivity of the disc is changed using a laser to represent the data. In either case, the disc is read with a laser and the computer interprets the reflection of the laser off the disc surface as 1s and 0s.

To accomplish this with molded or stamped optical discs, tiny depressions (when viewed from the top side of the disc) or bumps (when viewed from the bottom) are created on the disc's surface. These bumps are called *pits*; the areas on the disc that are not changed are called *lands*. Although many people think that each individual pit and land represents a 1 or 0, that idea is not completely accurate—it is actually the transition between a pit and land that represents a 1. When the disc is read, the amount of laser light reflected back from the disc changes when the laser reaches a transition between a pit and a land. When the optical drive detects a transition, it is interpreted as a 1; no transition for a specific period of time indicates a 0.

With a disc that is recorded using a DVD drive, the recording laser beam changes the reflectivity of the appropriate areas on the disc to represent the data stored there—dark, nonreflective areas are pits; reflective areas are lands, as illustrated in Figure 3-11. As with molded or stamped discs, the transition between a pit and a land represents a 1 and no transition for a specific distance along the track represents a 0. Different types of optical discs use different types of laser beams. Conventional **CD discs** use *infrared* lasers; conventional **DVD discs** use *red* lasers, which allow data to be stored more compactly on the same size disc; and high-definition **Blu-ray Discs (BDs)** use *blue-violet lasers*, which can store data even more compactly on a disc.

Optical Drives

Optical discs in each of the three categories (CD, DVD, and BD) can be read-only, recordable, or rewritable; they can use the + or − standard; and they can be either *single-layer* or *dual-layer* (*DL*) discs. Optical discs are designed to be read by **optical drives**, such as *CD*, *DVD*, and *BD drives*, and the type of optical drive being used must support the type of optical disc being used. Most optical drives today support multiple types of optical discs—some support all possible types. Optical drives are almost always *downward-compatible*, meaning they can be used with lower (older) types of discs but not higher (newer) ones. So, while a DVD drive would likely support all types of CD and DVD discs, it cannot be used with BD discs, but most BD drives today support all types of CD, DVD, and BD discs.

> **CD disc.** A low capacity (typically 700 MB) optical disc that is often used to deliver music and software, as well as to store user data.
> **DVD disc.** A medium capacity (typically 4.7 GB or 8.5 GB) optical disc that is often used to deliver software and movies, as well as to store user data. > **Blu-ray Disc (BD).** A high-capacity (typically 25 GB or 50 GB) disc that is often used to deliver high-definition movies, as well as to store user data. > **Optical drive.** A drive used with optical discs, such as CD or DVD discs.

To use an optical disc, it is inserted into an appropriate optical drive. Purchased optical discs often have a title and other text printed on one side; if so, they are inserted into the optical drive with the printed side facing up. Two-sided commercial discs typically identify each side of a disc by printing that information on the disc close to the inner circle.

The process of recording data onto a recordable or rewritable optical disc is called *burning*. To burn an optical disc, the optical drive being used must support burning and the type of disc being used. In addition, *CD-burning* or *DVD-burning* software is required. Many burning programs are available commercially, and recent versions of operating systems (including Windows and Mac OS) include burning capabilities. In addition, most CD and DVD drives come bundled with burning software. Some optical drives—such as *LightScribe-enabled drives*—are even capable of burning label information on the surface of a disc after the content has been recorded. (To do this, you first burn the data to the disc, and then you flip the disc over and burn the desired label information on the other side of the disc.) Most personal computers today come with an internal optical drive; however, netbooks and mobile devices typically do not include an optical drive. An *external optical drive* that connects via a USB port (see Figure 3-12) can be used with most computers and some media tablets whenever an optical drive is temporarily needed.

Courtesy Apricorn

FIGURE 3-12
External optical drives. Can be connected as needed, typically via a USB port, such as to the netbook shown here.

Optical Disc Shapes, Sizes, and Capacities

Standard-sized optical discs are 120-mm (approximately 4.7-inch) discs. There are also smaller 80-mm (approximately 3-inch) *mini discs*, which use either that smaller form factor or are surrounded by clear material to be the same physical size as a standard disc to better fit in optical disc drives. Because the track starts at the center of the disc and the track just stops when it reaches an outer edge of the disc, optical discs theoretically can be made into a variety of sizes and shapes—such as a heart, a triangle, an irregular shape, or a hockey-rink shape appropriate for *business card CDs* (discs with business card information printed on the outside that contain a résumé, portfolio, or other digital documents). However, an ongoing patent battle over changing the shape of any normally round storage media (a process an individual claims to have patented) has resulted in these custom shapes not being available by any CD or DVD manufacturer until the patent issue is resolved. The practice of using optical discs to replace ordinary objects, such as business cards and mailed advertisements, is becoming more common. In addition, *scented discs* that have a specific scent (such as a particular perfume, popcorn, pine trees, or a specific fruit) added to the label that is released when the surface of the disc is rubbed are available. Some examples of optical discs are shown in Figure 3-13.

FIGURE 3-13
Optical discs are available in a variety of sizes, appearances, and capacities.

Courtesy Adobe

STANDARD 120 MM (4.7 INCH) SIZED DISC

Copyright © 2015 Cengage Learning®

MINI 80 MM (3.1 INCH) SIZED DISC

Courtesy Megaladon

Back of disc

Front of disc

MINI 80 MM (3.1 INCH) SIZED DISC
(with a clear background to be standard size)

TYPE OF DISC	CAPACITIY	USED FOR
CD	700 MB	Audio music delivery; custom CDs containing music, photos, etc.
DVD DVD-DL	4.7 GB 8.5 GB	Movie and software delivery; custom DVDs containing videos, music, photos, etc.
BD BD-DL BDXL	25 GB 50 GB 100 GB (rewritable) or 128 GB (recordable)	Primarily movie delivery

FIGURE 3-14
Summary of optical discs.

FIGURE 3-15
High-definition movies are available on Blu-ray Discs (BDs).

One of the biggest advantages of optical discs is their large capacity (see Figure 3-14). To further increase capacity, many discs are available as *dual-layer discs* (also called *double-layer discs*) that store data in two layers on a single side of the disc, so the capacity is approximately doubled. For an even larger capacity, discs with more than two layers are in development. Standard-sized CD discs are normally single-layer and usually hold 700 MB (though some hold 650 MB), standard-sized DVD discs hold 4.7 GB (single-layer discs) or 8.5 GB (dual-layer discs), and standard-sized BD discs hold either 25 GB (single-layer discs) or 50 GB (dual-layer discs). Discs can also be *double sided*, which doubles the capacity; however, unlike hard disks, optical discs are only read on one side at a time and so must be turned over to access the second side. Double-sided discs are most often used with movies and other prerecorded content, such as to store a *widescreen version* of a movie on one side of a DVD disc and a *standard version* on the other side. Small optical discs have a smaller storage capacity than their larger counterparts: typically, single-layer, single-sided 3-inch mini CD, DVD, and BD discs hold about 200 MB, 1.4 GB, and 7.5 GB, respectively, and business card-sized CD and DVD discs hold about 50 MB and 325 MB, respectively.

As with magnetic disks, researchers are continually working to increase the capacity of optical discs without increasing their physical size. For instance, the new BD standard (*BDXL*), which uses more layers to boost capacity, supports capacities up to 128 GB, large enough to support *4K* (*Ultra HD*) versions of movies (4K is discussed in more detail in Chapter 4).

Read-Only Optical Discs: CD-ROM, DVD-ROM, and BD-ROM Discs

CD-ROM (*compact disc read-only memory*) **discs** and **DVD-ROM** (*digital versatile disc read-only memory*) **discs** are *read-only optical discs* that come prerecorded with commercial products, such as software programs, clip art and other types of graphics collections, music, and movies. For high-definition content (such as feature films), **BD-ROM** (*Blu-ray Disc read-only memory*) **discs** are available (see the 4K BD movie in Figure 3-15). There are also additional read-only disc formats for specific gaming devices, such as the proprietary discs used with the Wii, Xbox, and PlayStation gaming consoles. The data on a read-only disc cannot be erased, changed, or added to because the pits that are molded into the surface of the disc when the disc is produced are permanent.

Recordable Optical Discs: CD-R, DVD-R, DVD+R, and BD-R Discs

Recordable optical discs (also sometimes called *write-once discs*) can be written to, but the discs cannot be erased and reused. Recordable CDs are referred to as **CD-R discs**. Single-layer recordable DVDs are called either

DVD-R discs or **DVD+R discs**, depending on the standard being used, and dual-layer recordable DVDs are called *DVD+R DL* or *DVD-R DL discs*. Recordable BD discs are also available in single-layer, dual-layer, and XL discs (**BD-R discs**, *BD-R DL discs*, and *BD-R XL* discs, respectively). The capacities of recordable optical discs are the same as the read-only formats.

Instead of having physically molded pits, most recordable optical discs have a recording layer containing organic light-sensitive dye embedded between the disc's plastic and reflective layers. One exception to this is the BD-R disc, which has a recording layer consisting of inorganic material. When data is written to a recordable disc, the recording laser inside the recordable optical drive burns the dye (for CD and DVD discs) or melts and combines the inorganic material (for BD-R discs), creating nonreflective areas that function as pits. In either case, the marks are permanent so data on the disc cannot be erased or rewritten.

Recordable CDs are commonly used for backing up files, sending large files to others, and creating custom music CDs (for example, from MP3 files legally downloaded from the Internet or from songs located on a music album purchased on CD). DVD-Rs can be used for similar purposes when more storage space is needed, such as for backing up large files and for storing home movies, digital photos, and other multimedia files. BD-R discs can be used when an even greater amount of storage is needed, such as very large backups or high-definition multimedia files.

Rewritable Optical Discs: CD-RW, DVD-RW, DVD+RW, and BD-RE Discs

Rewritable optical discs can be written to, erased, and overwritten just like magnetic hard disks. The most common types of rewritable optical discs are **CD-RW**, **DVD-RW**, **DVD+RW**, and **BD-RE discs**; BD-RE discs are also available as dual-layer discs (*BD-RE DL discs*) and XL discs (*BD-RE XL*). The capacities of rewritable discs are typically the same as their read-only and recordable counterparts (BDXL discs are the exception). An additional, but not widely used, rewritable DVD format is *DVD-RAM*. DVD-RAM and DVD-RAM DL discs are supported by *DVD-RAM drives*, as well as by some DVD and BD drives.

To write to, erase, or overwrite rewritable optical discs, *phase change* technology is used. With this technology, the rewritable disc is coated with layers of a special metal alloy compound that can have two different appearances after it has been heated and then cooled, depending on the heating and cooling process used. With one process, the material *crystallizes* and that area of the disc is reflective. With another process, the area cools to a nonreflective *amorphous* state. Before any data is written to a rewritable optical disc, the disc is completely reflective. To write data to the disc, the recording laser heats the metal alloy in the appropriate locations on the spiral track and then uses the appropriate cooling process to create either the nonreflective areas (pits) or the reflective areas (lands). To erase the disc, the appropriate heating and cooling process is used to change the areas to be erased back to their original reflective state.

Rewritable optical discs are used for many of the same purposes as recordable optical discs. However, they are particularly appropriate for situations in which data written to the optical disc can be erased at a later time so the disc can be reused (such as for transferring large files from one computer to another or temporarily storing TV shows recorded on your computer that you will later watch using your living room TV and DVD player).

>**DVD-R/DVD+R discs.** Recordable DVDs. >**BD-R disc.** A recordable Blu-ray Disc. >**CD-RW disc.** A rewritable CD. >**DVD-RW/DVD+RW discs.** Rewritable DVDs. >**BD-RE disc.** A rewritable Blu-ray Disc.

TREND

DNA Data Storage

First we had magnetic tape and hard drives, then optical discs, and, finally, flash memory. What's next in storage developments? Think DNA.

Researchers are looking at DNA as a storage medium because of its capability for long-term high-density encoding. For instance, DNA for the long-extinct woolly mammoth has survived for tens of thousands of years. And researchers think they have figured it out. Recently, researchers from the United Kingdom encoded a variety of data—including Shakespeare's sonnets, a JPEG photo, and an MP3 recording of Martin Luther King Jr.'s "I Have a Dream" speech—into DNA material. They first translated the data into binary 0s and 1s, then converted the binary data to a ternary code of 0s, 1s, and 2s in order to add error correction, and then rewrote that data as strings of DNA's chemical bases and stored it in DNA.

Besides longevity and the belief that (possibly unlike magnetic and optical storage) scientists will always have the ability to read DNA material, another huge potential advantage is capacity. Currently, scientists are able to store data in DNA using densities that are at least 1,000 times greater than current media—about 2.2 PB per gram. At that rate, if you took everything human

beings have ever written (an estimated 50 PB of text) and stored it in DNA, it would weigh less than a granola bar.

One of the biggest obstacles to DNA storage at the present time is cost—about $12,400 per megabyte. However, as the technology improves and the cost for DNA synthesis goes down, it is possible that DNA storage may be cost-effective for some applications—such as data that needs to be archived for many years (DNA is not practical for regular data storage because the data cannot be overwritten and it is not possible at the present time to search for specific pieces of data). But researchers believe that DNA data storage may be a viable archiving option in less than 10 years.

FLASH MEMORY STORAGE SYSTEMS

As previously discussed, **flash memory** is a chip-based storage medium that represents data using electrons. It is used in a variety of storage systems, such as the SSDs and hybrid hard drives already discussed and the additional storage systems discussed next. For a look at a possibility for what might be the next new storage medium—*DNA data storage*—see the Trend box.

MEDIA TABLET
Contains 64 GB of embedded flash memory.

EMBEDDED FLASH MEMORY

Embedded Flash Memory

Embedded flash memory refers to flash memory chips embedded into products. Because flash memory media are physically very small, they are increasingly being embedded directly into a variety of consumer products—such as portable digital media players, digital cameras, handheld gaming devices, GPS devices, mobile phones, and even sunglasses and wristwatches—to provide built-in data storage. Flash memory is also increasingly being integrated into mobile devices, such as small tablet computers and smartphones. While embedded flash memory can take the form of small SSDs or memory cards, it is increasingly being implemented with small stand-alone chips, such as the one shown in Figure 3-16.

> **Flash memory.** Nonvolatile memory chips that can be used for storage by the computer or user; can be built into a computer or a storage medium.
> **Embedded flash memory.** Flash memory chips embedded into products, such as consumer devices.

Flash Memory Cards and Readers

One of the most common types of flash memory media is the **flash memory card**—a small card containing one or more flash memory chips, a controller chip, other electrical components, and metal contacts to connect the card to the device or reader being used. Flash memory cards are available in a variety of formats, such as *CompactFlash (CF)*, *Secure Digital (SD)*, *Secure Digital High Capacity (SDHC)*, *Secure Digital Extended Capacity (SDXC)*, *MultiMedia Card (MMC)*, *xD Picture Card (xD)*, *XQD*, and *Memory Stick (MS)* (see Figure 3-17). These formats are not interchangeable, so the type of flash memory card used with a device is determined by the type of flash media card that device can accept. Flash memory cards are the most common type of storage media for digital cameras, portable digital media players, mobile phones, and other portable devices. Flash memory cards can also be used to store data for a personal computer, as needed, as well as to transfer data from a portable device (digital camera, media tablet, smartphone, etc.) to a computer. Consequently, most personal computers and many mobile devices today come with a *flash memory card reader* capable of reading flash memory cards; an external flash memory card reader (such as the ones shown in Figure 3-17) that connects via a USB port can be used when the destination device doesn't have a built-in reader. The capacity of flash memory cards is continually growing and is up to 256 GB at the present time with even higher capacity cards expected in the near future.

One of the most widely used types of flash memory media—Secure Digital (SD)—is available in different physical sizes, as well as in different capacities. For instance, standard-sized SD cards are often used in digital cameras and computers; the smaller *miniSD* and *microSD* (about one-half and one-quarter the size of a standard SD card, respectively, as shown in Figure 3-17) are designed to be used with mobile phones and other mobile devices. When more storage space is needed, higher capacity *miniSDHC* and *microSDHC* cards can be used. MMC cards and memory sticks are also available in mobile sizes; adapters can be used with mobile-sized flash memory cards in order to use them in a larger, but compatible, memory card slot (such as the *microSD-to-SD adapter* shown in Figure 3-17).

TIP

Some computers come with a *multi-card reader* that has a variety of slots to support multiple types of cards—just be sure to use the proper slot for each card.

TIP

The speeds of SDHC cards are beginning to use class ratings to indicate their speed, such as *Class 4* cards and *Class 10* cards that have a minimum data transfer rate of 4 MB/second and 10 MB/second, respectively.

FIGURE 3-17
Some flash memory cards, readers, and adapters.

HAS SLOTS FOR 3 TYPES OF FLASH MEMORY CARDS HERE.

USB MULTI-CARD READER

COMPACTFLASH (CF) CARDS

MEMORY STICKS

MICROSD-TO-SD ADAPTER

USB MICROSD READER

SECURE DIGITAL (SD) CARDS

XD PICTURE CARDS

> **Flash memory card.** A small, rectangular flash memory medium, such as a CompactFlash (CF) or Secure Digital (SD) card; often used with digital cameras and other portable devices.

While general-purpose flash memory cards can be used for most applications, there are also flash memory cards designed for specific uses. For instance, *professional flash memory cards* designed for professional photographers are faster and more durable than consumer cards; *gaming flash memory cards* are specifically designed for gaming consoles and devices, such as the Nintendo Wii or Sony PSP; and *HD flash memory cards* are designed for capturing and transferring high-definition video. There are even Wi-Fi-enabled flash memory cards that can wirelessly upload digital photos taken with a camera using that card for storage, as discussed in the Technology and You box in Chapter 7.

Typically, flash memory media are purchased blank, but some flash-memory-based software (such as games, encyclopedias, and language translators) is available. A relatively new option for portable music is *slotMusic*—music albums that come stored on microSD cards. These cards can be used with any phone or portable digital media player that has a microSD slot and they typically contain extra storage space to add additional files as desired. Movies are also beginning to be delivered via flash memory media, such as microSD cards and USB flash drives. These new options for portable multimedia are geared toward individuals who would like access to this content via a mobile phone, hotel room television, netbook, or other device often used while on the go that has a flash memory card slot or a USB port.

USB Flash Drives

USB flash drives (sometimes called *USB flash memory drives*, *thumb drives*, or *jump drives*) consist of flash memory media integrated into a self-contained unit that connects to a computer or other device via a standard USB port and is powered via that port. USB flash drives are designed to be very small and very portable. In order to be appropriate for a wide variety of applications, USB flash drives are available in a host of formats—including those designed to be attached to backpacks or worn on a lanyard around the neck; those built into pens, necklaces, wristbands, or wristwatches; those thin enough to fit easily into a wallet; and those made into custom shapes for promotional or novelty purposes (see Figure 3-18). In fact, a growing trend with USB flash drives used for promotional purposes is completely custom-shaped drives made out of rubber, metal, plastic, or wood (such as the model car drive shown in Figure 3-18). When the USB flash drive is built into a consumer product (such as a watch, sunglasses, or a Swiss Army knife), a retractable cord is typically used

FIGURE 3-18
USB flash drives.

CONVENTIONAL DRIVE

Courtesy Kingston Technology Company, Inc.

CUSTOM CONVENTIONAL DRIVE

Courtesy CustomUSB.com

CUSTOM LANYARD DRIVE

Courtesy CustomUSB.com

CUSTOM WALLET DRIVE

Courtesy CustomUSB.com

> **USB flash drive.** A small storage device that plugs into a USB port and contains flash memory media.

TECHNOLOGY AND YOU

Thumb Drive PCs

We all know that USB flash drives are a great way to transport documents from one location to another, but what about using one to take a personalized computer with you wherever you go? It's possible and easy to do with the use of *portable applications* (also called *portable apps*)—computer programs that are designed to be used with portable devices like USB flash drives. When the device is plugged into the USB port of any computer, you have access to the software and personal data (including your browser bookmarks, calendar, e-mail and instant messaging contacts, and more) stored on that device, just as you would on your own computer. And when you unplug the device, none of your personal data is left behind because all programs are run directly from the USB flash drive. Many portable applications (such as PortableApps.com shown in the accompanying illustration) are free and include all the basics you might want in a single package. For instance, PortableApps.com includes a menu structure, as well as a built-in app store so you can find and install all the free apps you want including antivirus programs, Web browsers, messaging programs, games, the LibreOffice office suite, and more. To set up a USB flash drive as a portable computer, you need to perform the following steps:

1. Download your desired portable app program (such as PortableApps.com) to your desktop or notebook computer.

2. Plug in your USB flash drive and run the portable apps installation program, using your USB flash drive as the destination folder.

3. Open a file management program such as File Explorer or Windows Explorer for Windows computers, double-click your USB flash drive, and then launch your portable apps software to test it.

4. Download and install any additional portable apps you would like to use (it is a good idea to include an antivirus program to try to prevent the USB flash drive from becoming infected with a computer virus).

To use your thumb drive computer, plug it into the USB port of any computer—many portable apps will launch automatically and display a main menu, such as the one shown in the accompanying illustration. Portable apps can also be installed on an iPod or other portable digital media player (instead of on a USB flash drive) if you prefer to use that device as your portable computer.

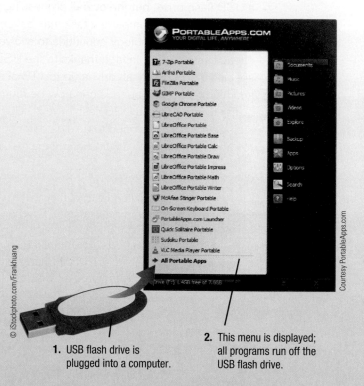

1. USB flash drive is plugged into a computer.

2. This menu is displayed; all programs run off the USB flash drive.

to connect the device to a computer when needed. Because they are becoming so widely used, additional hardware related to USB flash drives is becoming available, such as *USB duplicator systems* used by educators to copy assignments or other materials to and from a large collection of USB flash drives at one time.

To read from or write to a USB flash drive, you just plug it into a USB port. If the USB flash drive is being used with a computer, it is assigned a drive letter by the computer, just like any other type of attached drive, and files can be read from or written to the USB flash drive until it is unplugged from the USB port. The capacity of most USB flash drives today ranges from about 4 GB to 1 TB. USB flash drive use has become commonplace for individuals, students, and employees to transport files from one computer to another, as well as to quickly back up important files. For a look at how you can carry your personal computer with you on a USB flash drive, see the Technology and You box.

ASK THE EXPERT

Mark Tekunoff, Senior Technology Manager, Kingston Technology

Is it better to copy a file from a USB flash drive to a storage device like an SSD or HDD for extensive editing instead of working directly on the USB flash drive?

For performance processing work, it is better to process work on an SSD or HDD as they are better designed for this type of activity. Depending on the type of work being performed, it can be done on a USB flash drive, but the overall processing time or time it takes to complete a task may be longer—although flash technology continues to evolve and capacities increase. In fact, thanks to the USB 3.0 specification, USB flash drives up to 1TB of storage and high read/write speeds can now be found.

For most people, a USB flash drive is still a portable storage solution, designed to take data from one place to another, rather than a working storage medium.

In addition to providing basic data storage and data portability, USB flash drives can provide additional capabilities. For instance, they can be used to lock a computer and to issue Web site passwords; they can also include *biometric features*—such as a built-in fingerprint reader—to allow only authorized individuals access to the data stored on the USB flash drive or to the computer with which the USB flash drive is being used.

OTHER TYPES OF STORAGE SYSTEMS

Other types of storage systems used with personal and business computers today include *network/cloud storage*, *smart cards*, and *holographic storage*. There are also storage systems and technologies designed for large computer systems. These systems are discussed next.

Network and Cloud Storage Systems

Remote storage refers to using a storage device that is not connected directly to the user's computer; instead, the device is accessed through a local network or through the Internet. Using a remote storage device via a local network (referred to as **network storage**) works in much the same way as using *local storage* (the storage devices and media that are directly attached to the user's computer). To read data from or write data to a remote storage device (such as a hard drive being accessed via a network), the user just selects it (see Figure 3-19) and then performs the necessary tasks in the normal fashion. Network storage is common in businesses; it is also used by individuals with home networks for backup purposes or to share files with another computer in the home.

Because of the vast amount of data shared and made available over networks today, network storage has become increasingly important. Two common types of network storage used today are **network attached storage (NAS)** devices and **storage area networks (SANs)**. NAS devices are high-performance storage systems that are connected individually to a network to provide storage for the computers connected to that network. Some (such as the one shown in Figure 3-19) are designed for small business use; others are geared for home use instead. A growing trend, in fact, is home NAS devices designed to store multimedia data (such as downloaded music, recorded TV shows, and downloaded movies) to be distributed over a home entertainment network. NAS devices typically have room for two to eight hard disk drives and connect to the network via a wired or wireless networking connection; networking is explained in detail in Chapter 7.

A storage area network (SAN) also provides storage for a network, but it consists of a separate network of hard drives or other storage devices, which is connected to the main network. The primary difference between NAS (network attached storage) and a

TIP

NAS and SAN devices typically require an operating system to function; many also include software to provide additional features, such as automatic backups or security scans.

TIP

If the router used to connect devices to your home network includes a USB port, you can create a NAS by plugging a USB storage device (such as an external hard drive) directly into the router.

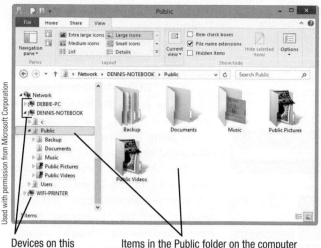

Devices on this network.

Items in the Public folder on the computer called DENNIS-NOTEBOOK.

SHARED FOLDERS
Shared folders on network computers appear and are accessed in a manner similar to local folders.

NETWORK ATTACHED STORAGE (NAS) DEVICES
This NAS device holds up to 16 TB of data and provides storage for all computers on the network.

FIGURE 3-19
Network storage.

SAN (storage area network) is how the storage devices interface with the network—that is, whether the storage devices act as individual network nodes, just like computers, printers, and other devices on the network (NAS), or whether they are located in a completely separate network of storage devices that is accessible via the main network (SAN). SANs can be more appropriate when a larger amount of network storage is needed; however, in terms of functionality, the distinction between NAS and SAN is blurring because they both provide storage services to the network. Typically, both NAS and SAN systems are scalable, so new devices can be added as more storage is needed, and devices can be added or removed without disrupting the network.

Remote storage services accessed via the Internet are often referred to as **cloud storage** or **online storage**. Cloud storage can be provided either as a stand-alone service or as part of a cloud computing service. For instance, most cloud applications (such as Google Docs, the Flickr photo sharing service, and social networking sites like Facebook) provide online storage for these services. There are also sites whose primary objective is to allow users to store documents online, such as *Box, Dropbox,*

ASK THE EXPERT

lenovo

Bill Hansen, Worldwide Product Manager, Network Storage Solutions, LenovoEMC

Do home networks today need network hard drives?

Definitely! Just as the Internet has changed the way we communicate, network hard drives are changing the way we share information in the home. By plugging a network hard drive into your home network, you can share files and folders easily with anyone on that network—no more walking a CD or USB flash drive around to every computer like in the past. Today's network hard drives are simple to set up and use, and they are designed to allow you to access and share your music, pictures, videos, or other files easily with the other devices on your home network. You can also use a network hard drive as a backup target for all of your computers. In a nutshell, network hard drives greatly enhance the ability to share and store your valuable digital files at home.

>**Cloud storage.** Refers to using a storage device that is accessed via the Internet; also called **online storage**.

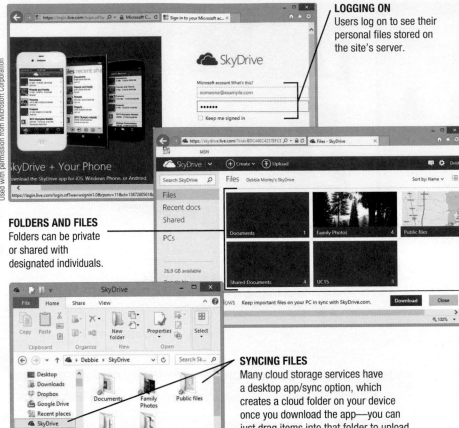

Used with permission from Microsoft Corporation

LOGGING ON
Users log on to see their personal files stored on the site's server.

FOLDERS AND FILES
Folders can be private or shared with designated individuals.

SYNCING FILES
Many cloud storage services have a desktop app/sync option, which creates a cloud folder on your device once you download the app—you can just drag items into that folder to upload them to your cloud account.

FIGURE 3-20
Cloud storage. This site provides 7 GB of free storage.

TIP

If you choose to sync your files with your cloud storage account, any files you delete from your cloud account will typically be deleted from the cloud folder on your computer, so be sure to back up those files to another location first if you will still need them.

TIP

The SIM cards used with mobile phones today are a special type of smart card.

Google Drive, or Microsoft *SkyDrive.* Typically, cloud storage sites are password protected (see Figure 3-20) and allow users to share uploaded files or folders with others via an e-mail message or a link to the shared content. Some sites go a step further, such as McAfee's *LiveSite,* which can grant access using *voice* or *face recognition* (discussed in Chapter 9).

The ability to store documents online (or "in the cloud") is growing in importance as more and more applications are becoming cloud based and as individuals increasingly want access to their files from anywhere with any Internet-enabled device, such as a portable computer, media tablet, or smartphone. Cloud storage is also increasingly being used for backup purposes—some sites have an automatic backup option that uploads the files in designated folders on your computer to your cloud account at regular specified intervals, as long as your computer is connected to the Internet. Many Web sites providing cloud storage to individuals offer the service for free (for instance, SkyDrive gives each individual 7 GB of free storage space); others charge a small fee, such as $10 per month for 25 to 100 GB of storage space.

Business cloud storage services are also available, such as those offered in conjunction with cloud computing services that allow subscribers to access a flexible amount of both storage and computing power as needed on demand. For instance, *Amazon Simple Storage Service* (*Amazon S3*)—one of the leaders in *enterprise cloud storage*—charges a monthly fee per GB of storage used plus a fee based on the amount of data transferred that month. This service can be used alone or in conjunction with Amazon's cloud computing service, *Amazon Elastic Compute Cloud* (*Amazon EC2*). In addition to these *public cloud storage services*, businesses can also create *private storage clouds* that are hosted in the business's data center and are designed to be accessed only by that business's designated users.

Smart Cards

A **smart card** is a credit card-sized piece of plastic that has built-in computer circuitry and components—typically a processor, memory, and storage. Smart cards today store a relatively small amount of data (typically 64 KB or less) that can be used for payment or identification purposes. For example, a smart card can store a prepaid amount of *digital cash*, which can be used for purchases at a smart card-enabled vending machine or computer—the amount of cash available on the card is reduced each time the card is used. Smart cards are also commonly used worldwide for national and student ID cards (for example,

>**Smart card.** A credit card-sized piece of plastic containing a chip and other circuitry that can store data.

Bangladesh recently implemented a smart card ID program for workers headed to other countries to prevent employment fraud), credit and debit cards (these typically adhere to the global *EMV* standard), and cards that store identification data for accessing facilities or computer networks. Although these applications have used conventional *magnetic stripe* technology in the past, the processor integrated into a smart card can perform computations—such as to authenticate the card, encrypt the data on the card to protect its integrity, and secure it against unauthorized access—and can allow data to be added to the card or modified on the card as needed. Smart cards can also store the identifying data needed to accelerate airport security and to link patients to the *electronic health records* (*EHRs*) increasingly being used by hospitals.

To use a smart card, it must either be inserted into a *smart card reader* (if it is the type of card that requires contact) or placed close to a smart card reader (if it is a *contactless* card) built into or attached to a computer, door lock, ATM machine, vending machine, or other device (see

LOGGING ONTO A COMPUTER VIA A CONTACT SMART CARD READER

MAKING A VENDING MACHINE PURCHASE VIA A CONTACT SMART CARD READER

ACCESSING A SECURE FACILITY VIA A CONTACTLESS SMART CARD READER

PURCHASING SUBWAY ACCESS VIA A CONTACTLESS SMART CARD READER

FIGURE 3-21
Common smart card applications.

Figure 3-21). Once a smart card has been verified by the card reader, the transaction—such as making a purchase or unlocking a door—can be completed. For an even higher level of security, some smart cards today store biometric data in the card and use that data to authenticate the card's user before authorizing the smart card transaction (biometrics, encryption, and other security procedures are discussed in more detail in Chapter 9). An emerging trend is the use of *mobile smart cards*—smart microSD cards that are designed to add smart card capabilities to any device that contains a microSD slot—though it is likely that *NFC* (*Near Field Communications*) will be the eventual technology of choice for mobile payments (as well as possibly for mobile access control), as discussed in later chapters.

Holographic Storage

Holographic storage is a type of three-dimensional (3D) storage system that, after many years of research and development, is now just about a reality. *Holographic drives* typically connect to a computer via a serial attached SCSI (SAS) or Fibre Channel interface. To record data onto a *holographic disc* or *holographic cartridge*, the holographic drive splits the light from a blue laser beam into two beams (a *reference beam* whose angle determines the address used to store data at that particular location on the storage medium and a *signal beam* that contains the data). The signal beam passes through a device called a *spatial light modulator* (*SLM*), which translates the data's 0s and 1s into a *hologram*—a

TIP

Researchers recently demonstrated the ability to store data in 5D in synthetic crystals—this technology may eventually result in discs that can store 360 TB each and that are stable enough to last essentially forever.

> **Holographic storage.** An emerging type of storage technology that uses multiple blue laser beams to store data in three dimensions.

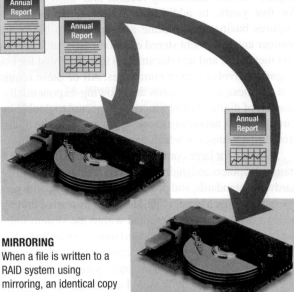

STRIPING
When a file is written to a RAID system using striping, it is split among two or more drives.

MIRRORING
When a file is written to a RAID system using mirroring, an identical copy of the file is sent to another drive in the system.

Copyright © 2015 Cengage Learning®

FIGURE 3-24
RAID. Two primary RAID techniques are striping and mirroring.

One disadvantage of RAID in the past is the difficulty traditionally involved with setting up and maintaining the system. New storage systems—such as *Drobo* storage systems (see Figure 3-25) and some of today's NASs—eliminate this concern. For instance, Drobo devices connect to an individual computer or a network similar to an external hard drive (such as via a USB, Thunderbolt, iSCSI, or Ethernet connection) and have up to 12 empty drive bays into which hard drives can be inserted for a total storage capacity of up to 36 TB. Like many RAID systems, Drobo systems offer continuous data redundancy, but they are much easier to use than conventional RAID systems and no special skills are needed to manage, repair, or upgrade them. For example, hard drives just slide in and out of Drobo devices to make it easy to replace a bad hard drive or to increase capacity, even while the devices are being used. When a drive is replaced, the system automatically copies data as needed to the new hard drive to restore the system back to its configuration before the hard drive failed or was removed. The new hard drives don't even have to match the others—they can be different types, speeds, capacities, and brands. In addition, Drobo has additional features (called *thin provisioning* and *automatic tiering*) that allow applications more control over the storage system than usual. This flexibility and ease of use makes the Drobo systems particularly appropriate for individuals and small businesses that need the security of data redundancy but have no IT personnel to assign to a RAID system.

Courtesy Drobo, Inc.

FIGURE 3-25
A Drobo storage system.

Magnetic Tape Systems

Magnetic tape consists of plastic tape coated with a magnetizable substance that represents the bits and bytes of digital data, similar to magnetic hard disks. Although magnetic tape is no longer used for everyday storage applications because of its sequential-access

>**Magnetic tape.** Storage media consisting of plastic tape with a magnetizable surface that stores data as a series of magnetic spots; typically comes as a cartridge.

property, it is still used today for business data archiving and backup. One advantage of magnetic tape is its low cost per terabyte.

Most computer tapes today are in the form of *cartridge tapes*, such as the one shown in Figure 3-26. Computer tapes are read by *tape drives*, which can be either an internal or an external piece of hardware. Tape drives contain one or more read/write heads over which the tape passes to allow the tape drive to read or write data. Cartridge tapes are available in a variety of sizes and formats; tape sizes and formats generally are not interchangeable. Tape cartridge capacity varies widely, up to 5 TB per cartridge. When an even larger capacity is required, *tape libraries*—devices that contain multiple tape drives—can be used to boost storage capacity up to 10 PB.

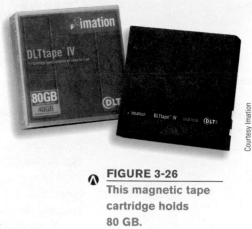

Courtesy Imation

FIGURE 3-26
This magnetic tape cartridge holds 80 GB.

EVALUATING YOUR STORAGE ALTERNATIVES

Storage alternatives are often compared by weighing a number of product characteristics and cost factors. Some of these product characteristics include speed, compatibility, storage capacity, convenience, and the portability of the media. Keep in mind that each storage alternative normally involves trade-offs. For instance, most systems with removable media are slower than those with fixed media, and external drives are typically slower than internal ones. Although cost is a factor when comparing similar devices, it is often not the most compelling reason to choose a particular technology. For instance, although USB flash drives are relatively expensive per GB compared to optical discs and external hard drives, many users find them essential for transferring files between work and home or for taking presentations or other files with them as they travel. For drives that use a USB interface, the type of USB port is also significant. For example, storage devices that connect via a USB port adhering to the original USB 1.0 standard transfer data at up to 12 Mbps—USB 2.0 devices are about 40 times faster and USB 3.0 devices are about 10 times as fast as USB 2.0 devices.

With so many different storage alternatives available, it is a good idea to research which devices and media are most appropriate for your personal situation. In general, most computer users today need a hard drive (for storing programs and data), some type of recordable or rewritable optical drive (for installing programs, backing up files, and sharing files with others), and a flash memory card reader (for transferring photos, music, and other content between portable devices and the computer). Users who plan to transfer music, digital photos, and other multimedia data on a regular basis between devices—such as a computer, digital camera, mobile phone, and printer—will want to select and use the flash memory media that are compatible with the devices they are using. They will also need to obtain any necessary adapters. Virtually all computer users today will also need at least one convenient free USB port to be used to connect external hard drives, USB flash drives, printers, mice, and other USB-based hardware, as well as USB devices that contain storage media, such as digital cameras and portable digital media players. Several convenient USB ports are even better, though a USB hub can be used to connect multiple devices to a single USB port, if needed.

Mobile device users have fewer options for storage alternatives, so users should consider the available options when selecting a mobile device to ensure it can perform the functions the user deems necessary, such as the ability to back up data and contacts in the cloud or on a medium the user can access with another device, the ability to transfer photos and other data to a computer or printer, and the ability to connect to any desired storage devices or other hardware. In addition, mobile device users will want to ensure that the device has the appropriate wireless connectivity (such as Wi-Fi and/or *cellular* ability) to connect to the desired wireless storage devices and other resources (these and other networking connections are discussed in detail in Chapter 7).

TIP

Because most netbooks don't come with an optical drive, netbook users may want to obtain an external DVD drive to use when needed.

HW

SUMMARY

STORAGE SYSTEMS CHARACTERISTICS

Storage systems make it possible to save programs, data, and processing results for later use. They provide nonvolatile storage, so when the power is shut off, the data stored on the storage medium remains intact. All storage systems involve two physical parts: a **storage device** (such as a DVD drive) and a **storage medium** (such as a DVD disc). Data is often stored *magnetically* or *optically* on storage media, and storage media are read by the appropriate types of drive. Drives can be *internal*, *external*, or *remote*. Drives are typically assigned letters by the computer; these letters are used to identify the drive.

Sequential access allows a computer system to retrieve the records in a file only in the same order in which they are physically stored. *Random access* (also called *direct access*) allows the system to retrieve records in any order. In either case, **files** (sometimes called *documents*) stored on a storage medium are given a **filename** and can be organized into **folders**. This is referred to as *logical file representation*. *Physical file representation* refers to how the files are physically stored on the storage medium by the computer.

HARD DRIVES

Hard drives are used in most computers to store programs and data. Conventional hard drives are **magnetic hard drives**; a newer type of hard drive that uses flash memory instead of magnetic disks is the **solid-state drive** (**SSD**). Hard drives can be *internal* or *external*; external hard drives can be full-sized or portable. **Hybrid hard drives** are a combination of a magnetic hard drive and an SSD, containing a large amount of flash memory that is used in conjunction with magnetic hard disks to provide increased performance while reducing power consumption.

Magnetic hard drives contain metal hard disks that are organized into concentric **tracks** encoded with magnetized spots representing 0s and 1s. **Sector** boundaries divide a magnetic disk surface into pie-shaped pieces. A **cluster**, which is the smallest amount of disk space that can be allocated to hold a file, contains one or more sectors. All tracks in the same position on all surfaces of all disks in a hard drive form a **cylinder**. A separate *read/write head* that corresponds to each disk surface is used to read and write data. Hard drives can be divided into multiple *partitions* (logical drives) for efficiency or to facilitate multiple users or operating systems. SSDs are increasingly used for portable computers and mobile devices because they are more shock-resistant and energy-efficient.

The total time it takes for a magnetic hard drive to read from or write to disks is called **disk access time**. **Disk caching**, which is the process of transferring data to memory whenever disk content is retrieved, can help to speed up access time. Hard drives connect to a computer using wireless networking or standards such as *serial ATA (SATA)*, *parallel ATA (PATA)*, *serial attached SCSI (SAS)*, *eSATA*, *Fibre Channel*, FireWire, Thunderbolt, or USB.

OPTICAL DISCS AND DRIVES

Optical discs, such as **CD discs**, **DVD discs**, and **Blu-ray Discs** (**BDs**), store data *optically* using laser beams, and they can store data much more densely than magnetic disks. They are divided into tracks and sectors like magnetic disks, but they use a single spiral track instead of concentric tracks. Data is represented by *pits* and *lands* permanently formed on the surface of the disk. Optical discs are available in a wide variety of sizes, shapes, and capacities and are read by **optical drives**, such as *CD* or *DVD drives*. **CD-ROM discs** come with data already stored on the disc. CD-ROM discs cannot be erased or overwritten—they are *read-only*. **DVD-ROM discs** are similar to CD-ROM discs, but they hold much more data (at least 4.7 GB instead of 700 MB). High-capacity read-only optical discs designed for high-definition content are **BD-ROM discs** (*BDXL* discs have an even greater capacity). *Recordable discs* (**CD-R**, **DVD-R/DVD+R**, and **BD-R discs**, for example) and *rewritable disks* (**CD-RW**, **DVD-RW/DVD+RW**, and **BD-RE discs**, for instance) can all be written to, but only rewritable discs can be erased and rewritten to, similar to a hard drive. Recordable CDs and DVDs store data by burning permanent marks onto the disc, similar to CD-ROM and DVD-ROM discs; rewritable discs typically use *phase change* technology to temporarily change the reflectivity of the disc to represent 1s and 0s.

FLASH MEMORY STORAGE SYSTEMS

Flash memory is used in a variety of storage systems. It can be **embedded flash memory**, which is embedded into products to provide storage capabilities, or it can take the form of *flash memory media* like *flash memory cards* and *USB flash drives*. **Flash memory cards**, one of the most common types of flash memory media, are commonly used with digital cameras, portable computers, and other portable devices, as well as with desktop computers. Flash memory cards come in a variety of formats—the most common are the various types of *Secure Digital (SD) cards*. **USB flash drives** connect to a computer or other device via a USB port and are a convenient method of transferring files between computers. They can also provide other capabilities, such as to lock a computer or control access to the data stored on the USB flash drive.

Chapter Objective 4:
Identify some flash memory storage devices and media and explain how they are used today.

OTHER TYPES OF STORAGE SYSTEMS

Remote storage involves using a storage device that is not directly connected to your computer. One example is using a **network storage** device, such as a **network attached storage (NAS)** or **storage area network (SAN)**. Another is **cloud storage** or **online storage**; that is, storage available via the Internet. **Smart cards** contain a chip or other circuitry usually used to store data or a monetary value. **Holographic storage**, which uses multiple blue laser beams to store data in three dimensions, is an emerging option for high-speed data storage applications.

Storage systems for larger computers implement many of the same standards as the hard drives used with personal computers. However, instead of a single set of hard disks inside a hard drive permanently installed within a system unit, a large *storage system* is often used. **RAID (redundant arrays of independent disks)** technology can be used to increase *fault tolerance* and performance. **Magnetic tape** systems store data on plastic tape coated with a magnetizable substance. Magnetic tapes are usually enclosed in cartridges and are inserted into a *tape drive* in order to be accessed. Magnetic tape is typically used today only for backup and archival purposes.

Chapter Objective 5:
List at least three other types of storage systems.

EVALUATING YOUR STORAGE ALTERNATIVES

Most personal computers today include a hard drive, some type of optical drive, a flash memory card reader, and multiple USB ports that can be used to connect USB-based storage devices, such as external hard drives and USB flash drives, as well as other USB hardware. The type of optical drive and any additional storage devices are often determined by weighing a number of factors, such as cost, speed, compatibility, storage capacity, removability, and convenience. Most devices will also include some type of wireless connectivity in order to access storage devices and other hardware via a wireless connection.

Chapter Objective 6:
Summarize the storage alternatives for a typical personal computer.

REVIEW ACTIVITIES

KEY TERM MATCHING

a. cloud storage

b. disk cache

c. file

d. flash memory card

e. folder

f. hard drive

g. holographic storage

h. RAID

i. solid-state drive (SSD)

j. storage area network (SAN)

Instructions: Match each key term on the left with the definition on the right that best describes it.

1. _____ A named place on a storage medium into which the user can place files in order to keep the files stored on that medium organized.

2. _____ A hard drive that uses flash memory media instead of metal magnetic hard disks.

3. _____ An emerging type of storage technology that uses multiple blue laser beams to store data in three dimensions.

4. _____ A small, rectangular flash memory medium, such as a CompactFlash (CF) or Secure Digital (SD) card; often used with digital cameras and other portable devices.

5. _____ A network of hard drives or other storage devices that provide storage for a network of computers.

6. _____ Refers to using a storage device that is accessed via the Internet.

7. _____ A storage method that uses several hard drives working together, typically to increase performance and/or fault tolerance.

8. _____ Memory used in conjunction with a magnetic hard drive to improve system performance.

9. _____ Something stored on a storage medium, such as a program, a document, or an image.

10. _____ The primary storage system for most computers; used to store most programs and data used with that computer.

SELF-QUIZ

Instructions: Circle **T** if the statement is true, **F** if the statement is false, or write the best answer in the space provided. **Answers for the self-quiz are located in the References and Resources Guide at the end of the book.**

1. **T F** A computer system with a C drive and a D drive must have two physical hard drives.

2. **T F** The smallest amount of space a file on a hard drive can use is one cluster.

3. **T F** External hard drives typically connect via a flash memory reader.

4. **T F** A CD-R disc can be written to by the user.

5. **T F** A hybrid hard drive contains both magnetic hard disks and optical discs.

6. The drive letter that would most likely be assigned to the primary hard drive on a typical personal computer is _____.

7. Storage media are not _____, meaning they do not lose their contents when the power is shut off.

8. CDs, DVDs, and BDs are examples of _____ discs.

9. A(n) _____ looks similar to a credit card but contains a chip and other circuitry that can store data.

10. Secure Digital (SD) cards are one type of _____ medium.

1. Assume, for simplicity's sake, that a kilobyte is 1,000 bytes, a megabyte is 1,000,000 bytes, and a gigabyte is 1,000,000,000 bytes. You have a 500-gigabyte hard drive with the following content:

ITEM	STORAGE SPACE USED
Operating system	15 GB
Other software	1,350 MB
Digital photos and videos	50 GB
Other documents	85 MB

How much storage space is currently being used? _____ How much is left? _____

2. Supply the missing words to complete the following statements.

   a. A(n) _____ disc typically holds either 25 GB or 50 GB and is designed for high-definition content, such as movies.

   b. *Thumb drive* is another name for a(n) _____.

   c. A hard drive that contains both a magnetic hard drive and flash memory is called a(n) _____ hard drive.

3. Explain why DVD-ROM discs are not erasable, but DVD+RW discs are.

4. List two possible advantages and two possible disadvantages for using cloud storage.

5. Which types of storage media would be appropriate for someone who needed to exchange large (5 MB to 75 MB) files with another person? List at least three different types, stating why each might be the most appropriate under specific conditions.

1. There are a number of types of flash memory cards available, such as SD, CF, XD, XQD, and memory stick. Is there an advantage to having multiple standards or would it be beneficial to consumers if there was only one flash memory standard, such as just the various sizes of SD cards? Would having a single standard be less expensive and more convenient for consumers? If so, will a single standard naturally evolve or should it be mandated by the storage industry or the government? If you use multiple types of flash memory cards with your devices, would you prefer they all used the same type? Why or why not?

2. People send their digital photos over the Internet in different ways. For instance, digital photos are often e-mailed to others, posted on Facebook pages and other social networking sites, and uploaded to a server (such as one belonging to Snapfish, Walmart, or Costco) in order to order prints, enlargements, or other photo-based items. If you have ever sent photos over the Internet, were you concerned about someone other than the intended recipient intercepting or viewing your photo files? If you have ever uploaded files to a processing service for printing, did you check to see if the Web server being used was secure? Should individuals be concerned about sending their personal photos over the Internet? There are a number of advantages, but are there privacy risks, as well?

PROJECTS

HOT TOPICS

1. **Tablet Storage** As discussed in the chapter How It Works box, most media tablets have a limited amount of storage and limited ways to connect additional storage.

   For this project, select a specific media tablet and determine how much internal storage it has and what type of connectivity it offers. Next, determine two options for expanding the storage for that tablet and locate at least one product for each option. Determine the amount of storage that can be added via your options, as well as the cost. If you owned this tablet, would you want to use either of your selected options for additional storage? Why or why not? At the conclusion of your research, prepare a one- to two-page summary of your findings and opinions and submit it to your instructor.

SHORT ANSWER/
RESEARCH

2. **Big Brother?** Some of the storage technology used today, such as smart cards, can help facilitate fast and secure access to locked facilities, can protect against the use of stolen credit card numbers, and, when used in conjunction with a biometric characteristic, can unequivocally identify an individual. They can also be used for employee monitoring, such as to identify the location of an employee carrying or wearing his or her smart card at any time. While some people find benefits to the applications just discussed, others worry that smart cards and other devices will be used to track our movements.

   For this project, write a short essay expressing your opinion about the use of smart cards and similar technology to identify individuals for various applications. Is the convenience of smart card technology worth the possible loss of privacy? Do you think employers or the government have the right to track individuals' movements? If so, under what conditions? What are some advantages and disadvantages for the government and your employer always knowing where you are? Have you ever used a smart card or been identified with a biometric system? If so, how do you rate the experience? Submit your opinion on this issue to your instructor in the form of a one-page paper.

HANDS ON

3. **Cloud Storage** There are a number of cloud storage services (such as ADrive, Microsoft SkyDrive, Google Drive, and Box) designed to allow individuals to back up files online and share specific files with others; specialty online storage services designed for digital photo sharing include Flickr, Photobucket, and Snapfish.

   For this project, visit at least one cloud storage site designed for backup and file exchange, and at least one site designed for digital photo sharing. You can try the sites listed above or use a search site to find alternative sites. Tour your selected sites to determine the features each service offers, the cost, the amount of storage space available, and the options for sending uploaded files to others. Do the sites password-protect your files, or are they available for anyone with an Internet connection to see? What are the benefits for using these types of storage services? Can you think of any drawbacks? Would you want to use any of the storage sites you visited? Why or why not? At the conclusion of this task, prepare a short summary of your findings and submit it to your instructor.

4. **Lost and Found** Portable computers, media tablets, mobile phones, USB flash drives, and other portable devices are lost all the time today. They can be dropped out of a pocket or bag, inadvertently left on a table, and so forth. If the owner has identifying information (name, phone number, or e-mail address, for instance) printed on the device, the individual who finds the device can attempt to return it to the owner. But what if there is no identifying information clearly visible on the device? Should the finder look at the contents of the device to try to determine the owner? If the device is lost in a location where there is a responsible party (such as an airplane or a restaurant), the finder can turn over the device to that authority (such as a flight attendant or manager), but is it ethical for the responsible party to look at the contents in order to identify the owner? If you lost a device, would you want someone to look at the contents to try to determine your identity? Why or why not? Is looking at the contents on a found device ever ethical? Should it be illegal?

For this project, form an opinion about the ethical ramifications of lost devices and be prepared to discuss your position (in class, via an online class discussion group, in a class chat room, or via a class blog, depending on your instructor's directions). You may also be asked to write a short paper expressing your opinion.

ETHICS IN ACTION

HW

5. **Flash Cards** There are a wide variety of flash memory card products available today and they can be used with a variety of devices.

For this project, find at least two different examples of flash memory card products in each of the following three categories: user storage; software, music, or movie delivery; and an interface for a peripheral device. Share your findings with the class in the form of a short presentation, including the products that you found, their purpose, what devices they are intended to be used with, and their cost. Be sure to also mention any additional categories or applications using flash cards (in addition to the three categories listed here) that you found doing your research. The presentation should not exceed 10 minutes and should make use of one or more presentation aids, such as a whiteboard, handouts, or a computer-based slide presentation (your instructor may provide additional requirements). You may also be asked to submit a summary of the presentation to your instructor.

PRESENTATION/ DEMONSTRATION

6. **Is E-Hording Bad for Us?** With large amounts of storage available to us at a reasonable cost or even for free, many computers users today are sloppy about deleting e-mails, old photos, and other digital data that they may no longer want or need. The average worker alone sends and receives more than 100 e-mails per day and about 90 billion spam e-mails are sent each day. With that kind of volume, it's hard for anyone to keep a clean Inbox. But should we try? Most workers are governed by policies regarding what e-mails and documents they are allowed to delete, but what about our personal documents? Is there anything wrong with saving everything in case it might be needed again? Or does having that much clutter create unnecessary stress and waste our time? If we have the necessary storage, are we prudent to keep everything in case we need it again? Or are we just lazy?

Pick a side on this issue, form an opinion and gather supporting evidence, and be prepared to discuss and defend your position in a classroom debate or in a 1–2 page paper, depending on your instructor's directions.

BALANCING ACT

chapter 4

Input and Output

After completing this chapter, you will be able to do the following:

1. Explain the purpose of a computer keyboard and the types of keyboards widely used today.

2. List several different pointing devices and describe their functions.

3. Describe the purposes of scanners and readers and list some types of scanners and readers in use today.

4. Explain what digital cameras are and how they are used today.

5. Understand the devices that can be used for audio input.

6. Describe the characteristics of a display device and explain some of the technologies used to display images.

7. List several types of printers and explain their functions.

8. Identify the hardware devices typically used for audio output.

OVERVIEW

In Chapter 2, we learned how data is processed by a computer. The focus of this chapter is on the hardware designed for inputting data into the computer and for outputting results to the user after the data has been processed. We begin with a look at input. First, we discuss the most common input devices used with computers and mobile devices today—mainly, keyboards, pointing devices (such as a mouse or pen), and touch devices. Next, we discuss hardware designed for capturing data in electronic form (such as scanners, barcode readers, and digital cameras), followed by an overview of audio input, including the voice input increasingly being used with mobile devices today.

The second part of this chapter explores output devices. Most output today occurs on a screen (via a display device) or on paper (via a printer). Display devices are covered first, including their basic properties and the various types of display devices that are in use today. Next, we discuss printers and then devices used for audio output. Due to the vast number of different types of input and output devices that can be used for various needs, this chapter focuses on the most common types of input and output devices in use today. ∎

KEYBOARDS

Most computers today are designed to be used with a **keyboard**—a device used to enter characters at the location on the screen marked by the *insertion point* or *cursor* (typically a blinking vertical line). Keyboards can be built into a device, attached by inserting the keyboard's wired cable or *wireless receiver* into a USB port, or connected via a wireless networking connection (such as *Bluetooth*, which is discussed in Chapter 7). A typical desktop computer keyboard is shown in Figure 4-1. Like most keyboards, this keyboard contains standard *alphanumeric keys* to input text and numbers, as well as additional keys used for various purposes. For instance, this keyboard contains a *numeric keypad* (for entering numbers), *function keys* (for issuing commands in some programs), *Delete* and *Backspace keys* (for deleting characters), *Ctrl* and *Alt keys* (for issuing commands in conjunction with other keys on the keyboard, such as Ctrl+S to save the current document in some programs), and *arrow keys* (for moving around within a document). Some keyboards also contain special keys that are used for a specific purpose, such as to control the speaker volume or DVD playback, or to launch an e-mail program or favorite Web site. To allow individuals to work under a variety of lighting conditions (such as in a dark living room or in an airplane), keyboards today are increasingly using *illuminated keys* to light up the characters on the keyboard.

Many computer keyboards today include *touch pads*, *scroll wheels*, and other components for easier control over some functions, such as *gesture input* (discussed shortly) or scrolling through documents. Some keyboards also include a *fingerprint reader* or other *biometric reader* that can be used for identification purposes, as discussed in more detail

> **TIP**
>
> A new trend is the availability of keyboards designed specifically to work with mobile devices, such as one Bluetooth keyboard designed for Apple devices that contains three Bluetooth buttons—by pressing the buttons you can automatically switch your target device, such as from typing on your Mac, to typing on your iPad, to typing on your iPhone.

> **Keyboard.** An input device containing numerous keys that can be used to input letters, numbers, and other symbols.

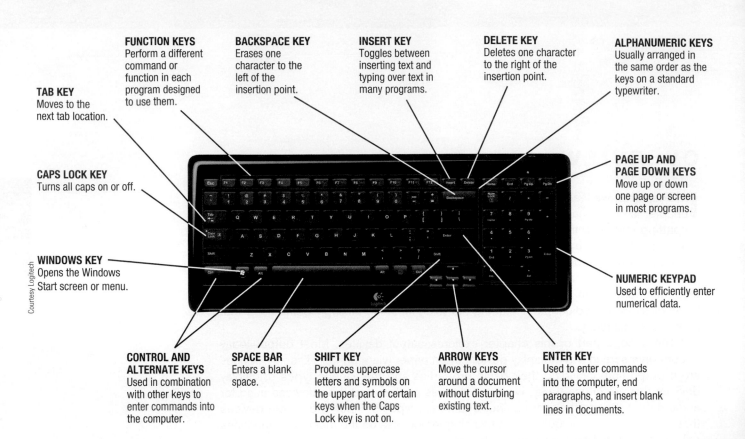

FUNCTION KEYS
Perform a different command or function in each program designed to use them.

BACKSPACE KEY
Erases one character to the left of the insertion point.

INSERT KEY
Toggles between inserting text and typing over text in many programs.

DELETE KEY
Deletes one character to the right of the insertion point.

ALPHANUMERIC KEYS
Usually arranged in the same order as the keys on a standard typewriter.

TAB KEY
Moves to the next tab location.

CAPS LOCK KEY
Turns all caps on or off.

PAGE UP AND PAGE DOWN KEYS
Move up or down one page or screen in most programs.

WINDOWS KEY
Opens the Windows Start screen or menu.

Courtesy Logitech

NUMERIC KEYPAD
Used to efficiently enter numerical data.

CONTROL AND ALTERNATE KEYS
Used in combination with other keys to enter commands into the computer.

SPACE BAR
Enters a blank space.

SHIFT KEY
Produces uppercase letters and symbols on the upper part of certain keys when the Caps Lock key is not on.

ARROW KEYS
Move the cursor around a document without disturbing existing text.

ENTER KEY
Used to enter commands into the computer, end paragraphs, and insert blank lines in documents.

FIGURE 4-1
A typical desktop keyboard.

later in this chapter and in Chapter 9. In addition, some keyboards are made for languages other than English and some keyboards are designed for special purposes, such as to allow easy input for specific systems (such as a library electronic card catalog or a company database), to input music into a computer (such as a *MIDI keyboard* used for piano compositions), or to be regularly and easily sterilized (such as keyboards used in hospitals).

Notebook and netbook computers usually have a keyboard that is similar to a desktop keyboard, but it is typically smaller, contains fewer keys (it often has no numeric keypad, for instance), and the keys are typically placed somewhat closer together. Notebook, netbook, and tablet computer users can also connect and use a conventional keyboard to make inputting data easier if their computer contains an appropriate port (such as a USB port) or Bluetooth capabilities.

Because of the increasing amount of data entered into mobile devices today, most mobile devices have either a built-in keyboard, such as a *slide-out keyboard* that can be revealed when needed and hidden when not in use or an *on-screen keyboard* that can be used with *touch* or *pen input*, as discussed shortly (see Figure 4-2). The order and layout of the keys on a mobile device may be different from the order and layout on a conventional keyboard, and the keyboard layout may vary from device to device. If a mobile device does not have a built-in keyboard, a *portable keyboard* (that folds or rolls up and connects to the device via a wired or wireless connection when needed) or a *keyboard dock* or *keyboard folio* to which the device is connected when the keyboard is needed (refer again to Figure 4-2) can often be used with the device for easier data entry. New input methods for mobile devices are under development as well. For instance, tiny keyboards (such as those used on smart watches) that automatically zoom in on the part of the keyboard you touch to allow you to touch a larger key for your final selection are in development. And the *Swype* app enables users with compatible on-screen keyboards to continuously drag through the letters in a word to spell that word, instead of having to type each letter separately. For instance, on the tablet shown in the middle image of Figure 4-2, the user dragged through the letters that spell *Seattle* to enter that data in the map app.

A keyboard is built into this portable case.

SLIDE-OUT KEYBOARDS   **ON-SCREEN KEYBOARDS**   **KEYBOARD FOLIO**

Courtesy Sprint

Courtesy Nuance

Courtesy Logitech

FIGURE 4-2
Keyboards for mobile devices.

POINTING AND TOUCH DEVICES

In addition to a keyboard, most computers today are used in conjunction with some type of **pointing device**. Pointing devices are used to select and manipulate objects, to input certain types of data (such as handwritten data), and to issue commands to the computer. The most common pointing devices are the *mouse*, the *pen/stylus*, and devices that use *touch input*. For a look at a possible input option for the future—*perceptual computing*—see the Trend box.

Mice

The **mouse** (see Figure 4-3) is the most common pointing device for a desktop computer. It typically rests on the desk or other flat surface close to the user's computer, and it is moved across the surface with the user's hand in the appropriate direction to point to and select objects on the screen. As it moves, an on-screen *mouse pointer*—usually an arrow—moves accordingly. Once the mouse pointer is pointing to the desired object on the screen, the buttons on the mouse are used to perform actions on that object (such as to open a hyperlink, to select text, or to resize an image). Similar to keyboards, mice today typically connect via a USB port or via a wireless connection.

Older *mechanical mice* have a ball exposed on the bottom surface of the mouse to control the pointer movement. Most mice today are *optical mice* or *laser mice* that track movements with light (*LED* or *laser light*, respectively). There are also mice that support two-dimensional gestures, such as *touch mice* (refer again to Figure 4-3) designed for Windows 8 devices. Instead of buttons, these mice include a touch surface on top of the mouse in order to support *finger swipes* and other movements for convenient navigation. In addition to being used with desktop

FIGURE 4-3
Mice.

TRADITIONAL MICE
Support pointing, clicking, and scrolling.

TOUCH MICE
Support swiping, tapping, and other navigational movements.

Courtesy Logitech

>**Pointing device.** An input device that moves an on-screen pointer, such as an arrow, to allow the user to select objects on the screen.
>**Mouse.** A common pointing device that the user slides along a flat surface to move a pointer around the screen and clicks its buttons to make selections.

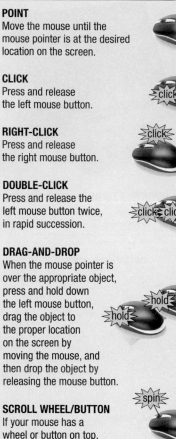

POINT
Move the mouse until the mouse pointer is at the desired location on the screen.

CLICK
Press and release the left mouse button.

RIGHT-CLICK
Press and release the right mouse button.

DOUBLE-CLICK
Press and release the left mouse button twice, in rapid succession.

DRAG-AND-DROP
When the mouse pointer is over the appropriate object, press and hold down the left mouse button, drag the object to the proper location on the screen by moving the mouse, and then drop the object by releasing the mouse button.

SCROLL WHEEL/BUTTON
If your mouse has a wheel or button on top, use it to scroll through the displayed document.

SWIPE
If your mouse supports gestures, swipe the surface in various directions with your fingers to scroll, flip, and zoom screen contents.

TAP
If your mouse supports gestures, tap on the mouse to perform clicks.

FIGURE 4-4
Common mouse operations.

computers, mice can also be used with portable computers (such as notebook and netbook computers), as long as an appropriate port (such as a USB port) is available or the mouse can connect via Bluetooth. There are also special *cordless presenter* mice that can be used by presenters to control on-screen slide shows.

Mice are used to start programs; open, move around, and edit documents; draw or edit images; and more. Some of the most common mouse operations are described in Figure 4-4.

Pens/Styluses

Many devices today, including computers, media tablets, and smartphones, can accept *pen input*; that is, input by writing, drawing, or tapping on the screen with a pen-like device called a **stylus**. Sometimes, the stylus (also called a *digital pen*, *electronic pen*, or *tablet pen*) is simply a plastic device with no additional functionality; other times, it is a pressure-sensitive device that transmits the pressure applied by the user to the device that the stylus is being used with in order to allow more precise input. These more sophisticated styluses are typically powered by the device with which it is being used, have a smooth rounded tip so they don't scratch the screen, and contain buttons or switches to perform actions such as erasing content or right-clicking.

The idea behind pen input and *digital writing* in general is to make using a computer or other device as convenient as writing with a pen, while adding the functionality that pen input can provide (such as converting handwritten pen input to editable typed text). Pen input is being used increasingly for photography, graphic design, animation, industrial design, document processing, and healthcare applications. In addition to supporting handwritten input (referred to as *inking*), digital pens can be used to navigate through a document and issue commands to the computer. Pens can also be used to provide easier touch input for mobile device users who have long fingernails, who wear gloves in the winter, or who have a device with a screen that is too small to have accurate touch input via a finger. Some of the most common devices that use pen input are discussed next.

Pen-Based Computers and Mobile Devices

Although their capabilities depend on the type of device and software being used, pen input can be used with a variety of computers and mobile devices today (see Figure 4-5). Most often, pens are used with mobile devices and tablet computers to both input handwritten text and sketches, and to manipulate objects (such as to select an option from a menu, select text, or resize an image). They can also be used with a desktop or notebook computer if the device supports pen input. Windows 8 supports both pen and touch input, but the display screen being used with the Windows 8 device must support this type of input in order for you to use it. To enable a regular Windows computer to function as a pen-enabled touch screen computer, new digital pens that use a USB receiver to transmit the pen's location information to a computer are becoming available. Depending on the software being used, handwritten input

---

> **Stylus.** An input device that is used to write electronically on the display screen.

TREND

Perceptual Computing

In the 2002 futuristic movie *Minority Report*, Tom Cruise changes the images on his display by gesturing with his hands. While it was fiction in the movie, it is now just about a reality. Enter the trend of *perceptual computing* where users control their devices with three dimensional (3D) gestures, voice commands, and facial expressions instead of with traditional input devices like the keyboard and mouse.

Gesture input itself isn't new—it's been used in various forms for several years with devices such as the Nintendo Wii, Xbox Kinect, and the Apple iPhone and in large screen consumer gaming and advertising applications; it is also an important component of the Windows 8 operating system. But the gesture-input systems of the future are expected to be much more sophisticated and combined with other types of input to allow users to more naturally control their computers and to allow the devices to adapt to each individual's need. For example, a computer or phone could offer to make a game easier if a player appears frustrated or could offer to turn the page on a tablet displaying a recipe if the hands of the person cooking are covered with flour.

One recent step in this direction is the *Leap 3D System* shown in the accompanying photograph. It is an iPod-sized box

that connects to a computer via a USB port and creates an eight-cubic-foot 3D interactive space inside which users can swipe, grab, pinch (refer again to the photo), and move objects around as if they were using a touch screen, except that they are not actually touching the screen. And noncontact systems such as this have additional advantages, such as being able to use 3D gestures instead of just 2D gestures, avoiding the fingerprint and germ issues related to public keyboard and touch screen use, allowing for full body input, and enabling input to be performed from a slight distance (such as from a nearby chair or through a glass storefront window).

Courtesy Leap Motion

can issue commands to the computer, be stored as an image, be stored as handwritten characters that can be recognized by the computer, or be converted to editable, typed text. For the latter two options, software with **handwriting recognition** capabilities must be used.

FIGURE 4-5
Pen-based computers and mobile devices.

| SMARTPHONES | TABLET COMPUTERS | DESKTOP COMPUTERS |

© iStockphoto.com/mkurtbas
Courtesy Motion Computing
Courtesy Wacom Technology Corp.

>**Handwriting recognition.** The ability of a device to identify handwritten characters.

ASK THE EXPERT

Microsoft **Stephen Rose,** Senior Community Manager for Windows Commercial OS, Microsoft

How is touch input changing personal computing today?

In the past, we were chained to a desk and our computers in order to have access to the services and resources required to do our jobs. As we moved into the laptop era, mobility and the opportunity to work from almost anywhere became the vision. We are now in the tablet era, where thin, light, mobile consumption devices allow us to truly work from anywhere. With these newer devices, the keyboard and mouse no longer make sense as the primary way to utilize the device. Hence the touch OS, which allows all users (including the elderly and small children) to gain access and use applications simply and easily. And touch interface tiles and icons (such as on Windows 8 devices) share information back to us, displaying the important information in our lives. For instance, when is my next meeting? Who called or texted? Is there an invoice to approve? Did my stock go up? All of this at a glance, without even launching a single app. In a nutshell, touch input gives us a more personalized, intimate computing experience not available in a non-touch environment.

horizontal position. Many touch screens today are *multi-touch*; that is, they can recognize input from more than one finger at a time, such as using two fingers to enlarge or rotate an image on the screen. Similar multi-touch products are used for large wall displays, such as for use in museums, government command centers, and newsrooms. For instance, news anchors can use large multi-touch screens to display maps, photos, videos, charts, and other data during broadcasts. Multi-touch systems are also featured in recent movies and television shows, such as the *Hawaii Five-0* TV series.

One new trend in touch screens is the *table PC*—a large screen computer either built into a table or designed to be used on a table (such as the 27-inch table PC shown in Figure 4-8) and that allows multi-touch input from multiple users. Table PCs can be used by several individuals at once to play games together, work together on a project, participate in an interactive museum display together, and so forth.

Touch screens are also used in consumer kiosks, restaurant order systems, and other point-of-sale (POS) systems, and they are useful for on-the-job applications (such as factory work) where it might be impractical to use a keyboard or mouse. A growing trend is to use touch screens that provide *tactile feedback*—a slight movement or other physical sensation in response to the users' touch so they know their input has been received by the computer. For a closer look at another emerging trend for mobile device displays—*augmented reality*—see the How It Works box. While touch screens make many devices today (such as computers, mobile phones, televisions, and many other consumer electronics) more convenient for the majority of individuals to use, there is also concern that these devices and their applications are not accessible to blind individuals, users with limited mobility, and other individuals with a disability. There are also concerns about the possible health ramifications of using vertical touch screens extensively. Ergonomic issues related to touch screens and other computing hardware, as well as accessibility issues, are discussed in detail in Chapter 16.

Other Pointing Devices

A few other common pointing devices are described next and shown in Figure 4-9. In addition to these and the other pointing devices discussed in this chapter, pointing devices specifically designed for users with limited mobility are available. These pointing devices—along with *ergonomic keyboards*, *Braille keyboards*, and other types of input devices designed for users with special needs—are discussed in Chapter 16.

Gaming Devices

A variety of gaming devices today (such as the ones shown in Figure 4-9) can be used as controllers to supply input to a computer. For instance, the stick of a *joystick* can be moved with the hand to move an on-screen object (such as a player or vehicle in a game) and the buttons pressed to perform their assigned functions (such as jumping or firing a

TIP

Google's new *Handwrite* feature allows you to use your finger to write out search queries on the device's screen in order to perform a mobile search more quickly than using an on-screen keyboard, and it is likely more accurate than using voice input. To use the Handwrite feature, just write your search terms anywhere on the Google home page displayed on your smartphone or tablet screen.

weapon). *Gamepads* perform similar functions but are held in the hand instead; *steering wheels* are also available for driving games. There are also input devices designed to be used with gaming devices, such as Wii, Xbox, and PlayStation gaming consoles. These include gamepads and steering wheels; guitars, drums, and other musical instruments; dance pads, balance boards, and other motion sensitive controllers; and proprietary controllers such as the Wii Remote, Xbox Kinect, and PlayStation Move.

Trackballs

Similar to an upside-down mechanical mouse, a *trackball* has the ball mechanism on top, instead of on the bottom. The ball is rotated with the thumb, hand, or finger to move the on-screen pointer. Because the device itself does not need to be moved, trackballs take up less space on the desktop than mice; they also are easier to use for individuals with limited hand or finger mobility.

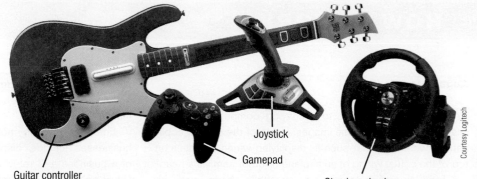

Guitar controller

Joystick

Gamepad

Steering wheel

Courtesy Logitech

GAMING DEVICES
Most often used for gaming applications.

Courtesy Logitech

TRACKBALLS
An alternative to a mouse that some individuals find easier to use.

© byggarn.se/Shutterstock.com; Courtesy Logitech

TOUCH PADS
Commonly found on notebook and netbook computers (left); also available as stand-alone devices (right).

FIGURE 4-9
Other common pointing devices.

Control Buttons and Wheels

Many consumer devices today, such as portable digital media players, GPS devices, and handheld gaming devices, use special control buttons and wheels to select items and issue commands to the device. For instance, a portable digital media player may contain buttons on the front and sides that are used to access music and other content stored on the device, navigate through songs, and adjust the volume.

Touch Pads

A **touch pad** is a rectangular pad across which a fingertip or thumb slides to move the on-screen pointer; tapping the touch pad (or one of its associated buttons) typically performs clicks and other mouse actions. Touch pads are the most common pointing device for notebook and netbook computers. They are used to point to and select objects, to scroll through documents or other content, and to perform gestures such as *swiping* and *pinching*. Because touch is so integrated into the newest operating systems (such as the most recent versions of Windows and OS X), there are also stand-alone touch pads available (see Figure 4-9) that can be used with computers that don't have a touch screen. Touch pads are also built into some keyboards.

>**Touch pad.** A small rectangular-shaped input device, often found on notebook and netbook computers, that is touched with the finger or thumb to control an on-screen pointer and make selections.

HOW IT WORKS

Augmented Reality

Augmented reality refers to overlaying computer-generated images on top of real-time images. Some of the earliest applications were industrial, such as displaying wiring diagrams on top of the actual wiring of an airplane or other item via a headset. Today, augmented reality is going mobile—being used with smartphones, as well as other mobile devices. To accomplish this, content is displayed over the images seen through the smartphone's camera and displayed on the smartphone. The content is typically based on the user's location (determined by the phone's GPS), the video feed from the smartphone's camera, a digital compass, and other data obtained from the smartphone. Displaying this information requires a *mobile AR browser* or an appropriate *mobile AR app*.

Some initial mobile augmented reality apps designed for consumers include overlaying home listing information (such as pricing and photos) over the video images displayed as a phone is pointing at houses in a neighborhood, displaying information (such as real-time game stats and player information) as a phone is pointing at a sporting event, and displaying activity opportunities (such as restaurant, movie, museum, or shopping information) as a phone is pointing at a business district (see the accompanying illustration). Travelers can use apps designed to overlay directions on top of a street map corresponding to what the camera sees, as well as apps to display sightseeing information as the camera is pointing at a historical building, a statue, or another landmark. Mobile augmented reality can also work indoors, such as identifying displays, concession stands, restrooms, and more at conventions or displaying exhibit information at museums.

Emerging mobile augmented reality opportunities for businesses include displaying the exact physical location of a business and relevant information or ads when an individual points his or her phone in the vicinity of the business. Information displayed could include room photos and pricing (for hotels), dining room photos and menus (for restaurants), or merchandise photos and specials (for stores). And augmented reality is moving beyond smartphones to glasses (such as *Google Glass*) and, eventually, it is expected to work in three dimensions, with devices that will be able to recognize objects and understand their physical properties.

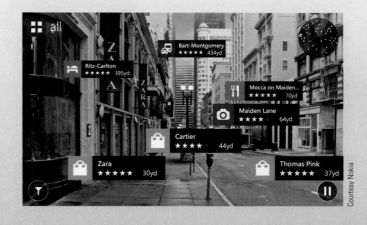

Courtesy Nokia

SCANNERS, READERS, AND DIGITAL CAMERAS

There are a variety of input devices designed to capture data in digital form so a computer can manipulate it. Some devices (such as *scanners* and *readers*) convert data that already exists in physical form (such as on *source documents* like photographs, checks, or product labels); other devices (such as *digital cameras*) capture data initially in digital form. Automating the data entry process is referred to as *source data automation* and can refer to capturing data electronically from a source document or entering data directly into a computer at the time and place the data is generated (see Figure 4-10).

Source data automation is widely used today because it can save a great deal of time and is much more accurate than recording the data on paper and then later entering it into a computer via a keyboard. It also allows the people who know the most about the events that the data represents to be the ones who input the data, which helps increase accuracy during the data entry process. For instance, an insurance adjuster or auto mechanic entering data directly into a computer about the condition of a car involved in an accident will likely have fewer input errors than if he or she records that data on paper, and then has an assistant key the data into a computer later.

Many devices used in source data automation are *scanning* or *reading devices*; that is, devices that scan or read printed text, codes, or graphics, and then translate the results into digital form. The next few sections discuss several different types of scanning and reading devices, followed by a look at *digital cameras*.

Scanners

A **scanner**, more officially called an *optical scanner*, captures an image of an object (usually a flat object, such as a printed document or photograph) in digital form, and then transfers that data to a computer. Typically, the entire document (including both text and images) is input as a single image that can be resized,

RECORDING DATA DIRECTLY INTO A COMPUTER

CAPTURING DATA FROM ITS SOURCE DOCUMENT

inserted into other documents, posted on a Web page, e-mailed to someone, printed, or otherwise treated like any other graphical image. The text in the scanned image, however, cannot be edited unless *optical character recognition* (*OCR*) software is used in conjunction with the scanner to input the scanned text as individual text characters.

Individuals frequently use scanners to input printed photographs and other personal documents into a computer. Businesses are increasingly using scanners to convert paper documents into electronic format for archival or document processing purposes. Most scanners scan in color and some are *duplex scanners*—that is, they can scan both sides of a document at one time. Scanners with networking capabilities can be used to scan images to other devices on that network, such as a media tablet or smartphone; some can scan directly to a cloud storage account, such as Google Drive. The most common types of scanners are discussed next.

FIGURE 4-10
Source data automation. Recording data initially in digital form or capturing data directly from a source document can help reduce data input errors and save time.

Types of Scanners

Flatbed scanners are designed to scan flat objects one page at a time, and they are the most common type of scanner. Flatbed scanners work in much the same way that photocopiers do—whatever is being scanned remains stationary while the scanning mechanism moves underneath it to capture the image (see Figure 4-11). Some scanners can scan slides and

FIGURE 4-11
Scanners.

FLATBED SCANNERS
Used to input photos, sketches, slides, book pages, and other relatively flat documents into the computer.

PORTABLE SCANNERS
Used to capture documents or other data while on the go; the data is typically transferred to a computer at a later time.

INTEGRATED SCANNERS
Built into other devices, such as into the ATM machine shown here to capture images of deposited checks.

>**Scanner.** An input device that reads printed text and graphics and transfers them to a computer in digital form. >**Flatbed scanner.** An input device that scans flat objects one at a time.

film negatives, in addition to printed documents. Scanners designed for high-volume business processing come with automatic document feeders so that large quantities of paper documents can be scanned (one page after the other) with a single command.

Portable scanners are designed to capture text and other data while on the go. Some are *full-page portable scanners* that can capture images of an entire document (such as a printed document or receipt); others (such as the one shown in Figure 4-11) are *handheld scanners* designed to capture text one line at a time. In either case, the scanner is typically powered by batteries, the scanned content is stored in the scanner, and the content is transferred to a computer (via a cable or a wireless connection) when needed. Some handheld scanners have OCR capabilities and some of these can also be used to translate scanned text from one language to another. One recent option is a scanner built into a mouse to enable users to switch between mouse actions and scanning as needed.

Multimedia, medical, and some business applications may require the use of a *three-dimensional (3D) scanner*, which can scan an item or person in 3D. Task-specific scanners, such as *receipt scanners* and *business card scanners*, are also available. In addition, scanning hardware is being incorporated into a growing number of products, such as ATM machines to scan the images of checks deposited into the machine (refer again to Figure 4-11); typically, the check images are printed on the deposit receipt and can be viewed online via online banking services.

> **TIP**
>
> Some scanners today include 3D scanning with 2D output; they typically use a camera on an adjustable arm to take multiple images of an object to create a composite 3D image that can then be saved or printed in 2D as usual.

⓿ FIGURE 4-12
Scanning resolution.

Copyright © 2015 Cengage Learning®

96 dpi
(833 KB)

300 dpi
(1,818 KB)

600 dpi
(5,374 KB)

RESOLUTION
Most scanners let you specify the resolution (in dpi) to use for the scan. High-resolution images look sharper but result in larger file sizes.

Scanning Quality and Resolution

The quality of scanned images is indicated by *optical resolution*, usually measured in the number of *dots per inch (dpi)*. When a document is scanned (typically using scanning software, though some application programs allow you to scan images directly into that program), the resolution of the scanned image can often be specified. The resolution can also be reduced if needed (such as to *compress* an image to reduce its file size before posting it on a Web page) using an image editing program. Scanners today usually scan at between 2,400 × 2,400 dpi and 4,800 × 9,600 dpi. A higher resolution results in a better image but also results in a larger file size, as illustrated in Figure 4-12. A higher resolution is needed, however, if the image (or a part of it) is to be enlarged significantly. The file size of a scanned image is also determined in part by the physical size of the image. Once an image has been scanned, it can usually be resized and then saved in the appropriate file format and resolution for the application with which the image is to be used.

Readers

A variety of *readers* are available to read the different types of codes and marks used today, as well as to read an individual's *biometric* characteristics. Some of the most common types of readers are discussed next.

Barcode Readers

A **barcode** is an *optical code* that represents data with bars of varying widths or heights. Two of the most familiar barcodes are *UPC (Universal Product Code)*, the type of barcode found on packaged goods in supermarkets and other retail stores, and *ISBN (International Standard Book Number)*, the type of barcode used with printed books (see Figure 4-13). A newer barcode designed for small consumer goods like fresh foods and jewelry is the *DataBar*, also shown in Figure 4-13. Businesses and organizations can also create and use custom barcodes to fulfill their unique needs. For instance, shipping organizations

---

> **Portable scanner.** A scanner designed to capture input while on the go. > **Barcode.** A machine-readable code that represents data as a set of bars.

(such as FedEx and UPS) use custom barcodes to mark and track packages, retailers (such as Target and Walmart) use custom barcodes added to customer receipts to facilitate returns, hospitals use custom barcodes to match patients with their charts and medicines, libraries and video stores use custom barcodes for checking out and checking in books and movies, and law enforcement agencies use custom barcodes to mark evidence. In fact, any business with a *barcode printer* and appropriate software can create custom barcodes for use with its products or to classify items (such as paper files or equipment) used within its organization. The most popular barcode for these types of nonfood use is *Code 39*, which can encode both letters and numbers. Examples of the Code 39 barcode and the *Intelligent Mail barcode* (used by the U.S. Postal Service to represent destination ZIP Codes, as well as shipper IDs and other identifying data specified by the shipper) are shown in Figure 4-13.

These conventional types of barcodes are referred to as *one-dimension (1D) barcodes* because they contain data in only one direction (horizontally). Newer *two-dimensional (2D) barcodes* store information both horizontally and vertically and can hold significantly more data—up to several hundred times more. One of the most common 2D barcodes—the *QR (Quick Response) code* that represents data with a matrix of small squares—is shown in Figure 4-13. Most, 2D barcodes today are designed to be used by consumers with smartphones. For instance, capturing the image of a QR barcode located on a magazine or newspaper ad, poster, or store display with a smartphone's camera could enable the consumer's smartphone to load a Web page, send a text message (to enter a contest or make a donation, for instance), display a video clip or photo (stored either in the code or online), *Like* a Facebook page, or download a coupon or ticket. QR codes can also be used to transfer contact information to a phone or add an event to an online calendar; they are also starting to become integrated into video games and other content. For instance, the *Animal Crossing: New Leaf* video game allows players to share their in-game creations with others via QR codes.

Barcodes are read with **barcode readers**. Barcode readers (see Figure 4-14) use either light reflected from the barcode or imaging technology to interpret the bars contained in the barcode as the numbers or letters they represent. Then, data associated with that barcode—typically identifying data, such as to uniquely identify a product, shipped package, or other item—can be retrieved. *Fixed* barcode readers are frequently used in point-of-sale (POS)

ISBN CODES

UPC (UNIVERSAL PRODUCT CODE) CODES

DATABAR CODES

INTELLIGENT MAIL CODES

CODE 39 CODES

QR CODES

FIGURE 4-13
Common types of barcodes.

FIGURE 4-14
Barcode readers.

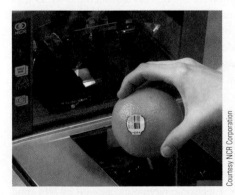

FIXED BARCODE READERS
Used most often in retail point-of-sale applications.

PORTABLE BARCODE READERS
Used when portability is needed.

INTEGRATED BARCODE READERS
Used most often for consumer applications.

>**Barcode reader.** An input device that reads barcodes.

systems; *portable* barcode readers are also available for individuals who need to scan barcodes while on the go, such as while walking through a warehouse, retail store, hospital, or other facility. In addition, most smartphones and media tablets today have barcode reading capabilities. With the proper app, these devices can be used to read both 1D and 2D barcodes, such as to access information and features offered by a QR code or to comparison shop for products by capturing UPC codes.

Radio Frequency Identification (RFID) Readers

Radio frequency identification (RFID) is a technology that can store, read, and transmit data located in **RFID tags**. RFID tags contain tiny chips and radio antennas (see Figure 4-15); they can be attached to objects, such as products, price tags, shipping labels, ID cards, assets (such as livestock, vehicles, computers, and other expensive items), and more. The data in RFID tags is read by **RFID readers**. Whenever an RFID-tagged item is within range of an RFID reader (from two inches to up to 300 feet or more, depending on the type of tag and the radio frequency being used), the tag's built-in antenna allows the information located within the RFID tag to be sent to the reader. Unlike barcodes, RFID tags only need to be within range (not within line of sight) of a reader. This enables RFID readers to read the data stored in many RFID tags at the same time and read them through cardboard and other materials—a definite advantage for shipping and inventory applications. Another advantage over barcodes is that the RFID tag attached to each item is unique (unlike UPC codes, for instance, that have the same code on all instances of a single product), so each tag can be identified individually and the data can be updated as needed. RFID technology is cost-prohibitive for low-cost items at the present time; however, the many advantages of RFID over barcodes make it possible that RFID may eventually replace barcodes on product labels and price tags—especially as the costs associated with RFID technology go down and its usage becomes even more commonplace. Because RFID technology can read numerous items at one time, it is also possible that, someday, RFID will allow a consumer to perform self-checkout at a retail store by just pushing a shopping cart past an RFID reader, which will ring up all items in the cart at one time.

RFID is used today for many different applications (see Figure 4-16 for some examples). Some of the initial RFID applications were tracking the movement of products and shipping containers during transit, managing inventory in retail stores, tagging pets and livestock, and tracking tractors and other large assets. Many of these applications use GPS technology in conjunction with RFID to provide location information for the objects to which the RFID tags are attached. For several years now, RFID has been used for *electronic toll collection* (automatically deducting highway tolls from a payment account when an RFID-tagged car drives past a tollbooth). More recent RFID applications include tracking patients at hospitals, increasing efficiency in ticketing applications (such as train passes, concert tickets, and ski lift tickets), and speeding up the identification process of travelers at border crossings. In the United States, for instance, several states are issuing *enhanced driver's licenses* that contain RFID chips, and all *U.S. Passports* and *U.S. Passport Cards* issued today contain RFID chips. RFID is also used extensively to facilitate *electronic payments* via RFID-enabled credit cards or smartphones that support *Near Field Communications* (*NFC*)—a short-range wireless communication standard used with some smartphones in conjunction with RFID. For security purposes, *high-frequency RFID chips* (which require the item containing the RFID chip to be within an inch or so of the reader) are used in electronic payment applications. Electronic payments, as well as NFC and other types of *mobile commerce*, are discussed in more detail in Chapter 11.

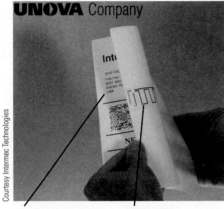

Courtesy Intermec Technologies

Label for shipping carton

RFID circuitry (chip and antenna)

FIGURE 4-15
RFID tags.

>**Radio frequency identification (RFID).** A technology used to store and transmit data located in RFID tags. >**RFID tag.** A device containing a tiny chip and a radio antenna that is attached to an object so it can be identified using RFID technology. >**RFID reader.** A device used to read RFID tags.

Another advantage of RFID chips is that they can be updated during the life of a product (such as to record information about a product's origin, shipping history, and the temperature range the item has been exposed to). Because that information can be read when needed (such as at a product's final destination), RFID is being used by prescription drug manufacturers to comply with government requirements that drugs be tracked throughout their life cycles. RFID is also used to track food products and sources. For instance, all cows, sheep, and goats in Australia are required to have RFID ear tags so that animals can be traced from birth to slaughter and diseased animals can be tracked back to their ranches.

A variety of RFID readers, including *handheld*, *portal*, and *stationary RFID readers*, are available to fit the various RFID applications in use today.

INVENTORY TRACKING
This portal RFID reader reads all of the RFID tags attached to all of the items on the palette at one time.

TICKETING APPLICATIONS
This stationary RFID reader is used to automatically open ski lift entry gates for valid lift ticket holders at a ski resort in Utah.

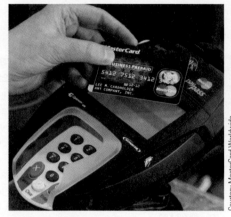

MOBILE PAYMENTS
This stationary RFID reader is used at checkout locations to process payments via RFID-enabled credit cards or NFC-enabled smartphones.

BORDER SECURITY
This stationary RFID reader is used at the U.S.-Mexico border crossing located in San Diego to reduce wait time.

FIGURE 4-16
RFID applications.

Handheld RFID readers are used by workers to read RFID tags on the go or to read RFID-enabled tickets at a venue entrance. Portal RFID readers are used to read all the RFID tags on all the products located inside sealed shipping boxes on a palette at one time when the palette passes through the portal. Stationary RFID readers are used at checkstands, border crossings, and other locations where RFID tags need to be read on a continual basis. A portal reader and three examples of stationary readers are shown in Figure 4-16.

Despite all its advantages, RFID growth in the retail industry has been slower than initially expected. This is primarily because of cost constraints and a number of privacy and security issues, such as concerns that others might be able to read the data contained in an RFID tag attached to your clothing, passport, or other personal item, or they might be able to make fraudulent charges via your smartphone. Precautions against fraudulent use—such as using high-frequency tags that need to be within a few inches of the reader, and requiring a *PIN code*, signature, or other type of authorization when an RFID payment system is used—are being developed. Currently, a price limit (such as $25) for completely automated purchases (without a signature or other authorization), similar to many credit cards today, is being debated as a compromise between convenience and security. Privacy advocates are concerned about linking RFID tag data with personally identifiable data contained in corporate databases, such as to track consumer movements or shopping habits. As of now, no long-term solution to this issue has been reached.

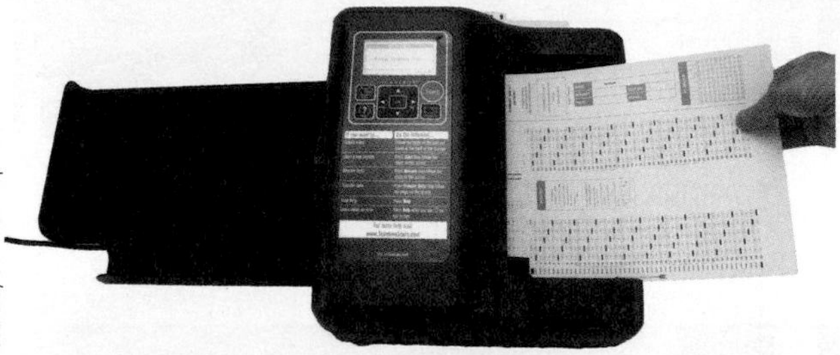

FIGURE 4-17

Optical mark readers (OMRs). OMRs are commonly used to score tests and tally questionnaires.

Courtesy Scantron Corporation®

Optical Mark Readers (OMRs)

Optical mark readers (*OMRs*) input data from special forms to score or tally exams, questionnaires, ballots, and so forth. Typically, you use a pencil to fill in small circles or other shapes on the form to indicate your selections, and then the form is inserted into an optical mark reader (such as the one shown in Figure 4-17) to be scored or tallied. The results can be input into a computer system if the optical mark reader is connected to a computer.

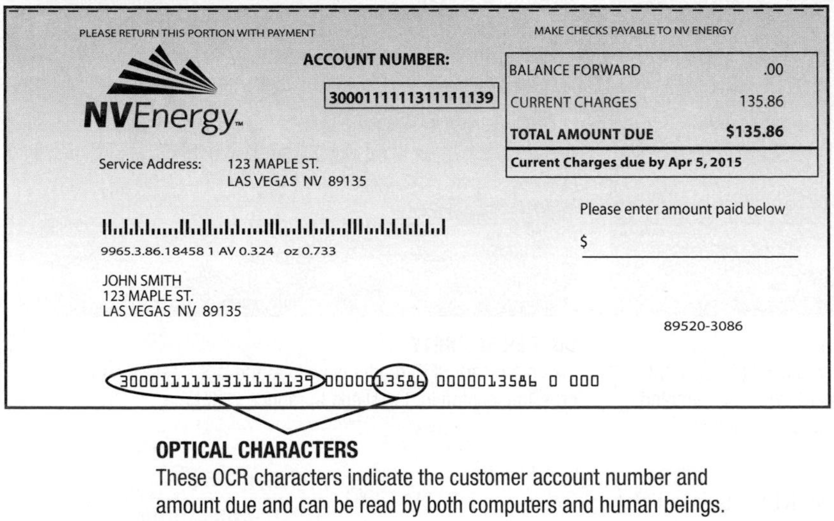

Courtesy NV Energy

PLEASE RETURN THIS PORTION WITH PAYMENT   MAKE CHECKS PAYABLE TO NV ENERGY

NVEnergy™

ACCOUNT NUMBER: 3000111111311111139

BALANCE FORWARD	.00
CURRENT CHARGES	135.86
TOTAL AMOUNT DUE	**$135.86**
Current Charges due by Apr 5, 2015	

Service Address: 123 MAPLE ST.
LAS VEGAS NV 89135

9965.3.86.18458 1 AV 0.324 oz 0.733

JOHN SMITH
123 MAPLE ST.
LAS VEGAS NV 89135

Please enter amount paid below

$ _____

89520-3086

3000111111311111139 0000013586 0000013586 0 000

OPTICAL CHARACTERS
These OCR characters indicate the customer account number and amount due and can be read by both computers and human beings.

FIGURE 4-18

Optical characters. The most common use of optical characters is in turnaround documents, such as on the utility bill shown here.

Optical Character Recognition (OCR) Devices

Optical character recognition (OCR) refers to the ability of a computer to recognize text characters printed on a document. The characters are read by a compatible scanning device, such as a flatbed scanner, barcode reader, or dedicated *OCR reader*, and then *OCR software* is used to identify each character and convert it to editable text. While OCR systems can recognize many different types of printed characters, *optical characters*—which are characters specifically designed to be identifiable by humans as well as by an OCR device—are often used on documents intended to be processed by an OCR system. For example, optical characters are widely used in processing *turnaround documents*, such as the monthly bills for credit card and utility companies (see Figure 4-18). These documents contain optical characters in certain places on the bill to aid processing when consumers send it back with payment—or "turn it around."

Magnetic Ink Character Recognition (MICR) Readers

Magnetic ink character recognition (*MICR*) is a technology used primarily by the banking industry to facilitate check processing. MICR characters (such as those located on the bottom of a check that represent the bank routing number, check number, and account number) are inscribed on checks with magnetic ink when the checks are first printed.

>**Optical character recognition (OCR).** The ability of a computer to recognize scanned text characters and convert them to electronic form as text, not images.

TECHNOLOGY AND YOU

Mobile Deposits

Though unheard of just a few years ago, *mobile deposit*—depositing checks via your smartphone—is quickly becoming the norm for many individuals.

Officially referred to as *mobile remote deposit capture* (or *mobile RDC*), this technology enables individuals to make deposits by transmitting check images taken with their smartphone's camera to their mobile banking service. In order to make a remote deposit via your smartphone, you need to have the appropriate mobile deposit app for your bank on your smartphone (virtually all banks today either have RDC or are in the process of implementing it). To make a remote deposit, you simply need to log on to your mobile banking service, and then you can enter the amount of the check and use your phone's camera to take a photo of the front and back of the check (see the accompanying photo). After the software optimizes the image and verifies it meets the Check 21 Law image standards, the check images and deposit data are transmitted to your bank and the check is deposited into your bank account.

© iStockphoto.com/PhotoInc

Smartphone cameras can be used to submit check images for remote deposit.

These characters can be read and new characters (such as to reflect the check's amount) can be added by an *MICR reader* (also called a *check scanner*) when needed. High-volume MICR readers are used by banks to process checks deposited at the bank. Smaller units (such as the one shown in Figure 4-19) are used by many businesses to deposit paper checks remotely (referred to as *remote deposit* and permitted by the *Check 21 Law*, which allows financial institutions to exchange digital check images and process checks electronically). To make a remote deposit using an MICR reader, the check is scanned and then the check data is transmitted to the bank electronically for payment. There are also MICR readers incorporated in most new ATM machines today to enable the MICR information located on checks inserted into the ATM machine to be read at the time of the deposit.

Remote deposit and electronic check processing is a growing trend. It is faster and more convenient for businesses and individuals. It also helps the environment because, according to one estimate, a paper check travels 48 miles during processing, which results in an annual cost to the environment for check processing of more than 80,000 tons of paper used and more than 160 million gallons of fuel consumed. In addition to MICR readers, remote deposit can be performed via your smartphone, as discussed in the Technology and You box.

Courtesy Epson America

FIGURE 4-19
Magnetic ink character recognition (MICR) readers are used primarily to process checks.

PERSONAL COMPUTERS
Often used to control access to the device (such as the notebook computer shown here), as well as to log on to secure Web sites.

Fingerprint reader

Fingerprint reader

MOBILE DEVICES
Often used to record or verify an individual's identity (such as with the device shown here that has fully integrated iris, face, fingerprint, and voice biometric capabilities).

FIGURE 4-20
Biometric readers.

✓ **TIP**

The *iPhone 5S*, released in late 2013, is the first iPhone with a *fingerprint reader*—the sensor is built into the phone's Home button.

✓ **TIP**

When comparing the zoom capabilities of a digital camera, look for *optical zoom*, not *digital zoom*, specifications. Optical zoom specifications reflect how much the camera can zoom without losing image quality.

Biometric Readers

Biometrics is the science of identifying individuals based on measurable biological characteristics. **Biometric readers** are used to read biometric data about a person so that the individual's identity can be verified based on a particular unique physiological characteristic (such as a fingerprint or a face) or personal trait (such as a voice or a signature). Biometric readers can be stand-alone or built into a computer or mobile device (see Figure 4-20); they can also be built into another piece of hardware, such as a keyboard, an external hard drive, or a USB flash drive. Biometric readers can be used to allow only authorized users access to a computer or facility or to the data stored on a storage device, as well as to authorize electronic payments, log on to secure Web sites, or punch in and out of work. Biometrics used for access control is covered in more detail in Chapter 9.

Digital Cameras

Digital cameras work much like conventional film cameras, but instead of recording images on film they record them on a digital storage medium, such as a flash memory card, built-in hard drive, or DVD disc. Digital cameras are usually designated either as *still* cameras (which take individual still photos) or *video* cameras (which capture moving video images), although many cameras today take both still images and video. In addition to stand-alone still and video cameras, digital camera capabilities are integrated into many portable computers and mobile devices today.

Digital Still Cameras

Digital still cameras are available in a wide variety of sizes and capabilities, such as inexpensive point-and-shoot digital cameras designed for consumers, professional digital cameras, and digital cameras integrated into mobile phones and other mobile devices (see Figure 4-21). Consumer digital cameras start at about $50; professional digital cameras can cost several thousand dollars each.

The primary appeal of digital still cameras is that the images are immediately available for viewing or printing, instead of having to have the film developed first as was the case with conventional film cameras. One disadvantage of digital cameras is the slight delay between when the user presses the button and when the camera takes the photo, which is especially important when taking action shots. Although not yet as quick as conventional film cameras, the delay typically associated with digital cameras is getting shorter. Digital still cameras most often use flash memory cards for storage; the number of digital photos that can be stored at one time depends on the capacity of the card being used, as well as the photo resolution being used.

> **Biometric reader.** A device used to input biometric data, such as an individual's fingerprint or voice. > **Digital camera.** An input device that takes pictures and records them as digital images.

Photos taken with a digital camera are typically transferred to a computer or printer via the flash memory card containing the images or by connecting the camera to the computer or printer using a wired or wireless connection. Some digital cameras and flash memory cards can connect directly to photo sharing Web sites via a *Wi-Fi* connection, as discussed in the Chapter 7 Technology and You box, to upload your photos automatically as they are taken. Once the photos have been transferred to a computer, they can be retouched with image editing software, saved, printed, posted to a Web page, or burned onto a CD or DVD disc, just like any other digital image. The images on the flash memory card or other storage medium being used with the camera can be deleted at any time to make room for more photos.

PREVIEWS
Virtually all digital cameras let you display and erase images.

STORAGE MEDIA
Most cameras use removable storage media in addition to, or instead of, built-in storage.

TYPICAL CONSUMER DIGITAL CAMERAS

PROFESSIONAL DIGITAL CAMERAS

DIGITAL CAMERAS INTEGRATED INTO MOBILE PHONES

FIGURE 4-21
Digital still cameras.

One factor affecting digital camera quality is the number of pixels (measured in *megapixels* or millions of pixels) used to store the data for each image. Today's cameras are typically between 5 and 35 megapixels. Although other factors—such as the quality of the lens and the technology used inside the camera to capture and process images—also affect the quality of digital photographs, the number of pixels does impact how large the digital photos can be printed. For instance, to print high-quality 8 by 10-inch or larger prints, a 5-megapixel camera is needed as a minimum.

Most mobile phones today have a built-in digital camera. This has many advantages, such as the ability to keep your friends up to date about your current activities (such as by uploading photos to Facebook or other social media); to take photos of car accidents and other incidents for authorities; and to read barcodes, remotely deposit checks, and facilitate gesture input, as discussed earlier in this chapter. However, they have also created new ethical problems in our society, such as the ability to take and distribute compromising photos of others, as well as to send compromising photos of oneself to others (a form of *sexting*, as discussed in more detail in Chapter 9).

ASK THE EXPERT

Louis Kaneshiro, Senior Technology Manager, Kingston Digital, Inc.

Is the speed of a flash memory card used with a digital camera important?

Faster SD card speed is only important if your device is designed to take advantage of it, and it is becoming more important with digital video cameras and the latest SLRs. If you're using a point & shoot camera, an ultra-zoom camera, or a camcorder, you're typically safe with a Class 6 card. Class 10 and the recent SDXC UHS-I capacity and speed specifications are designed for the newest DSLR cameras that require faster speeds for burst mode photography, RAW files, and HD video. We recommend that customers buy the speed class advised by the manufacturer in the device's manual, as this will typically satisfy the minimum requirements at the lowest cost.

Built-in video camera

DIGITAL CAMCORDERS
Typically store video on a built-in hard drive (as in this camera) or on DVD discs.

Courtesy Sony Electronics Inc.

U.S. Air Force photo/Staff Sgt. Levi Riendeau

PC VIDEO CAMERAS
Commonly used to deliver video over the Internet, such as during a video phone call as shown here.

⚓ **FIGURE 4-22**
Digital video cameras.

Digital Video Cameras

Digital video cameras (see Figure 4-22) include *digital camcorders* and small digital video cameras used in conjunction with computers and other devices. Digital video cameras are often built into portable computers and mobile devices; they are also available as stand-alone devices (commonly called *PC cams* or *webcams*) to connect to a desktop computer or a network. Digital camcorders are similar to conventional *analog* camcorders, but they store images on digital media—typically on built-in hard drives or rewritable DVDs for conventional-sized camcorders or on flash memory for pocket-sized camcorders. Video taken on a device with a built-in camera is typically stored on the device's internal storage. Once a video is recorded, it can be transferred to a computer, edited with software as needed, and saved to a DVD or other type of storage medium. It can also be *compressed* (made smaller), if needed, and then uploaded to social media sites, such as YouTube, Facebook, or *Vine*. Some digital video cameras today can take high-definition (HD) video, and some include wide angle lenses and microphones to facilitate *video phone calls* and *videoconferences* with multiple individuals.

Both individuals and businesses commonly use digital video cameras today. Both can set up a webcam to share a video feed of a scenic location, zoo, or other place with the public via a Web site. Typical personal applications include recording home movies with a digital camcorder and making video phone calls via a computer (as in Figure 4-22). An emerging personal application is using special *home surveillance video cameras* for security purposes—such as to monitor an empty house from work or keep an eye on a sleeping baby from another room in the home. Typically, these systems either transmit the video via the Internet to a computer or mobile device, or via a wireless connection to a special display device located in the home. Their use is growing and can give homeowners and parents the peace of mind of being able to watch their home surveillance video via the Internet in order to know that their home or children are safe, as well as give them the opportunity to notify the police immediately if they see their house is in the process of being burglarized or their children are being mistreated by a nanny or babysitter. Businesses also often use digital video cameras for security applications, as well as to create videos for marketing purposes and to perform videoconferences and *Webinars* (seminars that take place via the Web). Digital video cameras can also be used for identification purposes, such as with the *face recognition technology* used to authorize access to a secure facility or computer resource via an individual's face, as discussed in more detail in Chapter 9.

AUDIO INPUT

Audio input is the process of entering audio data into the computer. The most common types of audio input are voice and music.

Voice Input and Speech Recognition Systems

Voice input—inputting spoken words and converting them to digital form—is typically performed via a *microphone* or *headset* (a set of *headphones* with a built-in microphone). It can be used in conjunction with *sound recorder software* to store the voice in an audio file, such as to create a *podcast*—a recorded audio file that is distributed via the Internet—as well as with *Voice over IP systems* that allow individuals to place telephone calls from a computer over the Internet, as discussed in Chapter 8. It can also be used in conjunction with *speech recognition software* to provide spoken instructions to a computer.

Speech recognition systems enable the computer to recognize voice input as spoken words. It requires appropriate software, such as *Dragon NaturallySpeaking* or *Windows Speech Recognition*, in addition to a microphone. With speech recognition, voice input can be used to control the computer, such as opening and closing programs, selecting options from a menu or list, and moving the insertion point. It can also be used to input and edit text, including dictating text to be typed, selecting text to be formatted or edited, deleting text, correcting errors, and so forth. Speech recognition systems are used by individuals who cannot use a keyboard, as well as by individuals who prefer not to use a keyboard or who can generate input faster via a voice input system. For instance, medical and legal transcription is the most frequently used speech recognition application at the present time.

To enable hands-free operation, speech recognition capabilities are increasingly incorporated into smartphones, GPS systems, and other mobile devices. They are also commonly built into cars to enable hands-free control of navigation systems and sound systems, as well as to allow hands-free mobile phone calls to take place via the car's voice interface. Specialty speech recognition systems are frequently used to control machines, robots, and other electronic equipment, such as by surgeons during surgical procedures.

With a typical speech recognition system (see Figure 4-23), a microphone is used to input the spoken words into the computer, and then the sounds are broken into digital representations of *phonemes*—the basic elements of speech, such as *duh*, *aw*, and *guh* for the word *dog*. Next, the speech recognition software analyzes the content of the speech to convert the phonemes to words. Once words are identified, they are displayed on the screen. If a match is questionable or a homonym is encountered (such as the choice between *two*, *too*, and *to*), the program analyzes the context in which the word is used in an attempt to identify the correct word. If the program inserts a wrong word while converting the user's voice input to text, the user can correct it. To increase accuracy, most speech recognition software can be trained by individual users to allow the program to become accustomed to the user's speech patterns, voice, accent, and pronunciation.

FIGURE 4-23

Speech recognition systems.

The basic concept of speech recognition is also being applied to other audio input applications that enable computers and devices to recognize sounds other than voice. For instance, one type of *sound recognition system* located inside a computer could monitor the sound a hard drive is making to detect a possible malfunction before it happens, and another type could be used in conjunction with security systems to "listen" for the sound of a door opening or other suspicious sounds in order to alert security personnel.

1. The user speaks into a microphone that cancels out background noise and inputs the speech into the computer.

2. An analog-to-digital converter on the sound card located inside the system unit converts the spoken words to phonemes, the fundamental sounds in the language being used, and digitizes them.

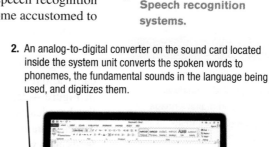

The patient exhibits signs of...

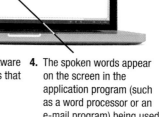

The patient exhibits signs of

3. Voice recognition software determines the words that were spoken.

4. The spoken words appear on the screen in the application program (such as a word processor or an e-mail program) being used.

© Ronen Boidek/Shutterstock.com

© Bombaert Patrick/Shutterstock.com; Used with permission from Microsoft Corporation

>**Speech recognition system.** A system, consisting of appropriate hardware and software, used to recognize voice input, such as dictation or audio computer commands.

MULTIPLE MONITORS
Can be used with a single computer to extend a desktop, which can increase productivity.

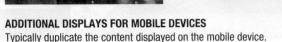

Image from the phone is duplicated on the second display.

ADDITIONAL DISPLAYS FOR MOBILE DEVICES
Typically duplicate the content displayed on the mobile device.

FIGURE 4-26
Flat-panel displays.

While CRT monitors are still in use, most computers today (as well as most television sets, mobile phones, and other consumer devices containing a display screen) use the thinner and lighter **flat-panel displays**. As discussed in more detail shortly, flat-panel displays form images by manipulating electronically charged chemicals or gases sandwiched between thin panes of glass or other transparent material. Flat-panel displays take up less desk space, which makes it possible to use multiple monitors working together to increase the amount of data the user can view at one time, increasing productivity without filling up an entire desk. Flat-panel displays also consume less power than CRTs and most use digital signals to display images (instead of the analog signals used with CRT monitors), which allows for sharper images. To use multiple monitors, you must have the necessary hardware to support it, such as the appropriate monitor ports, as discussed shortly. Multiple displays can be used with both desktop and portable computers; typically, you will use the displays to *extend* your desktop as in the left part of Figure 4-26, instead of duplicate it. There are displays for mobile devices, however, that are designed to duplicate the content so you can work on a larger screen when desired (see the right part of Figure 4-26).

Size and Aspect Ratio

Display device size is measured diagonally from corner to corner, in a manner similar to the way TV screens are measured. Most desktop computer monitors today are between 19 inches and 30 inches (though larger screens—up to 80 inches and more—are becoming increasingly common); notebook displays are usually between 14 inches and 17 inches; netbooks typically have 10-inch displays; and media tablet displays are typically between 7 inches and 10 inches. To better view DVDs and other multimedia content, many monitors today are *widescreen displays*, which conform to the *16:9 aspect ratio* of widescreen televisions, instead of the conventional *4:3 aspect ratio*.

Screen Resolution

Regardless of the technology used, the screen of a display device is divided into a fine grid of tiny pixels, as previously discussed. The number of pixels used on a display screen determines the *screen resolution*, which affects the amount of information that can be displayed on the screen at one time. When a higher resolution is selected, such as 1,600 pixels horizontally by 900 pixels vertically for a widescreen computer monitor (written as $1,600 \times 900$ and read as *1600 by 900*), more information can fit on the screen, but everything will be displayed smaller than with a lower resolution, such as $1,280 \times 768$. The screen resolution on many computers today can be changed by users to match their

---

TIP

High-resolution displays on Apple devices are dubbed *Retina* by Apple.

>**Flat-panel display.** A slim type of display device that uses electronically charged chemicals or gases instead of an electron gun to display images.

preferences and the software being used. On Windows computers, display options are changed using the Control Panel. When multiple monitors are used, typically the screen resolution of each display can be set independently of the others. Very high-resolution monitors are available for special applications, such as viewing digital X-rays.

Video Adapters, Interfaces, and Ports

The *video graphics card* installed inside a computer or the integrated graphics component built directly into the motherboard or the CPU of the computer houses the *graphics processing unit* (*GPU*)—the chip devoted to rendering images on a display device. The video graphics card or the integrated graphics component determines the graphics capabilities of the computer, including the screen resolutions available, the number of bits used to store color information about each pixel (called the *bit depth*), the total number of colors that can be used to display images, the number of monitors that can be connected to the computer via that video card or component, and the types of connectors that can be used to connect a monitor to the computer. Video cards typically contain a fan and other cooling components to cool the card. Most video cards also contain memory chips (typically called *video RAM* or *VRAM*)

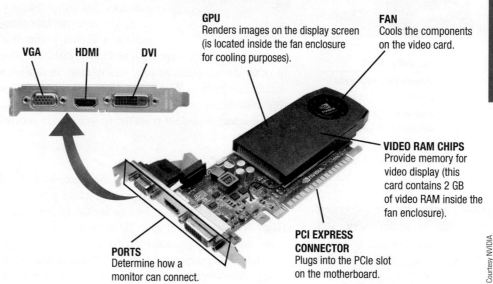

GPU
Renders images on the display screen (is located inside the fan enclosure for cooling purposes).

FAN
Cools the components on the video card.

VGA **HDMI** **DVI**

VIDEO RAM CHIPS
Provide memory for video display (this card contains 2 GB of video RAM inside the fan enclosure).

PORTS
Determine how a monitor can connect.

PCI EXPRESS CONNECTOR
Plugs into the PCIe slot on the motherboard.

Courtesy NVIDIA

to support graphics display, although some are designed to use a portion of the computer's regular RAM as video RAM instead. To support higher resolutions, higher bit depths, and a greater number of colors, a sufficient amount of video RAM is required. Most video cards today contain between 512 MB and 6 GB of video RAM. A typical video card is shown in Figure 4-27.

The three most common types of interfaces used to connect a monitor to a computer are *VGA* (*Video Graphics Array*), *DVI* (*Digital Visual Interface*), and *HDMI* (*High-Definition Multimedia Interface*), all shown in Figure 4-27. VGA uses a 15-pin D-shaped connector and it is commonly used with CRT monitors and many flat-panel monitors to transfer analog images to the monitor. DVI uses a more rectangular connector and it is frequently used with flat-panel displays to allow the monitor to receive clearer, more reliable digital signals than is possible with a VGA interface. HDMI is a newer type of digital connection that uses a smaller connector and can be used with display devices that support high-definition content. An even newer type of connector is *DisplayPort*, which is designed to eventually replace VGA and DVI ports on computers, video cards, and monitors. It is available in regular size, as well as the smaller *Mini DisplayPort* format. An adapter can be used to connect a VGA or DVI monitor to a DisplayPort connector.

A video card or an integrated video component in a desktop computer will have at least one port exposed through the system unit case to connect a monitor. Notebook computers and other computers with a built-in display typically contain a monitor port to connect a second monitor to the computer. A relatively new option for connecting additional monitors to a computer is using the computer's USB port. *USB monitors* (monitors designed to connect via a USB port) can be added to a computer even if that computer does not have a video card that supports multiple monitors. Conventional monitors can also connect to a computer via a USB port if a *USB display adapter* (see Figure 4-28) or a peripheral device (such as a docking station) that includes USB display capabilities is used. A USB connection has the

▲ **FIGURE 4-27**
Video cards. Provide a connection to a monitor, as well as determine video capabilities.

▼ **FIGURE 4-28**
A USB display adapter.

USB port connects the adapter to the computer.

DVI cable connects the display device.

Courtesy Kensington

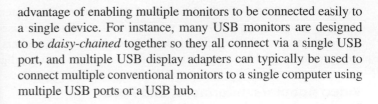

advantage of enabling multiple monitors to be connected easily to a single device. For instance, many USB monitors are designed to be *daisy-chained* together so they all connect via a single USB port, and multiple USB display adapters can typically be used to connect multiple conventional monitors to a single computer using multiple USB ports or a USB hub.

Courtesy HTC

FIGURE 4-29

Wireless displays.
Display content from a device (such as the smartphone shown here) to the display via a wireless signal.

Wired vs. Wireless Displays

Traditionally, computer monitors are *wired displays*; that is, monitors that are physically connected to the system unit via a cable. However, an increasing number of display devices today— including digital photo frames, e-readers, computer monitors, and television sets—are designed to be wireless. *Wireless displays* connect to a computer or other device (such as to a smartphone, as in Figure 4-29) using a wireless networking connection such as Wi-Fi, Bluetooth, or a special wireless standard designed for transmitting multimedia (as discussed in more detail in Chapter 7). Once connected, either all content or selected content from the source device is displayed on the wireless display.

2D vs. 3D Displays

While conventional displays are *two-dimensional* (*2D*) devices, recent improvements in flat-panel display technology and graphics processing have led to several emerging *three-dimensional* (*3D*) *output devices*, including *3D display screens* for computers. While traditional 3D displays (and most 3D televisions today) require special 3D glasses, the newest 3D computer display products use filters, prisms, multiple lenses, and other technologies built into the display screen to create the 3D effect and, as a result, do not require 3D glasses. Some 3D displays resemble conventional monitors; others are shaped differently, such as the dome-shaped *Perspecta* 3D display that is used primarily for medical imaging. 3D consumer products are increasingly available as well, such as the Nintendo 3DS handheld gaming device.

TIP

Researchers at Intel Labs predict that much of the Internet will use realistic-looking 3D applications by 2020.

Wearable Displays

While most displays are designed to be looked at from at least several inches away, some displays are designed to be wearable. A *wearable display* usually projects the image from a mobile device (such as a smartphone or media tablet) to a display screen built into the glasses via a wireless connection. Typically, the technology allows the user to see the image as if it is on a distant large screen display, and many wearable displays overlay the projected image on top of what the user is seeing in real time to provide augmented reality. For example, the *Google Glass* eyeglasses-based display shown in Figure 4-30 has a tiny display located where the right lens would be and users can see content projected on that screen in front of what they are seeing normally. Google Glass is typically connected (via Bluetooth) to a smartphone and then content (such as text messages, maps and directions, video calls, and Web pages) is streamed from that phone to the Google Glass display. Google Glass also has a built-in Web browser and can connect directly to a Wi-Fi hotspot when needed, has a touch-sensitive pad on the right side of the frame for input, and a bone-conductive audio output system so that audio output is heard only by the user. In addition to consumer wearable displays that have entertainment and productivity applications (such as being able to access GPS directions as needed or to monitor your e-mail during a meeting), there are also wearable displays designed for soldiers and other mobile workers.

Display is built into the Glass frames.

Content from a smartphone or the Internet appears in your line of vision.

Courtesy Google

FIGURE 4-30

Google Glass.

Touch and Gesture Capabilities

As discussed earlier in this chapter, it is increasingly common for monitors and display screens to support touch input. Touch screen displays are commonly used with personal computers, as well as with consumer kiosks, portable gaming devices, mobile phones, media tablets, and other consumer devices. Large screen (such as 55-inch) touch screen displays are also available for conference room and other group locations. Gesture input is widely used with these products, as well as with large screen interactive displays and smart TVs.

Flat-Panel Display Technologies

The most common flat-panel technologies include *liquid crystal display* (*LCD*), various types of *light emitting diode* (*LED*), and *gas plasma*. One emerging flat-panel technology is *interferometric modulator display* (*IMOD*). These display technologies are discussed next. Another technology used by some flat-panel displays (including e-readers, some digital signage systems, and the display on some wristwatches and USB flash drives) is *e-paper* technology, discussed in the Inside the Industry box.

Liquid Crystal Displays (LCDs)

A **liquid crystal display** (**LCD**) uses charged liquid crystals located between two sheets of clear material (usually glass or plastic) to light up the appropriate pixels to form the image on the screen. Several layers of liquid crystals are used, and, in their normal state, the liquid crystals are aligned so that light passes through the display. When an electrical charge is applied to the liquid crystals (via an electrode grid layer contained within the LCD panel), the liquid crystals change their orientation or "twist" so that light cannot pass through the display, and the liquid crystals at the charged intersections of the electrode grid appear dark. Color LCD displays use a color filter that consists of a pattern of red, green, and blue *subpixels* for each pixel. The voltage used controls the orientation (twisting) of the liquid crystals and the amount of light that gets through, affecting the color and shade of that pixel—the three different colors blend to make the pixel the appropriate color.

LCD displays can be viewed only with reflective light, unless light is built into the display. Consequently, LCD panels used with computer monitors typically include a light inside the panel, usually at the rear of the display—a technique referred to as *backlighting*. While fluorescent lamps were used to backlight conventional LCD screens, today's screens are increasingly using *LED* backlighting instead for increased energy efficiency. An emerging option is backlighting LCDs using *quantum dot technology*, a nanotechnology development that enables LCDs to display about 50% more color than conventional LCDs. Many newer LCDs use *IPS* (*In-Plane Switching*) technology to display images with a broader range of color and brightness, with a better viewing angle, and with less blurring when the display is touched. However, LCDs using the older *TN* (*Twisted Nematic*) technology are less expensive.

Light Emitting Diode (LED) and Organic Light Emitting Diode (OLED) Displays

LED (*light emitting diode*) *technology* is another flat-panel technology commonly used with consumer products, such as alarm clocks and Christmas lights, as well as to backlight LCD panels. Several emerging types of LEDs are discussed next.

Organic light emitting diode (**OLED**) **displays** use layers of organic material, which emit a visible light when electric current is applied. Because they emit a visible light, OLED

E-Paper

Electronic paper (*e-paper*) is a technology used with flat panel display devices that attempts to mimic the look of ordinary printed paper. The purpose of an *Electronic Paper Display* (*EPD*) is to give the user the experience of reading from paper, while providing them with the ability to update the information shown on the device electronically. EPDs display content in high-contrast, so they can be viewed in direct sunlight. They also require much less electricity than other types of displays because they don't require a backlight and they don't require power to maintain the content shown on the display—they only require power to change the content. Because the content stored in an EPD can be erased when it is no longer needed and then replaced with new content, EPDs are more environmentally friendly than conventional paper documents. An additional benefit is portability; an *e-reader* (such as the Amazon *Kindle* and the Barnes & Noble *Nook,* shown in the accompanying photograph), for instance, can hold thousands of books stored in electronic format in a device about the size of a paperback novel. In fact, with an e-reader, you could carry a small library in your backpack. New e-books are transferred to the e-reader via a flash memory card or a wireless (typically Wi-Fi or 3G) download. E-readers today typically have color displays and many support Web browsing, apps, and other functions in addition to displaying e-books.

E-paper is also widely used for *e-signs*, which look like ordinary paper signs but their text can be changed wirelessly. Their low power consumption means that e-signs can run off battery power for an extended period of time, even with moving data. Some e-signs don't even require a battery; instead, the wireless signal used to transmit data to the display is strong enough to update the sign content. Other retail applications currently on the market include e-paper shelf price tags that can communicate electronically with the store's database so the current price is always displayed, e-paper displays on wristwatches and USB flash drives, and destination displays on trains.

E-paper technology used with fabric, plastic, metal, and other materials is in development and is expected to be used to enable keyboards to be printed on military uniform sleeves, light switches to be printed onto wallpaper, and radio circuitry and controls to be printed onto clothing and other everyday objects. It may also allow e-paper to be used on billboards, T-shirts, and even paint for easy redecorating, as well as

regular-sized e-paper that can be inserted into a special computer printer to be printed electronically and then reused over and over. One improvement that has already occurred is the incorporation of touch and pen input with e-paper displays. For instance, both touch and pen input can be used with many e-readers today to flip the "pages" of the book and otherwise control the device, as well as to make notes on the pages or highlight passages of text.

So how does e-paper work? It is based on a display technology called *electrophoretic*, which was invented and is now manufactured and marketed by E Ink® Corporation. An electrophoretic display contains *electronic ink*—essentially charged ink that consists of millions of tiny beads or *microcapsules* about half the diameter of a human hair. For monochrome displays, these beads contain positively charged white particles and negatively charged black particles suspended in a clear fluid. When voltage is applied to the beads (through the circuitry contained within the display), either the white or the black particles rise to the top and the opposite colored particles are pulled to the bottom of the bead, depending on the polarity of the charge applied. Consequently, the beads in each pixel appear to be either white or black (see the accompanying illustration) and remain in that state until another transmission changes the pattern. Color e-ink displays work in a similar manner but typically include a color filter to make the images appear in color.

AN E-READER

The white particles are at the top, so this pixel appears white.

AN E-INK MICROCAPSULE

displays do not use backlighting. This characteristic makes OLEDs more energy efficient than conventional LCDs and LED-backlit LCDs and lengthens the battery life of portable devices using OLED displays. Other advantages of OLEDs are that they are thinner than LCDs, they have a wider viewing angle than LCDs and so displayed content is visible from virtually all directions, and their images are brighter and sharper than LCDs. OLED displays are incorporated into many digital cameras, mobile phones, portable digital media players, Google Glass, and other consumer devices (see Figure 4-31). They are also beginning to appear in television and computer displays.

There are also a few special types of OLEDs that support applications not possible with CRT, LCD, or traditional LED technology. For instance, *flexible OLED* (*FOLED*) displays—a technology developed by Universal Display Corporation—are OLED displays built on flexible surfaces, such as plastic or metallic foil. Flexible displays using FOLED technology—such as displays for portable computers and mobile devices that can roll up when not in use (see Figure 4-32)—are being developed by several companies. Other possible uses for flexible screens include making lighter displays for computers and mobile devices, integrating displays on military uniform sleeves, and allowing retractable wall-mounted large screen displays. White OLED displays are in development for use with lightbulbs.

Another form of OLED developed by Universal Display Corporation is *transparent OLED* (*TOLED*). TOLED displays are transparent and can emit light toward the top and bottom of the display surface. The portion of the display that does not currently have an image displayed (and the entire display device when it is off) is nearly as transparent as glass, so the user can see through the screen (refer again to Figure 4-32). TOLED technology opens up the possibility of displays on home windows, car windshields, helmet face shields, and other transparent items. A third type of OLED developed by Universal Display Corporation is *Phosphorescent OLED* or *PHOLED*. The term *phosphorescence* refers to a process that results in much more conversion of electrical energy into light instead of heat; with phosphorescence, OLEDs can be up to four times more efficient than without it. Consequently, PHOLED technology is especially appropriate for use on mobile devices, consumer electronics, and other devices where power consumption is an important concern.

FIGURE 4-31
How OLED displays work. Each pixel on an OLED display emits light in the necessary color.

Electron layers
Metal or silicon backing
Glass layer
One pixel
Light output
OLED display
Organic layers

Courtesy SanDisk Corporation; Copyright © 2015 Cengage Learning®

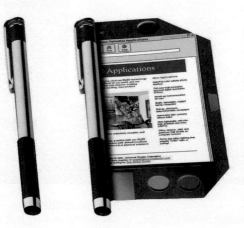

FOLEDS
Used to create flexible displays on plastic or another type of flexible material.

TOLEDS
Used to create transparent displays.

Courtesy of Universal Display Corporation

FIGURE 4-32
Special types of OLEDs.

Ⓐ FIGURE 4-33
An IMOD display is bright and readable, even in direct sunlight.

Ⓥ FIGURE 4-34
Data projectors.

Interferometric Modulator (IMOD) Displays

Another emerging flat-panel display technology is *interferometric modulator (IMOD) displays*. Designed initially for mobile phones and other portable devices, an IMOD display is essentially a complex mirror that uses external light—such as from the sun or artificial light inside a building—to display images. Because IMOD displays are utilizing light instead of fighting it the way LCD displays do, images are bright and clear even in direct sunlight (see Figure 4-33). And, because backlighting isn't used, power consumption is much less than what is needed for LCD displays. In fact, similar to e-paper, devices using IMOD displays use no power unless the image changes so they can remain on at all times without draining the device battery. Beginning to be used with mobile devices, IMODs could eventually be used for outdoor television screens, large digital signs, and other outdoor display devices that normally consume a great deal of power.

Plasma Displays

Plasma displays use a layered technology like LCD and OLED and look similar to LCD displays, but they use a layer of gas between two plates of glass, instead of liquid crystals or organic material. A phosphor-coated screen (with red, green, and blue phosphors for each pixel) is used, and an electron grid layer and electronic charges are used to make the gas atoms light up the appropriate phosphors to create the image on the screen. While plasma technology has traditionally been used with the very large displays used by businesses, as well as many large screen televisions, it is slowly being replaced by LCDs.

Data and Multimedia Projectors

A **data projector** is used to display output from a computer to a wall or projection screen. Projectors that are designed primarily to display movies and other multimedia are sometimes called *multimedia projectors*. Data projectors are often found in classrooms, conference rooms, and similar locations and can be portable units, freestanding larger units, or units that are permanently mounted onto the ceiling (see Figure 4-34). While larger data projectors typically connect via cable to a computer, *wireless projectors* that use a Wi-Fi

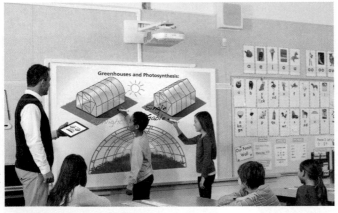

CONVENTIONAL DATA PROJECTORS
Frequently used for both business and classroom presentations; the projector shown here is ceiling mounted and Wi-Fi-enabled.

PICO PROJECTORS
Can be stand-alone or built into a mobile device; images from the mobile device (such as the smartphone shown here) are projected onto any surface.

> **Plasma display.** A type of flat-panel display that uses layers of gas to display images; most often used on large displays. > **Data projector.** A display device that projects all computer output to a wall or projection screen.

connection are available to more easily project content located on a company network, the Internet, a smartphone, or a media tablet. Some projectors include an *iPod dock* to connect an iPod in order to project videos stored on that device.

For projecting content to a small audience while on the go, small *pico projectors* are available. These pocket-sized projectors typically connect to a smartphone, portable computer, or other device to enable the device to project an image (such as a document, presentation, or movie) onto a wall or other flat surface from up to 12 feet away. Pico projectors typically create a display up to about 10 feet wide in order to easily share information stored on the device with others without having to crowd around a tiny screen. They are also beginning to be integrated directly into mobile devices (see the Samsung Beam *projector phone* shown in Figure 4-34). An emerging type of data projector is the *3D projector*. Some 3D projectors are designed to project 3D images that are viewed with 3D glasses, similar to 3D televisions. Others are designed to project actual 3D projections or *holograms*. For instance, holograms of individuals and objects can be projected onto a stage for a presentation and hologram display devices can be used in retail stores, exhibitions, and other locations to showcase products or other items in 3D.

PRINTERS

Instead of the temporary, ever-changing soft copy output that a monitor produces, **printers** produce *hard copy*; that is, a permanent copy of the output on paper. Most desktop computers are connected to a printer; portable computers can use printers as well.

Printer Characteristics

Printers differ in a number of important respects, such as the technology used, size, print quality, speed, and type of connection used. Some general printer characteristics are discussed next, followed by a look at the most common types of printers.

Printing Technology

Printers produce images through either impact or nonimpact technologies. *Impact printers*, like old ribbon typewriters, have a print mechanism that actually strikes the paper to transfer ink to the paper. For example, a *dot-matrix printer* (see Figure 4-35) uses a *printhead* consisting of pins that strike an inked ribbon to transfer the ink to the paper—the appropriate pins are extended (and, consequently, strike the ribbon) as the printhead moves across the paper in order to form the appropriate words or images. Impact printers are used today primarily for producing multipart forms, such as invoices, packing slips, and credit card receipts.

Most printers today are *nonimpact printers*, meaning they form images without the print mechanism actually touching the paper. Nonimpact printers usually produce higher-quality images and are much quieter than impact printers are. The two most common types of printers today—*laser printers* and *ink-jet printers*—are both nonimpact printers. As discussed in more detail shortly, laser printers form images with *toner powder* (essentially ink powder) and ink-jet printers form images with liquid ink. Both impact and nonimpact printers form images with dots, in a manner similar to the way monitors display images with pixels. Because of this, printers are very versatile and can print text in virtually any size, as well as print photos and other graphical images. In addition to paper, both impact and nonimpact printers can print on transparencies, envelopes, mailing labels, and more.

Courtesy InfoPrint Solutions Company

FIGURE 4-35
Dot-matrix printers.
Dot-matrix printers are impact printers; today they are typically high-speed printers used in manufacturing, shipping, or similar applications.

>**Printer.** An output device that produces output on paper.

© Paul Broadbent/Shutterstock.com

FIGURE 4-36

Color printing.
Color printers require multiple color cartridges or cartridges that contain multiple colors.

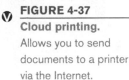

TIP

To save money, consider buying *recharged* (refilled) toner cartridges to replace your laser printer cartridge when it runs out of toner powder (give the used one back to be refilled if possible). Recharged cartridges typically cost about one-third less than new cartridges and last at least as long.

FIGURE 4-37

Cloud printing.
Allows you to send documents to a printer via the Internet.

Courtesy Epson America

Color vs. Black and White

Both *color printers* and *black-and-white printers* are available. Color printers work similarly to black-and-white printers, except that, instead of using just black ink or toner, they also use cyan (blue), magenta (red), and yellow ink or toner (see Figure 4-36). Color printers either apply all of the colors in one pass or go through the entire printing process multiple times, applying one color during each pass. Color printers are often used in homes (to print photographs, greeting cards, flyers, and more). Businesses may use black-and-white printers for output that does not need to be in color (because it is less expensive and faster to print in black and white) and color printers for output that needs to be in color (such as product brochures and other colorful marketing materials).

Print Resolution

Most printing technologies today form images with dots of liquid ink or flecks of toner powder. The number of dots per inch (dpi)—called the *print resolution*—affects the quality of the printed output. Printers with a higher print resolution tend to produce sharper text and images than printers with a lower resolution tend to produce, although other factors (such as the technology and number of colors used) also affect the quality of a printout. Guidelines for acceptable print resolution are typically 300 dpi for general-purpose printouts, 600 dpi for higher-quality documents, and 2,400 dpi for professional applications.

Print Speed

Print speed is typically measured in *pages per minute* (*ppm*). How long it takes a document to print depends on the actual printer being used, the selected print resolution, the amount of memory inside the printer, and the content being printed. For instance, pages containing photographs or other images typically take longer to print than pages containing only text, and full-color pages take longer to print than black-and-white pages. Common speeds for printers today range from about 15 to 65 ppm.

Personal vs. Network Printers

Printers today can be designated as *personal printers* (printers designed to be connected directly to a single computer) or *network printers* (printers designed to be connected directly to a home or an office network). Personal printers can be shared over a network if the computer to which the printer is connected is powered up and the printer is designated as a shared device. However, network printers are designed to connect directly to a network (instead of to a single computer) so they can be used by anyone connected to the network via a wired or wireless connection. Network printers are increasingly being used in homes as well as in businesses. Network printers can be accessed by any computer or device on the same network; they can also be accessed via the Internet using an appropriate app, an assigned e-mail address for that printer, or a *cloud printing* service such as *Google Cloud Print*. For instance, if your printer has Internet access, you can print content from your smartphone, media tablet, or other mobile device to your home or office printer from any location with Internet access (see Figure 4-37); you can also send printouts wirelessly to public printers, such as those located at airports, libraries, office stores, and shipping stores such as FedEx Office and the UPS Store. In addition, printers are often classified by print volume (such as *home/small business* or *enterprise printers*). Enterprise printers are designed for high-volume office printing, typically support multiple paper trays to print various sized documents, and often include other capabilities, such as to collate, staple, hole-punch, and print on both sides of the page (referred to as *duplex printing*). Networks are discussed in detail in Chapter 7.

Connection Options

Most personal printers today connect to a computer via a USB connection; many have the option of connecting via a wired or wireless networking connection as well. In addition, many personal printers can receive data to be printed via a flash memory card. As previously discussed, network printers are connected directly to a wired or wireless network and can be used by any device on the network, or via the Internet if cloud printing is available and enabled.

Multifunction Capabilities

Some printers today offer more than just printing capabilities. These units—referred to as **multifunction devices (MFDs)** or *all-in-ones*—typically copy, scan, fax, and print documents (see Figure 4-38). MFDs can be based on ink-jet printer or laser printer technology, and they are available as both color and black-and-white devices. Although multifunction devices have traditionally been desktop units used in small offices and home offices, it is common today for enterprise printers to be multifunction devices.

Courtesy Epson America

FIGURE 4-38
A multifunction device (MFD).

Laser Printers

Laser printers (see Figure 4-39) are the standard for business documents and come in both personal and network versions; they are also available as both color and black-and-white printers. To print a document, the laser printer first uses a laser beam to charge the appropriate locations on a drum to form the page's image, and then *toner powder* (powdered ink) is released from a *toner cartridge* and sticks to the drum. The toner is then

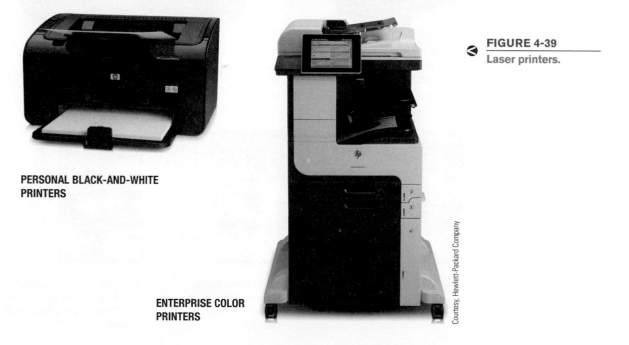

PERSONAL BLACK-AND-WHITE
PRINTERS

ENTERPRISE COLOR
PRINTERS

Courtesy, Hewlett-Packard Company

FIGURE 4-39
Laser printers.

transferred to a piece of paper when the paper is rolled over the drum, and a heating unit fuses the toner powder to the paper to permanently form the image. Laser printers print one entire page at a time and are typically faster and have better quality output than *ink-jet printers*, discussed next. Common print resolutions for laser printers are between 600 and 2,400 dpi; speeds range from about 10 to 70 ppm.

Ink-Jet Printers

Ink-jet printers form images by spraying tiny drops of liquid ink from one or more *ink cartridges* onto the page, one printed line at a time (see Figure 4-40). Some printers print with one single-sized ink droplet; others print using different-sized ink droplets and using multiple nozzles or varying electrical charges for more precise printing. The printhead for an ink-jet printer typically travels back and forth across the page, which is one reason why ink-jet printers are slower than laser printers (ink jets print up to about 30 ppm). However, some ink-jet printers use a printhead that is the full width of the paper, which allows the printhead to remain stationary while the paper feeds past it. These printers are very fast, printing up to 60 ppm for letter-sized paper.

Because they are relatively inexpensive, have good-quality output, and can print in color, ink-jet printers are often the printer of choice for home use. With the use of special photo paper, ink-jet printers can also print photograph-quality digital photos. Starting at less than $50 for a simple home printer, ink-jet printers are affordable, although the cost of the replaceable ink cartridges can add up, especially if you do a lot of color printing.

FIGURE 4-40
How ink-jet printers work.

Copyright © 2015 Cengage Learning®

Each ink cartridge is made up of multiple tiny ink-filled firing chambers; to print images, the appropriate color ink is ejected through the appropriate firing chamber.

INK-JET PRINTER

Courtesy, Hewlett-Packard Company

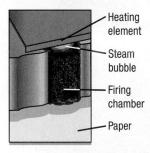

- Heating element
- Steam bubble
- Firing chamber
- Paper

1. A heating element makes the ink boil, which causes a steam bubble to form.

- Steam bubble
- Ink droplet

2. As the steam bubble expands, it pushes ink through the firing chamber.

- Steam bubble
- Ink droplet

3. The ink droplet is ejected onto the paper and the steam bubble collapses, pulling more ink into the firing chamber.

Copyright © 2015 Cengage Learning®

>**Ink-jet printer.** An output device that sprays droplets of ink to produce images on paper.

In addition to being used in computer printers, ink-jet technology is being applied to a number of other applications. For instance, ink-jet technology may eventually be used for dispensing liquid metals, aromas, computer chips and other circuitry, and even "printing" human tissue and other organic materials for medical purposes. At least one company is currently working on modifying ink-jet technology to print proteins instead of ink, with the goal of eventually allowing doctors to use a patient's own fat to print a customized breast implant. Some of these applications are *3D printing applications*; 3D printers are discussed in more detail shortly.

Special-Purpose Printers

Although both laser and ink-jet printers can typically print on a variety of media—including sheets of labels, envelopes, transparencies, photo paper, and even fabric, in addition to various sizes of paper—some printers are designed for a particular purpose. Some of the most common *special-purpose printers* are discussed next.

Barcode, Label, and Postage Printers

Barcode printers enable businesses and other organizations to print custom barcodes on price tags, shipping labels, and other documents for identification or pricing purposes. Most barcode printers can print labels in a variety of barcode standards; some can also encode RFID tags embedded in labels (see Figure 4-41). For other types of labels, such as for envelopes, packages, and file folders, regular *label printers* may come in handy. Some special-purpose label printers referred to as *postage printers* can print *electronic postage* (also called *e-stamps*). E-stamps are valid postage stamps that can be printed once a postage allotment has been purchased via the Internet or from an e-stamp vendor; postage values are deducted from your allotment as you print the e-stamps. Some e-stamp services also allow stamps to be printed directly onto shipping labels and envelopes using laser or ink-jet printers.

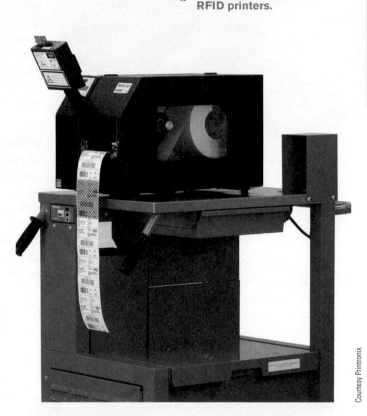

FIGURE 4-41
RFID printers.

Courtesy Printronix

Photo Printers

Photo printers are color printers designed to print photographs. They can be connected to a computer to print photos stored on the hard drive; most photo printers also can print photos directly from a digital camera, smartphone, or storage medium (such as a flash memory card) by connecting that device either physically or wirelessly to the printer. Often, photo printers have a preview screen to allow for minor editing and cropping before printing, but it is usually more efficient to do extensive editing on a computer. Some photo printers can print a variety of photo paper sizes; others—sometimes called *snapshot* or *pocket printers*—print only on standard 4 by 6-inch photo paper. In addition to photo printers designed for home use, there are also professional photo printers used by businesses and photo processing companies. Although home photo printers offer the convenience of printing digital photos at home and whenever the need arises, the cost per photo is typically higher than using a photo printing service at a retail store or an Internet photo printing service.

TIP

In addition to printing your digital photos, many retail and Internet photo services can print digital photos on shirts, mugs, playing cards, calendars, mouse pads—even valid U.S. postage stamps.

> **Barcode printer.** An output device that prints barcoded documents. > **Photo printer.** An output device designed for printing digital photographs.

© AP Photo/Mark Lennihan

FIGURE 4-42
Portable printers.
This printer uses ZINK
technology.

FIGURE 4-43
Wide-format
printers. Are used
to print documents
that are too large for a
standard-sized printer.

Courtesy, Hewlett-Packard Company

Portable and Integrated Printers

Portable printers are small, lightweight printers that can be used on the go, usually with a notebook computer or mobile device, and they connect via either a wired or wireless connection. Portable printers that can print on regular-sized (8.5 by 11-inch) paper are used by businesspeople while traveling; portable receipt, label, and barcode printers are used in some service professions. Printers can also be integrated into other devices, such as smartphones and other mobile devices. And some portable printers don't use conventional ink-jet or laser technology. For instance, the *ZINK printer* shown in Figure 4-42 uses a technology developed by *ZINK* (for "zero ink") *Imaging*. This printer uses no ink; instead, it uses special paper that is coated with special color dye crystals. Before printing, the embedded dye crystals are clear, so *ZINK Paper* looks like regular white photo paper. The ZINK printer uses heat to activate and colorize these dye crystals when a photo is printed, creating a full-color image.

Wide-Format Ink-Jet Printers

To print charts, drawings, maps, blueprints, posters, signs, advertising banners, and other large documents in one piece, a larger printer (such as the one shown in Figure 4-43) is needed. Today, most large format printers (sometimes called *plotters*) are *wide-format ink-jet printers*, which are designed to print documents from around 24 inches to 60 inches in width. Although typically used to print on paper, some wide-format ink-jet printers can print directly on fabric and other types of materials.

3D Printers

When 3D output is required, such as to print a 3D model of a new building or prototype of a new product, **3D printers** (see Figure 4-44) can be used. Instead of printing on paper, these printers typically form output in layers using molten plastic during series of passes to build a 3D version of the desired output—a process referred to as *additive manufacturing* because material is added instead of being taken away as in traditional *subtractive manufacturing*. Some printers can produce multicolor output; others print in only one color and need to be painted by hand if color output is desired. 3D printers are becoming available in a variety of sizes, from personal printers for printing smartphone cases, toys, jewelry, and other personal objects to professional printers for printing working product prototypes or custom manufacturing parts. They have even begun to be used to print medical implants using FDA-approved 3D material. Another area with great potential is space exploration. NASA is preparing to launch a 3D printer into space in 2014 in order to enable astronauts to print tools, spare parts, rocket pieces, and even small satellites using spools of plastic strands. One issue with the increased availability of

>**Portable printer.** A small, lightweight printer designed to be used while on the go. >**3D printer.** An output device designed to print three-dimensional objects, such as product prototypes.

3D printers is the risk of them being used to print dangerous or illegal items, such as working plastic guns. In fact, after a 3D-printed gun was recently demonstrated firing standard bullets, lawmakers are considering enacting legislation to ban 3D printers from making weapons.

AUDIO OUTPUT

Audio output includes voice, music, and other audible sounds. **Computer speakers**, the most common type of audio output device, connect to a computer and provide audio output for computer games, music, video clips and TV shows, Web conferencing, and other applications. Computer speaker systems resemble their stereo system counterparts and are available in a wide range of prices. Some speaker systems (such as the one shown in Figure 4-45) consist of only a pair of speakers. Others include additional speakers and a subwoofer to create better sound (such as surround sound) for multimedia content. Instead of being stand-alone units, the speakers for some desktop computers are built directly into, or permanently attached to, the monitor. Portable computers and mobile devices typically have speakers integrated into the device; these devices can also be connected to a home or car stereo system, portable speakers, or a consumer device (such as a treadmill) that contains a compatible *dock* and integrated speakers in order to play music stored on the device through those speakers. Typically, mobile devices are connected to a speaker system via the device's headphone jack, dock connection, USB port, or wireless connection.

Headphones can be used instead of speakers when you don't want the audio output to disturb others (such as in a school computer lab or public library). **Headsets** (see Figure 4-45) are headphones with a built-in microphone and are often used when dictating, making phone calls, or participating in Web conferences using a computer; wireless headsets are commonly used in conjunction with mobile phones. Even smaller than headphones are the *earphones* and *earbuds* often used with portable digital media players, handheld gaming devices, and other mobile devices.

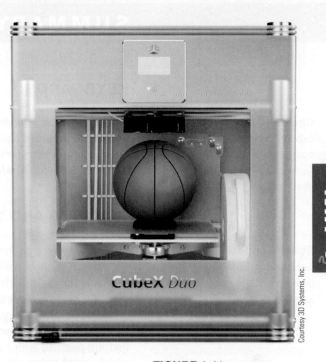

Courtesy 3D Systems, Inc.

FIGURE 4-44
3D printers. This printer can print objects up to the size of a standard basketball.

FIGURE 4-45
Audio output devices.

Courtesy Altec Lansing

COMPUTER SPEAKERS
Used to output sound from a computer.

Courtesy Altec Lansing

TABLET DOCK
Used to output sound from a media tablet.

Courtesy Nuance

HEADSETS
Used when both voice input and audio output are required.

>**Computer speakers.** Output devices connected to computers that provide audio output. >**Headphones.** A personal audio output device used by an individual so only he or she can hear the sound; headphones with a built-in microphone are typically referred to as **headsets**.

REVIEW ACTIVITIES

KEY TERM MATCHING

a. digital camera

b. ink-jet printer

c. laser printer

d. mouse

e. OLED display

f. optical character recognition (OCR)

g. RFID tag

h. scanner

i. stylus

j. touch screen

Instructions: Match each key term on the left with the definition on the right that best describes it.

1. _____ A common pointing device that the user slides along a flat surface to move a pointer around the screen and clicks its buttons to make selections.

2. _____ A device containing a tiny chip and a radio antenna that is attached to an object so it can be identified using radio frequency identification technology.

3. _____ A display device that is touched with the finger to issue commands or otherwise provide input to the connected device.

4. _____ An input device that reads printed text and graphics and transfers them to a computer in digital form.

5. _____ An input device that is used to write electronically on the display screen.

6. _____ An input device that takes pictures and records them as digital images.

7. _____ An output device that uses toner powder and technology similar to that of a photocopier to produce images on paper.

8. _____ A type of flat-panel display that uses emissive organic material to display brighter and sharper images than LCDs.

9. _____ An output device that sprays droplets of ink to produce images on paper.

10. _____ The ability of a scanning device to recognize scanned text characters and convert them to electronic form as text, not images.

SELF-QUIZ

Instructions: Circle **T** if the statement is true, **F** if the statement is false, or write the best answer in the space provided. **Answers for the self-quiz are located in the References and Resources Guide at the end of the book.**

1. **T** **F** A keyboard is an example of a pointing device.

2. **T** **F** Most digital still cameras store photos on flash memory media.

3. **T** **F** UPC is a type of barcode.

4. **T** **F** Consumer kiosks located in retail stores commonly use touch screens for input.

5. **T** **F** An ink-jet printer normally produces a better image than a laser printer.

6. With _____ software, pen-based computers can convert handwritten text into editable, typed text.

7. A(n) _____ can be used to convert flat printed documents, such as a drawing or photograph, into digital form.

8. The smallest colorable area in an electronic image (such as a scanned document, digital photograph, or image displayed on a display screen) is called a(n) _____.

9. Virtually all portable computers and mobile devices, and most desktop computers today, use _____ displays, which are smaller, thinner, and lighter than the _____ monitors used with desktop computers in the past.

10. Match each input device to its input application, and write the corresponding number in the blank to the left of the input application.

a. _____ Pen-based computing

b. _____ Media tablet

c. _____ Text-based data entry

d. _____ Secure facility access

e. _____ Tracking goods

1. Keyboard
2. Stylus
3. RFID tag
4. Biometric reader
5. Touch screen

EXERCISES

HW

1. For the following list of computer input and output devices, write the appropriate abbreviation (I or O) in the space provided to indicate whether each device is used for input (I) or output (O).

a. _____ Biometric reader

b. _____ Graphics tablet

c. _____ Speaker

d. _____ Photo printer

e. _____ Flat-panel display

f. _____ Digital camera

g. _____ Data projector

h. _____ Microphone

i. _____ OLED monitor

j. _____ Gaming controller

2. Write the number of the type of printer that best matches each of the printing applications in the blank to the left of each printing application.

a. _____ To print inexpensive color printouts for a wide variety of documents.

b. _____ To print all output for an entire office.

c. _____ To print receipts for jet-ski rentals at the beach.

d. _____ To print high-quality black-and-white business letters and reports at home.

1. Personal laser printer
2. Network laser printer
3. Ink-jet printer
4. Portable printer

3. List three advantages of RFID technology over barcode technology.

4. Would an OLED display or an LCD display use more battery power? Explain why.

5. List one personal or business application that you believe is more appropriate for a dot-matrix printer, instead of another type of printer, and explain why.

DISCUSSION QUESTIONS

1. While gaming and texting are both popular pastimes, it is possible to become injured by performing these activities. For instance, some Wii users have developed tennis elbow and other ailments from some Wii Sports games and heavy texters have developed problems with their thumbs. Think of the devices you use regularly. Have you ever become sore or injured from their use? If so, was it the design of the input device being used, overuse, or both? What responsibilities do hardware manufacturers have with respect to creating safe input devices? If a user becomes injured due to overuse of a device, whose fault it is? Should input devices come with warning labels?

2. The choice of an appropriate input device for a product is often based on both the type of device being used and the target market for that device. For instance, a device targeted to college students and one targeted to older individuals may use different input methods. Suppose that you are developing a device to be used primarily for Internet access that will be marketed to senior citizens. What type of hardware would you select as the primary input device? Why? What are the advantages and disadvantages of your selected input device? How could the disadvantages be minimized?

PROJECTS

1. **Biometrics and Personal Privacy** Biometric input devices, such as fingerprint readers and iris scanners, are increasingly being used for security purposes, such as to clock in and out of work, or to obtain access to locked facilities, a computer, or a computer network. Other uses of biometric technology are more voluntary, such as expedited airport-screening programs used by some frequent travelers and the fingerprint payment systems used at some retail stores. While viewed as a time-saving tool by some, other individuals may object to their biometric characteristics being stored in a database for this purpose. Is convenience worth compromising some personal privacy? What about national security? Would you be willing to sign up for a voluntary program, such as an airport-screening system or a fingerprint payment system, that relies on biometric data? Would you work at a job that required you to use a biometric input device on a regular basis? Do you think a national ID card containing hard-to-forge biometric data could help prevent terrorist attacks, such as the September 11, 2001, attacks? If so, do you think most Americans would support its use?

   For this project, research the use of biometric input devices today and form an opinion about their use and any potential impact their use may have on personal privacy. At the conclusion of your research, prepare a one-page summary of your findings and opinions and submit it to your instructor.

2. **Printer Shopping** Printers today have many more features than a few years ago. These features may include improved quality, more memory, photo printing capabilities, digital camera connectivity, built-in flash memory card readers, wireless connectivity, and faster speed.

   For this project, suppose you are in the market for a new personal printer. Make a list of the most important features needed to meet your needs, and then research printers to identify the best printer for your needs. Be sure to consider both the price of the printer and the price of consumables (such as paper and ink/toner) in your evaluation process. At the conclusion of your research, prepare a one-page summary of your findings and best options and submit it to your instructor.

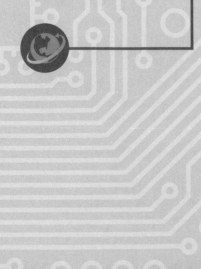

3. **Keyboarding Speed Test** Although voice and other alternative means of input are emerging, most data input today is still performed via the keyboard. Proper keyboarding technique can help increase speed and accuracy. Online keyboarding tests can help to evaluate your keyboarding ability.

   For this project, find a site (such as **Typingtest.com**) that offers a free online typing test and test your keyboarding speed and accuracy. At the conclusion of the test, rate your keyboarding ability and determine whether a keyboarding course or tutor program, or just keyboarding practice, will help you improve if your score is not at least 20 correct words per minute (cwpm). Take the test one more time to see if your speed improves now that you are familiar with how the test works. If your speed is fast, but accuracy is low, take the test once more, concentrating on accuracy. If you still test less than 20 cwpm, locate a free typing tutor program or Web site and evaluate it to see if it would help you to increase your speed and accuracy. At the conclusion of this task, prepare a short summary of your experience, including the typing test site used and your best score.

4. **Green Technology Mandates** The chapter Inside the Industry box discusses e-paper—an erasable, reusable alternative to traditional paper and ink. While e-paper has many societal benefits (such as reducing the use of traditional paper and ink, as well as the resources needed to create and dispose of them), it has been slow to catch on beyond e-readers. When a new technology, such as e-paper, that has obvious benefits to society is developed, who (if anyone) should be responsible for making sure it gets implemented in a timely fashion? Do we, as a society, have an ethical responsibility to ensure the new product succeeds? Should the government mandate the use of beneficial technology? Will businesses or individuals choose to use e-paper products if the only incentive is a cleaner environment? Would you be willing to switch to a new technology (such as e-paper) that is beneficial to society if it costs more than the existing technology? Is it ethical for an industry or the government to mandate the use of new technologies if they create an additional cost or inconvenience to individuals?

    For this project, form an opinion about the ethical obligations individuals, businesses, and the government have with respect to the development and implementation of beneficial new technologies and be prepared to discuss your position (in class, via an online class discussion group, in a class chat room, or via a class blog, depending on your instructor's directions). You may also be asked to write a short paper expressing your opinion.

ETHICS IN ACTION

HW

5. **Assistive Computing** In addition to the conventional input and output hardware mentioned in the chapter, there are a variety of assistive input and output devices that physically challenged individuals can use to make computing easier and more efficient.

    For this project, select one type of disability, such as being blind, deaf, paraplegic, quadriplegic, or having the use of only one arm or hand. Research the hardware and software options that could be used with a new computer for someone with the selected disability. Make a list of potential limitations of any standard computer hardware and the assistive hardware and software that would be appropriate for this individual. Research each assistive option, comparing the ease of use, cost, and availability, and then prepare a recommendation for the best computer system for your selected hypothetical situation. Share your findings with the class in the form of a short presentation. The presentation should not exceed 10 minutes and should make use of one or more presentation aids, such as a whiteboard, handouts, or a computer-based slide presentation (your instructor may provide additional requirements). You may also be asked to submit a summary of the presentation to your instructor.

PRESENTATION/ DEMONSTRATION

6. **Should Printers Be Used to Print Body Parts?** As discussed in this chapter, researchers are looking to ink-jet printers and 3D printers as a means to create body parts for the future. Possibilities include replacement joints, blood vessels, skin, muscles, organs, and implants. Instead of ink, these printers print with living cells. It is looking like this technology will eventually be feasible, but do we want it to be? Possible advantages include quickly printing new skin on a burn victim's wound, printing new organs on demand when needed, and creating custom implants from the patient's cells so they won't be as easily rejected. But what about the ethical ramifications, such as selling manufactured body parts or surgeons adding extra body parts (such as an extra ear or arm) on demand for a fashion statement or for added productivity? What if replacing our failing organs as needed leads to virtual immortality—will we end up an overcrowded society of essentially mutants? Or are the potential benefits worth the risks?

    Pick a side on this issue, form an opinion and gather supporting evidence, and be prepared to discuss and defend your position in a classroom debate or in a 1–2 page paper, depending on your instructor's directions.

BALANCING ACT

Hardware

Courtesy Logitech

Logitech

Ali Moayer is a Senior Director at Logitech and the head of engineering for developing audio/video communications products for the Unified Communications (UC) market. He has worked on many innovative ideas and designs, many of which were patented. Ali has more than 30 years of engineering experience and holds a Bachelor of Science degree in Electrical Engineering and an MBA in Technology Management.

A conversation with ALI MOAYER

Senior Director of Engineering, Logitech

> *"... augmented reality technology in products such as Google Glass will transform the way we look at the world and interact with each other."*

My Background . . .

I have been curious about technology from my childhood. I studied engineering and technology management in college and then started my career developing office messaging and networking equipment. I am now a Senior Director of Engineering in the Logitech for Business (LFB) group. As part of my responsibilities, I am the head of engineering for developing audio/video communications products for the Unified Communications (UC) market; my group also develops webcams and security cameras for the electronics retail market. Throughout my career, my college background, together with my work experiences developing medical imaging instruments, video cameras, and a wide variety of computer peripherals, has helped me be successful in the computer hardware industry. I also believe that my ability to understand electronics and consumer needs has been a contributing factor in my success in developing some of the best-in-class products for the PC peripheral market.

It's Important to Know . . .

The importance of input/output devices. Interface devices used with computers, such as audio/video capture and playback control devices and human interface control devices like mice and touch screens, are essential for providing a good user experience. We will continue to see computer interfaces enhanced with voice and gesture recognition, as well as new interfaces evolving to enable the human-to-machine interface to be more natural and intuitive.

Hardware will continue to shrink in size while increasing in capabilities. Computation power and memory capacity in devices will continue to increase and hardware systems will have access to remote sensors and robots. In addition, expect to see products that accommodate organic shapes with forms that no longer have to be rigid.

Our interactions with smart devices will intensify. We will rely on smart devices to act as our intelligent personal assistant and we will start to expect much more from computers to relieve us from mundane tasks. In addition, augmented reality technology in products such as Google Glass will transform the way we look at the world and interact with each other. However, before wearable products become mainstream, the industry will need to break technology barriers in the areas of miniature electronics, very low energy devices, and wireless connectivity.

How I Use this Technology . . .

Like most people, I use computer systems for my personal life and, in fact, feel detached from our world if I don't have my smartphone next to me. I use audio/video communications tools, such as Skype and FaceTime, with my computing devices to enable me to have closer relationships with people around the world. I also use my smartphone to capture audio/video clips and pictures to share on social networking sites, as well as to read the latest news and conduct business over interactive Web sites. At home, I am starting to build electronic control systems that will be accessed with my phone to make my home smarter and more energy efficient, and I imagine that we will all have smart digital homes in the near future that will save us money and make our lives easier.

What the Future Holds ...

Electronic systems will continue to expand in many sectors, such as wearable electronics, mobile phones and personal computers, smart home and business appliances, robotics, and Internet servers. The intelligence and capabilities of these systems will grow rapidly and be challenged with being energy efficient, compact, and low cost. Audio, video, and control interfaces for home and business appliances will improve and Internet servers will provide analytic capabilities for making decisions and monitoring and controlling our environment, in addition to storing, searching, and exchanging data.

Another difference in the future will be in the intelligence and fluidity of the interactions between users and computers. The Internet initially provided access to stored data and services that were provided by large organizations. Now the majority of information is authored and shared by individuals but is still in a pre-recorded or stored form. Soon it will be common for people to interact with each other and with computer-generated artificial intelligence in real-time.

One ongoing risk for the future is privacy. Our personal information is now mostly in the form of digital records, and our lives are being tracked by electronic sensors and cameras all over the world. We all need to understand that our private data can be accessed easily by hackers and we should try our best to secure it with passwords, data encryption, and firewalls. We should also all be careful not to post sensitive information about our personal lives and our family members on social networking websites, and should become educated about the "social engineering" techniques that criminals are increasingly using. Unfortunately, hackers have become creative in manipulating people as the human interactions shift more toward electronic systems and we all should do what we can to protect ourselves.

My Advice to Students ...

Participate in as many hands-on projects or internship programs that your time allows. This will help you to learn valuable problem-solving techniques, as well as retain the knowledge that you gain in school.

> *"Soon it will be common for people to interact with each other and with computer-generated artificial intelligence in real-time."*

Discussion Question

Ali Moayer believes that we will rely on smart devices to act as our intelligent personal assistant and relieve us from mundane tasks in the near future. Think about the routine tasks that you need to do on a daily basis—which tasks could be performed by a smart device? Are there any tasks that you wouldn't feel comfortable trusting to that device? If so, what technological improvements would need to be made in order for you to assign those tasks to your device? Would a more natural and intuitive human-to-computer interface make a difference? Are there some routine tasks that you don't see ever being turned over to your computer? Be prepared to discuss your position (in class, via an online class discussion group, in a class chat room, or via a class blog, depending on your instructor's directions). You may also be asked to write a short paper expressing your opinion.

> For more information about Logitech, visit www.logitech.com.

Module
Software

In Chapter 1, we looked at the basic software concepts involved with starting up and using a computer. We continue that focus in this module, discussing in more depth both system software—the software used to run a computer—and application software—the software that performs the specific tasks users want to accomplish using a computer.

Chapter 5 focuses on system software and how it enables the hardware of a computer system to operate and to run application software. Chapter 6 discusses application software, including some important basic concepts and characteristics, as well as an overview of some of the most common types of application software used today—namely, word processing, spreadsheet, database, presentation graphics, and multimedia software.

in this module

"...the computer is becoming just a vessel to connect you to the Internet and your data."

For more comments from Guest Expert **Stephen Rose** of Microsoft, see the **Expert Insight on . . . Software** feature at the end of the module.

chapter 5

System Software: Operating Systems and Utility Programs

After completing this chapter, you will be able to do the following:

1. Understand the difference between system software and application software.

2. Explain the different functions of an operating system and discuss some ways that operating systems enhance processing efficiency.

3. List several ways in which operating systems differ from one another.

4. Name today's most widely used operating systems for personal computers and servers.

5. State several devices other than personal computers and servers that require an operating system and list one possible operating system for each type of device.

6. Discuss the role of utility programs and outline several tasks that these programs perform.

7. Describe what the operating systems of the future might be like.

OVERVIEW

As you already know, all computers require software in order to operate and perform basic tasks. For instance, software is needed to translate your commands into a form the computer can understand, to open and close other software programs, to manage your stored files, and to locate and set up new hardware as it is added to a computer. The type of software used to perform these tasks is system software—the focus of this chapter. System software runs in the background at all times, making it possible for you to use your computer.

We begin this chapter by looking at the difference between system software and application software. System software, the primary topic of this chapter, is usually divided into two categories: operating systems and utility programs. First, we examine the operating system—the primary component of system software. We discuss the functions of and general differences between operating systems, and then we explore the specific operating systems most widely used today. Next, we look at utility programs. Utility programs typically perform support functions for the operating system, such as allowing you to manage your files, perform maintenance on your computer, check your computer for viruses, or uninstall a program you no longer want on your computer. Chapter 5 closes with a look at what the future of operating systems may hold. ∎

SYSTEM SOFTWARE VS. APPLICATION SOFTWARE

Computers run two types of software: system software and application software.

➤ **System software** consists of the operating system and utility programs that control your computer and allow you to use it. These programs enable the computer to boot, to launch application programs, and to facilitate important jobs, such as transferring files from one storage medium to another, configuring your computer to work with the hardware connected to it, connecting your computer to a network, managing files on your hard drive, and protecting your computer from unauthorized use.

➤ **Application software** includes all the programs that allow you to perform specific tasks on your computer, such as writing a letter, preparing an invoice, viewing a Web page, listening to a music file, checking the inventory of a particular product, playing a game, preparing financial statements, designing a home, and so forth. Application software is discussed in detail in Chapter 6.

In practice, the difference between system and application software is not always straightforward. Some programs, such as those used to burn DVDs, were originally viewed as utility programs. Today, these programs typically contain a variety of additional

---

>**System software.** Programs, such as the operating system, that control the operation of a computer and its devices, as well as enable application software to run on the computer. >**Application software.** Programs that enable users to perform specific tasks on a computer, such as writing a letter or playing a game.

features, such as the ability to organize and play music and other media files, transfer videos and digital photos to a computer, edit videos and photos, create DVD movies, copy CDs and DVDs, and create slide shows. Consequently, these programs now fit the definition of application software more closely. On the other hand, system software today typically contains several application software components. For example, the *Microsoft Windows* operating system includes a variety of application programs including a Web browser, a calculator, a calendar program, a painting program, a media player, a movie making program, an instant messaging program, and a text editing program. A program's classification as system or application software usually depends on the principal function of the program, and the distinction between the two categories is not always clear cut.

THE OPERATING SYSTEM

A computer's **operating system** is a collection of programs that manage and coordinate the activities taking place within the computer and it is the most critical piece of software installed on the computer. The operating system boots the computer, launches application software, and ensures that all actions requested by a user are valid and processed in an orderly fashion. For example, when you issue the command for your computer to store a document on your hard drive, the operating system must perform the following steps: 1) make sure that the specified hard drive exists, 2) verify that there is adequate space on the hard drive to store the document and then store the document in that location, and 3) update the hard drive's directory with the filename and disk location for that file so that the document can be retrieved again when needed. In addition to managing all of the resources associated with your local computer, the operating system also facilitates connections to the Internet and other networks.

In general, the operating system serves as an intermediary between the user and the computer, as well as between application programs and the computer system's hardware (see Figure 5-1). Without an operating system, no other program can run, and the computer cannot function. Many tasks performed by the operating system, however, go unnoticed by the user because the operating system works in the background much of the time.

Functions of an Operating System

Operating systems have a wide range of functions—some of the most important are discussed next.

FIGURE 5-1
The intermediary role of the operating system.

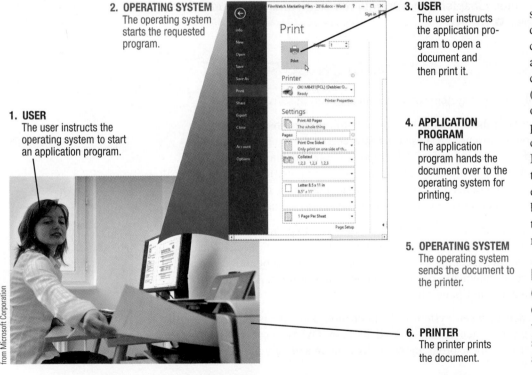

1. USER
The user instructs the operating system to start an application program.

2. OPERATING SYSTEM
The operating system starts the requested program.

3. USER
The user instructs the application program to open a document and then print it.

4. APPLICATION PROGRAM
The application program hands the document over to the operating system for printing.

5. OPERATING SYSTEM
The operating system sends the document to the printer.

6. PRINTER
The printer prints the document.

© Martin Novak/Shutterstock.com; Used with permission from Microsoft Corporation

>**Operating system.** The main component of system software that enables a computer to operate, manage its activities and the resources under its control, run application programs, and interface with the user.

Interfacing with Users

As Figure 5-1 illustrates, one of the principal roles of every operating system is to translate user instructions into a form the computer can understand. It also translates any feedback from hardware—such as a signal that the printer has run out of paper or that a new hardware device has been connected to the computer—into a form that the user can understand. The means by which an operating system or any other program interacts with the user is called the *user interface*; user interfaces can be *text-based* or *graphics-based*, as discussed in more detail shortly. Most, but not all, operating systems today use a *graphical user interface* (*GUI*).

Booting the Computer

As discussed in Chapter 1, the first task your operating system performs when you power up your computer is to *boot* the computer. During the boot process, the essential portion, or core, of the operating system (called the **kernel**) is loaded into memory. The kernel remains in memory the entire time the computer is on so that it is always available; other parts of the operating system are retrieved from the hard drive and loaded into memory when they are needed. Before the boot process ends, the operating system determines the hardware devices that are connected to the computer and configured properly, and it reads an opening batch of instructions. These startup instructions (which the user can customize to some extent when necessary) assign tasks for the operating system to carry out each time the computer boots, such as prompting the user to sign in to an instant messaging program or launching a security program to run continually in the background to detect possible threats.

Typically, many programs are running in the background all the time, even before the user launches any application software. The Windows *Task Manager* (shown in Figure 5-2) lists all the programs and *processes* (program tasks) currently running on a computer. Some of these programs are *startup* programs that are launched automatically by the operating system during the boot process; regardless of how programs are launched, they all consume memory and processing power. In Windows, users can see some of the application programs that are running in the background by looking at the icons in the *notification area* (see the bottom screen in Figure 5-2). To close one of these programs, right-click its icon and select the appropriate option. To view the programs that will run each time the computer boots or to remove a program from this *startup list*, Windows 8 users can use the *Startup* tab on the Task Manager, as shown in Figure 5-2 (with older versions of Windows, use the *msconfig* command to open the *Microsoft System Configuration Utility*). To avoid creating a problem with your computer, however, do not disable a program from the startup list without knowing absolutely what the program does and that it can be safely disabled. Other system configuration information is stored in the *Windows registry* files, which should be modified only by the Windows program itself or by advanced Windows users.

FIGURE 5-2
Windows Task Manager. Shows all running programs and processes and allows you to specify startup programs.

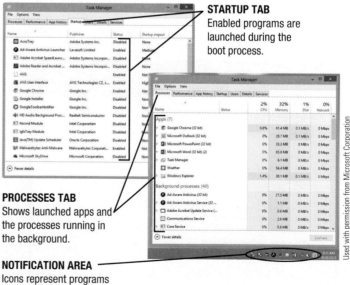

STARTUP TAB
Enabled programs are launched during the boot process.

PROCESSES TAB
Shows launched apps and the processes running in the background.

NOTIFICATION AREA
Icons represent programs running in the background.

Used with permission from Microsoft Corporation

>**Kernel.** The essential portion, or core, of an operating system.

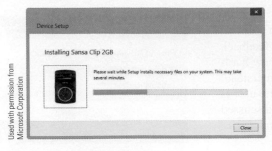

FIGURE 5-3

Finding new hardware. Most operating systems are designed to detect new hardware and to try to configure it automatically.

Configuring Devices

The operating system also configures all devices connected to a computer. Small programs called **device drivers** (or simply **drivers**) are used to communicate with peripheral devices, such as monitors, printers, portable storage devices, and keyboards. Most operating systems today include the drivers needed for the most common peripheral devices. In addition, drivers often come on a CD packaged with the peripheral device or they can be downloaded from the manufacturer's Web site. Most operating systems today look for and recognize new devices each time the computer boots. If a new device is found, the operating system typically tries to install the appropriate driver automatically in order to get the new hardware ready to use (see Figure 5-3)—a feature called *Plug and Play*. Because USB and FireWire devices can be connected to a computer when the computer is running, those devices are recognized and configured, as needed, each time they are plugged in to the computer.

Once a device and its driver have been installed properly, they usually work fine. If the device driver file is deleted, becomes *corrupted*, or has a conflict with another piece of software, then the device will no longer work. Usually, the operating system detects problems like this during the boot process and notifies the user, and then tries to reinstall the driver automatically. If the operating system is unable to correct the problem, the user can reinstall the driver manually. You may also need to update or reinstall some device drivers if you *upgrade* your operating system to a newer version. To keep your system up to date, many operating systems have an option to check for operating system updates automatically—including updated driver files—on a regular basis. Enabling these *automatic updates* is a good idea to keep your system running smoothly and protected from new threats (like the *computer viruses* discussed in Chapter 9).

FIGURE 5-4

Network connections. Most operating systems can repair network connections when needed.

Managing Network Connections

The operating system is also in charge of managing your network connections, such as a wired connection to a home or office network or wireless connections at home, school, work, or on the go. For instance, as you move into range of a wireless network, the operating system will notify you that a new wireless network is available and then either connect your device to that network or wait for your instruction to connect to the network, depending on your device's wireless network settings. If at any time you lose a network connection, the operating system can try to fix it, such as by resetting your device's network adapter (see Figure 5-4). If your device connects to a secure network, the operating system will prompt you for the appropriate password when needed and then connect your device to the network after verifying the password is correct.

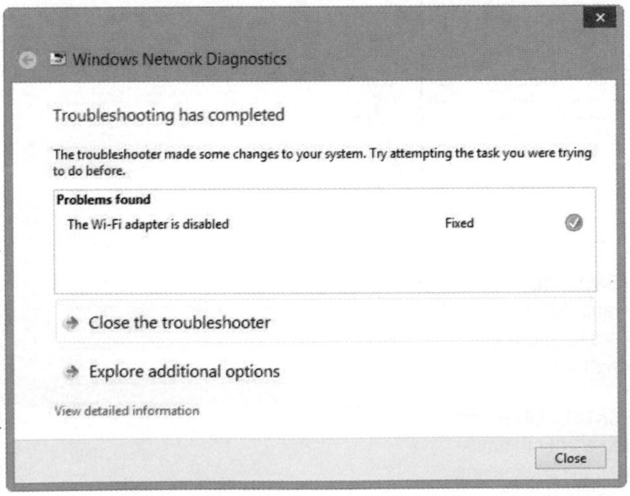

Managing and Monitoring Resources and Jobs

As you work on your computer, the operating system continuously manages your computer's resources (such as software, disk space, and memory) and makes them available to devices and programs when they are needed. If a problem occurs—such as a program stops functioning or too many programs are open for the amount of memory installed in the computer—the operating system notifies the user and tries to correct the problem, often by closing the offending program. If the problem cannot be corrected by the operating system, then the user typically needs to reboot the computer.

>**Device driver.** A program that enables an operating system to communicate with a specific hardware device; often referred to simply as a **driver**.

As part of managing system resources, the operating system schedules jobs (such as documents to be printed or files to be retrieved from a hard drive) to be performed using those resources. *Scheduling routines* in the operating system determine the order in which jobs are carried out, as well as which commands get executed first if the user is working with more than one program at one time or if the computer (such as a server or mainframe) supports multiple users.

File Management

Another important task that the operating system performs is *file management*—keeping track of the files stored on a computer so that they can be retrieved when needed. As discussed in Chapter 3, you can organize the files on a storage medium into folders to simplify file management. Usually the operating system files are stored inside one folder (such as a *Windows* folder), and each application program is stored in its own separate folder inside a main programs folder (such as *Program Files*). Other folders designed for storing data files are typically created by the operating system for each user (such as *My Documents*, *My Music*, and *My Pictures* folders); individuals may create additional folders, as desired, to keep their files organized. Folders can contain both files and other folders (called *subfolders*).

Files and folders are usually viewed in a hierarchical format; the top of the hierarchy for any storage medium is called the *root directory* (such as C: for the root directory of the hard drive C shown in Figure 5-5). The root directory typically contains both files and folders. To access a file, you generally navigate to the folder containing that file by opening the appropriate drive, folder, and subfolders. Alternatively, you can specify the *path* to a file's exact location. For example, as Figure 5-5 shows, the path

C:\My Documents\Letters\Mary

leads through the root directory of the C drive and the *My Documents* and *Letters* folders to a file named *Mary*. A similar path can also be used to access the files *John* and *Bill*. As discussed in Chapter 3, you specify a filename for each file when you initially save the file on a storage medium; there can be only one file with the exact same filename in any particular folder on a storage medium.

Filename rules vary with each operating system. For instance, Windows supports filenames that are from 1 to 260 characters long (the length includes the entire path to the file's location) and may include numbers, letters, spaces, and any special characters except \ / : * ? " < > and |. Filenames typically include a *file extension* (usually three or four characters preceded by a period) at the end of the filename, which indicates the type of file (see Figure 5-6). File extensions are automatically added to a filename by the program in which that file was created, although sometimes the user may have a choice of file extensions supported by a program.

File extensions should not be changed by the user because the operating system uses them to identify the program that should be used to open the file. For instance, if you issue a command to open a file named *Letter to Mom.docx*, the file will open using the Microsoft Word program (assuming a recent version of that program is

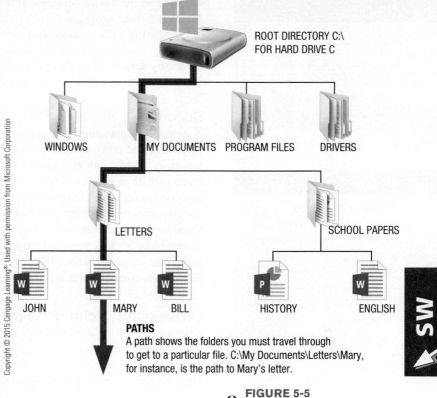

ROOT DIRECTORY C:\
FOR HARD DRIVE C

WINDOWS   MY DOCUMENTS   PROGRAM FILES   DRIVERS

LETTERS   SCHOOL PAPERS

JOHN   MARY   BILL   HISTORY   ENGLISH

PATHS
A path shows the folders you must travel through to get to a particular file. C:\My Documents\Letters\Mary, for instance, is the path to Mary's letter.

FIGURE 5-5
A sample hard drive organization.

FIGURE 5-6
Common file extensions.

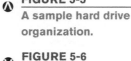

DOCUMENTS

.doc .docx .txt .rtf .htm .html

.mhtml .xml .xls .xlsx .mdb. .accdb

.ppt .pptx .pdf .sxc .sxi .odf

PROGRAMS

.com .exe

GRAPHICS

.bmp .tif .tiff .jpg .jpe .jpeg .eps

.gif .png .pcx .svg .dib

AUDIO

.wav .au .mp3 .snd .aiff .midi

.aac .wma .ra .m4a

VIDEO

.mpg .mp2 .mp4 .mpe .mov .avi

.rm .wmv .wm .asf

COMPRESSED FILES

.zip .sit .sitx .tar

installed on the device being used) because the *.docx* file extension is associated with the Microsoft Word program. Files can be opened, as well as moved, copied, renamed, and deleted, using a *file management program* such as *File Explorer*. You may not be able to see file extensions in your file management program, however, because they are usually hidden by default. The File Explorer file management program and other utilities typically included in an operating system are discussed near the end of this chapter.

Security

A computer's operating system can use *passwords*, *biometric characteristics* (such as fingerprints), and other security procedures to limit access to the computer and other system resources to only authorized users. Most operating systems also include other security features, such as an integrated *firewall* to protect against unauthorized access via the Internet or an option to download and install *security patches* (small program updates that correct known security problems) automatically from the operating system's manufacturer on a regular basis. Operating system passwords can also be used to ensure that *administrative level* operating system tasks (such as installing programs or changing system settings) are performed only by authorized users. Passwords, biometrics, and other security issues related to networks and the Internet are discussed in detail in Chapter 9.

Processing Techniques for Increased Efficiency

Operating systems often utilize various processing techniques in order to operate more efficiently and increase the amount of processing the computer can perform in any given time period. Some of the techniques most commonly used by operating systems to increase efficiency are discussed in the next few sections.

Multitasking

Multitasking refers to the ability of an operating system to have more than one program (also called a *task*) open at one time. For example, multitasking allows a user to edit a spreadsheet file in one window while loading a Web page in another window or to retrieve new e-mail messages in one window while a word processing document is open in another window. Without the ability to multitask, an operating system would require the user to close one program before opening another program. Virtually all computer operating systems support multitasking (operating systems for mobile devices tend to have more limited multitasking).

Although multitasking enables a user to work with multiple programs at one time, a single CPU core cannot execute more than one task at one time (unless Intel's Hyper-Threading Technology or another technology that allows a single core to function as two cores is used, as discussed in Chapter 2). Consequently, the CPU rotates between processing tasks, but it works so quickly that to the user it appears as though all programs are executing at the same time. However, CPUs with multiples cores can execute multiple tasks at one time, as discussed shortly.

Multithreading

A *thread* is a sequence of instructions within a program that is independent of other threads, such as spell checking, printing, and opening documents in a word processing program. Operating systems that support *multithreading* have the ability to rotate between multiple threads (similar to the way multitasking can rotate between multiple programs) so that processing is completed faster and more efficiently, even though only one thread is executed by a single core at one time. Most operating systems support multithreading.

> **Multitasking.** The capability of an operating system to run more than one program at one time.

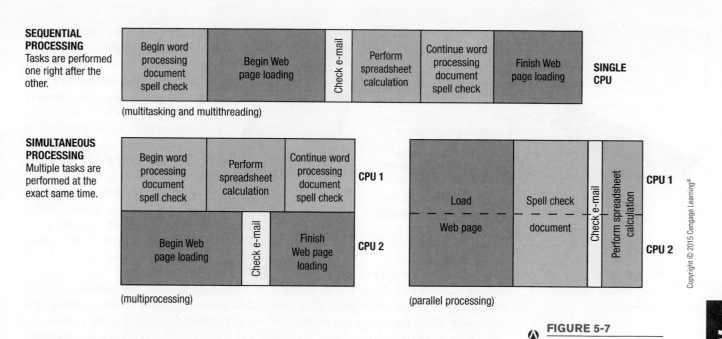

SEQUENTIAL PROCESSING
Tasks are performed one right after the other.

(multitasking and multithreading)

SIMULTANEOUS PROCESSING
Multiple tasks are performed at the exact same time.

(multiprocessing)

(parallel processing)

FIGURE 5-7
Sequential vs. simultaneous processing.

Multiprocessing and Parallel Processing

As discussed in Chapter 2, both multiprocessing and parallel processing involve using two or more CPUs (or multiple cores in a single CPU) in one computer to perform work more efficiently. The primary difference between these two techniques is that, with multiprocessing, each CPU or core typically works on a different job; with parallel processing, the CPUs or cores usually work together to complete one job more quickly. In either case, tasks are performed *simultaneously* (at exactly the same time); in contrast, multitasking and multithreading use a single CPU or core and process tasks *sequentially* (by rotating through tasks, as discussed previously). Figure 5-7 illustrates the difference between simultaneous and sequential processing, using tasks typical of a desktop computer.

Multiprocessing is supported by most operating systems and is used with personal computers that have multi-core CPUs (as discussed in Chapter 2), as well as with servers and mainframe computers that have multi-core CPUs and/or multiple CPUs. Parallel processing is used most often with supercomputers.

Memory Management

Because many of today's programs are memory intensive, good *memory management*, which involves optimizing the use of main memory (RAM), can help speed up processing. The operating system allocates RAM to programs as needed and then reclaims that memory when the program is closed. Because each additional running program or open window consumes memory, users can also help with memory management by limiting the number of startup programs to only the ones that are absolutely necessary, as well as by closing windows when they are no longer needed.

One memory-management technique frequently used by operating systems is **virtual memory**, which uses a portion of the computer's hard drive as additional RAM. All programs and data located in RAM are divided into fixed-length *pages* or variable-length *segments*, depending on the operating system being used. When the amount of RAM

TIP

Although memory used by a program or process is supposed to be released when it is no longer needed, this does not always happen. Referred to as a *memory leak*, this problem can cause your computer to run out of memory temporarily. When this occurs, reboot your computer to refresh its RAM.

> **Virtual memory.** A memory-management technique that uses hard drive space as additional RAM.

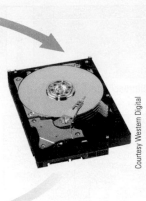

1. Pages of programs or data are copied from RAM to the virtual memory area of the hard drive.

2. Pages are copied back to RAM as they are needed for processing.

3. As more room in RAM is needed, pages are copied to virtual memory and then deleted from RAM.

4. The swapping process continues until the program finishes executing.

FIGURE 5-8
How virtual memory works.

required exceeds the amount of RAM available, the operating system moves pages from RAM to the virtual memory area of the hard drive (this area is called the *page file* or *swap file*). Consequently, as a program is executed, some of the program may be stored in RAM and some in virtual memory. As RAM gets full, pages are moved to virtual memory, and as pages stored in virtual memory are required, they are retrieved from virtual memory and moved to RAM (see Figure 5-8). This *paging* or *swapping* process continues until the program finishes executing. Virtual memory allows you to use more memory than is physically available on your computer, but using virtual memory is slower than just using RAM. Most operating systems today allow the user to specify the total amount of hard drive space to be used for virtual memory. Users with computers running recent versions of Windows can also use flash memory media (such as a USB flash drive) in conjunction with Windows' *ReadyBoost* feature to add more usable memory to a computer, which then is available for virtual memory.

Buffering and Spooling

Some input and output devices are exceedingly slow, compared to today's CPUs. If the CPU had to wait for these slower devices to finish their work, the computer system would experience a horrendous bottleneck. For example, suppose a user sends a 100-page document to the printer. Assuming the printer can output 20 pages per minute, it would take 5 minutes for the document to finish printing. If the CPU had to wait for the print job to be completed before performing other tasks, the computer would be tied up for 5 minutes.

To avoid this problem, most operating systems use *buffering* and *spooling*. A **buffer** is an area in RAM or on the hard drive designated to hold data that is used by different hardware devices or programs that may operate at different speeds. For instance, a *keyboard buffer* stores characters as they are entered via the keyboard, and a *print buffer* stores documents that are waiting to be printed. The process of placing items in a buffer so they can be retrieved by the appropriate device when needed is called **buffering** or **spooling**. The most common use of buffering and spooling is *print spooling*. Print spooling allows multiple documents to be sent to the printer at one time and to print, one after the other, in the background while the computer and user are performing other tasks. The documents waiting to be printed are said to be in a *print queue*, which designates the order the documents will be printed. While in the print queue, most operating systems allow the user to cancel print jobs and pause the printer (see Figure 5-9); some also allow the user to prioritize the documents in the print queue.

FIGURE 5-9
A print queue.

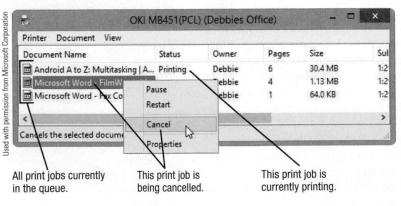

All print jobs currently in the queue.

This print job is being cancelled.

This print job is currently printing.

>**Buffer.** An area in RAM or on the hard drive designated to hold data that is used by different hardware devices or programs that may operate at different speeds. >**Buffering.** The process of placing items in a buffer so the appropriate device can retrieve them when needed; also called **spooling**, particularly when used in conjunction with a printer.

Although originally used primarily for keyboard input and print jobs, most computers and operating systems today use several other buffers to speed up operations. For instance, it is common today for computers to use buffers to assist in redisplaying images on the screen and to temporarily store data that is in the process of being burned onto a CD or DVD, or being streamed from the Internet (such as videos and other multimedia content).

Differences Among Operating Systems

There are different types of operating systems available to meet different needs. Some of the major distinctions among operating systems include the type of user interface utilized, the category of device the operating system will be used with, and the type of processing the operating system is designed for.

Command Line vs. Graphical User Interface

As mentioned earlier in this chapter, a user interface is the manner in which an operating system interacts with its users. Most operating systems today use a **graphical user interface** (**GUI**). The older *DOS* operating system and some versions of the *UNIX* and *Linux* operating systems use a **command line interface** (see Figure 5-10), although graphical versions of UNIX and Linux are available. Command line interfaces require users to input commands using the keyboard; graphical user interfaces allow the user to issue commands by selecting icons, buttons, menu items, and other graphical objects—typically with a mouse, stylus, or finger.

Categories of Operating Systems

Operating systems are typically designed for a particular type of device. For example, operating systems used with personal computers are typically referred to as **personal operating systems** (also called **desktop operating systems**) and they are designed to be installed on a single computer. In contrast, **server operating systems** (also called **network operating systems**) are designed to be installed on a network server to grant multiple users access to a network and its resources. Each computer on a network has its own personal operating system installed (just as with a stand-alone computer) and that operating system controls the activity on that computer, while the server operating system controls access to network resources. Computers on a network may also need special *client* software to access the network and issue requests to the server.

Server operating systems are typically used with large networks, such as those found in businesses and schools. Home networks don't require a server operating system, though some home network devices (such as a media server or NAS) come with networking software designed for that device. For both large and home networks, network resources (such as a shared network hard drive or printer) generally look like *local* (non-network) resources to any device that is connected to the network. For example, you will see a network hard drive listed with its own identifying letter (such as F or G) along with the drives located on your computer, and you will see a network printer included in your list of available printers whenever you open a Print dialog box. If you do not log on to

FIGURE 5-10
Command line vs. graphical user interfaces.

COMMAND LINE INTERFACE
Commands are entered using the keyboard.

GRAPHICAL USER INTERFACE
Objects (such as icons, buttons, menus, and tiles) are selected with the mouse, pen, or finger to issue commands to the computer.

Used with permission from Microsoft Corporation

Windows 8: Windows® is a registered trademark of Microsoft Corporation. © 2012 Microsoft.

>**Graphical user interface (GUI).** A graphically based interface that allows a user to communicate instructions to the computer easily.
>**Command line interface.** A user interface that requires the user to communicate instructions to the computer via typed commands. >**Personal operating system.** A type of operating system designed to be installed on a single personal computer; also called a **desktop operating system**.
>**Server operating system.** A type of operating system designed to be installed on a network server; also called a **network operating system**.

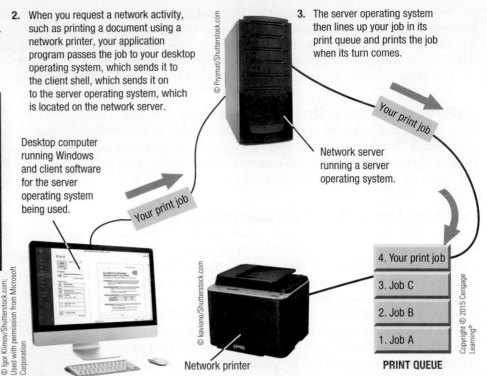

1. The client software provides a shell around your desktop operating system. The shell program enables your computer to communicate with the server operating system, which is located on the network server.

2. When you request a network activity, such as printing a document using a network printer, your application program passes the job to your desktop operating system, which sends it to the client shell, which sends it on to the server operating system, which is located on the network server.

3. The server operating system then lines up your job in its print queue and prints the job when its turn comes.

Client shell

Desktop operating system

Application software

Your print job

Desktop computer running Windows and client software for the server operating system being used.

Your print job

Your print job

Network server running a server operating system.

Your print job

4. Your print job

3. Job C

2. Job B

1. Job A

PRINT QUEUE

Network printer

© Igor Klimov/Shutterstock.com; Used with permission from Microsoft Corporation

© kaviona/Shutterstock.com

© Pryzmat/Shutterstock.com

Copyright © 2015 Cengage Learning®

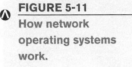
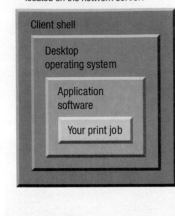

FIGURE 5-11
How network operating systems work.

the network or if the network is down, you cannot access network resources, such as to launch a program located on the network server, save a document to a network hard drive, print using a shared printer, or access the Internet via a shared Internet connection. However, you can still work locally on that computer, just as you would on a stand-alone computer. An overview of how a typical personal operating system and a server operating system interact on a business computer network is illustrated in Figure 5-11.

In addition to personal operating systems and server operating systems, there are **mobile operating systems** that are designed to be used with mobile phones and other mobile devices, and **embedded operating systems** that are built into consumer kiosks, cash registers, cars, consumer electronics, and other devices. Specific examples of personal, server, mobile, and embedded operating systems are covered later in this chapter.

The Types of Processors Supported

Most operating systems today are designed to be used with specific types of processors (such as mobile, desktop, or server processors), as well as with specific numbers of processors. In addition, most operating systems are designed for either 32-bit or 64-bit CPUs (most operating systems have a version for each). Because 64-bit processors can process up to twice as much data per clock cycle as 32-bit processors (depending on the extent to which the application being used supports 64-bit processing) and can address more than 4 GB of RAM, using a 64-bit operating system with a 64-bit computer can help to speed up processing. Operating systems that support 64-bit CPUs often include other architectural improvements that together may result in a more efficient operating system and, consequently, faster operations. Details about Windows, Mac OS, Linux, and other operating systems are discussed shortly.

>**Mobile operating system.** A type of operating system used with mobile phones and other mobile devices. >**Embedded operating system.** A type of operating system embedded into devices, such as cars and consumer devices.

TREND

Internet Monitors

The dilemma: How to offer visitors and customers easy-to-use entertainment and Web browsing without compromising your business's network or computers? The answer: *Internet monitors.*

There are many locations—such as lobbies, waiting rooms, hotels, airports, and restaurants—where it would be a beneficial service for the business to offer visitors and customers easy-to-use Web access. But the expense and hassle of setting up a computer for customers to use—and having to maintain that computer when someone changes the settings or the computer gets infected with malware—is too much for many businesses. The solution? New, locked-down, inexpensive, easy-to-set-up systems, such as Internet monitors.

Unlike conventional computers but similar to other *locked-down systems*, Internet monitors have restricted functionality; that is, users can only do what the system has been set up to allow them to do. While conventional computers can be locked down to make them safer for the general public to use, a number of new products are emerging that are designed specifically for this purpose. One example of an Internet monitor—essentially just a monitor that provides Internet access—is shown in the accompanying photo. Similar to an all-in-one computer, this device consists of just a monitor that also functions as a system unit. But the device is not a conventional computer. Instead, it contains a custom Linux-based operating system designed specifically for this device; the operating system displays the Home screen shown in the accompanying photo each time it boots or an app is closed.

Users select the app they want using a USB keyboard or mouse in order to listen to music, watch videos, browse the Web, or view photos (they can view their own content via the device's built-in USB ports and flash memory card reader). And the hosting business doesn't have to worry about users installing software on the device or changing the system settings because they can't. That makes "service with a smile" a lot easier to accomplish!

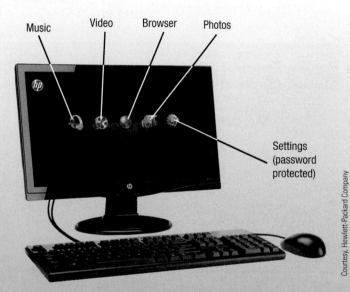

Users have just four apps available via the device's Home screen.

Courtesy, Hewlett-Packard Company

Support for Virtualization and Other Technologies

As new technologies or trends (such as new types of buses, virtualization, mobility, security concerns, power consumption concerns, touch and gesture input, and the move to cloud software) emerge, operating systems must be updated in order to support those new technologies or trends. For example, the latest version of Windows was created to support the touch and pen input used with mobile devices today, as well as support the keyboard and mouse input typically used with personal computers. On the other hand, as technologies become obsolete, operating system manufacturers need to decide when support for those technologies will cease. Alternatively, hardware manufacturers also need to respond to new technologies introduced by operating systems. For instance, because the latest versions of Windows and Mac OS support multi-touch input, a flurry of new devices that have touch screens and that support gesture input have been introduced. For a look at one new trend for businesses—*Internet monitors*—see the Trend box.

OPERATING SYSTEMS FOR PERSONAL COMPUTERS AND SERVERS

As previously discussed, many operating systems today are designed either for personal computers (such as desktop and notebook computers) or for network servers. The most widely used personal and server operating systems are discussed next. Mobile and embedded versions of these operating systems are discussed later in this chapter.

DOS

During the 1980s and early 1990s, **DOS (Disk Operating System)** was the dominant operating system for microcomputers. DOS traditionally used a command line interface, although later versions of DOS supported a menu-driven interface. There are two primary forms of DOS: *PC-DOS* and *MS-DOS*. PC-DOS was created originally for IBM PCs (and is owned by IBM), whereas MS-DOS was created for use with IBM-compatible PCs. Both versions were originally developed by Microsoft Corporation, but neither version is updated any longer. DOS is considered obsolete today because it does not utilize a graphical user interface and does not support modern processors and processing techniques. Some computers (such as computers running the Windows operating system), however, can still execute DOS commands and users can issue these commands using the *Command Prompt* window, as shown in Figure 5-12.

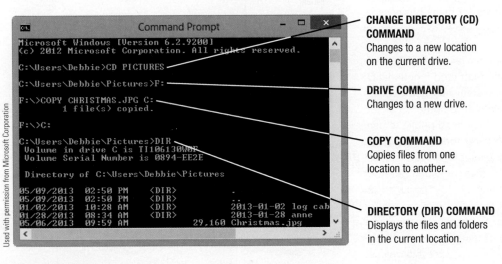

CHANGE DIRECTORY (CD) COMMAND
Changes to a new location on the current drive.

DRIVE COMMAND
Changes to a new drive.

COPY COMMAND
Copies files from one location to another.

DIRECTORY (DIR) COMMAND
Displays the files and folders in the current location.

FIGURE 5-12
DOS. Even though DOS has become technologically obsolete, Windows users can still issue DOS commands via the Command Prompt.

Windows

Microsoft Windows has been the predominant personal operating system for many years and still holds about 90% of the market. There have been many different versions of **Windows** over the years; the next few sections chronicle the main developments of this operating system.

Windows 1.0 Through Windows Vista

Microsoft created the original version of Windows—*Windows 1.0*—in 1985 in an effort to meet the needs of users frustrated by having to learn and use DOS commands. Windows 1.0 through *Windows 3.x* (*x* stands for the version number of the software, such as Windows 3.0, 3.1, or 3.11) were not, however, full-fledged operating systems. Instead, they were *operating environments* for the DOS operating system; that is, graphical shells that operated around the DOS operating system and were designed to make DOS easier to use.

In 1994, Microsoft announced that all versions of Windows after 3.11 would be full-fledged operating systems instead of just operating environments. The next three versions of Windows designed for personal computers were *Windows 95* (released in 1995), *Windows 98* (released in 1998), and *Windows Me* (*Millennium Edition*) (released in 2000). *Windows NT* (*New Technology*) was the first 32-bit version of Windows designed for high-end workstations and servers. It was built from the ground up using a different kernel than the other versions of Windows and was eventually replaced by *Windows 2000*. *Windows XP* replaced both Windows 2000 (for business use) and Windows Me (for home use). Throughout this progression of Windows releases, support for new hardware (such as DVD drives and USB devices), networking and the Internet, multimedia applications, and voice and pen input were included. While support for all of the early versions of Windows has been discontinued, Microsoft plans to support Windows XP until 2014.

Windows Vista replaced Windows XP. One of the most obvious initial changes in Windows Vista was the *Aero* interface, a visual graphical user interface that uses transparent windows and dynamic elements. Windows Vista also introduced the *Sidebar* feature that contains *gadgets*—small applications that are used to perform a variety of tasks, such as displaying weather information, a clock, a calendar, a calculator, and news headlines. Other features new to Vista included the *Windows Media Center* (which is used to access digital entertainment, such as recorded TV shows and downloaded music) and *Windows Speech Recognition* (which allows users to interact with their computers using their voice).

Windows 7

Windows 7, released in late 2009, is available in four main editions, including *Home Premium* (the primary version for home users) and *Professional* (the primary version for businesses). Windows 7 requires less memory and processing power than previous versions of Windows, and it is designed to start up and respond faster than Vista so it can run well on netbooks and media tablets.

The appearance of Windows 7 is similar to Windows Vista—many of the improvements in Windows 7 focus on making it faster and easier to use. For instance, you can now drag taskbar buttons to rearrange them in the order you prefer, and you can *pin* (lock) a program to the taskbar so it can be launched with a single click. In addition, you can preview thumbnails of all of an application's open windows by pointing to that program's taskbar button, and you can temporarily *peek* into that window by pointing to its taskbar thumbnail. You can also right-click a taskbar button (and some Start menu items) to bring up a *jump list* to show your most recent documents for that program (see Figure 5-13). Gadgets have moved from the Sidebar (as in Windows Vista) to the desktop in Windows 7 to free up the entire screen for documents and other content. Gadgets (and

SW

ASK THE EXPERT

Courtesy Strike Fighter Weapons School Pacific, NAS Lemoore

Tony Onorati, Former Naval Aviator and Former Commanding Officer, Strike Fighter Weapons School Pacific, NAS Lemoore

What computer experience is needed to be a U.S. Navy pilot?

While no computer experience is necessarily required to enter flight school, failure to have a solid knowledge of the Windows operating system will put the candidate well behind his/her contemporaries when they finally do reach the fleet as a pilot. All the tactical planning tools for preflight preparation, navigation, ordnance delivery, and mission planning, as well as all aircraft-specific publications, manuals, and training, are all computer based. For the FA-18 Hornet, all mission data is created on the computer, copied to a mission computer card, and plugged into the jet where it is downloaded into the aircraft's computer for use in flight. Becoming a naval aviator without computer skills is like entering flight school without ever having flown before—it can be done but it places you well behind the power curve.

LIBRARIES
Help users find related documents.

AERO INTERFACE
Windows are transparent and have dynamic elements.

GADGETS
Gadgets can be located on the desktop.

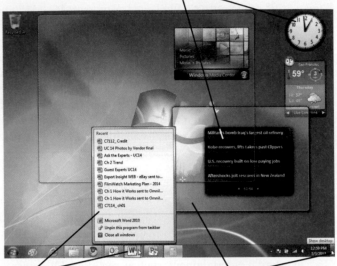

PROGRAM ICONS
Can be pinned to the taskbar.

TASKBAR BUTTONS
Can be rearranged by the user; pointing to a button displays *Live Thumbnails*.

JUMP LISTS
Right-click an icon to display the most recent documents for that program.

SHOW DESKTOP
Point to the Show Desktop button to make all windows temporarily transparent.

FIGURE 5-13
Windows 7.

other items located on the desktop) can be viewed easily by pointing to the *Show Desktop* button in the bottom far-right corner of the taskbar. This option temporarily makes all open windows transparent so items on the desktop are visible (as in the right image in Figure 5-13).

To help you better organize and locate your files, a new *Libraries* feature (shown in the left image in Figure 5-13) gives you virtual folders that display the content that you specify should be in that library (such as your documents, photos, music, or videos), regardless of where those files are physically located on your hard drive. In addition, Windows 7 includes a *HomeGroup* feature for improved home networking; one-click Wi-Fi connections; support for multi-touch, voice, and pen input; and improved accessory programs (such as a more versatile Calculator and a Paint program that uses the *Ribbon* interface found in recent versions of Microsoft Office).

Windows 8

The current version of Windows is **Windows 8**. According to Microsoft, it is a "reimaging of Windows, from the chip to the interface." It is designed to be used with a wide range of devices, from smartphones to desktop computers, as well as with or without a keyboard or mouse because it supports multi-touch input. The new Windows 8 *Start screen* (the initial screen you see when you boot your computer, though if you have a password you'll see the *lock screen* until you enter your password) uses **tiles** instead of the traditional Windows Start menu (see Figure 5-14). Tiles represent apps, Web sites, and more and are selected with the mouse or finger to launch the corresponding content.

>**Windows 8.** The current version of Windows. >**Tiles.** Components of the Windows 8 Start screen interface; tiles represent apps and are clicked to launch that app.

WINDOWS 8 START SCREEN

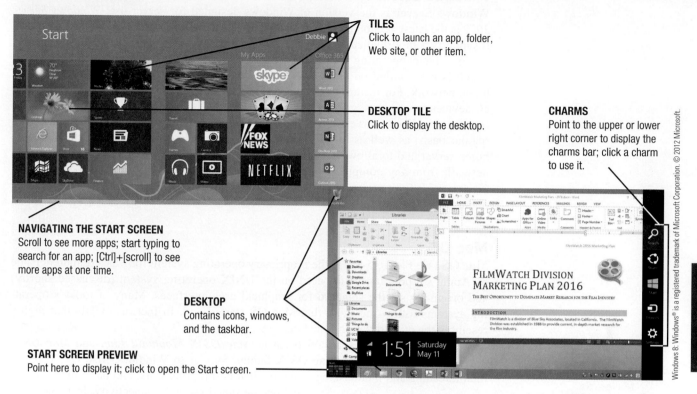

TILES
Click to launch an app, folder, Web site, or other item.

DESKTOP TILE
Click to display the desktop.

CHARMS
Point to the upper or lower right corner to display the charms bar; click a charm to use it.

NAVIGATING THE START SCREEN
Scroll to see more apps; start typing to search for an app; [Ctrl]+[scroll] to see more apps at one time.

DESKTOP
Contains icons, windows, and the taskbar.

START SCREEN PREVIEW
Point here to display it; click to open the Start screen.

Windows 8: Windows® is a registered trademark of Microsoft Corporation. © 2012 Microsoft.

WINDOWS 8 DESKTOP

Windows 8 apps run full-screen, though you can *snap* an app to run two apps side by side on the screen; conventional programs run inside windows that can be sized as in previous versions of Windows. Some tiles are *Live Tiles*, which show up-to-date information and notifications (such as social media activity, news, weather, and new e-mail messages). Both conventional programs and apps from the *Windows Store* are represented by tiles; users can pin and unpin apps to and from the Start screen, as well as rearrange and name groups of tiles. Although you have to launch programs via the Start screen, users can work with the more traditional Windows desktop if they prefer. To display the desktop from the Start screen, click the *Desktop tile*; to return to the Start screen, press the Windows key on the keyboard, click the bottom left corner of the screen, or use the *Start charm* (discussed shortly). The Windows 8 desktop works similar to previous versions of Windows, with a taskbar, taskbar buttons, and windows.

Another new feature of Windows 8 is *charms*. The *charms bar* (refer again to Figure 5-14) is displayed by pointing to the upper or lower right corner of the screen or by swiping in from the right edge of the screen. The *Search charm* allows you to search your computer, the Web, the Windows Store, and more for content related to your designated search terms. The *Share charm* allows to you to send links, photos, and other content to your friends from within a Windows 8 app. The *Start charm* takes you to the Start screen (or if you are on the Start screen, it takes you to your last app). The *Devices charm* helps you manage the devices that are connected to your computer. The *Settings charm* is used to configure settings (such as networks and speaker volume) and to shut down your PC. To easily launch other system management programs (such as the *Control Panel*, File Explorer, or the Command Prompt), point to the lower left corner of the screen to display the *Start screen preview* and then right-click.

Windows 8 has better graphics support and is faster overall than previous versions of Windows. Microsoft plans to release annual updates of Window; the initial update to Windows 8 (dubbed *Windows Blue*) became available in late 2013.

FIGURE 5-14
Windows 8.

TIP

There are both touch and mouse versions of Windows 8 commands. For instance, you can tap your finger or click the mouse on a tile to launch it, and you can slide your finger or scroll with the mouse to scroll through the tiles.

TIP

If you are using a recent version of Windows, use Libraries to give you access to common types of files (such as photos, documents, music, or videos), regardless of where those items are physically stored on your computer. Right-click a Library and select *Properties* to specify which folders on your computer that Library should include.

Windows Server and Windows Home Server

Windows Server is the version of Windows designed for server use. *Windows Server 2012* is the latest version and it is designed to be used with both small and large systems. It supports both virtualization and cloud computing.

A related operating system designed for home use is *Windows Home Server*, which is preinstalled on home server devices and designed to provide services for a home network. For instance, a home server can serve as a central storage location for all devices (computers, gaming consoles, portable digital media players, and so forth) in the home. Home servers also can be set up to back up all devices in the home on a regular basis, as well as to give users of the home network access to the data on the home server and to allow parents or other authorized individuals to control the home network from any computer via the Internet. The current version is *Windows Home Server 2011*; future versions will be incorporated into the *Windows Server Essentials* operating systems.

Mac OS

Mac OS (see Figure 5-15) is the proprietary operating system for Mac computers made by Apple Corporation. It is based on the UNIX operating system (discussed shortly) and originally set the standard for graphical user interfaces. Many of today's operating systems follow the trend that Mac OS started and, in fact, use GUIs that highly resemble the one used with Mac OS.

Recent versions of Mac OS (such as *Mac OS X Mountain Lion* and *Mac OS X Mavericks*) are part of the **Mac OS X** family. Similar to Windows, Mac OS X allows multithreading and multitasking, supports dual 64-bit processors, and has a high level of multimedia functions and connectivity. It includes the *Safari* Web browser, as well as a variety of built-in apps for e-mail, maps, messages, calendaring, videoconferencing, and more—additional apps are available at the *Mac App Store*.

Like previous versions of Mac OS X, Mavericks has a *Dock* to store your favorite apps (refer again to Figure 5-15); a *Notifications* feature that displays and lets you interact with notifications such as e-mail, messages, calendar alerts, Web site updates, and video calls, without leaving your current app; and a *Mission Control* feature that gives you a bird's-eye view of your open windows. In addition, Mac OS X Mavericks has a *Launchpad* used to launch apps, includes a *tagging* option to organize and find your files more easily, includes a *Keychain* feature to store and supply your Web site passwords, and can sync all your Apple devices via *iCloud*. It also supports multi-touch gestures; has a *Versions* feature, which saves the different versions of your documents as you work; and has a *Resume* feature to bring your programs back to how you left them when you restart your computer. **Mac OS X Server** is the server version of Mac OS X.

FIGURE 5-15
Mac OS X Mavericks.

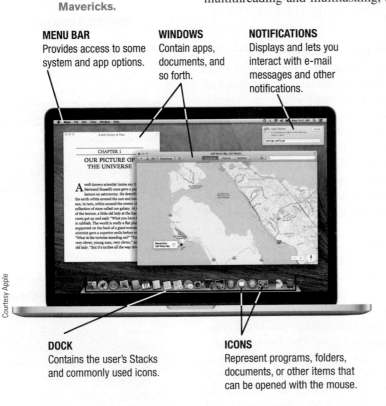

Courtesy Apple

MENU BAR
Provides access to some system and app options.

WINDOWS
Contain apps, documents, and so forth.

NOTIFICATIONS
Displays and lets you interact with e-mail messages and other notifications.

DOCK
Contains the user's Stacks and commonly used icons.

ICONS
Represent programs, folders, documents, or other items that can be opened with the mouse.

>**Windows Server.** The version of Windows designed for server use. >**Mac OS.** The operating system used on Apple computers; the most recent version is Mac OS X Mavericks. >**Mac OS X.** The family of current versions of Mac OS. >**Mac OS X Server.** The version of Mac OS X designed for server use.

UNIX

UNIX was originally developed in the late 1960s at AT&T Bell Laboratories as an operating system for midrange servers. UNIX is a multiuser, multitasking operating system. Computer systems ranging from microcomputers to mainframes can run UNIX, and it can support a variety of devices from different manufacturers. This flexibility gives UNIX an advantage over competing operating systems in some situations. However, UNIX is more expensive, requires a higher level of technical knowledge, and tends to be harder to install, maintain, and upgrade than most other commonly used operating systems.

There are many versions of UNIX available, as well as many other operating systems that are based on UNIX. These operating systems—such as Mac OS—are sometimes referred to as *UNIX flavors*. In fact, the term *UNIX*, which initially referred to the original UNIX operating system, has evolved to refer today to a group of similar operating systems based on UNIX. Many UNIX flavors are not compatible with each other, which creates some problems when a program written for one UNIX computer system is moved to another computer system running a different flavor of UNIX. To avoid this incompatibility problem, the *Open Group* open source consortium has overseen the development of the *Single UNIX Specification*—a standardized programming environment for UNIX applications—and certifies UNIX systems if they conform to the Single UNIX Specification. Both personal and server versions of UNIX-based operating systems are available.

Linux

Linux is an operating system developed by *Linus Torvalds* in 1991 when he was a student at the University of Helsinki in Finland. The operating system resembles UNIX but was developed independently from it. Linux was released to the public as *open source software*; that is, a program whose *source code* is available to the public and can be modified to improve it or to customize it to a particular application, as discussed in more detail in Chapter 6. Over the years, the number of Linux users has grown, and volunteer programmers from all over the world have collaborated to improve it, sharing their modified code with others over the Internet. Although Linux originally used a command line interface, most recent versions of Linux programs use a graphical user interface and operate similarly to other desktop operating systems, such as Windows and Mac OS. For instance, the version of Linux shown in Figure 5-16 (*Ubuntu*) has icons, menus, windows, and an app dock. Linux is widely available as a free download via the Internet; companies are also permitted to customize Linux and sell it as a retail product. Commercial Linux distributions come with maintenance and support materials (something that many of the free versions do not offer), making the commercial versions more attractive for corporate users.

Over the years, Linux has grown from an operating system used primarily by computer techies who disliked Microsoft to a widely accepted operating system with strong support from mainstream companies,

FIGURE 5-16

Linux. This version is Ubuntu, one of the most widely-used Linux operating systems.

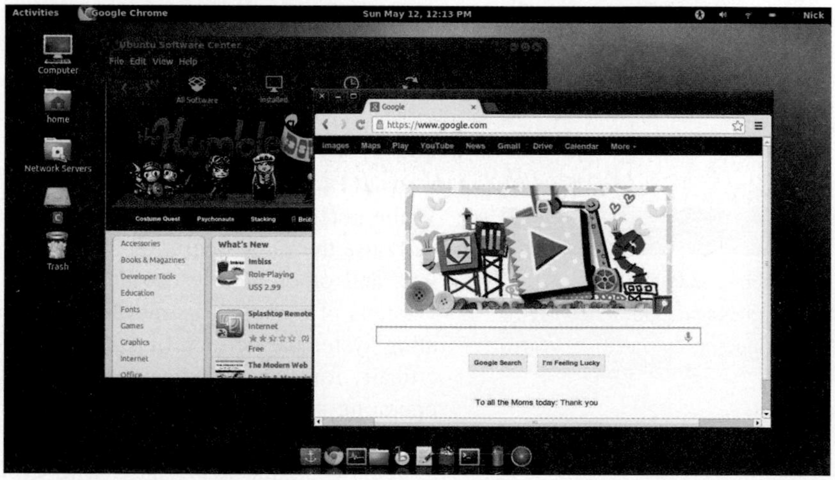

Courtesy Ubuntu; Courtesy Nick Morley

>**UNIX.** An operating system developed in the late 1960s for midrange servers and mainframes; many variations of this operating system are in use today. >**Linux.** An open source operating system that is available without charge over the Internet and is increasingly being used with mobile devices, personal computers, servers, mainframes, and supercomputers.

ASK THE EXPERT

Jim Zemlin, Executive Director, The Linux Foundation

Is there a downside to installing Linux on a personal computer?

We encourage people to install Linux on their personal computers. People who install Linux on their desktops learn by using Linux and grow to become the world's best Linux users and developers. Tinkering on your Linux desktop can translate into major breakthroughs for your personal computing experience and for the greater community at large; it can also lead to widespread recognition. And, even if you're not running Linux on your desktop today, you're using it every time you're using your browser because Linux runs Google, Amazon, Facebook, and most of the Internet. In addition, Chrome OS, Android, and other operating systems are based on Linux. We see no downside in sight and, furthermore, Linux offers you flexibility, customization, and choice on your desktop. This freedom is important, as your PC is your personal property and you should be able to use it exactly how you see fit. Linux allows you to do that.

such as IBM, NVIDIA, HP, Dell, and Novell. Linux is available in both personal and server versions; it is also widely used with mobile phones, as discussed shortly. The use of Linux with inexpensive personal computers is growing. In fact, one Linux-based operating system (*Android*) is widely used with media tablets and other mobile devices, as discussed shortly.

One reason individuals and organizations are switching to Linux and other open source software is cost. Typically, using the Linux operating system and a free or low-cost office suite, Web browser, and e-mail program can save several hundreds of dollars per computer. Other reasons include the ability to customize the user interface and to directly control the computer much more than is possible with Windows and OS X. In addition, Linux computers can run faster than Windows and OS X, due to Linux's much lower hardware requirements. For example, the Ubuntu version of Linux shown in Figure 5-16 requires only 64 MB of RAM and 5 GB of hard drive space versus the 1 GB of RAM and 16 GB of hard drive space required by Windows 8.

Chrome OS

Chrome OS is the first *cloud operating system*; that is, an operating system designed for devices that will be used entirely online. Chrome OS is essentially the Chrome Web browser redesigned to run a computer, in addition to accessing Web resources. It replaces traditional desktop operating systems like Windows but it is currently only available preinstalled on Chrome devices, such as *Chromebooks*.

> **TIP**
>
> Most mobile operating systems today are designed for touch screen input.

OPERATING SYSTEMS FOR MOBILE DEVICES

While notebook, hybrid notebook-tablets, and other portable personal computers typically use the same operating systems as desktop computers, mobile phones, media tablets, and other mobile devices usually use mobile operating systems—either mobile versions of personal operating systems (such as Windows 8 or Linux) or special operating systems (such as *Android, Apple iOS,* or *BlackBerry OS*) that are designed specifically for mobile devices. However, the current trend with both Microsoft and Apple operating systems is to make computers and mobile devices running their respective operating systems work more seamlessly together. There are also embedded operating systems designed to be used with everyday objects, such as home appliances, gaming consoles, digital cameras, e-readers, digital photo frames, ATMs, toys, watches, GPS systems, home medical devices, voting terminals, and cars (for a look at some of the features you may soon use in *smart cars*, see the Technology and You box). Most users select a mobile phone by considering the mobile provider, hardware, and features

TECHNOLOGY AND YOU

Smart Cars

Computers have been integrated into cars for years to perform specific tasks, such as assisting with gear shifting and braking. Lately, however, the use of computers in cars has skyrocketed because they are being used to add additional convenience and safety to the driving experience. Some features, such as GPS navigation systems and smart air bag systems that adjust the deployment of an air bag based on the weight of the occupant, are fairly standard today. Integrated *infotainment systems* that use Bluetooth and USB ports to tie mobile phones and portable digital media players to the car stereo system, as well as to steering wheel and voice control systems, are also now available. Some other new and emerging trends in smart cars are discussed next.

> *Self-driving systems*—use sensors, radar, and video cameras to drive the car via an autopilot system; prototypes are currently being demonstrated and self-driving vehicles are expected to be on the market by 2020.

> *Self-parking/parking assist systems*—use cameras and/or sensors to assist in parallel parking; the onboard computer completely controls the car's steering wheel during the parking process and instructs the driver when any action (such as changing gears) is needed in order to park the car correctly. Systems are currently in the prototype stage that enable drivers to control the parking system via a mobile app in order to have the car park itself after the passengers have left the vehicle or to have it pull out of a parking space to pick up its passengers (see the accompanying photo).

> *Lane departure systems*—use cameras to view the markings on the road and vibrate the steering wheel if the car begins to veer out of its lane.

> *Drowsiness detection systems*—use cameras to evaluate the driver's blinking pattern and eyelid movements and vibrate the seat or otherwise alert the driver if the driver becomes drowsy.

> *Blind spot detection systems*—use cameras mounted on the car's side mirrors to detect vehicles in the driver's blind spot and display a warning light near the mirror to notify the driver that something is in the blind spot (shown in Figure 1-12 in Chapter 1).

> *Adaptive cruise control and distance alert systems*—use a radar system installed on the front of the car to detect the speed and distance of the vehicle ahead of it, and then automatically decrease or increase the speed of the car to maintain a safe distance from that vehicle.

> *Windshield displays*—project images from car instruments, GPS systems, and infotainment systems to enable the driver to see instrument readings, maps, incoming calls, and more without looking away from the windshield; some systems can also read speed limit signs and display that information (along with notifications, such as excessive speed for the current conditions).

> *Collision warning and auto brake systems*—use radar and camera systems installed on the front of the car to warn the driver when they are too close to the car in front of them; if a collision is imminent, the brakes are automatically activated at that point. Some systems can detect pedestrians as well as other vehicles.

> *Keyless entry and ignition systems*—use the owner's fingerprint or a key fob to unlock and start the car; mobile phone applications that perform these tasks are beginning to become available.

> *Distraction-prevention systems*—delay or prevent mobile phone calls and other distractions while the car is in motion or during intense steering, braking, or acceleration, depending on the settings.

One of the biggest challenges for smart car technologies is the safe use of all the smart gadgets being incorporated into cars. The concern stems from studies consistently showing that distracted drivers are the cause of a vast majority of crashes. Voice-controlled dashboard components, mobile phones, and other devices help because they are hands-free, although studies have found that your risk of an accident requiring a trip to the hospital quadruples when you are talking on a mobile phone—hands-free or not.

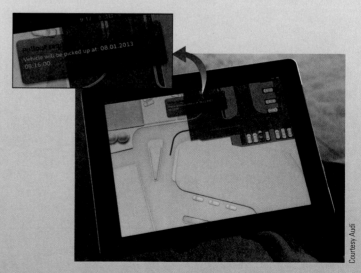

Courtesy Audi

Courtesy HTC; Windows 8: Windows® is a registered trademark of Microsoft Corporation. © 2012 Microsoft.

associated with the phone, instead of considering the operating system used. However, users should understand that the operating system used with a phone or other device determines some of the capabilities of the device, the interface used, and the applications that can run on that device. The most widely used mobile and embedded operating systems are discussed next.

Windows Phone 8, Windows RT, and Windows Embedded

There are both mobile and embedded versions of the Windows operating system, as discussed next.

FIGURE 5-17

Windows Phone 8 (left) and Windows RT (right).

Windows Phone 8 and Windows RT

Windows Phone is the latest version of Windows designed for smartphones; the current version, *Windows Phone 8*, is based on the Windows 8 operating system. There is also a version of Windows 8 designed for tablet use: **Windows RT**. Both Windows Phone 8 and Windows RT are optimized for mobile use but still have many of the same features as Windows 8 (see Figure 5-17). Windows Phone 8 and Windows RT devices already include some apps, such as Mail, Music, SkyDrive, and mobile versions of Microsoft Word, Excel, and PowerPoint; additional apps can be downloaded from the *Windows Phone Store* (for Windows Phone devices) or *Windows Store* (for Windows RT devices).

FIGURE 5-18

Android is used with both smartphones (left) and media tablets (right).

Windows Embedded

Windows Embedded is a family of operating systems based on Windows that is designed primarily for consumer and industrial devices that are not personal computers, such as cash registers, digital photo frames, GPS devices, ATM machines, medical devices, and robots. The current versions of Windows Embedded are based on Windows 8.

Courtesy HTC; Courtesy Samsung

Android

Android (see Figure 5-18) is a Linux-based operating system developed by the *Open Handset Alliance*, a group that includes Google and more than 30 technology and mobile companies. The most widely used mobile operating system in the United States, Android was built from the ground up with current mobile device capabilities in mind, which enables developers to create mobile applications that take full advantage of all the features a mobile device has to offer. It is an open platform, so

>**Windows Phone.** The version of Windows designed for mobile phones; the current version is *Windows Phone 8*. >**Windows RT.** The version of Windows 8 designed for media tablets. >**Windows Embedded.** A family of operating systems based on Windows that is designed for nonpersonal computer devices, such as cash registers and consumer electronic devices. >**Android.** A Linux-based operating system designed for mobile devices and developed by the Open Handset Alliance, which is a group of companies led by Google.

anyone can download and use Android, although hardware manufacturers must adhere to certain specifications in order to be called "Android compatible." The current version of Android is *Android 4.3*, also known as *Jelly Bean*. All Android devices have a customizable Home screen and a standard set of apps including a browser and apps for e-mail, messaging, music, search, and more. Android devices support multitasking, multiple cores, NFC mobile payment transactions, Internet phone calls, a variety of sensors (including gyroscopes and barometers), and the ability to select, copy, and paste text. Approximately one million apps have already been developed for Android (available via *Google Play*).

iOS

The mobile operating system designed for Apple mobile phones and mobile devices, such as the *iPhone* and the *iPad*, is **iOS** (see Figure 5-19). This operating system is based on Apple's Mac OS X operating system, supports multi-touch input, and has more than 900,000 apps available via the *App Store*. The current version of iOS is *iOS 7*. It supports multitasking and includes the Safari Web browser; the *Siri* intelligent assistant that lets users perform searches, place calls, and perform other tasks via voice commands; and apps for e-mail, messaging, music, search, and video calling via *FaceTime*. Features new to iOS 7 include *AirDrop*, which allows iOS users to send items (such as photos) to each other without having to launch a text or e-mail app, as well as improvements to Siri, such as using both male and female voices and the ability to perform Twitter searches.

FIGURE 5-19
iOS.

BlackBerry OS and BlackBerry PlayBook OS

BlackBerry OS is the operating system designed for BlackBerry devices. It supports multitasking and, like other mobile operating systems, it includes e-mail and Web browsing support, music management, video recording, calendar tools, and more. The latest version is *BlackBerry 10 OS*. Blackberry's tablet operating system is *BlackBerry PlayBook OS*. There is a wide range of software available for BlackBerry devices, from business and syncing software, to games and other apps available through *BlackBerry World*.

Mobile Linux

In addition to Android and iOS, there are other Linux-based mobile operating systems used with mobile devices today. For instance, Ubuntu has versions available for phones and tablets, and HP recently released its *webOS* product to open source—two current versions are *Enyo* and *Open webOS*. Two emerging mobile operating systems are *Firefox OS* and *Tizen*. Both are Linux-based operating systems and are geared toward smartphones running *HTML5* Web-based apps (HTML5 and other languages used for Web content is discussed in detail in Chapter 10).

OPERATING SYSTEMS FOR LARGER COMPUTERS

Larger computers—such as high-end servers, mainframes, and supercomputers—sometimes use operating systems designed solely for that type of system. For instance, IBM's *z/OS* is designed for IBM mainframes. In addition, many servers and mainframes today run conventional operating systems, such as Windows, UNIX, and Linux. Linux in particular is increasingly being used with both mainframes and supercomputers. Larger computers may also use a customized operating system based on a conventional operating system; for instance, many IBM mainframes and Cray supercomputers use versions of UNIX developed specifically for those computers. For a look at one supercomputer system being used to better predict the weather in the Swiss Alps, see the Inside the Industry box.

UTILITY PROGRAMS

FIGURE 5-20
Utility suites. Utility suites contain a number of related utility programs.

Courtesy Symantec

A **utility program** is a software program that performs a specific task, usually related to managing or maintaining a computer system. Many utility programs—such as programs for finding files, diagnosing and repairing system problems, cleaning up a hard drive, viewing images, playing multimedia files, and backing up files—are built into operating systems. There are also many stand-alone utility programs available as an alternative to the operating system's utility programs (such as a *backup program*) or to provide additional utility features not built into the operating system being used (such as a *registry cleaner* or a *file compression program*). Stand-alone utility programs are often available in a *suite* of related programs (such as a collection of *maintenance programs* or *security programs*, as shown in Figure 5-20). Some of the most commonly used integrated and stand-alone utility programs are discussed next.

File Management Programs

File management programs allow you to perform file management tasks such as looking to see which files are stored on a storage medium, as well as copying, moving, deleting, and renaming folders and files. The file management program incorporated into Windows 8 is **File Explorer** (previous versions of Windows use *Windows Explorer*); some common file management tasks using this program are summarized next.

Looking at the Folders and Files Stored on a Computer

Once a file management program is open, you can look at the folders and files stored on your computer. For instance, you can do the following in File Explorer (see Figure 5-21):

> ▶ To see the folders and files stored on your hard drive, USB flash drive, or any other storage medium, click the appropriate letter or name for that medium in the left pane (called the *Navigation pane*).

> ▶ To look inside a folder, click it (in the left pane) or double-click it (in the right pane). To go back to the previous location, click the Back toolbar button.

> **Utility program.** A type of software that performs a specific task, usually related to managing or maintaining a computer system. **>File management program.** A utility program that enables the user to perform file management tasks, such as copying and deleting files.
> **>File Explorer.** The file management program built into the Windows operating systems; older versions of Windows use *Windows Explorer*.

INSIDE THE INDUSTRY

Weather Forecasting in the Alps

Weather forecasting in the Alps is not easy. The Alps are very sensitive to climate change, due to their intense precipitation, glacial melting, steep mountains, and other factors. In fact, according to Thomas Schoenemeyer, associate director of the technology integration team of the *Swiss National Supercomputing Center* (*CSCS*), "Switzerland has one of the most complex topographies in the world."

One of the functions of the CSCS is to house the supercomputers needed to predict the weather in the Swiss Alps. It is currently implementing a new supercomputer system in order to give Switzerland's national weather system, *MeseoSwiss*, the ability to make more accurate forecasts—particularly for small valleys that current models can't discern.

The new supercomputer (shown in the accompanying photo) is called *Piz Daint* after one of Switzerland's mountain peaks. It is a Cray XC30 system, which uses Intel Xeon CPUs, NVIDIA GPUs, a Linux-based operating system, and runs at 750 teraflops. The combination of CPUs and GPUs is designed to facilitate better performance and will enable the system to run 30 slightly different weather forecasting models simultaneously, according to Schoenemeyer. Because of its parallel processing ability, larger and more complex scientific problems will be able to be addressed, such as in the fields of climatology, earth science, materials science, fluid dynamics, astrophysics, and life science. As an environmental plus, the system will use water from nearby Lake Lugano for cooling, and that water will later be reused to heat the CSCS building.

Courtesy CSCS

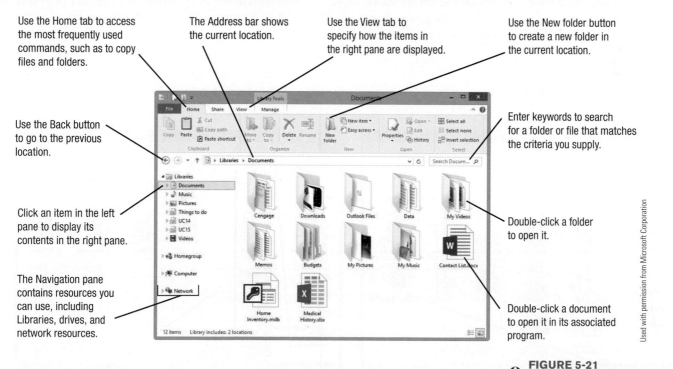

Use the Home tab to access the most frequently used commands, such as to copy files and folders.

The Address bar shows the current location.

Use the View tab to specify how the items in the right pane are displayed.

Use the New folder button to create a new folder in the current location.

Use the Back button to go to the previous location.

Enter keywords to search for a folder or file that matches the criteria you supply.

Click an item in the left pane to display its contents in the right pane.

Double-click a folder to open it.

The Navigation pane contains resources you can use, including Libraries, drives, and network resources.

Double-click a document to open it in its associated program.

Used with permission from Microsoft Corporation

FIGURE 5-21

Using File Explorer to look at the files stored on a computer.

➤ To open a file in its associated program, double-click it.

➤ To create a new folder in the current location, click the *New folder* button and then type the name for the new folder.

Copying and Moving Files and Folders

To copy or move a file or folder using a file management program, you first need to navigate to the drive and folder where the item is located and then select the desired file or folder. Next, issue either the *Copy command* (to copy the item) or the *Cut command* (to move the item), such as by using the File Explorer's Home tab, as shown in Figure 5-22, to copy or move that item to the *Clipboard* (a temporary location used for copying items). You then need to navigate to the drive and folder where you want the file to go, and use the *Paste command* to copy or move the item to that location. You can also copy or move more than one file at a time: Hold the Shift key down and click on the first and then the last file to select a group of adjacent files; hold the Ctrl key down while clicking files to select non-adjacent files. For a look at a shortcut for copying files in Windows—customizing the *Send-To menu*—see the How It Works box.

Renaming Files and Folders

You can also change the name of a file and folder using a file management program. To rename an item in File Explorer, select the item to be renamed, use the Home tab to issue the *Rename command* (or click a second time on the filename once the item is selected), and then retype or edit the filename.

Deleting Files and Folders

To delete a file or folder using a file management program, navigate to the drive and folder that contains the file or folder you want to delete, select the desired item, and then press the Delete key on the keyboard. You will need to select *Yes* when the Confirm File/Folder Delete dialog box opens to finish the deletion process. Deleting a folder deletes all of the contents located inside that folder.

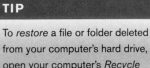

TIP

You can also copy, move, rename, or delete a file or folder in File Explorer by right-clicking the item and selecting the desired action from the shortcut menu that is displayed.

TIP

To *restore* a file or folder deleted from your computer's hard drive, open your computer's *Recycle Bin* and restore the file to its original location.

FIGURE 5-22
Using File Explorer to copy files.

2. Click *Copy* to copy the file to the Clipboard.

3. Navigate to the drive and folder where you want the file to go.

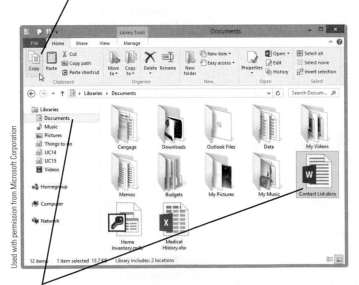

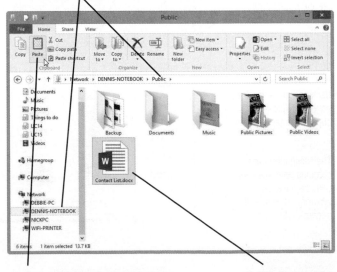

Used with permission from Microsoft Corporation

1. Navigate to the drive and folder containing the file you want to copy or move, and then select the file.

4. Click *Paste* to copy the file to the current location.

5. The file is copied.

Search Tools

As the amount of e-mail, photos, documents, and other important data individuals store on their computers continues to grow, **search tools**—utility programs that search for documents and other files on a user's hard drives—are becoming more important. Search tools are often integrated into file management programs and they are highly improved in recent versions of some operating systems, such as Mac OS and Windows. There are also a number of third-party search tools available.

Search tools typically are used to find files located somewhere on the specified storage medium that meet specific criteria, such as being in a certain folder, including certain characters in the filename, being of a particular type (a song, digital photo, or spreadsheet, for instance), and/or having a particular date associated with the file. If a document has been manually or automatically assigned *metadata tags* (information about the file, such as author, artist, or keywords), some search programs can search by those tags as well.

In Windows, for instance, users can use the *search box* located at the upper-right corner of the File Explorer window (refer again to Figure 5-21) to search for files and folders in the current location that match the keywords entered into the search box. You can also use the *Search charm* to display the Search box on the Start screen and start typing search terms to display matching content as shown in Figure 5-23 (the default search is Apps; click another option to search inside Settings, Files, Store, or any of the other displayed options).

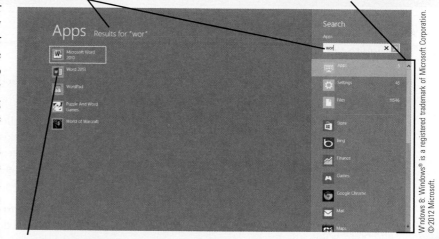

Start typing search terms to see matching content.

Click to select a different resource to search.

Click an app to launch it.

FIGURE 5-23
Using the Search charm in Windows 8.

Windows 8: Windows® is a registered trademark of Microsoft Corporation. © 2012 Microsoft.

Diagnostic and Disk Management Programs

Diagnostic programs evaluate your system, looking for problems and making recommendations for fixing any errors that are discovered. *Disk management programs* diagnose and repair problems related to your hard drive. Diagnostic and disk management utilities built into the Windows operating system (see Figure 5-24) include programs to check your hard drive for errors and programs to optimize your hard drive (by rearranging the data on the hard drive so all files are stored in contiguous locations—called *disk defragmentation*) so it works more efficiently. Third-party utility programs can perform these and other related tasks, as well.

FIGURE 5-24
Windows disk tools.

Uninstall and Cleanup Utilities

As programs are used, temporary data is often created. When programs are *uninstalled* (removed from the hard drive), this data and other remnants of that program can be left behind on the hard drive or in system files unless an *uninstall utility* is used. If a user removes programs by deleting the program's folder (which is not the recommended method for removing programs), the extraneous data is left behind, using up valuable disk space and, sometimes, slowing down the computer. Uninstall utilities remove the programs along with related extraneous data, such as references to those programs in your system files. Some uninstall capabilities are built into most operating systems; often an uninstall option is also included in a program's folder when that program is originally installed.

TI106130W0F (C:) Properties

General | Tools | Hardware | Sharing | Security | Quota

Error checking
This option will check the drive for file system errors.
Check

Optimize and defragment drive
Optimizing your computer's drives can help it run more efficiently.
Optimize

OK | Cancel | Apply

Used with permission from Microsoft Corporation.

>**Search tool.** A utility program designed to search for files on the user's hard drive.

HOW IT WORKS

Sending to the Cloud

The Windows *Send to* menu is a great shortcut for sending files to a USB flash drive, external hard drive, or other resource listed on the shortcut menu that is displayed when you right-click on a file or folder (see Step 1 in the accompanying illustration). But what if the resource you use all the time—like your cloud storage account—isn't listed? Simple. You add it.

To add a resource to the Send to menu, do the following:

1. Open a File Explorer window and type the following in the Address bar (see Step 2 in the accompanying illustration) and press Enter:

    %APPDATA%/Microsoft/Windows/SendTo

2. The SendTo folder will then be displayed showing the current available options for the Send to menu (see Step 3).

3. Copy the locations you would like to be on the menu to that folder, such as by dragging a cloud account from your Favorites list to the folder as in Step 3; choose *Copy* if a menu is displayed asking if you would like to copy or move the item.

4. The next time you right-click on an item, your new shortcuts will be displayed (see Step 4).

Step 1: Right-click an item to display the *Send to* menu.

Step 2: To open the SendTo folder, type this command in the Address bar.

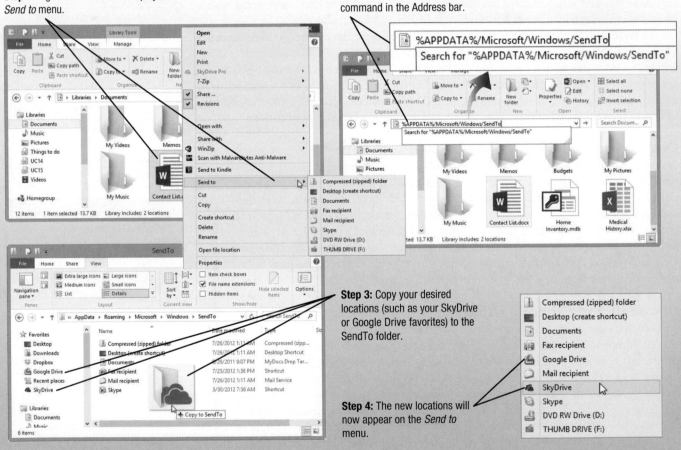

Step 3: Copy your desired locations (such as your SkyDrive or Google Drive favorites) to the SendTo folder.

Step 4: The new locations will now appear on the *Send to* menu.

Cleanup utilities (such as Windows *Disk Cleanup* shown in Figure 2-22 in Chapter 2) are designed to delete temporary files (such as deleted files still in the Recycle Bin, temporary Internet files, temporary installation files, and so forth) in order to free up disk space. Some specialty cleanup programs (called *registry cleaners*) are designed to locate unnecessary information in the Windows registry and other system files (such as from uninstalled programs) and delete it, making your computer run more efficiently.

CAUTION CAUTION CAUTION CAUTION CAUTION CAUTION CAU

To avoid deleting any system files used by other programs when uninstalling a program, be sure to keep all files (such as *.dll* files) that an uninstall utility asks you about and says might be needed by another program. As an extra precaution, you can create a *System Restore point* (using the *Recovery* tools) before uninstalling a program (if you are using a Windows computer) so you can roll the computer's settings back to that point if a problem occurs after the program is uninstalled.

File Compression Programs

File compression programs reduce the size of files so they take up less storage space on a storage medium or can be transmitted faster over the Internet. The most common format for user-compressed files in the Windows environment is the *.zip* or *.zipx* format, which is created by file compression programs such as *WinZip* and the free *7-Zip* program, and is used with the file compression features built into Windows 8 (see Figure 5-25). Mac users typically use *StuffIt* (which creates files in the *.sit* or *.sitx* format) or a similar program, although many file compression programs can open files compressed with other programs. A file compression program is required to both compress (*zip*) and decompress (*unzip*) files, unless the zipped file is made *executable*. Executable zipped files have the extension *.exe* and decompress automatically when they are opened, even if the appropriate file compression program is not installed on the recipient's computer. File compression programs can compress either a single file or a group of files into a single compressed file. When multiple files are compressed, they are separated back into individual files when the file is decompressed. Some file compression programs can also *encrypt* your zipped files so that a password is needed to unzip them. Encryption is discussed in detail in Chapter 9.

FIGURE 5-25
File compression. Reduces the size of files so they can be more efficiently stored or transmitted.

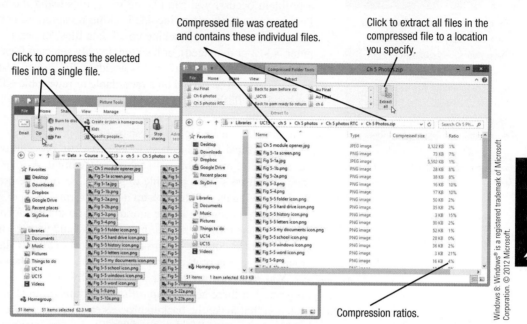

Click to compress the selected files into a single file.

Compressed file was created and contains these individual files.

Click to extract all files in the compressed file to a location you specify.

Compression ratios.

Windows 8: Windows® is a registered trademark of Microsoft Corporation. © 2012 Microsoft.

ASK THE EXPERT

Courtesy of DriveSavers Data Recovery www.drivesavers.com

Mike Cobb, Director of Engineering, DriveSavers Data Recovery

How important are disk-maintenance procedures—such as defragmenting a hard drive—in preventing a hard drive failure?

It's important to run a disk maintenance program occasionally to fix minor directory corruption and repair incorrect disk or file permissions. In addition, defragmenting files—or optimizing as it is sometimes called—can help improve the performance of a hard drive.

Computer users who create large high-resolution graphics, professional audio recordings, and video production files should defragment regularly; these users will see the most benefit from a regular defragmenting routine.

>**File compression program.** A program that reduces the size of files, typically to be stored or transmitted more efficiently.

Backup and Recovery Utilities

Virtually every computer veteran will warn you that, sooner or later, you will lose some critical files. This could happen due to a power outage (if the file you are working on has not yet been saved), a hardware failure (such as if your computer or hard drive stops functioning), a major disaster (such as a fire that destroys your computer), or a user error (such as accidentally deleting or overwriting a file).

Creating a **backup** means making a duplicate copy of important files so that when a problem occurs, you can restore those files using the backup copy to avoid data loss. Performing a backup can include backing up an entire computer (so it can be restored at a later date, if needed), backing up all data files (in order to restore them in case the computer is lost or damaged), or backing up only selected files (to make sure you have a clean copy of each file if the original is accidentally lost or destroyed). Depending on its size, backup data can be placed on a recordable or rewritable CD or DVD disc, an external hard drive, a USB flash drive, or virtually any other storage medium. To protect against fires and other natural disasters, backup media should be stored in a different physical location than your computer or inside a fire-resistant safe.

It is critical for a business to have backup procedures in place that back up all data on a frequent, regular basis—such as every night. A rotating collection of backup media should be used so it is possible to go back beyond the previous day's backup, if needed. While individuals tend to back up in a less formal manner, personal backups are becoming increasingly necessary as the amount of important information that users store digitally (such as home movies, music, digital photos, and tax returns) grows. Personal backups can be as simple as copying important documents to a USB flash drive or uploading them to a cloud storage site, or as comprehensive as backing up the entire contents of your computer.

You can perform backups by manually copying files using your file management program, but there are *backup utility* programs (both stand-alone and built into operating systems) that make the backup process easier, such as the *Windows Backup* program used in older versions of Windows and the *File History* program used in Windows 8 and shown in Figure 5-26 that can be used to automatically back up your libraries, favorites, and contacts so they can be restored if the originals are lost, corrupted, or accidentally deleted.

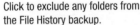

Ⓥ **FIGURE 5-26**
The Windows File History program.

Click to exclude any folders from the File History backup.

Click to select the drive to be used with File History.

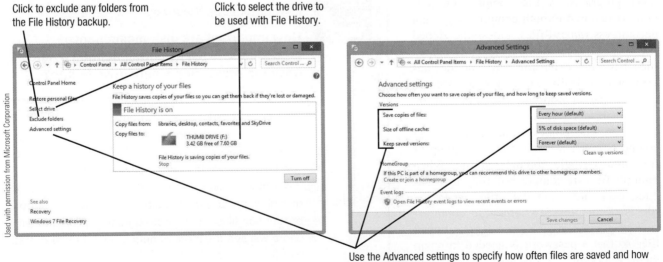

Used with permission from Microsoft Corporation

Use the Advanced settings to specify how often files are saved and how long they are kept.

>**Backup.** A duplicate copy of data or other computer content in case the original version is destroyed.

For convenience, many backup programs can be scheduled to back up specified files, folders, or drives on a regular basis (such as every night or every Friday night, depending on how important the contents of your computer are and how often you modify files)— with File History, you can select the frequency of the automatic backup, how long the backup files are kept, and any folders you would like to exclude from the backup (refer again to Figure 5-26). There are also online backup services that can back up your specified files automatically to a secure cloud server on a regular basis, provided you have a broadband Internet connection. Backups and *disaster recovery* are discussed in more detail in Chapter 15.

Antivirus, Antispyware, Firewalls, and Other Security Programs

As discussed in detail in Chapter 9, a *computer virus* is a software program that is designed to cause damage to a computer or perform some other malicious act, and *spyware* is a software program installed without the user's knowledge that secretly collects information and sends it to an outside party via the user's Internet connection. Other security concerns today include *phishing* schemes that try to trick users into supplying personal information that can be used for credit card fraud, *identity theft*, and other criminal acts. Because of these threats, it is critical that all computer users today protect themselves and their computers. There are many *security programs* available, such as *antivirus programs* and *antispyware programs* (that protect against malicious software being installed on your computer) and *firewall programs* (that protect against someone accessing your computer via the Internet or a wireless connection). Increasingly, operating systems are including security software integrated into the operating system. For instance, recent versions of Windows include *Windows Firewall* and *Windows Defender* (an antispyware program, shown in Figure 5-27). Because network and Internet security is such an important topic today, Chapter 9 is dedicated to these topics.

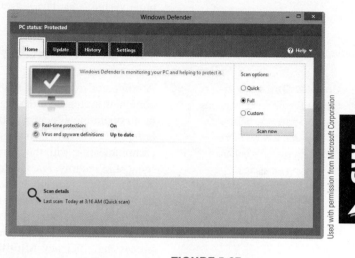

FIGURE 5-27
The Windows Defender program.

THE FUTURE OF OPERATING SYSTEMS

The future configuration of operating systems is anyone's guess, but it is expected that they will continue to become more user-friendly and, eventually, be driven primarily by a voice, touch, and/or gesture interface. Operating systems are also likely to continue to become more stable and self-healing, repairing or restoring system files as needed. In addition, they are expected to continue to include security and technological improvements as they become available.

Improvements will almost certainly continue to be made in the areas of synchronizing and coordinating data and activities among a person's various computing and communications devices, such as his or her personal computer and mobile phone. Desktop and mobile operating systems will also likely continue to converge into a single operating system as those devices continue to converge. In addition, with the pervasiveness of the Internet, operating systems in the future may be used primarily to access software available through the Internet or other networks, instead of accessing software on the local computer.

SUMMARY

SYSTEM SOFTWARE VS. APPLICATION SOFTWARE

System software consists of the programs that coordinate the activities of a computer system. The basic role of system software is to act as a mediator between **application software** (programs that allow a user to perform specific tasks on a computer, such as word processing, playing a game, preparing taxes, browsing the Web, and so forth) and the computer system's hardware, as well as between the computer and the user.

THE OPERATING SYSTEM

A computer's **operating system** is the primary system software program; it manages the computer system's resources and interfaces with the user. The essential portion, or core, of an operating system is called its **kernel**. The functions of the operating system include booting the computer, configuring devices and **device drivers** (often simply called **drivers**), communicating with the user, managing and monitoring computer resources, file management, and security. *File management programs* allow the user to manage the enormous collection of files typically found on a computer's hard drive by organizing files hierarchically into folders. To access a file in any directory, the user can specify the *path* to the file; the path identifies the drive and folders the user must navigate through in order to access the file.

A variety of processing techniques can be built into operating systems to help enhance processing efficiency. **Multitasking** allows more than one program to be open at one time; *multithreading* allows for rotation between program *threads*; and multiprocessing and parallel processing involve using two or more CPUs (or CPU cores) to perform work at the same time. Operating systems typically use **virtual memory** to extend conventional memory by using a portion of the hard drive as additional memory, and **buffering** and **spooling** free up the CPU from delays by storing data that is used by different hardware devices or programs that may operate at different speeds in a **buffer**.

Some of the differences among operating systems center around whether they use a **graphical user interface (GUI)** or **command line interface**, whether they are a **personal (desktop) operating system** designed for individual users or a **server (network) operating system** designed for multiple users, and the types and numbers of processors supported. Operating systems that are used with mobile devices or are embedded in other devices are called **mobile operating systems** or **embedded operating systems**, respectively.

OPERATING SYSTEMS FOR PERSONAL COMPUTERS AND SERVERS

One of the original operating systems for IBM and IBM-compatible personal computers was **DOS (Disk Operating System)**, which is still in existence but not widely used. Most desktop computers today run a version of **Windows**. *Windows 3.x*, the first widely used version of Windows, was an *operating environment* that added a GUI shell to DOS, replacing the DOS command line interface with a system of menus, icons, and screen boxes called *windows*. *Windows 95, Windows 98, Windows NT, Windows Me, Windows 2000, Windows XP, Windows Vista,* and *Windows 7*—all full-fledged operating systems and successors to Windows 3.x—each included an increasing number of enhancements, such as multitasking, a better user interface, and more Internet, multimedia, and communications functions. The current personal version of Windows is **Windows 8**, which uses a new **tile** interface; the current network version of Windows (**Windows Server**) is *Windows Server 2012*.

Chapter Objective 1:
Understand the difference between system software and application software.

Chapter Objective 2:
Explain the different functions of an operating system and discuss some ways that operating systems enhance processing efficiency.

Chapter Objective 3:
List several ways in which operating systems differ from one another.

Chapter Objective 4:
Name today's most widely used operating systems for personal computers and servers.

Mac OS is the operating system used on Apple computers. The current personal version is **Mac OS X** (and includes *Mac OS X Mountain Lion* and *Mac OS X Mavericks*); **Mac OS X Server** is designed for server use. **UNIX** is a flexible operating system that was originally developed for use with midrange servers, but is now available for a variety of devices. UNIX comes in many versions or *UNIX flavors* and is the basis of several other operating systems, including Mac OS. The open source **Linux** operating system has gathered popularity because it is distributed free over the Internet and can be used as an alternative to Windows and Mac OS. Linux has earned support as a mainstream operating system in recent years and is being used in computers of all sizes, from netbooks to supercomputers.

OPERATING SYSTEMS FOR MOBILE DEVICES

Mobile phones and mobile devices usually require a different operating system than a desktop computer or server, although many mobile operating systems are mobile versions of desktop operating systems. Widely used mobile operating systems include **Windows Phone**, **Windows RT**, **Android**, **iOS**, **BlackBerry OS**, and *Ubuntu*. Other everyday devices that contain a computer—such as cars, cash registers, and consumer electronics devices—typically use an embedded operating system, such as **Windows Embedded**.

OPERATING SYSTEMS FOR LARGER COMPUTERS

High-end servers, mainframes, and supercomputers may use an operating system designed specifically for that type of system, but are increasingly using customized versions of conventional operating systems, such as Windows, UNIX, and Linux.

UTILITY PROGRAMS

A **utility program** is a type of system software written to perform specific tasks usually related to maintaining or managing the computer system. **File management programs** enable users to perform file management tasks, such as copying, moving, and deleting files. The file management system built into Windows is **File Explorer**. **Search tools** are designed to help users find files on their hard drives; *diagnostic* and *disk management programs* are used mainly to diagnose and repair computer problems, such as hard drive errors and files deleted accidentally, as well as maintenance tasks, such as performing *disk defragmentation*. *Uninstall utilities* remove programs from a hard drive without leaving annoying remnants behind, **file compression programs** reduce the stored size of files so they can be more easily archived or sent over the Internet, and **backup** programs make it easier for users to back up the contents of their hard drive. There are also a number of security-oriented utility programs, such as *antivirus*, *antispyware*, and *firewall* programs.

THE FUTURE OF OPERATING SYSTEMS

In the future, operating systems will likely become even more user-friendly, voice-driven, and stable, repairing themselves when needed and causing errors and conflicts much less frequently. They will also likely continue to include improved security features, support for new technologies, and assistance for coordinating data and activities among a user's various computing and communications devices. They may also one day be designed primarily for accessing cloud applications.

Chapter Objective 5:
State several devices other than personal computers and servers that require an operating system and list one possible operating system for each type of device.

SW

Chapter Objective 6:
Discuss the role of utility programs and outline several tasks that these programs perform.

Chapter Objective 7:
Describe what the operating systems of the future might be like.

REVIEW ACTIVITIES

KEY TERM MATCHING

a. Android

b. backup

c. device driver

d. kernel

e. multitasking

f. operating system

g. spooling

h. utility program

i. virtual memory

j. Windows

Instructions: Match each key term on the left with the definition on the right that best describes it.

1. _____ A duplicate copy of data or other computer content for use in the event that the original version is destroyed.

2. _____ A Linux-based operating system designed for mobile devices and developed by the Open Handset Alliance, which is a group of companies led by Google.

3. _____ A memory-management technique that uses hard drive space as additional RAM.

4. _____ A program that enables an operating system to communicate with a specific hardware device.

5. _____ A type of software that performs a specific task, usually related to managing or maintaining a computer system.

6. _____ The capability of an operating system to run more than one program at one time.

7. _____ The essential portion, or core, of an operating system.

8. _____ The main component of system software that enables a computer to operate, manage its activities and the resources under its control, run application programs, and interface with the user.

9. _____ The primary personal computer operating system developed by Microsoft Corporation.

10. _____ The process of placing items in a buffer so the appropriate device (such as a printer) can retrieve them when needed.

SELF-QUIZ

Instructions: Circle **T** if the statement is true, **F** if the statement is false, or write the best answer in the space provided. **Answers for the self-quiz are located in the References and Resources Guide at the end of the book.**

1. **T   F**   Windows 8 is an example of an operating system.

2. **T   F**   Most operating systems today use a command line interface.

3. **T   F**   Mobile devices, such as media tablets and mobile phones, typically require an operating system.

4. **T   F**   File Explorer is an operating system designed for mobile phones.

5. **T   F**   Windows Phone is a versatile operating system designed to be used on a variety of computer types, such as mainframes, servers, personal computers, and mobile phones.

6. _____ refers to the ability of an operating system to have more than one program open at one time.

7. _____ is the operating system used with iPhones and iPads.

8. To decrease the size of a file, a(n) _____ utility program can be used.

9. To guard against losing your data if a computer problem occurs, you should _____ your data files on a regular basis.

10. Match each device to the most appropriate operating system and write the corresponding number in the blank to the left of the device.

a. _____ Home office computer

b. _____ Mainframe computer

c. _____ Media tablet

d. _____ ATM machine

1. Windows Embedded

2. Android

3. Windows 8

4. UNIX

EXERCISES

1. For the following path, identify the drive the document is located on, the name of the file (including its file extension), and whether or not the document is stored inside a folder. If the file is stored inside one or more folders, list the folder name(s).

   C:\ My Documents\Resume.docx

2. Match each program or processing technique with the appropriate term and write the corresponding number in the blank to the left of each term.

a. _____ Zipped file

b. _____ Printer

c. _____ Swap file

d. _____ Folder

1. Spooling

2. File management program

3. File compression program

4. Virtual memory

3. Would a new notebook computer typically have Windows XP, Windows 8, Windows Phone 8, or Windows Server 2012 installed as its operating system? Explain your answer.

4. What type of utility program is designed to automatically make duplicate copies of your hard drive content for safekeeping?

5. Identify the purpose of each of the following types of utility programs.

a. File management program _____

b. Uninstall utility _____

c. File compression program _____

d. Antivirus program _____

SW

DISCUSSION QUESTIONS

1. There are a few companies, such as Microsoft and Google, that have moved into many different areas of computing, such as operating systems, application software, cloud software, search, and more, and both of these companies have been accused of monopolistic procedures. Is there a risk for the consumer or for businesses if one company is involved with so many different aspects of computing? Should this be prohibited or should the natural order of the free market be trusted to prevent areas of computing from being monopolized by one company?

2. As discussed in the chapter, many everyday devices—including cars and other vehicles—are controlled by operating systems. There are advantages, such as avoiding possible driver errors and the ability to change the speed of or reroute trains automatically to avoid collisions. But are there potential risks, as well? For example, Thailand's Finance Minister once had to be rescued from inside his limousine after the onboard computer malfunctioned, leaving the vehicle immobilized and the door locks, power windows, and air conditioning not functioning. Do you think the benefits of increased automation of devices that could put us in danger if they malfunction outweigh the risks? What types of safeguards should be incorporated into computer-controlled cars, subway trains, and other automated vehicles? What about medication dispensers and other automated medical devices?

PROJECTS

1. **New OSs** There have been a number of new operating systems developed in the past few years, such as Android, Windows RT, and Google Chrome OS.

   For this project, select one new or emerging operating system and research it. What is the purpose and targeted market for this operating system? What advantages does it have over any current competition for this market? If the operating system was developed to fulfill a new need, are there other operating systems that are being adapted or being developed as a result? Do you think your selected operating system will succeed? Why or why not? At the conclusion of your research, prepare a one- to two-page summary of your findings and opinions and submit it to your instructor.

2. **File Compression** As described in the chapter, compression programs can be used to reduce the size of files before they are stored or sent over the Internet. The most common compression programs create files with the file extensions *.zip*, *.sit*, *.sitx*, and *.exe*. Self-extracting compressed files decompress automatically when you download them, while compressed files must be decompressed with a version of the program that compressed them.

   For this project, identify compression programs associated with each of the file extensions listed above and determine which extensions represent a self-extracting format, as well as which extensions are associated with the Windows and Mac OS operating systems. For the type of computer you use most often, find at least two compression programs that you might use and compare their costs and capabilities. At the conclusion of your research, prepare a one-page summary of your findings and submit it to your instructor.

3. **File Practice** As discussed in the chapter, all operating systems have a file management system, such as the File Explorer program illustrated in Figures 5-21 and 5-22.

   For this project, obtain a removable storage medium (such as a USB flash drive) appropriate for a computer you have access to, connect it to that computer, and perform the following tasks.

   a. Open the file management program and select the icon representing the removable storage medium being used to display its contents. Are there any files on the storage medium? How much room is available on the storage medium?

   b. Open any word processing program available on your computer (such as Word or Notepad for a Windows computer). Create a new document consisting of just your name, then save the document to your storage medium (be sure to change the save location to the appropriate drive and use an appropriate filename). In the file management program, view the content of your storage medium to see the new document. What is the file size and how much room is now left on your storage medium?

   c. Prepare a short summary of your work to submit to your instructor, listing the software programs and storage medium used, the name and size of the file, and the amount of space left on your storage medium once the file was stored on it.

   d. Return to your file management program and delete the file from your storage medium.

4. **Operating System Bugs** Most software, including operating systems, is not error free when it is first released. Some programs, in fact, contain thousands of problems, called *bugs*. Software companies regularly release fixes (called *patches*) to correct known issues with released software. Is it ethical for software companies to release products that have known problems? Many hackers and other criminals target these bugs with computer viruses or other attacks, frequently on the day a new vulnerability is announced—called a *zero-day attack*. Obviously, the acts by these criminals are not ethical, but what responsibility does a software company have to consumers if they are put at risk due to the company's carelessness or rush to market? What responsibility do consumers have to make sure they keep their computers patched against new vulnerabilities?

   For this project, form an opinion about the ethical ramifications of software bugs and be prepared to discuss your position (in class, via an online class discussion group, in a class chat room, or via a class blog, depending on your instructor's directions). You may also be asked to write a short paper expressing your opinion.

ETHICS IN ACTION

5. **OS Support** No matter which operating system you have, it's likely you will eventually need to get some help resolving a problem. Support options typically include the following: searchable knowledge bases, technical support phone numbers and e-mail addresses, online chat, FAQs, and user discussion groups.

   For this project, select one operating system and go to the manufacturer's Web site to determine which of the support options listed in the previous paragraph are available. Select one support option and find out how it is used and what type of information can be obtained. Share your findings with the class in the form of a short presentation. The presentation should not exceed 10 minutes and should make use of one or more presentation aids, such as a whiteboard, handouts, or a computer-based slide presentation (your instructor may provide additional requirements). You may also be asked to submit a summary of the presentation to your instructor.

PRESENTATION/ DEMONSTRATION

6. **Are Computerized Cars a Cyber Threat?** As discussed in this chapter, cars are continually getting smarter and these features are supposed to help make us safer. But do they put us at risk as well? Today's cars are essentially computers on wheels and computers can be hacked. What if a hacker infects a car with malware and takes control of the car's speed, braking, and other vital systems? Researchers have already shown that such an attack is possible. There are a number of access points available to hackers, such as the car's entertainment system, the car's Internet connection—even the tire pressure monitoring system. Could hackers be hired as hit men to murder selected individuals by taking control of their cars? What about terrorists introducing a virus to large numbers of cars as a terrorist act? Do we need new laws to make hacking cars illegal? Should security companies be developing antivirus software for cars? Will we get to the point where we'll need to run a virus scan before we can safely use our vehicles? Are the benefits of computerized cars worth the potential risks?

   Pick a side on this issue, form an opinion and gather supporting evidence, and be prepared to discuss and defend your position in a classroom debate or in a 1–2 page paper, depending on your instructor's directions.

BALANCING ACT

SW

chapter 6

Application Software

After completing this chapter, you will be able to do the following:

1. Describe what application software is, the different types of ownership rights, and the difference between installed and cloud software.

2. Detail some concepts and commands that many software programs have in common.

3. Discuss word processing and explain what kinds of documents are created using this type of program.

4. Explain the purpose of spreadsheet software and the kinds of documents created using this type of program.

5. Identify some of the vocabulary used with database software and discuss the benefits of using this type of program.

6. Describe what presentation graphics and electronic slide shows are and when they might be used.

7. List some types of graphics and multimedia software that consumers use frequently.

8. Name several other types of application software programs and discuss what functions they perform.

outline

OVERVIEW

As discussed in previous chapters, application software consists of programs designed to perform specific tasks or applications. Today, a wide variety of application software is available to meet virtually any user need. Individuals and businesses use software to perform hundreds of tasks, including to write letters, keep track of their finances, participate in videoconferences, watch videos, learn a foreign language, entertain themselves or their children, create music CDs or home movie DVDs, manage business inventories, create greeting cards and flyers, make business presentations, process orders, prepare payrolls and tax returns, touch up digital photos, and access Web-based resources.

This chapter begins with a discussion of some general characteristics of application software. Then we look at five of the most widely used types of application software: word processing, spreadsheet, database, presentation graphics, and graphics/ multimedia software. The chapter concludes with an overview of some of the other types of application software you may encounter in your personal and professional life. ■

THE BASICS OF APPLICATION SOFTWARE

All computer users should be familiar with the basic characteristics and concepts related to **application software (apps)**—for instance, the different possible ownership rights and delivery methods used with application software, how software for personal computers and mobile devices differs, and the basic commands that are common to most types of application software. Although these topics are discussed next in the context of application software, they also apply to other types of software, such as system software (discussed in Chapter 5) and programming languages (discussed in Chapter 13).

Software Ownership Rights

The *ownership rights* of a software program specify the allowable use of that program. After a software program is developed, the developer (typically an individual or an organization) holds the ownership rights for that program and decides whether or not the program can be sold, shared with others, or otherwise distributed. When a software program is purchased, the buyer is not actually buying the software. Instead, the buyer is acquiring a **software license** that permits him or her to use the software. This license specifies the conditions under which a buyer can use the software, such as the number of computers on which it may be installed. In fact, many software licenses permit the software to be installed on only one computer. In addition to being included in printed form inside the packaging of most software programs, the licensing agreement is usually displayed and must be agreed to by the end user at the beginning of the software installation process (see Figure 6-1).

>**Application software.** Programs that enable users to perform specific tasks on a computer, such as writing a letter or playing a game; frequently referred to as **apps**. >**Software license.** An agreement, either included in a software package or displayed on the screen when the software is installed or launched, that specifies the conditions under which the program can be used.

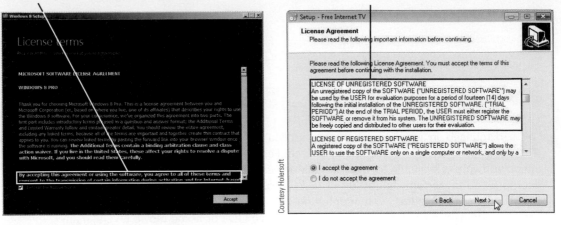

This statement explains that you are accepting the terms of the license agreement by installing the software.

This statement explains that the program can be tried for 14 days and then it needs to be either registered or uninstalled.

Used with permission from Microsoft Corporation

Courtesy Holersoft

COMMERCIAL SOFTWARE PROGRAM

SHAREWARE PROGRAM

FIGURE 6-1

Software licenses.
Most software programs display their licensing agreements at the beginning of the installation process.

There are four basic categories of software: *commercial software*, *shareware*, *freeware*, and *public domain software* (see Figure 6-2). Each of these types of software has different ownership rights, as discussed next. In addition, software that falls into any of these four categories can also be **open source software**, which are programs made up of source code that is available to the public. An open source program can be copyrighted, but individuals and businesses are allowed to modify the program and redistribute it—the only restrictions are that changes must be shared with the open source community and the original copyright notice must remain intact. For more information about open source software, see the Inside the Industry box.

FIGURE 6-2

Software ownership rights.

Commercial Software

Commercial software is software that is developed and sold for a profit. When you buy a commercial software program (such as *Microsoft Office*, *TurboTax*, or *GarageBand*), it typically comes with a *single-user license*, which means you cannot legally make copies of the installation CD or file to give to your friends and you cannot legally install the software on their computers using your copy. You cannot even install the software on a second computer that you own, unless allowed by the license. For example, some software licenses state that the program can be installed on one desktop computer and one portable computer belonging to the same individual. To determine which activities are allowable for a particular commercial software program, refer to its software license. Schools or businesses that need to install software on a large number of computers or need to have the software available to multiple users over a network can usually obtain a *site license* or *network license* for the number of users needed.

TYPE OF SOFTWARE	EXAMPLES
Commercial software	Microsoft Office (office suite) Norton AntiVirus (antivirus program) Adobe Photoshop (image editing program) Minecraft - Pocket Edition (game)
Shareware	WinZip (file compression program) Video Edit Magic (video editing program) Image Shrinker (image optimizer) Deluxe Ski Jump 3 (game)
Freeware	Chrome (Web browser) LibreOffice (office suite) QuickTime Player (media player) Evernote (notetaking/archiving software)
Public domain software	Lynx (text-based Web browser) Quake 3 (game)

Copyright © 2015 Cengage Learning®

>**Open source software.** Software programs made up of source code that is made available to the public. >**Commercial software.** Copyrighted software that is developed, usually by a commercial company, for sale to others.

INSIDE THE INDUSTRY

Open Source Software

The use of open source software has grown over the past few years, primarily for cost reasons. One of the first widely known open source programs was the Linux operating system, which was discussed in Chapter 5. However, there are also low-cost or no-cost open source alternatives for a wide selection of application programs today. For instance, the free *LibreOffice* office suite can be used as an alternative to Microsoft Office, and the free *GIMP* program (see the accompanying screenshot) can be used to retouch photos instead of Adobe Photoshop or another pricey image editing program. In addition to saving you money, these alternative programs often require less disk space and memory than their commercial software counterparts require.

Other possible benefits of using open source software include increased stability and security (because they are tested and improved by a wide variety of programmers and users), and the ability to modify the application's source code. Perceived risks of using open source software include lack of support and compatibility issues. However, both Linux and open source application programs are continuing to gain acceptance and their use is growing. Some insiders feel that the open source movement is finally gathering the momentum it deserves.

A recent survey of executives found that most executives view open source as beneficial to both innovation and collaboration. It also revealed that more than half of all software purchased five years from now is expected to be open source, with the top factors driving this increased popularity of open source software being improved quality and flexibility of software libraries.

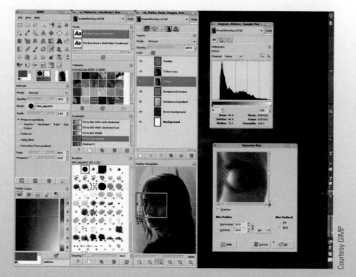

Courtesy GIMP

The GNU Image Manipulation Program (GIMP).

In addition to their full versions, some commercial software is available in a *demo* or *trial version*. Typically, these versions can be used free of charge and distributed to others, but often they are missing some key features (such as the ability to save or print a document) or they will not run after the trial period expires. Because these programs are not designed as replacements for the fee-based version, it is ethical to use them only to determine if you would like to buy the full program. If the decision is made against purchasing the product, the demo or trial version should be uninstalled from your computer.

Recent trends in computing—such as multiprocessing, virtualization, mobile computing, and cloud computing, all discussed in earlier chapters of this book—are leading to new software licensing issues for commercial software companies. For example, software companies must decide whether the number of installations allowed by the license is counted by the number of computers on which the software is installed or by the total number of processors or CPU cores used by those computers, as well as decide whether to charge per user or per device for software use. Some Microsoft software, for instance, is licensed per processor, regardless of the number of cores each processor has. And, for some server software used within a virtual environment, Microsoft computes the number of users based on a *per running instance*—that is, the number of software instances (installed or virtual) being used at any given time—instead of how many virtual environments the software is actually available to. Another software vendor (Altair Engineering) uses *license tokens* that are drawn from a central license server when the application is running and returned to the server when the application is finished. This system allows the number of tokens used

> **TIP**
>
> Ownership rights for original creative works are referred to as *copyrights* and are discussed in more detail in Chapter 16.

> **TIP**
>
> Businesses should periodically audit their software licenses to ensure they are paying only for the number of installs actually being used. They should also consider negotiating new types of licensing agreements that best fit the company, such as concurrent-user pricing instead of per-computer pricing.

ASK THE EXPERT

Stacy Reed, Software Librarian and Editor, Tucows

Why should an individual or business pay for shareware?

Ethically and legally, it's the right thing to do. Software publishers offer trial versions of their software for free because it allows users ample opportunity to evaluate the software to ensure it meets their needs. After the trial period expires, you should either uninstall the software or pay for the full version so the developer can continue to provide technical support and product enhancements. Some software may disable or cripple functionality after the trial has ended; others may remind you to pay by displaying nag screens, watermarks, or advertisements. Though there are sneaky ways to circumvent licensing, doing so is copyright infringement and it is illegal. Conviction could include jail time and/or fines for each infringement and, if you or your company willfully profit from stolen software, you stand to face maximum penalties—in some countries, that could mean hundreds of thousands of dollars in fines per instance or several years in prison.

by an individual computer to vary depending on the computing hardware (such as number of cores) being used, but still ensures that the number of users accessing the software at any one time does not exceed the limits specified in the software license. Software vendors are expected to continue to develop and implement new licensing models to address these and other trends in the future.

Shareware

Shareware programs are software programs that are distributed on the honor system. Most shareware programs are available to try free of charge, but typically require a small fee if you choose to use the program regularly (refer again to the shareware license in Figure 6-1). By paying the requested registration fee, you can use the program for as long as you want to use it and may be entitled to product support, updates, and other benefits. You can legally and ethically copy shareware programs to pass along to friends and colleagues for evaluation purposes, but those individuals are expected to pay the shareware fee if they decide to keep the product.

Many shareware programs have a specified trial period, such as one month. Although it is not illegal to use shareware past the specified trial period, it is unethical to do so. Ethical use of shareware dictates either paying for the program or uninstalling it from your computer at the end of the trial period. Shareware is typically much less expensive than commercial versions of similar software because it is often developed by a single programmer and because it uses the shareware marketing system to sell directly to consumers (typically via a variety of software download sites, such as the one shown in Figure 6-3) with little or no packaging or advertising expenses. Shareware authors stress that the ethical use of shareware helps to cultivate this type of software distribution. Legally, shareware and demo versions of commercial software are similar, but shareware is typically not missing key features.

Ⓥ **FIGURE 6-3**
Download sites.
Typically offer a variety of software, including shareware and freeware.

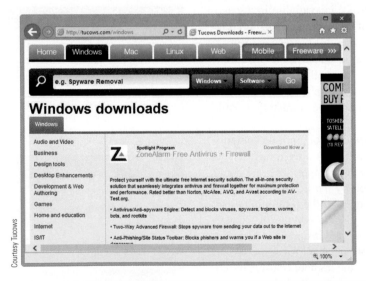

Freeware

Freeware programs are software programs that are given away by the author for others to use free of charge. Although freeware is available without charge and can be shared with others, the author retains the ownership rights

---

> **Shareware.** Copyrighted software that is distributed on the honor system; consumers should either pay for it or uninstall it after the trial period.
> **Freeware.** Copyrighted software that may be used free of charge.

to the program, so you cannot do anything with it—such as sell it or modify it—that is not expressly allowed by the author. Freeware programs are frequently developed by individuals; commercial software companies sometimes release freeware as well. Like shareware programs, freeware programs are widely available over the Internet. In fact, many apps available at the *app stores* used with mobile devices (see Figure 6-4) are freeware.

Public Domain Software

Public domain software is not copyrighted; instead, the ownership rights to the program have been donated to the public domain. Consequently, it is free and can be used, copied, modified, and distributed to others without restrictions.

Desktop vs. Mobile Software

Notebook computers, tablet computers, netbooks, and other portable computers typically run the same application software as desktop computers. However, mobile phones and other mobile devices (such as iPads and other media tablets) typically require *mobile software* (also called *mobile apps*); that is, software specifically designed for a specific type of mobile phone or other mobile device, such as an Apple or Android device. A wide variety of apps is available today. For instance, there are mobile versions of popular programs like Word or PowerPoint, games and other entertainment apps, business and reference tools, calendars and communications apps, location-based apps, financial and banking apps, health and fitness apps, Web browsers, and more (see Figure 6-5). In fact, there are approximately one million Android apps available via the *Google Play* store (shown in Figure 6-4), and the Apple *App Store*, which has over 900,000 apps, hit its 50 billionth download in mid 2013. Many mobile apps are available free of charge or for a minimal cost, such as 99 cents. For a look at a new trend in mobile apps—mobile ticketing—see the Technology and You box.

In addition to having a more compact, efficient appearance, many mobile apps include features for easier data input, such as an on-screen keyboard, a phrase list, voice input capabilities, or handwriting recognition capabilities. Some mobile apps are designed to be compatible with popular *desktop software*, such as Microsoft Office, to facilitate sharing documents between the two platforms. The desktop versions of the most common Microsoft Office programs are illustrated later in this chapter.

Installed vs. Cloud Software

Software also differs in how it is accessed by the end user. It can be installed on and run from the end user's computer (or installed on and run from a network server in a network setting), or it can be cloud software that is accessed by the end user over the Internet.

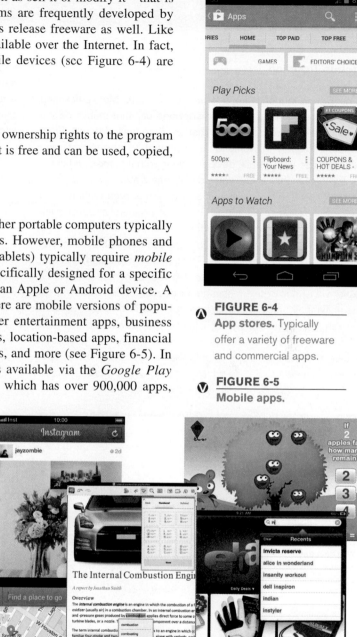

FIGURE 6-4

App stores. Typically offer a variety of freeware and commercial apps.

FIGURE 6-5

Mobile apps.

> **Public domain software.** Software that is not copyrighted and may be used without restriction.

TECHNOLOGY AND YOU

Mobile Ticketing

A new trend in mobile apps is *mobile ticketing*. Mobile ticketing goes beyond just using your smartphone or other mobile device to locate and purchase tickets that are then mailed to you. From concerts to sporting events to transportation to movie tickets, you can now use your mobile device as your actual admission ticket.

To buy a mobile ticket, you typically use a mobile app, such as an individual app for a particular application or organization (such as the *Fandango app* for movie tickets) or a generalized app (such as *StubHub*) for tickets to sporting events, concerts, and more. In either case, you use the app to make the applicable selections (such as the desired event, date, time, and seat location) and pay, and then your tickets are either sent to your smartphone or media tablet via e-mail or text message, or you use a link to download them. Typically, mobile tickets have a barcode on them; to enter the venue, you just display the ticket on your device, an attendant scans it, and you're in. For example, the *mobile boarding pass* shown in the accompanying photo allows you to use your smartphone or media tablet as your airline boarding pass at airport security checkpoints or at the gate during boarding.

There are also Web sites (such as *MogoTix*) that allow you to easily sell and distribute mobile tickets to custom events, such as a fundraiser or conference. You just publish an event (including details, ticket prices, and payment options) on the ticketing Web site and you're in business!

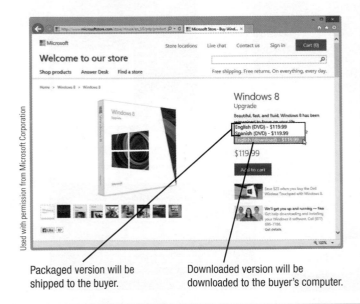

FIGURE 6-6

Installed software.

Is often purchased via the Internet.

Packaged version will be shipped to the buyer.

Downloaded version will be downloaded to the buyer's computer.

Installed Software

Installed software must be installed on a computer before it is run. Desktop software can be purchased in physical form (such as on a CD or DVD) or downloaded from the Internet (see Figure 6-6); mobile software is almost always downloaded from an *app store*, such as the App Store or Google Play (shown in Figure 6-4). In either case, the program is installed using its *installation program* (which typically runs automatically when the software CD or DVD is inserted into the drive or when the downloaded program is opened). Once the software is installed, it is ready to use. Whether or not installed software requires a fee depends on whether the program is a commercial, demo/trial, shareware, freeware, or public domain program. For a look at how custom installed apps are being used to help American Airlines pilots and flight attendants during flights, see the Trend box.

Cloud Software

Instead of being available in an installed format, some software is run directly from the Internet as **cloud software**, also referred to as **Software as a Service (SaaS)** and **cloudware**.

>**Installed software.** Software that must be installed on a computer in order to be used. >**Cloud software.** Software that is delivered on demand via the Web; also referred to as **Software as a Service (SaaS)** and **cloudware**.

BUSINESS SAAS APPLICATIONS
This program allows you to share documents and collaborate on projects online.

Google Docs

Office on Demand

WEB DATABASE APPLICATIONS
This application allows you to retrieve property information, such as home values and homes for sale.

CLOUD PRODUCTIVITY APPLICATIONS
These programs allow you to create documents online.

Courtesy Soonr; Courtesy Zillow; Google screenshot © Google Inc. and used with permission.; Used with permission from Microsoft Corporation

SW

Cloud software is delivered on demand via the Web to wherever the user is at the moment, provided he or she has an Internet connection (and has paid to use the software if a payment is required). The use of cloud software is growing rapidly and research firm IDC estimates that the enterprise SaaS market alone will exceed $67 billion by 2016. Typically, documents created using cloud software are stored online so that they are accessible via any Internet-enabled device.

There is a wide range of both free and fee-based cloud software available (see Figure 6-7). For instance, many free interactive games are available through Web sites and there are several free online *office suites* (such as *Google Docs, ThinkFree Online, CloudOn,* and *Zoho Docs*) that can be used on computers and mobile devices as an alternative to the Microsoft Office office suite (discussed in more detail shortly). Some software is offered in both installed and cloud versions. For instance, the latest version of Microsoft Office is available as a traditional installed version (*Office 2013*) or a subscription-based cloud version (*Office 365*); Office 365 users can install and use the program on their computers, as well as stream the program over the Internet via the *Office on Demand* feature (shown

FIGURE 6-7
Cloud software. Is commonly used with both computers and mobile devices.

TIP

Android and iOS versions of Microsoft Office are expected by the end of 2014.

TREND

Airline Apps

A more personalized in-flight experience is just about a reality for some airline passengers. American Airlines is currently in the process of outfitting all 17,000 cabin crew members with Samsung Galaxy Note tablets in order to provide better and additional services to passengers during flights. Using the device equipped with customized software, flight attendants will have immediate access to customer data, such as seat assignments, loyalty program status, meal and beverage preferences for premium class customers, and special assistance needs. Pending FAA approval, they will also be able to connect to the airplane's Wi-Fi connection to provide passengers with up-to-the minute information about connecting flight gate locations, weather, and flight delays, as well as complete customer food purchases and other in-flight transactions.

The Samsung Galaxy Note was chosen based on flight attendant feedback after months of testing various devices. The device includes a 5.3-inch touch screen display and was preferred because it is thin, portable, and easy to read—a device that flight attendants can carry in one hand, use, and then slip in a pocket. The software on all 17,000 devices can be updated remotely and American plans to add additional capabilities (such as replacing the flight attendant paper manual with an electronic version) over time. Not to be left out, American Airlines pilots are receiving 8,000 iPads to replace the heavy paper manuals, maps, and other documents pilots are required to carry with them (see the accompanying photo). American Airlines is the first airline to deploy these *Electronic Flight Bags* (*EFB*)

throughout its entire fleet, and the company estimates that this change will save more than 400,000 gallons of fuel (and more than $1 million in fuel costs) per year.

American Airlines planes now have approximately 25,000 media tablets being used in-flight today. Talk about "cloud" computing...

Courtesy American Airlines

American Airlines pilots have replaced 35 pounds of paper documents with 1.35-pound iPads.

in Figure 6-7). In addition, many business software services are offered as SaaS, including applications geared for collaboration, scheduling, customer service, accounting, project management, and more. Typically, business SaaS applications use a subscription (often per user, per month) pricing scheme; companies that deliver SaaS are sometimes referred to as *application service providers* (*ASPs*). As it evolves, cloud software is beginning to move from single stand-alone applications to groups of products that can work together to fulfill a wide variety of needs. For instance, the Google Docs Home page provides access to the Google Docs applications, but it also allows easy access to other Google online services, such as Gmail, Calendar, Photos, and Web search.

One advantage of cloud software over installed software is that the programs and your files can be accessed from any computer with an Internet connection regardless of the type of computer or operating system used; some can also be accessed via a smartphone, media tablet, or other type of Internet-enabled mobile device. This makes cloud software especially appropriate for applications like shared scheduling and collaboration applications that are time-critical because documents and other data can be shared regardless of an individual's location or device. Other advantages of cloud software include ease of implementation, potential lower cost of ownership, improved collaboration capabilities, and always working with the most current version of the software without having to perform software updates on company computers. In addition, cloud applications can easily interface with existing online databases, such as online maps and property records (for instance, the real estate applications accessible via the Zillow Web site shown in Figure 6-7 utilize maps, property record information, and real estate listing information pulled from various online databases).

Some potential disadvantages of cloud software are that online applications tend to run more slowly than applications stored on a local hard drive, that many online applications have a limit regarding the file size of the documents you create, and that the cost may eventually exceed the cost of buying a similar installed software program. In addition, you cannot access cloud software and your data if the server on which they reside goes down or if you are in a location with no Internet access, such as while traveling or in a rural area. To eliminate this last concern, a growing trend is for online applications to also function, at least in part, offline. For instance, Google Docs includes offline capabilities so that users can access the Google Docs applications and their documents locally on their computers, when needed. Edits are stored locally on the computer when a user is offline and, when the user reconnects to the Internet, the changes are synchronized with the documents stored on the Google Docs servers.

Software Suites

Sometimes, related software programs (such as a group of graphics programs, utility programs, or office-related software) are sold bundled together as a **software suite**. Businesses and many individuals often use *office suites*, sometimes called *productivity software suites*, to produce written documents. Typically, office suites contain the following programs; many also contain additional productivity tools—such as a calendar, an e-mail or a messaging program, or collaboration tools.

> *Word processing software*—allows users to easily create and edit complex text-based documents that can also include images and other content.

> *Spreadsheet software*—provides users with a convenient means of creating documents containing complex mathematical calculations.

> *Database software*—allows users to store and organize vast amounts of data and retrieve specific information when needed.

> *Presentation graphics software*—allows users to create visual presentations to convey information more easily to others.

One of the most widely used office software suites is **Microsoft Office**. The latest version is Microsoft Office 2013 (called Office 365 when purchased as an online subscription). Similar suites are available from Corel (*WordPerfect Office*) and Apple (*iWork*) (see Figure 6-8). Free alternative installed office suites are *LibreOffice* and *Apache OpenOffice*; as already mentioned, free cloud office suites include Google Docs and CloudOn. Many office suites are available in a variety of versions, such as a home or student version that contains fewer programs than a professional version. Not all software suites are available for all operating systems, however. For example, Microsoft Office is available for both Windows and Mac OS computers; iWork is available only for Mac OS computers; and both LibreOffice and Apache OpenOffice are available for Windows, Linux, and Mac OS computers. Apache OpenOffice is also available in more than 30 different languages.

The primary advantages of using a software suite include a common interface among programs in the suite and a total cost that is lower than buying the programs individually. Although most programs written for the same operating system (such as Windows or

SW

FIGURE 6-8

Office suites. Three of the most common commercial office suites are Microsoft Office, Corel WordPerfect Office, and Apple iWork.

Mac OS) use similar interfaces and commands, the entire command interface for a software suite is usually very similar from program to program. This similarity is not only for basic commands (such as *Save* and *Print*) but also for all commands (such as adding borders and shading or inserting a row or column) that appear in more than one program in the suite. The standardization of the user interface across all programs in a suite means that once you are familiar with how to use one program in a suite, you will probably find it easy to learn another program in that suite.

Common Software Commands

One of the greatest advantages of using software instead of paper and pencil to create a document is that you do not have to recreate the entire document when you want to make changes to it. This is because the document is created in RAM and then saved on a storage medium, instead of being created directly on paper. Consequently, the document can be retrieved, modified, saved, and printed as many times as needed. The types of commands used to perform these tasks are similar in most application programs; the most common ways to issue commands to application programs are discussed next.

FIGURE 6-9
Common application software commands.

Toolbars, Menus, Keyboard Shortcuts, and the Ribbon

Most commands in an application program are issued through *menus*, *keyboard shortcuts*, or *command buttons* located on a *toolbar* or *Ribbon*. As shown in Figure 1-10 in Chapter 1, the *menu bar* appears at the top of many windows and contains text-based lists (menus), which provide access to commands that can be selected to perform actions in that program. Many programs also have toolbars—sets of *icons* or command buttons that are clicked with the mouse to issue commands. **Keyboard shortcuts** are key combinations that correspond to specific commands, such as Ctrl+S for the Save command (this keyboard shortcut is issued by holding down the Ctrl key and pressing the S key). A list of common keyboard shortcuts used in Microsoft Office and many other programs is shown in Figure 6-9, along with examples of the command buttons typically used to perform these operations.

COMMAND	COMMAND BUTTON	KEYBOARD SHORTCUT	DESCRIPTION
Open		Ctrl+O	Opens a dialog box so you can choose a saved document to open from a storage medium so it can be edited or printed.
Save		Ctrl+S	Saves the current version of the document to a storage medium.
Print		Ctrl+P	Prints the current version of the document onto paper.
Cut		Ctrl+X	Moves the selected item to the Clipboard.
Copy		Ctrl+C	Copies the selected item to the Clipboard.
Paste		Ctrl+V	Pastes the last item copied or cut to the Clipboard to the current location.
Undo		Ctrl+Z	Undoes the last change to the document.
Close		Alt+F4	Closes the document. Any changes made to the document are lost if the document wasn't saved first.

>**Keyboard shortcut.** A combination of keyboard keys that are pressed in unison to issue a specific software command.

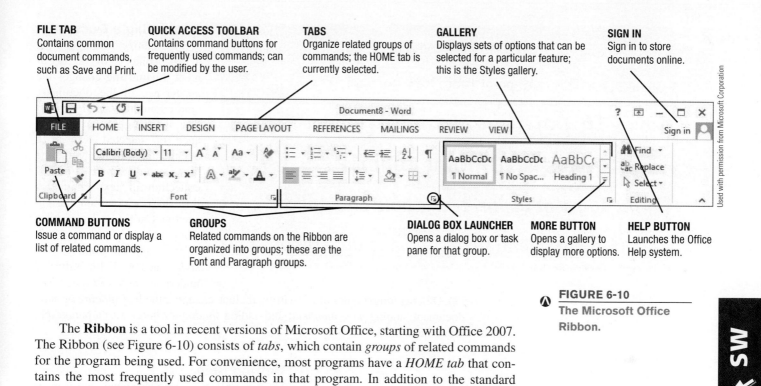

FILE TAB
Contains common document commands, such as Save and Print.

QUICK ACCESS TOOLBAR
Contains command buttons for frequently used commands; can be modified by the user.

TABS
Organize related groups of commands; the HOME tab is currently selected.

GALLERY
Displays sets of options that can be selected for a particular feature; this is the Styles gallery.

SIGN IN
Sign in to store documents online.

COMMAND BUTTONS
Issue a command or display a list of related commands.

GROUPS
Related commands on the Ribbon are organized into groups; these are the Font and Paragraph groups.

DIALOG BOX LAUNCHER
Opens a dialog box or task pane for that group.

MORE BUTTON
Opens a gallery to display more options.

HELP BUTTON
Launches the Office Help system.

Used with permission from Microsoft Corporation

FIGURE 6-10
The Microsoft Office Ribbon.

The **Ribbon** is a tool in recent versions of Microsoft Office, starting with Office 2007. The Ribbon (see Figure 6-10) consists of *tabs*, which contain *groups* of related commands for the program being used. For convenience, most programs have a *HOME tab* that contains the most frequently used commands in that program. In addition to the standard Ribbon tabs that are available whenever the program is open, additional *contextual tabs* are displayed as needed, depending on the action being taken. For instance, selecting a picture or other graphic in Word displays the *PICTURE TOOLS tab* that contains commands you might use to edit a picture, such as to crop, resize, rotate, or recolor the picture. Clicking a command button on the Ribbon either carries out that command or displays a *gallery* of choices from which the user can select the desired action. The *FILE tab* replaces the Microsoft Office Button and the File menu used in older versions of Office and opens the *Backstage view*, which contains commands commonly used with all documents, such as to open, save, print, send, and publish a document.

Editing a Document

Editing a document refers to changing the content of the document, such as adding or deleting text. Most application programs that allow text editing have an **insertion point** that looks like a blinking vertical line on the screen and shows where the next change will be made to the document currently displayed on the screen. To insert text, just start typing and the text will appear at the insertion point location. To delete text, press the Delete key to delete one character to the right of the insertion point or press the Backspace key to delete one character to the left of the insertion point. If the insertion point is not in the proper location for the edit, it must be moved to the appropriate location in the document by using the arrow keys on the keyboard or by pointing and clicking with the mouse. To select an object or block of text, click the object or drag the mouse over the text. Usually, once an object or some text is selected, it can be manipulated, such as to be moved, deleted, copied, or *formatted*.

>**Ribbon.** A feature found in recent versions of Microsoft Office that uses tabs to organize groups of related commands. >**Editing.** Changing the content of a document, such as inserting or deleting words. >**Insertion point.** An on-screen character that looks like a blinking vertical line; indicates the current location in a document, which is where the next change will be made.

This is 10-point Arial.

This is 12-point Times New Roman.

This is 16-point Lucida Handwriting.

This is 20-point Calibri.

This 16-point Calibri text is bold and italic.

This 16-point Calibri text is red and underlined.

FIGURE 6-11

Fonts. The font face, size, style, and color used with text can be specified in many application programs.

Formatting a Document

While editing changes the actual content of a document, **formatting** changes the appearance of the document. One common type of formatting is changing the appearance of selected text in a document. You can change the *font face* or *typeface* (a named collection of text characters that share a common design, such as Calibri or Times New Roman), *font size* (which is measured in *points*), *font style* (such as bold, italic, or underline), and *font color* (see Figure 6-11). Other common types of formatting include changing the *line spacing* or *margins* of a document; adding *page numbers*; and adding *shading* or *borders* to a paragraph, image, or other item.

ASK THE EXPERT

LibreOffice
The Document Foundation

Cor Nouws, Founding Member and Volunteer Contributor, The Document Foundation

Can a student use the free LibreOffice office suite at home and the Microsoft Office suite at school for the same documents?

Yes, absolutely. You can save LibreOffice documents in many different formats, including Microsoft Office (such as .docx or .doc for word processing documents or .xlsx or .xls for spreadsheet files), as well as CorelDraw and Visio. While some formatting can be lost in the translation process between file formats, most features that you use in LibreOffice are also found in Office.

For complex documents, you can use styles, tables, and other formatting features to help your work look the same in both programs. You can also save your documents in either suite using the OpenDocument (ODF) file formats.

Getting Help

Most people have an occasional question or otherwise need some help as they work with a software program. There are various options for getting help when you need it. For instance, most application programs have a built-in help feature, typically available through a *Help button* or a *Help* option on a menu. The type and amount of built-in help available varies from program to program, but typically includes one or more of the following forms.

➤ *Table of Contents*—works much like the table of contents in a book; that is, with related help topics organized under main topics. With most help systems, selecting a main topic reveals the subtopics related to that main topic; subtopics can then be selected until the desired help topic is displayed. Selecting a help topic displays information related to that topic on the screen.

➤ *Browsing*—allows you to click hyperlinks related to major help categories, similar to a Table of Contents but each time a topic is clicked, a new page containing links appears, similar to the way Web pages work. Clicking a link representing a help topic displays information related to that topic on the screen.

>**Formatting.** Changing the appearance of a document, such as changing the margins or font size.

➤ *Search*—allows you to search for help topics by typing a keyword or phrase, and then the help system displays a list of links to possible matching help topics; clicking a help topic link displays information related to that topic on the screen (see Figure 6-12).

Some help systems automatically search for online help from the manufacturer's Web site if the program detects an Internet connection. In addition, there is a vast amount of additional information about application software programs available via the Web, such as online articles, tutorials, and *message boards* for particular software programs, and e-mail support from software companies. Of course, online and offline books are also available for many software programs.

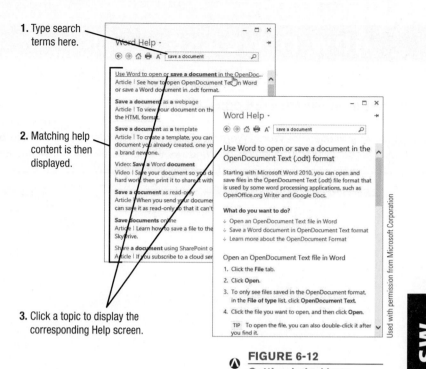

1. Type search terms here.

2. Matching help content is then displayed.

3. Click a topic to display the corresponding Help screen.

Used with permission from Microsoft Corporation

◬ FIGURE 6-12

Getting help. Most application programs have built-in help systems.

WORD PROCESSING CONCEPTS

Word processing is one of the most widely used application programs today. Although the actual commands and features vary somewhat from program to program, it is important to be familiar with the general concept of what word processing enables you to do, as well as the basic features of word processing. The following sections discuss these concepts and features.

What Is Word Processing?

Word processing refers to using a computer and **word processing software** to create, edit, save, and print written documents, such as letters, contracts, manuscripts, newsletters, invoices, marketing material, and reports. At its most basic level, word processing is used to do what was done on a typewriter before computers were commonplace. Many documents created with word processing software also include content that was not possible to create using a typewriter, such as photos, drawn objects, clip art images, hyperlinks, video clips, and text in a variety of sizes and appearances. Like any document created with software instead of paper and pencil, word processing documents can be retrieved, modified, and printed as many times as needed.

Word processing programs today typically include improved collaboration, security, and *rights-management tools* (tools used to protect original content from misuse by others). Rights management and intellectual property rights are discussed in more detail in Chapter 16; *digital signatures*, *encryption*, and other security tools that can be used to secure word processing documents are discussed in Chapter 9. Word processing programs today also typically include a variety of Web-related tools, as well as support for speech, pen, and touch input. For a look at how to use gesture input with Microsoft Word and other Microsoft Office programs on a Windows 8 touch screen computer, see the How It Works box.

TIP

To get help for a question about an application program, enter your question in a search box on your favorite search site to see a list of Web pages that may contain the answer to your question.

TIP

When selecting font size in a document, 72 points equals one-inch-tall text.

HOW IT WORKS

Gesture Input with Microsoft Office

The newest versions of Word (Word 2013) and other Microsoft Office products support gestures on Windows 8 touch screens.

You may wonder if using touch can be handy in Office applications. The answer is yes. But, before you can use touch gestures in Office programs, you need to master a few basic gestures (see the following table and the illustrations below).

GESTURE	HOW TO PERFORM	USE IN OFFICE
Tap	Using one finger, tap the screen in the appropriate location (tap twice for a *double-tap*).	Similar to clicking with the mouse. Examples: ➤ Move the insertion point (to the location where you tap). ➤ Select/open what you tap (such as a Ribbon tab or button, or the Show Keyboard button). ➤ Select text (tap in the desired text and then drag a selection handle). ➤ Select multiple objects (tap and hold the first object, then tap other objects). ➤ Resize/rotate an object (tap and then drag the resize/ rotate handle).
Press and hold	Press one finger down on the screen and leave it there for a few seconds.	Similar to right-clicking with the mouse. Examples: ➤ Show information about the selected item. ➤ Open a menu specific to the item and what you are doing.
Slide	Using one finger, touch the appropriate location on the screen and move your finger across the screen.	Similar to scrolling or dragging with the mouse. Examples: ➤ Scroll the contents of the screen. ➤ Move an object (tap and hold on an object and then drag it to the appropriate new location).
Swipe	Using one finger, touch the appropriate location on the screen and move your finger across the screen a short distance.	Show more options/items (such as when swiping a Gallery).
Pinch	Using two or more fingers (often your thumb and index finger), touch the appropriate location on the screen and move your fingers closer together.	Zoom in on your document.
Stretch	Using two or more fingers (often your thumb and index finger), touch the appropriate location on the screen and move your fingers farther apart.	Zoom out on your document.

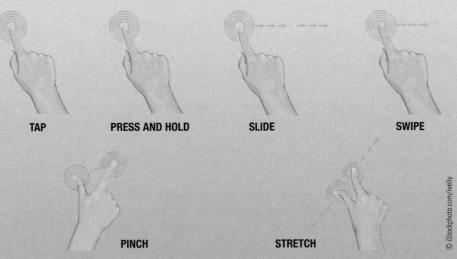

TAP PRESS AND HOLD SLIDE SWIPE

PINCH STRETCH

Virtually all formal writing today is performed using a word processing program. Among today's most frequently used word processing programs are *Microsoft Word*, *Corel WordPerfect*, and *Apple Pages*—all part of the software suites mentioned earlier in this chapter. Most word processing programs offer hundreds of features, but virtually all support a core group of features used to create, edit, and format documents. Some of these basic features are described in the next few sections, using Microsoft Word 2013 as the example. Recent versions of Word save documents using the *.docx* extension by default, although other file formats (including the original *.doc* Word 97–2003 format for files that can be opened in older versions of Word, the more universal *Rich Text Format* (*.rtf*), and several Web page formats) can be used instead when needed.

Creating a Word Processing Document

Every word processing program contains an assortment of operations for creating and editing documents, including commands to insert text, graphics, and other items, and then move, copy, delete, or otherwise edit the content, as needed. Some features in a typical word processing program are shown in Figure 6-13.

When entering text in a word processing document, it is important to know when to press the Enter key. Word processing programs use a feature called **word wrap**, which means the insertion point automatically moves to the beginning of the next line when the

FIGURE 6-13
Some features in a typical word processing program.

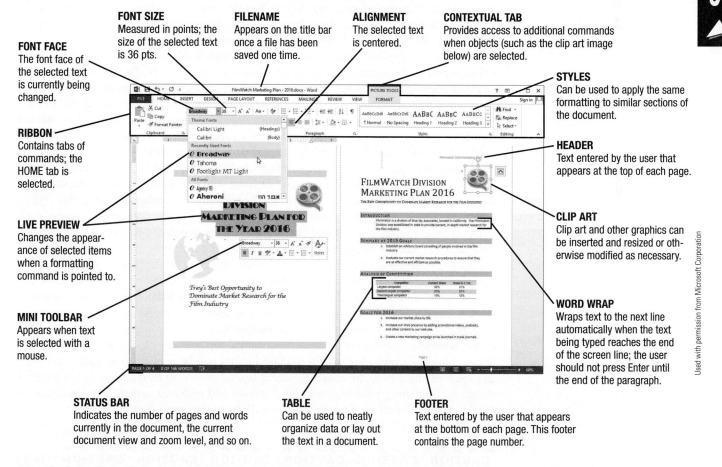

FONT SIZE Measured in points; the size of the selected text is 36 pts.

FILENAME Appears on the title bar once a file has been saved one time.

ALIGNMENT The selected text is centered.

CONTEXTUAL TAB Provides access to additional commands when objects (such as the clip art image below) are selected.

FONT FACE The font face of the selected text is currently being changed.

RIBBON Contains tabs of commands; the HOME tab is selected.

LIVE PREVIEW Changes the appearance of selected items when a formatting command is pointed to.

MINI TOOLBAR Appears when text is selected with a mouse.

STATUS BAR Indicates the number of pages and words currently in the document, the current document view and zoom level, and so on.

TABLE Can be used to neatly organize data or lay out the text in a document.

FOOTER Text entered by the user that appears at the bottom of each page. This footer contains the page number.

STYLES Can be used to apply the same formatting to similar sections of the document.

HEADER Text entered by the user that appears at the top of each page.

CLIP ART Clip art and other graphics can be inserted and resized or otherwise modified as necessary.

WORD WRAP Wraps text to the next line automatically when the text being typed reaches the end of the screen line; the user should not press Enter until the end of the paragraph.

Used with permission from Microsoft Corporation

>**Word wrap.** The feature in a word processing program that automatically returns the insertion point to the next line when the end of the screen line is reached.

end of the screen line is reached. Consequently, the Enter key should not be pressed until it is time to begin a new paragraph or leave a blank line. With word wrap, when changes are made to the document—such as adding, modifying, or deleting text or changing the text size or page margins—the program will automatically adjust the amount of text on each screen line, as long as the Enter key was not pressed at the end of each line.

In most word processing programs, formatting can be applied at the character, paragraph, and document levels. *Character formatting* changes the appearance of individual characters, such as to change the font face, size, style, or color. To format characters, you usually select them with the mouse, and then apply the appropriate format. In recent versions of Word, for instance, you can use the command buttons on the Ribbon's HOME tab or the *Mini toolbar* (which appears when text is selected and is designed to allow easy text formatting). To see additional character formatting options, click the *Font Dialog Box Launcher* (a small arrow at the lower-right corner of the *Font group* on the HOME tab) to open the *Font dialog box*. As shown in Figure 6-13, Word includes a *Live Preview* feature, which allows the user to see the results of many formatting commands before they are applied, such as watching selected text change as the user scrolls through a list of font faces or sizes.

Paragraph formatting changes an entire paragraph at one time, such as specifying the *line spacing* for a particular paragraph. To format paragraphs, you usually select the paragraph with the mouse, and then apply the appropriate format. In Word, for instance, you can use the command buttons in the *Paragraph group* on the Ribbon's HOME tab or you can click the *Paragraph Dialog Box Launcher* to open the *Paragraph dialog box*. The most common types of paragraph formatting include *line spacing*, *indentation*, and *alignment*. Line spacing is the amount of blank space between lines of text—usually set to 1 for single spacing or 2 for double spacing. Indentation is the distance between the paragraph and the left or right margin. Alignment indicates how the paragraph is aligned in relation to the left and right margins of the document, such as *left*, *center*, *right*, or *justify* (flush with both the left and right edges of the document as in this textbook). *Tabs* are set locations to which the insertion point is moved when the Tab key on the keyboard is pressed. Usually the tab settings are preset to every one-half inch, but the tab settings can be changed by the user. *Styles*—named format specifications—can also be applied on a paragraph-by-paragraph basis. Styles are used to keep a uniform appearance for related parts of a document. Once a paragraph has been assigned a style (such as one of Word's predefined styles, like Heading 1, or a new style defined by the user), all other paragraphs formatted with that style will appear the same and any formatting changes made to the style will be applied to all paragraphs using that style.

Most word processing programs also have a variety of *page formatting* options, such as changing the *margins*, the *paper size* being used, and whether you want the page to use the traditional *portrait orientation* (8.5 inches wide by 11 inches tall on standard paper) or the wider *landscape orientation* (11 inches wide by 8.5 inches tall on standard paper). In recent versions of Word, most page formatting options are found on the *PAGE LAYOUT tab* on the Ribbon. You can also use the *INSERT tab* on the Ribbon to add page numbers at the top or bottom of the page, or to specify a *header* or *footer*. As shown in Figure 6-13, a header or a footer is specified text or images that print automatically on every page unless otherwise specified; a header appears at the top of every page and a footer appears at the bottom of every page. Many of these options can be applied to an individual page as page formatting or to the entire document (called *document formatting*). Other types of document formatting include generating *footnotes* and *endnotes*, a *table of contents*, or an *index*, as well as applying a *background* or a *theme* to the entire document.

CAUTION CAUTION CAUTION CAUTION CAUTION CAUTION CAUT

To avoid the embarrassment of distributing a document with hidden text, internal comments, personal information, and other data you may not want to pass on to others, click *FILE*, *Info*, *Check for Issues*, and then *Prepare for Sharing* to check for and remove this data before distribution.

INSERT TAB
Used to insert a table, picture, shape, or other object into the document.

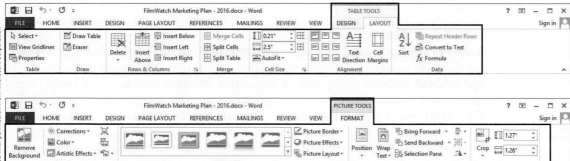

TABLE TOOLS CONTEXTUAL TABS
Used to change the design or layout of a table; available only when a table is selected.

PICTURE TOOLS CONTEXTUAL TAB
Used to format a picture object, such as to crop it or change its size, color, or border; available only when an image is selected.

Used with permission from Microsoft Corporation

FIGURE 6-14
Ribbon tabs used to insert and modify tables and images.

Tables, Graphics, and Templates

Most word processing programs today have advanced features to help users create documents or add special features to documents. For instance, a *table* feature allows content to be organized in a table consisting of *rows* and *columns*. Tables can be used as basic data tables, such as the one shown in Figure 6-13; they can also be used to lay out documents, such as when creating a newsletter, résumé, or Web page. Once a table has been created, shading, borders, and other formatting can be applied to the table and/or its contents, and rows and columns can be inserted or deleted, as needed. There are a number of Ribbon tabs that can be used in Word to help users insert and modify tables. For instance, the INSERT tab (shown in Figure 6-14) is used to insert tables (as well as pictures, shapes, charts, text boxes, and other objects). Once a table is created and selected, the *TABLE TOOLS* contextual tabs (*DESIGN* and *LAYOUT*—LAYOUT is the active tab in Figure 6-14) appear on the Ribbon and contain commands that can be used to modify the table.

Graphics or *drawing* features are also commonly found in word processing programs. Virtually all word processing programs allow images (such as a photograph, a drawing from another program, a geometric shape, or a *clip art image* like the one in Figure 6-13) to be inserted into a document. Once an image is inserted into a document, it can be modified (such as changing the brightness or contrast of a digital photo, cropping an image, converting a color image to grayscale, compressing an image to reduce the file size of the document, or adding borders). The *PICTURE TOOLS* contextual tab, which is used in Word for these purposes and is displayed on the Ribbon whenever an image is selected, is shown in Figure 6-14. Once images are inserted into a document, they can be copied, moved, deleted, or otherwise modified, just like any other object in the document.

To help users create new documents quickly, many word processing programs have a variety of *templates* available. A template is a document that is already created and formatted to fit a particular purpose, such as a fax cover sheet, résumé, memo, calendar, invoice, newsletter, or Web page. Usually placeholder text is included for text that can be customized so that all the user needs to do is to replace that text with the appropriate content.

Word Processing and the Web

Most word processing programs today include Web-related features, such as the ability to send a document as an e-mail message or post to a blog via the word processing program, the inclusion of Web page hyperlinks in documents, and the ability to create or modify Web pages. The latest versions of Office also include the ability to collaborate with others online, as well as stream Office apps from and store Office documents in the cloud.

TIP

When using a table for layout purposes, change the table borders to *None* after the document is finished to make the table outline invisible.

TIP

Additional templates are often available free of charge through software manufacturer Web sites, such as Microsoft's *Office.com* Web site.

TIP

To open the Web page associated with a hyperlink included in a document (assuming you have an active Internet connection), hold down the Ctrl key and then click the hyperlink.

SPREADSHEET CONCEPTS

Another widely used application program is *spreadsheet software*. Spreadsheet software is commonly used by a variety of businesses and employees, including CEOs, managers, assistants, analysts, and sales representatives. Basic spreadsheet concepts and features are described next.

What Is a Spreadsheet?

A **spreadsheet** is a group of values and other data organized into rows and columns, similar to the ruled paper worksheets traditionally used by bookkeepers and accountants. **Spreadsheet software** is the type of application software used to create computerized spreadsheets, which typically contain a great deal of numbers and mathematical calculations. Most spreadsheets include *formulas* that are used to compute calculations based on data entered into the spreadsheet. All formula results are updated automatically whenever any changes are made to the data. Consequently, no manual computations are required, which increases accuracy. In addition, the automatic recalculation of formulas allows individuals to modify spreadsheet data as often as necessary either to create new spreadsheets or to experiment with various possible scenarios (called *what-if analysis*, as discussed shortly) to help make business decisions. Spreadsheet software typically includes a variety of data analysis tools, as well as the ability to generate charts.

The most widely used spreadsheet programs today are *Microsoft Excel*, *Corel Quattro Pro*, and *Apple Numbers*—again, all are part of their respective software suites mentioned near the beginning of this chapter. Some of the basic features supported by all spreadsheet programs are described in the next few sections, using Microsoft Excel 2013 as the example. Recent versions of Excel save spreadsheet files with the *.xlsx* extension by default.

Creating a Spreadsheet

A single spreadsheet document is often called a **worksheet**. Most spreadsheet programs allow multiple worksheets to be saved together in a single spreadsheet file, called a **workbook**. Worksheets are divided into **rows** and **columns**. The intersection of a row and a column is called a **cell**. Each cell is identified by its *cell address*, which consists of the column letter followed by the row number, such as B4 or E22. The *cell pointer* is used to select a cell; the selected cell is called the *active cell* or *current cell* and has a border around it so it is easy to identify. You can enter content into the active cell, as well as apply formatting to content already in the active cell. The cell pointer can be used to select more than one cell; if so, the selected cells are called a *range* or *block*. Ranges are always rectangular and are identified by specifying two opposite corners of the range, such as D8 through E9 for the four cells in the range shown in Figure 6-15 (and usually typed as *D8:E9* or *D8..E9*, depending on the spreadsheet program being used). As with Word, the Excel interface uses the Ribbon, contextual tabs, the Mini toolbar, and Live Preview for editing and formatting.

Entering Data into a Spreadsheet Cell

Data is entered directly into worksheet cells by clicking a cell to make it the active cell and then typing the data to be contained in that cell. The contents of the active cell can be erased by pressing the Delete key or by typing new content, which replaces the old contents of that cell. The data entered into a cell is usually a *label*, a *constant value*, a *formula*,

>**Spreadsheet.** A document containing a group of values and other data organized into rows and columns. >**Spreadsheet software.** Application software used to create spreadsheets, which typically contain a great deal of numbers and mathematical computations organized into rows and columns. >**Worksheet.** A single spreadsheet document in a spreadsheet program. >**Workbook.** A collection of worksheets saved in a single spreadsheet file. >**Row.** In a spreadsheet program, a horizontal group of cells on a worksheet. >**Column.** In a spreadsheet program, a vertical group of cells on a worksheet. >**Cell.** The location at the intersection of a row and column on a worksheet into which data can be typed.

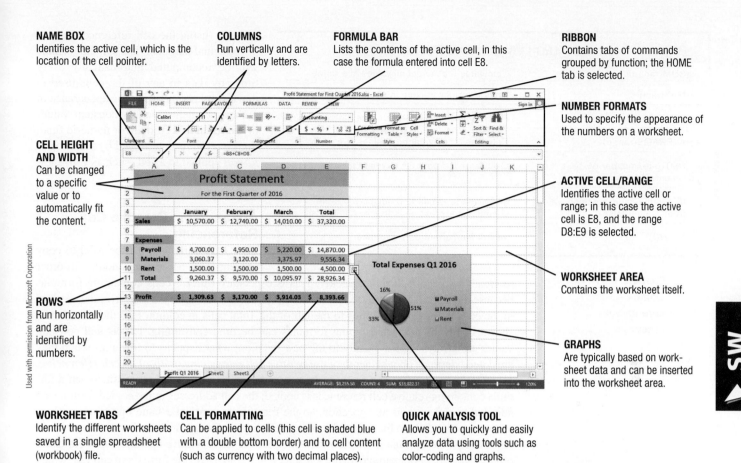

NAME BOX
Identifies the active cell, which is the location of the cell pointer.

COLUMNS
Run vertically and are identified by letters.

FORMULA BAR
Lists the contents of the active cell, in this case the formula entered into cell E8.

RIBBON
Contains tabs of commands grouped by function; the HOME tab is selected.

NUMBER FORMATS
Used to specify the appearance of the numbers on a worksheet.

CELL HEIGHT AND WIDTH
Can be changed to a specific value or to automatically fit the content.

ACTIVE CELL/RANGE
Identifies the active cell or range; in this case the active cell is E8, and the range D8:E9 is selected.

ROWS
Run horizontally and are identified by numbers.

WORKSHEET AREA
Contains the worksheet itself.

GRAPHS
Are typically based on worksheet data and can be inserted into the worksheet area.

WORKSHEET TABS
Identify the different worksheets saved in a single spreadsheet (workbook) file.

CELL FORMATTING
Can be applied to cells (this cell is shaded blue with a double bottom border) and to cell content (such as currency with two decimal places).

QUICK ANALYSIS TOOL
Allows you to quickly and easily analyze data using tools such as color-coding and graphs.

FIGURE 6-15
Some features in a typical spreadsheet program.

FIGURE 6-16
Universal mathematical operators.

or a *function*. **Labels** are words, column headings, and other nonmathematical data, such as *Profit Statement* and *January* in Figure 6-15. **Constant values** are numbers (such as *105* or *12740.25*) and are entered into a cell without any additional characters (such as a dollar sign or comma). A **formula** performs mathematical operations using the content of other cells (such as adding or multiplying the values in the specified cells) and displays the result in the cell containing the formula. A **function** is a named, preprogrammed formula, such as to compute the average of a group of cells or to calculate a mortgage payment amount. There are literally hundreds of functions that can be used in spreadsheets for statistical, date and time, engineering, math, logical, and text-based computations. The standard mathematical operators used in formulas and functions are shown in Figure 6-16; some examples of commonly used spreadsheet functions are listed in Figure 6-17.

When entering a formula or function into a cell, most spreadsheet programs require that you begin with some type of mathematical symbol—usually the equal sign (=). You can then enter the cell addresses and mathematical operators to create the formula, or you can type the appropriate function name and *arguments* (such as a cell or range address). When creating formulas and functions, it is important to always use the cell addresses of the numbers you want to include in the calculation (such as =B8+C8+D8 for the formula used to calculate the value displayed in cell E8 in Figure 6-15), rather than the numbers themselves (such as =4700+4950+5220). If the actual numbers are used in a formula instead of the cell addresses, the result of that formula (such as the total in cell E8) will not be correctly updated if one of the numbers (such as January payroll expenses in cell B8) is changed. When a proper

SYMBOL	OPERATION
+	Addition
−	Subtraction
*	Multiplication
/	Division
^	Exponentiation

>**Label.** A text-based entry in a worksheet cell that identifies data on the worksheet. >**Constant value.** A numerical entry in a worksheet cell.
>**Formula.** An entry in a worksheet cell that performs computations on worksheet data and displays the results. >**Function.** A named formula that can be entered into a worksheet cell to perform some type of calculation or to extract information from other cells in the worksheet.

EXAMPLES OF FUNCTIONS

=SUM(range)	Calculates the sum of all values in a range.
=MAX(range)	Finds the highest value in a range.
=MIN(range)	Finds the lowest value in a range.
=AVERAGE(range)	Calculates the average of values in a range.
=PMT(rate, number of payments, loan amount)	Calculates the periodic payment for a loan.
=IF(conditional expression, value if true, value if false)	Supplies the values to be displayed if the conditional expression is true or if it is false.
=NOW( )	Inserts the current date and time.

FIGURE 6-17
Common spreadsheet functions.

FIGURE 6-18
Relative vs. absolute cell referencing.

formula (using the cell references instead of the actual numbers) is used, the formula will be recomputed automatically every time any data in any of the cells used in that formula is changed. The appearance of numeric content (such as constant values or the result of a formula or numeric function) in a cell is determined by the *number format* applied to a cell (such as *Currency*, *Comma*, or *Percent*).

Absolute vs. Relative Cell Referencing

The Copy command can be used to copy content from one cell to another, in order to create a spreadsheet more quickly. This is especially true for cells containing formulas because the cells in a column or row often contain similar formulas (such as to add the values in the cells in the three columns to the left of the Total cells in column E in the spreadsheet shown in Figure 6-15) and typing formulas can be time consuming. Labels and constant values are always copied exactly to the new location; what happens to formulas when they are copied depends on whether they use *relative cell referencing* or *absolute cell referencing*.

Relative cell references are used in most spreadsheet programs by default. When a formula containing relative cell references is copied, the cell addresses in the copied formula are adjusted to reflect their new location, so the formula performs the same operation (such as adding the two cells to the left of the cell containing the formula) but in the new location. In other words, the formula in the new location does the same *relative* operation as it did in the original location. For example, in the left screen in Figure 6-18, the formula in cell D2 (which uses relative cell references to add the two cells to the left of the cell containing the formula) is copied to cells D3 and D4. Because the cell references are all relative, when the formula is copied to the new cells, the cell references are adjusted to continue to add the two cells to the left of the formula cell. For instance, the formula in cell D3 is updated automatically to

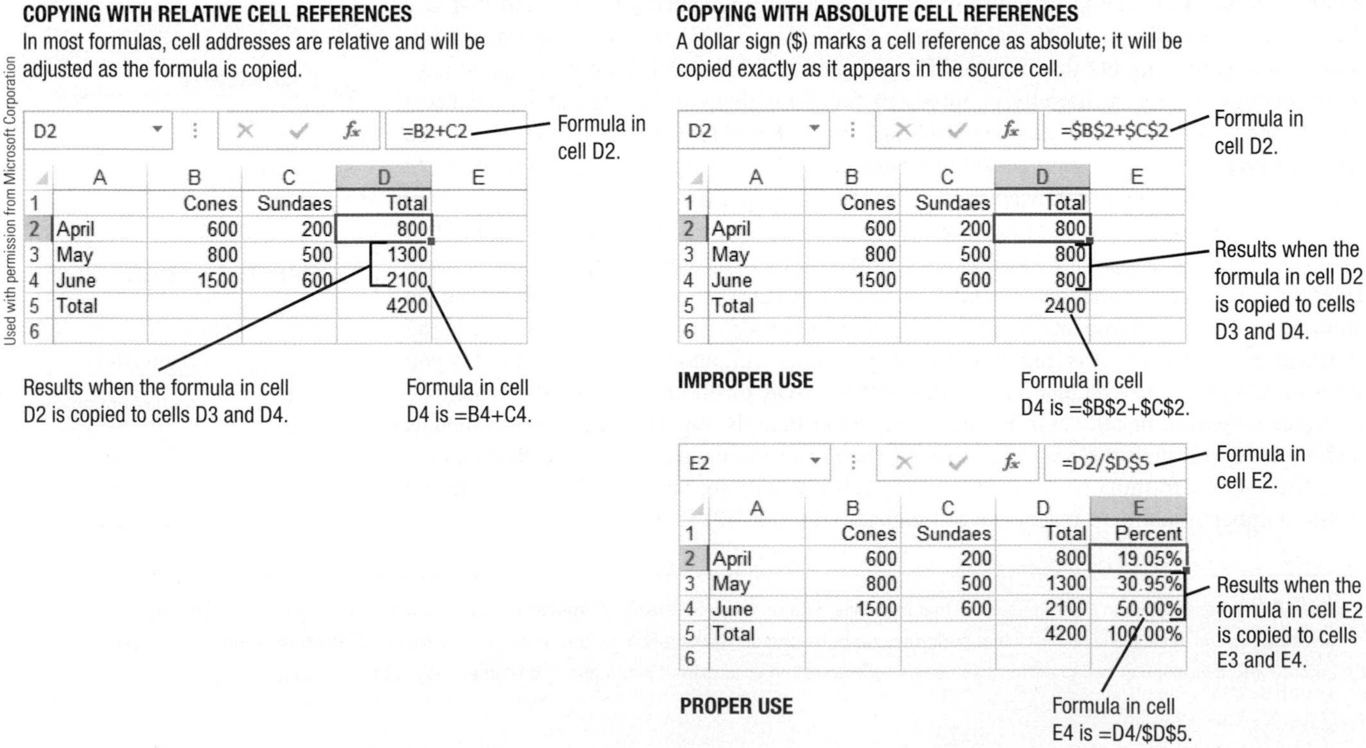

COPYING WITH RELATIVE CELL REFERENCES
In most formulas, cell addresses are relative and will be adjusted as the formula is copied.

D2 | fx =B2+C2 — Formula in cell D2.

	A	B	C	D	E
1		Cones	Sundaes	Total	
2	April	600	200	800	
3	May	800	500	1300	
4	June	1500	600	2100	
5	Total			4200	
6					

Results when the formula in cell D2 is copied to cells D3 and D4.

Formula in cell D4 is =B4+C4.

COPYING WITH ABSOLUTE CELL REFERENCES
A dollar sign ($) marks a cell reference as absolute; it will be copied exactly as it appears in the source cell.

D2 | fx =$B$2+$C$2 — Formula in cell D2.

	A	B	C	D	E
1		Cones	Sundaes	Total	
2	April	600	200	800	
3	May	800	500	800	
4	June	1500	600	800	
5	Total			2400	
6					

Results when the formula in cell D2 is copied to cells D3 and D4.

IMPROPER USE

Formula in cell D4 is =$B$2+$C$2.

E2 | fx =D2/$D$5 — Formula in cell E2.

	A	B	C	D	E
1		Cones	Sundaes	Total	Percent
2	April	600	200	800	19.05%
3	May	800	500	1300	30.95%
4	June	1500	600	2100	50.00%
5	Total			4200	100.00%
6					

Results when the formula in cell E2 is copied to cells E3 and E4.

PROPER USE

Formula in cell E4 is =D4/$D$5.

=B3+C3 and the formula in cell D4 is updated automatically to =B4+C4. Relative cell references are also adjusted automatically when a row or column is inserted or deleted.

In contrast, when *absolute cell references* are used, formulas are copied exactly as they are written (see the rightmost screens in Figure 6-18). It is appropriate to use an absolute cell reference when you want to use a specific cell address in all copies of the formula—such as always multiplying by a constant value (perhaps a sales tax rate located in a particular cell on the worksheet) or always dividing by a total in order to compute a percentage. In other words, whenever you do not want a cell address to be adjusted when the formula is copied, you must use an absolute cell reference in the formula. To make a cell reference in a formula absolute, a special symbol—usually a dollar sign ($)—is placed before each column letter and row number that should not change. For example, both of the cell references in the formula in cell D2 in the upper-right screen in Figure 6-18 are absolute, resulting in the formula =$B$2+$C$2 being placed in both cells (D3 and D4) when the formula is copied. Obviously, this is not the correct formula for these cells—the formula in cell D2 needs to use relative cell references for both cell references in order to display the proper totals in cells D3 and D4 when the formula is copied to those cells. In cells E2 through E4 in the lower-right screen, however, an absolute cell reference is correctly used for cell D5 (and written as $D$5) in order to divide the total sales for each month (located in cells D2, D3, and D4, respectively) by the total sales for all three months (located in cell D5) to compute the percent of total sales. The reference to cell D5 must be absolute if the formula in cell E2 is to be copied to other cells because the denominator in that formula should always be the value in D5.

Charts and What-If Analysis

Most spreadsheet programs include some type of *charting* or *graphing* capability. Because the data to be included in many business charts is often already located on a spreadsheet, using that program's charting feature eliminates reentering that data into another program. Instead, the cells containing the data to be charted are selected, and then the type of chart—as well as titles and other customizations—can be specified. Charts are inserted into an Excel spreadsheet using the commands in the *Charts group* on the INSERT tab on the Ribbon. Finished charts (like the one in Figure 6-15) can be moved like other graphical objects to the desired location on the worksheet. Selecting an existing chart displays three *CHART TOOLS* contextual tabs on the Ribbon. These three tabs can be used to change the design, layout, or format of the chart.

Because spreadsheet programs automatically recalculate all formulas on a worksheet every time the content of a cell on the worksheet is edited, spreadsheet programs are particularly useful for *what-if analysis* (also called *sensitivity analysis*)—a tool frequently used to help make business decisions. For example, suppose you want to know *what* profit would have resulted for January in Figure 6-15 *if* sales had been $15,000 instead of $10,570. You can simply enter the new value (15000) into cell B5, and the spreadsheet program automatically recalculates all formulas, allowing you to determine (from looking at the new value in cell B13) that the profit would have been $5,739.63. This ability to enter new numbers and immediately see the result allows businesspeople to run through many more possibilities in a shorter period of time before making decisions than in the past when all such calculations had to be performed by hand. Another type of sensitivity analysis (called *goal seeking* in Microsoft Excel) involves having the spreadsheet compute the amount a constant value would need to be in order for the result of a particular formula to become a specified amount (such as the total sales required to obtain a January profit of $5,000 if all of the expenses stayed the same).

Spreadsheets and the Web

As with word processors, most spreadsheet programs have built-in Web capabilities. Although they are used less commonly to create Web pages, many spreadsheet programs include the option to save the current worksheet as a Web page, and hyperlinks can be inserted into worksheet cells. Microsoft Excel includes the ability to send a workbook as an e-mail message and to collaborate online; ranges of cells can also be copied to a Web publishing or word processing program to insert spreadsheet data into a document as a table.

TIP

Recent versions of Excel include the *Sparklines* feature (located on the Insert menu) that allows you to create tiny charts (such as column or line charts) in a single cell to illustrate trends between data located in a range of cells.

DATABASE CONCEPTS

People often need to retrieve specific data rapidly while on the job. For example, a customer service representative may need to locate a customer's order status quickly while the customer is on the telephone. The registrar at a university may have to look up a student's grade point average or rapidly determine if the student has any outstanding fees before processing his or her class registration. A clerk in a video store may need to determine if a particular DVD is available for rental and, if not, when it is scheduled to be returned. The type of software used for such tasks is a *database management system*. Computer-based database management systems are rapidly replacing the paper-based filing systems that people used in the past to find information. The most common type of database used with personal computers today is a *relational database*. The basic features and concepts of this type of database software are discussed next. Other types of database programs are discussed in Chapter 14.

What Is a Database?

A **database** is a collection of related data that is stored on a computer and organized in a manner that enables information to be retrieved as needed. A *database management system (DBMS)*—also called **database software**—is the type of program used to create, maintain, and organize data in a database, as well as to retrieve information from it. Typically data in a database is organized into *fields*, *records*, and *files*. A **field** (today more commonly called a **column**) is a single type of data, such as last name or telephone number, to be stored in a database. A **record** (today more commonly called a **row**) is a collection of related fields—for example, the ID number, name, address, and major of Phyllis Hoffman (see Figure 6-19).

FIGURE 6-19

Paper-based vs. computerized databases. Data is organized into fields (columns), records (rows), and tables.

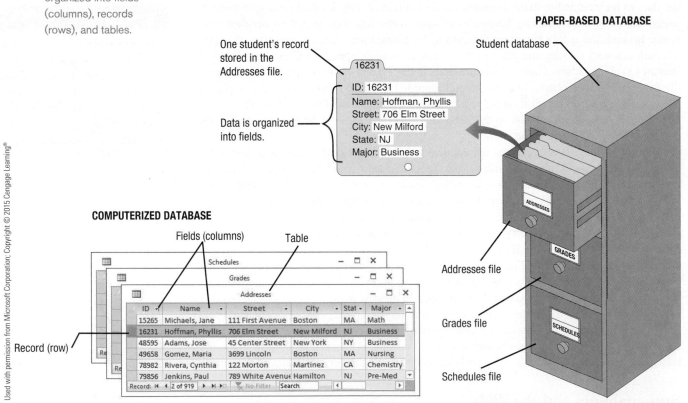

>**Database.** A collection of related data that is stored in a manner enabling information to be retrieved as needed; in a relational database, a collection of related tables. >**Database software.** Application software that allows the creation and manipulation of an electronic database. >**Field.** A single category of data to be stored in a database, such as a person's last name or phone number; also called a **column**. >**Record.** A collection of related fields in a database; also called a **row**.

A **table** is a collection of related records (such as all student address data, all student grade data, or all student schedule data). One or more related tables can be stored in a database file.

The most commonly used *relational database management systems* (*RDBMSs*) include *Microsoft Access* (part of the Microsoft Office software suite), *Corel Paradox, Oracle Database,* and IBM's *DB2*. Some of the basic features of relational database programs in general are described in the next few sections, using Microsoft Access 2013 as the example. Recent versions of Access save database files with the *.accdb* extension by default.

Creating a Database

An Access database can contain a variety of *objects*. *Tables* are the objects that contain the database data. Other types of objects (such as *forms*, *queries*, and *reports*, discussed shortly) can be created and used in conjunction with tables when needed. As shown in Figure 6-20, a list of the various objects stored in a database file is displayed when the file is opened. However, you do not see the content of a database object until you open that object.

To create a database, you create the database file first, and then you create the database objects you want that database to contain. Each time Access is launched, you have the option of creating a new blank database file, creating a database file from a template, or opening an existing database file. If you choose to create a new blank database file, a new blank table opens in *Datasheet view* (which displays the table in rows and columns similar to a spreadsheet—see the left screen in Figure 6-21).

DATABASE FILE
Contains the Inventory database objects.

RIBBON
Contains tabs of commands grouped by function; the CREATE tab, which is used to create new database objects, is selected.

DATABASE OBJECTS
Include Tables (for storing data), Forms (for viewing and editing table data), and Queries and Reports (for retrieving information from tables).

FIGURE 6-20
Typical database objects. Common database objects include tables, forms, queries, and reports. The first object to be created is the table.

FIGURE 6-21
Creating a database table.

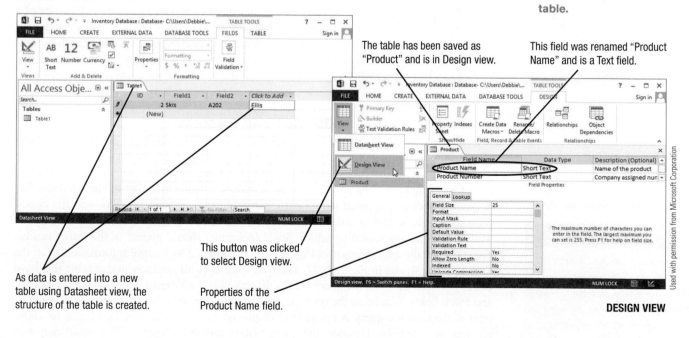

DATASHEET VIEW

The table has been saved as "Product" and is in Design view.

This field was renamed "Product Name" and is a Text field.

This button was clicked to select Design view.

As data is entered into a new table using Datasheet view, the structure of the table is created.

Properties of the Product Name field.

DESIGN VIEW

> **Table.** In a relational database, a collection of related records.

Used with permission from Microsoft Corporation

<div>

TIP

Unlike word processing and spreadsheet documents, the database file is automatically saved for you. However, you must save individual objects as they are created and modified in order for them to be included in the database file.

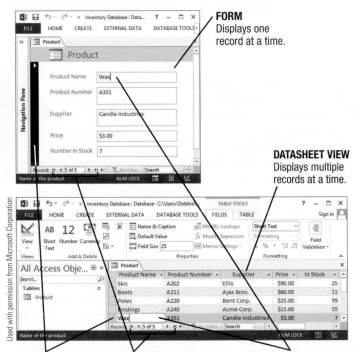

FORM
Displays one record at a time.

DATASHEET VIEW
Displays multiple records at a time.

Click to the left of a form or table record to select that record.

Click the Record buttons to display other records.

Click in a field to edit it.

FIGURE 6-22
Table data can be modified using a form or the Datasheet view.

TIP

To see your table data in both Form view and Datasheet view at the same time (in order to more quickly find a record using Datasheet view and then edit it using Form view, for example), create a *Split Form*.

As data is entered into a new table using Datasheet view, the *structure* of the table (the fields and their properties) is created. Each column becomes a new field and is given a temporary *field name* (a unique identifying name, such as *Field1*) and is assigned an appropriate *data type* (which identifies the type of data to be contained in the field; for example, text, a number, or a date) based on the data initially entered into that field. These properties can be changed by selecting the field and using the commands on the *FIELDS tab* on the *TABLE TOOLS* contextual tab on the Ribbon (such as selecting the *Name & Caption* option in the *Properties* group to rename the field or selecting a different data type using the *Data Type* option in the *Formatting* group). Each field should be given a descriptive field name and the data type should be changed if the default data type is not correct. A field can also be declared a *required* field if it cannot be left blank. Other field properties include the *field size* (the maximum number of characters allowed for the content of that field), the *default value* (the initial content of that field that remains until it is changed), the field *description*, and the *format* (how the field content should be displayed, such as including commas or dollar signs with numeric data). *Design view* (shown in the right screen in Figure 6-21) can also be used to create a table and change field properties. When the table is saved, it is given a name by the user and both the table data and structure are saved in that table object.

To add new data to an existing table, to edit data, or to delete data, either a *form* or Datasheet view can be used. As shown in Figure 6-22, a form (which is created by the user for a particular table) typically displays one record at a time, while Datasheet view displays several records at one time. However, either Datasheet view or a form can be used to change the data in the table. Data can be edited by clicking inside the appropriate field and then making the necessary edits. A record can be deleted by clicking to the left of the first field in the appropriate Datasheet row or on the left edge of a form to select that record, and then pressing the Delete key. A field can be deleted in Datasheet view by selecting the appropriate field (column), and then pressing the Delete key. The *Record buttons* at the bottom of the form or Datasheet view window can be used to move through the records as needed.

Queries and Reports

To retrieve information from a database, *queries* and *reports* are used. A *query* is a question, or, in database terms, a request for specific information from the database. Like other database objects, each query object is created and then saved using an appropriate name as a part of the database file. A query object is associated with a particular table and contains *criteria*—specific conditions that must be met in order for a record (row) to be included in the query results—as well as instructions regarding which fields (columns) should appear in the query results. For instance, the query shown in Figure 6-23 is designed to retrieve information from the Product table shown in Figure 6-22. The query retrieves all products in that table that have prices less than $25, and the query results display only the Product Name, Product Number, and Price fields. Whenever the query is opened, only the records meeting the specified criteria at the time the query is opened are displayed, and only the specified fields for those records are listed. For instance, the query results shown in Figure 6-23 contain only two records from the Product table in Figure 6-22 because only two records in that table contain products with prices less than $25. If a new product priced less than $25 is added to the database, three records will be displayed the next time the query is opened.

When a more formal output is required, *reports* are used. Reports can contain page and column headings, as well as a company logo or other graphics, and can be formatted and customized as desired. Reports are associated with a database table or query and can be easily created using the *Report button* or *Report Wizard button* on the *CREATE tab* on the Ribbon. Existing reports can be modified using the *Report Design button*. Whenever a report object is opened, the corresponding data is displayed in the specified location in the report. Consequently, just as with queries, reports always display the data contained in a table at the time the report is generated. Queries and reports are discussed in more detail in Chapter 14.

Databases and the Web

Databases are often used on the Web. Many Web sites use one or more databases to keep track of inventory; to allow searching for people, documents, or other information; to place real-time orders; and so forth. For instance, any time you type keywords in a search box on a search site or hunt for a product on a retail store's Web site using its search feature, you are using a Web database. Web databases are explained in more detail in Chapter 14.

PRESENTATION GRAPHICS CONCEPTS

If you try to explain to others what you look like, it may take several minutes. Show them a color photograph, on the other hand, and you can convey the same information within seconds. The saying "a picture is worth a thousand words" is the cornerstone of *presentation graphics*. The basic concepts and features of presentation graphics are discussed in the next few sections.

What Is a Presentation Graphic?

A **presentation graphic** (see Figure 6-24) is an image designed to enhance a presentation (such as an *electronic slide show* or a printed report) visually, typically to convey information more easily to people. A variety of software (including spreadsheet programs, *image editing programs*, and *presentation graphics software*) can be used to create presentation graphics. Presentation graphics often take the form of electronic **slides** containing images, text, video, and more that are displayed

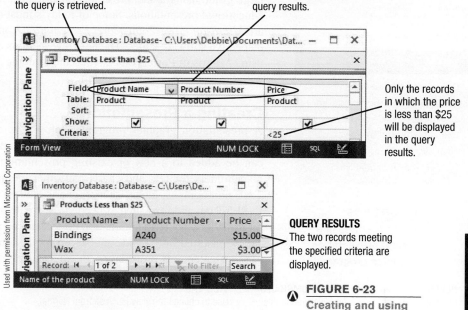

QUERY DESIGN SCREEN
This query will display only the records that meet the specified criteria each time the query is retrieved.

Only these three fields will be displayed in the query results.

Only the records in which the price is less than $25 will be displayed in the query results.

Used with permission from Microsoft Corporation

QUERY RESULTS
The two records meeting the specified criteria are displayed.

Ⓐ **FIGURE 6-23**
Creating and using a database query.

Ⓥ **FIGURE 6-24**
Examples of presentation graphics.

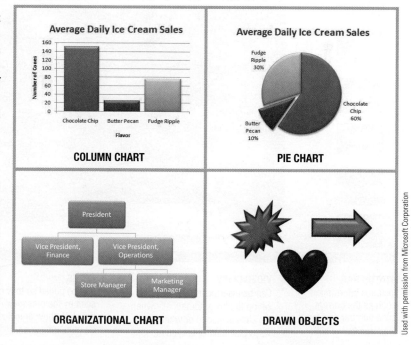

COLUMN CHART

PIE CHART

ORGANIZATIONAL CHART

DRAWN OBJECTS

Used with permission from Microsoft Corporation

SW

>**Presentation graphic.** An image, such as a graph or drawn object, designed to visually enhance a presentation. >**Slide.** A one-page presentation graphic that can be displayed in a group with others to form an electronic slide show.

one after the other in an **electronic slide show**. Electronic slide shows are created with **presentation graphics software** and can be run on individual computers or presented to a large group using a data projector; for instance, they are frequently used for business and educational presentations. Some of today's most common presentation graphics programs are *Microsoft PowerPoint*, *Corel Presentations*, and *Apple Keynote*—again, all part of their respective software suites. The next few sections discuss creating an electronic slide show, using Microsoft PowerPoint 2013 as the example. Recent versions of PowerPoint save files with the *.pptx* extension by default.

Creating a Presentation

A presentation graphics program, such as the one shown in Figure 6-25, contains an assortment of tools and operations for creating and editing slides. For instance, new slides can be added to a new or existing presentation (preformatted *slide layouts* containing placeholders for text and charts and other elements in a slide can be used, if desired). Text, photographs, tables, shapes, charts, and more can then be added to slides using the INSERT tab and formatted as needed. To create more exciting and dynamic presentations, multimedia objects and animation effects can be used. For instance, video and audio clips can be inserted into a slide and set up to play automatically each time the slide containing those elements is displayed, or, alternatively, to play when certain objects on the slide

TIP

Before inserting audio or video files into a PowerPoint slide, be sure those files are saved in a format supported by PowerPoint, such as .mp4 or .mpg for video files, or .wmv for audio files.

FIGURE 6-25
Some features in a typical presentation graphics program.

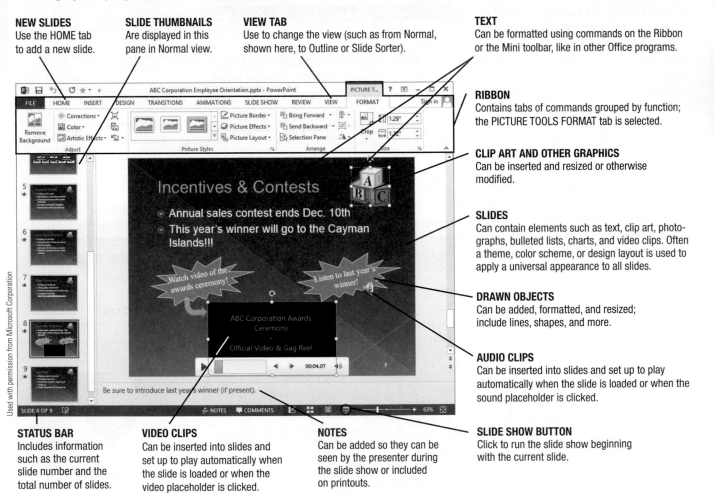

NEW SLIDES
Use the HOME tab to add a new slide.

SLIDE THUMBNAILS
Are displayed in this pane in Normal view.

VIEW TAB
Use to change the view (such as from Normal, shown here, to Outline or Slide Sorter).

TEXT
Can be formatted using commands on the Ribbon or the Mini toolbar, like in other Office programs.

RIBBON
Contains tabs of commands grouped by function; the PICTURE TOOLS FORMAT tab is selected.

CLIP ART AND OTHER GRAPHICS
Can be inserted and resized or otherwise modified.

SLIDES
Can contain elements such as text, clip art, photographs, bulleted lists, charts, and video clips. Often a theme, color scheme, or design layout is used to apply a universal appearance to all slides.

DRAWN OBJECTS
Can be added, formatted, and resized; include lines, shapes, and more.

AUDIO CLIPS
Can be inserted into slides and set up to play automatically when the slide is loaded or when the sound placeholder is clicked.

STATUS BAR
Includes information such as the current slide number and the total number of slides.

VIDEO CLIPS
Can be inserted into slides and set up to play automatically when the slide is loaded or when the video placeholder is clicked.

NOTES
Can be added so they can be seen by the presenter during the slide show or included on printouts.

SLIDE SHOW BUTTON
Click to run the slide show beginning with the current slide.

Used with permission from Microsoft Corporation

>**Electronic slide show.** A group of electronic slides that are displayed one after the other on a computer monitor or other display device.
>**Presentation graphics software.** Application software used to create presentation graphics and electronic slide shows.

are clicked. Text or other objects can be *animated* so that a special effect (such as *flying* the text in from the edge of the screen or *dissolving* the text in or out on a slide) is used to display that text or object each time the slide is viewed. *Animation settings* can be specified to indicate the sequence in which objects are displayed (such as to build a bulleted list one item at a time), whether or not a video loops continuously, and more.

Once the basic slides in a presentation have been created, the overall appearance of the entire slide show can be changed by applying a *theme* (a combination of colors, fonts, and effects that can be applied to an entire slide show at one time) to the presentation using the *DESIGN tab*. In addition, *transitions*—special effects used between slides—can be applied to specific slides, or random transitions can be selected for the entire slide show. In PowerPoint, animations and transitions are specified using the *ANIMATIONS tab* and *TRANSITIONS tab,* respectively.

Finishing a Presentation

Once all of the slides in a slide show have been created and the desired animation and transition effects have been applied, the slide show is ready to be finalized. To preview the slides and rearrange them if needed, presentation graphics programs typically have a special view, such as PowerPoint's *Slide Sorter view*, that shows thumbnails of all the slides in a presentation. Using this view, slides can easily be rearranged by dragging them with the mouse to their new location in the presentation. When the slide show is run, the slides are displayed in the designated order. The slides advance either automatically or manually, depending on how the presentation is set up. For an *automatic slide show*, the amount of time each slide should be displayed is specified using the *SLIDE SHOW tab* on the Ribbon before the presentation is saved. For a *manual slide show*, the speaker (or person viewing the slide show, for a stand-alone presentation) moves to the next slide by pressing the spacebar or by clicking anywhere on the screen using the mouse. If desired, PowerPoint allows narration to be recorded and played back when the slide show is run, and *speaker notes* can be added to the slides, as needed.

PowerPoint, like many other presentation software programs, also has a variety of *speaker tools*. For instance, the speaker can choose a laser pointer, pen, or highlighter tool and point to items or "write" on the slides while the slide show is running, perhaps to circle a particular sentence for emphasis or to draw an arrow pointing to one part of the slide. Recent versions of PowerPoint also include a *Presenter View* (see Figure 6-26) that can be used when two display devices are available (such as when a data projector is connected to the notebook computer being used to run the presentation). The regular slide show is projected in full screen for the audience on one display device (such as onto a large screen via the data projector), while a special Presenter View version of the slide show (containing a smaller version of the current slide along with speaker notes, a preview of the next slide, a timer, and so forth) is displayed for the presenter on the second display device (such as on the notebook computer's display screen). Most presentation software programs can also print the speaker notes, as well as the slides (either full-sized or miniature versions printed several to a page) to create overhead transparencies or audience handouts.

Presentation Graphics and the Web

As with the other application programs discussed so far, presentation graphics programs can be used to generate Web pages or Web page content, and slides can include hyperlinks. When a slide show is saved as a series of Web pages and displayed using a Web browser, generally forward and backward navigational buttons are displayed on the slides to allow the user to control the presentation.

FIGURE 6-26
Running an electronic slide show.

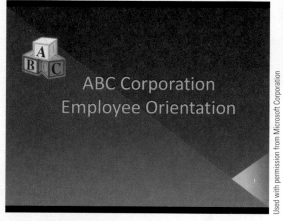

Used with permission from Microsoft Corporation

SLIDE SHOW VIEW
Displays the slide show for the audience in full screen with the software interface hidden. Slides can be advanced at predetermined intervals or by clicking the mouse or pressing the spacebar.

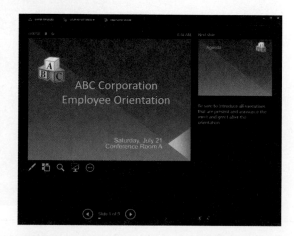

PRESENTER VIEW
Seen only by the presenter on a different display device; includes a preview of the next slide, a timer, speaker notes, annotation tools, and so forth.

GRAPHICS AND MULTIMEDIA CONCEPTS

Graphics are graphical images, such as digital photographs, clip art, scanned drawings, and original images created using a software program. *Multimedia* technically refers to any application that contains more than one type of media (as discussed in Chapter 10), but is often used to refer to audio and video content. There are a variety of software programs designed to help individuals create or modify graphics, edit digital audio or video files, play media files, burn CDs and DVDs, and so forth, as discussed next. Some programs focus on just one task; others are designed to perform multiple tasks, such as to import and edit images, audio, and video, and then create a finished DVD.

Graphics Software

Graphics software—also called *digital imaging software*—is used to create or modify images. Graphics software programs are commonly distinguished by whether they are primarily oriented toward painting, drawing, or image editing, although these are general categories, not strict classifications, and some products fit into more than one category.

Painting programs traditionally create *bitmap images*, which are created by coloring the individual pixels in an image. One of the most common painting programs is *Microsoft Paint* (shown in Figure 6-27). Painting programs are often used to create and modify simple

FIGURE 6-27
Graphics software.

PAINTING PROGRAMS
Typically create images pixel by pixel so images cannot be layered or resized.

DRAWING PROGRAMS
Typically create images using mathematical formulas so images can consist of multiple objects that can be layered, and the images can be resized without distortion.

PHOTO EDITING PROGRAMS
Allow users to edit digital photos from their computer (left) or mobile device (right).

Used with permission from Microsoft Corporation; Courtesy Corel Corporation; Courtesy Adobe Systems

> **Graphics software.** Application software used to create or modify images.

images, but, unless the painting program supports *layers* and other tools discussed shortly, use for these programs is relatively limited. This is because when something is drawn or placed on top of a bitmap image, the pixels in the image are recolored to reflect the new content so whatever was beneath the new content is lost. In addition, bitmapped images cannot be enlarged and still maintain their quality, because the pixels in the images just get larger, which makes the edges of the images look jagged. Some painting programs today do support layers and so are more versatile. Painting tools are also increasingly included in other types of software, such as in office suites and the drawing programs discussed next.

Drawing programs (also referred to as *illustration programs*) typically create *vector graphics*, which use mathematical formulas to represent image content instead of pixels. Unlike bitmap images, vector images can be resized and otherwise manipulated without loss of quality. Objects in drawing programs can also typically be *layered* so, if you place one object on top of another, you can later separate the two images if desired. Drawing programs are often used by individuals and small business owners to create original art, logos, business cards, and more; they are also used by professionals to create corporate images, Web site graphics, and so forth. Popular drawing programs include *Adobe Illustrator*, *CorelDRAW*, and *Corel Painter* (shown in Figure 6-27).

ASK THE EXPERT

Courtesy Ben Bardens

Ben Bardens, Professional Animator and Motion Graphics Artist

What computer skills should an individual obtain to prepare for a career in computer animation?

First and foremost, a solid understanding of different operating systems and how to navigate and manage files within them is crucial. It is not uncommon for digital artists to be expected to work proficiently on both Macintosh and Windows platforms and sometimes switch between the two.

Second, all digital artists (including graphic designers, motion graphics artists, animators, illustrators, and photographers) should be proficient with Adobe Photoshop. Photoshop is considered by many to be the foundation computer graphics program, and it has a broad range of uses and applications within several related fields. Any aspiring computer animator or artist should start by learning Photoshop. Once a student knows how to create and edit composite images within Photoshop, it is much easier to transition to learning other computer graphics and animation programs, such as Adobe Illustrator, After Effects, or Flash.

Image editing or *photo editing programs* are drawing or painting programs that are specifically designed for touching up or modifying images, such as original digital images and digital photos. Editing options include correcting brightness or contrast, eliminating red eye, cropping, resizing, and applying filters or other special effects. Most programs also include options for *optimizing* images to reduce the file size. Optimization techniques include reducing the number of colors used in the image, reducing the resolution of the image, and converting the image to another file format. Some of the most widely used consumer image editing and photo editing programs are *Adobe Photoshop Elements*, *Adobe Photoshop Express* (shown in Figure 6-27), *Apple iPhoto*, *Corel PaintShop Pro* (also shown in Figure 6-27), and the free *Picasa* program. For professional image editing, the full *Adobe Photoshop* program is the leading program.

> **TIP**
>
> You can often do some photo editing in apps designed to be used with smartphone photos; for instance, with *Instagram*, you can straighten a crooked photo, crop it, or apply a filter before sharing it online.

Audio Capture and Editing Software

For creating and editing audio files, *audio capture* and *audio editing* software is used. To capture sound from a microphone, *sound recorder* software is used; to capture sound from a CD, *ripping software* is used. In either case, once the audio is captured, it can then be modified, as needed. For instance, background noise or pauses can be removed, portions of the selection can be edited out, multiple segments can be spliced together, and special effects such as fade-ins and fade-outs can be applied. There are also specialized audio capture and editing programs designed for specific applications, such as creating podcasts

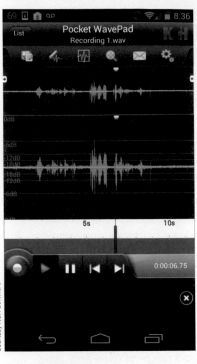

FIGURE 6-28
**Audio editing
software.**

FIGURE 6-29
**Video editing
software.** Often
includes both video
editing and DVD
authoring capabilities.

or musical compositions. Professional audio capture and editing software (such as *Sony Creative Software Sound Forge Pro* and *Adobe Audition*) is used to create professional audio for end products, Web pages, commercial podcasts, presentations, and so forth. Common consumer audio capture and editing programs include *Windows Sound Recorder*, *Apple GarageBand*, and the free *Audacity* program. The *WavePad Free Audio Editor* mobile app that can be used to record and edit voice recordings while you are on the go is shown in Figure 6-28.

Video Editing and DVD Authoring Software

It is common today for individuals to want to create finished videos, such as to create a video to upload to YouTube or to edit home videos and transfer them to a DVD. Businesses also often find the need for *video editing*, such as to prepare video clips for presentations, Web sites, or the company's YouTube channel. Most video capture today is in digital form; if so, the video can be imported directly into a video editing program by connecting the camera to the computer or by inserting the storage media containing the video (such as a DVD) into the computer. Once the video has been imported, video editing tasks (such as deleting or rearranging scenes, adding voice-overs, and adding other special effects) can be performed (see Figure 6-29). Some video editing software today can edit video in high-definition format. There are also mobile apps (such as *Vine* and *Instagram*) designed to help you create and share short videos taken with a smartphone.

DVD authoring refers to organizing content to be transferred to DVD, such as importing video clips and then creating the desired menu structure for the DVD to control the playback of those videos. *DVD burning* refers to recording data (such as a collection of songs or a finished video) on a recordable or rewritable DVD. DVD authoring and burning capabilities are commonly included with video editing capabilities in *video editing software*. There are also stand-alone *DVD authoring programs*, and DVD burning

VIDEO EDITING
Allows users to import and edit video; the finished video can be stored in a file or included in a DVD presentation.

Click to burn the finished presentation to a DVD.

The DVD includes the video clips and uses the titles and appearance designated by the user.

Video clips can be edited as needed; the timeline is used to crop out sections of the current video clip.

DVD AUTHORING
Allows users to import and organize photos, video, and music into a finished DVD presentation.

capabilities are often preinstalled on computers containing a recordable or rewritable optical drive. Some file management programs and *media players* (discussed next) include CD and DVD burning capabilities, as well.

Consumer video editing software includes *Adobe Premiere Elements, Serif MoviePlus* (shown in Figure 6-29), *Roxio Creator, Apple iMovie, Windows Movie Maker,* and *Sony Creative Software Movie Studio.* Professional products include *Adobe Premiere Pro, Corel VideoStudio Pro,* and *Sony Creative Software Vegas Pro.*

Media Players

Media players are programs designed to play audio and video files. They are used to play media available via your computer—such as music CDs, downloaded music, or video streamed from the Internet. Many media players are available for free, such as *RealPlayer, iTunes* (see Figure 6-30), *Windows Media Player,* and *QuickTime Player.* Media players typically allow you to arrange your stored music and videos into *playlists,* and then transfer them to CDs or portable digital music players. Some players also include the ability to download video from the Web and/or purchase and download music via an associated *music store.*

Use to view the media files stored on your computer.

Use to buy more media or review your purchases.

Use to access content on a CD or portable device.

Use to view or access your playlists.

Courtesy Apple

FIGURE 6-30
A typical media player program.

It is important when using digital music to adhere to copyright laws, such as only transferring music from CDs that you have purchased and only downloading digital music files from sites that are authorized to distribute the music. While most music download sites today are legal and charge around $1 per title, illegal *peer-to-peer* (*P2P*) MP3 file exchanges do exist. Copyrights and P2P networks are discussed in more detail in later chapters.

Graphics, Multimedia, and the Web

Graphics and multimedia software are often used by individuals and businesses to create content to be included on a Web site or to be shared via the Web. For instance, company logos, Web site banners, games, tutorials, videos, demonstrations, and other multimedia content available on the Web are created with multimedia software. Multimedia elements and creating multimedia Web sites are the focus of Chapter 10.

OTHER TYPES OF APPLICATION SOFTWARE

There are many other types of application software available today. Some are geared for business or personal productivity; others are designed for entertainment or educational purposes. Still others are intended to help users with a particular specialized application, such as preparing financial reports, issuing prescriptions electronically, designing buildings, controlling machinery, and so forth. A few of the most common types of application software not previously covered are discussed next.

TIP

More cloud applications are featured in Chapter 8; security software is discussed in Chapter 9.

Desktop and Personal Publishing Software

Desktop publishing refers to using a personal computer to combine and manipulate text and images to create attractive documents that look as if they were created by a professional printer. Although many desktop publishing effects can be produced using a word processing

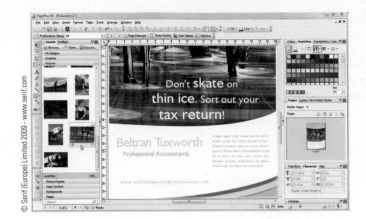

program, users who frequently create publication-style documents usually find a desktop publishing program a more efficient means of creating those types of documents. Some popular desktop publishing programs are *Adobe InDesign*, *Microsoft Publisher*, and *Serif PagePlus* (see Figure 6-31). *Personal publishing* refers to creating desktop-publishing-type documents—such as greeting cards, invitations, flyers, calendars, certificates, and so forth—for personal use. There are also specialized personal publishing programs for particular purposes, such as to create scrapbook pages, cross-stitch patterns, CD and DVD labels, and so forth. Many publishing programs (as well as *Adobe Acrobat* and Microsoft Word 2013) can create *PDF files* for distributing documents that look the same, regardless of the device being used to view them.

FIGURE 6-31

Desktop publishing software. Allows users to create publication-quality documents.

Educational, Entertainment, and Reference Software

A wide variety of educational and entertainment application programs are available. *Educational software* is designed to teach one or more skills, such as reading, math, spelling, a foreign language, or world geography, or to help prepare for standardized tests. *Entertainment software* includes games, simulations, and other programs that provide amusement. A hybrid of these two categories is called *edutainment*—educational software that also entertains. *Reference software* includes encyclopedias, dictionaries, atlases, mapping/travel programs, cookbook programs, nutrition or fitness programs, and other software designed to provide valuable information. Although still available as stand-alone software packages, reference information today is also obtained frequently via the Internet.

FIGURE 6-32

Note taking software. Allows individuals to record and organize important data.

Note Taking Software and Web Notebooks

Note taking software is used by both students and businesspeople to take notes during class lectures, meetings, and similar settings. It is used most often with tablet computers and other devices designed to accept pen input. Typically, note taking software (such as Microsoft *OneNote* or the Circus Ponies *Notebook* program shown in Figure 6-32) supports both typed and handwritten input; handwritten input can usually be saved in its handwritten form as an image or converted to typed text. The Notebook program also includes a voice recorder so you can record a lecture or meeting—tapping the speaker icon next to a note replays the voice recorded at the time that particular note was taken. Note taking software typically contains features designed specifically to make note taking—and, particularly, retrieving information from the notes—easier. Like a paper notebook, tabbed sections can usually be created (such as one tab per course) and files, notes, Web links, and any other data are stored under the appropriate tabs. In addition, search tools that allow you to find the information you need quickly and easily are usually included. Online versions of these programs (such as *Zoho Notebook* and *Evernote*) are sometimes referred to as *Web notebooks*. Web notebooks are designed to help organize your online research (including text, images, Web links, search results, and Web page resources), as well as other content (including notes, documents, and scanned images) that you want to save.

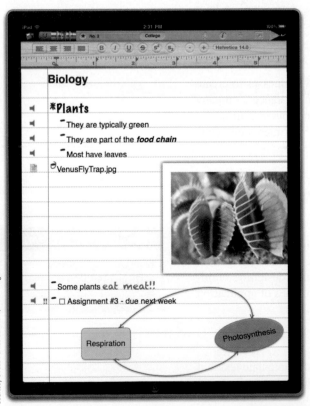

CAD and Other Types of Design Software

As discussed in more detail in Chapter 12, *computer-aided design* (*CAD*) *software* enables designers to design objects on the computer. For example, engineers or architects can create designs of buildings or other objects and modify the designs as often as needed. Increasingly, CAD programs are including capabilities to analyze designs in terms of how well they meet a number of design criteria, such as testing how a building design will hold up during an earthquake or how a car will perform under certain conditions. Besides playing an important role in the design of finished products, CAD is also useful in fields such as art, advertising, law, architecture, and movie production. In addition to professional CAD programs, there are also design programs intended for home and small business use, such as for designing new homes, and for making remodeling plans, interior designs, and landscape designs.

Accounting and Personal Finance Software

Accounting software is used to automate some of the accounting activities that need to be performed on a regular basis. Common tasks include recording purchases and payments, managing inventory, creating payroll documents and checks, preparing financial statements, keeping track of business expenses, and creating and managing customer accounts and invoices (see Figure 6-33). *Personal finance software* is commonly used at home by individuals to write checks and balance checking accounts, track personal expenses, manage stock portfolios, and prepare income taxes. Increasingly, personal finance activities are becoming Web-based, such as the *online banking* and *online portfolio management* services available through many banks and brokerage firms and discussed in more detail in Chapter 8.

Project Management, Collaboration, and Remote Access Software

Project management software is used to plan, schedule, track, and analyze the tasks involved in a project, such as the construction of a building or the schedule for preparing a large advertising campaign for a client. Project management capabilities are often included in *collaboration software*—software that enables a group of individuals to work together on a project—and are increasingly available as cloud software programs.

Remote access software enables individuals to access content on another computer they are authorized to access, via the Internet. Some programs allow you to control the remote computer directly; others allow you to access your media files (such as recorded TV shows or music) from any Web-enabled device while you are away from home. For instance, the *Slingbox* product gives you access to and control over your cable box and DVR via the Internet (as discussed in Chapter 7), and *TeamViewer* software (see Figure 6-34) allows you to access a computer (such as a home or an office PC), including controlling the computer and accessing files, from any Web-enabled device while you are away from home (you need to have the remote access software running on your PC first and then launch your mobile app). Other remote access software automatically backs up all data files on your main computer to a secure Web server so they can be accessed from any Web-enabled device (such as a portable computer, mobile phone, or media tablet), as well as shared with others for collaboration purposes. Some companies (such as Microsoft) offer a remote access feature for technical support, where the technician will access your computer remotely to resolve your problem if you grant permission.

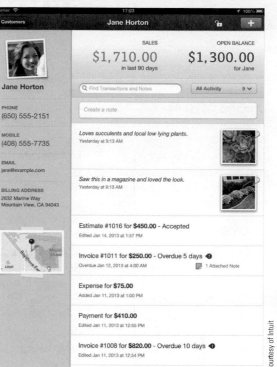

FIGURE 6-33
Accounting software. This QuickBooks Online for iPad app allows you to create and keep track of customer invoices while on the go.

FIGURE 6-34
Remote access software. Allows you to use a computer from a remote Internet-enabled device.

This Windows 8 computer is being accessed remotely via this smartphone.

SUMMARY

THE BASICS OF APPLICATION SOFTWARE

Application software (or an **app**) is software designed to carry out a specific task. Common types of application software include games, Web browsers, word processing programs, multimedia software, and more. Many application software programs today are **commercial software** programs that are developed and sold for a profit. When a software program is purchased, individual users receive a **software license** authorizing them to use the software. Some commercial software is available in a *demo* or *trial version*. Other software is available as **shareware**, **freeware**, or **public domain software**. **Open source software** is the term for programs whose source code is available to the general public. Software is designed as either *desktop software* or *mobile software*. **Installed software** is installed on a local computer or network server; **cloud software**, which is also called **Software as a Service (SaaS)** and **cloudware**, is run from the Internet instead. Organizations that provide cloud software are referred to as *application service providers* (*ASPs*).

Many office-oriented programs are sold bundled together as a **software suite**. One of the most widely used software suites is **Microsoft Office**. Although they are used for different purposes, most application software programs share some of the same concepts and functions, such as similar document-handling operations and help features. For instance, documents are commonly *opened, saved, printed, edited,* and *formatted* in a similar manner. **Editing** a document changes its content; **formatting** a document changes its appearance (such as by changing the *font face, font size,* or *font style* of text or by changing the *line spacing* or *margins*). Commands can be issued via a variety of methods, such as by using *menus, toolbars,* **keyboard shortcuts**, or the Microsoft Office **Ribbon**—the **insertion point** typically looks like a blinking vertical line and identifies the current position in a document. Online help is available in many programs.

WORD PROCESSING CONCEPTS

Word processing refers to using a computer and **word processing software** to create, manipulate, and print written documents, such as letters, contracts, and so forth. When creating or editing a word processing document, the **word wrap** feature automatically moves the insertion point to the next line when the end of the screen line is reached. Formatting can be applied at the character, paragraph, or document level. Other enhancements found in most word processing programs include the ability to include graphical images and *tables,* and to use *styles, templates,* or *wizards* for more efficient document creation. Documents can also include hyperlinks and be saved as Web pages in many programs. Most word processors also include a spelling and grammar check feature and other useful tools.

SPREADSHEET CONCEPTS

Spreadsheet software is used to create documents (**spreadsheets** or **worksheets**) that typically include a great deal of numbers and mathematical computations; a collection of worksheets stored in the same spreadsheet file is called a **workbook**. A worksheet is divided into **rows** and **columns** that intersect to form **cells**, each of which can be accessed through a *cell address,* such as B3. A rectangular group of cells is referred to as a *range.*

Content is entered into individual cells and may consist of **labels**, **constant values**, **formulas**, or **functions**. Formulas can be typed using *relative cell* or *absolute cell references,* depending on the type of computation required. Once created, the content of individual cells may be edited and formatted. *Numeric formats* are used to change the appearance of numbers, such as adding a dollar sign or displaying a specific number of decimal places. Spreadsheet programs commonly include a *charting* or *graphing* feature and the ability to perform *what-if analysis*. Some spreadsheet programs allow worksheets to be saved in the form of a Web page and the inclusion of hyperlinks in cells.

DATABASE CONCEPTS

A *database management system* (*DBMS*) or **database software** program enables the creation of a **database**—a collection of related data stored in a manner so that information can be retrieved as needed. In a relational DBMS (the most common type found on personal computers), a **field** or **column** is a collection of characters that make up a single piece of data, such as a name or phone number; a **record** or **row** is a collection of related fields; and a **table** is a collection of related records. One or more tables can be stored in a database file.

A relational database typically contains a variety of *objects*, such as tables, *forms* to input or view data, *queries* to retrieve specific information, and *reports* to print a formal listing of the data stored in a table or the results of a query. When a table is created, the table fields are specified along with their characteristics, such as *field name*, *field size*, and *data type*. This structure, as well as the data, are saved in the table and can be modified when needed. Databases are commonly integrated into the Web, such as to keep track of inventory and to facilitate online ordering.

Chapter Objective 5:
Identify some of the vocabulary used with database software and discuss the benefits of using this type of program.

PRESENTATION GRAPHICS CONCEPTS

Presentation graphics are images used to visually enhance the impact of information communicated to other people. **Presentation graphics software** can be used to create presentation graphics and **electronic slide shows** consisting of electronic **slides**. The individual slides in the slide show are created, and then they can be edited and formatted, as can the overall appearance of the presentation. Multimedia elements, such as images and video clips, can also be included. After all slides have been created for a presentation, the order of the slides can be rearranged and *transitions* between the slides can be specified. It is becoming increasingly common to find slide-based presentations available through the Web. Web-based slide shows can include multimedia elements, as well as hyperlinks and other navigational buttons.

Chapter Objective 6:
Describe what presentation graphics and electronic slide shows are and when they might be used.

GRAPHICS AND MULTIMEDIA CONCEPTS

Graphics are graphical images, such as digital photographs, clip art, and original art. *Multimedia* refers to applications that include more than one type of media, but often refers to audio and video content. To create graphics, **graphics software**—such as a *painting*, a *drawing*, or an *image editing program*—can be used. *Audio editing*, *video editing*, and *DVD authoring software* are common types of multimedia programs, as are the *media player* programs used to play audio and video files. *CD* and *DVD burning software* can be used to burn songs or other data on a CD or DVD disc.

Chapter Objective 7:
List some types of graphics and multimedia software that consumers use frequently.

OTHER TYPES OF APPLICATION SOFTWARE

Other types of application software include *desktop publishing* and *personal publishing* programs, *computer-aided design* (*CAD*) and other types of *design software*, *accounting software*, *personal finance software*, and *project management software*. The use of *collaboration*, *remote access*, and *note taking software* is growing. *Educational*, *entertainment*, and *reference software* are very popular with home users.

Chapter Objective 8:
Name several other types of application software programs and discuss what functions they perform.

REVIEW ACTIVITIES

KEY TERM MATCHING

a. cell

b. database

c. field

d. formula

e. label

f. public domain software

g. record

h. shareware

i. software license

j. workbook

Instructions: Match each key term on the left with the definition on the right that best describes it.

1. _____ A collection of related data that is stored in a manner enabling information to be retrieved as needed.

2. _____ A collection of related fields in a database; also called a row.

3. _____ A collection of worksheets saved in a single spreadsheet file.

4. _____ An agreement, either included in a software package or displayed on the screen when the software is installed or launched, that specifies the conditions under which the program can be used.

5. _____ An entry in a worksheet cell that performs computations on worksheet data and displays the results.

6. _____ A single category of data to be stored in a database, such as a person's name or phone number; also called a column.

7. _____ A text-based entry in a worksheet cell that identifies data on the worksheet.

8. _____ Copyrighted software that is distributed on the honor system; consumers should either pay for it or uninstall it after the trial period.

9. _____ Software that is not copyrighted and may be used without restriction.

10. _____ The location at the intersection of a row and column on a worksheet into which data can be typed.

SELF-QUIZ

Instructions: Circle **T** if the statement is true, **F** if the statement is false, or write the best answer in the space provided. **Answers for the self-quiz are located in the References and Resources Guide at the end of the book.**

1. **T   F**   Microsoft Office is one example of a software suite.

2. **T   F**   Changing the font size in a document is an example of a formatting operation.

3. **T   F**   In a word processing document, the Enter key is always pressed at the end of each screen line to move down to the next line.

4. **T   F**   The formula =A2+B2 located in cell C2 would multiply the two cells to the left of cell C2.

5. **T   F**   Typically, a single software program can be installed on both a computer and a mobile device.

6. With a(n) _____ program, the source code for the program is made available to the public and so can be modified by others.

7. The blinking vertical line displayed on the screen that indicates the current location in a document, such as where the next change will be made to the document in a word processing program, is called the _____.

8. A named formula (such as @SUM) in a spreadsheet program is called a(n) _____.

9. In a relational database, the database object that contains the actual data is the _____.

10. Match each application with its type of application program, and write the corresponding number in the blank to the left of each application.

a. _____ Listening to a music CD.

b. _____ Creating a child's birthday invitation.

c. _____ Creating a home movie DVD.

1. DVD authoring software
2. Media player
3. Personal publishing software

---

1. List the programs included in the Microsoft Office software suite that fit in the following categories.

   a. Spreadsheet software _____

   b. Presentation graphics software _____

   c. Word processing software _____

   d. Database software _____

2. Match each spreadsheet element with its term and write the corresponding number in the blank to the left of each term.

   a. _____ An absolute cell address

   b. _____ A relative cell address

   c. _____ A function

   1. =SUM(A1:A2)
   2. $D$4
   3. B6

3. For a customer database containing 50 customers and recording data about the customer's number, last name, street, city, state, ZIP code, and current balance, answer the following questions.

   a. How many records are in the database? _____

   b. How many fields are in the database? _____

   c. To display a list of all customers who live in Texas and have a current balance of less than $10, what database tool should be used? _____

4. Write the number of the presentation graphic that best matches each of the following possible uses in the blank to the left of each use.

   a. _____ Adding an arrow to highlight a point located on a slide.

   b. _____ Illustrating the percent of sales coming from each sales territory.

   c. _____ Conveying the key points in an educational lecture.

   1. Pie chart
   2. Slide
   3. Drawn object

5. Would rearranging the paragraphs in a document using a word processing program be an editing operation or a formatting operation? Explain your answer.

---

1. There are an increasing number of cloud applications available and the current version of Office is available in both installed and cloud versions. What are the advantages and disadvantages of cloud software? Which do you prefer to use for school-related documents? Why? If you prefer installed software, what would have to change about cloud software in the future to change your opinion?

2. Open source software is usually reviewed and improved at no cost. Proponents of open source software believe that if programmers who are not concerned with financial gain work on an open source program, they will produce a more useful and error-free product much faster than the traditional commercial software development process. As open source use continues to grow, will it force existing commercial software companies to cut costs to better compete with open source products? Or will they strive to produce products that are better and more reliable than open source competitors? Or will commercial software companies simply go out of business? Will commercial software manufacturers be justified in raising their prices to make up for revenue lost to open source competitors? Do you think open source software will have an overall positive or negative impact on the quality of software?

PROJECTS

1. **Natural Input** As pen, touch, gesture, and voice input technologies continue to improve, these types of more natural input methods are increasingly being supported by software programs.

    For this project, select one type of input method besides the keyboard or mouse (such as pen, gesture, touch, or voice). Research its use in conjunction with application software. How frequently is it used today with desktop and portable computers? With mobile devices? Select one office application (such as a word processor or spreadsheet program) and determine what hardware or software is needed to use your selected method of input. What are the advantages of your input method? The disadvantages? Would you prefer to use a keyboard and mouse or your selected method of input with this program? Explain. At the conclusion of your research, prepare a one- to two-page summary of your findings and opinions and submit it to your instructor.

2. **Software Search** Just as with toys, movies, and music, the price of a software program can vary tremendously, based on where you buy it, sales, rebates, and more. Although most software has a manufacturer's suggested retail price, it is almost always possible to beat that price—sometimes by a huge amount—with careful shopping.

    For this project, select one software program (such as an office suite or a security suite) that you might be interested in buying and research it. By reading the program specifications either in a retail store or on a Web page, determine the program's minimum hardware and software requirements. By checking in person, over the phone, or via the Internet, locate three price quotes for the program, including any sales tax and shipping, and check availability and estimated delivery time. Do any of the vendors have the option to download the software? If so, do you have to register the program online or enter a code to activate the product after it is downloaded? At the conclusion of this task, prepare a one-page summary of your research and submit it to your instructor. Be sure to include a recommendation of where you think it would be best to buy your chosen product and why.

3. **Online Tours** There are many online tours and tutorials for application programs. Some are available through the software company's Web site; others are located on third-party Web sites. Many are free.

    For this project, select one common software program (such as Word, Excel, PowerPoint, Chrome, Google Docs, or Paint). Locate a free online tour or tutorial for the program you selected and work your way through one tour or tutorial. How useful is it? Is it easy to use and understand? Did you learn anything new? Did you encounter any errors or other problems? Are there multiple versions for varying levels of difficulty? Would you recommend this tour or tutorial to others? At the conclusion of this task, prepare a one-page summary of your efforts and submit it to your instructor.

4. **Emotion Recognition Software** An emerging application is *emotion recognition software*, which uses camera input to try to read a person's current emotion. The first expected application of such a system is for ATM machines because they already have cameras installed. Possibilities include changing the advertising display based on the customer's emotional response to displayed advertising, and enlarging the screen text if the customer appears to be squinting. Is it ethical for businesses using emotion recognition software to read the emotions of citizens without their consent? Proponents of the technology argue that it is no different than when human tellers or store clerks interpret customers' emotions and modify their treatment of the customer accordingly. Do you agree? Why or why not? Is this a worthy new technology or just a potential invasion of privacy? Would you object to using an ATM machine with emotion recognition capabilities? Why or why not?

For this project, form an opinion about the ethical ramifications of emotion recognition systems and be prepared to discuss your position (in class, via an online class discussion group, in a class chat room, or via a class blog, depending on your instructor's directions). You may also be asked to write a short paper expressing your opinion.

ETHICS IN ACTION

5. **Compatibility** Files created by an application program are often upward compatible, but not always downward compatible. For example, a *.docx* file created in Microsoft Word 2013 cannot be opened in Word 2003, but a Word 2003 *.doc* file can be opened in Word 2013. Most application programs feature a "Save As" option that can be used to save a file in one of several formats.

For this project, select one widely used software program and determine in which file formats the program can save documents and which file formats the program can open. If there are older versions of the program, are documents upward compatible? Downward compatible? Research *plain text (.txt)*, *Portable Document Format (PDF)*, and the *Rich Text Format (.rtf)* and determine their purposes, the programs in which documents saved in each of these formats can be opened, and any disadvantages for using these formats. Have you ever experienced a compatibility problem with a document? If so, how was the problem resolved? Share your findings with the class in the form of a short presentation. The presentation should not exceed 10 minutes and should make use of one or more presentation aids, such as a whiteboard, handouts, or a computer-based slide presentation (your instructor may provide additional requirements). You may also be asked to submit a summary of the presentation to your instructor.

PRESENTATION/ DEMONSTRATION

SW

6. **Should Computers Grade Essay Tests?** Using computers and other automated tools to grade true-false and multiple-choice tests is widespread, but grading essays has been reserved for instructors. Until now. Software developed by a nonprofit enterprise founded by Harvard and MIT recently released software that can grade student essays and short written answers. Students answer online instead of in a blue book and immediately receive their grade after clicking a Send button. The software uses artificial intelligence (it initially "learns" how to grade an instructor's test by reviewing 100 essay exams that the instructor scored) and is designed to free up professors for other tasks, as well as give students the opportunity to immediately revise their graded essays for an improved grade. But does the system work? Are the automated grades similar to what a human grader would award? Skeptics (including the National Council of Teachers of English) say no. Objections include a lack of tests to support the validity of the grading system and the inability of the software to leave in-depth comments in the margin of a paper like a professor would. But does the immediate feedback, as well as the ability to improve your writing and grade, offset these objections? Would you prefer that your essays be graded immediately via software or wait for a human score? Is this an advancement in education or a mistake?

Pick a side on this issue, form an opinion and gather supporting evidence, and be prepared to discuss and defend your position in a classroom debate or in a 1–2 page paper, depending on your instructor's directions.

BALANCING ACT

expert insight on...
Software

A conversation with STEPHEN ROSE

Senior Product Marketing and Community Manager, Windows Commercial, Microsoft

Courtesy Microsoft, Inc.

:: Microsoft

Stephen Rose is the Senior Product Marketing and Community Manager for the Windows Commercial team at Microsoft. Before joining Microsoft, he was the Senior Tech Correspondent for Fast Company Magazine and an IT consultant. He has been a Microsoft Certified Systems Engineer and Microsoft Certified Trainer for 20 years, as well as a two-time Microsoft Most Valuable Professional (MVP). Stephen has a Bachelor of Arts degree and holds multiple technical certifications, including MCSE, MCP+I, MCT, MCTIP, A+, Net+, Security+, Linux+, Project+, and PMI.

" . . . The fact that people want their data to synch across multiple devices from the cloud is a huge game changer."

My Background . . .

It's funny how things work out. I received a bachelor's degree in Film and Video production from Columbia College in Chicago in the late '80s. By 1996, I was burned-out and decided to follow my passion for computers and IT by becoming a technical trainer with New Horizons. Within two years I got my MCT and MCSE, and I started my own IT consulting company that designed, built, and managed software and services for companies worldwide (including many Fortune 500 companies) for 15 years. I'm now the Senior Product Marketing and Community Manager for the Windows Commercial team at Microsoft. There are 22.6 million IT pros in the world and my job is to help support them within the workplace. I oversee and manage the Windows content on Microsoft TechNet, as well as on a number of forums, newsletters, and blogs. I also speak at conferences, roundtables, and the North American and European Springboard Series Tours.

It's Important to Know . . .

Apps are moving to the cloud. While individuals have used Web mail and other cloud products for some time, businesses are now moving into the cloud, which will dramatically change the business model for many companies. With Web-based apps, virtualized desktops, and more, the computer is becoming just a vessel to connect you to the Internet and your data. Understanding the cloud, as well as where and when it makes sense to use it, is key to being a successful IT pro.

Software is not always a one-size-fits-all situation. Apps will need to run on many different form factors, such as phones, tablets, and touch-based devices, in addition to laptops and desktops. And these devices are not interchangeable. In addition, an overblown app on a device without a keyboard can be hard to use—if an app is difficult to use, no one will adopt it.

Computers are inherently secure. It is the choices that users make (such as clicking on links in e-mails and downloading music, movies, and software illegally) that make them unsecure. If users use their best judgment when surfing the Web, they will be safer. If something sounds too good to be true, it usually is. At Microsoft, we are adding many new features to our operating system and browser to help users make smart decisions.

How I Use this Technology . . .

I travel around the world and need my computing resources as I travel. One of my favorite features in Windows 8 is Direct Access, which automatically connects me to my company intranet without having to log into a secure VPN connection with tokens and pin numbers. For instance, I recently sat down at a Starbucks in Prague, turned on my Windows 8 laptop, and within seconds I was not only connected to the Wi-Fi network but also to my key internal Web sites. From Prague to Redmond in a matter of seconds without doing anything but turning on my PC. It is a seamless experience. As I have heard from so many end users over the years, "I don't care how it works. I just want it to work." I also use several laptops, so products like OneNote and Sharepoint are key to ensuring that all my data is on multiple devices and synched automatically.

What the Future Holds . . .

The cloud is one of the major technologies changing our future. It is going to dramatically change how we do business and how we perceive data. The physical PC is no longer part of the equation and the idea of "my data anywhere on the planet from any computer" is very powerful. Not storing data locally reduces risk, lowers costs, and adds more productivity via flexibility. In addition, cloud computing—along with new form factors, the need for social media accessibility, the emergence of location-aware applications, and the increased availability of app stores—have changed how we view devices. The lines between tablets, smartphones, and PCs are already blurring. With the addition of system on a chip (SoC), there will be an increase in the amount and types of devices that the end user is impacted by.

Cloud computing will also impact software development. The fact that people want their data to synch across multiple devices from the cloud is a huge game changer. Knowing HTML5 will be critical in the development of apps located in the cloud. HTML5 will also have a big impact on end users.

Tablets and smartphones are currently replacing laptops for many tasks and I expect that trend to continue in the future. These smart devices allow us to be more informed on many aspects of our life. They allow us to be more nimble and to take advantage of opportunities that 10 years ago were unheard of.

> *". . . technology shapes us but, like any tool, it's how we leverage it and use it for the better that is important."*

My Advice to Students . . .

Remember that technology shapes us but, like any tool, it's how we leverage it and use it for the better that is important.

Discussion Question

Stephen Rose believes that cloud computing will impact both individuals and businesses and change how we perceive data and do business. Think about the computing and communications tasks you use today. What is the benefit of being able to perform them via the cloud? Are there any disadvantages? Do you currently use multiple devices to access your data and apps? If so, are the data and apps stored in the cloud, on each device, or both? If not, would the ability to access your data and apps via any device, anywhere, be an advantage in your life? Would a cloud-based world change how you use data or apps on a daily basis? If a person or business decides not to utilize the cloud, will this be a disadvantage for that person or business? Why or why not? Be prepared to discuss your position (in class, via an online class discussion group, in a class chat room, or via a class blog, depending on your instructor's directions). You may also be asked to write a short paper expressing your opinion.

>**For more information about Microsoft, visit www.microsoft.com. For resources for Windows and other Microsoft software, visit www.microsoft.com/springboard and windowsteamblog.com/windows/b/springboard. Follow the Springboard Series on TechNet via Twitter @MSSpringboard.**

Networks and the Internet

From telephone calls, to home and business networks, to Web surfing and online shopping, networking and the Internet are deeply embedded in our society today. Because of this, it is important for individuals to be familiar with basic networking concepts and terminology, as well as with the variety of activities that take place today via networks—including the Internet, the world's largest network. It is also important for all individuals to be aware of the potential problems and risks associated with networks and our networked society.

The purpose of Chapter 7 is to introduce basic networking principles, including what a computer network is, how it works, and what it can be used for. The Internet and World Wide Web are the topics of Chapter 8. Although they were introduced in Chapter 1, Chapter 8 explains in more detail how the Internet and World Wide Web originated, and looks more closely at common Internet activities, including how to search the Web effectively for information. This chapter also discusses the various options for connecting to the Internet, as well as how to select an Internet service provider (ISP). Chapter 9 takes a look at some of the risks related to network and Internet use, and explains measures computer users can take to lessen these risks.

in this module

"What is associated with your digital identity becomes associated with you..."

For more comments from Guest Expert **Greg Hampton** of McAfee, see the **Expert Insight on . . . Networks and the Internet** feature at the end of the module.

chapter 7

Computer Networks

After completing this chapter, you will be able to do the following:

1. Define a computer network and its purpose.

2. Describe several uses for networks.

3. Understand the various characteristics of a network, such as topology, architecture, and size.

4. Understand characteristics about data and how it travels over a network.

5. Name specific types of wired and wireless networking media and explain how they transmit data.

6. Identify the most common communications protocols and networking standards used with networks today.

7. List several types of networking hardware and explain the purpose of each.

OVERVIEW

The term *communications*, when used in a computer context, refers to *telecommunications*; that is, data sent from one device to another using communications media, such as telephone lines, privately owned cables, and the airwaves. Communications usually take place over a private (such as a home or business) computer network, the Internet, or a telephone network, and are an integral part of our personal and professional lives today.

The purpose of Chapter 7 is to introduce you to the concepts and terminology associated with computer networks. First, a computer network is defined, followed by a look at some common networking applications. Next, a number of technical issues related to networks are discussed, including general characteristics of data and data transmission, as well as the types of transmission media in use today. We then proceed to an explanation of the various communications protocols and networking standards, which help explain the ways networked devices communicate with one another. The chapter closes with a look at the various types of hardware used with a computer network. ■

WHAT IS A NETWORK?

A *network*, in general, is a connected system of objects or people. As discussed in Chapter 1, a **computer network** is a collection of computers and other hardware devices connected together so that network users can share hardware, software, and data, as well as communicate with each other electronically. Today, computer networks are converging with *telephone networks* and other *communications networks*, with both data and voice being sent over these networks. Computer networks range from small private networks to the Internet and are widely used by individuals and businesses today (see Figure 7-1).

In most businesses, computer networks are essential. They enable employees to share expensive resources, access the Internet, and communicate with each other, as well as with business partners and customers. They facilitate the exchange and collaboration of documents and they are often a key component of the ordering, inventory, and fulfillment systems used to process customer orders. In homes, computer networks enable individuals to share resources, access the Internet, and communicate with others. In addition, they allow individuals to access a wide variety of information, services, and entertainment, as well as share data (such as digital photos, downloaded movies, and music) among the networked

FIGURE 7-1
Common uses for computer networks.

USES FOR COMPUTER NETWORKS
Sharing an Internet connection among several users.
Sharing application software, printers, and other resources.
Facilitating Voice over IP (VoIP), e-mail, videoconferencing, messaging, and other communications applications.
Working collaboratively; for example, sharing a company database or using collaboration tools to create or review documents.
Exchanging files among network users and over the Internet.
Connecting the computers and the entertainment devices (such as TVs, gaming consoles, and stereo systems) located within a home.

Copyright © 2015 Cengage Learning®

> **Computer network.** A collection of computers and other hardware devices that are connected together to share hardware, software, and data, as well as to communicate electronically with one another.

those employees can use their work mobile phone to receive and place calls via Wi-Fi when they are in range of a Wi-Fi network, and via a cellular network when they are out of range of the Wi-Fi network.

Another, but less common, type of mobile phone is the **satellite phone** (refer again to Figure 7-2), which communicates via *satellite technology*, also described in detail later in this chapter. Although more expensive than cellular service, satellite phone coverage is typically much broader, often on a country-by-country basis, and some satellite phone services cover the entire earth. Consequently, satellite phones are most often used by individuals—such as soldiers, journalists, wilderness guides, and researchers—traveling in remote areas where continuous cellular service might not be available. They are also useful during times when cellular service might be interrupted, such as during a hurricane or other emergency. An emerging option is the *cellular/satellite dual-mode phone* that can be used with cellular service when it is available and then switches to satellite service when cellular service is not available.

Television and Radio Broadcasting

Two other original communications networks are *broadcast television networks* and *radio networks*. These networks are still used to deliver TV and radio content to the public, though some of this content is also available via the Internet today. Other networks involved with television content delivery are *cable TV networks*, *satellite TV networks*, and the private *closed-circuit television* (*CCTV*) systems used by businesses for surveillance and security purposes. Cable and satellite TV networks are also used today to provide access to the Internet.

Global Positioning System (GPS) Applications

The **global positioning system** (**GPS**) network consists of 24 Department of Defense *GPS satellites* (in orbit approximately 12,000 miles above the earth) that are used for location and navigation purposes. A *GPS receiver* measures the distance between the receiver and four GPS satellites simultaneously to determine the receiver's exact geographic location; these receivers are accurate to within 3 meters (less than 10 feet).

GPS receivers (see some examples in Figure 7-3) are commonly used by individuals to determine their geographic location while hiking and to obtain driving directions while traveling. GPS receivers are also commonly used on the job, such as by surveyors, farmers, fishermen, and public safety personnel. In addition to relaying location information, GPS can be used to guide vehicles and equipment (for example, to locate and dispatch ambulances, police cars, and other emergency vehicles, or to guide bulldozers and other construction equipment automatically using that device's preprogrammed instructions). GPS is used by the military to guide munitions and trucks, as well as to track military aircraft, ships, and submarines. Most smartphones today include GPS capabilities, which allow the use of location-specific services and applications such as using your location in Web searches, social media activities, and self-guided tours (see the Fresno State tour app in Figure 7-3). These services and applications are referred to as *geobrowsing*, which is discussed in more detail in Chapter 8. GPS capabilities are also built into consumer devices that are designed for specific purposes, such as fitness devices that use GPS technology to record workout data for runners or bicyclists.

>**Satellite phone.** A mobile phone that communicates via satellite technology. >**Global positioning system (GPS).** A system that uses satellites and a receiver to determine the exact geographic location of the receiver.

HANDHELD GPS RECEIVERS   **CAR-MOUNTED GPS RECEIVERS**

GPS RECEIVERS INTEGRATED INTO SMARTPHONES

One recent concern regarding GPS technology is the possibility that the aging GPS satellites might fail (and, consequently, interrupt GPS services) before new replacement satellites can be launched. However, there are 30 GPS satellites currently in orbit—six more than the 24 GPS satellites required to have at least four satellites in view from anywhere on the planet. The next generation GPS system (*GPS III*) is currently under development and will be more powerful and more accurate than the current system. The first GPS III satellite is scheduled to launch by 2015.

FIGURE 7-3
GPS receivers.
Allow people to determine their exact geographical location, usually for safety or navigational purposes.

Monitoring Systems

Monitoring systems use networking technology to determine the current location or status of an object. Some monitoring systems in use today use the RFID tags and RFID readers discussed in Chapter 4 to monitor the status of the objects (such as shipping boxes, livestock, or expensive equipment) to which the RFID tags are attached. Other monitoring systems use GPS technology. For instance, many law enforcement *ankle bracelet monitoring systems* use GPS to detect if the offender has left his or her authorized areas, and the *OnStar* system built into many GM cars uses GPS to locate vehicles when the occupant activates the service or when sensors indicate that the car was involved in an accident. There are also *vehicle monitoring systems* that are installed in cars by parents and employers to monitor the location and use of the vehicles (by children or employees, respectively) using networking technology; *child monitoring systems* allow parents to monitor the physical locations of their children. Both types of monitoring systems typically record a location history; many also allow the location of a vehicle or child to be tracked in real time via a Web site or mobile app (see Figure 7-4). Some systems can even be used to set up a "virtual fence" for a child or a car or a maximum allowable car speed; the parent or employer is notified (usually via a text message) anytime the child or vehicle leaves the prescribed geographical area or the vehicle being monitored (or that the child being monitored is riding in) exceeds the designated speed. Child monitoring systems often include additional features, such as the ability to have the child's location pushed to the parent's device at regular intervals, the ability to have the parent notified if the child is within 500 feet of a registered sex offender, and an "SOS" button that the child can press if he or she is lost or afraid. The child monitoring system shown in Figure 7-4 also is available as a smartphone app for teenagers. Similar GPS systems are designed to be used to track elderly parents or by individuals who are hiking or traveling so they can be located if they become lost or injured.

FIGURE 7-4
GPS-based child monitoring systems.
Allow parents to track their children in real time.

Locations of registered offenders.

Child's current (green) and past (red) locations.

Courtesy Nest Labs

FIGURE 7-5

Smart themostats.

This thermostat (left) contains a variety of sensors and can be controlled remotely via a mobile app (right).

TIP

It has been predicted that 50 billion devices (essentially anything with an on-off switch) will be connected by 2020, creating an *Internet of Things* (*IoT*), discussed more in Chapter 8.

FIGURE 7-6

Placeshifting.

Products like the Slingbox are used to placeshift multimedia content to the user's current location.

1. Slingbox device is connected to the user's home DVR, cable set-top box, or satellite receiver.

2. SlingPlayer software allows the user to watch and control his or her home TV system from anywhere with an Internet connection.

Courtesy Sling Media

Another area in which monitoring systems are frequently used is home healthcare. With the U.S. population aging, a variety of home medical monitoring systems are available to monitor elderly or infirm individuals and to notify someone if a possible problem is detected. For instance, *electronic medical monitors* take the vital signs of an individual (such as weight, blood-sugar readings, or blood pressure) or prompt an individual to answer questions (such as if he or she has eaten yet that day or has taken prescribed medication). These monitors then transfer readings or the individual's responses to a healthcare provider via the Internet or a telephone network for evaluation and feedback and to detect potential problems as early as possible.

Other monitoring systems use *sensors*—devices that respond to a stimulus (such as heat, light, or pressure) and generate an electrical signal that can be measured or interpreted. The sensors are usually small and lightweight; contain the necessary hardware and software to sense and record the appropriate data, as well as transmit the data to other devices in the network; and include a power source (typically a battery). Sensors can be included in a network anytime there is a situation with measurable criteria that needs precise, automatic, and continual monitoring. For example, *sensor networks* can be used during transport to monitor the temperature inside cargo containers to ensure that products stay within the allowable temperature range, in pharmaceutical plants to monitor temperature and relative humidity in the drug development process, and in homes to manage and control devices such as smart appliances and heating/cooling systems. For example, the thermostat shown in Figure 7-5 contains temperature, humidity, activity, and light sensors; can be controlled via a mobile app; and can be programmed based on your activity within the home. IBM expects to see the use of sensor technology expanding to additional areas in the future, such as nano-sized sensors embedded in paint that help manage the energy use of a building or as a coating applied to plumbing systems to detect leaks and other potential problems.

Multimedia Networking

A growing use of home networks is to deliver digital multimedia content (such as digital photos, digital music, home movies, downloaded movies, and recorded TV shows) to devices (such as computers, mobile devices, televisions, and home entertainment systems) on that network. Home networks are also used to connect smart TVs to the Internet. While sometimes the necessary networking capabilities are built into the devices being used (such as smart TVs with wireless technology built in), a *multimedia networking* device (such as a *digital media receiver* or *digital media streamer*) can be used to connect a conventional television to your home network to deliver content from your networked devices or the Internet to that television. The most common multimedia networking standards available today are discussed later in this chapter.

Other multimedia networking devices (such as the *Slingbox* shown in Figure 7-6) are designed to *placeshift* multimedia content; that is, to allow individuals to view their multimedia content at a more convenient location. For instance, an individual with a Slingbox installed at home can both control and view programs from their home TV via a portable computer or mobile device, in order to watch local news while out of town, watch a recorded TV show while at the beach, or start recording a TV show from the office. The newest Slingboxes also allow you to wirelessly transfer photos and videos from your mobile device to your home TV via your home network.

Videoconferencing, Collaborative Computing, and Telecommuting

Videoconferencing is the use of networking technology to conduct real-time, face-to-face meetings between individuals physically located in different places. Videoconferencing can take place between individuals using their personal computers and the Internet (as discussed in more detail in Chapter 8) or it can take place using two mobile phones or other mobile devices with videoconferencing (sometimes called *video calling* or *video chat*) capabilities. Larger business videoconferences often take place via a dedicated videoconferencing setup using *telepresence videoconferencing*, which more closely mimics a real-time meeting environment. Although telepresence videoconferencing setups are expensive, with travel becoming increasingly more expensive and time consuming, many businesses view videoconferencing as a viable replacement for face-to-face meetings. Telepresence videoconferencing is also used in educational settings (for instance, the system shown in Figure 7-7 is installed at the Wharton School campuses in both Philadelphia and San Francisco to hold bicoastal classes) and in public locations such as airports and hospitals to provide language translation services for nonverbal languages such as American Sign Language.

Networking technology is also widely used today with collaborative software tools to enable individuals to work together on documents and other project components. This trend toward online collaboration is usually called *workgroup computing* or *collaborative computing*. For many industries, collaboration is a very important business tool. For example, engineers and architects commonly collaborate on designs; advertising firms and other businesses often route proposals and other important documents to several individuals for comments before preparing the final version of a client presentation; and newspaper, magazine, and book editors must read and edit drafts of articles and books before they are published. Instead of these types of collaborations taking place on paper, as in the not-too-distant past, collaboration tools (such as the Microsoft Office *markup tools* and specialized *collaboration software*) are used in conjunction with networking technology (typically a company network or the Internet) to allow multiple individuals to edit and make comments in a document without destroying the original content. Once a document has been reviewed by all individuals, the original author can read the comments and accept or reject changes that others have made. Some collaboration software also includes shared calendars, project scheduling, and videoconferencing tools.

Students in this classroom see a life-sized projected image of the professor.

The instructor sees a projected image of these students, who appear to be seated behind the students physically located in the professor's classroom.

FIGURE 7-7
Telepresence videoconferencing.

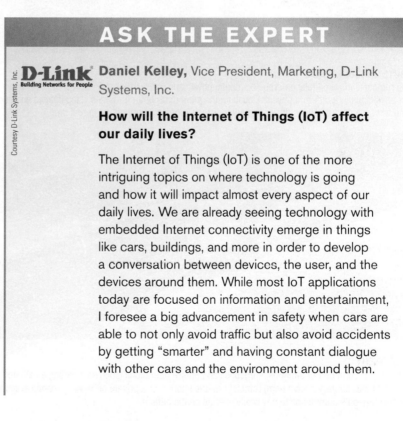

ASK THE EXPERT

Daniel Kelley, Vice President, Marketing, D-Link Systems, Inc.

How will the Internet of Things (IoT) affect our daily lives?

The Internet of Things (IoT) is one of the more intriguing topics on where technology is going and how it will impact almost every aspect of our daily lives. We are already seeing technology with embedded Internet connectivity emerge in things like cars, buildings, and more in order to develop a conversation between devices, the user, and the devices around them. While most IoT applications today are focused on information and entertainment, I foresee a big advancement in safety when cars are able to not only avoid traffic but also avoid accidents by getting "smarter" and having constant dialogue with other cars and the environment around them.

The availability of videoconferencing, collaborative computing, and other tools (such as the Internet, e-mail, and mobile phones) has made **telecommuting** a viable option for many individuals. With telecommuting, individuals work from a remote location (typically their home) and communicate with their place of business and clients via networking technologies. Telecommuting allows the employee to be flexible, such as to work nontraditional hours or remain with the company after a relocation. It also enables a company to save on office and parking space, as well as office-related expenses such as utilities. As an environmental plus, telecommuting helps cut down on the traffic and pollution caused by traditional work commuting. In addition, it gives a business the possibility to continue operations during situations that may affect an employee's ability to get to the office, such as during hurricanes, during a bridge or highway closure, or during a flu outbreak. As a result, many experts suggest businesses include telecommuting procedures in their *business continuity plans*, even if they don't intend to use telecommuting on a regular basis. Business continuity plans and disaster recovery are discussed in detail in Chapter 15.

FIGURE 7-8
Examples of telemedicine applications.

REMOTE CONSULTATIONS
Using remote-controlled teleconferencing robots, physicians can "virtually" consult with patients or other physicians in a different physical location; the robot (left photo) transmits video images and audio to and from the doctor (via his or her computer or mobile device, right photo) in real time.

TELESURGERY
Using voice or computer commands, surgeons can perform operations (such as inserting a catheter during the heart surgery shown here) remotely via the Internet or a private network; a robotic system uses the surgeon's commands to physically operate on the patient.

Telemedicine

Telemedicine is the use of networking technology to provide medical information and services. At its simplest level, it includes Web sites that patients can access to contact their physicians, make appointments, view lab results, and more. However, more complex telemedicine systems are often used to provide care to individuals who may not otherwise have access to that care, such as allowing individuals living in remote areas to consult with a specialist. For instance, physicians can use videoconferencing robots to communicate remotely with other physicians or with hospitalized patients (see Figure 7-8). Physicians can also use telemedicine to perform remote diagnosis of patients (for example, healthcare workers at rural locations, childcare facilities, and other locations can use video cameras, electronic stethoscopes, and other devices to send images and vital statistics of a patient to a physician located at a medical facility).

Another example of telemedicine is **telesurgery**—a form of *robot-assisted surgery* (where a robot controlled by a physician operates on the patient) in which at least one of the surgeons performs the operation by controlling the robot remotely over the Internet or another network (refer again

>**Telecommuting.** The use of computers and networking technology to enable an individual to work from a remote location. >**Telemedicine.** The use of networking technology to provide medical information and services. >**Telesurgery.** A form of robot-assisted surgery in which the doctor's physical location is different from the patient's and robot's physical location; the doctor controls the robot remotely over the Internet or another network.

to Figure 7-8). Robot-assisted surgery systems typically use cameras to give the human surgeon an extremely close view of the surgical area. As a result, robot-assisted surgery is typically more precise and results in smaller incisions than those made by a human surgeon, allowing for less invasive surgery (for example, not having to crack through the rib cage to access the heart) and resulting in less pain for the patient, a faster recovery time, and fewer potential complications.

Telemedicine has enormous potential for providing quality medical care to individuals who live in rural or underdeveloped areas and who do not have access to sufficient medical care. Telemedicine will also be necessary for future long-term space explorations—such as a trip to Mars and back that may take two years or more—because astronauts will undoubtedly need medical care while on the journey. In fact, NASA astronauts and physicians have performed telesurgery experiments in the Aquarius Undersea Laboratory 50 feet below the ocean surface to help in the development of a robotic unit that will eventually allow physicians to perform surgery remotely on patients who are in outer space. Some individuals envision the eventual use of portable robot-assisted telesurgery units in space, war zones, and other environments where access to surgeons is extremely limited.

NETWORK CHARACTERISTICS

Networks can be identified by a variety of characteristics, including whether they are designed for wired or wireless access, their *topology*, their *architecture*, and their *size* or *coverage area*. These topics are described in the next few sections.

Wired vs. Wireless Networks

Networks can be designed for access via *wired* and/or *wireless* connections. With a **wired network** connection, the computers and other devices on the network are physically connected (via cabling) to the network. With a **wireless network** connection, wireless (usually radio) signals are used to send data through the air between devices, instead of using physical cables. Wired networks include conventional telephone networks, cable TV networks, and the wired networks commonly found in schools, businesses, and government facilities. Wireless networks include conventional television and radio networks, cellular telephone networks, satellite TV networks, and the wireless networks commonly found in homes, schools, and businesses. Wireless networks are also found in many public locations (such as coffeehouses, businesses, airports, hotels, and libraries) to provide Internet access to users while they are on the go via public *wireless hotspots*. For a look at how wireless networks are being used at baseball and football stadiums today, see the Trend box.

Many networks today are accessible via both wired and wireless connections. For instance, a business may have a wired main company network to which the computers in employee offices are always connected, as well as provide wireless access to the network for visitors and employees to use while in waiting rooms, conference rooms, and other locations within the office building. A home network may have a wired connection between the devices needed to connect the home to the Internet (such as a *modem* and *router*), plus wireless access for the devices in the home (such as computers, printers, televisions, and gaming devices) that will access the home network wirelessly.

Wired networks tend to be faster and more secure than wireless networks, but wireless networks have the advantage of allowing easy connections in locations where physical wiring is impractical or inconvenient (such as inside an existing home or outdoors), as

NET

>**Wired network.** A network in which computers and other devices are connected to the network via physical cables. >**Wireless network.** A network in which computers and other devices are connected to the network without physical cables; data is typically sent via radio waves.

TREND

Stadium Wireless Networks

Beginning with the 2004 Opening Day of the San Francisco Giants baseball team, when AT&T Park became the first professional sports venue to provide continuous universal wireless access to fans in all concourses and seating areas, wireless networks and sports stadiums have been intertwined. Today, AT&T Park has 334 wireless access points within the park for fans to use free of charge. In addition to allowing baseball fans access to apps like the *Giants Digital Dugout* (which enables fans to watch video replays, review player profiles and standings, buy tickets to future games, and more) and send social media updates, the Wi-Fi network allows busy Silicon Valley businesspeople to send e-mails and perform other necessary business tasks while attending home games. And fans are using the network—the wireless network has been overhauled nearly every year to increase its capacity and it had about 870,000 unique visitors during the 2012 season. Other improvements are ongoing, such as the current plan to include mobile device charging stations at the ballpark.

Technology is also a big factor when designing new stadiums today. The new $1.2 billion Levi's Stadium, which is under construction in Santa Clara and will be the new home to the San Francisco 49ers football team, is one example of cutting-edge technology being integrated into new stadium design. Scheduled to open in 2014 and be the host stadium for Super Bowl 50 in 2016, the stadium (see the accompanying illustration) will seat 70,000 fans and include stadium-wide Wi-Fi, media tablet holders on the seats,

in-game apps, and high-definition video boards measuring over 13,000 square feet total. This technology-rich stadium has kick-started discussion about including consumer-oriented technology in stadiums across the country. According to Baltimore Ravens President Dick Cass, "It's what our fans want. They want the ability to take out their tablet, send a Facebook picture, and check the fantasy football scores, so we have to provide that." Based on recent trends, they likely will.

An artist rendering of the new San Francisco 49er Levi's Stadium.

---

well as giving users much more freedom regarding where they can use their computers. With wireless networking, for example, you can surf the Web on your notebook computer from anywhere in your house, access the Internet with your media tablet or smartphone while you are on the go, and create a home network without having to run wires among the rooms in your house.

Network Topologies

The physical *topology* of a computer network indicates how the devices in the network are arranged. Three of the most common physical topologies are *star*, *bus*, and *mesh* (see Figure 7-9).

> ➤ **Star network**—used in traditional mainframe environments, as well as in small office, home, and wireless networks. All the networked devices connect to a central device (such as a server or a *switch*, discussed later in this chapter) through which all network transmissions are sent. If the central device fails, then the network cannot function.

> **Star network.** A network that uses a host device connected directly to several other devices.

➤ **Bus network**—uses a central cable to which all network devices connect. All data is transmitted down the bus line from one device to another so, if the bus line fails, then the network cannot function.

➤ **Mesh network**—uses a number of different connections between network devices so that data can take any of several possible paths from source to destination. With a *full mesh topology* (such as the one shown in Figure 7-9), each device on the network is connected to every other device on the network. With a *partial mesh topology*, some devices are connected to all other devices, but some are connected only to those devices with which they exchange the most data. Consequently, if one device on a mesh network fails, the network can still function, assuming there is an alternate path available. Mesh networks are used most often with wireless networks.

Many networks, however, don't conform to a standard topology. Some networks combine topologies and connect multiple smaller networks, in effect turning several smaller networks into one larger one. For example, two star networks may be joined together using a bus line.

Network Architectures

Networks also vary by their *architecture*; that is, the way they are designed to communicate. The two most common network architectures are *client-server* and *peer-to-peer (P2P)*.

Client-Server Networks

Client-server networks include both *clients* (computers and other devices on the network that request and utilize network resources) and *servers* (computers that are dedicated to processing client requests). Network servers are typically powerful computers with lots of memory and a very large hard drive. They provide access to software, files, and other resources that are being shared via the network. Servers typically perform a variety of tasks. For example, a single server can act as a *network server* to manage network traffic, a *file server* to manage shared files, a *print server* to handle printing-related activities, and/or a *mail server* or *Web server* to manage e-mail and Web page requests, respectively. For instance, there is only one server in the network illustrated in Figure 7-10, and it is capable of performing all server tasks for that network. When a client retrieves files from a server, it is called *downloading*; transferring data from a client to a server is called *uploading*.

Peer-to-Peer (P2P) Networks

With a *peer-to-peer (P2P) network*, a central server is not used (see Figure 7-11). Instead, all the computers on the network work at the same functional level, and users have direct access to the computers and other devices attached to the network. For instance, users can access files stored on a peer computer's hard drive and print using a peer computer's printer, provided those devices have been designated as *shared devices*. Peer-to-peer networks are less expensive and less complicated to implement than client-server networks because there are no dedicated servers, but they may not have the same performance as client-server

STAR NETWORKS
Use a central device to connect each device directly to the network.

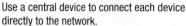

BUS NETWORKS
Use a single central cable to connect each device in a linear fashion.

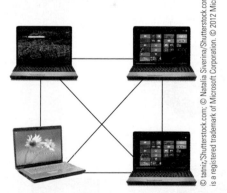

MESH NETWORKS
Each computer or device is connected to multiple (sometimes all of the other) devices on the network.

FIGURE 7-9
Basic network topologies.

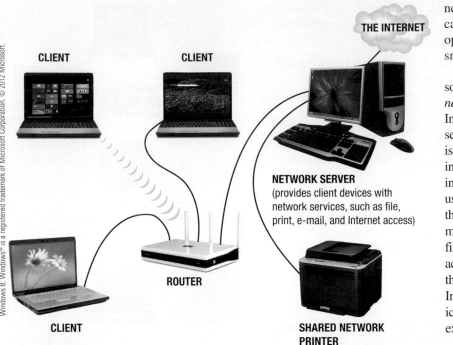

CLIENT

CLIENT

THE INTERNET

NETWORK SERVER
(provides client devices with
network services, such as file,
print, e-mail, and Internet access)

ROUTER

CLIENT

SHARED NETWORK PRINTER

© Natalia Siverina/Shutterstock.com; © tatniz/Shutterstock.com; © 300dpi/Shutterstock.com; Courtesy D-Link Systems, Inc.; © kavione/Shutterstock.com; Used with permission from Microsoft Corporation; Windows 8: Windows® is a registered trademark of Microsoft Corporation. © 2012 Microsoft.

Ⓐ **FIGURE 7-10**
Client-server networks.
Client computers
communicate through one
or more servers.

Ⓥ **FIGURE 7-11**
Peer-to-peer networks.
Computers communicate
directly with one another.

P2P HOME NETWORKS
Devices connect and communicate via the
home network.

THE INTERNET

INTERNET P2P NETWORKS
Devices connect and communicate
via the Internet.

© Natalia Siverina/Shutterstock.com; Courtesy D-Link Systems, Inc.; © kavione/Shutterstock.com; © tatniz/Shutterstock.com; Windows 8: Windows® is a registered trademark of Microsoft Corporation. © 2012 Microsoft.; Copyright © 2015 Cengage Learning®

networks under heavy use. Peer-to-peer capabilities are built into many personal operating systems and are often used with small office or home networks.

Another type of peer-to-peer networking—sometimes called *Internet peer-to-peer (Internet P2P) computing*—is performed via the Internet. Instead of placing content on a Web server for others to view via the Internet, content is exchanged over the Internet directly between individual users via a peer-to-peer network. For instance, one user can copy a file from another user's hard drive to his or her own computer via the Internet. Internet P2P networking is commonly used for exchanging music and video files with others over the Internet—an illegal act if the content is copyright-protected and the exchange is unauthorized, although legal Internet P2P networks exist. Copyright law, ethics, and other topics related to peer-to-peer file exchanges are covered in Chapter 16.

CAUTION CAUTION CAUTION CAUTION CAUTION CAUTION CAUT

Do not enable sharing for folders that you do not want others on your network to see. And, if you choose to use a P2P network, be sure to designate the files in your shared folder as *read-only* to prevent your original files from being overwritten by another P2P user.

Network Size and Coverage Area

One additional way networks are classified is by the size of their coverage area. This also impacts the types of users the network is designed to service. The most common categories of networks are discussed next; these networks can use both wired and wireless connections.

Personal Area Networks (PANs)

A **personal area network (PAN)** is a small network of two or more personal devices for one individual

> **Personal area network (PAN).** A network that connects two or more of an individual's personal devices when they are located close together.

(such as a computer, mobile phone, headset, media tablet, portable speakers, smart watch, fitness gadget, and printer) that is designed to enable those devices to communicate and share data. PANs can be set up on demand or set up to work together automatically as soon as the devices get within a certain physical distance of each other. For instance, a PAN can be used to synchronize a mobile device automatically with a personal computer whenever the devices are in range of each other, to connect a media tablet to a portable speaker, or to connect a mobile phone to a headset and/or smart watch (see Figure 7-12). *Wireless PANs* (*WPANs*) are more common today than wired PANs and are typically implemented via *Bluetooth* or another short-range networking standard (discussed shortly) or via the Internet using Google or another cloud service.

Local Area Networks (LANs)

A **local area network (LAN)** is a network that covers a relatively small geographical area, such as a home, an office building, or a school. LANs allow users on the network to exchange files and e-mail, share printers and other hardware, and access the Internet. The client-server network shown in Figure 7-10 is an example of a LAN.

Metropolitan Area Networks (MANs)

A **metropolitan area network (MAN)** is a network designed to service a metropolitan area, typically a city or county. Most MANs are owned and operated by a city or by a network provider in order to provide individuals in that location access to the MAN. Some wireless MANs (often referred to as *municipal Wi-Fi* projects) are created by cities (such as Riverside, California—see Figure 7-13) or large organizations (such as Google in Mountain View, California) to provide free or low-cost Internet access to area residents. In addition, some Internet service providers (such as Comcast) are experimenting with setting up free wireless MANs in select metropolitan areas for their subscribers to use for Internet access when they are on the go.

FIGURE 7-12
WPANs. This smart watch connects wirelessly to a smartphone to access GPS information, as well as display incoming phone calls, e-mails, and text messages.

FIGURE 7-13
Municipal Wi-Fi. This MAN covers downtown Riverside, California.

Wide Area Networks (WANs)

A **wide area network (WAN)** is a network that covers a large geographical area. Typically, a WAN consists of two or more LANs that are connected together using communications technology. The Internet, by this definition, is the world's largest WAN. WANs may be publicly accessible, like the Internet, or they may be privately owned and operated. For instance, a company may have a private WAN to transfer data from one location to another, such as from each retail store to the corporate headquarters. Large WANs, like the Internet, typically use a mesh topology.

Intranets and Extranets

An **intranet** is a private network (such as a company LAN) that is designed to be used by an organization's employees and is set up like the Internet (with data posted on Web pages that are accessed with a Web browser). Consequently, little or no employee training is required to use an intranet, and intranet content can be accessed using a variety of devices. Intranets today are used for many purposes, including coordinating internal e-mail and communications, making company publications (such as contact information,

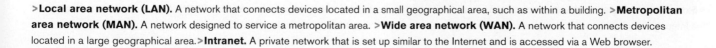

>**Local area network (LAN).** A network that connects devices located in a small geographical area, such as within a building. >**Metropolitan area network (MAN).** A network designed to service a metropolitan area. >**Wide area network (WAN).** A network that connects devices located in a large geographical area. >**Intranet.** A private network that is set up similar to the Internet and is accessed via a Web browser.

ASK THE EXPERT

Marian Merritt, Internet Safety Advocate, Symantec Corporation

How can an individual surf safely at a public Wi-Fi hotspot?

First, install Internet security software that includes antivirus, local firewall, and intrusion protection. Next, know the name of your Wi-Fi provider, create a unique username for that connection, and use a complex password comprised of random letters and numbers. When connecting through a logon page, view the site's certificate presented by the browser to verify that the site is operated by the expected organization.

In addition, turn off file and printer sharing to make it harder for a stranger to check your wireless activities, and avoid sending any confidential information (Social Security numbers, bank account passwords, and so on) over a Wi-Fi connection. If you can delay doing your online shopping or banking until you are back at home or the office, then do so! Unless you are connected to the Internet over an encrypted connection, assume that someone could potentially gain access to your personal information. Lastly, when possible, use a Virtual Private Network (VPN), which provides stronger protection against a variety of risks.

manuals, forms, job announcements, and so forth) available to employees, facilitating collaborative computing, and providing access to shared calendars and schedules.

A company network that is accessible to authorized outsiders is called an **extranet**. Extranets are usually accessed via the Internet, and they can be used to provide customers and business partners with access to the data they need. Access to intranets and extranets is typically restricted to employees and other authorized users, similar to other company networks.

Virtual Private Networks (VPNs)

A **virtual private network (VPN)** is a private, secure path across a public network (usually the Internet) that is set up to allow authorized users private, secure access to the company network. For instance, a VPN can allow a traveling employee, business partner, or employee located at a satellite office or public wireless hotspot to connect securely to the company network via the Internet. A process called *tunneling* is typically used to carry the data over the Internet; special *encryption* technology is used to protect the data so it cannot be understood if it is intercepted during transit (encryption is explained in Chapter 9). Essentially, VPNs allow an organization to provide secure, remote access to the company network without the cost of physically extending the private network.

DATA TRANSMISSION CHARACTERISTICS

Data transmitted over a network has specific characteristics, and it can travel over a network in various ways. These and some other characteristics related to data transmission are discussed next.

Bandwidth

As discussed in Chapter 2, the term *bandwidth* (also called *throughput*) refers to the amount of data that can be transferred (such as over a certain type of networking medium) in a given time period. Text data requires the least amount of bandwidth; video data requires the most. Just as a wide fire hose allows more water to pass through it per unit of time than a narrow garden hose allows, a networking medium with a high bandwidth allows more data to pass through it per unit of time than a networking medium with a low bandwidth. Bandwidth is usually measured in the number of *bits per second* (*bps*), *Kbps* (thousands of bits per second), *Mbps* (millions of bits per second), or *Gbps* (billions of bits per second).

>**Extranet.** An intranet that is at least partially accessible to authorized outsiders. >**Virtual private network (VPN).** A private, secure path over the Internet that provides authorized users a secure means of accessing a private network via the Internet.

Analog vs. Digital Signals

Data can be represented as either *analog* or *digital* signals. Voice and music data in its natural form, for instance, is analog, and data stored on a computer is digital. Most networking media send data using **digital signals**, in which data is represented by only two *discrete states*: 0s and 1s (see Figure 7-14). **Analog signals**, such as those used by conventional telephone systems, represent data with *continuous waves*. The data to be transmitted over a networking medium must match the type of signal (analog or digital) that the medium supports; if it doesn't originally, then it must be converted before the data is transmitted. For instance, analog data that is to be sent using digital signals (such as analog music broadcast by a digital radio station) must first be converted into digital form, and digital data to be sent using analog signals (such as computer data sent over a conventional analog telephone network) must be converted into analog form before it can be transmitted. The conversion of data between analog and digital form is performed by networking hardware.

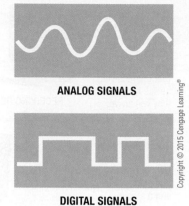

ANALOG SIGNALS

DIGITAL SIGNALS

FIGURE 7-14
Analog vs. digital signals.

Transmission Type and Timing

Networking media can also use either *serial transmission* or *parallel transmission*. With **serial transmission**, data is sent one bit at a time, one after the other along a single path (see Figure 7-15). When **parallel transmission** is used, the message is sent at least one byte at a time, with each bit in the byte taking a separate path (refer again to Figure 7-15). While parallel transmission is frequently used within computer components (such as buses) and is used for some wireless networking applications, networking media typically use serial transmission.

When data is sent using serial transmission, a technique must be used to organize the bits being transferred so the data can be reconstructed after it is received. Three ways of timing serial transmissions are by using *synchronous*, *asynchronous*, and *isochronous* connections (see Figure 7-16). Although all three of these methods send data one bit at a time, the methods vary with respect to how the bits are organized for transfer.

- ➤ *Synchronous transmission*—data is organized into groups or blocks of data, which are transferred at regular, specified intervals. Because the transmissions are synchronized, both devices know when data can be sent and when it should arrive. Most data transmissions within a computer and over a network are synchronous transmissions.

- ➤ *Asynchronous transmission*—data is sent when it is ready to be sent, without being synchronized. To identify the bits that belong in each byte, a *start bit* and *stop bit* are used at the beginning and end of the byte, respectively. This overhead makes asynchronous transmission less efficient than synchronous transmission and so it is not as widely used as synchronous transmission.

- ➤ *Isochronous transmission*—data is sent at the same time as other related data to support certain types of real-time applications that require the different types of data to be delivered at the proper speed for that application. For example, when transmitting a video file, the audio data must be received at the proper time in order for it to be played with its corresponding video data. To accomplish this with isochronous transmission, the sending and receiving devices first communicate to determine the bandwidth and other factors needed for the transmission, and then the necessary bandwidth is reserved just for that transmission.

FIGURE 7-15
Serial vs. parallel transmissions.

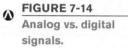
01000001

SERIAL TRANSMISSIONS
All the bits in one byte follow one another over a single path.

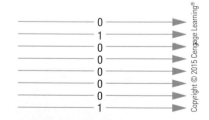

PARALLEL TRANSMISSIONS
The eight bits in each byte are transmitted over separate paths at the same time.

> **Digital signal.** A type of signal where the data is represented by 0s and 1s. > **Analog signal.** A type of signal where the data is represented by continuous waves. > **Serial transmission.** A type of data transmission in which the bits in a byte travel the same path one after the other. > **Parallel transmission.** A type of data transmission in which bytes of data are transmitted at one time, with the bits in each byte taking a separate path.

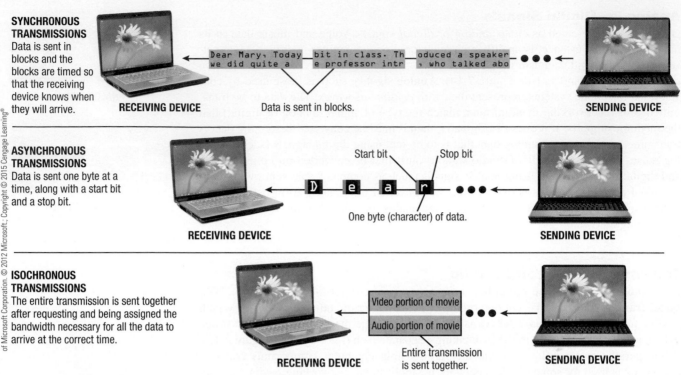

SYNCHRONOUS TRANSMISSIONS
Data is sent in blocks and the blocks are timed so that the receiving device knows when they will arrive.

Dear Mary. Today bit in class. Th oduced a speaker
we did quite a e professor intr , who talked abo

RECEIVING DEVICE

Data is sent in blocks.

SENDING DEVICE

ASYNCHRONOUS TRANSMISSIONS
Data is sent one byte at a time, along with a start bit and a stop bit.

Start bit   Stop bit

D e a r

RECEIVING DEVICE

One byte (character) of data.

SENDING DEVICE

ISOCHRONOUS TRANSMISSIONS
The entire transmission is sent together after requesting and being assigned the bandwidth necessary for all the data to arrive at the correct time.

Video portion of movie
Audio portion of movie

RECEIVING DEVICE

Entire transmission is sent together.

SENDING DEVICE

FIGURE 7-16

Transmission timing. Most network transmissions use synchronous transmission.

Another distinction between types of transmissions is the direction in which transmitted data can move.

> *Simplex transmission*—data travels in a single direction only (like a doorbell). Simplex transmission is relatively uncommon in data transmissions because most devices that are mainly one-directional, such as a printer, can still transmit error messages and other data back to the computer.

> *Half-duplex transmission*—data can travel in either direction, but only in one direction at a time (like a walkie-talkie where only one person can talk at a time). Some network transmissions are half-duplex.

> *Full-duplex transmission*—data can move in both directions at the same time (like a telephone). Many network and most Internet connections are full-duplex; sometimes two connections between the sending device and receiving device are needed to support full-duplex transmissions.

Delivery Method

When data needs to travel across a large network (such as a WAN), typically one of three methods is used (see Figure 7-17). With *circuit switching*, a dedicated path over a network is established between the sender and receiver and all data follows that path from the sender to the receiver. Once the connection is established, the physical path or circuit is dedicated to that connection and cannot be used by any other device until the transmission is finished. The most common example of a circuit-switched network is a conventional telephone system.

The technique used for data sent over the Internet is *packet switching*. With packet switching, messages are separated into small units called *packets*. Packets contain information about the sender and the receiver, the actual data being sent, and information about how to reassemble the packets to reconstruct the original message. Packets travel along the network separately, based on their final destination, network traffic, and other network conditions. When the packets reach their destination, they are reassembled in the proper order. Another alternative is *broadcasting*, in which data is sent out (typically in packets) to all nodes on a network and is retrieved only by the intended recipient. Broadcasting is used primarily with LANs.

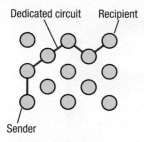

Dedicated circuit   Recipient

Sender

**CIRCUIT-SWITCHED
NETWORKS**
Data uses a dedicated path
from the sender to the
recipient.

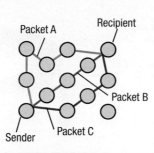

Packet A   Recipient

Packet B

Packet C

Sender

**PACKET-SWITCHED
NETWORKS**
Data is sent as individual packets,
which are assembled at the
recipient's destination.

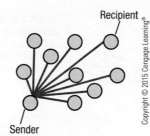

Recipient

Sender

BROADCAST NETWORKS
Data is broadcast to all
nodes within range; the
designated recipient
retrieves the data.

FIGURE 7-17
Circuit-switched,
packet-switched,
and broadcast
networks.

Copyright © 2015 Cengage Learning®

NETWORKING MEDIA

To connect the devices in a network, either *wired media* (physical cables) or *wireless media* (typically radio signals) can be used. The most common wired and wireless networking media are discussed next.

Wired Networking Media

The most common types of wired networking media are *twisted-pair*, *coaxial*, and *fiber-optic cable*.

Twisted-Pair Cable

A **twisted-pair cable** is made up of pairs of thin strands of insulated wire twisted together (see Figure 7-18). Twisted-pair is the least expensive type of networking cable and has been in use the longest. In fact, it is the same type of cabling used inside most homes for telephone communications. Twisted-pair cabling can be used with both analog and digital data transmission and is commonly used for LANs. Twisted-pair cable is rated by *category*, which indicates the type of data, speed, distance, and other factors that the cable supports. *Category 3 (Cat 3)* twisted-pair cabling is regular telephone cable; higher speed and quality cabling—such as *Category 5 (Cat 5)*, *Category 6 (Cat 6)*, and *Category 7 (Cat 7)*—is frequently used for home or business networks. The pairs of wires in twisted-pair wire are twisted together to reduce interference and improve performance. To further improve performance, it can be *shielded* with a metal lining. Twisted-pair cables used for networks have different connectors than those used for telephones. Networking connectors are typically *RJ-45* connectors, which look similar to, but are larger than, telephone *RJ-11* connectors.

Coaxial Cable

Coaxial cable (also known as *coax*) was originally developed to carry a large number of high-speed video transmissions at one time, such as to deliver cable TV service. A coaxial cable (see Figure 7-18) consists of a relatively thick center wire surrounded by insulation and then covered with a shield of braided wire to block electromagnetic signals from entering the cable. Coaxial cable is commonly used today in computer networks, for

NET

>**Twisted-pair cable.** A networking cable consisting of wire strands twisted in sets of two and bound into a cable. >**Coaxial cable.** A networking cable consisting of a center wire inside a grounded, cylindrical shield, capable of sending data at high speeds.

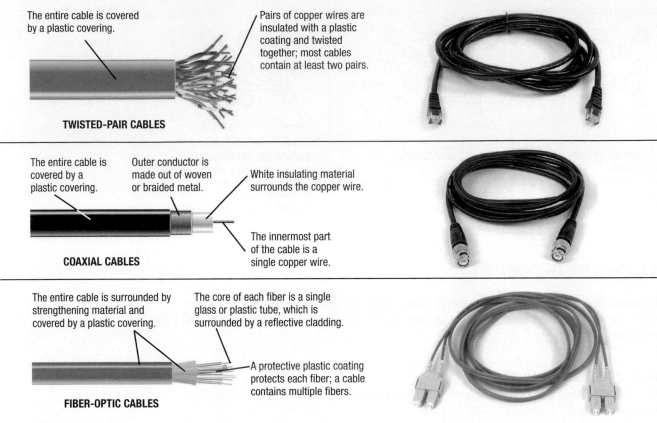

The entire cable is covered by a plastic covering.

Pairs of copper wires are insulated with a plastic coating and twisted together; most cables contain at least two pairs.

TWISTED-PAIR CABLES

The entire cable is covered by a plastic covering.

Outer conductor is made out of woven or braided metal.

White insulating material surrounds the copper wire.

The innermost part of the cable is a single copper wire.

COAXIAL CABLES

The entire cable is surrounded by strengthening material and covered by a plastic covering.

The core of each fiber is a single glass or plastic tube, which is surrounded by a reflective cladding.

A protective plastic coating protects each fiber; a cable contains multiple fibers.

FIBER-OPTIC CABLES

Courtesy of Black Box Corporation; Courtesy Belkin International, Inc.

FIGURE 7-18
Wired network transmission media.

short-run telephone transmissions outside of the home, and for cable television delivery. Although more expensive than twisted-pair cabling, it is much less susceptible to interference and can carry more data more quickly. While not used extensively for networking home computers at the moment, that may change with the relatively new option of networking via the existing coax in a home. Coax is also used with home multimedia networks. The most common types of connectors used with coaxial cable are the slotted *BNC connectors* that are turned once to lock or unlock them into place (and are on the cable shown in Figure 7-18) and the threaded *F connectors* frequently used with cable TV and antenna applications.

Fiber-Optic Cable

Fiber-optic cable is the newest and fastest of these three types of wired transmission media. It contains multiple (sometimes several hundred) clear glass or plastic fiber strands, each about the thickness of a human hair (refer again to Figure 7-18). Fiber-optic cable transfers data represented by light pulses at speeds of billions of bits per second. Each strand has the capacity to carry data for several television stations or thousands of voice conversations, but each strand can only send data in one direction so two strands are needed for full-duplex data transmissions.

Fiber-optic cable is commonly used for the high-speed backbone lines of a network, such as to connect networks housed in separate buildings or for the Internet infrastructure. It is also used for telephone backbone lines and, increasingly, is being installed by telephone companies all the way to the home or business to provide super-fast connections

> **Fiber-optic cable.** A networking cable that utilizes hundreds of thin transparent fibers over which lasers transmit data as light.

directly to the end user. The biggest advantage of fiber-optic cabling is speed; the main disadvantage of fiber-optic cabling is the initial expense of both the cable and the installation. Fiber-optic connectors are less standardized than connectors for other types of wired media, so it is important to use cables with the connectors that match the hardware with which the cable will be used. Common connectors include the push-pull *SC connector* (shown in Figure 7-18) and the tabbed *SC* and slotted *ST connectors*.

Wireless Networking Media

Wireless networks usually use *radio signals* to send data through the airwaves. Depending on the networking application, radio signals can be short range (such as when used to connect a wireless keyboard or mouse to a computer), medium range (such as when used to connect a computer to a wireless LAN or public hotspot), or long range (such as when used to provide Internet access or cell phone coverage to a relatively large geographic area or to broadcast TV or radio shows). The radio signals used in wireless networks and the types of technologies used to transmit them are discussed next.

The Electromagnetic and Wireless Spectrums

All wireless applications in the United States—such as wireless networks, mobile phones, radio and TV broadcasts, sonar and radar applications, and GPS systems—use specific *frequencies* as assigned by the *Federal Communications Commission (FCC)*. Frequencies are measured in *hertz (Hz)* and the frequencies that make up the *electromagnetic spectrum*—the range of common *electromagnetic radiation* (energy)— are shown in Figure 7-19. Different parts of the spectrum have different properties (including the distance a signal can travel, the amount of data a signal can transmit in a given period of time, and the types of objects a signal can pass through), which make certain frequencies more appropriate for certain applications. As illustrated in this figure, most wireless networking applications use frequencies located in the *radio frequency (RF)* band at the low end (up to 300 GHz) of the electromagnetic spectrum—this range is sometimes referred to as the *wireless spectrum*.

The frequencies assigned to an application, such as FM radio or cell phone service, typically consist of a range of frequencies to be used as needed for that application. For instance, FM radio stations broadcast on frequencies from 88 MHz to 108 MHz and each radio station in a particular geographic area is assigned its own frequency. Most radio frequencies in the United States are licensed by the FCC and can only be used for that specific application by the licensed individuals in their specified geographic areas. However, the 900 MHz, 2.4 GHz, 5 GHz, and 5.8 GHz frequencies used by many cordless landline phones, garage door openers, and other consumer devices—as well as for *Wi-Fi*, *WiMAX*, and *Bluetooth* wireless networking—fall within an unlicensed part of the spectrum and, therefore, can be used by any product or individual. A frequency range can be further broken down into multiple *channels*, each of which can be used simultaneously by different users. There are also ways to combine multiple signals to send them over a transmission medium at one time to allow more users than would otherwise be possible.

TIP

The emerging standard for *next-generation Wi-Fi* (discussed later in this chapter) uses the higher, but still unlicensed, 60 GHz band.

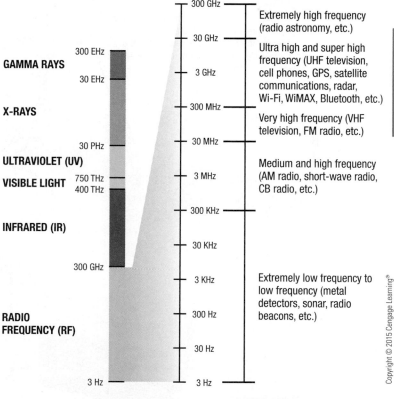

NET

FIGURE 7-19
The electromagnetic spectrum. Each type of communication is assigned specific frequencies within which to operate.

Copyright © 2015 Cengage Learning®

Because the number of wireless applications is growing all the time and there is a limited amount of the parts of the spectrum appropriate for today's wireless networking applications, the wireless spectrum is relatively crowded and frequencies are in high demand. One benefit of the 2009 switch from analog to digital television broadcasts is that it freed up some of the VHF and UHF frequencies for other applications. As a new part of the spectrum becomes available, it is assigned a function (such as the recent addition of 195 MHz of the 5 GHz band for Wi-Fi use) or auctioned off (such as the 700 MHz band auction that ended in 2011). The next auction—in the 600 MHz band—is scheduled for 2014. The FCC is continually working to free up spectrum for the rapidly growing mobile broadband market. In fact, it is currently looking into a proposal to free up more spectrum for in-flight Internet use for airline passengers.

Cellular Radio Transmissions

Cellular radio transmissions are used with cell phones and are sent and received via *cellular (cell) towers*—tall metal towers with antennas on top. Cellular service areas are divided into honeycomb-shaped zones called *cells*; each cell contains one cell tower (see Figure 7-20). When a cell phone user begins to make a call, it is picked up by the appropriate cell tower (the one that is located in the cell in which the cell phone is located and that is associated with the user's wireless provider). That cell tower then forwards the call to the wireless provider's *Mobile Telephone Switching Office (MTSO)*, which routes the call to the recipient's telephone via his or her mobile or conventional telephone service provider (depending on the type of phone being used by the recipient). When a cell phone user moves out of the

FIGURE 7-20

How cellular phones work.

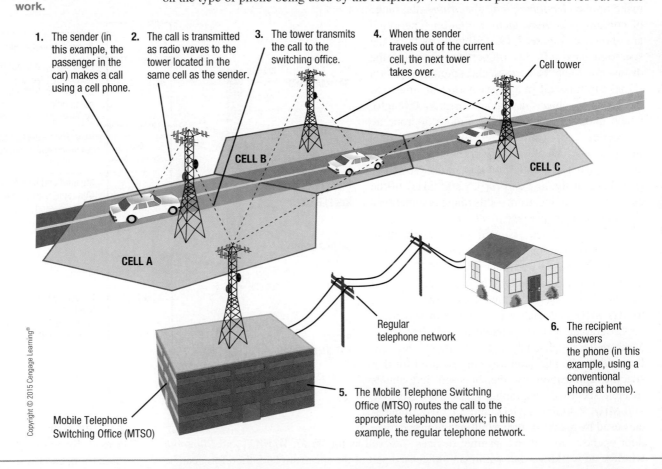

1. The sender (in this example, the passenger in the car) makes a call using a cell phone.

2. The call is transmitted as radio waves to the tower located in the same cell as the sender.

3. The tower transmits the call to the switching office.

4. When the sender travels out of the current cell, the next tower takes over.

Cell tower

CELL B

CELL A

CELL C

Mobile Telephone Switching Office (MTSO)

Regular telephone network

5. The Mobile Telephone Switching Office (MTSO) routes the call to the appropriate telephone network; in this example, the regular telephone network.

6. The recipient answers the phone (in this example, using a conventional phone at home).

Copyright © 2015 Cengage Learning®

> **Cellular radio.** A form of broadcast radio designed for use with cellular telephones that broadcasts using antennas located inside honeycomb-shaped cells.

current cell into a new cell, the call is passed automatically to the appropriate cell tower in the cell that the user is entering. Data (such as e-mail and Web page requests) sent via cell phones works in a similar manner. The speed of cellular radio transmissions depends on the type of *cellular standard* being used, as discussed later in this chapter.

Microwave and Satellite Transmissions

Microwaves are high-frequency radio signals that can send large quantities of data at high speeds over long distances. Microwave signals can be sent or received using *microwave stations* or *communications satellites*, but they must travel in a straight line from one station or satellite to another without encountering any obstacles because microwave signals are *line of sight*. **Microwave stations** are earth-based stations that can transmit microwave signals directly to each other over distances of up to about 30 miles. To avoid buildings, mountains, and the curvature of the earth obstructing the signal, microwave stations are usually placed on tall buildings, towers, and mountaintops. Microwave stations typically contain both a dish-shaped *microwave antenna* and a transceiver. When one station receives a transmission from another, it amplifies it and passes it on to the next station. Microwave stations can exchange data transmissions with *communications satellites*, discussed next, as well as with other microwave stations. Microwave stations designed specifically to communicate with satellites (such as those used to provide satellite TV and satellite Internet services) are typically called *satellite dishes*. Satellite dishes are usually installed permanently where they are needed, but they can also be mounted on trucks, boats, RVs, and other types of transportation devices when portable transmission capabilities are necessary or desirable, such as when used for military or recreational applications.

Communications satellites are space-based devices launched into orbit around the earth to receive and transmit microwave signals to and from earth (see the satellite Internet example in Figure 7-21). Communications satellites were originally used to facilitate microwave transmission when microwave stations were not economically viable (such as over large, sparsely populated areas) or were physically impractical (such as over large bodies of water) and were used primarily by the military and communications companies (such as for remote television news broadcasts). Today, communications satellites are used to send and receive transmissions to and from a variety of other devices, such as personal satellite dishes used for satellite television and Internet service, GPS receivers, satellite radio receivers, and satellite phones. They are also used for *earth observation* (*EO*) applications, including weather observation, mapping, and government surveillance.

FIGURE 7-21
How satellite Internet works.

3. An orbiting satellite receives the request and beams it down to the satellite dish at the ISP's operations center.

2. The request is sent up to a satellite from the individual's satellite dish.

1. Data, such as a Web page request, is sent from the individual's computer to the satellite dish via a satellite modem.

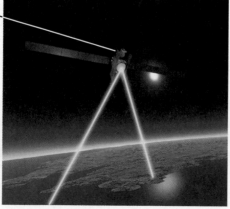

4. The ISP's operations center receives the request (via its satellite dish) and transfers it to the Internet.

THE INTERNET

5. The request travels over the Internet as usual. The requested information takes a reverse route back to the individual.

> **Microwave station.** An earth-based device that sends and receives high-frequency, high-speed radio signals. > **Communications satellite.** An earth-orbiting device that relays communications signals over long distances.

Traditional communications satellites maintain a *geosynchronous* orbit 22,300 miles above the earth and, because they travel at a speed and direction that keeps pace with the earth's rotation, they appear (from earth) to remain stationary over any given spot. Because these satellites are so far above the surface of the earth, there is a slight delay while the signals travel from earth, to the satellite, and back to earth again. This delay—less than one half-second—is not normally noticed by most users (such as individuals who receive Internet or TV service via satellite) but it does make geosynchronous satellite transmissions less practical for voice, gaming, and other real-time communications. Because of this delay factor, *low earth orbit* (*LEO*) satellite systems were developed for use with satellite telephone systems. LEO satellites typically are located anywhere from 100 to 1,000 miles above the earth and, consequently, provide faster transmission than traditional satellites. *Medium earth orbit* (*MEO*) systems typically use satellites located about 1,000 to 12,000 miles above the earth and are used most often for GPS.

Infrared (IR) Transmissions

One type of wireless networking that does not use signals in the RF band of the electromagnetic spectrum is **infrared (IR) transmission**, which sends data as infrared light rays over relatively short distances. Like an infrared television remote control, infrared technology requires line-of-sight transmission. Because of this limitation, many formerly infrared devices (such as wireless mice and keyboards) now use RF radio signals instead. Infrared transmissions are still used with remote controls (such as for computers that contain TV tuners). They are also used to beam data between some mobile devices, as well as between some game consoles, handheld gaming devices, and other home entertainment devices.

COMMUNICATIONS PROTOCOLS AND NETWORKING STANDARDS

A *protocol* is a set of rules to be followed in a specific situation; in networking, for instance, there are *communications protocols* that determine how devices on a network communicate. The term *standard* refers to a set of criteria or requirements that has been approved by a recognized standards organization (such as the *American National Standards Institute* (*ANSI*), which helps to develop standards used in business and industry, or *IEEE*, which develops networking standards) or is accepted as a de facto standard by the industry. Standards are extremely important in the computer industry because they help hardware and software manufacturers ensure that the products they develop can work with other computing products. *Networking standards* typically address both how the devices in a network physically connect (such as the types of cabling that can be used) and how the devices communicate (such as the communications protocols that can be used). Communications protocols and the most common wired and wireless networking standards are discussed in the next several sections.

TCP/IP and Other Communications Protocols

The most widely used communications protocol today is **TCP/IP**. TCP/IP is the protocol used for transferring data over the Internet and actually consists of two protocols: *Transmission Control Protocol* (*TCP*), which is responsible for the delivery of data, and *Internet Protocol* (*IP*), which provides addresses and routing information. TCP/IP uses packet switching to transmit data over the Internet; when the packets reach their destination, they are reassembled in the proper order (see Figure 7-22). Support for TCP/IP is built into operating systems,

---

>**Infrared (IR) transmissions.** A wireless networking medium that sends data as infrared light rays. >**TCP/IP.** A networking protocol that uses packet switching to facilitate the transmission of messages; the protocol used with the Internet.

and IP addresses are commonly used to identify the various devices on computer networks.

The first widely used version of IP was *Internet Protocol Version 4* (*IPv4*), which was standardized in the early 1980s. IPv4 uses 32-bit addresses and so allows for 2^{32} (4.3 billion) possible unique addresses. While still in use today, IPv4 was never designed to be used with the vast number of devices that access the Internet today and IPv4 addresses are running out. Consequently, a newer version of IP (*IPv6*) was developed and is in the process of being implemented. IPv6 uses 128-bit addresses (and so allows for 2^{128} possible unique addresses). It provides enough addresses so that all devices can have their own direct public IP

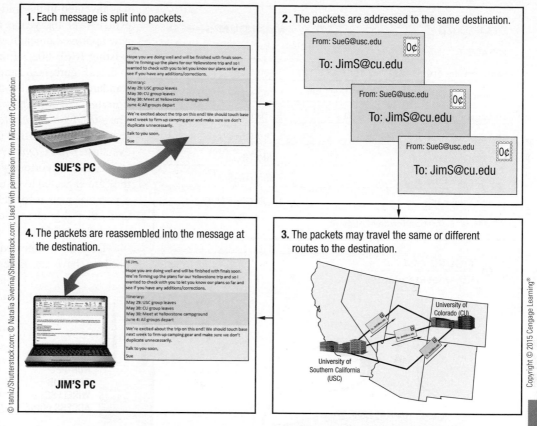

1. Each message is split into packets.

SUE'S PC

2. The packets are addressed to the same destination.

From: SueG@usc.edu   0¢
To: JimS@cu.edu

From: SueG@usc.edu   0¢
To: JimS@cu.edu

From: SueG@usc.edu   0¢
To: JimS@cu.edu

4. The packets are reassembled into the message at the destination.

JIM'S PC

3. The packets may travel the same or different routes to the destination.

University of Colorado (CU)

University of Southern California (USC)

FIGURE 7-22
How TCP/IP works.
TCP/IP networks (like the Internet) use packet switching.

address. Using IPv6 addressing, your devices can be accessible on the Internet directly via their own IP address, instead of all the devices in your home being identified by your *router's* IP address (which requires the router to relay the appropriate traffic to and from each device). The use of IPv6 addressing will make applications such as home automation and gaming easier to implement. It is expected that external systems (such as company Web sites) will switch over to IPv6 first and that IPv4 and IPv6 will coexist for several years. However, in some countries (such as China) where IPv4 address are scare, end users are expected to switch over faster. In the United States, the government has mandated that all federal agencies be capable of switching to IPv6 and to purchase only IPv6-compatible new hardware and software. Experts suggest that businesses perform a network audit to determine what hardware and software changes will be needed to switch to IPv6 so that the business is prepared when the change is necessary.

While TCP/IP is used to connect to and communicate with the Internet, other protocols are used for specific Internet applications. For instance, as discussed in Chapter 1, *HTTP* (*Hypertext Transfer Protocol*) and *HTTPS* (*Secure Hypertext Transfer Protocol*) are protocols used to display Web pages, and *FTP* (*File Transfer Protocol*) is a protocol used to transfer files over the Internet. Protocols used to deliver e-mail over the Internet include *SMTP* (*Simple Mail Transfer Protocol*) and *POP3* (*Post Office Protocol*).

Ethernet (802.3)

Ethernet (802.3) is the most widely used standard for wired networks. It is typically used with LANs that have a star topology (though it can also be used with WANs and MANs) and can be used in conjunction with twisted-pair, coaxial, or fiber-optic cabling. Ethernet

TIP
Examples of the networking adapters used with the various networking standards are included later in this chapter.

> **Ethernet (802.3).** A widely used wired LAN networking standard.

STANDARD	MAXIMUM SPEED
10BASE-T	10 Mbps
Fast Ethernet (100BASE-T or 100BASE-TX)	100 Mbps
Gigabit Ethernet (1000BASE-T)	1,000 Mbps (1 Gbps)
10 Gigabit Ethernet (10GBASE-T)	10 Gbps
40 Gigabit Ethernet	40 Gbps
100 Gigabit Ethernet	100 Gbps
400 Gigabit Ethernet*	400 Gbps
Terabit Ethernet*	1,000 Gbps (1 Tbps)

*Under consideration for development

FIGURE 7-23
Ethernet standards.

PoE SWITCH

NON-PoE OUTDOOR WIRELESS ACCESS POINT

PoE ADAPTER

PoE CAMERA

—— POWER CABLE
—— ETHERNET CABLE

FIGURE 7-24
With Power over Ethernet (PoE), devices are powered through the Ethernet connection.

TIP

The ongoing development of faster Ethernet standards is necessary because Internet traffic is expected to quadruple in the next five years and networks need to be able to handle the increased traffic.

was invented in the mid-1970s and has continued to evolve over the years; about every three years the new approved amendments are incorporated into the existing IEEE 802.3 Ethernet standard to keep it up to date. Figure 7-23 summarizes the various Ethernet standards; of these, the most common today are *Fast Ethernet*, *Gigabit Ethernet*, and *10 Gigabit Ethernet*. The *40 Gigabit Ethernet* and *100 Gigabit Ethernet* standards were ratified in 2010. Development of the even faster *400 Gigabit Ethernet* and *Terabit Ethernet* standards are currently being explored; if ratified, they are expected to be used for connections between servers, as well as for delivering video, digital X-rays and other digital medical images, and other high-speed, bandwidth-intensive networking applications.

Devices connected to an Ethernet network need to have an Ethernet port either built in or added using an expansion card. Ethernet networks can contain devices using multiple Ethernet speeds, but the slower devices will only operate at their respective speeds.

A relatively new Ethernet development is *Power over Ethernet* (*PoE*), which allows electrical power to be sent along the cables in an Ethernet network (often referred to as *Ethernet cables*) along with data (see Figure 7-24). Consequently, PoE devices are not plugged into an electrical outlet. PoE is most often used in business networks with remote wired devices (such as outdoor networking hardware, security cameras, and other devices) that are not located near a power outlet. It can also be used to place networked devices near ceilings or other locations where a nearby power outlet may not be available, and in homes to connect wired devices (such as security cameras) to a home network without running new electrical wiring. Regular Ethernet-enabled devices can be powered via PoE if a *PoE adapter*, such as the one shown in Figure 7-24, is used.

Phoneline, Powerline, G.hn, and Broadband over Powerline (BPL)

Two alternatives to the Ethernet standard for wired home networks are the *Phoneline* and *Powerline standards*. Phoneline (also called the *HomePNA standard*) allows computers to be networked through ordinary telephone wiring and telephone jacks, as well as over existing home coaxial cable wiring. The newest version of this standard—*HomePNA 3.1*—supports speeds up to 320 Mbps and is designed to network both the computers and the home entertainment devices within a home. The Powerline (also called *HomePlug*) standard allows computers to be networked over existing power lines using conventional electrical outlets. Similar to Phoneline networks, Powerline networks are quick and easy to set up and are relatively fast (up to 200 Mbps). In addition, they have the advantage that houses usually have many more power outlets than phone outlets. Similar to the newest Phoneline standard, the Powerline standard—named *HomePlug AV*—can be used to network home entertainment devices in addition to computers. Products adhering to the even newer *HomePlug AV2* standard are 5 times faster than HomePlug AV, which allows them to support streaming HD video throughout the home. Both Phoneline and Powerline networks require network adapters to go between the devices on the network and the phone jack (for Phoneline) or power outlet (for Powerline). An emerging trend is using the Powerline standard to facilitate home automation. For instance, the *WeMo Light Switch* shown in Figure 7-25 replaces an existing light switch in the home and enables the homeowner to control that light with a smartphone (via the home's Wi-Fi network); appliances plugged into a *WeMo Switch* adapter (that plugs into an electrical outlet) can also be controlled remotely.

The *G.hn* standard is a new standard designed as a unified worldwide standard for creating home networks over any existing home wiring—phone lines, power lines, and coaxial cable. G.hn is viewed as the next-generation standard for wired home networking and may eventually replace the Powerline and Phoneline standards. G.hn is fast—up to 1 Gbps—and adapters and other products are expected to be available soon.

A technology based on the Powerline standard that has been under development for several years and that is designed to deliver broadband Internet to homes via the existing outdoor power lines (with the addition of some new hardware at the power poles) is *broadband over powerline (BPL)*. BPL service is typically available through the local power company and has great potential for delivering broadband Internet to any home or business that has access to electricity, but momentum for BPL appears to be slowing.

Courtesy Belkin International, Inc.

Ⓐ FIGURE 7-25
WeMo. Allows you to remotely control your lights with your smartphone; works over existing power lines.

Wi-Fi (802.11)

One of the most common networking standards used with wireless LANs is **Wi-Fi (802.11)**—a family of wireless networking standards that use the IEEE 802.11 standard. Wi-Fi (sometimes called *wireless Ethernet* because it is designed to easily connect to a wired Ethernet network) is the current standard for wireless networks in the home or office, as well as for public Wi-Fi hotspots. Wi-Fi hardware is built into virtually all portable computers and most mobile devices today. Wi-Fi capabilities are also becoming increasingly integrated into everyday products, such as printers, digital cameras, portable digital media players, external hard drives, baby monitors, gaming consoles and devices, digital photo frames, e-readers, home medical monitors, home audio systems, appliances, televisions, Blu-ray Disc players, and even bathroom scales (see Figure 7-26), to allow those devices to wirelessly network with other devices or to access the Internet. For a look at a Wi-Fi-enabled consumer product you can use to automatically upload digital photos to your favorite photo-sharing sites—Wi-Fi flash memory cards—see the Technology and You box.

The speed of a Wi-Fi network and the area it can cover depend on a variety of factors, including the *Wi-Fi standard* and hardware being used, the number of solid objects (such as walls, trees, or buildings) between the access point and the computer or other device being used, and the amount of interference from cordless phones, baby monitors, microwave ovens, and other devices that also operate on the same radio frequency as Wi-Fi (usually 2.4 GHz). In general, Wi-Fi is designed for medium-range data transfers—typically between 100 and 300 feet indoors and 300 to 900 feet outdoors. Usually both speed and distance degrade with interference. The distance of a Wi-Fi network can be extended using additional *antennas* and other hardware designed for that purpose, as discussed shortly.

Ⓥ FIGURE 7-26
Smart scales.
This scale transmits readings to a smartphone via Wi-Fi.

Scale

Courtesy Withings

>**Wi-Fi (802.11).** A widely used networking standard for medium-range wireless networks.

TECHNOLOGY AND YOU

Wi-Fi SD Cards

One interesting relatively new Wi-Fi product is the *Wi-Fi SD card*. These cards (such as the *Eye-Fi cards* shown in the accompanying illustration) are designed to upload photos wirelessly and automatically from your camera to your computer or mobile device via a Wi-Fi network. Some cards can also *geotag* your photos with location information (based on geographic coordinates) as you take them in order to show where the photos were taken; others can automatically upload your photos to your favorite Web sites like Flickr, Facebook, and Picasa.

For instance, all three Eye-Fi cards in the accompanying photo wirelessly transfer your photos from your digital camera to your home computer as soon as the camera is within range of your home Wi-Fi network. They can also wirelessly upload photos to your favorite photo and video sharing Web sites, as well as to your smartphone. *Eye-Fi Pro X2* cards also automatically geotag your photos. In addition, the Eye-Fi Pro X2 card can upload the *RAW* files often used by professional photographers. All cards automatically sync photos and videos to the user's Eye-Fi cloud storage account; content can be accessed for 7 days for regular users (there is no time limit for users with a premium account).

In addition to allowing you to share your photos immediately with others (while on a vacation or at a special event, for example), using a Wi-Fi SD card for your digital photos can also give you the peace of mind that your photos are backed up on your home computer and/or online. This is especially beneficial if your camera is stolen or the card becomes damaged. In fact, using an Eye-Fi card enabled one woman to catch the individual who stole her camera gear while she was on vacation—her photos, along with images of the thief with the camera gear, were uploaded to her home computer and the police were able to apprehend the thief and recover the stolen gear.

Courtesy Eye-Fi

A summary of the different Wi-Fi standards in use today is shown in Figure 7-27; of these, the most widely used today are *802.11g*, *802.11n*, and *802.11ac*. Beginning with the 802.11n standard, *MIMO (multiple in, multiple out) antennas* are used to transfer multiple streams of data at one time. As a result of this and other improvements, 802.11n allows for data transmissions typically about five times as fast as 802.11g and about twice the range; 802.11ac, which is expected to be ratified soon and already has compatible hardware available, is designed for faster speeds and is about three times as fast as 802.11n.

Typically, the various types of Wi-Fi products can be used on the same network as long as they operate on the same frequencies. Wi-Fi products are backward compatible (so computers using older 802.11g hardware can connect to 802.11n networks but they will only connect at 802.11g speeds, and 802.11n devices can be used on an 802.11ac network, but the 802.11n devices will work at 802.11n speeds). Updates, called *extensions*, to the 802.11 standard are developed on a regular basis; for instance, to facilitate mesh networks (*802.11s*), to facilitate networking with devices that are not preauthorized (*802.11u*), and to add security mechanisms that reduce the possibility of network disruption

FIGURE 7-27
Common Wi-Fi standards.

WI-FI STANDARD	DESCRIPTION
802.11b	An early Wi-Fi standard; supports data transfer rates of 11 Mbps.
802.11a	Supports data transfer rates of 54 Mbps, but uses a different radio frequency (5 GHz) than 802.11b/g (2.4 GHz), making the standards incompatible.
802.11g	A current Wi-Fi standard; supports data transfer rates of 54 Mbps and uses the same 2.4 GHz frequency as 802.11b, so their products are compatible.
802.11n	A current Wi-Fi standard; supports speeds up to about 300 Mbps and has twice the range of 802.11g. It can use either the 2.4 GHz or 5 GHz frequency.
802.11ac	The newest Wi-Fi standard expected to be ratified in 2014; supports speed up to about three times faster than 802.11n and uses the 5 GHz frequency (though virtually all 802.11ac routers also support 2.4 GHz devices for backward compatibility).

(802.11w). To ensure that hardware from various vendors will work together, consumers can look for products that are *Wi-Fi CERTIFIED* by the *Wi-Fi Alliance* (see Figure 7-28).

The Wi-Fi Alliance is also developing a new certification program for very fast (up to 7 Gbps) short-range wireless networking. This next-generation technology (called **WiGig** or **802.11ad**) works in the 60 GHz band, though some WiGig devices may be Wi-Fi-compatible and also support the current (2.4 and 5 GHz) Wi-Fi standards. Because it has a much shorter range than Wi-Fi (essentially just within one room), the technology is designed to complement, not replace, Wi-Fi, and it is expected to be used primarily for applications (such as transferring video from one device to another or streaming video to a wireless display) that require multigigabit speeds.

While Wi-Fi is very widely used today, it does have some limitations—particularly its relatively limited range. For instance, an individual using a Wi-Fi hotspot inside a Starbucks coffeehouse will lose that Internet connection when he or she moves out of range of that network and will need to locate another hotspot at his or her next location. In addition, many businesses may be physically too large for a Wi-Fi network to span the entire organization. While hardware can be used to extend a Wi-Fi network, another possibility for creating larger wireless networks is *WiMAX*, discussed next.

FIGURE 7-28
Wi-Fi CERTIFIED logo.

TIP

A competing 60 GHz standard—*WirelessHD*—is discussed shortly.

WiMAX (802.16)

WiMAX (802.16) is a series of standards designed for longer range wireless networking connections, typically MANs. Similar to Wi-Fi, *fixed WiMAX* (also known as *802.16a*) is designed to provide Internet access to fixed locations (sometimes called *hotzones*), but the coverage is significantly larger (a typical hotzone radius is between 2 and 6 miles, though WiMAX can transmit data as far as 10 miles or more). With fixed WiMAX, it is feasible to provide coverage to an entire city or other geographical area by using multiple WiMAX towers (see Figure 7-29), similar to the way cell phone cells overlap to provide continuous cell phone service. WiMAX can use licensed radio frequencies, in addition to unlicensed frequencies like Wi-Fi, to avoid interference issues. *Mobile WiMAX (802.16e)* is the mobile version of the WiMAX wireless networking standard. It is designed to deliver broadband wireless networking to mobile users via a mobile phone, portable computer, or other WiMAX-enabled device. Mobile WiMax is capable of speeds of approximately 70 Mbps, but speeds of 1 to 6 Mbps are more typical.

WiMAX capabilities are beginning to be built into portable computers and other devices, and WiMAX is currently being used to provide Internet access to more than 1 billion people in about 150 countries. In the United States, for instance, WiMAX leader Clearwire (now owned by Sprint) offers both fixed and mobile WiMAX-based Internet service to businesses and individuals in more than 75 cities. The newest version of mobile WiMAX (*802.16m* or *WiMAX Release 2*) supports speeds up to approximately 120 Mbps.

Copyright © 2015 Cengage Learning®

● WiMAX hotzone
● Wi-Fi hotspot

NET

FIGURE 7-29
WiMAX vs. Wi-Fi.
A WiMAX hotzone is larger than a Wi-Fi hotspot and so has a greater range; it can provide service to anyone in the hotzone, including mobile users.

Cellular Standards

Cellular standards have evolved over the years to better fulfill the demand for mobile Internet, mobile multimedia delivery, and other relatively recent mobile trends. The original *first-generation phones* were analog and designed for voice data only. Starting with

ASK THE EXPERT

Jim Sappington Senior Vice President, Chief Information Officer, McDonald's Corporation

How has the emergence of Wi-Fi affected companies such as McDonalds?

The emergence of Wi-Fi has fueled our customers' expectations of having immediate access to information. Our customers and employees love the convenience and relevance of McDonald's "hotspots." Through wireless connectivity, Wi-Fi is creating a more modern and relevant experience for our customers. The ability to conveniently check e-mail, Facebook, or browse the Internet can be a deciding factor in choosing a place to eat—a trend we don't see ending anytime soon.

FIGURE 7-30
Connecting to a 4G cellular network with a notebook.

> **TIP**
>
> The *SmartGlass* app that enables you to use your smartphone or media tablet as a second Xbox 360 screen can connect via either Wi-Fi or a 3G/4G cellular network.

second-generation (*2G*) *phones*, cell phones are digital, support both data and voice, and are faster. Common *2G wireless standards* include *GSM* (*Global System for Mobile communications*) and *CDMA* (*Code Division Multiple Access*). Both of these standards are designed for voice traffic and both support speeds up to 14.4 Kbps, though some wireless providers have developed technologies such as *EDGE* (*Enhanced Data Rates for GSM Evolution*) that can be used with 2G networks to provide faster service (for instance, EDGE supports speeds up to 135 Kbps). These interim developments are sometimes referred to as *2.5G cellular standards*. GSM and CDMA are not compatible with each other, although some dual-mode phones are available that can be used with both standards.

The current standards for cellular networks today in the United States and many other countries are *3G* (*third generation*) and *4G* (*fourth generation*). 3G and 4G networks use packet-switching (like TCP/IP) instead of circuit-switching (like conventional telephones and earlier mobile phones). Typically, 3G speeds are between 1 and 4 Mbps; 4G speeds currently range from about 3 to 15 Mbps. While the original specification for 4G called for speeds of 100 Mbps, the term *4G* is currently being used to describe cellular phone service that is significantly faster (typically 4 to 10 times as fast) than current 3G service. Users of both 3G and 4G smartphones and other mobile devices can access broadband Internet content (such as online maps, music, games, TV, videos, and more) and many cell phones today can switch between 3G and 4G, in order to use a 3G network in a location where a 4G network is not within range. Because 3G and 4G speeds are equivalent to the speeds many home broadband Internet users experience, Internet access via a 3G or 4G network is often referred to as *mobile broadband*. Increasingly, 4G capabilities are being integrated into both media tablets and computers so users can connect to the Internet via their cell service when needed (see Figure 7-30).

Virtually all wireless providers today have both a 3G and a 4G network, though 4G service may not be available in all areas. The 3G standard used with a network depends on the type of cellular network. For instance, GSM mobile networks (like AT&T Wireless and T-Mobile) typically use the *HSDPA* (*High Speed Downlink Packet Access*)/*UMTS* (*Universal Mobile Telecommunications System*) 3G standards for their 3G networks; CDMA networks (like Verizon Wireless and Cricket Wireless) typically use the *EV-DO* (*Evolution Data Optimized*) 3G standard instead. There are two primary standards for 4G networks today: the mobile WiMAX standard already discussed and *Long Term Evolution* (*LTE*), supported by AT&T Wireless, Verizon Wireless, and T-Mobile. LTE is currently the fastest 4G standard and the *Phase 2 LTE network* currently being implemented by AT&T is expected to double 4G speeds. While mobile WiMAX is not technically a cellular standard, it is being used by some companies (such as Sprint) to provide 4G wireless service to subscribers.

Bluetooth, Ultra Wideband (UWB), and Other Short-Range Wireless Standards

There are several wireless networking standards in existence or being developed that are designed for short-range wireless networking connections. Most of these are used to facilitate PANs or very small, special-purpose home networks, such as connecting home entertainment devices or appliances within a home. The most common of these standards are discussed next.

Bluetooth, Wireless USB, and Wi-Fi Direct

Bluetooth is a wireless standard that was originally designed for very short-range (10 meters, approximately 33 feet, or less) connections (though there is no maximum range and some industrial products have a range of 300 feet). Bluetooth is designed to replace cables between devices, such as to connect a wireless keyboard or mouse to a desktop computer, to send print jobs wirelessly from a portable computer to a printer, or to connect a mobile phone to a wireless headset (see Figure 7-31). Bluetooth devices automatically recognize and network with each other when they get within transmission range. For instance, Bluetooth enables a wireless keyboard and mouse to be connected to a computer automatically as soon as the computer is powered up. Bluetooth signals can transmit through clothing and other nonmetallic objects, so a mobile phone or other device in a pocket or briefcase can connect with Bluetooth hardware (such as a headset) without having to be removed from the pocket or briefcase. One of the key enhancements in the newest Bluetooth specification (*Bluetooth 4.0*, also called *Bluetooth Smart*) is low energy, which enables small devices to run for years on a single button-sized battery. Consequently, Bluetooth is increasingly being used with consumer devices, such as to connect health and fitness devices to a watch or mobile phone; to connect a mobile phone to a smart watch (for example, the smart watch shown in Figure 7-12 connects via Bluetooth); and to connect 3D glasses to a 3D television set.

Bluetooth works using radio signals in the frequency band of 2.4 GHz, the same as Wi-Fi, and the latest Bluetooth specifications can utilize 802.11 technology when transferring large amounts of data to support transfers up to 24 Mbps. Once two Bluetooth-enabled devices come within range of each other, their software identifies each other (using their unique identification numbers) and establishes a link. Because there may be many Bluetooth devices within range, up to 10 individual Bluetooth networks (called *piconets*) can be in place within the same physical area at one time. Each piconet can connect up to eight devices, for a maximum of 80 devices within any 10-meter radius. To facilitate this, Bluetooth divides its allocated radio spectrum into multiple channels of 1 MHz each. Each Bluetooth device can use the entire range of frequencies, jumping randomly (in unison with the other devices in that piconet) on a regular basis to minimize interference between piconets, as well as from other devices (such as garage-door openers, Wi-Fi networks, and some cordless phones and baby monitors) that use the same frequencies. Because Bluetooth transmitters change frequencies 1,600 times every second automatically, it is unlikely that any two transmitting devices will be on the same frequency at the same time.

Another standard that is designed to connect peripheral devices, similar to Bluetooth, but that transfers data more quickly is **wireless USB**. The speed of wireless USB depends on the distance between the devices being used, but it is approximately 100 Mbps at 10 meters (about 33 feet) or 480 Mbps at 3 meters (about 10 feet). While Bluetooth and wireless USB can be used for similar applications, it is possible they might coexist. For example, wireless USB might be used to connect computer hardware in more permanent setups, while Bluetooth might be used in short-range mobile situations with portable computers and mobile devices.

The desktop computer, keyboard, and mouse form a piconet to communicate with each other. The headset and cell phone (not shown in this photo) belong to another piconet.

The headset and cell phone form a piconet when they are within range to communicate with each other.

© iStockphoto.com/Ben Blankenburg

© Stockbyte/Getty Images

FIGURE 7-31
Bluetooth. Bluetooth is designed for short-range wireless communications between computers or mobile devices and other hardware.

NET

TIP

If your computer doesn't have Bluetooth capability built in, you can add it via a USB *Bluetooth adapter*.

>**Bluetooth.** A networking standard for very short-range wireless connections; the devices are automatically connected once they get within the allowable range. >**Wireless USB.** A wireless version of USB designed to connect peripheral devices.

Wi-Fi Direct phone is a hotspot.

Wi-Fi phones can connect to that hotspot.

Courtesy Nick Morley

FIGURE 7-32
Wi-Fi Direct. Allows Wi-Fi devices to connect directly to one another.

A newer standard also designed to connect devices for short-range communications is **Wi-Fi Direct**. Wi-Fi Direct enables Wi-Fi devices to connect directly to each other without needing a router or an access point. Connections can be one-to-one (such as to transfer photos from one mobile device to another or to send a document from a smartphone to a printer) or one-to-many (such as to connect mobile or gaming devices together for a multiplayer game). A compatible app is required for many tasks, though a Wi-Fi Direct device can often create a Wi-Fi hotspot for other Wi-Fi devices just by using the phone's Wi-Fi settings to *tether* those devices to the Wi-Fi Direct device's Internet connection (see Figure 7-32). Wi-Fi Direct is not designed to replace traditional Wi-Fi networks, but it is considered a competitor to Bluetooth because it has the advantage of faster speeds (up to 250 Mbps) and a greater range (up to 600 feet).

Ultra Wideband (UWB), WirelessHD (WiHD), and TransferJet

There are several wireless technologies being developed to transfer multimedia content quickly between nearby devices, such as between televisions and video cameras, DVD players, or gaming consoles, or between computers and mobile devices, digital cameras, or TVs. **Ultra Wideband (UWB)** utilizes a wider band of frequencies and so has less interference issues than some other standards. UWB speeds vary from 100 Mbps at 10 meters (about 33 feet) to 480 Mbps at 2 meters (about 6.5 feet). **WirelessHD (WiHD)** is also designed for fast transfers of high-definition video between home consumer electronic devices, but it is faster. Backed by seven major electronics companies, WiHD is designed to transfer full-quality uncompressed high-definition audio, video, and data within a single room at speeds up to 28 Gbps. Similar to the WiGig standard previously discussed, WiHD operates at 60 GHz and incorporates a smart antenna system that allows the system to steer the transmission, allowing for non-line-of-sight communications.

A wireless standard designed for very fast transfers between devices that are extremely close together (essentially touching each other) is **TransferJet**. Developed by Sony, TransferJet is designed to quickly transfer large files (such as digital photos, music, and video) between devices as soon as they come in contact with each other (such as to transfer data between mobile phones or between digital cameras, to download music or video from a consumer kiosk or digital signage system to a mobile phone or other mobile device, or to transfer images or video from a digital camera to a TV or printer). At a maximum speed of 560 Mbps, TransferJet is fast enough to support the transfer of video files.

ZigBee and Z-Wave

One networking standard designed for inexpensive and simple short-range networking (particularly sensor networks) is *ZigBee (802.15)*. ZigBee is intended for applications that require low data transfer rates and several years of battery life. For instance, ZigBee can be used for home and commercial automation systems to connect a wide variety of devices (such as appliances and lighting, heating, and security systems). ZigBee is also used in industrial manufacturing, personal home healthcare, device tracking, telecommunications, and wireless sensor networks. ZigBee is designed to accommodate more than 65,000 devices on a single network and supports speeds from 20 Kbps to 250 Kbps, depending on the frequency being used (several different frequencies are available for ZigBee networks). ZigBee has a range of 10 to 100 meters (about 33 to 328 feet) between devices, depending on power output and environmental characteristics; a wireless mesh configuration can be used to greatly extend the range of the network.

Another wireless networking standard designed primarily for home automation is *Z-Wave*. Devices with Z-Wave capabilities built-in or connected via a Z-Wave module can

>**Wi-Fi Direct.** A standard for connecting Wi-Fi devices directly, without using a router or an access point. >**Ultra Wideband (UWB).** A networking standard for very short-range wireless connections among multimedia devices. >**WirelessHD (WiHD).** A wireless networking standard designed for very fast transfers between home electronic devices. >**TransferJet.** A networking standard for very short-range wireless connections between devices; devices need to touch in order to communicate.

HOW IT WORKS

Smart Homes

Home automation is taking off. For example, systems using *Z-Wave* technology are available that enable you to control your lights and door locks, as well as be notified of door/window/ motion sensor activation, via your smartphone. The systems typically have a central hub that connects to your home Internet connection and you can program a sequence of events to occur, such as turning on an indoor light whenever the front door is unlocked.

Another home automation option is using your smartphone as your door key. For example, *Kevo* (a system made by Kwikset using technology developed by UniKey—see the accompanying illustration) uses proximity sensors and Bluetooth 4.0 in conjunction with an iPhone app to allow you to unlock your door by just touching the lock, provided your phone is within range of your door. If you misplace your phone, you can use a key fob instead of your iPhone, or the actual door key. However, using your iPhone has additional advantages—including the ability to send virtual keys to others (permanent keys to friends and family members

and temporary keys to others who need access to your home on a certain date and time, for instance) so they can use their phones as a key, as well as the ability to check the status of your locks and virtual keys online. And, because the system uses battery power and Bluetooth, it functions even if your power or Internet connection is out. In addition, you can have multiple keys stored in your phone, which means no more fumbling with keys on a keyring!

Courtesy UniKey Technologies

communicate with each other and can be controlled via home control modules, as well as remotely via a computer or smartphone. There can be up to 232 devices on a single Z-Wave network and each device (a lamp, thermostat, television set, garage door opener, or pool control, for instance) has its own unique code. Devices can control each other (such as having your garage door opener programmed to turn on your house lights when you arrive home) and sequences of actions can be programmed to be performed with a single button (such as turning off the house lights, activating the security system, locking the doors, and programming the coffeepot for breakfast when a single button designated for bedtime is pressed). Z-Wave signals have a range of about 90 feet indoors.

For a look at how short-range wireless networking is changing home automation, see the How It Works box. For a summary of the wireless networking standards just discussed, see Figure 7-33.

NET

▼ **FIGURE 7-33**
Summary of common wireless networking standards.

CATEGORY	EXAMPLES	INTENDED PURPOSE	APPROXIMATE RANGE
Short range	Bluetooth Wireless USB	To connect peripheral devices to a mobile phone or computer.	33 feet–200 feet
	Ultra Wideband (UWB) WirelessHD (WiHD) TransferJet WiGig	To connect and transfer multimedia content between home consumer electronic devices (computers, TVs, DVD players, etc.).	1 inch–33 feet
	ZigBee Z-Wave	To connect a variety of home, personal, and commercial automation devices.	33 feet–328 feet
Medium range	Wi-Fi (802.11)	To connect computers and other devices to a local area network.	100–300 feet indoors; 300–900 feet outdoors
	Wi-Fi Direct	To connect computers and other devices directly together.	600 feet
Long range	WiMAX Mobile WiMAX	To provide Internet access to a large geographic area for fixed and/or mobile users.	6 miles non-line of sight; 30 miles line of sight
	Cellular standards	To connect mobile phones and mobile devices to a cellular network for telephone and Internet service.	10 miles

NETWORKING HARDWARE

Various types of hardware are necessary to create a computer network, to connect multiple networks together, or to connect a computer or network to the Internet. The most common types of networking hardware used in home and small office networks are discussed next.

Network Adapters and Modems

A **network adapter**, also called a **network interface card** (**NIC**) when it is in the form of an expansion card, is used to connect a computer to a network (such as a home or business network). A **modem** (derived from the terms *modulate* and *demodulate*) is used to connect a computer to a network over telephone lines. Technically, to be called a *modem*, a device must convert digital signals (such as those used by a computer) to modulated analog signals (such as those used by conventional telephone lines) and vice versa. However, in everyday use, the term *modem* is also used to refer to any device that connects a computer to a broadband Internet connection, such as a *cable modem* used for cable Internet service. In addition, the term *modem* is often used interchangeably with *network adapter* when describing devices used to obtain Internet access via certain networks, such as cellular or WiMAX networks.

Most computers and mobile devices today come with a network adapter and/or modem built into the device, typically as a network interface card, as a chip included on the motherboard, or as circuitry built directly into the CPU. The type of network adapter and modem used depends on the type of network (such as Ethernet, Wi-Fi, or cellular) and Internet access being used. For instance, to connect a computer to an Ethernet network, an Ethernet network adapter is used. To connect a computer to a cable Internet connection, typically both a cable modem (such as the NETGEAR modem shown in Figure 7-34)

FIGURE 7-34
Network adapters and modems.

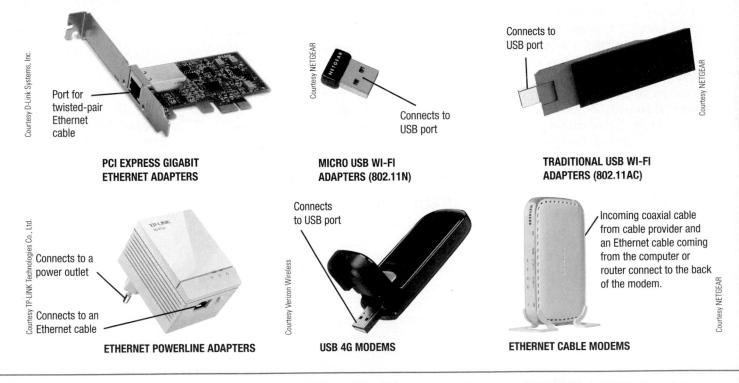

PCI EXPRESS GIGABIT ETHERNET ADAPTERS   **MICRO USB WI-FI ADAPTERS (802.11N)**   **TRADITIONAL USB WI-FI ADAPTERS (802.11AC)**

ETHERNET POWERLINE ADAPTERS   **USB 4G MODEMS**   **ETHERNET CABLE MODEMS**

>**Network adapter.** A network interface, such as an expansion card or external network adapter. >**Network interface card (NIC).** An expansion card through which a computer can connect to a network. >**Modem.** A device that enables a computer to communicate over analog networking media, such as to connect that computer to the Internet via telephone lines.

and an Ethernet network adapter are used. To connect a computer to a cellular, Wi-Fi, or WiMAX network, a cellular, Wi-Fi, or WiMAX network adapter, respectively, is used. Some examples of network adapters and modems are shown in Figure 7-34.

When a new type of networking connectivity is needed (such as wanting to use a newer Wi-Fi standard, wanting to add 4G capabilities, or switching to a different type of Internet connection), an external adapter or modem can be obtained. The network adapter or modem needs to be for the appropriate type of network, as well as support the type of networking media (such as twisted-pair cabling, coaxial cabling, or wireless signal) being used.

TIP

When using any type of wireless router, it is very important to secure it against unauthorized access. This and other security precautions are discussed in Chapter 9.

Switches, Routers, and Other Hardware for Connecting Devices and Networks

A variety of networking hardware are used to connect the devices on a network, as well as to connect multiple networks together. For instance, as mentioned earlier in this chapter, networks using the star topology need a central device to connect all of the devices on the network. In a wired network, this device was originally a *hub*. A hub transmits all data received to all network devices connected to the hub, regardless of which device the data is being sent to, so the bandwidth of the network is shared and the network is not very efficient. Today, the central device in a wired network is usually a **switch**. A switch contains ports to which the devices on the network connect (typically via networking cables) and facilitates communications between the devices, similar to a hub. But, unlike a hub, a switch identifies which device connected to the switch is the one the data is intended for and sends the data only to that device, rather than sending data out to all connected devices. Consequently, switches are more efficient than hubs. An emerging trend is *software defined networking* (*SDN*) in which outside software is used to control network traffic, instead of the software built into the networking hardware (such as hubs and switches).

To connect multiple networks (such as two LANs, two WANs, or a LAN and the Internet), a **router** is used. Routers pass data on to the intended recipient only and can plan a path through the network to ensure the data reaches its destination in the most efficient manner possible, and they are used to route traffic over the Internet.

A **wireless access point** is a device used to grant network access to wireless client devices. In home and small business networks, typically the capabilities of a switch, router, and wireless access point are integrated into a single **wireless router** device. A wireless router (see Figure 7-35) is commonly used to connect both wireless (via Wi-Fi) and wired (via Ethernet cables) devices to a network and to connect that network to an Internet connection via the appropriate broadband modem. As shown in Figure 7-35, there are travel-sized wireless routers designed for use in hotels and other locations. Some broadband modems today include wireless router capabilities, which you can use to create a wireless network and obtain Internet access using a single piece of hardware. To connect just two LANs together, a **bridge** can be used. The most common use for a bridge in a home network is to wirelessly connect a wired device (such as a home audio/video system, DVR, or gaming console) to a home network via a wireless connection.

▼ **FIGURE 7-35**
Wireless routers.
Provide wireless users access to each other and an Internet connection.

Wired devices can connect here.

Modem providing Internet access connects here.

USB devices (such as a printer or external hard drive) can connect here.

CONVENTIONAL WIRELESS ROUTERS
This 802.11ac router also includes a switch and wireless access point.

A wired Internet connection connects here.

A wired device can connect here.

A USB 3G or 4G modem connects here.

TRAVEL WIRELESS ROUTERS
This 802.11a/b/g/n router enables multiple devices to share a single wired Internet connection.

MOBILE BROADBAND ROUTERS
This 3G/4G router enables multiple devices to share a mobile broadband connection.

Courtesy Belkin International, Inc.; Courtesy TP-LINK Technologies Co., Ltd.

>**Switch.** A device used to connect multiple devices on a single (typically wired) network; forwards packets to only the intended recipient.
>**Router.** A device that connects multiple networks together; routes packets to their next location in order to efficiently reach their destination.
>**Wireless access point.** A device on a wireless network that connects wireless devices to that network. >**Wireless router.** A router with a built-in wireless access point; most often used to connect wireless devices to a network and an Internet connection and often contains a built-in switch. >**Bridge.** A device used to bridge or connect two LANs; most often used to connect wired devices wirelessly to a network.

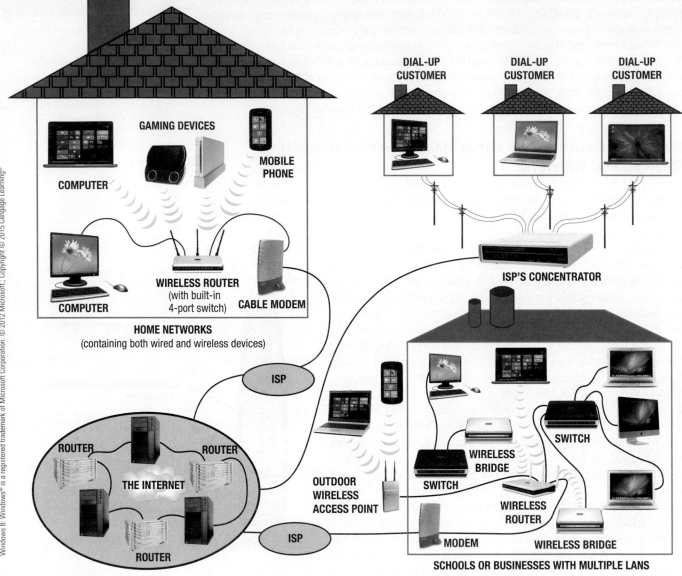

FIGURE 7-36

Networking hardware. As shown in this example, many different types of hardware are used to connect networking devices.

There are also routers and other devices used to connect multiple devices to a cellular network. For instance, *mobile broadband routers* are used to share a mobile wireless Internet connection with multiple devices (such as a cell phone, personal computer, and handheld gaming device)—essentially creating a Wi-Fi hotspot that connects to your 3G or 4G Internet connection. Small mobile broadband routers (such as the one shown in Figure 7-35) are designed to enable you to easily create a *mobile hotspot* when you are on the go. Other devices (sometimes called *femtocells*) can be used to route cell phone calls over a broadband network in order to provide better cellular coverage while indoors.

Figure 7-36 provides an example of how the devices discussed in this section, as well as the other networking hardware discussed in the next section, might be used in a network.

Other Networking Hardware

Additional networking hardware is often needed to extend the range of a network and to share networking media, as discussed next.

Repeaters, Range Extenders, and Antennas

Repeaters are devices that amplify signals along a network. They are necessary whenever signals have to travel farther than would be otherwise possible over the networking medium being used. Repeaters are available for both wired and wireless networks; repeaters for a wireless network are often called **range extenders**. Range extenders usually connect wirelessly to the network and repeat the wireless signal to extend coverage of that network outside or to an additional floor of a building, or to eliminate *dead spots*—areas within the normal network range that don't have coverage. Some *WDS (Wireless Distribution System)* wireless access points can be used as range extenders by extending the network coverage from one access point to another.

Another alternative for increasing the range of a Wi-Fi network is using a *higher-gain* (stronger) **antenna**. The MIMO antennas used by many 802.11n and 802.11ac routers allow for faster connections and a greater range than older wireless networks, but sometimes this still isn't enough. Using a network adapter designed for the router being used typically helps the network range to some extent; so does replacing the antenna on the router with a higher-gain antenna or adding an *external antenna* to a networking adapter, if the adapter contains an antenna connector.

Antennas come in a variety of formats and are classified as either *directional antennas* (antennas that concentrate the signal in a particular area) or *omnidirectional antennas* (antennas that are equally effective in all directions). Directional antennas have a greater range than omnidirectional antennas, but they have a more limited delivery area. The strength of an antenna is measured in *decibels (dB)*. For applications where a large Wi-Fi coverage area is needed (such as in a large business or a hotel), high-gain outdoor antennas can be used (in conjunction with outdoor range extenders and access points, if needed) to enable the network to span a larger area than the hardware would normally allow.

Multiplexers and Concentrators

High-speed communications lines are expensive and almost always have far greater capacity than a single device can use. Because of this, signals from multiple devices are often combined and sent together to share a single communications medium. A *multiplexer* combines the transmissions from several different devices and sends them as one message. For instance, multiple analog signals can be sent at one time by using multiple frequencies, and multiple optical signals can be sent at one time by using multiple wavelengths. Regardless of how the signals are sent, when the combined signal reaches its destination, the individual messages are separated from one another. Multiplexing is frequently used with fiber-optic cables and other high-capacity media to increase data throughput. For instance, if eight signals are multiplexed and sent together over each fiber in one fiber-optic cable, then the throughput of that cable is increased by a factor of eight.

A *concentrator* is a type of multiplexer that combines multiple messages and sends them via a single transmission medium in such a way that all the individual messages are simultaneously active, instead of being sent as a single combined message. For example, ISPs often use concentrators to combine the signals from their conventional dial-up modem customers to be sent over faster communications connections to their Internet destinations.

TIP
There are also range extenders and antennas designed to extend the range of a cellular network, such as to boost reception inside a home in order to use a cell phone as a primary home telephone.

TIP
When buying an external antenna for a device, be sure they are compatible. For instance, 802.11n MIMO routers with three antennas cannot use a single antenna designed for 802.11g devices.

>**Repeater.** A device on a network that amplifies signals. >**Range extender.** A repeater for a wireless network. >**Antenna.** A device used for receiving or sending radio signals; often used to increase the range of a network.

SUMMARY

WHAT IS A NETWORK?

Chapter Objective 1:
Define a computer network and its purpose.

Communications refers to data being sent from one device to another over a distance—such as over long-distance phone lines, via privately owned cables, or by satellite. A **computer network** is a collection of computers and other hardware devices that are connected together to share hardware, software, and data, as well as to facilitate electronic communications. Computer networks include home networks, business networks, and the Internet.

NETWORKING APPLICATIONS

Chapter Objective 2:
Describe several uses for networks.

Some of the oldest networking applications are conventional telephone service and television and radio broadcasting. Many of today's networking applications take place via the Internet. There are, however, a variety of other important business and personal applications that utilize networks. For making phone calls while on the go, **mobile phones**—namely, **cellular** (**cell**) and **satellite phones**—are used; **dual-mode phones** can utilize more than one network, such as to place calls via both a cellular and Wi-Fi network. There are a variety of **global positioning system** (**GPS**) and monitoring system applications used by individuals and businesses; many homes today also have a *multimedia network*. To communicate and work with others remotely, **videoconferencing**, *collaborative computing*, and **telecommuting** applications are used; **telesurgery** and other **telemedicine** applications can be used to provide remote medical care.

NETWORK CHARACTERISTICS

Chapter Objective 3:
Understand the various characteristics of a network, such as topology, architecture, and size.

Networks can be either **wired networks** (where devices are physically connected) or **wireless networks** (where devices are connected with wireless signals). Wired networks are found in businesses and some homes; wireless networks are becoming very common in both businesses and homes, and are frequently found in public locations to provide a wireless connection to the Internet. Networks can be classified in terms of their *topology* or physical arrangement (such as a **star network**, **bus network**, or **mesh network**). They can also be classified according to their *architecture* (such as *client-server* networks, which consist of *server* devices that provide network services to *client* computers, or *peer-to-peer* (*P2P*) networks, in which the users' computers and the shared peripherals in the network communicate directly with one another instead of through a server). With *Internet peer-to-peer* (*P2P*) *computing*, files are exchanged directly with other peers via the Internet.

Networks can also be classified by size. **Personal area networks** (**PANs**) connect the devices immediately around an individual; **local area networks** (**LANs**) connect geographically close devices, such as within a single building; **metropolitan area networks** (**MANs**) provide Internet access to cities; and **wide area networks** (**WANs**) span relatively wide geographical areas. Networks classified as **intranets** are private networks that implement the infrastructure and standards of the Internet and the World Wide Web, **extranets** are private networks accessible to authorized outsiders, and **virtual private networks** (**VPNs**) are used to transfer private information over a public communications system.

DATA TRANSMISSION CHARACTERISTICS

Chapter Objective 4:
Understand characteristics about data and how it travels over a network.

Data that travels over a network can use **analog signals** (where data is sent as continuous waves) or **digital signals** (where data is coded as 0s and 1s). Data transmissions can also be characterized by their *bandwidth* (the amount of data that can be transferred at one time), whether it uses **serial transmission** or **parallel transmission**, how serial transmissions are timed (namely, *synchronous*, *asynchronous*, or *isochronous transmission*), and whether it transmits in *simplex*, *half-duplex*, or *full-duplex* directions. Data can also be transferred using *circuit switching*, *packet switching*, or *broadcasting*.

NETWORKING MEDIA

Networking media used with wired networks include **twisted-pair**, **coaxial**, and **fiber-optic cable**. Wireless networks typically send messages through the air in the form of *radio signals* and typically use the frequencies in the *radio frequency* (*RF*) band of the *electromagnetic spectrum*. Wireless signals can be sent using **cellular radio** transmissions (which send and receive data via *cell towers* located within designated areas or *cells*), using **microwave stations** and/or **communications satellites** (which send and receive data to and from microwave stations and satellites), or using **infrared** (**IR**) **transmissions** (which send data over short distances as infrared light rays).

Chapter Objective 5:
Name specific types of wired and wireless networking media and explain how they transmit data.

COMMUNICATIONS PROTOCOLS AND NETWORKING STANDARDS

A *communications protocol* determines how the devices on a network communicate; a networking standard typically addresses both how the devices connect and the communications protocols used. The most common communications protocol is **TCP/IP**—the protocol used with the Internet. The most common networking standard for wired networks is **Ethernet** (**802.3**), which is available in a variety of speeds, as well as the *Power over Ethernet* (*PoE*) standard, which allows both power and data to be transferred via an Ethernet network. Alternatives for wired networks increasingly being used within the home include the *Phoneline* and *Powerline* standards and the emerging universal *G.hn* standard. *Broadband over powerline* (*BPL*) can be used to deliver Internet via the existing power pole infrastructure.

The most common networking standard for home and business wireless LANs is **Wi-Fi** (**802.11**). Wi-Fi is designed for medium-range wireless transmissions, and there are various versions of the standard that support different speeds and distances. When a network with a greater range is needed, **WiMAX** (**802.16**) can be used. **Wi-Fi Direct** enables Wi-Fi devices to be connected directly, without additional hardware. There are a variety of *cellular standards* used with mobile phones; the newest and fastest are *3G* and *4G standards*. For very short-range applications (such as to connect a keyboard to a computer), **Bluetooth** can be used. Other standards used to connect devices wirelessly include **WiGig** (**802.11ad**), **Ultra Wideband** (**UWB**), and **WirelessHD** (**WiHD**), which are most often used to connect home electronic devices; **wireless USB**, which is a wireless version of USB used to connect peripheral devices to a computer; and **TransferJet**, which is used to transfer data between devices as they are touched together.

Chapter Objective 6:
Identify the most common communications protocols and networking standards used with networks today.

NETWORKING HARDWARE

Computer networks require a variety of hardware. Computers usually connect to a network through either a **network adapter** (called a **network interface card** (**NIC**) when it is in the form of an expansion card); a **modem** is used to connect to a network via telephone lines, though many devices that connect a computer to the Internet today are commonly referred to as *modems*. The type of network adapter or modem used depends on the type of computer, connection, and networking media being used.

A **switch** is used to connect multiple (typically wired) devices to a network. **Routers** connect multiple devices together; **wireless routers** typically include a router, switch, and **wireless access point** to connect both wireless and wired devices to a network and the Internet. A **bridge** can be used to connect two LANs or a wired device to a wireless network. **Repeaters**, **range extenders**, and **antennas** can be used to extend the range of a network; *multiplexers* and *concentrators* are most commonly used with larger networks.

Chapter Objective 7:
List several types of networking hardware and explain the purpose of each.

REVIEW ACTIVITIES

KEY TERM MATCHING

a. antenna

b. Bluetooth

c. computer network

d. digital transmission

e. Ethernet (802.3)

f. global positioning system (GPS)

g. mesh network

h. switch

i. TCP/IP

j. WiMAX (802.16)

Instructions: Match each key term on the left with the definition on the right that best describes it.

1. _____ A collection of computers and other hardware devices that are connected together to share hardware, software, and data, as well as to communicate electronically with one another.

2. _____ A device used for receiving or sending radio signals; often used to increase the range of a network.

3. _____ A device used to connect multiple devices on a single (typically wired) network; forwards packets to only the intended recipient.

4. _____ A networking standard for very short-range wireless connections; the devices are automatically connected once they get within the allowable range.

5. _____ A network in which there are multiple connections between the devices on the network so that messages can take any of several possible paths.

6. _____ A wireless networking standard that is faster and has a greater range than Wi-Fi.

7. _____ A networking protocol that uses packet switching to facilitate the transmission of messages; the protocol used with the Internet.

8. _____ A system that uses satellites and a receiver to determine the exact geographic location of the receiver.

9. _____ A type of data transmission where the data is represented by 0s and 1s.

10. _____ A widely used wired LAN networking standard.

SELF-QUIZ

Instructions: Circle **T** if the statement is true, **F** if the statement is false, or write the best answer in the space provided. **Answers for the self-quiz are located in the References and Resources Guide at the end of the book.**

1. **T   F**   GPS systems are used only by the government.

2. **T   F**   With serial transmissions, each bit of data is sent individually.

3. **T   F**   The Internet is an example of a LAN.

4. **T   F**   The type of cable used inside most homes for telephone service is twisted-pair wire.

5. **T   F**   A router is a type of modem.

6. With a(n) _____ network topology, all devices are connected in a line to a central cable.

7. A(n) _____ phone can be used with more than one communications network, such as when used with both a cellular and Wi-Fi network.

8. A small network designed to connect the personal devices for an individual (such as via Bluetooth) is called a(n) _____.

9. A(n) _____ is a network that transfers private information securely over the Internet or other public network.

10. Match each description to its networking application, and write the corresponding number in the blank to the left of the description.

a. _____ To diagnose a patient from a distance.

b. _____ To work for a company in New York when you live in California.

c. _____ To watch a TV show in the living room that is recorded on your computer.

d. _____ To receive telephone calls while you are out shopping.

e. _____ To determine your physical location while hiking in the mountains.

1. Multimedia networking
2. GPS
3. Telemedicine
4. Telecommuting
5. Cellular phone

EXERCISES

1. Match each description to its networking hardware, and write the corresponding number in the blank to the left of each description.

a. _____ A device used to connect network devices via cabling.

b. _____ A device that enables a computer to communicate over telephone lines.

c. _____ A device used to connect wireless devices to a wired network.

d. _____ A device used to amplify signals on a network.

1. Repeater
2. Modem
3. Switch
4. Wireless access point

2. Match each description to the networking standard most suited for this purpose, and write the corresponding number in the blank to the left of each description.

a. _____ To connect a portable computer to a wireless hotspot.

b. _____ To connect a wireless keyboard to a computer.

c. _____ To create a wired home or business network.

d. _____ To wirelessly connect home entertainment devices.

1. Bluetooth
2. Wi-Fi
3. WirelessHD
4. Ethernet

3. If you need to transfer a 35 MB file from one computer to another over a Fast Ethernet network that supports data transfer rates of 100 Mbps, how long should it take to download the file? What real-world conditions might affect this download time?

4. What is the most common use of the TCP/IP networking standard?

5. Explain the difference between Wi-Fi and Bluetooth, including speed, range, and the purpose of each networking standard.

DISCUSSION QUESTIONS

1. As discussed in the chapter, Internet peer-to-peer (P2P) networking involves sharing files and other resources directly with other computers via the Internet. While some content is legally exchanged via an Internet P2P network, some content (such as movies and music) is exchanged illegally. Should Internet P2P networks be regulated to ensure they are used for only legal activities? Why or why not? If a P2P network set up for legitimate use is used for illegal purposes, should the organization or person who set up the P2P network be responsible? Would you want to use an Internet P2P network?

2. Interference with wireless devices is happening much more often than in the past. For instance, unlicensed walkie-talkies used on TV sets have interfered with police radios, and British air traffic control transmissions have been interrupted by transmissions from nearby baby monitors. If devices that use unlicensed radio frequencies interfere with each other, whose fault is it? The individual for buying multiple products that use the same radio frequency? The manufacturers for not ensuring their products can switch channels as needed to use a free channel? The government for allowing unregulated airwaves? Is there a solution to this problem? Who, if anyone, should be responsible for fixing this problem?

PROJECTS

HOT TOPICS

1. **WiMAX vs. Wi-Fi** As discussed in the chapter, WiMAX and Wi-Fi are both wireless networking standards that can be used to connect computers and other devices (such as smartphones and media tablets) to the Internet.

   For this project, research WiMAX and Wi-Fi to determine their current status and the differences between the two standards. Are they designed for the same or different purposes? Explain. How are they being used today? Are they designed for the same types of devices? Do you think the standards will coexist in the future, or will one eventually replace the other? At the conclusion of your research, prepare a one-page summary of your findings and opinions and submit it to your instructor.

SHORT ANSWER/ RESEARCH

2. **Unwired** As discussed in the chapter, home networks—particularly wireless home networks— are becoming very common today to connect computers, printers, and other devices together, as well as to provide Internet access to computers, smartphones, smart TV, and other devices.

   For this project, suppose that you have a home desktop computer and you are planning to buy a notebook computer to use at home, as well as on the go. You would like to network the two computers wirelessly. Determine the hardware you will need to accomplish this. Create a labeled sketch of the network and a list of the hardware you would need to acquire. Next, research the approximate cost of the hardware to determine the overall cost of the network. Does the cost seem reasonable for the benefits? Would you want to network your home computers in this manner? If you also wanted to use a printer with both computers, would you need any additional hardware? Why or why not? At the conclusion of your research, prepare a one-page summary of your findings and submit it to your instructor, along with your sketch and list of hardware.

HANDS ON

3. **Geocaching** Geocaching is a GPS application that is essentially a form of high-tech hide and seek—someone hides a water-tight container filled with a "treasure" (usually toys or cheap collectors' goodies) and posts the location of the cache (in GPS coordinates) on a geocaching Web site. Other individuals use their GPS equipment to find the cache and then sign a log (if one is included in the cache), take an item from the cache, and put another object into the cache as a replacement.

   For this project, find out how to geocache, including the required equipment and any "rules" or courtesies common among geocachers regarding listing or finding a cache, by searching online or visiting a geocaching Web site (such as **www.geocaching.com**). Next, use a geocaching site to find information about a cache currently hidden close to your city and determine what you would need to do in order to find it. At the conclusion of your research, prepare a one-page summary of your findings and submit it to your instructor.

4. **Net Neutrality and Your ISP** The term *net neutrality* refers to the equality of data as it is transferred over the Internet. For instance, the data from an individual and the data from Microsoft are treated the same. A recent controversy surrounding the cable giant Comcast brought up the possibility of ISPs interfering with the delivery of Internet data. According to complaints by customers, Comcast has been blocking the use of P2P sites like BitTorrent to download movies, music, and other large files. Comcast, like most ISPs, includes a statement in its terms of service that allows it to use tools to "efficiently manage its networks," in order to prevent those customers using a higher than normal level of bandwidth from interfering with the access of other customers. However, the Comcast issue was considered by many to be a blatant net neutrality issue—blocking access to multimedia from sources other than its own cable sources. Do you think the actions taken by Comcast were ethical? Does an ISP have a right to block selected Internet traffic? Why or why not? Was there a more ethical way Comcast could have handled the problem of some users consuming a higher than normal level of bandwidth?

For this project, form an opinion about the ethical ramifications of ISPs blocking selected Internet traffic and be prepared to discuss your position (in class, via an online class discussion group, in a class chat room, or via a class blog, depending on your instructor's directions). You may also be asked to write a short paper expressing your opinion.

5. **Wired Home Network** If you have two or more computers at home and want to share files, an Internet connection, or a printer, you will need to set up a home network. Although a wireless network is an option, wired networks still exist and new options for wired networks are emerging.

For this project, suppose that you want to set up a wired home network. Create a scenario (real or fictitious) that describes the number of computers and other devices involved, where each item is located, and the tasks for which the network will be used. Select a wired networking option (such as Ethernet, Powerline, or Phoneline) and determine the steps and equipment necessary to implement that network for your scenario. Be sure to include the cost of the necessary hardware and how the network would be physically installed. Share your findings (including a diagram of your proposed network) with your class in the form of a presentation. The presentation should not exceed 10 minutes and should make use of one or more presentation aids, such as a whiteboard, handouts, or a computer-based slide presentation (your instructor may provide additional requirements). You may also be asked to submit a summary of the presentation to your instructor.

6. **Is It Ever Ethical to Wi-Fi Piggyback?** Wi-Fi piggybacking refers to using an unsecured Wi-Fi network to access the Internet without authorization. Some people piggyback on a stranger's Wi-Fi network for a quick Google search or e-mail check; others use a neighbor's Wi-Fi connection on a regular basis. According to a recent poll, about one-third of individuals have piggybacked at one time or another. The legality of Wi-Fi piggybacking varies from location to location and it is illegal in the United Kingdom and in some states in the United States. Individuals have been arrested and prosecuted for Wi-Fi piggybacking—typically for using the network for illegal activities, such as downloading child pornography. Does the appropriateness of Wi-Fi piggybacking change based on the type of network being used (business or home, for instance)? What about the type or amount of use, such as checking e-mail or viewing a map while traveling versus using your neighbor's Internet connection on a daily basis? When a Wi-Fi network is left unsecured, does that mean that outside use is invited? Or, similar to an unlocked front door, is it ethical to enter only with their permission? What if the piggybacking results in an individual's Internet service being canceled as a result of violating their Internet provider's terms of use—would that impact your opinion? How would you feel if someone piggybacked on your Wi-Fi network?

Pick a side on this issue, form an opinion and gather supporting evidence, and be prepared to discuss and defend your position in a classroom debate or in a 1–2 page paper, depending on your instructor's directions.

chapter 8

The Internet and the World Wide Web

After completing this chapter, you will be able to do the following:

1. Discuss how the Internet evolved and what it is like today.

2. Identify the various types of individuals, companies, and organizations involved in the Internet community and explain their purposes.

3. Describe device and connection options for connecting to the Internet, as well as some considerations to keep in mind when selecting an ISP.

4. Understand how to search effectively for information on the Internet and how to cite Internet resources properly.

5. List several ways to communicate over the Internet, in addition to e-mail.

6. List several useful activities that can be performed via the Web.

7. Discuss censorship and privacy and how they are related to Internet use.

OVERVIEW

With the prominence of the Internet in our personal and professional lives today, it is hard to believe that there was a time not too long ago that few people had even heard of the Internet, let alone used it. But technology is continually evolving and, in fact, it is only relatively recently that it has evolved enough to allow the use of multimedia applications—such as downloading music and movies, watching TV and videos, and playing multimedia interactive games—over the Internet to become everyday activities. Today, the Internet and the World Wide Web are household words, and, in many ways, they have redefined how people think about computers, communications, and the availability of news and information.

Despite the popularity of the Internet, however, many users cannot answer some important basic questions about it. What makes up the Internet? Is it the same thing as the World Wide Web? How did the Internet begin, and where is it heading? What is the most effective way to use the Internet to find specific information? This chapter addresses these types of questions and more.

Chapter 8 begins with a discussion of the evolution of the Internet, followed by a look at the many individuals, companies, and organizations that make up the Internet community. Next, the chapter covers different options for connecting to the Internet, including the types of devices, Internet connections, and ISPs that are available today. Then, one of the most important Internet skills you should acquire— efficient Internet searching—is discussed. To help you appreciate the wide spectrum of resources and activities available over the Internet, we also take a brief look at some of the most common applications available via the Internet. The chapter closes with a discussion of a few of the important societal issues that apply to Internet use. ■

EVOLUTION OF THE INTERNET

The **Internet** is a worldwide collection of separate, but interconnected, networks accessed daily by millions of people using a variety of devices to obtain information, disseminate information, access entertainment, or communicate with others. While *Internet* has become a household word only during the past two decades or so, it has actually operated in one form or another for much longer than that.

From ARPANET to Internet2

The roots of the Internet began with an experimental project called *ARPANET*. The Internet we know today is the result of the evolution of ARPANET and the creation of the *World Wide Web* (WWW).

>**Internet.** The largest and most well-known computer network, linking millions of computers all over the world.

ARPANET

The U.S. Department of Defense *Advanced Research Projects Agency* (*ARPA*) created **ARPANET** in 1969. One objective of the ARPANET project was to create a computer network that would allow researchers located in different places to communicate with each other. Another objective was to build a computer network capable of sending or receiving data over a variety of paths to ensure that network communications could continue even if part of the network was destroyed, such as in a nuclear attack or by a natural disaster.

Initially, ARPANET connected four supercomputers and enabled researchers at a few dozen academic institutions to communicate with each other and with government agencies. As the project grew during the next decade, students were granted access to ARPANET as hundreds of college and university networks were connected to it. These networks consisted of a mixture of different computers so, over the years, protocols were developed for tying this mix of computers and networks together, for transferring data over the network, and for ensuring that data was transferred intact. Additional networks soon connected to ARPANET, and this *internet*—or network of networks—eventually evolved into the present day Internet.

The Internet infrastructure today can be used for a variety of purposes, such as researching topics of interest; exchanging e-mail and other messages; participating in videoconferences and making telephone calls; downloading software, music, and movies; purchasing goods and services; watching TV and video online; accessing computers remotely; and sharing files with others. Most of these activities are available through the primary Internet resource—the *World Wide Web* (*WWW*).

The World Wide Web

In its early years, the Internet was used primarily by the government, scientists, and educational institutions. Despite its popularity in academia and with government researchers, the Internet went virtually unnoticed by the public and the business community for over two decades because 1) it required a computer and 2) it was hard to use (see the left image in Figure 8-1). As always, however, computer and networking technology improved and new applications quickly followed. Then, in 1989, a researcher named *Tim Berners-Lee* proposed the idea of the **World Wide Web** (**WWW**). He envisioned the World Wide Web as a way to organize information in the form of pages linked together through selectable text or images (which are today's hyperlinks) on the screen. Although the introduction of Web pages did not replace all other Internet resources (such as e-mail and collections of downloadable files), it became a popular way for researchers to provide written information to others.

In 1993, a group of professors and their students at the University of Illinois *National Center for Supercomputing Applications* (*NCSA*) released the *Mosaic* Web browser. Soon after,

FIGURE 8-1

Using the Internet: Back in the "old days" versus now.

EARLY 1990s
Even at the beginning of the 1990s, using the Internet for most people meant learning how to work with a cryptic sequence of commands. Virtually all information was text-based.

TODAY
Today's Web organizes much of the Internet's content into easy-to-read pages that can contain text, graphics, animation, video, and interactive content that users access via hyperlinks.

> **ARPANET.** The predecessor to the Internet, named after the Advanced Research Projects Agency (ARPA), which sponsored its development.
> **World Wide Web (WWW).** The collection of Web pages available through the Internet.

use of the World Wide Web began to increase dramatically because Mosaic's graphical user interface (GUI) and its ability to display images on Web pages made using the World Wide Web both easier and more fun than in the past. Today's Web pages are a true multimedia, interactive experience (see the *Rookie Blue* Web site shown in Figure 8-1). They can contain text, graphics, animation, sound, video, and three-dimensional virtual reality objects.

A growing number of today's Web-based applications and services are referred to as *Web 2.0* applications. Although there is no precise definition, Web 2.0 generally refers to applications and services that use the Web as a platform to deliver rich applications that enable people to collaborate, socialize, and share information online. Some Web 2.0 applications (such as cloud computing) have been discussed in previous chapters; others (such as *social networking sites*, *RSS feeds*, *podcasts*, *blogs*, and *wikis*) are covered later in this chapter.

Although the Web is only part of the Internet, it is by far the most widely used part. Today, most companies regard their use of the Internet and their World Wide Web presence as indispensable competitive business tools, and many individuals view the Internet—and especially the Web—as a vital research, communications, and entertainment medium.

One remarkable characteristic of both the Internet and World Wide Web is that they are not owned by any person or business, and no single person, business, or organization is in charge. Web pages are developed by individuals and organizations, and are hosted on Web servers owned by individuals, schools, businesses, or other entities. Each network connected to the Internet is privately owned and managed individually by that network's administrator, and the primary infrastructure that makes up the *Internet backbone* is typically owned by communications companies, such as telephone and cable companies. In addition, the computers and other devices used to access the Internet belong to individuals or organizations. So, while individual components of the Internet are owned by individuals and organizations, the Internet as a whole has no owner or network administrator. The closest the Internet comes to having a governing body is a group of organizations that are involved with issues such as establishing the protocols used on the Internet, making recommendations for changes, and encouraging cooperation between and coordinating communications among the networks connected to the Internet.

Internet2

Internet2 is a consortium of researchers, educators, and technology leaders from industry, government, and the international community that is dedicated to the development of revolutionary Internet technologies. Internet2 uses high-performance networks linking over 200 member institutions to deploy and test new network applications and technologies. Internet2 is designed as a research and development tool to help develop technologies that ensure the Internet in the future can handle tomorrow's applications, and it is now being used to deploy advanced applications and technologies that might not be possible otherwise with today's Internet. Much of Internet2 research is focused on speed. In fact,

ASK THE EXPERT

Jim Sappington, Senior Vice President, Chief Information Officer, McDonald's Corporation

How important is it for a business to have a Web site today if it doesn't sell products and services online?

At McDonald's, our online presence is about extending the McDonald's experience to our customers. Our Web sites (www.aboutmcdonalds.com and www.mcdonalds.com) allow our customers another channel to engage with our brand without ever entering a restaurant. Through our Web sites, customers can find promotions and nutritional information on all of our products. On the Open for Discussion blog, customers are talking about McDonald's corporate sustainability efforts. In addition, customers can download podcasts about food safety.

For McDonald's, our Web sites allow us the opportunity to connect with our customers on topics that are important to them and in the way that they want to connect. In addition, in some parts of the world you can order off the menu located on our Web site and have it delivered to your door. As our customers demand even more convenience and control over the "ordering process," this may become even more prevalent, and mobile, in the future.

NET

the Internet2 backbone network was recently upgraded to support 8.8 Tbps. This network is the first national network to use 100 Gigabit Ethernet over its entire footprint; it will be used to support high bandwidth applications, such as telemedicine and distance learning, to schools, libraries, hospitals, and other organizations.

The Internet Community Today

The Internet community today consists of individuals, businesses, and a variety of organizations located throughout the world. Virtually anyone with a computer or other Web-enabled device can be part of the Internet, either as a user or as a supplier of information or services. Most members of the Internet community fall into one or more of the following groups.

Users

Users are people who use the Internet to retrieve content or perform online activities, such as to look up a telephone number, read the day's news headlines or top stories, browse through an online catalog, make an online purchase, download a music file, watch an online video, make a phone call, or send an e-mail message. According to the Pew Internet & American Life Project, more than 80% of U.S. adults (and 95% of all U.S. teens) are Internet users, using the Internet at work, home, school, or another location. The availability of low-cost computers, low-cost or free Internet access (such as at libraries, schools, and other public locations), smartphones, and bundled pricing for obtaining Internet service in conjunction with telephone and/or television service has helped Internet use begin to approach the popularity and widespread use of telephones and TVs.

Internet Service Providers (ISPs)

Internet service providers (**ISPs**) are businesses or other organizations (see some examples in Figure 8-2) that provide Internet access to others, typically for a fee. ISPs (sometimes called *wireless ISPs* or *WISPs* when referring to ISPs that offer service via a wireless network) include most communications and media companies, such as conventional and wireless phone providers, cable providers, and satellite providers. Some ISPs (such as cable and cellular phone companies) offer Internet service over their private networks; other ISPs provide Internet service over the regular telephone lines or the airwaves. While many ISPs (such as AT&T and EarthLink) provide service nationwide, others provide service to a more limited geographical area. Regardless of their delivery method and geographical coverage, ISPs are the onramp to the Internet, providing their subscribers with access to the World Wide Web, e-mail, and other Internet resources. In addition to Internet access, some ISPs provide proprietary online services available only to their subscribers. A later section of this chapter covers ISPs in more detail, including factors to consider when selecting an ISP.

(V) FIGURE 8-2

Companies that provide Internet access today include telephone, cable, and satellite companies.

Internet Content Providers

Internet content providers supply the information that is available through the Internet. Internet content providers can be commercial businesses, nonprofit organizations, educational institutions, individuals, and more. Some examples of Internet content providers are listed next.

➤ A photographer who posts samples of her best work on a Web page.

➤ An individual who publishes his opinion on various subjects to an online journal or *blog*.

>**Internet service provider (ISP).** A business or other organization that provides Internet access to others, typically for a fee. >**Internet content provider.** A person or an organization that provides Internet content.

➤ A software company that creates a Web site to provide product information and software downloads.

➤ A national news organization that maintains an online site to provide up-to-the-minute news, feature stories, and video clips.

➤ A television network that develops a site for its TV shows, including episode summaries, cast information, and links to watch past episodes online.

Application Service Providers (ASPs) and Web Services

Application service providers (ASPs) are companies that manage and distribute Web-based software services to customers over the Internet. Instead of providing access to the Internet like ISPs do, ASPs provide access to software applications via the Internet. In essence, ASPs rent access to software programs to companies or individuals—typically, customers pay a monthly or yearly fee to use each application. As discussed in Chapter 6, this software can be called *cloud software*, *Software as a Service (SaaS)*, and *cloudware*. Common ASP applications for businesses include office suites, collaboration and communications software, accounting programs, and e-commerce software.

One type of self-contained business application designed to work over the Internet or a company network is a **Web service**. A Web service can be added to Web pages to provide a service that would otherwise not be feasible (such as the inclusion of mapping information on a Web site or in a Web application using Microsoft's *MapPoint .NET Web service*). For example, Web developers for secure Web sites (such as Zappos.com, shown in Figure 8-3) can use a new Web service by Amazon to allow their customers to log onto those secure Web sites by using their Amazon, Facebook, or Google account logon information. A Web service can also be used to provide a service via a user's computer and the Internet. For instance, the *FedEx QuickShip Web service* allows users to create a shipment to any Microsoft Outlook contact from within Microsoft Outlook. It is important to realize that Web services are not stand-alone applications— they are simply a standardized way of allowing different applications and computers to share data and processes via a network so they can work together with other Web services and be used with many different computer systems. A company that provides Web services is sometimes referred to as a *Web services provider*.

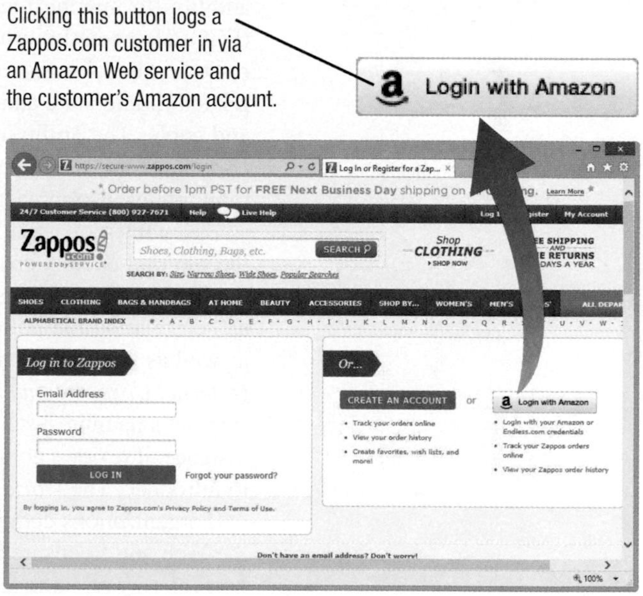

FIGURE 8-3

Web services. This Web service enables Web developers to use Amazon's authentication system for users.

Clicking this button logs a Zappos.com customer in via an Amazon Web service and the customer's Amazon account.

Courtesy Zappos.com

Infrastructure Companies

Infrastructure companies are the enterprises that own or operate the paths or "roadways" along which Internet data travels, such as the Internet backbone and the communications networks connected to it. Examples of infrastructure companies include conventional and mobile phone companies, cable companies, and satellite Internet providers.

Hardware and Software Companies

A wide variety of hardware and software companies make and distribute the products used with the Internet and Internet activities. For example, companies that create or sell the software used in conjunction with the Internet (such as Web browsers, e-mail programs, e-commerce

>**Application service provider (ASP).** A company that manages and distributes software-based services over the Internet. >**Web service.** A self-contained business application that operates over the Internet.

and multimedia software, and Web development tools) fall into this category. So, too, do the companies that make the hardware (network adapters, modems, cables, routers, servers, computers, and smartphones, for instance) that is used with the Internet.

The Government and Other Organizations

Many organizations influence the Internet and its uses. Governments have the most visible impact; their laws can limit both the information made available via Web servers located in a particular country and the access individuals residing in that country have to the Internet. For example, in France, it is illegal to sell items or post online content related to racist groups or activities; in China there are tight controls imposed on what information is published on Web servers located in China, as well as on the information available to its citizens. And in the United States, anything illegal offline (illegal drugs, child pornography, and so forth) is also illegal online.

Legal rulings also can have a large impact on the communications industry in general. For example, the 1968 *Carterfone Decision* allowed companies other than AT&T to utilize the AT&T infrastructure and the 1996 *Telecommunications Act* deregulated the entire communications industry so that telephone companies, cable TV and satellite operators, and firms in other segments of the industry were free to enter each other's markets. In addition to making these types of decisions, the Federal Communications Commission (FCC) also greatly influences the communications industry through its ability to allocate radio frequencies (as discussed in Chapter 7) and to implement policies and regulations related to interstate and international communications via radio, television, wire, satellite, and cable. The ability of the government to approve or block potential mergers between communications companies and to break apart companies based on antitrust law to prevent monopolies also impacts the Internet and communications industry.

Key Internet organizations are responsible for many aspects of the Internet. For example, the *Internet Society* provides leadership in addressing issues that may impact the future of the Internet. It also oversees the groups responsible for Internet infrastructure standards, such as determining the protocols that can be used and how Internet addresses are constructed, as well as facilitating and coordinating Internet-related initiatives around the world. *ICANN* (*Internet Corporation for Assigned Names and Numbers*) coordinates activities related to the Internet's naming system, such as IP address allocation and domain name management. For instance, it reviews nominations for new top-level domains and determines which new TLDs to introduce. The *World Wide Web Consortium* (*W3C*) is an international community of over 450 organizations dedicated to developing new protocols and specifications to be used with the Web and to ensure its interoperability. In addition, many colleges and universities support Internet research and manage blocks of the Internet's resources.

Myths About the Internet

Because the Internet is so unique in the history of the world—and its content and applications keep evolving—several widespread myths about it have surfaced.

Myth 1: The Internet Is Free

This myth stems from the fact that there has traditionally been no cost associated with accessing online content—such as news and product information—or with e-mail exchange, other than what the Internet users pay their ISPs for Internet access. And many people—such as students, employees, and consumers who opt for free Internet service or use free access available at public libraries or other public locations—pay nothing for Internet access. Yet it should also be obvious that someone, somewhere, has to pay to keep the Internet up and running.

Businesses, schools, public libraries, and most home users pay Internet service providers flat monthly fees to connect to the Internet. In addition, businesses, schools, libraries, and other large organizations might have to lease high-capacity communications lines (such as from a telephone company) to support their high level of Internet traffic.

Mobile users that want Internet access while on the go typically pay hotspot providers or wireless providers for this access. ISPs, phone companies, cable companies, and other organizations that own part of the Internet infrastructure pay to keep their parts of the Internet running smoothly. ISPs also pay software and hardware companies for the resources they need to support their subscribers. Eventually, most of these costs are passed along to end users through ISP fees. ISPs that offer free Internet access typically obtain revenue by selling on-screen ads that display on the screen when the service is being used.

Another reason the idea that the Internet is free is a myth is the growing trend of subscription or per-use fees to access Web-based resources. For instance, downloadable music and movies are very common today (see Figure 8-4) and some journal or newspaper articles require a fee to view them online. In fact, many newspapers and magazines have moved entirely online and most charge a subscription fee to view the level of content that was previously published in a print version. In lieu of a mandatory fee, some Web sites request a donation for use of the site. Many experts expect the use of fee-based Internet content to continue to grow at a rapid pace.

FIGURE 8-4
Fee-based Web content. The use of fee-based Web content, such as streaming movies via Netflix as shown here, is growing.

Myth 2: Someone Controls the Internet

As already discussed, no single group or organization controls the Internet. Governments in each country have the power to regulate the content and use of the Internet within their borders, as allowed by their laws. However, legislators often face serious obstacles getting legislation passed into law—let alone getting it enforced. Making governmental control even harder is the "bombproof" design of the Internet itself. If a government tries to block access to or from a specific country or Web site, for example, users can use a third party (such as an individual located in another country or a different Web site) to circumvent the block. This occurred in Iran when the Iranian government blocked access to social networking sites after the 2009 elections—some Iranian citizens were able to send and read Twitter updates via third-party sites.

Myth 3: The Internet and the World Wide Web Are Identical

Because you can now use a Web browser to access most of the Internet's resources, many people think the Internet and the Web are the same thing. Even though in everyday use many people use the terms *Internet* and *Web* interchangeably, they are not the same thing. Technically, the Internet is the physical network, and the Web is the collection of Web pages accessible over the Internet. A majority of Internet activities today take place via Web pages, but there are Internet resources other than the Web that are not accessed via a Web browser. For instance, files can be uploaded and downloaded using an *FTP (File Transfer Protocol) program* and conventional e-mail can be accessed using an e-mail program.

GETTING SET UP TO USE THE INTERNET

Getting set up to use the Internet typically involves three decisions—determining the type of device you will use to access the Internet, deciding which type of connection is desired, and selecting the Internet service provider to be used. Once these determinations have been made, your computer can be set up to access the Internet.

TIP

Many people use multiple devices to access the Internet; according to Cisco, there will be nearly three times as many Internet-enabled devices than people in the world by 2017.

Type of Device

The Internet today can be accessed using a variety of devices. The type of device used depends on a combination of factors, such as the devices available to you, if you need

INSIDE THE INDUSTRY

Mobile Data Caps

Mobile data use has increased tremendously recently as individuals are watching TV and videos, downloading music and movies, playing online multiplayer games, participating in video phone calls, and otherwise performing high-bandwidth activities using their smartphones and media tablets. This has created the issue of wireless carriers potentially running out of bandwidth available for customers, resulting in outages or delays. In response, many wireless carriers have implemented *data caps* and have eliminated unlimited data plans (though many plans still have unlimited talk and texts). With a data cap, customers either temporarily lose high-speed Internet access (such as being slowed down from 4G to 2G speeds—called *data throttling*) or are charged an additional fee if they exceed their download limit (often 2 GB per month).

One explanation for the increased data usage is speed—4G data speeds are significantly faster than 3G service and the results (such as faster Web pages and smoother streaming videos) make it easier for users to go through a large amount of bandwidth in a relatively short period of time. One potential solution under consideration by wireless carriers is allowing content providers or app developers to pay carriers so that their services don't count against a customer's monthly data limit—essentially buying traffic for their content. However, the Internet is designed for all content and services to be treated equally. Because this solution would give larger companies an unfair advantage over upstarts, it is viewed by some as a *net neutrality* issue.

So how do you avoid the expensive or annoying ramifications associated with going over your data cap? The best way is to not go over your limit in the first place. To help with this, use Wi-Fi for large downloads instead of your cellular connection. It is also prudent to monitor your data usage to make sure you stay under your data cap (you can also use this information to decide if you need to consider upgrading to a higher plan if your usage is typical but still over your data cap). Some smartphones have an option for viewing your total data usage for the current billing period, as well as usage per app or Web site to help you see where you are using the most data.

Another useful tool is third-party apps designed to help you monitor your bandwidth usage. One such app is *Onavo Extend*, shown in the accompanying illustration. It gives you a breakdown of consumption by app, so you know your worst bandwidth offenders. As a bonus, it compresses your incoming data by up to 500% so you can do up to five times more with your data plan without going over. Five times more data for free? It's about time!

Courtesy Onavo Mobile Ltd.

access just at home or while on the go, and what types of Internet content you want to access. Some possible devices are shown in Figure 8-5 and discussed next.

Personal Computers
Most users who have access to a personal computer (such as a desktop or notebook computer) at home, work, or school will use it to access the Internet. One advantage of using personal computers for Internet access is that they have relatively large screens for viewing Internet content and keyboards for easier data entry. They can also be used to view or otherwise access virtually any Web page content, such as graphics, animation, music, games, and videos. In addition, they typically have a large hard drive and are connected to a printer so Web pages, e-mail messages, and downloaded files can be saved and/or printed easily.

Smartphones, Media Tablets, and Other Mobile Devices
Smartphones and other mobile devices are increasingly being used to view Web page content, exchange e-mail and other messages, and download music and other online content. In fact, mobile Web use—or *wireless Web*, as it is sometimes called—is one of the fastest

TIP

According to market research firm IDC, more people will access the Internet through their mobile devices than through their personal computers by 2015.

PERSONAL COMPUTERS   SMARTPHONES   SMART TVS

growing uses of the Internet today (more than half of American adults now own smart-phones). While smartphones are convenient to use on the go, they typically have a relatively small display screen; media tablets typically have a larger screen size for easier viewing. Some mobile devices include a built-in or sliding keyboard for easier data entry; others utilize pen, voice, or touch input instead.

FIGURE 8-5
A variety of devices can be used to access the Internet.

Gaming Devices and Televisions

Another option is using a gaming device (such as a gaming console or handheld gaming device) to access Web content, in addition to using that device to play games. For instance, the Sony PlayStation, Sony PSP, Nintendo Wii, and Nintendo 3DS all have Web browsers that can be used to access Web content. Smart TVs have built-in Internet capabilities in order to display Web pages and other Web content (such as interactive polls and other show-specific information, social networking updates, and shopping opportunities, as shown in Figure 8-5) without any additional hardware. It is estimated that 400 million households worldwide will have smart TVs by 2016.

Type of Connection and Internet Access

In order to use the Internet, you need to connect a computer or other device to it. Typically, this occurs by connecting the device you are using to a computer or a network (usually belonging to your ISP, school, or employer) that is connected continually to the Internet. As discussed in Chapter 7, there are a variety of wired and wireless ways to connect to another device. Most types of connections today are *broadband* or high-speed connections. In fact, 90% of all home Internet connections in the United States are broadband connections, according to a recent study. As applications requiring high-speed connections continue to grow in popularity, access to broadband Internet speeds is needed in order to take full advantage of these applications. For instance, high-definition video, video chat, video-on-demand (VOD), and other multimedia applications all require broadband connections (see Figure 8-6). For a look at an issue related to the increased use of multimedia Internet content—*mobile data caps*—see the Inside the Industry box.

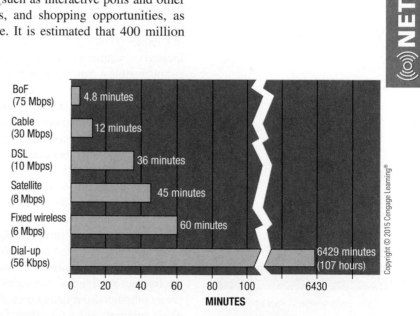

FIGURE 8-6
Approximate time to download a 2.7 GB (about 2-hour HD) movie using different home Internet options.

The difference between *dial-up* and *direct* Internet connections is discussed next, followed by an overview of the most common types of Internet connections used for personal use today; these types of Internet connections are also summarized in Figure 8-7. Many providers today offer bundles (such as cable TV, telephone, and Internet service) to lower an individual's overall total cost for the services. Similar to the mobile data caps discussed in the Inside the Industry box, some home broadband Internet services have data caps (you typically either

TYPE OF INTERNET CONNECTION	AVAILABILITY	APPROXIMATE MAXIMUM SPEED*	APPROXIMATE MONTHLY PRICE
Conventional dial-up	Anywhere there is telephone service	56 Kbps	Free–$20
Cable	Virtually anywhere cable TV service is available	3–100 Mbps	$30–110
DSL	Within 3 miles of a switching station that supports DSL	1–25 Mbps	$20–65
Satellite	Anywhere there is a clear view of the southern sky and where a satellite dish can be mounted and receive a signal	5–15 Mbps	$40–100
Fixed wireless	Selected areas where service is available	1–12 Mbps	$35–75
Broadband over fiber (BoF)	Anywhere fiber has been installed to the building	15–150 Mbps	$45–130
Mobile wireless (3G/4G)	Virtually anywhere cellular phone service is available	1–30 Mbps	Varies greatly; often bundled with mobile phone service

* Download speed; most connections have slower upload speeds.

Copyright © 2015 Cengage Learning®

FIGURE 8-7

Typical home Internet connection options.

are throttled down significantly or are charged an additional fee when you go over your limit), while others offer unlimited Internet.

Dial-Up vs. Direct Connections

While some Internet connections are *dial-up connections* (in which your computer dials up and connects to your ISP's computer only when needed), most are *direct* (or *always-on*) *connections* (in which you have a continuous connection to your ISP).

Dial-up connections work over standard telephone lines. To connect to the Internet, your computer dials its modem and then connects to a modem attached to a computer belonging to your ISP via the telephone lines. While you are connected to your ISP, your computer can access Internet resources. To end your Internet session, you disconnect from your ISP. One advantage of a dial-up connection is security. Because you are not continually connected to the Internet, it is much less likely that anyone (such as a *hacker*, as discussed in Chapter 9) will gain access to your computer via the Internet, either to access the data located on your computer or, more commonly, to use your computer in some type of illegal or unethical manner. However, dial-up connections are significantly slower than other types of connections; they are also inconvenient because you have to instruct your computer to dial up your ISP every time you want to connect to the Internet. Also, your telephone line will be tied up while you are accessing the Internet, unless you have a second phone line. The most common type of dial-up Internet service is *conventional dial-up*.

Direct connections keep you continually connected to your provider and, therefore, continually connected to the Internet. With a direct connection (such as *cable*, *DSL*, *satellite*, or *fixed wireless*), you access the Internet simply by opening a Web browser, such as Internet Explorer, Chrome, Safari, or Firefox. Direct Internet connections are broadband connections, are often available in different *tiers* (which means you have a choice of speeds and the price varies accordingly), are commonly used in homes and businesses, and are often connected to a LAN to share the Internet connection with multiple devices within the home or business. Because direct connections keep your computer connected to the Internet at all times (as long as your computer is powered up), it is important to protect your computer from unauthorized access or hackers. Consequently, all computers with a direct Internet connection should use a *firewall* program. Firewall programs block access to a computer from outside computers and enable each user to specify which programs on his or her computer are allowed to have access to the Internet. Firewalls, as well as other network and Internet security precautions, are discussed in more detail in Chapter 9.

>**Dial-up connection.** A type of Internet connection in which the computer or other device must dial up and connect to a service provider's computer via telephone lines before being connected to the Internet. >**Direct connection.** A type of Internet connection in which the computer or other device is connected to the Internet continually.

Conventional Dial-Up

Conventional dial-up Internet access uses a conventional dial-up modem connected to a standard telephone jack with regular twisted-pair telephone cabling. Conventional dial-up Internet service is most often used with home computers for users who don't need, or do not want to pay for, broadband Internet service. Advantages include inexpensive hardware, ease of setup and use, and widespread availability (including remote areas). The primary disadvantage is slow connection speed—a maximum of 56 Kbps.

Cable

Cable Internet access uses a direct connection and is the most widely used type of home broadband connection, with over half of the home broadband market. Cable connections are very fast (typically between 15 and 50 Mbps, though faster services up to 100 Mbps are available in some areas for a premium fee) and are available wherever cable TV access is available, provided the local cable provider supports Internet access. Consequently, cable Internet is not widely available in rural areas. Cable Internet service requires a cable modem.

DSL

DSL (Digital Subscriber Line) Internet access is a type of direct connection that transmits via standard telephone lines, but it does not tie up your telephone line. DSL requires a DSL modem and is available only to users who are relatively close (within three miles) to a telephone switching station and who have telephone lines capable of handling DSL. DSL speeds are slower than cable speeds and the speed of the connection degrades as the distance between the modem and the switching station gets closer to the three-mile limit. Consequently, DSL is usually only available in urban areas. Download speeds can be up to about 25 Mbps, but are more typically between 1 and 15 Mbps.

Satellite

Satellite Internet access uses a direct connection, but it is slower and more expensive than cable or DSL access (between 5 and 15 Mbps, though around 10 Mbps is typical) and almost always has a data cap. However, it is often the only broadband option for rural areas. In addition to a satellite modem, it requires a *transceiver* satellite dish mounted outside the home or building to receive and transmit data to and from the satellites being used. Installation requires an unobstructed view of the southern sky (to have a clear line of sight between the transceiver and appropriate satellite), and performance might degrade or stop altogether during very heavy rain or snowstorms.

Fixed Wireless

Fixed wireless Internet access uses a direct connection and is similar to satellite Internet in that it uses wireless signals, but it uses radio transmission towers (either stand-alone towers like the one shown in Figure 8-8 or transmitters placed on existing cell phone towers) instead of satellites. Fixed wireless Internet access requires a modem and, sometimes, an outside-mounted transceiver. Fixed wireless companies typically use WiMAX technology to broadcast the wireless signals to customers. Speeds are typically up to about 12 Mbps, though the speed depends somewhat on the distance between the

TIP

Before using a dial-up access number to connect to the Internet, verify that it is a local telephone number; if it is not, you will incur long-distance charges.

FIGURE 8-8
WiMAX towers. This tower is installed at the peak of Whistler Mountain in British Columbia.

>**Conventional dial-up Internet access.** Dial-up Internet access via standard telephone lines. >**Cable Internet access.** Fast, direct Internet access via cable TV lines. >**DSL (Digital Subscriber Line) Internet access.** Fast, direct Internet access via standard telephone lines. >**Satellite Internet access.** Fast, direct Internet access via the airwaves and a satellite dish. >**Fixed wireless Internet access.** Fast, direct Internet access available in some areas via the airwaves.

tower and the customer, the types and number of obstacles in the path, and the type and speed of the connection between the wireless transmitter and the Internet.

Broadband over Fiber (BoF)

A relatively new type of very fast direct connection available to homes and businesses in areas where there is fiber-optic cabling available all the way to the building is generically called **broadband over fiber** (**BoF**) or **fiber-to-the-premises** (**FTTP**) **Internet access**, with other names being used by individual providers, such as Verizon's *fiber-optic service* (*FiOS*). These fiber-optic networks are most often installed by telephone companies in order to upgrade their overall infrastructures and, where installed, are used to deliver telephone and TV service in addition to Internet service. Where available, download speeds for BoF service typically range between 15 Mbps and 150 Mbps, though some areas offer speeds as fast as 1 Gbps. BoF requires a special networking terminal installed at the building to convert the optical signals into electrical signals that can be sent to a computer or over a LAN.

Mobile Wireless

Mobile wireless Internet access is the type of direct connection most commonly used with smartphones and media tablets to keep them connected to the Internet via a cellular network, even as they are carried from place to place. Some mobile wireless services can be used with computers as well as with mobile devices. To add Internet access to a mobile device, typically a *data plan* is needed. As discussed in Chapter 7, the speed of mobile wireless depends on the cellular standard being used—3G networks typically have speeds between 1 and 4 Mbps; 4G networks are often between 3 and 15 Mbps, with speeds up to 30 Mbps available in some areas. Costs for mobile wireless Internet access vary widely, with some packages (typically 4G WiMAX services) including unlimited Internet, some charging by the number of minutes of Internet use, and some charging by the amount of data transferred. A growing trend is *prepaid* and *pay as you go plans*, in which you purchase service month to month (or day to day), instead of committing to a lengthy contract.

FIGURE 8-9

Wi-Fi hotspots.

Hotspots are used to wirelessly connect to the Internet via the Internet connection belonging to a business, city, school, or other organization.

COFFEEHOUSES AND OTHER PUBLIC LOCATIONS
Often fee-based, though some are available for free.

© iStockphoto.com/LuckyBusiness

HOTELS AND CONFERENCE CENTERS
Often free for guests.

© iStockphoto.com/YanLev

HOSPITALS, BUSINESSES, AND OTHER ORGANIZATIONS
Usually designed for employees but are sometimes also available free to visitors.

© Burlingham/Shutterstock.com

COLLEGE CAMPUSES
Usually designed for students and faculty; sometimes used directly in class, as shown here.

© iStockphoto.com/CEFutcher

Wi-Fi Hotspots

While not typically used for primary home Internet access, another option for Internet access is a **Wi-Fi hotspot**—a location with a direct Internet connection and a wireless access point that allows users to connect wirelessly (via Wi-Fi) to the hotspot to use its Internet connection (see Figure 8-9). Public Wi-Fi

---

>**Broadband over fiber (BoF) Internet access.** Very fast, direct Internet access via fiber-optic networks; also referred to as **fiber-to-the-premises (FTTP) Internet access**. >**Mobile wireless Internet access.** Internet access via a mobile phone network. >**Wi-Fi hotspot.** A location that provides wireless Internet access to the public.

hotpots are widely available today, including at many coffeehouses and restaurants; at hotels, airports, and other locations frequented by business travelers; and in or nearby public areas such as libraries, subway stations, and parks. Some public Wi-Fi hotspots are free; others charge per hour, per day, or on a subscription basis. College campuses also typically have Wi-Fi hotspots to provide Internet access to students; many businesses and other organizations have Wi-Fi hotspots for use by employees in their offices, as well as by employees and guests in conference rooms, waiting rooms, lunchrooms, and other on-site locations.

TIP

Unlike most home Internet connections, mobile wireless service is typically tied to a particular device, though *family plans* are often available to give discounted rates for additional devices and mobile hotspots and tethering can often be used to share a single connection temporarily when needed, as discussed in Chapter 7.

Selecting an ISP and Setting Up Your Computer

Once the type of Internet access to be used is determined, the final steps to getting connected to the Internet are selecting an ISP and setting up your system. While this discussion is geared primarily toward a home Internet connection used with a personal computer, some of the concepts apply to business or mobile users as well.

Selecting an ISP

The type of device used (such as a personal computer or mobile device), the type of Internet connection and service desired (such as cable Internet or mobile wireless), and your geographical location (such as metropolitan or rural) will likely determine your ISP options. The pricing and services available often vary within a single ISP, as well as from one ISP to the next. The questions listed in Figure 8-10 can help you narrow your ISP choices and determine the questions you want answered before you decide on an ISP and a service package. A growing trend is for ISPs to offer a number of *tiers*; that is, different combinations of speeds and/or data caps for different prices so users requiring faster service or a more generous data plan can get it, but at a higher price.

FIGURE 8-10
Choosing an ISP.
Some questions to ask before making your final selection.

AREA	QUESTIONS TO ASK
Services	Is the service compatible with my device?
	Is there a monthly bandwidth limit? If so, do I have a choice of tiers?
	How many e-mail addresses can I have?
	What is the size limit on incoming and outgoing e-mail messages and attachments?
	Do I have a choice between conventional and Web-based e-mail?
	Are there any special member features or benefits?
	Does the service include Web site hosting?
Speed	How fast are the maximum and usual downstream (ISP to my PC) speeds?
	How fast are the maximum and usual upstream (my PC to ISP) speeds?
	How much does the service slow down under adverse conditions, such as high traffic or poor weather?
Support	Is telephone technical support available?
	Is Web-based technical support (such as via e-mail) available?
	Is there ever a charge for technical support?
Cost	What is the monthly cost for the service? Is it lower if I prepay a few months in advance? Are different tiers available?
	Is there a setup fee? If so, can it be waived with a long-term agreement?
	What is the cost of any additional hardware needed, such as modem or transceiver? Can the fee be waived with a long-term service agreement?
	Are there any other services (telephone service, or cable or satellite TV, for instance) available from this provider that can be combined with Internet access for a lower total cost?

Setting Up Your Computer

The specific steps for setting up your computer to use your selected type of Internet connection depend on the type of device, the type of connection, and the ISP you have chosen to use. Some types of Internet connections, such as satellite and broadband over fiber, require professional installation, after which you will be online; with other types, you can install the necessary hardware (typically a modem that connects to your computer or wireless router via an Ethernet cable) yourself (mobile device setup usually doesn't require any additional hardware). You will usually need to select a username and your desired payment method at some point during the ordering or setup process; this username is typically used in your e-mail address that will be associated with that Internet service.

After one computer is successfully connected to the Internet, you may need to add additional hardware to connect other computers and devices that you want to be able to access the Internet.

NET

For instance, to share a broadband connection, you can connect other computers directly to the modem (via an Ethernet cable or Wi-Fi connection) if the modem contains a built-in switch or wireless router. If the modem does not include switching or wireless routing capabilities, you will need to connect a switch or wireless router to the modem (typically via an Ethernet cable) and then connect your devices to the switch or router in order to share the Internet connection with those devices.

SEARCHING THE INTERNET

Most people who use the Internet turn to it to find specific information. For instance, you might want to find out the lowest price of the latest *Star Trek* DVD, the flights available from Los Angeles to New York on a particular day, a recipe for clam chowder, the weather forecast for the upcoming weekend, a video of the last presidential inaugural address, or a map of hiking trails in the Grand Tetons. The Internet provides access to a vast array of interesting and useful information, but that information is useless if you cannot find it when you need it. Consequently, one of the most important skills an Internet user can acquire today is how to search for and locate information on the Internet successfully. Basic Internet searching was introduced in Chapter 1, but understanding the various types of search sites available and how they work, as well as some key searching strategies, can help you perform more successful and efficient Internet searches. These topics are discussed next.

Search Sites

Search sites (such as *Google, Bing, Yahoo! Search, Ask.com*, and so forth) are Web sites designed specifically to help you find information on the Web. Most search sites use a **search engine**—a software program—in conjunction with a huge database of information about Web pages to help visitors find Web pages that contain the information they are seeking. Search site databases are updated on a regular basis; for example, Google estimates that its entire index is updated about once per month. Typically, this occurs using small, automated programs (often called *spiders* or *web crawlers*) that use the hyperlinks located on Web pages to *crawl* (jump continually) from page to page. At each Web page, the spider program records important data about the page into the search site's database, such as the page's URL, its title, the keywords that appear frequently on the page, and the keywords and descriptive information added to the page's code by the Web page author when the page was created. Spider programs can be tremendously fast, visiting millions of pages per day. In addition to spider programs, search site databases also obtain information from Web page authors who submit Web page URLs and keywords associated with their Web sites to the search site, as discussed more in Chapter 11. The size of the database used varies with each particular search site, but typically includes information collected from several billion Web pages.

To begin a search using a search site, type the URL for the desired search site in the Address bar of your browser (alternately, many Web browsers allow you to type search terms in the Address bar instead of a URL and the search will be performed using whichever search site is specified as the default search site). Most search sites today are designed for *keyword searches*; some sites allow *directory searches* as well. These two types of searches are discussed next. In addition, as the ability to search becomes more and more important, new types of searching are being developed. One

> **Search site.** A Web site designed to help users search for Web pages that match specified keywords or selected categories. > **Search engine.** A software program used by a search site to retrieve matching Web pages from a search database.

emerging possibility is *real-time search engines* that search the Web live, instead of relying on a search site database (one such service—called *MyLiveSearch*—is currently in development). Another emerging search site—*ChaCha Search*—uses human guides that you can chat with via the ChaCha Search page if you can't find the information you are looking for.

Keyword Search

The most common type of Internet search is the **keyword search**—that is, when you type appropriate **keywords** (one or more key terms) describing what you are looking for into a search box. The site's search engine then uses those keywords to return a list of Web pages (called *hits*) that match your search criteria; you can view any one of these Web pages by clicking its corresponding hyperlink (see Figure 8-11). Search sites differ in determining how close a match must be between the specified search criteria and a Web page before a link to that page is displayed, so the number of hits from one search site to another may vary. To reduce the number of hits displayed, good search strategies (discussed shortly) can be used. Search sites also differ with respect to the order in which the hits are displayed. Some sites list the most popular sites (usually judged by the number of Web pages that link to it) first; others list Web pages belonging to organizations that pay a fee to receive a higher rank (typically called *sponsored links*) first.

The keyword search is the most commonly used search type. It is used not only on conventional search sites like the Google search site shown in Figure 8-11, but also on many other Web sites. For instance, many types of Web pages include a keyword search box like the one shown in Figure 8-12 so visitors can search that Web site to find information (such as items for sale via the site or specific documents or Web pages located on that site). These Web site searches are typically powered by search engine technology, such as by *Google Site Search* or the open source *Lucene* search application.

Directory Search

An alternate type of Internet search available on some search sites is the **directory search**, which uses lists of categories instead of a search box. To perform a directory search, click the category that best matches what you are looking for in order to display a list of more specific subcategories within the main category. You can then click specific subcategories to drill down to more specific topics until you see hyperlinks to Web pages matching the information you are looking for.

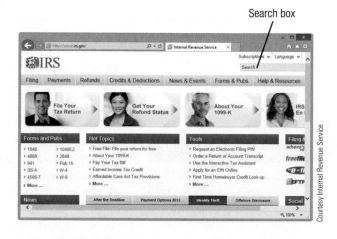

FIGURE 8-11
Using a search site.

FIGURE 8-12
Web page keyword searches. Allow users to search the Web site for the desired content.

Search Site Tools

Many search sites contain a variety of tools that can be used to find specific types of information. For instance, many search sites include links next to the search box that allow you to search for items other than Web pages, such as music files, videos, images, maps, news articles, products for sale—even files on your computer. Google is one of the most versatile search sites at the present time and is continually adding new search options. In addition to the options just listed, Google allows a variety of special searches to be conducted by typing specific search criteria in its search box to find other useful information, such as to quickly track a shipped package, look up a telephone number, check on the status of an airline flight, or make a calculation or conversion. Some examples of search tools that can be performed using the Google search box are listed in Figure 8-13.

FUNCTION	EXPLANATION
Calculator	Enter a mathematical expression or a conversion to see the result.
Currency converter	Enter an amount and currency types (such as *10 Euro in USD*) to see the corresponding value.
Dictionary	Enter the term *define* followed by a term to view definitions for that term from online sources.
Earthquakes	Enter the term *earthquake* to see recent earthquake activity around the world.
Flight information	Enter an airline and a flight number to see status information.
Movie showtimes	Enter the term *movie* followed by a ZIP Code to view movies showing in that area.
Number search	Enter a UPS, FedEx, or USPS tracking number; an area code; or a UPC code to view the associated information.
Sports scores	Enter a team name or league name to see scores, schedules, and other information.
Sunrise/sunset	Enter the term *sunrise* or *sunset* followed by a city name to see the time of the sunrise or sunset in that city.
Street maps	Enter an address to find a map to that location.
Time	Enter the term *time* followed by a city name to see the current time in that city.
Weather	Enter the term *weather* followed by a city name or ZIP Code to view the weather for that location.
Yellow pages	Enter a type of business and city name or ZIP Code to view businesses in that local area.

EXAMPLES:

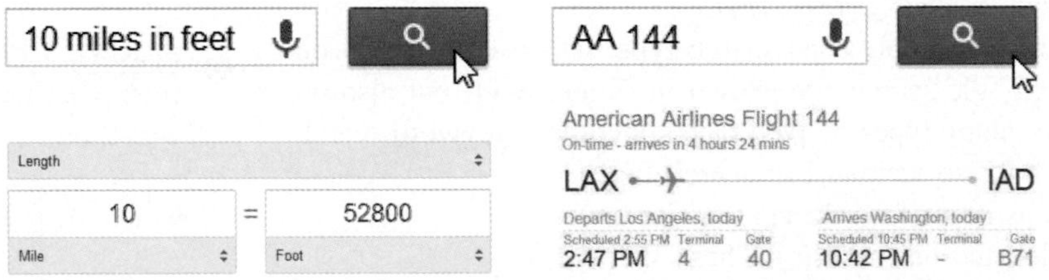
10 miles in feet
Length
10
=
52800
Mile
Foot
AA 144
American Airlines Flight 144
On-time - arrives in 4 hours 24 mins
LAX
IAD
Departs Los Angeles, today
Scheduled 2:55 PM Terminal Gate
2:47 PM 4 40
Arrives Washington, today
Scheduled 10:45 PM Terminal Gate
10:42 PM - B71

FIGURE 8-13
Google search tools.

Search Strategies

There are a variety of strategies that can be used to help whittle down a list of hits to a more manageable number (some searches can return billions of Web pages). Some search strategies can be employed regardless of the search site being used; others are available only on certain sites. Some of the most useful search strategies are discussed next.

TIP

If there is an uncommon word that relates to your search, use it to help improve your results.

Using Phrases

One of the most straightforward ways to improve the quality of the hits returned is to use *phrase searching*—essentially typing more than one keyword in a keyword search. Most search engines automatically list the hits that include all the keywords first, followed by hits matching most of the keywords, continuing down to hits that fit only one of the keywords. To force this type of sorting, virtually all search engines allow you to use some type of character—often quotation marks—to indicate that you want to search for the entire phrase together. Because search options vary from site to site, it is best to look for a search tips link on the search site you are using; the search tips should explain all of the search options available for that site. Examples of the results based on different search phrases to find Web pages about hand signals used with dogs and conducted at two search sites are listed in Figure 8-14. Notice that while the last two search phrases shown in Figure 8-14

SEARCH PHRASE USED	SEARCH SITE	NUMBER OF PAGES FOUND	TITLE OF FIRST TWO NONSPONSORED PAGES FOUND*
dogs	Google	1,420,000,000	Dogs – Wikipedia, the free encyclopedia Dog: Dog Breeds, Adoption, Bringing a Dog Home and Care
	Bing	53,200,000	Dog – Wikipedia, the free encyclopedia Dog Supplies | Dog Accessories & Dog Products – Dog.com
hand signals	Google	26,300,000	Hand Signals – Wikipedia, the free encyclopedia California Driver Handbook – Safe Driving Practices
	Bing	17,400,000	Hand Signals – Wikipedia, the free encyclopedia Hand Signs Part 1
dog hand signals	Google	1,830,000	DDEAF Training Hand Signs – Deaf Dog Education Action Fund Dog Training Hand Signals – Dog Training Excellence
	Bing	6,500,000	How to Teach a Dog Hand Signals | eHow.com Dog Training Hand Signals, A Different Type of Communication
"dog hand signals"	Google	51,500	DDEAF Training Hand Signs – Deaf Dog Education Action Fund Utilize Dog Hand Signals in Your Training: Dog Obedience Training
	Bing	6,490	How to Teach a Dog Hand Signals | eHow.com Dog Training Hand Signals, A Different Type of Communication

* Highlighted entries indicate Web pages about dog hand signals.

both returned relevant (and similar) Web pages, the number of Web pages found varied dramatically (thousands of pages versus millions).

Using Boolean Operators

To further specify exactly what you want a search engine to find, *Boolean operators*—most commonly AND, OR, and NOT—can often be used in keyword searches. For example, if you want a search engine to find all documents that cover *both* the Intel and AMD microprocessor manufacturers, you can use the search phrase *Intel AND AMD* if the search engine supports Boolean operators. If, instead, you want documents that discuss *either* of these companies, the search phrase *Intel OR AMD* can be used. On the other hand, if you want documents about microprocessors that are cataloged with no mention of Intel, *microprocessors NOT Intel* can be used. Just as with other operators, the rules for using Boolean operators might vary from search site to search site (for instance, Google automatically assumes the AND operator as the default operator any time more than one search term is listed and Google uses a minus sign (–) instead of the word *NOT*). Be sure to check the search tips for the search site that you are using to see what operators can be used on that site. Some search sites also include an *Advanced Search* option that helps you specify Boolean conditions and other advanced search techniques using a fill-in-the-blank form.

Using Multiple Search Sites

Most users have a favorite search site that they are most comfortable using. However, as illustrated in Figure 8-14, different search sites can return different results. It is important to realize that sometimes a different search site might perform better than the one you use regularly. If you are searching for something and are not making any progress with one search site, then try another search site.

Using Appropriate Keywords, Synonyms, Variant Word Forms, and Wildcards

When choosing the keywords to be used with a search site, it is important to select words that represent the key concept you are searching for. For example, if you want to find out about bed and breakfasts located in the town of Leavenworth, Washington, a keyword phrase (such as *Leavenworth Washington bed and breakfast*) should return appropriate

FIGURE 8-14
Examples of phrase searching. Using different search phrases and different search sites can significantly change the search results.

NET

TIP

When searching, be efficient—if an appropriate Web page is not included among the first page or two of hits, redo the search using more specific criteria, a different search site, or a different search strategy.

FIELD TYPE	EXAMPLE	EXPLANATION
Title	title: "tax tips"	Searches for Web pages containing the words "tax tips" in the page title.
Text	text: "tax tips"	Searches for Web pages containing "tax tips" in the text of the page.
Site	forms site:irs.gov	Searches for Web pages associated with the keyword "forms" that are located only on the irs.gov Web site.
Domain	tax tips site:*.gov	Searches for Web pages associated with the keywords "tax tips" that are located on government Web sites (they can have anything for the first part of the domain name, but must have a .gov TLD).

FIGURE 8-15

Field searching.

Field searches limit search results to just those pages that match specific field criteria, in addition to any specified search criteria.

✓ **TIP**

To search for a search term and its synonyms at the same time in Google, type the tilde symbol (~) immediately in front of your search term, such as *~bed and breakfast* to have Google search for *bed and breakfast*, as well as automatically also search for *hotels*, *motels*, and other synonymous terms.

results. If your initial search does not produce the results you are hoping for, you can try *synonyms*—words that have meanings similar to other words. For example, you could replace *bed and breakfast* with *hotel* or *lodging*. To use synonyms in addition to the original keywords, Boolean operators can be used, such as the search phrase *"bed and breakfast" OR hotel OR lodging AND Leavenworth AND Washington.*

Variant—or alternate—word forms are another possibility. Try to think of a different spelling or form of your keywords if your search still does not work as desired. For example, *bed and breakfast* could be replaced or supplemented with the variants *bed & breakfast* and *B&B*, and the *hand signals* keywords used in Figure 8-14 could be replaced with the variants *hand signal* and *hand signaling*. Using alternative spellings is a form of this strategy, as well. Another strategy that is sometimes used with keywords is the *wildcard* approach. A wildcard is a special symbol that is used in conjunction with a part of a word to specify the pattern of the terms you want to search for. For instance, the asterisk wildcard (*) is used to represent one or more letters at the asterisk location, so on many sites searching for *hand sign** would search for *hand sign*, *hand signal*, *hand signals*, *hand signaling*, and any other keywords that fit this specific pattern.

Using Field Searches

Another strategy that can be used when basic searching is not producing the desired results is *field searching*. A field search limits the search to a particular search characteristic (or *field*), such as the page title, URL, page text, top-level domain, or Web site (see Figure 8-15). When a field search is performed, only the hits associated with the Web pages that match the specified criteria in the specified field are displayed. You can also use field searching in conjunction with regular search terms, such as to search for a particular keyword on just Web sites that use a specific domain. Many, but not all, search engines support some type of field searching. Check the search tips for the particular search site you are using to see if it has that option.

Evaluating Search Results

Once a list of Web sites is returned as the result of a search, it is time to evaluate the sites to determine their quality and potential for meeting your needs. Two questions to ask yourself before clicking a link in the search results are as follows:

➤ Does the title and listed description sound appropriate for the information you are seeking?

➤ Is the URL from an appropriate company or organization? For example, if you want technical specifications about a particular product, you might want to start with information on the manufacturer's Web site. If you are looking for government publications, stick with government Web sites.

After an appropriate Web page is found, the evaluation process is still not complete. To determine if the information can be trusted, you should evaluate both the author and the source to decide if the information can be considered reliable and whether or not it is biased. Be sure to also check for a date to see how up to date the information is—many online

TYPE OF RESOURCE	CITATION EXAMPLE
Web page article (magazine)	Dvorak, J. (2013, June 3). The Google assumption engine. *PC Magazine*. Retrieved from http://www.pcmag.com/article2/0,2817,2419867,00.asp
Web page article (journal)	Dickens, C. (2013, June). Health literacy and nursing: An update. *American Journal of Nursing, 113(6)*, 52–57. Retrieved from http://journals.lww.com/ajnonline/Fulltext/2013/06000/Health_Literacy_and_ Nursing___An_Update.29.aspx
Web page article (not appearing in a periodical)	Elias, P. (2013, June 01). Judge orders Google to turn over data to FBI. Retrieved from http://www.nbcnews.com/technology/judge-orders-google-turn-over-data-fbi-6C10157219
Web page content (not an article)	*Security 101 - Internet Security Glossary	Norton.* (n.d.) Retrieved from http://us.norton.com/ security-101
E-mail (cited in text, not reference list)	M. Rodriquez (personal communication, March 28, 2014)

articles are years old. If you will be using the information in a report, paper, or other document in which accuracy is important, try to verify the information with a second source.

Citing Internet Resources

According to the online version of the Merriam-Webster Dictionary, the term *plagiarize* means "to steal and pass off the ideas or words of another as one's own" or to "use another's production without crediting the source." To avoid plagiarizing Web page content, you need to credit Web page sources—as well as any other Internet resources—when you use them in papers, on Web pages, or in other documents.

The guidelines for citing Web page content are similar to those for written sources. In general, the author, date of publication, and article or Web page title are listed along with a "Retrieved" statement listing the URL of the Web page used to retrieve the article. Some citation examples based on the guidelines obtained from the *American Psychological Association (APA)* Web site are shown in Figure 8-16. If in doubt when preparing a research paper, check with your instructor as to the style manual (such as APA, *Modern Language Association (MLA)*, or *Chicago Manual of Style*) he or she prefers you to follow and refer to that guide for direction.

BEYOND BROWSING AND E-MAIL

In addition to basic browsing and e-mail (discussed in Chapter 1), there are a host of other activities that can take place via the Internet. Some of the most common of these Web-based applications are discussed next.

Other Types of Online Communications

Many types of online communications methods exist. E-mail, discussed in Chapter 1, is one of the most common; other types of online communications are discussed in the next few sections. While the programs that supported the various types of online communications discussed next were originally dedicated to a single task, today's programs can typically be used for a variety of types of online communications. For instance, the *Skype* online communications program shown in Figure 8-17 can be used to exchange *instant messages (IMs)*, make voice and video calls via *Voice over Internet Protocol (VoIP)*, and exchange files with your online contacts; the Gmail Web mail service can be used to exchange instant messages and make voice and video calls (using Google's *Hangouts* communications app), in addition to sending

FIGURE 8-16
Citing Web sources.
These examples follow the American Psychological Association (APA) citation guidelines.

FIGURE 8-17
Skype. This app can be used for a variety of online communications.

Click to return to your Home page to select another contact.

The messages from both you and your contact appear here.

Click to start a video or voice call to this contact.

Type a new message here.

Courtesy WhatsApp Inc.

FIGURE 8-18

Group messaging.
Works the same as traditional IM, just with more people.

and receiving e-mail messages. Some e-mail programs (such as Microsoft Outlook) can also display your contact's social networking updates. This online communications convergence trend is found in both personal and business applications; in business, it is referred to as *unified communications* (*UC*). With UC, all of a business's communications (such as e-mail, instant messaging, videoconferencing, customer service center communications, and telephone calls via both in-office landlines and mobile phones) are tied together and work with a single unified mailbox and interface—often via a cloud UC provider.

Instant Messaging (IM) and Text Messaging

Instant messaging (**IM**), also commonly referred to as **chat**, allows you to exchange real-time typed messages with people on your *contact list* or *buddy list*—a list of individuals (such as family, friends, and business associates) that you specify or with whom you have already exchanged messages. Instant messages (IMs) can be sent via computers and smartphones via *messaging programs* or *apps* (such as *AIM, Yahoo! Messenger*, the Skype program shown in Figure 8-17, or the *WhatsApp* mobile app shown in Figure 8-18) or via Web pages (such as TV show Web sites and social networking sites like Facebook and Google+) that support instant messaging. Originally a popular communications method among friends, IM has also become a valuable business tool.

In order to send an IM, you must be signed in to your IM service. You can then select a contact and send an IM, which then appears immediately on your contact's device. You can also typically engage in other types of activities with your contact via the IM program, such as sending a photo or file, starting a voice or video conversation, or starting a *group call* or *conversation* (refer again to Figure 8-18). Instant messaging capabilities are also often integrated into Web pages, such as to ask questions of a customer service representative or to start a conversation with one of your friends via a social networking site.

Because IM applications typically display the status of your buddies (such as if they are online or if they have set their status to "Busy" or "In a meeting"), IM is an example of an application that uses *presence technology*—technology that enables one computing device to identify the current status of another device. Presence technology is increasingly being integrated into devices and applications and is discussed in more detail in Chapter 15. For a look at a growing presence application—*geofencing*—see the How It Works box.

Text messaging is a form of messaging frequently used by mobile phone users. Also called *Short Message Service* or *SMS*, text messaging is used to send short (less than 160 character) text-based messages via a cellular network. If the messages also include photos, audio, or video, *Multimedia Message Service* or *MMS* is used instead. In either case, the messages are typically sent to the recipient via his or her mobile phone number or e-mail address (you can also send text messages to a mobile phone from your computer's e-mail program—just use the recipient's mobile phone number and the appropriate domain for their wireless carrier such as *111-555-0000@txt.att.net*). Individuals may incur a fee for exchanging IMs and text messages, if these services are not included in their wireless plan.

While e-mail is still important for business online communications, messaging is beginning to replace e-mail for personal communications—particularly with teenagers and other individuals who carry a moble phone with them at all times. According to the director of engineering at Facebook, "The future of messaging is more real time, more conversational, and more casual."

Twittering and Social Networking Updates

Twittering refers to posting short (up to 140 character) updates (called *tweets*) about what you are doing or thinking about at any moment to the *Twitter* social network. The updates

HOW IT WORKS

Geofencing

Using your smartphone's location to deliver Web content—sometimes referred to as *geobrowsing*—is nothing new. Some geobrowsing applications and services (such as *Foursquare*) allow you to broadcast your current location to friends or *check in* to share your current location with friends; others (such as *Eventful*) are designed to find entertainment and live events that are close to your current location.

Location-based marketing and *geofencing* take geobrowsing one step further by enabling developers to deliver ads, offers, and other marketing resources to users based on their current physical location. For instance, a business could set up *geofences* (prescribed geographical areas) so it is notified when a customer is close to a particular store location, as well as when the customer enters and exits the store, in order to send appropriate messages and offers to that customer via his or her smartphone. Google recently released tools to help developers create these types of applications—the tools can determine more accurate locations faster and without draining the smartphone's battery; can determine if the user is walking, cycling, or driving; and can set up location-based triggers when someone enters or exists a geofenced area.

While *mobile marketing* is a common use for geofencing, the same technology can be used by individuals for geofences they set up for themselves (such as the geofence shown being added in the accompanying illustration). For example, you can use a geofencing app to turn off your Wi-Fi when you are out of range of a network

(for security reasons and to save your battery) or an app to remind you of tasks you need to accomplish when you enter or exit a specific geofence. And a new *Nearby* service from Wikipedia displays Wikipedia articles based on people's current location in hopes that these individuals will upload photos and otherwise update content using their smartphones. Geofencing possibilities are growing and appear to be only limited by developers' imaginations.

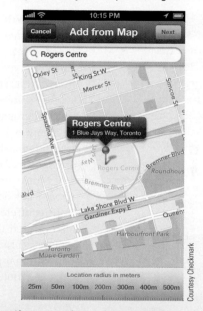

Creating a geofence from a map location.

---

can be sent via text message or the Twitter Web site. Individuals see the tweets of people they *follow* on their Twitter home page; they can view other tweets by searching Twitter for key terms or *hashtags* (key terms used on Twitter and that are preceded by the symbol #), as shown in Figure 8-19. You can also send *direct messages* to one of your followers, which are then seen only by you and the recipient.

Features similar to Twitter tweets (generally referred to as *status updates*) are available on some social networking sites (most notably, Facebook) to keep your friends up to date on your current activities, as discussed shortly. The use of Twitter and status updates is changing the way some people communicate online. Twitter is used today to get updates on the weather, to ask for assistance with problems or to conduct information searches—even for personal safety purposes. For instance, as shown in Figure 8-19, the U.S. State Department uses Twitter to issue traveling advisories. Increasingly, people turn to Twitter to comment on newsworthy events—such as terrorist attacks, natural disasters, and breaking news—as they occur.

FIGURE 8-19

Twitter. Allows individuals to post and view tweets.

Click to see the tweets of the people you follow.

Type a hashtag in the form #*keyword* here to display tweets that use that hashtag.

State Dept. tweets; click to follow.

Forums

For asking questions of, making comments to, or initiating discussions with a large group of individuals, **forums** (also called *discussion groups* and *message boards*) can be used. Forums are Web pages designed to facilitate written discussions on specific subjects, such as TV shows, computers, movies, investing, gardening, music, photography, or politics. They typically have a *moderator* who monitors the forum to remove inappropriate posts. When a participant posts a message, it is displayed for anyone accessing the forum to read and respond to. Messages are usually organized by topics (called *threads*); participants can post new messages in response to an existing message and stay within that thread, or they can start a new thread. Forum participants do not have to be online at the same time so participants can post and respond to messages at their convenience.

Voice over Internet Protocol (VoIP)

Internet telephony is the original industry term for the process of placing telephone calls over the Internet. Today, the standard term for placing telephone calls over the Internet or any other type of data network is **Voice over Internet Protocol** (**VoIP**) and it can take many forms. At its simplest level, VoIP calls can take place from computer to computer, such as by starting a voice conversation with an online contact using a messaging program and a headset or microphone. Computer to computer calls (such as via the popular Skype service shown in Figure 8-17, as well as via messaging programs that support voice calls) are generally free. Often calls can be received from or made to conventional or mobile phones for a small fee, such as 2 cents per minute or $2.99 per month for unlimited calling for domestic calls.

More permanent VoIP setups (sometimes referred to as *digital voice* or *broadband phone*) are designed to replace conventional landline phones in homes and businesses. VoIP is offered through some ISPs, such as cable, telephone, and wireless providers; it is also offered through dedicated VoIP providers, such as *Vonage*. Permanent VoIP setups require a broadband Internet connection and a *VoIP phone adapter* that goes between a conventional phone and a broadband router, as shown in Figure 8-20. Once your phone calls are routed through your phone adapter and router to the Internet, they travel to the recipient's phone, which can be another VoIP phone, a mobile phone, or a landline phone. VoIP phone adapters are typically designed for a specific VoIP provider. With these more permanent VoIP setups, most users switching from landline phone service can keep their existing telephone number.

The biggest advantage of VoIP is cost savings, such as unlimited local and long-distance calls for as little as $25 per month, or basic cable and VoIP services bundled together for about $50 per month. One of the biggest disadvantages of VoIP at the present time is that it does not function during a power outage or if your Internet connection (such as your cable connection for cable Internet users) goes down.

Web Conferences and Webinars

As discussed in Chapter 7, the term *videoconferencing* refers to the use of computers or mobile devices, video cameras, microphones, and other communications

Ⓥ **FIGURE 8-20**
Voice over IP (VoIP).
Permanent VoIP setups allow telephone calls to be placed via a broadband Internet connection using a conventional telephone.

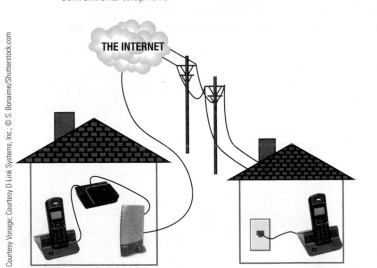

Courtesy Vonage; Courtesy D-Link Systems, Inc.; © S. Bonaime/Shutterstock.com

1. A conventional phone is plugged into a VoIP adapter, which is connected to a broadband modem.

2. Calls coming from the VoIP phone travel over the Internet to the recipient's phone.

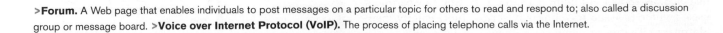

> **Forum.** A Web page that enables individuals to post messages on a particular topic for others to read and respond to; also called a discussion group or message board. > **Voice over Internet Protocol (VoIP).** The process of placing telephone calls via the Internet.

technologies to conduct real-time, face-to-face meetings between people in different locations. Videoconferencing that takes place via the Internet is often called *Web conferencing* or *online conferencing*. **Web conferences** typically take place via a personal computer or mobile device (see Figure 8-21) and are used by businesses and individuals. As previously discussed, many free messaging programs or services (such as Skype, Google Hangouts, and *Apple FaceTime*) support video phone calls. While some of these programs support group calls and other more advanced features, business Web conferences that require multiple participants or other communications tools (such as a shared whiteboard or the ability for attendees to share the content on their computer screens) may need to use a *Web conferencing service* (such as *WebEx*) or a premium service from Skype or another messaging service instead. Business Web conferencing is often used for meetings between individuals located in different geographical locations, as well as for employee training, sales presentations, customer support, and other business applications.

Webinars (Web seminars) are similar to Web conferences, but typically have a designated presenter and an audience. Although interaction with the audience is usually included (such as question-and-answer sessions), a Webinar is typically more one-way communication than a Web conference. A completely one-way presentation (such as a recorded Webinar played back on demand) is sometimes referred to as a *Webcast*.

Courtesy Cisco Systems

FIGURE 8-21
Web conferencing.
Allows individuals to talk with and see each other in real time.

Social Networking/Social Media

A **social networking site** can be loosely defined as any site that creates a community of individuals who can communicate with and/or share information with one another; the collection of social networking sites and other communications channels used to transmit or share information with a broad audience is referred to as **social media**. Some examples of social networking sites are *MySpace*, *Facebook*, and *Google+* that allow users to post information about themselves for others to read; *Meetup* that connects people in specific geographic areas with common hobbies and interests; *Flickr* and *Fotki* and other photo sharing sites; *Pinterest* that allows individuals to share ideas and snippets from Web pages, organized by topic; and *YouTube* and other video sharing sites. Social networking can be performed via personal computers, though the use of *mobile social networking*—social networks accessed with a smartphone or other mobile device—is more common today, making social networking a real-time, on-the-go activity. Some reasons for this include that

ASK THE EXPERT

THROW THE FIGHT **Ryan Baustert**, Guitarist, Throw the Fight

What impact has the Internet and social networking sites had on your band's success?

The Internet has had a major impact on us. The best marketing is when the distance between artist and audience is short and direct. Due to sites like MySpace, Purevolume, and Facebook, we are able to stay better connected and interact with our fans on a more personal level. We can also gauge how our music is received by peoples' reactions and comments online.

It's much easier to promote shows, tours, and album releases, as well. More recently, with the explosion of Twitter, we can go one step further and give fans more insight into what is going on in our lives behind the scenes. This, in turn, helps us build brand loyalty.

NET

>**Web conference.** A face-to-face meeting taking place via the Web; typically uses video cameras and microphones to enable participants to see and hear each other. >**Webinar.** A seminar presented via the Web. >**Social networking site.** A site that enables a community of individuals to communicate and share information. >**Social media.** The collection of social networking sites and other communications channels used to transmit or share information with a broad audience.

Courtesy ABC.com; Courtesy YouTube

LOGIN
Log in to a Web site using social network credentials.

SHARE
Share Web content via online communications or social networks.

Ⓐ **FIGURE 8-22**
Social networks are integrated into many Web sites.

Ⓥ **FIGURE 8-23**
Social networking sites. Allow individuals to exchange posts, photos, videos, messages, and more with their friends.

Courtesy Facebook; Courtesy Throw the Fight www.facebook.com/throwthefight, www.throwthefight.com.

most individuals carry a mobile phone with them all the time, many individuals like to communicate with others via the Web while they are on the go, and smartphones enable location applications to be integrated into the social networking experience.

Social networking is also increasingly being integrated with other online activities. For instance, you can exchange messages or have video calls with your friends from within Google+ or Facebook; you can share YouTube videos via an e-mail message, a video call, or one of your social networking pages from a YouTube video page; and you can view your friends' Facebook updates in Skype. In addition, many Web sites include *Like* buttons on their site to allow a visitor to Like the business's Facebook page, Like content (such as a video) on the business's Web site, or share content from the business's Web site on the visitor's Facebook page. A Web site can also integrate an *Activity Feed* to show visitors Likes and comments about the site made by the visitor's *Facebook friends*. In addition, a Web site can allow visitors to easily log in to its Web site using the visitor's logon credentials from Facebook or another social network (see Figure 8-22).

Social networking sites are used most often to communicate with existing friends. Facebook, for instance (shown in Figure 8-23), allows you to post photos, videos, music, status updates, and other content for your *Facebook friends* (individuals you have chosen to communicate with via Facebook) to view. You can also chat with your Facebook friends who are currently online, and *Like* or comment on the posts shown on your friends' Facebook pages or in the *news feed* on your Facebook page. For privacy purposes, you can limit access to your Facebook page to the individuals you identify (such as just to your Facebook friends).

In addition to being used to communicate with existing friends, social networking sites are also used to learn about individuals you currently don't know. For instance, college-bound students can use social media to meet other incoming freshmen before the school year starts, "facestalk" (view the profiles of) other students in their graduating class, look up the profiles of their dorm roommates, find fellow students with common interests, and more—all before actually setting foot on campus. They are also used to share information during natural disasters, such as New Yorkers sharing transportation updates and gas station availability via Twitter during the power outages following Hurricane Sandy.

In addition to being used for personal use, social networking sites today are also viewed as a business marketing tool. For instance, Twitter, Facebook, and YouTube are often used by businesses, political candidates, emerging musicians, and other professionals or professional organizations to increase their online presence. There are also business social networking sites designed for business networking. Some of these sites (such as *LinkedIn*) are used for recruiting new employees, finding new jobs, building professional contacts, and other business activities. Others (such as *StartupNation*) are designed to help entrepreneurs connect with business owners and resources, and exchange ideas. Other specialized social networking sites include sites designed for children (these usually work in a manner similar to Facebook, but they have safeguards in place to prevent personal information from being posted, to monitor language, and so forth) and families (such as to exchange messages, view online tasks lists, and access a shared family calendar).

When using a social networking site, adults and children should be cautious about revealing too much personal information via these sites, both for personal safety reasons and to prevent the information from being used in personalized, targeted *spear phishing* attacks, discussed in Chapter 9. In addition, social networking content is increasingly being monitored by colleges (to find inappropriate behavior by students and to research college applicants) and employers (to find unprofessional behavior by current employees and to research potential job candidates). Because of this, all individuals should be careful about the types of photos and other content they post online. There have been numerous cases over the past few years of students being disciplined or not admitted to a college, and individuals being fired or not hired, due to content posted to a social networking site. Consequently, it is a good idea for individuals to take a close look at their online posts and photos and remove anything that might be potentially embarrassing if viewed by current or future employers, a future partner, or other people important to them now or in the future.

Another emerging issue is what happens to social networking content when someone dies unexpectedly because family members and heirs cannot access the sites without logon information or access to the deceased's e-mail for password recovery purposes. In response, some special services have emerged to help individuals store information about their online assets (such as logon information) and to designate a beneficiary—the person designated to receive that information or to whom the account ownership will be transferred upon the individual's death. Some services can also distribute e-mail messages to designated individuals when the member dies, as well as update the person's bio or change his or her status update to one predesignated by the member. An alternative is for individuals to leave the necessary online contact and access information, as well as instructions regarding how to notify online friends and sites, with a trusted friend or relative who is instructed to use the information only in the event of the individual's death.

Online Shopping and Investing

Online shopping and *online investing* are examples of *e-commerce*—online financial transactions. It is very common today to order products, buy and sell stock, pay bills, and manage financial accounts online. However, because *online fraud*, *credit card fraud*, and *identity theft* (a situation in which someone gains enough personal information to pose as another person) are continuing to grow at a rapid pace, it is important to be cautious when participating in online financial activities. To protect yourself, use a credit card or *online payment service* such as *PayPal* (discussed in Chapter 11) whenever possible when purchasing goods or services online so that any fraudulent activities can be disputed. Also, be sure to enter your payment information only on a *secure Web page* (look for a URL that begins with *https* instead of *http*) and don't perform any financial transactions via a public Wi-Fi hotspot. Online financial accounts should also be protected with *strong user passwords* that are changed frequently. Internet security and strong passwords are discussed in detail in Chapter 9, and e-commerce is the topic of Chapter 11.

Online Shopping and Online Auctions

Online shopping is commonly used to purchase both physical products (such as clothing, books, DVDs, shoes, furniture, and more) and downloadable products (such as software, movies, music, and e-books) via Web pages. Typically, shoppers locate the items

NET

>**Online shopping.** Buying products or services over the Internet.

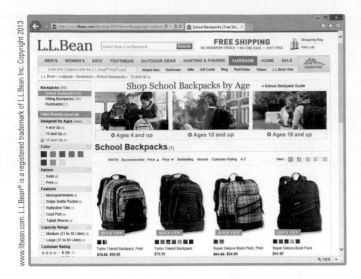

FIGURE 8-24

Online shopping.

Allows you to purchase goods and services online.

they would like to purchase using an online shopping site (such as the L.L. Bean Web site shown in Figure 8-24), and then they add those items to their online *shopping carts* or *shopping bags*. The site's *checkout* process—including supplying the necessary billing and shipping information—is then used to complete the sale. After the payment is processed, the item is either shipped to the customer (if it is a physical product), or the customer is given instructions on how to download it (if it is a downloadable product). Forrester Research predicts that U.S. online sales will reach approximately $370 billion by 2017.

Online auctions are one of the most common ways to purchase items online from other individuals. Sellers list items for sale on an auction site (such as *eBay*) and pay a small listing fee if required, and then pay a commission to the auction site if the item is sold. Individuals can visit the auction site and enter bids on auction items until the end of the auction. At that time, the person with the highest bid is declared the successful bidder (provided the minimum selling price, if one was established, was met) and arranges payment for and delivery of the item directly with the seller. Online auctions are described in more detail in Chapter 11. Another common way to purchase items from other individuals is via online classified ads, such as those posted on the popular *Craigslist* site.

Online Banking and Online Investing

Many banks today offer **online banking** as a free service to their customers to enable customers to check balances on all their accounts (such as checking, credit cards, mortgage, and investment accounts), view cashed checks and other transactions, transfer funds between accounts, pay bills electronically, and perform other activities related to their bank accounts. Online banking is continually growing and can be performed via a computer or a mobile device. In fact, most banks today allow users to view balances, transfer funds, make remote check deposits, and more via a mobile Web site, mobile banking app, or text message (see Figure 8-25).

Buying and selling stocks, bonds, mutual funds, and other types of securities is referred to as **online investing**. Although it is common to see stock quote capabilities on many search and news sites, trading stocks and other securities requires an *online broker*. The biggest advantages of online investing include lower transaction fees and the ability to quickly buy or sell stock when desired, without having to make a phone call—a convenience for those investors who do a lot of trading. Common online investing services include the ability to order sales and purchases; access performance histories, corporate news, and other useful investment information; and set up an *online portfolio* that displays the status of the stocks you specify. On some Web sites, stock price data is delayed 20 minutes; on other sites, real-time quotes are available. Like other Web page data, stock price data is current at the time it is retrieved via a Web page, but it may not be updated (and you will not see current quotes, for instance) until you reload the Web page using your browser's Refresh or Reload toolbar button.

FIGURE 8-25

Mobile banking.

>**Online auction.** An online activity where bids are placed for items, and the highest bidder purchases the item. >**Online banking.** Performing banking activities via the Web. >**Online investing.** Buying and selling stocks or other types of investments via the Web.

Online Entertainment

There are an ever-growing number of ways to use the Web for entertainment purposes, such as listening to music, watching TV and videos, and playing online games. Some applications can be accessed with virtually any type of Internet connection; others are only practical with a broadband connection. Many online entertainment applications require the use of a *media player program* or *plug-in* (such as *QuickTime Player* or *Silverlight*) to deliver multimedia content.

Online Music

There are a number of options available today for **online music**, such as listening to live radio broadcasts via an *online radio station*, watching music videos on *MTV.com* or *Yahoo! Music*, listening to or downloading music on demand via a monthly *online music subscription service*, or downloading music from *online music stores*, such as the *iTunes Music Store* or *Amazon MP3*. Music can be listened to or downloaded via a computer, mobile phone, or portable digital media player. Music files downloaded to your computer can be played from your computer's hard drive; they can also be copied to a CD to create a custom music CD or transferred to a portable digital media player or mobile phone provided the download agreement does not preclude it. Most online music is accessed via a mobile device and online subscription services are viewed as the fastest growing online music market. In fact, Juniper Research predicts the number of mobile online music subscribers will hit 178 million users by 2015.

Online TV, Videos, and Movies

Watching TV shows, videos, and movies online is another very popular type of online entertainment (see Figure 8-26). **Online videos** (such as news videos and movie trailers, videos posted to Web sites belonging to businesses and other organizations, personal

FIGURE 8-26
TV, videos, and movies are commonly watched online.

ONLINE TV AND MOVIES
TV shows and movies can be watched online for free via a variety of Web sites.

VIDEO-ON-DEMAND
Rented or purchased TV shows and movies can be delivered to your computer, TV, or mobile device.

>**Online music.** Music played or obtained via the Web. >**Online video.** Video watched or downloaded via the Web.

TECHNOLOGY AND YOU

High-Tech Workouts

Got a smartphone or media tablet? You now have a personal trainer. From apps that remind you when it's time to work out, to apps that use the accelerometer on your smartphone to chart your workout progress, to apps that provide you with a personal video workout, mobile video workouts are hot.

A leader in the area of mobile video workouts is *PumpOne*, which offers mobile personal training (see the accompanying illustration). Video workouts are available on demand in a variety of areas, such as strength training, weight loss, toning, overall conditioning, cardio, flexibility, and sports conditioning. Workouts are streamed to the appropriate device, range from 10 minutes to over an hour, and can be purchased on an unlimited basis or subscribed to on a month-to-month basis (selected workouts are free). Other options include the ability to share workouts with others and ask questions of a personal trainer.

Other popular high-tech workout tools include dumbbells that attach to a Wii remote and nunchuk to add resistance training to Wii Fit workouts; wristbands and watches that track your pace, distance, time, and calories burned on a run and that can upload this data in order to chart your programs online; and scales that record your weight and BMI and then upload this data to a Web site so you can view your weight history via a computer or smartphone.

© www.pumpone.com

A PumpOne iPad video workout.

videos posted to blogs and social networking pages, and videos shared via YouTube) are widely available (YouTube alone streams one billion video views per day). For a look at how online video can be used to help you with your workouts, see the Technology and You box.

Another option is **online TV** and **online movies**. Both are available from wireless providers, TV networks, and third-party Web sites. TV shows and movies can be watched *live*, which means they are available at the time they are being aired (such as news broadcasts and sporting events) or they can be downloaded or viewed at the user's convenience. For example, many wireless providers offer *mobile TV*, which delivers live sports, live news, primetime TV shows, and children's TV shows to your smartphone. A wide variety of recorded TV content (such as episodes of current TV shows after they have been aired) is also available through the respective television network Web sites for viewing online. Both TV shows and movies are available through a number of Web sites, such as *Hulu* (shown in Figure 8-26), *TV.com*, *Xfinity TV*, and

> **Online TV.** Live or recorded TV shows available via the Web. > **Online movies.** Feature films available via the Web.

Zap2It. In addition, YouTube and the *Internet Movie Database* (*IMDb*) have full-length TV shows and movies that visitors can watch for free, and Amazon has thousands of TV shows and movies that *Amazon Prime* members can stream at no charge to their Kindles and other devices. A new trend is the development of TV shows that are only available online (such as the recent seasons of *Arrested Development* that are only available on Netflix and Hulu, and the recent revival of cancelled soap operas, like *All My Children* and *One Life to Live*, that are only available via the Web). Typically, online TV and online movies are streaming media, in which the video plays from the server when it is requested. Consequently, you need an Internet connection in order to view the video.

While much of the online TV, videos, and movies already mentioned are available free of charge (one exception is mobile TV, which is often available on a subscription basis), renting movies and TV shows that are delivered to your device at your request—referred to as **video-on-demand** (**VOD**)—is another option. VOD can be ordered through an individual's cable or satellite TV company or, more commonly today, through a cloud VOD provider such as *CinemaNow*, *iTunes*, *BLOCKBUSTER OnDemand*, or *Amazon Instant Video*). Rentals typically cost $4.99 or less; purchasing a movie costs around $15. In either case, the movies are streamed or downloaded to a computer, to a DVR or other device (such as a digital media player, a Blu-ray player, or a gaming console) that is connected to your TV, or to a smartphone or media tablet (refer again to Figure 8-26). Rented movies can usually be viewed only for a limited time; some services allow movies downloaded to a computer to be transferred to a portable digital media player or other mobile device during the allowable viewable period. One popular VOD option is *Netflix*, which offers unlimited video streaming to a TV, gaming console, computer, or mobile device for $8 per month.

With the arrival of today's smart TVs, TV shows and movies can now be delivered via the Internet directly to your television, along with other features such as interactive polls related to the TV show being viewed (as shown in Figure 8-5 earlier in this chapter), or *widgets* or *gadgets*—small pieces of current information such as sport scores, news headlines, or product information.

Online Gaming

Online gaming refers to games played over the Internet. Many sites—especially children's Web sites—include games for visitors to play. There are also sites whose sole purpose is hosting games that can be played online. Some of the games are designed to be played alone or with just one other person. Others, called *online multiplayer games*, are designed to be played online against many other online gamers. Online multiplayer games (such as *Doom*, *EverQuest*, *Final Fantasy*, and *City of Heroes*) are especially popular in countries, such as South Korea, that have readily available high-speed Internet connections and high levels of Internet use in general. Internet-enabled gaming consoles (such as recent versions of the PlayStation, Xbox, and Wii consoles) and portable gaming devices (such as the Sony PSP and Nintendo 3DS) that have built-in Internet connectivity can also be used for multiplayer online gaming. Online gaming is also associated quite often with *Internet addiction*—the inability to stop using the Internet or to prevent extensive use of the Internet from interfering with other aspects of one's life. Internet addiction is a growing concern and is discussed in more detail in Chapter 16.

> **TIP**
> To view streaming video without it appearing choppy, Internet service that delivers a minimum download speed of 1.5 Mbps is recommended.

> **TIP**
> According to a recent Sandvine report, 33% of peak downstream Internet traffic in the United States is attributed to Netflix.

> **TIP**
> An emerging trend is *gamification*; that is, using gaming elements (like the ability to earn points or rewards) in a non-entertainment context, such as for customer and employee engagement.

>**Video-on-demand (VOD).** The process of downloading movies and television shows, on demand, via the Web. >**Online gaming.** Playing games via the Web.

Online News, Reference, and Information

There is an abundance of news and other important information available through the Internet. The following sections discuss some of the most widely used news, reference, and information resources.

News and Reference Information

News organizations, such as television networks, newspapers, and magazines, nearly always have Web sites that are updated on a continual basis to provide access to current local and world news, as well as sports, entertainment, health, travel, politics, weather, and other news topics (see the *ABC News* Web site in Figure 8-27). Many news sites also have searchable archives to look for past articles, although some require a fee to view back articles. Once articles are displayed, they can typically be saved, printed, or sent to other individuals via e-mail. A growing trend is for newspapers and magazines to abandon print subscriptions and to provide Web-only service—primarily for cost reasons. Although some subscribers miss the print versions, there are some advantages to digital versions, such as the ability to easily search through content in some digital publications. Other online news resources include news radio programs that are broadcast over the Internet, as well as the wide variety of news video clips available through many Web sites.

Online news is commonly read on home or business computers, as well as on smartphones and media tablets. However, reading full news articles on a small device is sometimes difficult and, consequently, has resulted in the development of news apps (such as *Summly*, recently acquired by Yahoo!) that summarize the news you want to see, such as by news sources or by topics, for easier reading on your mobile device. News can also be delivered via headlines displayed on smart TVs, as well as via an app (such as the Windows 8 *News* live tile) that can be clicked to display that news story.

Reference sites are designed to provide users access to specific types of useful information. For example, reference sites can be used to generate maps (see the *MapQuest* Web site in Figure 8-27), check the weather forecast, look up the value of a home, or provide access to encyclopedias, dictionaries, ZIP Code directories, and telephone directories. One potential downside to the increased availability of online reference sites is use by criminals. For instance, one California lawmaker has introduced a bill requiring mapping sites to blur out details of schools, churches, and government buildings after being informed that some terrorists have used these maps to plan bombings and other attacks.

Ⓥ FIGURE 8-27

Online news and reference Web sites.

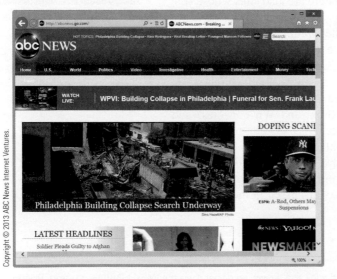

NEWS SITES
News organizations typically update their sites several times per day to provide access to the most current news and information.

REFERENCE SITES
Reference Web sites provide access to specific types of useful information, such as the maps and driving directions available via this Web site.

Portal Pages, RSS Feeds, and Podcasts

Portal Web pages are Web pages designed to be selected as a browser's home page and used as a launching pad to access other Web pages. Portal pages (such as the *MSN* page for Windows 8 shown in Figure 8-28) typically include search capabilities, news headlines, weather, and other useful content, and can often be customized by users to display their requested content. Once a portal page is customized, the specified information is displayed each time the user visits the portal page. Popular portals include *My Yahoo!*, *MSN*, and *AOL.com*.

RSS (Really Simple Syndication) is an online tool designed for delivering news articles, *blogs* (discussed shortly), and other content regularly published to a Web site. Provided the content has an associated *RSS feed*, individuals can *subscribe* (usually for free) to that feed and then the content will be delivered as it becomes available. You can subscribe to an RSS feed by clicking a *subscribe* link on the associated Web page to add the feed content to your browser *feed list*; if you are using an *RSS reader* (such as *Feedly* shown in Figure 8-29), you can typically search for new feeds using that program. To view the feed content, either select that feed from your browser's feed list (such as on the *Feeds* tab in the Favorites list in Internet Explorer) or click the appropriate link in your RSS reader. RSS readers often allow you to organize your feed into categories, as shown in Figure 8-29. In either case, as new content for the subscribed feed becomes available, it will be accessible via the feed links. In the future, we will likely see RSS feeds delivered directly to watches, refrigerators, and other consumer devices that have a display screen.

Another Web resource that can provide you with useful information is a **podcast**—a recorded audio or video file that can be downloaded via the Internet. The term *podcast* is derived from the iPod portable digital media player (the first widely used device for playing digital audio files), although podcasts today can also be listened to using a computer or mobile phone.

Podcasting (creating a podcast) enables individuals to create self-published, inexpensive Internet radio broadcasts in order to share their knowledge, express their opinions on particular subjects, or share original poems, songs, or short stories with interested individuals. Originally created and distributed by individuals, podcasts are now also being created and distributed by businesses. For instance, some commercial radio stations are making portions of their broadcasts available via podcasts, and a growing number of news sites and corporate sites now have regular podcasts available. In fact, some view podcasts as the new and improved radio because it is an easy way to listen to your favorite radio broadcasts on your own schedule. Podcasts are also used for educational purposes. Podcasts are typically uploaded to the Web on a regular basis, and RSS feeds can be used to notify subscribers when a new podcast is available.

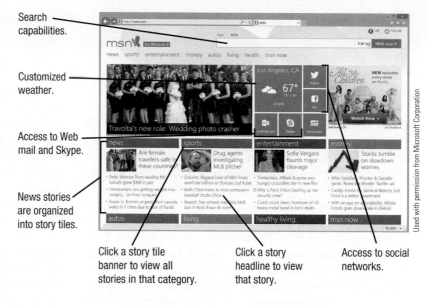

Search capabilities.

Customized weather.

Access to Web mail and Skype.

News stories are organized into story tiles.

Click a story tile banner to view all stories in that category.

Click a story headline to view that story.

Access to social networks.

Used with permission from Microsoft Corporation

FIGURE 8-28
Portal pages. Portal pages can contain a wide variety of customized news and information.

FIGURE 8-29
RSS readers. RSS feeds (right) can often be organized into categories (left).

Courtesy feedly

>**Portal Web page.** A Web page designed to be designated as a browser home page; typically can be customized to display personalized content.
>**RSS (Really Simple Syndication).** A tool used to deliver selected Web content to subscribers as the content is published to a Web site.
>**Podcast.** A recorded audio or video file that can be played or downloaded via the Web.

TREND

The Internet of Things (IoT)

One of the hottest Internet topics today is the *Internet of Things* (*IoT*). The Internet of Things refers to a world where everyday physical objects are connected to, and uniquely identifiable on, the Internet so they can communicate with other devices. Also called *Machine-to-Machine* (*M2M*) because it involves primarily machines talking directly to one another, the IoT is expected to greatly impact our lives and the way we get information and control objects. The IoT will be created by turning formerly dumb objects into smart devices (using sensors and other technology) that can send data to a system for analysis. These smart devices can range from sensors in your shoes, to smart fitness devices, to healthcare monitors, to home automation systems, to smart farm equipment, to smart freeways and traffic lights. These smart devices will communicate with each other (such as over low-power Bluetooth Smart technology) to, in theory, provide advantages such as making our lives more convenient, saving us money, and providing us with better healthcare and other services. Businesses will benefit from getting feedback from equipment (being notified when a machine in the field needs service or refilling, for instance, without an employee having to physically monitor it), being able to automate more processes, and getting faster and more accurate feedback about point-of-sale purchases.

One example of a personal application of IoT is home automation—enabling the appliances and other devices in your home (such as your alarm system, door locks, and sprinklers) to communicate with you and each other so the devices operate according to your stated preferences or observed habits, as well as be able to give you the power to control devices remotely via your smartphone, as discussed in the Chapter 7 How It Works box. Fitness systems are another example. For instance, the *Nike+ FuelBand* uses a sports-tested accelerometer to track your daily activity—including running, walking, dancing, and basketball (professional basketball player Kevin Durant is wearing a *Nike+* FuelBand in the accompanying photo)—in steps, time of day, and calories burned. It converts your activity into *NikeFuel*, a universal measurement of activity, and syncs the data with your PC or mobile device. You can set a personal goal for yourself (and monitor your progress toward that goal by viewing the lights on the edge of the band, as well as by looking at your stats on your PC or phone). You can also share your data with others via Facebook and Twitter. Other Nike+ products can be used for more sports-specific tracking, such as for running (via the *Nike+ SportWatch GPS*) or basketball (via sensors embedded in the soles of the *Nike+ Basketball* shoes). While the IoT is larger than just home automation and *wearable* technology, these two initial IoT applications may be the ones that impact individuals the most.

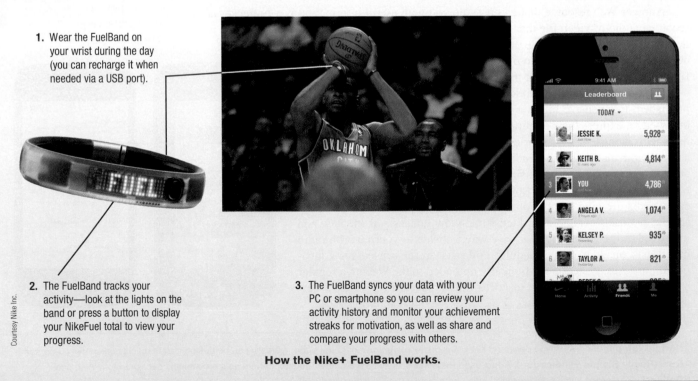

1. Wear the FuelBand on your wrist during the day (you can recharge it when needed via a USB port).

2. The FuelBand tracks your activity—look at the lights on the band or press a button to display your NikeFuel total to view your progress.

3. The FuelBand syncs your data with your PC or smartphone so you can review your activity history and monitor your achievement streaks for motivation, as well as share and compare your progress with others.

Courtesy Nike Inc.

How the Nike+ FuelBand works.

Product, Corporate, Government, and Other Information

The Web is a very useful tool for locating product and corporate information. Manufacturer and retailer Web sites often include product specifications, instruction manuals, and other information that is useful to consumers before or after they purchase a product. There are also numerous consumer review sites (such as *Epinions.com*) to help purchasers evaluate their options before buying a product online or in a physical store; many online stores (such as Amazon.com) also include customer reviews on product pages. For investors and consumers, a variety of corporate information is available online, from both company Web sites and sites (such as *Hoovers.com*) that offer free or fee-based corporate information. For a look at an emerging Internet trend that is beginning to impact both business and individuals—the *Internet of Things* (*IoT*)—see the Trend box.

⚠ FIGURE 8-30
FactCheck.org. This Web site can be used to check the accuracy of political statements.

Government information is also widely available on the Internet. Most state and federal agencies have Web sites to provide information to citizens, such as government publications, archived documents, forms, and legislative bills. You can also perform a variety of tasks, such as downloading tax forms and filing your tax returns online. In addition, many cities, counties, and states allow you to pay your car registration fees, register to vote, view property tax information, or make an appointment to renew your driver's license online.

There is also a wide variety of information available from various organizations, such as nonprofit organizations, conservation groups, political parties, and more. For instance, many sites dedicated to energy conservation and saving the environment have emerged over the past few years to bring awareness to this issue, and there are numerous online resources for learning the positions of political candidates and other information important to voters. For example, the nonpartisan *FactCheck.org* Web site shown in Figure 8-30 is dedicated to monitoring the factual accuracy of what is being said by major U.S. political candidates and elected officials and reporting it, in an attempt to reduce the level of deception and confusion in U.S. politics.

Online Education and Writing

Online education—using the Internet to facilitate learning—is a rapidly growing Internet application. The Internet can be used to deliver part or all of any educational class or program; it can also be used to supplement or support traditional education. In addition, many high school and college courses use Web content—such as online syllabi, schedules, discussion boards, podcasts, and tutorials—as required or suggested supplements. For example, the Web site that supplements this book contains

ASK THE EXPERT

IHG InterContinental Hotels Group

Nick Ayres, Manager, Social Marketing, IHG

How important is it for a business to have a social media presence today?

Today, customers across every industry and geography expect brands to meet them where they are. Social media has become table stakes for doing business in the 21st century and is no longer a "nice to have" marketing tool.

A social media footprint that spans the right social channels is an important step toward meeting these expectations. Importantly, however, this social media footprint is only the first step because its primary relevance comes in its ability to deliver a mechanism by which we can activate a robust customer engagement and dialog strategy.

Ultimately, we at IHG win when we find ways to deliver seamless, interactive, and dynamic hotel brand experiences—both on and offline—whether it's an InterContinental® resort or a city-center Holiday Inn® hotel, as that is increasingly what our customers expect and deserve. And while this is no small task, we believe success in this arena can produce a sustainable competitive advantage.

((•)) NET

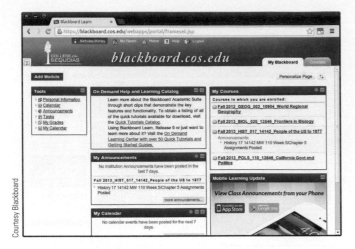

FIGURE 8-31

Blackboard. This learning management system can be used to view and complete assignments, view grades and announcements, and more.

✓ **TIP**

Some distance learning classes today use *synchronous* or *live online learning*, where students and instructors are online at the same time; this has the benefit of encouraging interaction, questions and answers, and other types of instant feedback.

✓ **TIP**

Online courses that have no tuition and are open to anyone via the Internet are sometimes referred to as *Massive Open Online Courses* (*MOOCs*).

an online study guide, online quizzes, online hands-on labs, Web links, downloadable audio and video podcasts, streaming videos, and other online resources for students taking a course that uses this textbook. There are also Web-based *learning management systems* (such as *Blackboard*, shown in Figure 8-31) that are often used to deliver course content, manage assignments and grades, and more; and the use of *student response systems*—where students use a special device or their mobile phone to respond to surveys or review questions during in-class lectures is growing. The next few sections take a look at some of the most widely used online education applications.

Web-Based Training and Distance Learning

The term **Web-based training** (**WBT**) refers to any instruction delivered via the Web. It is commonly used for employee training, as well as for delivering instruction in an educational setting. **Distance learning** occurs whenever students take classes from a location—often home or work—which is different from the one where the delivery of instruction takes place. Distance learning today typically includes Web-based training or other online learning tools (and so is also called *online learning* and *e-learning*) and is available through many high schools, colleges, and universities, as well as organizations that provide professional certifications. Distance learning can be used to learn just one task or new skill; it can also be used to complete an *online course* or an entire degree online via an accredited college or university. Typically the majority of distance learning coursework is completed over the Internet via class Web pages, YouTube videos, Webinars, podcasts, discussion groups, e-mail, and learning management systems like Blackboard (refer again to Figure 8-31), although schools might require some in-person contact, such as sessions for orientation and testing.

The biggest advantage of Web-based training and distance learning is that they are typically experienced individually and at the user's own pace. Online content for Web-based training components is frequently customized to match the pace of each individual user and can be completed at the user's convenience. Web-based content can be updated as needed and online content and activities (such as exercises, exams, and animations) typically provide immediate feedback to the student. One disadvantage is the possibility of technological problems—because students need a working device and Internet connection to access the material, they cannot participate if they have no access to a computer or an appropriate mobile device, or if their device, their Internet connection, or the Web server hosting the material goes down. Another concern among educators is the lack of face-to-face contact, and security issues—such as the difficulty in ensuring that the appropriate student is completing assignments or taking exams. Some possible solutions for this latter concern are discussed in the next section.

Online Testing

In both distance learning and traditional classes, *online testing*—which allows students to take tests via the Internet—is a growing trend. Both objective tests (such as those containing multiple choice or true/false questions) and performance-based exams (such as those given in computer classes to test student mastery of software applications) can be administered and taken online. For instance, there are *SAM* (*Skills Assessment Manager*) tests available for use in conjunction with this textbook to test both Microsoft Office software skills and computer concepts. Typically online tests are graded automatically, providing fast feedback to the students, as well as freeing up the instructor's time for other activities. One recent debate focuses on the use of computers to automatically grade essay tests, as discussed in the Balancing Act project at the end of Chapter 6.

One challenge for online testing is ensuring that an online test is taken by the appropriate individual and in an authorized manner in order to avoid cheating. Some distance learning programs require students to go physically to a testing center to take the test or to find an acceptable test proctor (such as an educator at a nearby school or a commanding officer for military personnel). Other options are using smart cards, fingerprint scans, and other means to authenticate students taking an online exam from a remote location. For instance, one secure testing solution being used at a number of schools nationwide to enable students to take online tests from their remote locations while still ensuring the integrity of the exams is the *Remote Proctor PRO* system shown in Figure 8-32. The Remote Proctor PRO device first authenticates the individual taking the test via a fingerprint scan, and then captures real-time audio and video during the exam. The device's camera points to a reflective ball, which allows it to capture a full 360-degree image of the room, and the recording is uploaded to a server so it can be viewed by the instructor from his or her location. The Remote Proctor PRO software locks down the computer so that it cannot be used for any purpose not allowed during the test (such as performing an Internet search). It also flags suspicious behavior (such as significant noises or movements) in the recording so that the instructor can review those portions of the recording to see if any unauthorized behavior (such as leaving the room or making a telephone call) occurred during the testing period.

1. The device authenticates the individual via a fingerprint scan before the exam can begin.

2. The device captures real-time audio and video during the exam.

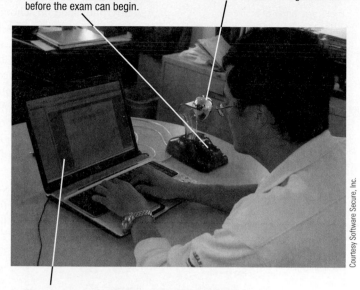

3. The computer is locked down during the exam so it can only be used for authorized activities.

FIGURE 8-32
Secure online testing.

FIGURE 8-33
Blogs. Allow individuals to post entries to an online personal journal.

Blogs, Wikis, and Other Types of Online Writing

Some types of online writing, such as e-mail, instant and text messaging, and social networking updates, were discussed earlier in this chapter. A few additional types of online writing are discussed next.

A **blog**—also called a *Web log*—is a Web page that contains short, frequently updated entries in chronological order, typically as a means of expression or communication (see the food blog shown in Figure 8-33). In essence, a blog is an online personal journal accessible to the public that is usually created and updated by one individual. Blogs are written by a wide variety of individuals—including ordinary people, as well as celebrities, writers, students, and experts on particular subjects—and can be used to post personal commentary, research updates, comments on current events, political opinions, celebrity gossip, travel diaries, television show recaps, and more.

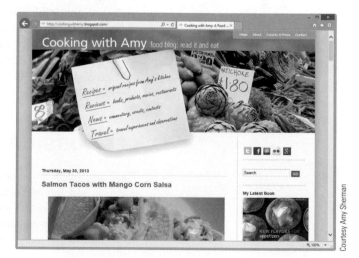

>**Blog.** A Web page that contains short, frequently updated entries in chronological order, typically by just one individual.

Blogging software, which is available via blogging sites such as Blogger.com, is often used to easily create and publish blogs and blog updates to the Web. Blogs are also frequently published on school, business, and personal Web sites. Blogs are usually updated frequently, and entries can be posted via computers, e-mail, and mobile devices. Blogs often contain text, photos, and video clips. With their increased use and audiences, bloggers and the *blogosphere* (the complete collection of blogs on the Internet) are beginning to have increasing influence on businesses, politicians, and individuals today. One new ethical issue surrounding blogging relates to bloggers who are paid to blog about certain products. Although some Web sites that match up bloggers with advertisers require that the blogger reveal that he or she receives payment for "sponsored" posts, some believe that commercializing blogging will corrupt the blogosphere. Others, however, view it as a natural evolution of word-of-mouth advertising.

Another form of online writing sometimes used for educational purposes is the **wiki**. Wikis, named for the Hawaiian phrase *wiki wiki* meaning *quick*, are a way of creating and editing collaborative Web pages quickly and easily. Similar to a blog, the content on a wiki page can be edited and republished to the Web just by pressing a Save or Submit button. However, wikis are intended to be modified by others and so are especially appropriate for collaboration, such as for class Web pages or group projects. To protect the content of a wiki from sabotage, the entire wiki or editing privileges for a wiki can be password protected.

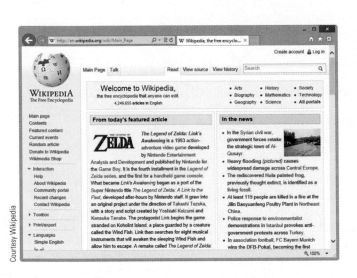

Courtesy Wikipedia

⚠ **FIGURE 8-34**

Wikis. Wikis, such as the Wikipedia collaborative online encyclopedia shown here, can be edited by any authorized individual.

One of the largest wikis is *Wikipedia* (shown in Figure 8-34), a free online encyclopedia that contains over 25 million articles written in 287 languages, is updated by volunteer contributors, and is visited by more than half a billion individuals every month. While most Wikipedia contributors edit articles in a responsible manner, there are instances erroneous information being added to Wikipedia pages intentionally. As with any resource, visitors should carefully evaluate the content of a Wikipedia article before referencing it in a report, Web page, or other document, as discussed earlier in this chapter.

An **e-portfolio**, also called an *electronic portfolio* or *digital portfolio*, is a collection of an individual's work accessible through a Web site. Today's e-portfolios are typically linked to a collection of student-related information, such as résumés, papers, projects, and other original works. Some e-portfolios are used for a single course; others are designed to be used and updated throughout a student's educational career, culminating in a comprehensive collection of information that can be used as a job-hunting tool.

CENSORSHIP AND PRIVACY ISSUES

There are many important societal issues related to the Internet. One important issue—network and Internet security—is covered in Chapter 9. Two other important issues—*censorship* and *privacy*—are discussed next, in the context of Internet use. Other societal issues—including computer security, ethics, health, and the environment—related to computer use are discussed in further detail in Chapters 15 and 16.

>**Wiki.** A collaborative Web page that is designed to be edited and republished by a variety of individuals. >**E-portfolio.** A collection of an individual's work accessible via the Web.

Censorship

The issue of Internet censorship affects all countries that have Internet access. In some countries, Internet content is filtered by the government, typically to hinder the spread of information from political opposition groups, to filter out subjects deemed offensive, or to block information from sites that could endanger national security. Increasingly, some countries are also blocking information (such as blogs and personal Web pages) from leaving the country, and have occasionally completely shut down Internet access to and from the country during political protests to stop the flow of information in and out of that country. For instance, all Internet and cell phone service was shut down in Egypt for about one week in 2011 because of mounting political unrest in that country.

In the United States, the First Amendment to the U.S. Constitution guarantees a citizen's right to free speech. This protection allows people to say things to others without fear of arrest. But how does the right to free speech relate to potentially offensive or indecent materials available over the Internet where they might be observed by children or by people who do not wish to see them? There have been some attempts in the United States and other countries to regulate Internet content—what some would view as *censorship*—in recent years, but the courts have had difficulty defining what is "patently offensive" and "indecent" as well as finding a fair balance between protection and censorship. For example, the *Communications Decency Act*, which was signed into law in 1996, made it a criminal offense to distribute patently indecent or offensive material online in order to protect children from being exposed to inappropriate Web content. In 1997, however, the Supreme Court overturned the portion of this law pertaining to indecent material on the basis of free speech, making this content legal to distribute via the Internet and protecting Web sites that host third-party content from being liable for that content.

Another example of legislation designed to protect children from inappropriate Web content is the *Children's Internet Protection Act (CIPA)*. CIPA requires public libraries and schools to implement Internet safety policies and technologies to block children's access to inappropriate Web content in order to receive certain public funds. While this law was intended to protect children, it was fought strenuously by free speech advocacy groups and some library associations on the basis that limiting access to some Internet content violates an individual's First Amendment rights to free speech. While CIPA was ruled unconstitutional by a federal court in 2002, the Supreme Court reversed the lower court decision in 2003 and ruled that the law is constitutional because the need for libraries to prevent minors from accessing obscene materials outweighs the free speech rights of library patrons and Web site publishers. However, the Court also modified the law to require a library to remove the technologies for an adult library patron at the patron's request.

One technology commonly used to conform to CIPA regulations, as well as by parents and employees, is **Internet filtering**—the act of blocking access to particular Web pages or types of Web pages. It can be used on home computers or mobile devices by individuals to protect themselves from material they would view as offensive or by parents to protect their children from material they feel is inappropriate. It is also commonly used by employers to keep employees from accessing non-work-related sites, by some ISPs and search sites to block access to potentially objectionable materials, and by many schools and libraries to control the Web content that children are able to view in order to be in compliance with CIPA. Internet filtering typically restricts access to Web pages that contain offensive language, sex/pornography, racism, drugs, or violence

>**Internet filtering.** Using a software program or browser option to block access to particular Web pages or types of Web pages.

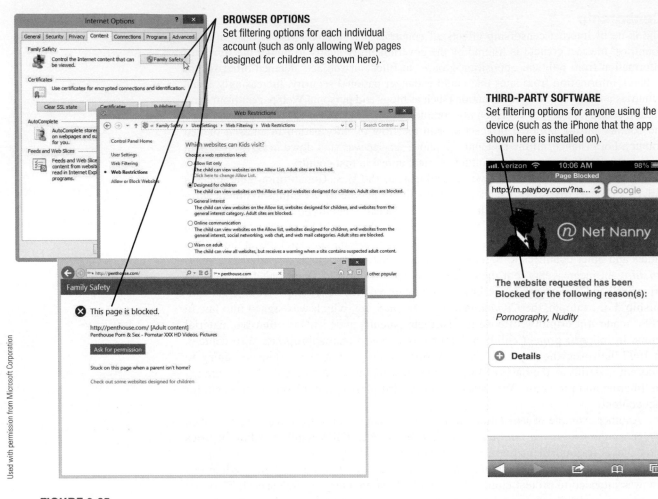

BROWSER OPTIONS
Set filtering options for each individual account (such as only allowing Web pages designed for children as shown here).

THIRD-PARTY SOFTWARE
Set filtering options for anyone using the device (such as the iPhone that the app shown here is installed on).

FIGURE 8-35
Internet filtering.

(based on either the keywords contained on each site or a database of URLs containing restricted content). It can also be used to block access to specific sites (such as social networking sites, YouTube, or eBay), as well as to restrict the total number of hours or the time of day that the Internet can be used.

Most browsers include some Internet filtering options. For instance, Internet Explorer's *Family Safety* options (see Figure 8-35) can be used to filter the Web sites displayed for specific users of a particular computer (although blocked Web sites can be viewed if the user knows the administrator password). More comprehensive Internet filtering can be obtained with stand-alone filtering programs, such as *NetNanny* (also shown in Figure 8-35) or *Safe Eyes* for parents, or *Netsweeper* for schools and businesses.

Web Browsing Privacy

Privacy, as it relates to the Internet, encompasses what information about individuals is available, how it is used, and by whom. As more and more transactions and daily activities are being performed online, there is the potential for vast amounts of private information to be collected and distributed without the individual's knowledge or permission. Therefore, it is understandable that public concern regarding privacy and the Internet is on the rise. Although personal privacy is discussed in more detail in Chapter 15, a few issues that are of special concern to Internet users regarding Web browsing privacy and e-mail privacy are discussed in the next few sections.

Cookies

Many Web pages today use **cookies**—small text files that are stored on your hard drive by a Web server—to identify return visitors and their preferences. Some cookies are *session based* (which means they are erased when you close your browser) and about half of *persistent cookies* (those that are stored on your hard drive) are *first-party cookies*. First-party cookies belong to the Web site you are visiting and are only read by that site. So, while some individuals view cookies as a potential invasion of privacy, they can provide some benefits to consumers. For example, cookies can enable a Web site to remember preferences for customized Web site content (such as on a portal page), as well as to save a shopping cart or remember a site password. Some Web sites also use cookies to keep track of which pages on their Web sites each person has visited in order to recommend products on return visits that match that person's interests. A use of cookies that is more objectionable to some is the use of *third-party cookies* (cookies placed on your hard drive by a company other than the one associated with the Web page that you are viewing—typically a Web advertising company). Third-party cookies target advertisements to Web site visitors based on their activities on the site (such as products viewed or advertisements clicked).

The information stored in a cookie file typically includes the name of the cookie, its expiration date, and the domain that the cookie belongs to. In addition, a cookie contains either personal information that you have entered while visiting the Web site or an ID number assigned by the Web site that allows the Web site's server to retrieve your personal information from its database. Such a database can contain two types of information: *personally identifiable information* (*PII*) and *non-personally identifiable information* (*Non-PII*). Personally identifiable information is connected with a specific user's identity—such as his or her name and address—and is typically given during the process of ordering goods or services. Non-personally identifiable information is anonymous data—such as which product pages were viewed or which advertisements located on the site were clicked—that is not directly associated with the visitor's name or another personally identifiable characteristic.

Cookies stored on your computer's hard drive can be looked at, if desired, although sometimes deciphering the information contained in a cookie file is difficult. Internet Explorer users can view and/or delete cookies and other temporary files by using Internet Explorer's Internet Options dialog box (see Figure 8-36) and selecting *Delete* in the *Browsing history* section on the General tab to delete all temporary files or *Settings* to have the option to view cookie files. The Privacy tab in this dialog box (also shown in Figure 8-36) can be used to

FIGURE 8-36
Browser cookie management in Internet Explorer.

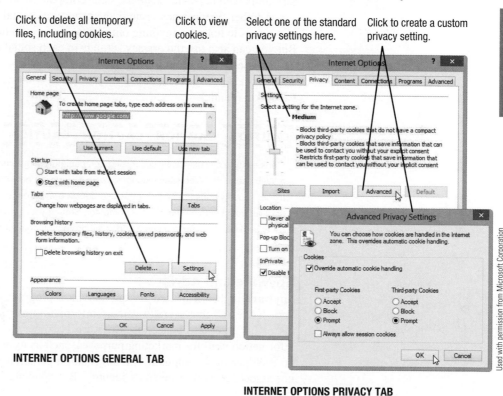

Click to delete all temporary files, including cookies.

Click to view cookies.

Select one of the standard privacy settings here.

Click to create a custom privacy setting.

INTERNET OPTIONS GENERAL TAB

INTERNET OPTIONS PRIVACY TAB

Used with permission from Microsoft Corporation

>**Cookie.** A small file stored on a user's hard drive by a Web server; commonly used to identify personal preferences and settings for that user.

Web sites requesting cookie use.

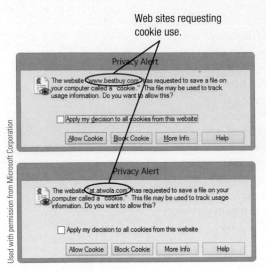

FIGURE 8-37

Cookie prompts.

After selecting the "Prompt" option in the cookie settings, you will have to accept or reject each cookie request.

specify which type of cookies (if any) are allowed to be used, such as permitting the use of regular cookies, but not third-party cookies or cookies using personally identifiable information. A growing trend (such as with Apple's Safari browser) is to not allow third-party cookies at all.

Turning off cookies entirely might make some features—such as a shopping cart—on some Web sites inoperable. The *Medium High* privacy option in Internet Explorer is a widely used setting because it allows the use of regular cookies but blocks many types of third-party cookies. Users who want more control over their cookies can choose to accept or decline cookies as they are encountered in most browsers. Although this option interrupts your Web surfing almost continually, it is interesting to see the cookies generated from each individual Web site. For example, the two cookie prompts shown in Figure 8-37 were generated while visiting the BestBuy.com Web site. Although the top cookie request is from the BestBuy.com Web site directly, the other is a third-party cookie from an online marketing company. An alternative to managing cookies within your browser is using third-party *cookie management software*.

Another alternative is the *private browsing* option available with many Web browsers, including Internet Explorer, Chrome, and Safari. As discussed more in Chapter 15, this option allows you to browse the Web without leaving any history (including browsing history, form data, cookies, usernames, and passwords) on the computer you are using. Private browsing is useful for individuals using school, library, or other public computers to visit password-protected sites, research medical information, or perform other tasks that the user may prefer to keep private. Individuals using a computer to shop for gift or other surprises for family members who share the same computer may find the feature useful, as well.

Another Web privacy issue is the privacy of social media data. The best preventative measure is to not post anything online that you would not want the general public to view. But you can also use the privacy settings in each social network that you utilize to specify who can see what in your profile. For instance, Facebook allows you to specify what content can be seen by the "Public" (anyone) and what can only be seen by "Friends" (your Facebook friends).

CAUTION CAUTION CAUTION CAUTION CAUTION CAUTION CAUT

Cookies (typically placed by advertising companies) that attempt to track your activities across a Web site or the Web sites belonging to an advertising network are referred to as *tracking cookies*. If your security software includes tracking cookie protection, be sure it is enabled to avoid these cookies from being stored on your computer. Setting your browser's privacy settings to block third-party cookies can offer you some additional protection against tracking cookies.

Spyware and Adware

Spyware is the term used for any software program that is installed without the user's knowledge and that secretly gathers information about the user and transmits it through his or her Internet connection. Spyware is sometimes used to provide advertisers with information used for marketing purposes, such as to help select advertisements to display on each person's computer. The information gathered by the spyware software is usually not associated with a person's identity. But spyware is a concern for privacy advocates

> **Spyware.** A software program that is installed without the user's permission and that secretly gathers information to be sent to others.

because it is typically installed without a user's direct knowledge (such as at the same time another program is installed, often when a program is downloaded from a Web site or a P2P service) and conveys information about a user's Internet activities. Spyware can also be used by criminals to retrieve personal data stored on your computer for use in criminal activities, as discussed in more detail in Chapter 9.

Unfortunately, spyware use is on the rise and can affect the performance of a computer (such as slowing it down or causing it to work improperly), in addition to its potential security risks. And the problem will likely become worse before it gets any better. Some spyware programs—sometimes referred to as *stealthware*—are getting more aggressive, such as delivering ads regardless of the activity you are doing on your computer, changing your browser home page or otherwise altering your browser settings (referred to as *browser hijacking*), and performing other annoying actions. The worst spyware programs rewrite your computer's main instructions—such as the Windows registry—to change your browser settings back to the hijacked settings each time you reboot your computer, undoing any changes you may have made to your browser settings.

A related type of software is *adware*, which is free or low-cost software that is supported by on-screen advertising. Many free programs that can be downloaded from the Internet include some type of adware, which results in on-screen advertising. The difference between spyware and adware is that adware typically does not gather information and relay it to others via the Internet (although it can), and it is not installed without the user's consent. Adware might, however, be installed without the user's direct knowledge because many users do not read licensing agreements before clicking OK to install a new program. When this occurs with a program that contains adware, the adware components are installed without the user's direct knowledge.

Both spyware and adware can be annoying and use up valuable system resources, in addition to revealing data about individuals. As discussed in detail in Chapter 9, *firewalls* and *antispyware programs* can be used to protect against spyware.

E-Mail Privacy

Many people mistakenly believe that the e-mail they send and receive is private and will never be read by anyone other than the intended recipient. Because it is transmitted over public media, however, only *encrypted* (electronically scrambled) e-mail can be transmitted safely, as discussed in Chapter 9. Although unlikely to happen to your personal e-mail, *nonencrypted* e-mail can be intercepted and read by someone else. Consequently, from a privacy standpoint, a nonencrypted e-mail message should be viewed more like a postcard than a letter (see Figure 8-38).

It is also important to realize that your employer and your ISP have access to the e-mail you send through those organizations. Businesses and ISPs typically archive (keep copies of) e-mail messages that travel through their servers and are required to comply with subpoenas from law enforcement agencies for archived e-mail messages.

FIGURE 8-38
You cannot assume e-mail messages are private, unless they are encrypted.

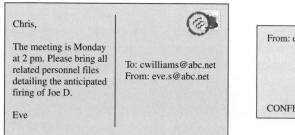

Chris,

The meeting is Monday at 2 pm. Please bring all related personnel files detailing the anticipated firing of Joe D.

Eve

To: cwilliams@abc.net
From: eve.s@abc.net

REGULAR (NONENCRYPTED E-MAIL) = POSTCARD

From: eve.s@abc.net

To: cwilliams@abc.net

CONFIDENTIAL

ENCRYPTED E-MAIL = SEALED LETTER

SUMMARY

EVOLUTION OF THE INTERNET

The origin of the **Internet**—a worldwide collection of interconnected networks that is accessed by millions of people daily—dates back to the late 1960s. At its start and throughout its early years, the Internet was called **ARPANET**. It was not until the development of the **World Wide Web** (**WWW**) that public interest in the Internet began to soar. Most companies have Web sites today and consider the Web to be an indispensable business tool. While the Web is a very important and widely used Internet resource, it is not the only one. Over the years, *protocols* have been developed to download files, send e-mail messages, and perform other tasks, in addition to using Web pages. Today, the term *Internet* has become a household word and, in many ways, has redefined how people think about computers and communications. The next significant improvement to the Internet infrastructure may be the result of projects such as *Internet2*.

The Internet community is made up of individual *users*; companies, such as **Internet service providers (ISPs)**, **Internet content providers**, **application service providers** (**ASPs**), *infrastructure companies*, and a variety of software and hardware companies; the government; and other organizations. Virtually anyone with a computer with communications capability can be part of the Internet, either as a user or supplier of information or services. **Web services** are self-contained business functions that operate over the Internet.

Because the Internet is so unique in the history of the world—and it remains a relatively new and ever-changing phenomenon—several widespread myths about it have surfaced. Three such myths are that the Internet is free, that it is controlled by some central body, and that it is synonymous with the World Wide Web.

GETTING SET UP TO USE THE INTERNET

Most Internet connections today are **direct connections** (always connected to the Internet), though some are **dial-up connections** (which need to dial up and connect to the Internet to provide access). Dial-up connections are typically **conventional dial-up Internet access**; common types of direct Internet connections include **cable**, **DSL (Digital Subscriber Line)**, **satellite**, **fixed wireless**, **mobile wireless**, and **broadband over fiber** (**BoF**)—also called **fiber-to-the-premises** (**FTTP**)—**Internet access**. Individuals can also connect to the Internet via a **Wi-Fi hotspot**. When preparing to become connected to the Internet, you need to decide which type of device (personal computer or mobile phone, for instance), which type of Internet connection, and which specific Internet service provider to use. Once all these decisions are made, you can acquire the proper hardware and software and set up your system for Internet access.

SEARCHING THE INTERNET

Search sites are Web sites that enable users to search for and find information on the Internet. They typically locate pages using a **keyword search** (in which the user specifies **keywords** for the desired information)—a **search engine** retrieves the list of matching Web pages from a database. A **directory search** (in which the user selects categories corresponding to the desired information) is another possibility. Search site databases are generally maintained by automated *spider* programs.

There are a variety of search strategies that can be used, including typing phrases instead of single keywords; using *Boolean operators*; trying the search at multiple search sites; and using *synonyms*, *variant word forms*, *wildcards*, and *field searches*. Once a list of links to Web pages matching the search criteria is displayed, the hits need to be evaluated for their relevancy. If the information found on a Web page is used in a paper, report, or other original document, the source should be credited appropriately.

BEYOND BROWSING AND E-MAIL

The Internet can be used for many different types of activities in addition to basic Web browsing and e-mail exchange. Common types of online communications include **instant messaging** or **IM** (also commonly referred to as **chat**) and **text messaging** (sending real-time typed messages via a computer or mobile phone, respectively), **Twittering** (sending short status updates via Twitter), **forums** (online locations where people post messages on a particular topic for others to read and respond to), **Web conferences** (real-time meetings taking place via the Web that typically use video cameras and microphones to enable participants to see and hear each other), and **Webinars** (seminars presented over the Web). **Social networking sites** (part of the collection of **social media** available today) also allow the members of an online community to communicate and exchange information. **Voice over Internet Protocol** (**VoIP**) refers to making voice telephone calls over the Internet.

Common Web activities for individuals include a variety of consumer *e-commerce* activities, such as **online shopping**, **online auctions**, **online banking**, and **online investing**. When performing any type of financial transaction over the Internet, it is very important to use only *secure* Web pages.

Online entertainment applications include **online gaming**, downloading music files and other types of **online music**, and **online TV**, **online movies**, and other types of **online video**. Selecting and receiving TV shows and movies via the Web is called **video-on-demand** (**VOD**). A wide variety of news, reference, government, product, and corporate information are available via the Web as well. News, reference, and search tools are commonly found on **portal Web pages**; **RSS** (**Really Simple Syndication**) feeds can be used to deliver current news, **podcasts**, and other Web content to individuals as it becomes available.

Online education options include **Web-based training** (**WBT**) and **distance learning**. *Online testing* can be used for both objective and performance-based exams and can be secured by a variety of means. Online writing includes **blogs** (Web pages that contain frequently updated entries by individuals), **wikis** (Web pages designed to be created and edited by multiple individuals), and **e-portfolios** (collections of an individual's work).

CENSORSHIP AND PRIVACY ISSUES

Among the most important societal issues relating to the Internet are *censorship* and *privacy*. Web content is not censored as a whole, but **Internet filtering** can be used by parents, employers, educators, and anyone wishing to prevent access to sites they deem objectionable on computers for which they have control. *Privacy* is a big concern for individuals, particularly as it relates to their Web activity. **Cookies** are typically used by Web sites to save customized settings for that site and can also be used for advertising purposes. Another item of possible concern is **spyware** (software installed without the user's permission that sends information to others). Unless an e-mail message is *encrypted*, it should not be assumed to be completely private.

Chapter Objective 5:
List several ways to communicate over the Internet, in addition to e-mail.

Chapter Objective 6:
List several useful activities that can be performed via the Web.

NET

Chapter Objective 7:
Discuss censorship and privacy and how they are related to Internet use.

REVIEW ACTIVITIES

KEY TERM MATCHING

a. cookie

b. dial-up connection

c. direct connection

d. distance learning

e. Internet

f. keyword

g. podcast

h. search engine

i. social media

j. World Wide Web (WWW)

Instructions: Match each key term on the left with the definition on the right that best describes it.

1. _____ A learning environment in which the student is physically located away from the instructor and other students; commonly, instruction and communications take place via the Web.

2. _____ A type of Internet connection in which the computer or other device is connected to the Internet continually.

3. _____ A small file stored on a user's hard drive by a Web server; commonly used to identify personal preferences and settings for that user.

4. _____ A software program used by a search site to retrieve matching Web pages from a search database.

5. _____ A type of Internet connection in which the computer or other device must dial up and connect to a service provider's computer via telephone lines before being connected to the Internet.

6. _____ A recorded audio or video file that can be played or downloaded via the Web.

7. _____ A word typed in a search box on a search site to locate information on the Internet.

8. _____ The collection of social networking sites and other communications channels used to transmit or share information with a broad audience.

9. _____ The collection of Web pages available through the Internet.

10. _____ The largest and most well-known computer network, linking millions of computers all over the world.

SELF-QUIZ

Instructions: Circle **T** if the statement is true, **F** if the statement is false, or write the best answer in the space provided. **Answers for the self-quiz are located in the References and Resources Guide at the end of the book**.

1. **T F** When the Internet was first developed, it was called Mosaic.

2. **T F** On the Internet, an *access provider* and a *content provider* are essentially the same thing.

3. **T F** With a direct connection, you need only open your browser to start your Internet session.

4. **T F** A Wi-Fi hotspot is used to provide Internet access to individuals via a wireless connection.

5. **T F** A Webinar is a Web site designed to allow individuals to easily create and publish blogs.

6. _____ is a type of always-on broadband Internet service that transmits data over standard telephone lines but does not tie up your phone line.

7. With a(n) _____ search, keywords are typed into the search box; with a(n) _____ search, users select categories to find matching Web pages.

8. A(n) _____ is a Web site (such as Facebook) designed to enable a community of individuals to communicate and exchange information.

9. With a(n) _____ , people bid on products over the Internet, and the highest bidder purchases the item.

10. Match each Internet application to its possible situation, and write the corresponding number in the blank to the left of each situation.

   a. _____ To communicate with a friend in a different state.

   b. _____ To pay only as much as you specify for an item purchased through the Internet.

   c. _____ To pay a bill without writing a check.

   d. _____ To find Web pages containing information about growing your own Bonsai trees.

   1. Online banking
   2. E-mail
   3. Internet searching
   4. Online auction

EXERCISES

1. Match each type of Internet access to its description, and write the corresponding number in the blank to the left of each description.

   a. _____ A common type of home broadband connection; does not use standard phone lines.

   b. _____ Provides access to the Internet via a very fast fiber-optic network.

   c. _____ Accesses the Internet via standard phone lines and ties up your phone; the maximum speed is 56 Kbps.

   1. Conventional dial-up
   2. BoF
   3. Cable

2. What would each of the following searches look for?

   a. hot AND dogs _____

   b. snorkel* _____

   c. text: "Internet privacy" domain:*.gov _____

3. List three different sets of keywords that could be used to search for information on how to maintain a trumpet.

4. Explain the difference between a blog, a wiki, and a podcast.

5. List one advantage and one disadvantage of the use of Web site cookies.

DISCUSSION QUESTIONS

1. Twittering became virtually an overnight sensation, but some question its usefulness. Do you want to know the routine activities your friends (or other individuals you choose to follow) are doing during the day? Is it useful information to tweet that your bus is stuck in traffic or having a bad day? Do you follow anyone on Twitter or tweet regularly? Why or why not? Because Twitter updates have to be very short, some may think that twittering on the job does not take up enough time to be a concern, but what about the distraction factor? Should employers allow employees to use Twitter, Facebook, and other popular online activities during work hours? Why or why not?

2. Some courtrooms today are becoming high-tech, such as using videoconferencing systems to allow defendants and witnesses to participate in proceedings from remote locations. Allowing defendants to participate remotely from the jail facility saves travel time and expense, as well as eliminates any risk of flight. Remote testimony from witnesses can save both time and money. But, could having defendants and witnesses participate remotely affect the jury's perspective? If the videoconference takes place via the Internet, can it be assured that proceedings are confidential? Do you think the benefits of these systems outweigh any potential disadvantages?

NET

PROJECTS

HOT TOPICS

1. **Social Network Addiction** As discussed in the chapter, social networks (such as Facebook and Google+) are very popular with individuals. However, it has become apparent recently that some individuals are moving from casual social networking use to compulsive or addictive behavior.

    For this project, investigate either Facebook addiction or Internet addiction. How common is it? What are some of the warning signs? Is there an actual medical disorder associated with it? If so, what is it and how is it treated? Find one example in a news or journal article of a person who was "addicted" to using a social networking site or other online activity—why was their behavior considered addictive? Were they able to modify their behavior? Have you ever been concerned about becoming addicted to any Internet activities? At the conclusion of your research, prepare a one-page summary of your findings and opinions and submit it to your instructor.

SHORT ANSWER/ RESEARCH

2. **Online Travel Planning** Planning and booking travel arrangements online is a very popular Internet activity today and there are a number of sites that can be used.

    For this project, review two popular travel sites, such as Expedia.com and Travelocity.com, to see what services they offer and how easy it is to locate the information needed to plan and book a flight via those sites. Select a destination and use one of the sites to obtain a quote for a particular flight on a particular day. Next, go to the Web site for the airline of the flight and use the site to obtain a quote for the same flight. Is there a difference in price or flight availability? Could you make a reservation online through both sites? Would you feel comfortable booking an entire vacation yourself online, or are there services that a travel agent could provide that you feel would be beneficial? Do you think these sites are most appropriate for making business travel plans or vacation plans, or are they suited to both? At the conclusion of your research, prepare a one-page summary of your findings and submit it to your instructor.

HANDS ON

3. **Web Searching** Search sites can be used to find Web pages containing specific information, and there are strategies that can be used to make Web searching an efficient and useful experience.

    For this project, go to the Google search site and perform the following searches, then submit your results and printouts to your instructor. (Note: Some of the answers will vary from student to student.)

    a. Search for *rules*. How many pages were found? What is the name of the first page in the list of hits? Next, search for *backgammon rules*. How many pages were found? Use the hits to find a picture of how a backgammon board is initially set up, then, print that page.

    b. Search to find a recipe for Buffalo Chicken Wings; a map of where your house, apartment, or dorm is located; and the ZIP Code for 200 N. Elm Street, Hinsdale, IL and print the pages containing this information.

    c. Go to the Advanced Search option. Use the form fields to perform a search for Web pages that contain all of the words *hiking trails Sierras*, do not contain the word *horse*, and have the domain *.gov*. After the hits are displayed, record the actual search phrase that is listed in the search box along with the name and URL of the first page displayed in the list of hits.

4. **Paid Bloggers** Blogs are traditionally online personal journals where the blogger expresses his or her opinion on desired topics. Unlike professional journalists, bloggers typically post because they want to, not because they have been hired to do so. However, as discussed in the chapter, bloggers are increasingly being paid or "sponsored" to blog. Is this ethical? If a blogger is paid to post his or her honest opinion about a product or service, does that lessen the credibility of that post? Does it change your opinion if the blogger reveals that it is a sponsored blog? If you based a purchase on a review posted in a blog that you later found out was sponsored, would you feel misled? How, if at all, do sponsored posts affect the blogosphere as a whole?

   For this project, form an opinion about the ethical ramifications of paid blogging and be prepared to discuss your position (in class, via an online class discussion group, in a class chat room, or via a class blog, depending on your instructor's directions). You may also be asked to write a short paper expressing your opinion.

ETHICS IN ACTION

5. **Advanced Search** Most search sites today include advanced features to help you more efficiently find the information you are searching for.

   For this project, select one search site (such as Google or Bing) and research the advanced search options the site supports. How does the advanced search work—do you have to type special symbols or is there a form that can be used? What operators does the site support? Are you able to search for only pages that were recently updated? Are you able to find pages that link to a specified Web page? Can you search for specified file types, such as images or videos? Do you find the advanced search options for your selected site useful? Share your findings and opinions with the class in the form of a short presentation. The presentation should not exceed 10 minutes and should make use of one or more presentation aids, such as a whiteboard, handouts, or a computer-based slide presentation (your instructor may provide additional requirements). You may also be asked to submit a summary of the presentation to your instructor.

PRESENTATION/ DEMONSTRATION

6. **In a Cyber War, Is it Ethical to Kill Enemy Hackers?** Cyber wars are heating up. Foreign governments (particularly China) are continually being accused of trying to hack into the computer systems of both the U.S. government and high-tech companies. Cybersecurity is a very important issue today and is a source of ongoing discussion between countries such as the United States and China. For instance, cybersecurity was high on the agenda for the meeting between President Obama and Chinese President Xi Jinping in 2013 following a government report that found nearly 40 Pentagon weapons programs and almost 30 other defense technologies were compromised by cyber intrusions from China. And, earlier that year, a cybersecurity firm linked a secret Chinese military unit to years of cyberattacks against U.S. companies. While China's government denies any involvement and the countries are not officially at war, how do actual wars and cyber wars differ? Is a country hacking into another country's computer systems an act of war? If so, should those hackers be fair targets for retaliation? Just as the military is permitted to kill enemy soldiers attacking its country or its citizens, should they also kill enemy hackers? Is cyber warfare any less of an actual conflict than ground or air-based physical combat? What about computer programmers that control the drones and missles used in combat—are they fair targets?

   Pick a side on this issue, form an opinion and gather supporting evidence, and be prepared to discuss and defend your position in a classroom debate or in a 1–2 page paper, depending on your instructor's directions.

BALANCING ACT

NET

chapter 9

Network and Internet Security

After completing this chapter, you will be able to do the following:

1. Explain why computer users should be concerned about network and Internet security.

2. List several examples of unauthorized access and unauthorized use.

3. Explain several ways to protect against unauthorized access and unauthorized use, including access control systems, firewalls, and encryption.

4. Provide several examples of computer sabotage.

5. List how individuals and businesses can protect against computer sabotage.

6. Discuss online theft, identity theft, spoofing, phishing, and other types of dot cons.

7. Detail steps an individual can take to protect against online theft, identity theft, spoofing, phishing, and other types of dot cons.

8. Identify personal safety risks associated with Internet use.

9. List steps individuals can take to safeguard their personal safety when using the Internet.

10. Discuss the current state of network and Internet security legislation.

OVERVIEW

As discussed in the last few chapters, networks and the Internet help many of us be more efficient and effective workers, as well as add convenience and enjoyment to our personal lives. However, there is a downside, as well. The widespread use of home and business networks and the Internet increases the risk of unauthorized computer access, theft, fraud, and other types of computer crime. In addition, the vast amount of business and personal data stored on computers accessible via company networks and the Internet increases the chances of data loss due to crime or employee errors. Some online activities can even put your personal safety at risk, if you are not careful.

This chapter looks at a variety of security concerns stemming from the use of computer networks and the Internet in our society, including unauthorized access and use, computer viruses and other types of sabotage, and online theft and fraud. Safeguards for each of these concerns are also covered, with an explanation of precautions that can be taken to reduce the chance that these security problems will happen to you. Personal safety issues related to the Internet are also discussed, and the chapter closes with a look at legislation related to network and Internet security. ∎

WHY BE CONCERNED ABOUT NETWORK AND INTERNET SECURITY?

From a *computer virus* making your computer function abnormally, to a *hacker* using your personal information to make fraudulent purchases, to someone harassing you online in a discussion group, a variety of security concerns related to computer networks and the Internet exist. Many Internet security concerns today can be categorized as **computer crimes**. Computer crime—sometimes referred to as *cybercrime*—includes any illegal act involving a computer. Many computer crimes today are committed using the Internet or another computer network and include theft of financial assets or information, manipulating data (such as grades or account information), and acts of sabotage (such as releasing a computer virus or shutting down a Web server). Cybercrime is an important security concern today. It is a multibillion-dollar business that is often performed by seasoned criminals. In fact, according to the FBI, organized crime organizations in many countries are increasingly turning to computer crime to target millions of potential victims easily, and *phishing attacks* and other *Internet scams* (discussed shortly) are expected to increase in reaction to the recent troubled economy. These and other computer crimes that are carried out via the Internet or another computer network are discussed in this chapter. Other types of computer crime (such as using a computer to create counterfeit currency or make illegal copies of a DVD) are covered in Chapter 15.

> **TIP**
>
> According to a recent Norton Cybercrime Report, the total cost of cybercrime is now estimated to be $110 billion per year worldwide and nearly $21 billion in the United States alone with an average loss of $290 per person.

>**Computer crime.** Any illegal act involving a computer.

With some security concerns, such as when a spyware program changes your browser's home page, the consequence may be just an annoyance. In other cases, such as when someone steals your identity and purchases items using your name and credit card number, the consequences are much more serious. And, with the growing use of wireless networks, social media, cloud computing, mobile computing, and individuals accessing company networks remotely—paired with an increasing number of security and privacy regulations that businesses need to comply with—network and Internet security has never been more important. Consequently, all computer users should be aware of the security concerns surrounding computer network and Internet use, and they should take appropriate precautions. The most common types of security risks related to network and Internet use, along with some corresponding precautions, are discussed throughout this chapter.

UNAUTHORIZED ACCESS AND UNAUTHORIZED USE

Unauthorized access occurs whenever an individual gains access to a computer, mobile device, network, file, or other resource without permission—typically by *hacking* into the resource. **Unauthorized use** involves using a computing resource for unauthorized activities. Often, they happen at the same time, but unauthorized use can occur when a user is authorized to access a particular computer or network but is not authorized for the particular activity the user performs. For instance, while a student may be authorized to access the Internet via a campus computer lab, some use—such as viewing pornography—would likely be deemed off-limits. If so, viewing that content from a school computer would be considered unauthorized use. For employees of some companies, checking personal e-mail or visiting personal Facebook pages at work might be classified as unauthorized use.

FIGURE 9-1
A sample code of conduct.

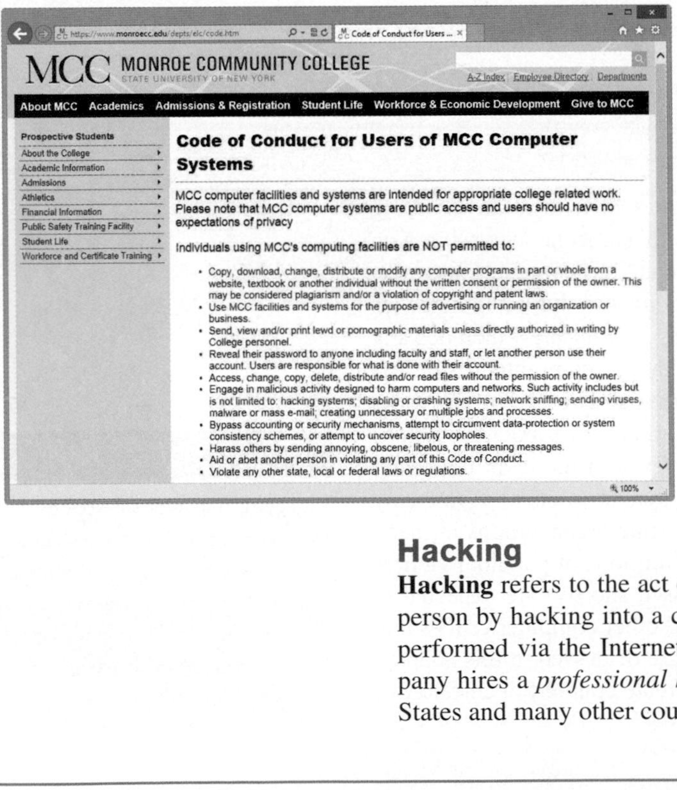

Unauthorized access and many types of unauthorized use are criminal offenses in the United States and many other countries. They can be committed by both *insiders* (people who work for the company whose computers are being accessed) and *outsiders* (people who do not work for that company). Whether or not a specific act constitutes unauthorized use or is illegal depends on the circumstances, as well as the specific company or institution involved. To explain acceptable computer use to their employees, students, or other users, many organizations and educational institutions publish guidelines for behavior, often called *codes of conduct* (see Figure 9-1). Codes of conduct typically address prohibited activities, such as playing games, installing personal software, violating copyright laws, causing harm to computers or the network, and snooping in other people's files.

Hacking

Hacking refers to the act of breaking into a computer or network. It can be performed in person by hacking into a computer the *hacker* has physical access to, but it is more often performed via the Internet or another network. Unless authorized (such as when a company hires a *professional hacker* to test the security of its system), hacking in the United States and many other countries is a crime.

>**Unauthorized access.** Gaining access to a computer, mobile device, network, file, or other resource without permission. >**Unauthorized use.** Using a computing resource for unapproved activities. >**Hacking.** Using a computer to break into another computer system.

Typically, the motivation for hacking is to steal data, sabotage a computer system, or perform some other type of illegal act. In particular, the theft of consumer data (such as credit card numbers) has increased dramatically over the past several years—more than 1,600 data breaches were discovered in 2012. Some of the most notable recent breaches include the 2013 theft of prepaid debit card numbers, which were then programmed with large balances and used in simultaneous ATM withdrawals by a gang of hackers and which resulted in a $45 million global heist; the 2012 theft of 3.6 million Social Security numbers, along with names, addresses, credit card numbers, and other sensitive information, from the South Carolina Department of Revenue computer system; and the 2012 *Zappos.com* data breach, which resulted in hackers gaining access to the names, addresses, phone numbers, and the last four digits of credit card numbers of 24 million customers. Another growing trend is to hack into a computer and "hijack" it for use in an illegal or unethical act, such as taking over an individual's computer, spying via a Web cam, generating spam, or hosting pornographic Web sites. Hackers are also increasingly aiming attacks at very specific individuals, such as product designers and other individuals who have access to valuable corporate data.

In addition to being a threat to individuals and businesses, hacking is also considered a very serious threat to national security in the United States. The increased number of systems that are controlled by computers and are connected to the Internet, along with the continually improving abilities of hackers, has led to an increased risk of *cyberterrorism*—where terrorists launch attacks via the Internet. Current concerns include attacks by individual terrorists, as well as by other countries, against the computers controlling vital systems; vital systems include the nation's power grids, banks, and water filtration facilities, as well as computers related to national defense, the airlines, and the stock market. In fact, President Obama and Chinese President Xi Jinping began serious discussion about cybersecurity in 2013 following a government report that found nearly 40 Pentagon weapons programs and almost 30 other defense technologies were compromised by cyber intrusions from China. President Obama has declared that "cyber threat is one of the most serious economic and national security challenges we face as a nation."

Today, hackers often gain access via a wireless network. This is because wireless networks are widely used and they are easier to hack into than wired networks. As discussed in Chapter 7, it is possible to gain access to a wireless network just by being within range (about 100 to 300 feet, depending on the Wi-Fi standard being used) of a wireless access point, unless the access point is sufficiently protected. Although security features are built into wireless routers and other networking hardware, they are typically not enabled by default. As a result, many wireless networks belonging to businesses and individuals are left unsecured. Securing a Wi-Fi network is discussed shortly.

ASK THE EXPERT

Courtesy ACM

Moshe Vardi, Rice University, Co-Chair of the ACM Globalization and Offshoring of Software Taskforce

Is there a national security risk to outsourcing/ offshoring software development?

Offshoring magnifies existing risks and creates new and often poorly understood threats. When businesses offshore work, they increase not only their own business-related risks (e.g., intellectual property theft) but also risks to national security and to individuals' privacy. While it is unlikely these risks will deter the growth of offshoring, businesses and nations should employ strategies to mitigate the risks. Businesses have a clear incentive to manage these new risks to suit their own interests, but nations and individuals often have little awareness of the exposures created. For example, many commercial off-the-shelf (COTS) systems are developed offshore, making it extremely difficult for buyers to understand all of the source and application code in the systems. This creates the possibility that a hostile nation or nongovernmental hostile agent (such as a terrorist or criminal) could compromise these systems. Individuals are also often exposed to loss of privacy or identity theft due to the number of business processes being offshored today and managed under laws that are much less restrictive than in most developed countries.

NET

War Driving and Wi-Fi Piggybacking

Unauthorized use of a Wi-Fi network is called **war driving** or **Wi-Fi piggybacking**, depending on the location of the hacker at the time. War driving typically involves driving in a car with a portable device looking for unsecured Wi-Fi networks to connect to. Wi-Fi piggybacking refers to accessing someone else's unsecured Wi-Fi network from the hacker's current location (such as inside his or her home, outside a Wi-Fi hotspot location, or near a local business). Both war driving and Wi-Fi piggybacking are ethically—if not legally—questionable acts. They can also lead to illegal behavior, such as individuals deciding to use data (credit card numbers, for instance) they run across while war driving for fraudulent purposes, as was the case with two men who illegally accessed a Lowe's wireless network during a war drive and later decided to steal credit card numbers via that network. War driving and Wi-Fi piggybacking can also have security risks, both for the hacker and the owner of the Wi-Fi network that is being used. For instance, they both risk the introduction of computer viruses (either intentionally or unintentionally) and unauthorized access of the data located on their computers. In addition, the owner may experience reduced performance or even the cancellation of his or her Internet service if the ISP limits bandwidth or the number of computers allowed to use a single Internet connection.

In some countries, such as the UK, the laws are clear that unauthorized access of a Wi-Fi connection is illegal. In the United States, federal law is not as clear, although some states (such as Michigan) have made using a Wi-Fi connection without permission illegal. In fact, a Michigan man was found guilty, fined, and sentenced to community service in 2007 for using the free Wi-Fi service offered to customers at a local café because he was using the service from his parked car located on the street outside the café to check his e-mail on a regular basis. And, at the time of this writing, Google was being accused, via a privacy class-action lawsuit, of collecting and storing private data (including e-mails, usernames, passwords, and documents) from unsecured home Wi-Fi networks in the United States and Europe while capturing data for its Street View mapping system.

Advocates of war driving and Wi-Fi piggybacking state that, unless individuals or businesses protect their access points, they are welcoming others to use them. Critics compare that logic to that of an unlocked front door—you cannot legally enter a home just because the front door is unlocked. Some wireless network owners do leave their access points unsecured on purpose and some communities are creating a collection of wireless access points to provide wireless Internet access to everyone in that community. However, it is difficult—if not impossible—to tell if an unsecured network is that way intentionally, unless the hotspot information states that it is a free public Wi-Fi hotspot. To help you locate public Wi-Fi hotspots, a number of services are available, such as browser-based mapping applications and smartphone apps that identify free and fee-based hotspots for a specific geographical location (see the Wi-Fi Finder app in Figure 9-2). Mobile apps have the advantage of automatically determining your geographical location to display information about hotspots in your current geographical area.

Some feel the ethical distinction of using an unsecured wireless network is determined by the amount of use, believing that it is acceptable to borrow someone's Internet connection to do a quick e-mail check or Google search, but that continually using a neighbor's Internet connection to avoid paying for your own is crossing over the line. Others feel that allowing outsiders to share an Internet connection is acceptable use, as long as the subscriber does not charge the outsider for that access. Still others believe that an Internet connection is intended for use only by the subscriber and that sharing it with others is unfair to the subscriber's ISP. This issue is beginning to be addressed by the courts and ISPs, and some answers regarding the legality of "Wi-Fi borrowing" and

FIGURE 9-2
Wi-Fi finders. Online mapping services and smartphone apps can show you the available Wi-Fi hotspots for a particular geographic area.

© Chardchanin/Shutterstock.com; Courtesy of JiWire

>**War driving.** Driving around an area with a Wi-Fi-enabled computer or mobile device to find a Wi-Fi network to access and use without authorization. >**Wi-Fi piggybacking.** Accessing an unsecured Wi-Fi network from your current location without authorization.

Internet connection sharing will likely be forthcoming in the near future. However, the ethical questions surrounding this issue may take longer to resolve.

Interception of Communications

Instead of accessing data stored on a computer via hacking, some criminals gain unauthorized access to data, files, messages, VoIP calls, and other content as it is being sent over the Internet. For instance, *unencrypted* (unsecured) messages, files, logon information, and more sent over a wireless network (such as while using a public Wi-Fi hotspot or over an unsecured home or business Wi-Fi network) can be captured and read by anyone within range using software designed for that purpose. Once intercepted, the data can be used for unintended or fraudulent purposes.

Although it is unlikely that anyone would be interested in intercepting personal e-mail or text messages sent to friends and relatives, proprietary corporate information and sensitive personal information (such as credit card numbers and Web site logon information) is at risk if it is sent unsecured over the Internet or over a wireless home or corporate network. The widespread use of wireless networks with both home and office computers, as well as with smartphones and other portable devices, has opened up new opportunities for data interception. For instance, the data on mobile devices with Bluetooth capabilities enabled can be accessed by other Bluetooth devices that are within range and any sensitive data stored on a smartphone can be accessed by a hacker if the phone is connected to an unsecured Wi-Fi network. With an increasing number of smartphone owners storing sensitive data (such as passwords for online banking and social networking sites, and credit card account numbers) on their devices (and less than half of owners securing their mobile devices with a *password*, according to one estimate), the risk of that data being intercepted is increasing.

A relatively recent trend is criminals intercepting credit and debit card information during the card verification process; that is, intercepting the data from a card in real time as a purchase is being authorized. Often, this occurrs via *packetsniffing* software installed at payment terminals (such as restaurant cash registers or gas station credit/debit card readers) by hackers—the packetsniffing software gathers data during transactions and then sends it to the hackers, who may then use it for fraudulent purposes.

PROTECTING AGAINST UNAUTHORIZED ACCESS AND UNAUTHORIZED USE

The first step in protecting against unauthorized access and unauthorized use of a computer system is controlling access to an organization's facilities and computer networks to ensure that only authorized individuals are granted access. In addition, steps need to be taken to ensure that authorized individuals access only the resources that they are supposed to access.

Access Control Systems

Access control systems are used to control access to facilities, devices, computer networks, company databases, Web site accounts, and other assets. They can be *identification systems*, which verify that the person trying to access the facility or system is listed as an authorized user, and/or *authentication systems*, which determine whether or not the person attempting access is actually who he or she claims to be. In businesses, access control systems are often integrated into a comprehensive *identity management (IDM) system* designed to manage users' access to enterprise systems, such as to grant them secure and appropriate access to the systems they are allowed to access in as convenient a manner as possible. An emerging trend is to use *single sign-on (SSO)* systems that grant employees access to a number of secure resources with a single authentication. The three most common types of access control systems are discussed next, followed by a discussion of additional considerations for controlling access to wireless networks. Some emerging control systems are discussed in the Trend box later in this chapter.

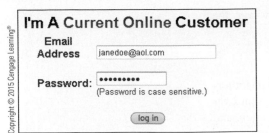

I'm A Current Online Customer

Email
Address   janedoe@aol.com

Password: ●●●●●●●●
            (Password is case sensitive.)

[log in]

Ⓐ **FIGURE 9-3**
Passwords.
Passwords are used
to log on to computers,
networks, Web sites,
and other computing
resources.

Ⓥ **FIGURE 9-4**
**Strategies for
creating strong
passwords.**

Possessed Knowledge Access Systems

A **possessed knowledge access system** is an identification system that requires the individual requesting access to provide information that only the authorized user is supposed to know. *Passwords* and *cognitive authentication systems* fall into this category.

Passwords, the most common type of possessed knowledge, are secret words or character combinations associated with an individual. They are typically used in conjunction with a *username* (often a variation of the person's first and/or last names or the individual's e-mail address). Username/password combinations are often used to restrict access to networks, computers, Web sites, routers, and other computing resources—the user is granted access only after supplying the correct information. While usernames and e-mail addresses are not secret, passwords are and, for security purposes, typically appear as asterisks or dots as they are being entered so they cannot be viewed (see Figure 9-3). For some applications (such as ATM machines), a *PIN* or *personal identification number*—a secret combination of numeric digits selected by the user—is used instead of a password. Numeric passwords are also referred to as *passcodes*. Instead of traditional passwords, some systems (such as Windows 8 devices and smartphone *lock screens*) can use *picture passwords*—typically gestures or patterns drawn on top of an image, such as a grid of dots or a photograph.

One of the biggest disadvantages of password-based systems is that any individual possessing the proper password will be granted access to the system because the system recognizes the password, regardless of whether or not the person using the password is the authorized user, and passwords can be guessed or deciphered by a hacker or a hacker's computer easily if secure password selection strategies are not applied. For example, many hackers are able to access networking hardware and databases because the system administrator passwords for those resources are still the default passwords (the ones assigned during manufacturing) and so are commonly known; some insiders gain unauthorized access to systems using passwords written down on sticky notes attached to a user's monitor. In addition, passwords can be forgotten. Consequently, it is important to select passwords that are *strong passwords* but are also easy to remember without writing them down. Strong passwords are passwords that are at least eight characters long; use a combination of letters, numbers, and symbols; and do not form words found in the dictionary or that match the username that the password is associated with. Some strategies for creating strong passwords are listed in Figure 9-4.

A growing trend in possessed knowledge access systems is the use of *cognitive authentication systems* instead of, or

PASSWORD STRATEGIES

Make the password at least eight characters and include both uppercase and lowercase letters, as well as numbers and special symbols.

Choose passwords that are not in a dictionary—for instance, mix numbers and special characters with abbreviations or unusual words you will remember but that do not conform to a pattern a computer can readily figure out.

Do not use your name, your kids' or pets' names, your address, your birthdate, or any other public information as your password.

Determine a *passphrase* that you can remember and use corresponding letters and symbols (such as the first letter of each word) for your password. For instance, the passphrase "My son John is five years older than my daughter Abby" could be used to remember the corresponding strong password "Msji5yotMd@".

Develop a system using a basic password for all Web sites plus site-specific information (such as the first two letters of the site and a number you will remember) to create a different password for each site, but still ones you can easily remember. For instance, you can combine your dog's name with the site initials followed by a number that is significant to you to form a password such as "RoverAM27" for Amazon.com.

Do not keep a written copy of the password in your desk or taped to your monitor. If you need to write down your password, create a password-protected file on your computer that contains all your passwords or use a password manager program.

Use a different password for your highly sensitive activities (such as online banking or stock trading) than for other Web sites. If a hacker determines your password on a low-security site (which is easier to break into), he or she can use it on an account containing sensitive data if you use the same password on both accounts.

Change your passwords frequently—at least every 6 months.

>**Possessed knowledge access system.** An access control system that uses information only the individual should know to identify that individual.
>**Password.** A secret combination of characters used to gain access to a computer, computer network, or other resource.

in conjunction with, usernames and passwords. Cognitive authentication systems use information that an individual should know or can remember easily. Some systems use personal information about the individual (such as his or her city of birth, first school attended, or amount of home mortgage) that was pulled from public databases or the company database and the individual must supply the correct answer in order to be granted access. Other systems (such as the password recovery systems used by many secure Web sites to verify individuals when they forget their password) allow the individual to supply answers to questions when the account is created and then the individual can supply those answers again for authentication purposes when needed.

CAUTION CAUTION CAUTION CAUTION CAUTION CAUTION CAUT

Don't select answers for the cognitive authentication questions used in the password recovery process of many Web sites that a hacker may be able to guess based on information found on your Facebook page or other online source. Instead, supply answers that you can remember but that also follow secure password rules. For instance, if your dog's name is Spot, you could enter *MDN1s$pOT* as the answer to a question about your pet's name and remember it as "My dog's name is Spot."

Possessed knowledge systems are often used in conjunction with the *possessed object access systems* and *biometric access systems* that are discussed next. Using two different methods to authenticate a user is called **two-factor authentication**. Typically, the methods used are some type of possessed knowledge (something you know) along with either a *possessed object* (something you have) or a *biometric feature* (something you are). Two-factor authentication adds an additional level of security to an access control system because hackers are much less likely to be able to gain access to two different required factors. One emerging type of two-factor authentication uses a conventional username/password combination in conjunction with a *soft token* (an electronic object available via something you already carry with you, such as a smartphone or credit card, instead of using a *hard token*, such as a *USB key token*). A soft token can be generated by a mobile app or by pressing a button on a credit card; it can also be sent via text message. A soft token supplies a *one-time password* (*OTP*), which must be entered in conjunction with your username/password in order to log on to the account. Two-factor authentication systems are common in many countries and their use is growing in the United States. For instance, many banks offer two-factor authentication for online and mobile banking, and it is an option for Google, Twitter, and Facebook users. In Facebook, for example, once two-factor authentication (called *Login Approvals*) is enabled, you will see the security code screen shown in Figure 9-5 whenever you log in with your Facebook logon information using a new browser or device; you will need to enter the OTP sent to your phone before you will be logged into your Facebook account. The disadvantage of two-factor authentication for businesses is that only one individual can access the account, unless the site (like Facebook) supports multiple users for a single account.

FIGURE 9-5
Facebook two-factor authentication. The first time you log on with a new device, you must supply the OTP sent to your mobile phone in addition to your conventional username/password combination.

1. An OTP is sent to your phone.

2. Enter that code here when prompted.

Facebook © 2013

NET

TIP

To enable Facebook Login Approvals, go to your *Security Settings* on that site.

Possessed Object Access Systems

Possessed object access systems use physical objects for identification purposes and they are frequently used to control access to facilities (called *physical access*) and computer systems (called *logical access*). Common types of possessed objects are smart

>**Two-factor authentication.** Using two different methods to authenticate a user. >**Possessed object access system.** An access control system that uses a physical object an individual has in his or her possession to identify that individual.

PHYSICAL ACCESS
The object (in this case a mobile phone containing an appropriate microSD card) is read by a reader to provide access to a facility.

LOGICAL ACCESS
The object (in this case a smart card employee badge) is read by a reader (this reader is integrated into the computer) to provide access to that computer system.

FIGURE 9-6

Possessed objects.
Can grant access to both facilities and computer resources (including computers, networks, and Web sites).

cards, RFID-encoded badges, magnetic cards, and smartphones that are swiped through or placed close to a reader to be read (see Figure 9-6)—emerging options include the use of an *NFC-enabled ring* or a Bluetooth app (as discussed in Chapter 15) to automatically lock and unlock your devices when they are within range. Possessed objects also include *USB security keys* or *tokens* (USB flash drives that are inserted into a computer to grant access to a network, to supply Web site usernames and passwords, or to provide other security features), access cards, smartphones, and other devices used to supply the OTPs used to log on to Web sites. An emerging option is integrating OTP capabilities into the hardware of devices, such as laptops that include Intel *Identity Protection Technology* (*IPT*), in order to automatically authenticate the devices being used to log on to participating Web sites.

One disadvantage of using possessed objects is that they can be lost or, like passwords, can be used by an unauthorized individual if that individual has possession of the object. This disadvantage can be overcome by using a second factor, such as a username/password combination or a fingerprint or other type of *biometric* data.

Biometric Access Systems

Biometrics is the study of identifying individuals using measurable, unique physiological or behavioral characteristics. **Biometric access systems** typically identify users by a particular unique biological characteristic (such as a fingerprint, a hand, a face, veins, or an iris), although personal traits are used in some systems. For instance, some systems today use *keystroke dynamics* to recognize an individual's unique typing pattern to authenticate the user as he or she types in his or her username and password; other systems identify an individual via his or her voice, signature, or gait. Because the means of access (usually a part of the body) cannot typically be used by anyone other than the authorized individual, biometric access systems can perform both identification and authentication. Biometric access systems are used for both physical and logical access (see Figure 9-7).

To identify and authenticate an individual, biometric access systems typically use a biometric reader (such as a *fingerprint reader, finger* or *palm vein reader*, or a *hand geometry reader*) to identify an individual based on his or her fingerprint, veins, or hand image, or a digital camera to identify an individual based on his or her face or iris, in conjunction with software and a database. The system matches the supplied biometric data with the biometric data that was stored in the database when the individual was enrolled in the system and authenticates the individual if the data matches. To speed up the process, many biometric access systems require users to identify themselves first (such as by entering a username or swiping a smart card), and then the system uses that identifying information to verify that the supplied biometric data matches the identified person.

>**Biometric access system.** An access control system that uses one unique physical characteristic of an individual (such as a fingerprint, a face, veins, or a voice) to authenticate that individual.

Biometric access systems are used to control access to secure facilities (such as corporate headquarters and prisons); to log users on to computers, networks, and secure Web sites (by using an external reader or camera or one built into the computer); to punch employees in and out of work; and to confirm consumers' identities at ATM machines and check-cashing services. Biometric readers are also increasingly being built into smartphones, external hard drives, USB flash drives, and other hardware to prevent unauthorized use of those devices.

In addition to being used to control access to computers, networks, and other resources, biometrics are an important part of the systems used by law enforcement agencies and the military to identify individuals. For instance, the border control systems in many countries use biometrics to identify citizens, travelers, criminal suspects, and potential terrorists, and biometric identification systems are used extensively by law enforcement agencies and the military in areas of conflict. For example, the Egyptian Hospital at Bagram Airfield in Afghanistan uses biometrics (fingerprints and iris scans—see Figure 9-7) to identify and track the records of incoming patients. In addition, *face recognition systems* (biometric systems that use cameras and a database of photos to attempt to identify individuals as they walk by the cameras) are used in many airports and other public locations to help identify known terrorists and criminal suspects.

FINGERPRINT READERS
Typically used to protect access to work facilities or computers, to log on to secure Web sites, for law enforcement identification, and to pay for products or services.

VEIN READERS
Beginning to replace hand geometry readers to control access to facilities (such as government offices, prisons, and military facilities) and to punch in and out of work.

FACE RECOGNITION SYSTEMS
Typically used to control access to highly secure areas, to identify individuals for law enforcement purposes, and to log on to devices or apps, as shown here.

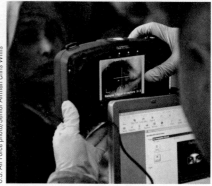

IRIS RECOGNITION SYSTEMS
Typically used to control access to highly secure areas and by the military, such as to identify Afghan patients as shown here.

FIGURE 9-7
Types of biometric access and identification systems.

Biometric access systems are very accurate. In fact, the odds of two different individuals having identical irises is 1 in 10^{78} and the statistical probability of two different irises being declared a match are 1 in 1.2 million—even identical twins (who have the same DNA structure) have different fingerprints and irises. Systems based on biological characteristics (such as a person's iris, hand geometry, face, or fingerprint) tend to be more accurate than those based on a personal trait (such as a person's voice or written signature) because biological traits do not change, but physical traits might change (such as an individual's voice, which might be affected by a cold, or a written signature, which might be affected by a broken wrist). In addition, biometric characteristics cannot be lost (like an access card), cannot be forgotten (like a password), and do not have to be pulled out of a briefcase or pocket (like an access card or other type of possessed object).

The primary disadvantages of biometric access systems are that much of the necessary hardware and software is expensive, and the data used for authentication (such as a fingerprint or an iris image) cannot be reset if it is compromised. In addition, fingerprint and hand geometry systems typically require contact with the reader device (which some users might object to)—vein systems (that use infrared LED light in conjunction with a digital camera to identify individuals based on the veins in their fingers or palms) can be contactless systems.

TIP

Fingerprint biometrics is an integral part of Windows 8.1, supporting both *touch* and *swipe fingerprint readers* for a variety of authentication functions.

Because the SSID is being broadcast, the user can select the network from the list.

The user must supply the appropriate network key or passphrase in order to connect to the network.

If the SSID isn't broadcast, the user must add the network manually by using its SSID in order to log on.

Used with permission from Microsoft Corporation

FIGURE 9-8

Accessing a Wi-Fi network. To access a secure network, the appropriate passphrase must be supplied.

Controlling Access to Wireless Networks

As already discussed, wireless networks—such as Wi-Fi networks—are less secure, in general, than wired networks. There are Wi-Fi security procedures, however, that can be used to protect against unauthorized use of a wireless network and to *encrypt* data sent over the network so that it is unreadable if it is intercepted. The original Wi-Fi security standard was *WEP* (*Wired Equivalent Privacy*). WEP is now considered insecure and has been replaced with the more secure *WPA* (*Wi-Fi Protected Access*) and the even more secure *WPA2* standards. However, Wi-Fi security features only work if they are enabled. Most Wi-Fi hardware today is shipped with the security features either switched off or enabled with a *default password* that is public knowledge; many network owners never change the default settings, leaving those networks unsecured.

To protect against unauthorized access, Wi-Fi network owners should secure their networks by changing the router or access point settings to enable one of the encryption standards and to assign a *network key* or *passphrase* (essentially a password) that must be supplied in order to access the secured network. In addition, the name of the network (called the *SSID*) can be hidden from view by switching off the SSID broadcast feature. While hiding the network name will not deter serious hackers, it may reduce the number of casual war drivers or neighbors accessing the network. Once a network is secured, users who want to connect to that network need to either select or supply the network SSID name (depending on whether or not the SSID is being broadcast) and then enter the network key assigned to that network (see Figure 9-8). For an overview of how you can secure your wireless home router, see the How It Works box.

Firewalls, Encryption, and Virtual Private Networks (VPNs)

In addition to the access control systems just discussed, there are a number of other tools that can be used to prevent access to an individual computer or to prevent data from being intercepted in an understandable form during transit. These tools are discussed next.

Firewalls

A **firewall** is a security system that essentially creates a barrier between a computer or a network and the Internet in order to protect against unauthorized access. Firewalls are typically two-way, so they check all incoming (from the Internet) and outgoing (to the Internet) traffic and allow only authorized traffic to pass through the firewall. *Personal firewalls* are software programs designed to protect home computers from hackers attempting to access those computers through their Internet connections. All computers with direct Internet connections (such as DSL, cable, satellite, or fixed wireless Internet access) should use a firewall (computers using dial-up Internet access only are relatively safe from hackers). Personal firewalls can be stand-alone programs (such as the free *ZoneAlarm* program or the free *Comodo Firewall* program shown in Figure 9-9); they are also built into many operating systems (such as the *Windows Firewall* program). Many routers, modems, and other pieces of networking hardware also include built-in firewall capabilities to help secure the networks these devices are used with. Firewalls designed to protect business networks may be software-based, hardware-based, or a combination of the two. They can typically be used both to prevent network access by hackers and other outsiders, as well as to control employee Internet access.

> **Firewall.** A collection of hardware and/or software intended to protect a computer or computer network from unauthorized access.

HOW IT WORKS

Securing a Wireless Home Router

If you have a home wireless network, it is important to secure it properly so it cannot be used by unauthorized individuals. To open your router's configuration screen to check or modify the security settings, type the IP address assigned to that device (such as 192.168.0.1—check your router's documentation for its default IP address and username) in your browser's Address bar. Use the default password to log on the first time, and then change the password using the configuration screen to prevent unauthorized individuals from changing your router settings. To secure the router, enter the network name (SSID) you want to have associated with the router, select the appropriate security mode (such as WPA or WPA2) to be used, and then type a secure passphrase to be used in order to log on to the network.

For additional security, *MAC (Media Access Control) address filtering* can be used to allow only the devices whose network adapter MAC addresses you enter into your router's settings access to the network. While MAC address filtering should not be considered an alternative to using WPA or WPA2 encryption, it does add another layer of protection. Other precautions include designating specific times (such as when you are away from home) that the router will deny access to any device, and reducing the strength of the wireless signal if its current strength reaches farther than you need.

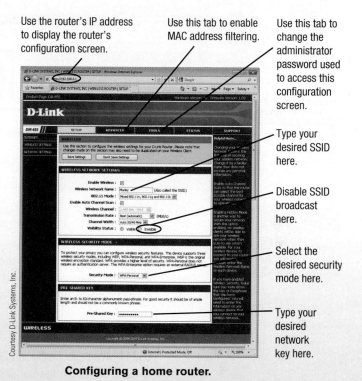

Use the router's IP address to display the router's configuration screen.

Use this tab to enable MAC address filtering.

Use this tab to change the administrator password used to access this configuration screen.

Type your desired SSID here.

Disable SSID broadcast here.

Select the desired security mode here.

Type your desired network key here.

Courtesy D-Link Systems, Inc.

Configuring a home router.

Firewalls work by closing down all external *communications port addresses* (the electronic connections that allow a computer to communicate with other computers) to unauthorized computers and programs. While business firewalls are set up by the network administrator and those settings typically cannot be changed by end users, individuals may choose to change the settings for their personal firewall. For example, the user can choose to be notified when any application program on the computer is trying to access the Internet, to specify the programs that are allowed to access the Internet, or to block all incoming connections temporarily. In addition to protecting your computer from outside access, firewall programs also protect against any spyware, computer viruses, or other malicious programs located on your computer that are designed to send data from your computer

FIGURE 9-9
A personal firewall.

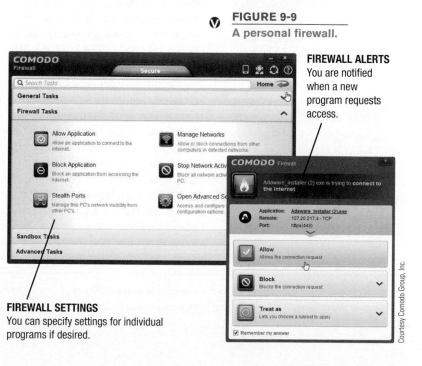

FIREWALL ALERTS
You are notified when a new program requests access.

FIREWALL SETTINGS
You can specify settings for individual programs if desired.

Courtesy Comodo Group, Inc.

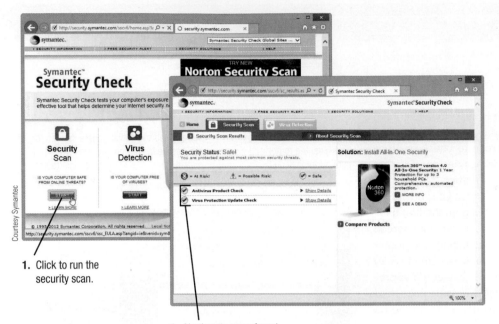

1. Click to run the security scan.

2. No threats were found.

FIGURE 9-10
Online security scans can check your system for vulnerabilities.

Courtesy Symantec

(such as credit card numbers, Web site passwords, and other sensitive data stored on your hard drive) to a hacker at the hacker's request.

A related type of security system increasingly being used by businesses today and included in many security suites is an *intrusion prevention system* (*IPS*). Whereas a firewall tries to block unauthorized traffic, an IPS continuously monitors and analyzes the traffic allowed by the firewall to try to detect possible attacks as they are occurring. If an attack is in progress, IPS software can immediately block it.

After installing and setting up a firewall (and an IPS if needed), individuals and businesses should test their systems to determine if vulnerabilities still exist. Individuals can use online security tests—such as the *Symantec Security Check* shown in Figure 9-10 or the tests at Gibson Research's *ShieldsUP!* site—to check their computers; businesses may want to hire an outside consultant to perform a comprehensive security assessment.

Encryption

Encryption is a way of temporarily converting data into a form, known as a *cipher*, which is unreadable until it is *decrypted* (unscrambled) in order to protect that data from being viewed by unauthorized individuals. As previously discussed, secure Wi-Fi networks use encryption to secure data that is transferred over the network. **Secure Web pages** use encryption so that sensitive data (such as credit card numbers) sent via the Web page is protected as it travels over the Internet. The most common security protocols used with secure Web pages are *Secure Sockets Layer* (*SSL*) and *Extended Validation Secure Sockets Layer* (*EV SSL*). The URL for Web pages using either form of SSL begins with *https:* instead of *http:*.

Some Internet services, such as *Skype* (for VoIP calls) and *Hushmail* (for Web-based e-mails), use built-in encryption. Encryption can also be added manually to a file or an e-mail message before it is sent over the Internet to ensure that the content is unreadable if the file or message is intercepted during transit. In addition to securing files during transit, encryption can be used to protect the files stored on a hard drive so they will be unreadable if opened by an unauthorized person (such as if a hacker accesses a file containing sensitive data or if a computer containing sensitive files is lost or stolen). Increasingly, computers and storage devices (particularly those used with portable computers) are *self-encrypting*; that is, encrypting all data automatically and invisibly to the user. Windows, Mac OS, and other current operating systems support encryption and businesses are increasingly turning to encryption to prevent data loss if a data breach should occur.

> **Encryption.** A method of scrambling the contents of an e-mail message or a file to make it unreadable if an unauthorized user intercepts it.
> **Secure Web page.** A Web page that uses encryption to protect information transmitted via that Web page.

The two most common types of encryption in use today are *public key encryption* (often used with content being transmitted over the Internet, such as secure Web pages and encrypted e-mail) and *private key encryption* (most often used to encrypt files or the content of a hard drive or other device). **Private key encryption**, also called *symmetric key encryption*, uses a single secret *private key* (essentially a password) to both encrypt and decrypt the file or message. It is often used to encrypt files stored on an individual's computer because the individual who selects the private key is likely the only one who will need to access those files. Private key encryption can also be used to send files securely to others, provided both the sender and recipient agree on the private key that will be used to access the file. Private key encryption capabilities are incorporated into a variety of programs today, including Microsoft Office, the WinZip file compression program, and Adobe Acrobat (the program used to create PDF files). To encrypt a document in Microsoft Word 2013, for instance, you select *Info* on the FILE tab, click *Protect Document* and select *Encrypt with Password*, type the desired password (private key) when prompted, and then save the file. To open that document again (or any copies of the file, such as those sent via e-mail), the password assigned to that file must be entered correctly.

Public key encryption, also called *asymmetric key encryption*, utilizes two encryption keys to encrypt and decrypt documents. Specifically, public key encryption uses a pair of keys (a private key and a *public key*) that are related mathematically to each other and have been assigned to a particular individual. An individual's public key is not secret and is available for anyone to use, but the corresponding private key is secret and is used only by the individual to whom it was assigned. Documents or messages encrypted with a public key can only be decrypted with the matching private key.

Public/private key pairs are generated by the program being used to perform the encryption or they are obtained via the Internet through a *Certificate Authority*, such as VeriSign or Thawte. Once obtained, encryption keys are stored in your browser, e-mail program, and any other program with which they will be used—this is typically done automatically for you when you obtain your key pairs. Obtaining a business public/private key pair usually requires a fee, but free key pairs for personal use are available through some Certificate Authorities. If a third-party encryption program is used (such as *Pretty Good Privacy* or *PGP*), the program typically takes care of obtaining and managing your keys for you.

To send someone an encrypted e-mail message or file using public key encryption, you need his or her public key. If that person has previously sent you his or her public key (such as via an e-mail message), it was likely stored by your e-mail program in your address book or contacts list, or by your encryption program in a central key directory used by that program. In either case, that public key is available whenever you want to send that person an encrypted document. If you do not already have the public key belonging to the individual to whom you want to send an encrypted e-mail or file, you will need to request it from that individual. Once the recipient's public key has been used to encrypt the file or e-mail message and that document is received, the recipient uses his or her private key to decrypt the encrypted contents (see Figure 9-11).

To avoid the need to obtain the recipient's public key before sending that person an encrypted e-mail, *Web-based encrypted e-mail* can be used. Web-based encrypted e-mail works similarly to regular Web-based e-mail (in which e-mail is composed and viewed on a Web page belonging to a Web-based e-mail provider), but Web-based encrypted e-mail systems use secure Web servers to host the Web pages that are used to compose and read e-mail messages. Some Web-based encrypted e-mail systems—such as the popular free *Hushmail* service that automatically encrypts all e-mail sent through the

NET

>**Private key encryption.** A type of encryption that uses a single key to encrypt and decrypt the file or message. >**Public key encryption.** A type of encryption that uses key pairs to encrypt and decrypt the file or message.

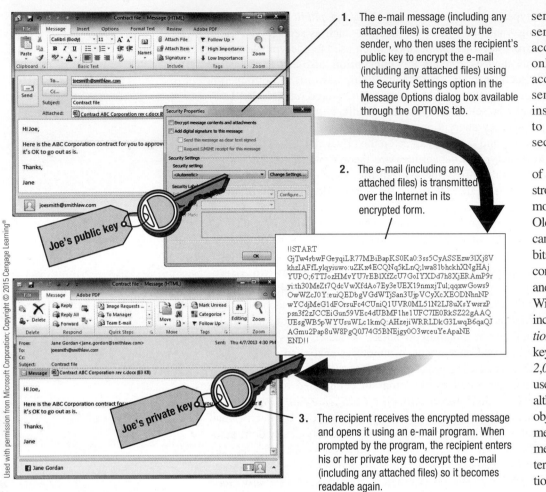

1. The e-mail message (including any attached files) is created by the sender, who then uses the recipient's public key to encrypt the e-mail (including any attached files) using the Security Settings option in the Message Options dialog box available through the OPTIONS tab.

2. The e-mail (including any attached files) is transmitted over the Internet in its encrypted form.

3. The recipient receives the encrypted message and opens it using an e-mail program. When prompted by the program, the recipient enters his or her private key to decrypt the e-mail (including any attached files) so it becomes readable again.

service—require both the sender and recipient to have accounts. Others require only the sender to have an account and the recipient is sent an e-mail containing instructions regarding how to view the message on a secure Web page.

There are various strengths of encryption available; the stronger the encryption, the more difficult it is to crack. Older 40-bit encryption (which can only use keys that are 40 bits or 5 characters long) is considered *weak encryption* and is no longer supported by Windows. Stronger encryption includes *strong 128-bit encryption* (which uses 16-character keys) and *military-strength 2,048-bit encryption* (which uses 256-character keys), although not without some objections from law enforcement agencies and the government because they state that terrorists routinely use encryption methods to communicate.

FIGURE 9-11
Using public key encryption to secure an e-mail message in Microsoft Outlook.

Virtual Private Networks (VPNs)

While e-mail and file encryption can be used to transfer individual messages and files securely over the Internet, a **virtual private network (VPN)** is designed to be used when a continuous secure channel over the Internet is needed. A VPN provides a secure private tunnel from the user's computer through the Internet to another destination and is most often used to provide remote employees with secure access to a company network. VPNs use encryption and other security mechanisms to ensure that only authorized users can access the remote network and that the data cannot be intercepted during transit. Because it uses the Internet instead of an expensive private physical network, a VPN can provide a secure environment over a large geographical area at a manageable cost. Once a VPN is set up, the user just needs to log on (such as with a username/password combination or a security token) in order to use the VPN.

VPNs are often used by both businesses and individuals at public Wi-Fi hotspots to prevent data interception when connecting to the Internet via the hotspot. While businesspeople will typically use a VPN set up by their companies, individuals can create *personal VPNs* using software designed for that purpose. This software automatically encrypts all inbound and outbound Internet traffic, including Web pages, e-mail messages, IMs, VoIP calls, and

TIP

Unless it is absolutely necessary and you are using a VPN, do not perform sensitive transactions (such as shopping or banking) at a public hotspot.

> **Virtual private network (VPN).** A private, secure path over the Internet that provides authorized users a secure means of accessing a private network via the Internet.

so forth, and also acts as a personal firewall. Using a personal VPN at a public hotspot can help individuals from becoming the victim of a hacker or an *evil twin*—a fake Wi-Fi hotspot set up to look like a legitimate hotspot.

Additional Public Hotspot Precautions

The precautions already discussed (such as using firewall software, secure Web pages, VPNs, and encryption) are a good start for protecting against unauthorized access and unauthorized use at a public Wi-Fi hotspot. However, there are additional precautions individuals can use to avoid data (both that which is on their devices and that which is being sent over the Internet) from being compromised. These precautions are listed in Figure 9-12.

Sensible Employee Precautions

While only about 20% of business security breaches are committed by insiders (according to a recent Data Breach Investigations Report), they are responsible for the majority (66.7%) of exposed records. In addition, these breaches are typically malicious in nature, with an employee deliberately performing the act (though other times the breach occurs because the employee makes a mistake, such as losing a portable computer or removable storage medium, or inadvertently providing access to sensitive data). In either case, employers should be cautious. Some suggestions to avoid security breaches by employees are listed next.

Screen Potential New Hires Carefully

Employers should carefully investigate the background of all potential employees. Some people falsify résumés to get jobs. Others may have criminal records or currently be charged with a crime. One embarrassing mistake made by Rutgers University was to hire David Smith, the author of the *Melissa* computer virus, as a computer technician when he was out on bail following the arrest for that crime.

Watch for Disgruntled Employees and Ex-Employees

The type of employee who is most likely to commit a computer crime is one who has recently been terminated or passed over for a promotion, or one who has some reason to want to "get even" with the organization. Limiting access for each employee to only the resources needed for his or her job (referred to as the *Principle of Least Privilege*) and monitoring any attempts to access off-limit resources can help prevent some types of problems, such as unauthorized access of sensitive files, unintentional damage like deleting or changing files inadvertently, or sabotage like deleting or changing company files intentionally. In addition, it is vital that whenever an employee leaves the company for any reason, all access to the system for that individual (username, password, e-mail address, and so forth) should be removed immediately. For employees with high levels of system access, simultaneously removing access while the termination is taking place is even better. Waiting even a few minutes can be too late because just-fired employees have been known to barricade themselves in their office immediately after being terminated in order to change passwords, sabotage records, and perform other malicious acts. For example, on the day he was fired, one computer programmer at Fannie Mae embedded malicious code into a routine program on his company laptop before turning it in. The code, designed to destroy all data (including financial, securities, and mortgage information), was transmitted to nearly 5,000 Fannie Mae servers. The code was discovered before it was executed and the man was sentenced to more than three years in prison for computer intrusion.

PUBLIC HOTSPOT PRECAUTIONS

Turn off automatic connections and pay attention to the list of available hotspots to make sure you connect to a legitimate access point (not an evil twin).

Use a personal firewall to control the traffic going to and coming from your device and temporarily use it to block all incoming connections.

Use a virtual private network (VPN) to secure all activity between your device and the Internet.

Only enter passwords, credit card numbers, and other data on secure Web pages using a VPN.

If you're not using a VPN, encrypt all sensitive files before transferring or e-mailing them.

If you're not using a VPN, avoid online shopping, banking, and other sensitive transactions.

Turn off file sharing so others can't access the files on your hard drive.

Turn off Bluetooth and Wi-Fi when you are not using them.

Disable *ad hoc* capabilities to prevent another device from connecting to your device directly without using an access point.

Use antivirus software and make sure your operating system and browser are up to date.

FIGURE 9-12
Sensible precautions for public Wi-Fi hotspot users.

INSIDE THE INDUSTRY

Securing BYOD

One growing trend today is *BYOD* or *Bring Your Own Device* (where students or employees bring their own smartphones, media tablets, or other devices to use instead of using issued devices—see the accompanying photo). Some businesses view BYOD as a cost-effective way of supplying employees with the devices they want to use; many IT departments view BYOD as a potential security nightmare. But it's here and not going away—research firm Gartner predicts that about half the world's companies will no longer provide computing devices to their employees by 2017.

BYOD is also changing the way many individuals perceive their work—no longer as a place, but as an activity that is independent of both location and specific technology. Consequently, it makes sense (and is more convenient) for individuals to carry with them at all times the devices that allow them to perform both work and personal functions as needed. For businesses, however, that brings the challenge of managing those devices. Disadvantages of BYOD from a company perspective include the risk of a *malware* infection via a BYOD device, as well as the potential exposure of company data via unsecured or lost personal devices or personal cloud storage systems (sometimes referred to as *Bring Your Own Cloud* or *BYOC*). Potential disadvantages from the employee perspective include having company-mandated restrictions on their personal devices (such as not using certain applications or cloud services and agreeing to allow the company to erase or reset the device remotely if it is lost or stolen), as well as the employer having access to personal data or activities performed via the phone. In addition, space on the device may be tied up for company data or apps that are used only for work.

While some companies use mobile device management (MDM) software to control the use of personal devices with corporate networks, one emerging solution is to completely separate the business and personal use of the device. For instance, software that supports *sandboxing* or *containerization* can create an isolated virtual environment on the user's device within which corporate data and applications can safely reside. With this method, the company would mandate control policies for just that portion of the device. An option for Windows 8 Enterprise companies is to use the *Windows To Go* feature, which uses a bootable USB flash drive to create a complete, managed Windows 8 environment on whatever device the USB flash drive is plugged into. Consequently, employees can use the Windows To Go environment on their personal devices at work, and then shut down the Windows To Go environment after work to use their devices as solely personal devices.

© Syda Productions/Shutterstock.com

Develop Policies and Controls

All companies should develop policies and controls regarding security matters. As already mentioned, employees should be granted the least amount of access to the company network that they need to perform their job. Employees should be educated about the seriousness and consequences of hacking, data theft, and other computer crimes, and they should be taught what to do when they suspect a computer crime has been committed. Employees should also be instructed about proper device usage policies—such as whether or not downloading software on company devices is allowed, whether or not employees are responsible for updating their devices, and the types of removable storage media that may be used with company devices—in order to avoid inadvertently creating a security problem. Policies for removing computers and storage media containing sensitive data from the premises should also be implemented, enforced, and updated as needed, and sensitive documents should be shredded when they are no longer needed.

Employees who work from home or otherwise access the company network via the Internet also need to be educated about security policies for remote access and the proper precautions that need to be taken. These precautions include keeping their operating system and security software up to date and using only encrypted storage devices (such as self-encrypting USB flash drives) when transporting documents between work and home.

In addition, telecommuting workers and outside contractors should not be allowed to have peer-to-peer (P2P) software on computers containing company documents because data is increasingly being exposed through the use of P2P networks. For instance, classified data about the U.S. presidential helicopter discovered on a computer in Iran was traced back to a P2P network and the computer of a military contractor in Maryland; and the Social Security numbers and other personal data belonging to about 17,000 current and former Pfizer workers were once leaked onto a P2P network after an employee installed unauthorized P2P software on a company notebook computer provided for use at her home.

Use Software to Manage Employee Devices and Prevent Data Leaks

As employees are increasingly bringing portable devices (such as smartphones and USB flash drives) that can interact with business networks to the office, the challenge of securing these *BYOD* (*Bring Your Own Device*) devices (and the company network) has grown. While some companies prohibit all portable devices and others allow only company-issued portable devices so they can ensure appropriate security measures (such as encryption, password protection, and the ability to wipe the device clean remotely if it is lost or stolen) are implemented, the use of BYOD is growing, as discussed in the Inside the Industry box.

To protect against employees copying or sending confidential data to others either intentionally or accidentally, *data-leakage* (also called *data-loss*) *prevention systems* can be used. Data-leakage prevention systems are available as software and/or hardware systems, and have a range of capabilities, but the overall goal is to prevent sensitive data from exposure. For instance, some systems control which devices (such as USB flash drives and smartphones) can be connected to an employee's computer in order to prevent sensitive data from being taken home inadvertently or intentionally. *Mobile device management* (*MDM*) *software* (see Figure 9-13) goes one step further by including other protections, such as specifying what apps and Web sites can be used with the device, protecting against unauthorized access and *malware*, facilitating remote access (to update software or erase a lost device, for instance), and locating a lost or stolen device. Other data-leakage prevention systems—sometimes also called *outbound-content monitoring systems*—scan all outgoing communications (e-mail, transferred files, and so forth) for documents containing Social Security numbers, intellectual property, and other confidential information and block them if they might contain prohibited content. Some can also continually scan network devices to locate documents containing sensitive data to ensure that sensitive files are not on the computer of an employee who should not have access to them. For even stronger protection of confidential company documents, *enterprise rights-management software*, which encrypts confidential documents and limits functions such as printing, editing, and copying the data to only authorized users with the appropriate password, can be used.

TIP

Deploying a centrally managed security solution to all endpoints (all user devices connected to the company network) is referred to as *endpoint security*.

FIGURE 9-13
Mobile device management (MDM) software. Secures and manages the mobile devices used in an organization.

Courtesy Airwatch

Ask Business Partners to Review Their Security

In this networked economy, many organizations provide some access to internal resources for business partners. If those external companies are lax with their security measures, however, attacks through the business partners' computers (such as via an employee or hacker) are possible. Consequently, businesses should make sure that their business partners maintain adequate security policies and controls. Regulations increasingly require businesses to ensure that adequate controls are in place to protect stored data. This impacts outside companies—such as business partners and *outsourcing companies* (outside vendors for specific business tasks, as discussed in Chapter 12)—if they have access to sensitive corporate data. Companies that utilize cloud computing also need to ensure that the cloud vendor's security and privacy policies match the company's requirements.

COMPUTER SABOTAGE

Computer sabotage—acts of malicious destruction to a computer or computer resource—is another common type of computer crime today. Computer sabotage can take several forms, including launching a *computer virus* or a *denial of service (DoS) attack*, altering the content of a Web site, or changing data or programs located on a computer. A common tool used to perform computer sabotage is a *botnet*, discussed next. Computer sabotage is illegal in the United States, and acts of sabotage are estimated to cost individuals and organizations billions of dollars per year, primarily for labor costs related to correcting the problems caused by the sabotage, lost productivity, and lost sales.

Botnets

A computer that is controlled by a hacker or other computer criminal is referred to as a **bot** or *zombie computer*; a group of bots that are controlled by one individual and can work together in a coordinated fashion is called a **botnet**. Millions of U.S. computers are part of a botnet—in 2013, one operation alone (*Operation b54*) performed by Microsoft working with the FBI cut the communications among 1,462 *Citadel* botnets (one of the largest botnets in existence and responsible for about half a billion dollars in losses) and their 5 million or more infected computers. Criminals (called *botherders*) are increasingly creating botnets to use for computer sabotage, such as to spread *malware* and to launch *denial of service (DoS) attacks*, discussed shortly. Botherders also often sell their botnet services to send spam and launch Internet attacks on their clients' behalf, as well as to steal identity information, credit card numbers, passwords, corporate secrets, and other sensitive data, which are then sold to other criminals or otherwise used in an illegal manner. Bots are also used to perform *click fraud*—automatically clicking on Internet ads to increase the fees that a company must pay, as discussed in Chapter 11.

Computer Viruses and Other Types of Malware

Malware is a generic term that refers to any type of malicious software. Malware programs are intentionally written to perform destructive acts, such as damaging programs, deleting files, erasing an entire hard drive, or slowing down the performance of a computer. This damage can take place immediately after a computer is *infected* (that is, the malware software is installed) or it can begin when a particular condition is met. A malware program that activates when it detects a certain condition, such as when a particular keystroke is pressed or an employee's name is deleted from an employee file, is called a *logic bomb*. A logic bomb that is triggered by a particular date or time is called a *time bomb*.

Writing a computer virus or other type of malware or even posting the malware code on the Internet is not illegal, but it is considered highly unethical and irresponsible behavior. Distributing malware, on the other hand, is illegal, and virus writers who release their malware are being vigorously prosecuted. Malware can be very costly in terms of the labor costs associated with removing the viruses and correcting any resulting damage, as well as the cost of lost productivity of employees. One type of malware often used by computer

---

> **TIP**
>
> A group of major U.S. ISPs recently committed to work together to combat three major cybersecurity threats, including bots; the FCC predicts this effort will have a significant positive effect on Internet security.

ASK THE EXPERT

Courtesy Symantec

Norton by Symantec

Marian Merritt, Internet Safety Advocate, Symantec Corporation

Does a smartphone need virus protection?

Yes, it is increasingly important to secure your smartphone. Begin with a screen lock passcode to protect against snooping. Tape a recovery phone number to the back of the phone so a finder can contact you. Install or enable tracking software to enable you to locate or lock a lost or stolen phone. And get mobile security software to keep you from installing bad apps or clicking on a dangerous link.

> **Computer sabotage.** An act of malicious destruction to a computer or computer resource. > **Bot.** A computer that is controlled by a hacker or other computer criminal. > **Botnet.** A group of bots that are controlled by one individual. > **Malware.** Any type of malicious software.

criminals to send sensitive data secretly from infected computers to the criminal—spyware—was discussed in Chapter 8. The most common other types of malware are discussed next.

Computer Viruses

One type of malware is the **computer virus**—a software program that is installed without the permission or knowledge of the computer user, that is designed to alter the way a computer operates, and that can replicate itself to infect any new media it has access to. Computer viruses are often embedded into program or data files (often games, videos, and music files downloaded from Web pages or shared via a P2P service). They are spread whenever the infected file is downloaded, is transferred to a new computer via an infected removable storage medium, or is e-mailed to another computer (see Figure 9-14). Viruses can also be installed when a recipient clicks a link in an e-mail message (often in an unsolicited e-mail message that resembles a legitimate e-mail message that normally contains a link, such as an electronic greeting card e-mail that contains a link to view the card); runs a Web app that either contains a virus or exploits a vulnerability in Java, Flash, or another common Web technology; or clicks a link in a message posted on a social networking site like Facebook. Viruses have also been found embedded in photos of bogus Craigslist items sent to potential buyers. Regardless of how it is obtained, once a copy of the infected file reaches a new computer it typically embeds itself into program, data, or system files on the new computer and remains there, affecting that computer according to its programmed instructions, until it is discovered and removed.

FIGURE 9-14
How a computer virus or other type of malicious software might spread.

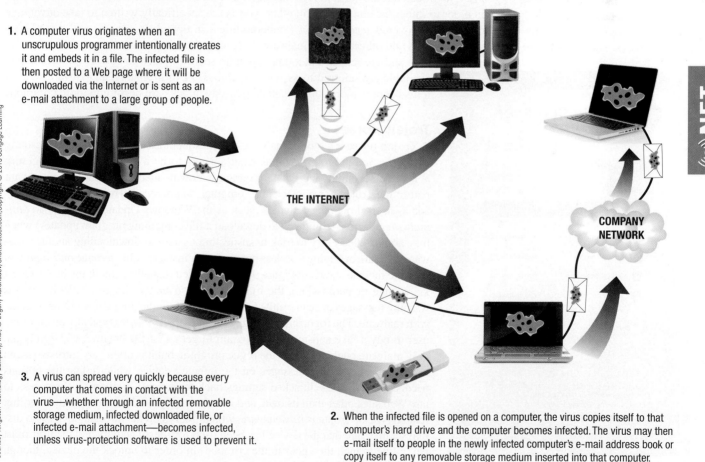

1. A computer virus originates when an unscrupulous programmer intentionally creates it and embeds it in a file. The infected file is then posted to a Web page where it will be downloaded via the Internet or is sent as an e-mail attachment to a large group of people.

THE INTERNET

COMPANY NETWORK

3. A virus can spread very quickly because every computer that comes in contact with the virus—whether through an infected removable storage medium, infected downloaded file, or infected e-mail attachment—becomes infected, unless virus-protection software is used to prevent it.

2. When the infected file is opened on a computer, the virus copies itself to that computer's hard drive and the computer becomes infected. The virus may then e-mail itself to people in the newly infected computer's e-mail address book or copy itself to any removable storage medium inserted into that computer.

> **Computer virus.** A software program installed without the user's knowledge and designed to alter the way a computer operates or to cause harm to the computer system.

Computer Worms

Another common form of malware is the **computer worm**. Like a computer virus, a computer worm is a malicious program that is typically designed to cause damage. Unlike a computer virus, however, a computer worm does not infect other computer files on the infected computer in order to replicate itself; instead, it spreads by creating copies of its code and sending those copies to other computers via a network. Often, the worm is sent to other computers as an e-mail attachment. Usually after the infected e-mail attachment is opened by an individual, the worm inflicts its damage and then automatically sends copies of itself to other computers via the Internet or a private network, typically using addresses in the e-mail address book located on the newly infected computer. When those e-mail messages and their attachments are opened, the new computers become infected and the cycle continues. Because of its distribution method, a worm can spread very rapidly. For instance, the *Mydoom* worm (which was released in 2004 and is considered one of the fastest spreading worms ever) spread so rapidly that, at one point, one out of every 10 e-mails contained the worm, and the persistent *Conficker* worm has infected a total of more than 12 million computers since it was released in 2008 and it is still active today.

Typically, worms do not require any action by the users (such as opening an e-mail attachment) to infect their computers. Instead, a worm scans the Internet looking for computers that are vulnerable to that particular worm and sends a copy of itself to those computers to infect them. Other worms just require the user to view an infected e-mail message or insert an infected removable storage medium (such as a USB flash drive) into the computer in order to infect the computer. Still other worms are specifically written to take advantage of newly discovered *security holes* (vulnerabilities) in operating systems and e-mail programs. Worms and other types of malware that are designed to take advantage of a security hole and are released at a time when no security patch to correct the problem is available are referred to as *zero-day attacks*. Unfortunately, as malware writing tools become more sophisticated, zero-day attacks are becoming more common.

FIGURE 9-15

Rogue anti-malware apps. These programs try to trick victims into purchasing subscriptions to remove nonexistent malware supposedly installed on their devices.

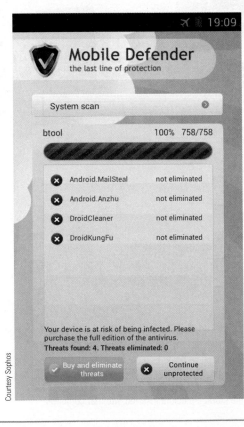

Courtesy Sophos

Trojan Horses

A **Trojan horse** is a type of malware that masquerades as something else—usually an application program (such as what appears to be a game or utility program). When the seemingly legitimate program is downloaded or installed, the malware part of the Trojan horse infects the computer. Many recent Trojan horses masquerade as normal ongoing activities (such as the Windows Update service or an *anti-malware program* telling you to download a file containing program updates) when they are installed to try to trick unsuspecting users into downloading another malware program or buying a useless program. For instance, after a *rogue anti-malware app* like the one shown in Figure 9-15 is installed (usually without the user's direct knowledge or permission), the malware takes over the device displaying bogus warning messages or scan results (see Figure 9-15) indicating the device is infected with malware. The rogue program (an example of *scareware*) typically prompts the user to buy a fake anti-malware program to get rid of the "malware." Usually the only malware on the device is the rogue program, but it is often very intrusive (such as displaying constant messages on the infected device while hiding the options needed to change the hijacked settings back to normal), it often blocks access to any Web sites other than its own, and it is extremely hard to remove. An emerging related type of Trojan is *ransomware*, which freezes up the infected device and displays a message that the device has been used for illegal activity and the user must pay a fine (which then goes to the criminal) in order to unlock the device, though

---

>**Computer worm.** A malicious program designed to spread rapidly to a large number of computers by sending copies of itself to other computers.
>**Trojan horse.** A malicious program that masquerades as something else.

paying the fine doesn't necessarily result in the device being returned to a usable state. Other *rogue apps* are spreading through social networks like Facebook and Twitter, primarily in the form of fake offers (such as for a free iPad) that request access to your social network information when you click the link—if granted, the scammer can then post that and additional scams (and collect information about others) via your account.

Unlike viruses and worms, Trojan horses cannot replicate themselves. Trojan horses are usually spread by being downloaded from the Internet, though they may also be sent as an e-mail attachment, either from the Trojan horse author or from individuals who forward it, not realizing the program is a Trojan horse. Some Trojan horses today act as spyware and are designed to find sensitive information about an individual (such as a Social Security number or a bank account number) or about a company (such as corporate intellectual property like mechanical designs, electronic schematics, and other valuable proprietary information) located on infected computers and then send that information to the malware creator to be used in illegal activities. One emerging type of Trojan horse is called a *RAT* (*Remote-Access Trojan*). RATs are typically installed via small files obtained from an Internet download, such as free software, games, or electronic greeting cards. Once installed, RATs are designed to record every keystroke made on the infected computer and then send the sensitive information they recorded (such as account numbers and passwords) to criminals.

Mobile Malware

In addition to computers, malware also can infect smartphones, media tablets, printers, and other devices that contain computing hardware and software. While more than 90% of today's mobile malware (according to a recent report) is spread via malicious links, smartphones with Bluetooth capabilities can also be infected just by being within range of an infected device. Some *mobile malware* is designed to be a nuisance by changing icons or otherwise making the device more difficult to use, but most (including half of mobile malware created in 2012) is designed to steal information or track the movement or activities of the user. Still other malware is money-oriented, such as malware that is designed to steal credit card data located on a smartphone and malware that places calls or sends text messages to premium rate numbers owned by the thief (for which the owner of the device is charged)—sometimes called *chargeware*. According to IBM, more malware will continue to be directed to smartphones and other devices—such as cars—that contain embedded computers as those devices continue to incorporate more software components and, consequently, become more vulnerable to malware. And mobile malware is getting more sophisticated—in 2013, Kaspersky Lab discovered the first ever Android malware app designed to infect any PCs or other devices the phone connects to. While the app was removed from Google Play, several thousand users had already downloaded it.

Denial of Service (DoS) Attacks

A **denial of service (DoS) attack** is an act of sabotage that attempts to flood a network server or Web server with so many requests for action that it shuts down or simply cannot handle legitimate requests any longer, causing legitimate users to be denied service. For example, a hacker might set up one or more computers to request nonexistent information continually or to *ping* (contact) a server continually with a request to send a responding ping back to a false return address. If enough useless traffic is generated, the server has no resources left to deal with legitimate requests (see Figure 9-16). An emerging trend is DoS attacks aimed at mobile wireless networks. These attacks typically involve repeatedly establishing and releasing connections with the goal of overloading the network to disrupt service.

> **TIP**
>
> About 94% of mobile malware today is written for Android phones (though Apple devices are still vulnerable).

> **TIP**
>
> The 2013 DDoS attacks on The Spamhaus Project created a staggering 300 Gbps of traffic.

> **Denial of service (DoS) attack.** An act of sabotage that attempts to flood a network server or a Web server with so much activity that it is unable to function.

1. Hacker's computer sends several simultaneous requests; each request asks to establish a connection to the server but supplies false return information. In a distributed DoS attack, multiple computers send multiple requests at one time.

Hello? I'd like some info...

2. The server tries to respond to each request but can't locate the computer because false return information was provided. The server waits for a short period of time before closing the connection, which ties up the server and keeps others from connecting.

I can't find you, I'll wait and try again...

3. The hacker's computer continues to send new requests so, as a connection is closed by the server, a new request is waiting. This cycle continues, which ties up the server indefinitely.

Hello? I'd like some info...

Hello? I'd like some info...

I'm busy, I can't help you right now.

LEGITIMATE COMPUTER

HACKER'S COMPUTER

4. The server becomes so overwhelmed that legitimate requests cannot get through and, eventually, the server usually crashes.

WEB SERVER

FIGURE 9-16

How a denial of service (DoS) attack might work.

DoS attacks today are often directed toward popular or controversial sites and typically are carried out via multiple computers (referred to as a *distributed denial of service attack* or *DDoS attack*). DDoS attacks are typically performed by botnets created by hackers; the computers in the botnet participate in the attacks without the owners' knowledge. Because home devices today typically use direct Internet connections but tend to be less protected than school and business computers, hackers are increasingly targeting home devices for botnets used in DDoS attacks and other forms of computer sabotage.

Denial of service attacks can be very costly in terms of business lost (such as when an e-commerce site is shut down), as well as the time and expense required to bring the site back online. Networks that use VoIP are particularly vulnerable to DoS attacks since the real-time nature of VoIP calls means their quality is immediately affected when a DoS attack slows down the network.

Data, Program, or Web Site Alteration

Another type of computer sabotage occurs when a hacker breaches a computer system in order to delete data, change data, modify programs, or otherwise alter the data and programs located there. For example, a student might try to hack into the school database to change his or her grade; a hacker might change a program located on a company server in order to steal money or information; or a disgruntled or former employee might perform a vengeful act, such as altering programs so they work incorrectly, deleting customer records or other critical data, or randomly changing data in a company's database. Like other forms of computer sabotage, data and program alteration is illegal.

Data on Web sites can also be altered by hackers. For instance, social media accounts are being increasingly targeted by hackers. In 2013, for instance, the Associated Press Twitter account was hacked and used to tweet that the president had been injured by explosions at the White House—the stock market tumbled in response. It is also becoming more common for hackers to compromise legitimate Web sites and then use those sites to perform malware attacks. Typically, a hacker alters a legitimate site to display an official-looking message that informs the user that a particular software program must be downloaded, or the hacker posts a rogue banner ad on a legitimate site that redirects the user to a malware site instead of the site for the product featured in the banner ad. According to a report by security company Websense, more than half of the Web sites classified as malicious are actually legitimate Web sites that have been compromised.

PROTECTING AGAINST COMPUTER SABOTAGE

One of the most important protections against computer sabotage is using *security software*, and ensuring that it is kept current.

Security Software

To protect against becoming infected with a computer virus or other type of malware, all computers and other devices used to access the Internet or a company network in both homes and offices should have **security software** installed. Security software typically includes a variety of security features, including a firewall, protection against spyware and bots, and protection against some types of *online fraud*, discussed shortly. Some also include a spam filter, parental controls, password managers, diagnostic software, and backup features; mobile security software also often includes *antitheft software*, discussed in more detail in Chapter 15. One of the most important components of security software is **antivirus software**, which protects against computer viruses and other types of malware.

Like most security software components, antivirus software typically runs continuously whenever the computer is on to perform real-time monitoring of the computer and incoming e-mail messages, instant messages, Web page content, and downloaded files, in order to prevent malicious software and other threats from executing. Many antivirus programs also automatically scan any devices as soon as they are connected to a USB port in order to guard against infections from a USB flash drive, a portable digital media player, or other USB device. Antivirus software helps prevent malware from being installed on your devices because it deletes or *quarantines* (safely isolates) any suspicious content (such as potentially infected e-mail attachments, downloaded files, or apps) as they arrive; regular full system scans can detect and remove any viruses or worms that find their way onto your computer (see Figure 9-17).

According to a recent Panda Security report, there are approximately 125 million malware threats in existence, and about 27 million new malware strains were discovered in 2012 alone. Consequently, it is vital that you keep your security software up to date. Security software is usually set up to download new *threat definitions* automatically from its associated Web site on a regular basis, as often as several times per day—a very important precaution. Most fee-based security

FIGURE 9-17
Security software. Different security programs will typically find different types of malware.

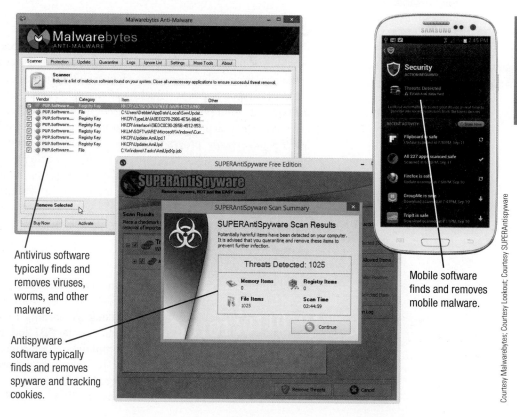

Antivirus software typically finds and removes viruses, worms, and other malware.

Antispyware software typically finds and removes spyware and tracking cookies.

Mobile software finds and removes mobile malware.

Courtesy Malwarebytes; Courtesy Lookout; Courtesy SUPERAntispyware

NET

> **Security software.** Software, typically a suite of programs, used to protect your computer against a variety of threats. > **Antivirus software.** Software used to detect and eliminate computer viruses and other types of malware.

VIRUS PREVENTION STRATEGIES

Use antivirus software to check incoming e-mail messages and files, and download updated virus definitions on a regular basis.

Limit the sharing of flash memory cards, USB flash drives, and other removable storage media with others.

Only download files from reputable sites.

Only open e-mail attachments that come from people you know and that do not have an executable file extension (such as .exe, .com, .bat, or .vbs); double-check with the sender before opening an unexpected, but seemingly legitimate, attachment.

For any downloaded file you are unsure of, upload it to a Web site (such as VirusTotal.com) that tests files for viruses before you open them.

Keep the preview window of your e-mail program closed so you will not view messages until you determine that they are safe to view.

Regularly download and install the latest security patches available for your operating system, browser, Java and other plug-ins, and e-mail programs.

Avoid downloading files from P2P sites.

FIGURE 9-18
Sensible precautions can help protect against computer virus infections.

TIP

If you suspect your computer is infected with a malware program that your regular antivirus software cannot detect or remove, try a software program that specializes in removing hard-to-remove malware, such as the free *Malwarebytes Anti-Malware* program shown in Figure 9-17.

software comes with a year of access to free updates; users should purchase additional years after that to continue to be protected or they should switch to a free antivirus program, such as *AVG Free*, that can be updated regularly at no cost. Schools and businesses should also ensure that students and employees connecting to the campus or company network with personal devices are using up-to-date antivirus software so they will not infect the network with malware inadvertently. Some colleges now require new students to go through a *quarantine process*, in which students are not granted access to the college network until they complete a security process that checks their computers for security threats, updates their operating systems, and installs antivirus software. Some additional virus-prevention strategies are listed in Figure 9-18.

Many ISPs and Web mail providers today also offer some malware protection to their subscribers. Typically, antivirus software scans all incoming e-mail messages at the mail server level to filter out messages containing a virus. If a message containing a virus is detected, it is usually deleted and the recipient is notified that the message contained a virus and was deleted. App stores can help remove a contaminated app when one is identified (by removing the app from the store and remotely wiping the app from phones), though that won't undo any damage already done to the phone by the malware.

Other Security Precautions

Individuals and businesses can protect against some types of computer sabotage (such as program, data, or Web site alteration) by controlling access to their computers and networks, as discussed earlier in this chapter. Intrusion protection systems can help businesses detect and protect against denial of service (DoS) attacks; some personal security software includes intrusion protection as well. For additional protection against spyware, rogue antivirus programs, and other specialized malware, specialized security programs (such as the *SUPERAntispyware* program shown in Figure 9-17) can be used. In addition, most Web browsers have security settings that can be used to help prevent programs from being installed on a computer without the user's permission, such as prompting the user for permission whenever a download is initiated. Enabling these security settings is a wise additional precaution.

ONLINE THEFT, ONLINE FRAUD, AND OTHER DOT CONS

A booming area of computer crime involves online fraud, theft, scams, and related activities designed to steal money or other resources from individuals or businesses—these are collectively referred to as **dot cons**. According to a report by the *Internet Crime Complaint Center (IC3)*, a joint venture of the FBI and the National White Collar Crime Center that receives cybercrime complaints from consumers and reports them to the appropriate law enforcement agency, IC3 received and processed more than 24,000 complaints per month in 2012 with reported losses more than 8% higher than in 2011. Some of the most common types of dot cons are discussed next.

> **Dot con.** A fraud or scam carried out through the Internet.

TREND

Beyond Fingerprint Readers—Digital Tattoos and More

Think passwords—even the newer types of passwords that use pictures or patterns instead of characters—are ho-hum? Well, you're in luck. A number of new alternatives that can be used to protect access to your device or log on to your Web sites are about to become available.

One option that Google is developing uses *facial gestures*, such as unlocking your phone by smiling or winking at it. Instead of using a static image (as with face recognition, which has been circumvented on phone unlocking systems by using a photograph of the authorized user), this new technology includes a "Liveness Check" where the user has to prove that he or she is alive and not a photo by blinking. In addition, the system requires a match of a facial landmark (such as an eye, mouth, or nose) in two different but related facial gestures (such as smiling and not smiling).

Two other more unusual alternatives recently demonstrated by Motorola are *electronic tattoos* and *authentication pills*. The tattoos (called *Biostamps* and originally developed for remote medical monitoring of patients) contain flexible electronic circuits that are attached to the wearer's skin (see the accompanying photo) using a rubber stamp and which then can be covered with a spray-on bandage for additional waterproofing if needed. The pills (called the *Proteus Digital Health pill* and already approved by the U.S. FDA for medication monitoring) are swallowed and then send signals from the stomach. Both devices already work with smartphones

and researchers propose that both technologies could be adapted to become authentication systems, automatically logging individuals on to their phones or computers and to secure Web sites. The downside is that both systems are temporary and would have to be replaced on a regular basis, which could lead to hackers stealing additional tattoos and pills not yet used and circumventing whatever activation system is in place or even kidnapping individuals to use their bodies to log in to secure systems.

Next up? *Thought-based authentication* where you can automatically log on to your wearable devices using only your brainwaves.

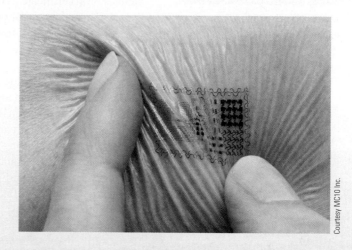

Courtesy MC10 Inc.

Theft of Data, Information, and Other Resources

Data theft or *information theft* is the theft of data or information located on or being sent from a computer. It can be committed by stealing an actual computer (as discussed in more detail in Chapter 15); it can also take place over the Internet or a network by an individual gaining unauthorized access to that data by hacking into the computer or by intercepting the data in transit. (For a look at some emerging biometric systems that may soon be used to help protect access to your PC and your Web sites, see the Trend box.) Common types of data and information stolen via the Internet or another network include customer data (such as Web site passwords or credit card information) and proprietary corporate information. As previously discussed, data breaches today frequently result in stolen customer and credit card data. Stolen consumer data is often used in fraudulent activities, such as *identity theft*, as discussed shortly.

Money is another resource that can be stolen via a computer. Company insiders sometimes steal money by altering company programs to transfer small amounts of money—for example, a few cents' worth of bank account interest—from a very large number of transactions to an account controlled by the thieves. This type of crime is sometimes called *salami shaving*. Victims of salami-shaving schemes generally are unaware that their funds have been accessed because the amount taken from each individual is very small. However, added together, the amounts can be substantial. Another example of monetary theft performed via computers involves hackers electronically transferring money illegally from online bank accounts, traditional bank accounts, credit card accounts, or accounts at online payment services (such as *PayPal*, which is discussed more in Chapter 11).

Identity Theft, Phishing, Social Media Hacks, and Pharming

A growing dot con trend is obtaining enough information about an individual to perform fraudulent financial transactions. Often, this is carried out in conjunction with *identity theft*; techniques frequently used to obtain the necessary personal information to commit identity theft are *phishing*, *spear phishing*, *social media hacking*, and *pharming*.

Identity Theft

Identity theft occurs when someone obtains enough information about a person to be able to masquerade as that person—usually to buy products or services in that person's name (see Figure 9-19). Typically, identity theft begins when a thief obtains a person's name, address, and Social Security number, often from a discarded or stolen document (such as a preapproved credit card application that was sent in the mail), from information obtained via the Internet (such as from a résumé posted online), or from information located on a computer (such as on a stolen computer or hacked server, or information sent from a computer via a computer virus or spyware program installed on that computer). The thief may then order a copy of the individual's birth certificate, obtain a "replacement" driver's license, make purchases and charge them to the victim, and/or open credit or bank accounts in the victim's name.

Assuming the thief requests a change of address for these new accounts after they are opened, it may take quite some time—often until a company or collections agency contacts the victim about overdue bills—for the victim to become aware that his or her identity has been stolen. Although identity theft often takes place via a computer today, information used in identity theft can also be gathered from trash dumpsters, mailboxes, and other locations. Other commonly used techniques are *skimming* and *social engineering*. Skimming involves stealing credit card or debit card numbers by using an illegal device attached to a credit card reader or an ATM machine that reads and stores the card numbers (and used in conjunction with a hidden camera to capture ATM PIN numbers) to be retrieved by the thief at a later time. Social engineering involves pretending—typically via phone or e-mail—to be a bank officer, potential employer, or other trusted individual in order to get the potential victim to supply personal information. Today, social engineering schemes often use social media to obtain the needed information and gain the trust of a victim. Because of this, *social engineering tests* are often included when a company runs a security evaluation of its company and employees, as discussed in Chapter 15.

FIGURE 9-19
How identity theft works.

1. The thief obtains information about an individual from discarded mail, employee records, credit card transactions, Web server files, or some other method.

2. The thief makes purchases, opens new credit card accounts, and more in the victim's name. Often, the thief changes the address on the account to delay discovery.

3. The victim usually finds out by being denied credit or by being contacted about overdue bills generated by the thief. Clearing one's name after identity theft is time consuming and can be very difficult and frustrating for the victim.

> **Identity theft.** Using someone else's identity to purchase goods or services, obtain new credit cards or bank loans, or otherwise illegally masquerade as that individual.

Unfortunately, identity theft is a very real danger to individuals today. According to the Federal Trade Commission (FTC), millions of Americans have their identity stolen each year and identity theft has topped the list of consumer complaints for 13 straight years. Identity theft can be extremely distressing for victims, can take years to straighten out, and can be very expensive. Some identity theft victims, such as Michelle Brown, believe that they will always be dealing with their "alter reality" to some extent. For a year and a half, an identity thief used Brown's identity to obtain over $50,000 in goods and services, to rent properties—even to engage in drug trafficking. Although the culprit was eventually arrested and convicted for other criminal acts, she continued to use Brown's identity and was even booked into jail using Brown's stolen identity. As a final insult after the culprit was in prison, U.S. customs agents detained the real Michelle Brown when she was returning from a trip to Mexico because of the criminal record of the identity thief. Brown states that she has not traveled out of the country since, fearing an arrest or some other serious problem resulting from the theft of her identity, and estimates she has spent over 500 hours trying to correct all the problems related to the identity theft.

Phishing and Spear Phishing

Phishing (pronounced "fishing") is the use of a *spoofed* communications (typically an e-mail message, such as one appearing to come from eBay, PayPal, Google, Bank of America, or another well-known legitimate organization, but is actually sent from a phisher) to trick the recipient into revealing sensitive personal information (such as Web site logon information or credit card numbers). Once obtained, this information is used in identity theft and other fraudulent activities. A phishing e-mail typically looks legitimate and it contains links in the e-mail that appear to go to the Web site of the legitimate business, but these links go to the phisher's Web site that is set up to look like the legitimate site instead—an act called *Web site spoofing*. Phishing e-mails are typically sent to a wide group of individuals and usually include an urgent message stating that the individual's credit card or account information needs to be updated and instructing the recipient of the e-mail to click the link provided in the e-mail in order to keep the account active. If the victim clicks the link and supplies the requested information via the spoofed site, the criminal gains access to all information provided by the victim, such as account numbers, credit card numbers, and Web site passwords. Phishing attempts can occur today via IM, text messages (called *smishing*), fake messages sent via eBay or Facebook, Twitter tweets, pop-up security alert windows, and phone calls, in addition to e-mail. Phishers also frequently utilize spyware; typically

Courtesy Symantec

ASK THE EXPERT

Norton by Symantec **Marian Merritt,** Internet Safety Advocate, Symantec Corporation

What is the single most important thing computer users should do to protect themselves from online threats?

The single most important step to protect computer users from online threats is to make sure their Internet security solution is current and up to date. There are several all-in-one security solutions available, such as Symantec's Norton 360, which combine PC security, antiphishing capabilities, backup, and tuneup technologies.

It's also pivotal to maintain a healthy wariness when receiving online communications. Do not click on links in suspicious e-mails or instant messages (IMs). These links will often direct you to sites that will ask you to reveal passwords, PINs, or other confidential data. Genuine organizations or institutions do not send such e-mails, nor do they ask for confidential data (like your Social Security number) for ordinary business transactions. If you're unsure whether or not an e-mail is legitimate, type the URL directly in your browser or call the institution to confirm they sent you that e-mail. Finally, do not open attachments in e-mails of questionable origin because they may contain viruses.

NET

> **Phishing.** The use of spoofed communications (typically e-mail messages) to gain credit card numbers and other personal data to be used for fraudulent purposes.

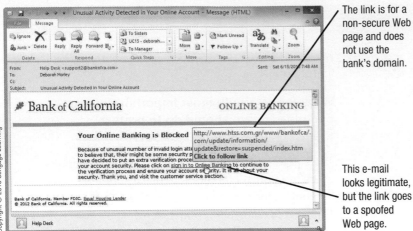

The link is for a non-secure Web page and does not use the bank's domain.

This e-mail looks legitimate, but the link goes to a spoofed Web page.

FIGURE 9-20

Phishing. Phishing schemes typically use legitimate-looking e-mails to trick users into providing private information.

✓ **TIP**

Spear phishing attacks are expected to increase as a result of the Epsilon data breach, which exposed names and e-mail addresses of individuals along with businesses that they patronize, such as banks, hotels, and stores.

clicking the link in the phishing e-mail installs the spyware on the victim's computer, and it will remain there (transmitting passwords and other sensitive data to a phisher) until it is detected and removed.

To fool victims into using the spoofed Web site, phishing e-mails and the spoofed Web sites often look legitimate (see Figure 9-20). To accomplish this, phishers typically use copies of the spoofed organization's logo and other Web site content from the legitimate Web site. For spoofed banking Web pages and other pages where the victim would expect to see a secure Web page, some criminals use a secure connection between the victim and the criminal's server so the Web page looks secure with an *https:* in the Address bar. The domain name of the legitimate company (such as *ebay* for an eBay phishing page) is also often used as part of the URL of the phishing link (such as a URL starting with the text *ebay* even though the URL's domain is not ebay.com) to make it appear more legitimate. Other phishing schemes use a technique called *typosquatting*, which is setting up spoofed Web sites with addresses slightly different from legitimate sites. For example, a spoofed Web site using the URL www.amazon.com might be used to catch shoppers intending to reach the Amazon.com Web site located at www.amazon.com in hopes that customers making this error when typing the URL will not notice it and will supply logon information via the spoofed site when they arrive.

Another recent trend is the use of more targeted, personalized phishing schemes, known as **spear phishing**. Spear phishing e-mails are directly targeted to a specific individual and typically appear to come from an organization or person that the targeted individual has an association with. They also often include personalized information (such as the potential victim's name, employer, and other information frequently found on social networking sites and other public resources) to make the spear phishing e-mails seem even more legitimate. Some attacks use spoofed logon pages for social networking sites to obtain an individual's logon information and password. Because many individuals use the same logon information for a variety of sites, once a scammer has a valid username/password combination, he or she can try it on a variety of common e-commerce sites, such as shopping sites, online banking sites, and online payment services like PayPal.

Spear phishers also target employees of selected organizations by posing as someone within the company, such as a human resource or technical support employee. These spear phishing e-mails often request confidential information (such as logon IDs and passwords) or direct the employee to click a link to supposedly reset his or her password. The goal for corporate spear phishing attacks is usually to steal intellectual property, such as software source code, design documents, or schematics. It can also be used to steal money. For instance, in one recent case, a grocery store chain received fraudulent e-mails that appeared to come from two approved suppliers. The e-mails instructed the grocery store chain to send future payments to new bank accounts listed in the e-mail—the grocery store chain deposited more than $10 million into two fraudulent bank accounts before the scam was discovered.

Social Media Hacks

The use of phishing e-mails declined dramatically in 2012, as thieves appeared to shift to other online communications, such as social networks, according to a recent Symantec

> **Spear phishing.** A personalized phishing scheme targeted at an individual.

Internet Security Threat Report. In addition to obtaining information from social networks that can be used in phishing schemes, **social media hacks** can provide phishers with social media logon information that can be used by the phishers to log on to the victim's account and then *hijack* it—posting comments or sending messages containing phishing links (posing as the victim) to the victim's friends, who are much more likely to click on the links because they appear to come from a friend. In addition to individuals' social networking accounts being hacked, business accounts have been recent targets as well. For example, the Twitter accounts of several businesses (including Burger King and Jeep) were hacked in 2013 and erroneous information posted (Burger King being purchased by McDonald's was one tweet made by the hackers). While hacking into a business's social media account and hijacking it temporarily is often a public embarrassment, sometimes (like when the stock market dipped after the recent AP Twitter hack that there was an explosion at the White House), the consequences of business social media hacking are more severe.

Pharming and Drive-By Pharming

Pharming is another type of scam that uses spoofing—specifically spoofed domain names used to obtain personal information for use in fraudulent activities. With pharming, the criminal reroutes traffic intended for a commonly used Web site to a spoofed Web site set up by the pharmer. Sometimes pharming takes place via malicious code sent to a computer via an e-mail message or other distribution method. More often, however, it takes place via changes made to a *DNS server*—a computer that translates URLs into the appropriate IP addresses needed to display the Web page corresponding to a URL. This type of pharming can take place at one of the 13 *root DNS servers* (the DNS servers used in conjunction with the Internet), but it more often takes place at a *company DNS server* (the DNS server for that company used to route Web page requests received via company Web site URLs to the appropriate company server). After hacking into a company DNS server (typically for a company with a commonly used Web site), the pharmer changes the IP addresses used in conjunction with a particular company URL (called *DNS poisoning*) so any Web page requests made via the legitimate company URL is routed (via the company's poisoned DNS server) to a phony spoofed Web page located on the pharmer's Web server. So, even though a user types the proper URL to display the legitimate company Web page in his or her browser, the spoofed page is displayed instead.

Because spoofed sites are set up to look like the legitimate sites, the user typically does not notice any difference, and any information sent via that site is captured by the pharmer. To avoid suspicion, some pharming schemes capture the user's account name and password as it is entered the first time on the spoofed site, and then display a password error message. The spoofed site then redirects the user back to the legitimate site where he or she is able to log on to the legitimate site, leaving the user to think that he or she must have just mistyped the password the first time. But, by then, the pharmer has already captured the victim's username and password and can use that information to gain access to the victim's account.

A recent variation of pharming is *drive-by pharming*. The goal is still to redirect victims to spoofed sites; however, the pharmer accomplishes this by changing the victim's designated DNS server (which often belongs to the individual's ISP and is specified in the victim's router settings) to the pharmer's DNS server in order to direct the victim to spoofed versions of legitimate Web sites when the victim enters the URLs for those sites. Typically, the pharmer uses malicious JavaScript code placed on a Web page to changes the victim's DNS settings to use the pharmer's DNS server; this change can only occur on a router in which the default administrator password was not changed.

NET

TIP

In 2013, the Department of Homeland Security began recommending disabling Java on Web browsers due to security flaws; while not possible for all users, try it— if your Web sites function fine without it, leave it disabled.

> **Social media hack.** The act of accessing someone else's social media account to make changes to the content or to perform an activity as that individual. > **Pharming.** The use of spoofed domain names to obtain personal information in order to use that information in fraudulent activities.

Online Auction Fraud

Online auction fraud (sometimes called *Internet auction fraud*) occurs when an online auction buyer pays for merchandise that is never delivered, or that is delivered but it is not as represented. It can also occur when an online buyer receives the proper items but falsely claims that they never arrived. Like other types of fraud, online auction fraud is illegal, but similar to many types of Internet cons, prosecution is difficult for online auction fraud because multiple jurisdictions are usually involved. Although most online auction sites have policies that suspend sellers with a certain number of complaints lodged against them, it is very easy for those sellers to come back using a new e-mail address and identity.

Other Internet Scams

There is a wide range of other scams that can occur via Web sites or unsolicited e-mails. The anonymity of the Internet makes it very easy for con artists to appear to be anyone they want to be, including a charitable organization or a reputable-looking business. Common types of scams include loan scams, work-at-home cons, pyramid schemes, bogus credit card offers and prize promotions, and fraudulent business opportunities and franchises. These offers typically try to sell potential victims nonexistent services or worthless information, or they try to convince potential victims to voluntarily supply their credit card details and other personal information. Some scammers hack into a system to obtain e-mail addresses to use as targets for a scam that is based on something those individuals have in common in order to increase the odds of a potential victim falling for the scam. Others send messages to a potential victim impersonating a distant friend or old classmate (typically found via a social networking site) and requesting money (such as by saying they are traveling out of the country and were just robbed).

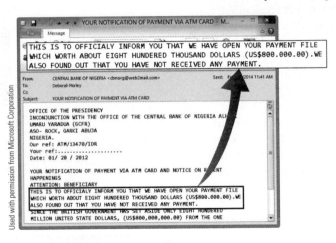

One ongoing Internet scam is the *Nigerian letter fraud* scheme. This scheme involves an e-mail message that appears to come from the Nigerian government and that promises the potential victim a share of a substantial amount of money in exchange for the use of the victim's bank account. Supposedly the victim's bank account information is needed to facilitate a wire transfer (but the victim's account is emptied instead) and/or up-front cash is needed to pay for nonexistent fees (but that is kept by the con artist). The scams often change to fit current events, such as the war in Iraq or a recent natural disaster. However, the scams always involve a so-called fortune that is inaccessible to the con artist without the potential victims' help (see Figure 9-21) and the victims always lose any money they provide.

Other schemes involve con artists who solicit donations for charitable organizations after disasters and other tragic events, but who keep the donations instead. Another common scam involves setting up a pornographic site that requires a valid credit card, supposedly to prove that the visitor is an adult, but which is then used for credit card fraud. A relatively new type of scam involves posting fake job listings on job search sites to elicit personal information (such as Social Security numbers) from job seekers. An even more recent twist is to hire individuals through online job sites for seemingly legitimate positions involving money handling (such as bookkeeping or accounting positions), but then use those individuals—often without their knowledge—to facilitate Internet auction scams and other monetary scams.

FIGURE 9-21
A Nigerian letter fraud e-mail.

>**Online auction fraud.** When an item purchased through an online auction is never delivered after payment, or the item is not as specified by the seller.

PROTECTING AGAINST ONLINE THEFT, ONLINE FRAUD, AND OTHER DOT CONS

In a nutshell, the best protection against many dot cons is protecting your identity; that is, protecting any identifying information about you that could be used in fraudulent activities. There are also specific precautions that can help protect against online theft, identity theft, online auction fraud, and other types of dot cons, as discussed next. With any dot con, it is important to act quickly if you think you have been a victim. For instance, you should work with your local law enforcement agency, credit card companies, and the three major consumer credit bureaus (*Equifax*, *Experian*, and *TransUnion*) to close any accessed or fraudulent accounts, place fraud alerts on your credit report, and take other actions to prevent additional fraudulent activity while the fraud is being investigated.

Arrests and prosecutions by law enforcement agencies may also help cut down on cybercrimes. Prosecution of online scammers has been increasing and sentences are not light. For instance, two Romanian citizens were recently sentenced for their involvement in a phishing scheme (the first time the United States has sentenced a foreigner for phishing)—one received 80 months in federal prison; the other received 27 months.

Protecting Against Data and Information Theft

Businesses and individuals can both help to prevent some types of data and information theft. For instance, businesses should use good security measures to protect the data stored on their computers. Individuals should be vigilant about protecting their private information by sending sensitive information via secure Web servers only and not disclosing personal information—especially a Social Security number or a mother's maiden name—unless it is absolutely necessary and they know how the information will be used and that it will not be shared with others. In addition, individuals should never give out sensitive personal information to anyone who requests it over the phone or by e-mail—businesses that legitimately need bank account information, passwords, or credit card numbers will not request that information via phone or e-mail. Encrypting computers and other hardware containing sensitive information, so it will not be readable if the hardware is lost or stolen, is another important precaution.

Protecting Against Identity Theft, Phishing, Social Media Hacks, and Pharming

Some precautions already discussed (such as disclosing your personal information only when necessary and only via secure Web pages) can help reduce your risk of identity theft. So can using security software (and keeping it up to date) to guard against malware that can send information from your computer or about your activities (the Web site passwords that you type, for example) to a criminal. In addition, to prevent someone from using the preapproved credit card offers and other documents containing personal information that are mailed to you, shred them before throwing them in the trash. To prevent the theft of outgoing mail containing sensitive information, don't place it in your mailbox—mail it at the post office or in a USPS drop box.

To avoid phishing schemes, never click a link in an e-mail message to go to a secure Web site—always type the URL for that site in your browser (not necessarily the URL shown in the e-mail message) instead. Phishing e-mails typically sound urgent and often contain spelling and grammatical errors—see Figure 9-22 for some tips to help

NET

▼ **FIGURE 9-22**
Tips for identifying phishing e-mail messages.

A PHISHING E-MAIL OFTEN . . .

Tries to scare you into responding by sounding urgent, including a warning that your account will be cancelled if you do not respond, or telling you that you have been a victim of fraud.

Asks you to provide personal information, such as your bank account number, an account password, credit card number, PIN number, mother's maiden name, or Social Security number.

Contains links that do not go where the link text says it will go (point to a hyperlink in the e-mail message to view the URL for that link to see the actual domain being used—a phisher would have to use a URL like microsoft.phisher.com, not microsoft.com).

Uses legitimate logos from the company the phisher is posing as.

Appears to come from a known organization, but one you may not have an association with.

Appears to be text or text and images but is actually a single image; it has been created that way to avoid being caught in a spam filter (a program that sorts e-mail based on legitimate e-mail and suspected spam) because spam filters cannot read text that is part of an image in an e-mail message.

Contains spelling or grammatical errors.

TIPS FOR AVOIDING IDENTITY THEFT

Protect your Social Security number—give it out only when necessary.

Be careful with your physical mail and trash—shred all documents containing sensitive data.

Secure your computer—update your operating system and use up-to-date security (antivirus, antispyware, firewall, etc.) software.

Be cautious—never click on a link in an e-mail message or respond to a too-good-to-be-true offer.

Use strong passwords for your computer and online accounts.

Verify sources before sharing sensitive information—never respond to e-mail or phone requests for sensitive information.

Be vigilant while on the go—safeguard your wallet, smartphone, and portable computer.

Watch your bills and monitor your credit reports—react immediately if you suspect fraudulent activity.

Use security software or browser features that warn you if you try to view a known phishing site.

FIGURE 9-23

Tips to reduce your risk of identity theft.

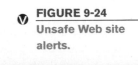

TIP

You can order your free credit reports online quickly and easily via Web sites like *AnnualCreditReport.com*.

FIGURE 9-24

Unsafe Web site alerts.

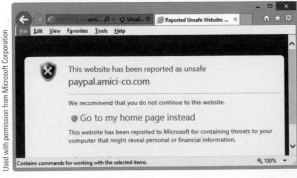

you recognize phishing e-mails. Remember that spear phishing schemes may include personalized information (such as your name)—do not let that fool you into thinking the phishing e-mail is legitimate. If you think an unsolicited e-mail message requesting information from you may be legitimate (for instance, if the credit card you use to make an automatic payment for an ongoing service is about to expire and you receive an e-mail message asking you to update your credit card information), type the URL for that site in your browser to load the legitimate site and then update your account information. To prevent a drive-by pharming attack, all businesses and individuals should change the administrator password for routers, access points, and other networking hardware from the default password to a strong password. Individuals can also change the DNS server for their router to one (such as *OpenDNS*) that uses filtering to block malicious sites and protect against pharming attempts.

Keeping a close eye on your credit card bills and credit history is also important to make sure you catch any fraudulent charges or accounts opened by an identity thief as soon as possible. Make sure your bills come in every month (some thieves will change your mailing address to delay detection), and read credit card statements carefully to look for unauthorized charges. Be sure to follow up on any calls you get from creditors, instead of assuming it is just a mistake. Most security experts also recommend ordering a full credit history on yourself a few times a year to check for accounts listed in your name that you did not open and any other problems. The *Fair and Accurate Credit Transactions Act (FACTA)* enables all Americans to get a free copy of their credit report, upon request, each year from the three major consumer credit bureaus. Ideally, you should request a report from one of these bureaus every four months to monitor your credit on a regular basis. These reports contain information about inquiries related to new accounts requested in your name, as well as any delinquent balances or other negative reports. For another tool that you can use to help detect identity theft—*online financial alerts*—see the Technology and You box. You can also use browser-based *antiphishing* tools and *digital certificates* to help guard against identity theft and the phishing and pharming schemes used in conjunction with identity theft, as discussed next. Some additional tips for minimizing your risk of identity theft are listed in Figure 9-23.

Antiphishing Tools

Antiphishing tools are built into many e-mail programs and Web browsers to help notify users of possible phishing Web sites. For instance, some e-mail programs will disable links in e-mail messages identified as questionable, unless the user overrides them; most recent browsers warn users when a Web page associated with a possible phishing URL is requested (see Figure 9-24); and antiphishing capabilities are included in many recent security suites.

In addition, some secure Web sites are adding additional layers in security to protect against identity thieves. For example, some online banking sites analyze users' habits to look for patterns that vary from the norm, such as accessing accounts online at an hour unusual for that individual or a higher than normal level of online purchases. If a bank suspects the account may be compromised, it contacts the owner for verification. Bank of America and some other financial institutions have also added an additional step in their logon process—displaying an image or word preselected by the user and stored on the bank's server—to prove

TECHNOLOGY AND YOU

Online Financial Alerts

Want to know ASAP when a transaction that might be fraudulent is charged to your credit card or deducted from your checking account? Well, *online financial alerts* might be the answer.

Many online banking services today allow users to set up e-mail alerts for credit card and bank account activity over a certain amount, low balances, and so forth. For individuals wishing to monitor multiple accounts, however, online money management aggregator services (such as *Mint.com*) make it easier. Once you have set up a free Mint.com account with your financial accounts (including credit cards and checking, savings, and PayPal accounts) and their respective passwords, you can see the status of all your accounts through the Mint.com interface. You can also set up alerts for any of the accounts based on your desired criteria, such as any fee charged or an unusual transaction (see the accompanying photo). The alerts are sent to you via e-mail or text message, depending on your preference, to help notify you as soon as possible if a suspicious activity occurs. And timeliness is of the essence, because the sooner identity theft is discovered, the less time the thief has to make additional fraudulent transactions. For security purposes, Mint.com doesn't store online banking usernames and passwords; instead, a secure online financial services

provider is used to connect Mint.com to the appropriate financial institutions to update your activity. In addition, the Mint.com Web site cannot be used to move money out of or between financial accounts—it can be used only to view information.

to the user that the site being viewed is the legitimate (not a phishing) site. In addition, if the system does not recognize the computer that the user is using to log on to the system, the user is required to go through an authentication process (typically by correctly answering cognitive authentication questions) before being allowed to access the system via that computer. The questions used are specifically designed to be "out of wallet" questions—easy for the individual to answer but difficult for hackers to guess the correct answer or find in a stolen wallet. Bank of America is also one bank offering customers the option of adding the use of one-time passwords (autogenerated by a security token like the one shown in Figure 9-5 or sent via text message to the individual's mobile phone) to their online banking logon procedure.

Digital Certificates and Digital Signatures

The purpose of a **digital certificate** (also called a **digital ID**) is to authenticate the identity of an individual or organization. Digital certificates are granted by Certificate Authorities and typically contain the name of the person, organization, or Web site being certified along with a certificate serial number and an expiration date. Digital certificates also include a public/private key pair. In addition to being used by the certificate holder to encrypt files and e-mail messages (as discussed earlier in this chapter), these keys and the digital certificate are used with secure Web pages to guarantee the Web pages are secure and actually belong to the stated organization (so users can know for sure who their credit

>**Digital certificate.** A group of electronic data that can be used to verify the identity of a person or organization; includes a key pair that can be used for encryption and digital signatures (also called a **digital ID**).

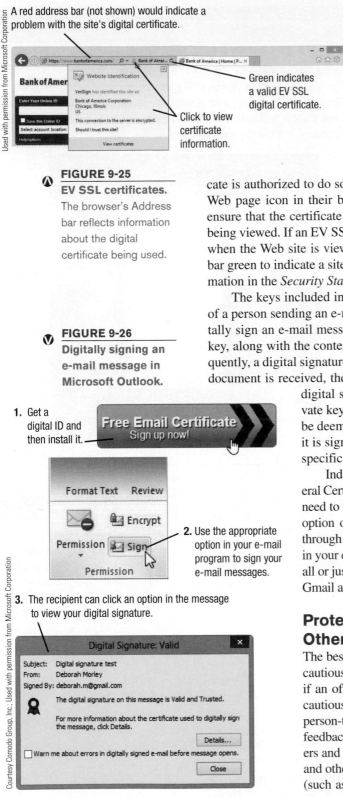

A red address bar (not shown) would indicate a problem with the site's digital certificate.

Green indicates a valid EV SSL digital certificate.

Click to view certificate information.

FIGURE 9-25

EV SSL certificates.
The browser's Address bar reflects information about the digital certificate being used.

FIGURE 9-26

Digitally signing an e-mail message in Microsoft Outlook.

1. Get a digital ID and then install it.

2. Use the appropriate option in your e-mail program to sign your e-mail messages.

3. The recipient can click an option in the message to view your digital signature.

card number or other sensitive data is really being sent to in order to protect against some online scams).

Secure Web sites can obtain either a normal *SSL digital certificate* or a newer *Extended Validation* (*EV*) *SSL digital certificate* that was developed to provide consumers with a higher level of trust while online. While both digital certificates require an application process, the verification process to obtain an EV SSL digital certificate is more thorough, requiring the use of reputable third-party sources to verify that the company has the right to use the Web site domain name in question and that the business requesting the certificate is authorized to do so. With both types of certificates, individuals can click the secure Web page icon in their browser window to view that site's digital certificate in order to ensure that the certificate is valid and issued to the company associated with the Web site being viewed. If an EV SSL certificate is used, however, additional information is displayed when the Web site is viewed in an EV-compliant browser, such as recoloring the Address bar green to indicate a site using a valid EV SSL certificate and displaying certificate information in the *Security Status bar* to the right of the Address bar, as shown in Figure 9-25.

The keys included in a digital certificate can also be used to authenticate the identity of a person sending an e-mail message or other document via a **digital signature**. To digitally sign an e-mail message or other document, the sender's private key is used and that key, along with the contents of the document, generates a unique digital signature; consequently, a digital signature is different with each signed document. When a digitally signed document is received, the recipient's computer uses the sender's public key to verify the digital signature. Because the document is signed with the sender's private key (that only the sender should know) and the digital signature will be deemed invalid if even one character of the document is changed after it is signed, digital signatures guarantee that the document was sent by a specific individual and that it was not tampered with after it was signed.

Individuals can obtain a free digital certificate for personal use from several Certificate Authorities (such as *Comodo*). Once you obtain one, you will need to install it on your computer (Windows users can use the *Certificates* option on the Content tab in the Internet Properties dialog box available through the Control Panel), and then you can use the digital signature option in your e-mail program (such as Microsoft Outlook, see Figure 9-26) to sign all or just selected messages. At this time, most Web mail programs (such as Gmail and Outlook.com) do not support the use of digital signatures.

Protecting Against Online Auction Fraud and Other Internet Scams

The best protection against many dot cons is common sense. Be extremely cautious of any unsolicited e-mail messages you receive and realize that if an offer sounds too good to be true, it probably is. You should also be cautious when dealing with individuals online through auctions and other person-to-person activities. Before bidding on an auction item, check out the feedback rating of the seller to see comments written by other auction sellers and buyers as well as the sellers' return policy. Always pay for auctions and other online purchases using a credit card or an online payment service (such as PayPal) that accepts credit card payments so you can dispute the

>**Digital signature.** A unique digital code that can be attached to a file or an e-mail message to verify the identity of the sender and guarantee the file or message has not been changed since it was signed.

transaction through your credit card company, if needed. Using an online payment service that bills the charge to your credit card, instead of allowing the seller to charge your credit card, has the extra advantage of keeping your credit card information private. In addition, some auction sites and online payment services offer free buyer protection against undelivered items or auction items that are significantly different from their description. For instance, most eBay purchases paid for via PayPal have at least $200 of buyer protection coverage at no additional cost. For expensive items, consider using a reputable *escrow service*, which allows you to ensure that the merchandise is as specified before your payment is released to the seller.

PERSONAL SAFETY ISSUES

In addition to being expensive and inconvenient, cybercrime can also be physically dangerous. Although most of us may not ordinarily view using the Internet as a potentially dangerous activity, cases of physical harm due to Internet activity do happen. For example, children and teenagers have become the victims of pedophiles who arranged face-to-face meetings by using information gathered via e-mail, online games, social networking sites, or other online sources. There are also a growing number of incidents in which children are threatened by classmates via e-mail, social media posts, or text messages. Adults have fallen victim to unscrupulous or dangerous individuals who misrepresent themselves online, and the availability of personal information online has made it more difficult for individuals to hide from people who may want to do them harm, such as abused women trying to hide from their abusive husbands. Two of the most common ways individuals are harassed online—*cyberbullying* and *cyberstalking*—are discussed next.

Cyberbullying and Cyberstalking

Children and teenagers bullying other children or teenagers via the Internet—such as through e-mail, a text message, a social networking site, a blog, or other online communications method—is referred to as **cyberbullying**. Unfortunately, cyberbullying is common today—it affects more than one-half of all U.S. teenagers, according to a recent report. Cyberbullying can take place via direct online communications (such as with an e-mail or a text message), as well as via more subtle means. For instance, there have been cases of students posting videos on YouTube of other students being bullied or shown in compromising situations, as well as cases of individuals hacking into a student's social networking account and changing the content on the student's pages to harass that student. Unfortunately, there are also several instances where teenagers have committed suicide because of cyberbullying, which have prompted many states and schools to look at harassment statutes and bullying policies. Several antibullying campaigns have been initiated by school districts and government organizations (see Figure 9-27) and most states have implemented new laws or amended existing harassment laws to address electronic harassment. And Web sites (along with the individuals or companies responsible for them) that provide the means for the harassment may also be at risk for prosecution. In Italy, three Google executives were given suspended jail terms for ignoring a parent's request to remove a video of a boy being bullied, and at the time of this writing, Italian prosecutors were investigating whether to sue Facebook for not removing harrassing messages that led to a teenage girl's suicide.

While incidents of online harrassment between adults can be referred to as *cyber-harassment*, repeated threats or other malicious behavior that poses a credible threat of harm carried out online between adults is referred to as **cyberstalking**. Cyberstalkers sometimes find their victims online; for instance, someone who makes a comment on a

Courtesy National Crime Prevention Council

FIGURE 9-27
An anti-cyberbullying Web banner.

NET

> **Cyberbullying.** Children or teenagers bullying other children or teenagers via the Internet. > **Cyberstalking.** Repeated threats or harassing behavior between adults carried out via e-mail or another Internet communications method.

social networking site that the cyberstalker does not like, or bloggers who are harassed and threatened because of their blogging activities. Other times, the attack is more personal, such as employers who are stalked online by ex-employees who were fired or otherwise left their position under adverse conditions, and celebrities who are stalked online by fans.

Cyberstalking typically begins with online harassment—such as sending harassing or threatening e-mail messages or unwanted files to the victim, posing as the victim in order to sign the victim up for pornographic or otherwise offensive e-mail newsletters, publicizing the victim's home address and telephone number, or hacking into the victim's social networking pages to alter the content. Cyberstalking can also lead to offline stalking and possibly physical harm to, and sometimes even the death of, the victim. While there are as yet no specific federal laws against cyberstalking, all states have made it illegal (and it is being increasingly prosecuted), and some federal laws do apply if the online actions include computer fraud or another type of computer crime, suggest a threat of personal injury, or involve sending obscene e-mail messages. Many cyberstalkers are not caught, however, due in part to the anonymity of the Internet, which assists cyberstalkers in concealing their true identities.

Online Pornography

A variety of controversial and potentially objectionable material is available on the Internet. Although there have been attempts to ban this type of material from the Internet, they have not been successful. For example, the *Communications Decency Act*, signed into law in 1996—which made it a criminal offense to distribute patently indecent or offensive material online—was ruled unconstitutional in 1997 by the U.S. Supreme Court. However, like its printed counterpart, online pornography involving minors is illegal. Because of the strong link they believe exists between child pornography and child molestation, many experts are very concerned about the amount of child pornography that can be found and distributed via the Internet. They also believe that the Internet makes it easier for sexual predators to act out, such as by striking up "friendships" with children online and convincing these children to meet them in real life. And this can have devastating consequences, as it did for a 13-year-old girl from Connecticut who was strangled to death in 2002 by a 25-year-old man she met originally online and eventually in person.

PROTECTING AGAINST CYBERBULLYING, CYBERSTALKING, AND OTHER PERSONAL SAFETY CONCERNS

The growing increase in attention to cyberbullying and cyberstalking is leading to more efforts to improve safeguards for children. For instance, social networking sites have privacy features that can be used to protect the private information of their members. In addition, numerous states in the United States have implemented cyberbullying and cyberstalking laws. While there is no surefire way to protect against cyberbullying, cyberstalking, and other online dangers completely, some common-sense precautions can reduce the chance of a serious personal safety problem occurring due to online activities.

Safety Tips for Adults

It is wise to be cautious and discreet online—especially in online profiles, Twitter tweets, forums, and other online locations where individuals communicate with strangers. To protect yourself against cyberstalking and other types of online harassment, use gender-neutral, nonprovocative identifying names, such as *jsmith*, instead of *janesmith* or *iamcute*. Be careful about the types of photos you post of yourself online and do not reveal personal information—such as your real name, address, or telephone number—to people you meet online. In addition, do not respond to any insults or other harassing comments you may receive online. You may also want to request that your personal information be removed from online directories—especially those associated with your e-mail address or other online identifiers.

TIP

Search for yourself using search sites and online telephone books to see what personal information is available about you on the Internet.

TIP

Both adults and children should avoid including personal information on their social networking pages that could be used by an online stalker.

Safety Tips for Children and Teens

Most experts agree that the best way to protect children from online dangers is to stay in close touch with them as they explore the Internet. Parents should monitor their children's computer and mobile phone activities, and children and teenagers should be told which activities are allowed, which types of Web sites are off-limits, and why. In addition, it should be made clear that they are never to reveal personal information about themselves online without a parent's permission. They should also be instructed to tell a parent (or teacher if at school) if an individual ever requests personal information or a personal meeting, or threatens or otherwise harasses the child, via any type of online communications medium. Older children should also be cautioned about sending compromising photos of themselves or sexually explicit messages to others—a growing practice referred to as *sexting*. Part of the problem is that many young people don't realize they lose control of photos and other compromising content once that information has been sent to others. The issue is also complicated by *sextortion*—where someone who sees a teen's explicit photo in a text message or on the Internet threatens to expose the teen's behavior unless the teen sends more explicit photos. Sexting can result in child pornography charges being filed against teens, though some states are passing legislation to make it illegal but have lesser charges for a minor's first offense.

TIP

One controversial bill under consideration is *CISPA* (*Cyber Intelligence Sharing and Protection Act*), which would allow for voluntary information sharing between private companies and the government in the event of a cyber attack.

NETWORK AND INTERNET SECURITY LEGISLATION

Although new legislation is introduced frequently to address new types of computer crimes, it is rarely passed due to differences in opinion regarding the balance of protection vs. civil liberties. In addition, there are both domestic and international jurisdictional issues because many computer crimes affect businesses and individuals located in geographic areas other than the one in which the computer criminal is located, and hackers can make it appear that activity is coming from a different location than it really is. Nevertheless, computer crime legislation continues to be proposed and computer crimes are being prosecuted. A list of selected federal laws concerning network and Internet security is shown in Figure 9-28.

FIGURE 9-28
Computer network and Internet security legislation.

DATE	LAW AND DESCRIPTION
2004	**Identity Theft Penalty Enhancement Act** Adds extra years to prison sentences for criminals who use identity theft (including the use of stolen credit card numbers) to commit other crimes.
2003	**CAN-SPAM Act** Implements regulations for unsolicited e-mail messages.
2003	**Fair and Accurate Credit Transactions Act (FACTA)** Amends the Fair Credit Reporting Act (FCRA) to require that the three nationwide consumer reporting agencies (Equifax, Experian, and TransUnion) provide consumers, upon request, a free copy of their credit report once every 12 months.
2003	**PROTECT Act** Includes provisions to prohibit virtual child pornography.
2003	**Health Insurance Portability and Accountability Act (HIPAA)** Includes a Security Rule that sets minimum security standards to protect health information stored electronically.
2002	**Homeland Security Act** Includes provisions to combat cyberterrorism, including protecting ISPs against lawsuits from customers for revealing private information to law enforcement agencies.
2002	**Sarbanes-Oxley Act** Requires archiving a variety of electronic records and protecting the integrity of corporate financial data.
2001	**USA PATRIOT Act** Grants federal authorities expanded surveillance and intelligence-gathering powers, such as broadening the ability of federal agents to obtain the real identity of Internet users, intercept e-mail and other types of Internet communications, follow online activity of suspects, expand their wiretapping authority, and more.
1998	**Identity Theft and Assumption Deterrence Act of 1998** Makes it a federal crime to knowingly use someone else's means of identification, such as name, Social Security number, or credit card, to commit any unlawful activity.
1997	**No Electronic Theft (NET) Act** Expands computer piracy laws to include online distribution of copyrighted materials.
1996	**National Information Infrastructure Protection Act** Amends the Computer Fraud and Abuse Act of 1984 to punish information theft crossing state lines and to crack down on network trespassing.
1984	**Computer Fraud and Abuse Act of 1984** Makes it a crime to break into computers owned by the federal government. This act has been regularly amended over the years as technology has changed.

SUMMARY

Chapter Objective 1:
Explain why computer users
should be concerned about
network and Internet security.

WHY BE CONCERNED ABOUT NETWORK AND INTERNET SECURITY?

There are a number of important security concerns related to computers and the Internet. Many of these are **computer crimes**. Because computers and networks are so widespread and many opportunities for criminals exist, all computer users should be aware of the risks of using networks and the Internet so they can take appropriate precautions.

Chapter Objective 2:
List several examples of
unauthorized access and
unauthorized use.

UNAUTHORIZED ACCESS AND UNAUTHORIZED USE

Two risks related to networks and the Internet are **unauthorized access** and **unauthorized use**. **Hacking** is using a computer to break into a computer. **War driving** and **Wi-Fi piggybacking** refer to the unauthorized use of an unsecured Wi-Fi network. Data can be intercepted as it is transmitted over the Internet or a wireless network.

PROTECTING AGAINST UNAUTHORIZED ACCESS AND UNAUTHORIZED USE

Chapter Objective 3:
Explain several ways to
protect against unauthorized
access and unauthorized
use, including access control
systems, firewalls, and
encryption.

Access control systems are used to control access to a computer, network, or other resource. These include **possessed knowledge access systems** that use **passwords** or other types of possessed knowledge; **possessed object access systems** that use physical objects; and **biometric access systems** that identify users by a particular unique biological characteristic, such as a fingerprint. Passwords should be *strong passwords*; **two-factor authentication** systems that use multiple factors are more effective than single-factor systems.

To protect wireless networks, they should be secured; **firewalls** protect against unauthorized access. Sensitive transactions should be performed only on **secure Web pages**; sensitive files and e-mails should be secured with **encryption**. **Public key encryption** uses a private key and matching public key; **private key encryption** uses only a private key. A **virtual private network (VPN)** can be used to provide a secure remote connection to a company network, as well as to protect individuals at public Wi-Fi hotspots. Employers should take appropriate precautions with current and former employees to limit the risk of unauthorized access and use, as well as accidental exposure of sensitive information.

COMPUTER SABOTAGE

Computer sabotage includes **malware** (**computer viruses**, **computer worms**, and **Trojan horses** designed to cause harm to computer systems), **denial of service (DoS) attacks** (designed to shut down a Web server), and data and program alteration. Computer sabotage is often performed via the Internet, increasingly by the **bots** in a **botnet**.

PROTECTING AGAINST COMPUTER SABOTAGE

Chapter Objective 5:
List how individuals
and businesses can
protect against computer
sabotage.

Protection against computer sabotage includes using appropriate access control systems to keep unauthorized individuals from accessing computers and networks, as well as using **security software**. In particular, **antivirus software** protects against computer viruses and other types of malware. It is important to keep your security software up to date.

ONLINE THEFT, ONLINE FRAUD, AND OTHER DOT CONS

There are a variety of types of theft, fraud, and scams related to the Internet—collectively referred to as **dot cons**—that all Internet users should be aware of. Data, information, or money can be stolen from individuals and businesses. A common crime today is **identity theft**, in which an individual poses as another individual—typically to steal money or make purchases posing as the victim. The information used in identity theft is often gathered via **phishing**, **spear phishing**, **social media hacking**, and **pharming**. **Online auction fraud** is another common dot con.

Chapter Objective 6:
Discuss online theft, identity theft, spoofing, phishing, and other types of dot cons.

PROTECTING AGAINST ONLINE THEFT, ONLINE FRAUD, AND OTHER DOT CONS

To protect against identity theft, individuals should guard their personal information carefully. To check for identity theft, watch your bills and credit history. When interacting with other individuals online or buying from an online auction, it is wise to be conservative and use a credit card whenever possible. To avoid other types of dot cons, be very wary of responding to unsolicited offers and e-mails, and steer clear of offers that seem too good to be true. Never click a link in an e-mail message to update your personal information. To verify a Web site, a **digital certificate** (also called a **digital ID**) can be used. To verify the sender of a document, a **digital signature** can be used. Digital certificates include key pairs that can be used to both digitally sign documents and to encrypt files.

Chapter Objective 7:
Detail steps an individual can take to protect against online theft, identity theft, spoofing, phishing, and other types of dot cons.

PERSONAL SAFETY ISSUES

There are also personal safety risks for both adults and children stemming from Internet use. **Cyberbullying** and **cyberstalking**—online harassment that frightens or threatens the victim—is more common in recent years, even though most states have passed laws against it. Cyberbully is a growing risk for children, as are the risks of potential exposure to online pornography and other materials inappropriate for children, as well as the growing *sexting* and *sextortion* trends.

Chapter Objective 8:
Identify personal safety risks associated with Internet use.

PROTECTING AGAINST CYBERBULLING, CYBERSTALKING, AND OTHER PERSONAL SAFETY CONCERNS

To protect their personal safety, adults and children should be cautious in online communications. They should be wary of revealing any personal information or meeting online acquaintances in person. To protect children, parents should keep a close watch on their children's online activities, and children should be taught never to reveal personal information to others online without a parent's consent.

Chapter Objective 9:
List steps individuals can take to safeguard their personal safety when using the Internet.

NETWORK AND INTERNET SECURITY LEGISLATION

The rapid growth of the Internet and jurisdictional issues have contributed to the lack of network and Internet security legislation. However, computer crime legislation continues to be proposed and computer crimes are actively prosecuted.

Chapter Objective 10:
Discuss the current state of network and Internet security legislation.

REVIEW ACTIVITIES

KEY TERM MATCHING

a. computer virus

b. denial of service (DoS) attack

c. dot con

d. encryption

e. firewall

f. hacking

g. identity theft

h. password

i. phishing

j. Trojan horse

Instructions: Match each key term on the left with the definition on the right that best describes it.

1. _____ A collection of hardware and/or software intended to protect a computer or computer network from unauthorized access.

2. _____ A fraud or scam carried out through the Internet.

3. _____ A malicious program that masquerades as something else.

4. _____ A method of scrambling the contents of an e-mail message or a file to make it unreadable if it is intercepted by an unauthorized user.

5. _____ A secret combination of characters used to gain access to a computer, computer network, or other resource.

6. _____ A software program installed without the user's knowledge and designed to alter the way a computer operates or to cause harm to the computer system.

7. _____ An act of sabotage that attempts to flood a network server or a Web server with so much activity that it is unable to function.

8. _____ The use of spoofed communications (typically e-mail messages) to gain credit card numbers and other personal data to be used for fraudulent purposes.

9. _____ Using a computer to break into another computer system.

10. _____ Using someone else's identity to purchase goods or services, obtain new credit cards or bank loans, or otherwise illegally masquerade as that individual.

SELF-QUIZ

Instructions: Circle **T** if the statement is true, **F** if the statement is false, or write the best answer in the space provided. **Answers for the self-quiz are located in the References and Resources Guide at the end of the book.**

1. **T F** A computer virus can only be transferred to another computer via a storage medium.

2. **T F** An access control system that uses passwords is a possessed knowledge access system.

3. **T F** Using a password that is two characters long is an example of two-factor authentication.

4. **T F** Secure Web pages use encryption to securely transfer data sent via those pages.

5. **T F** Cyberstalking is the use of spoofed e-mail messages to gain credit card numbers and other personal data to be used for fraudulent purposes.

6. Driving around looking for a Wi-Fi network to access is referred to as _____.

7. _____ access control systems use some type of unique physical characteristic of a person to authenticate that individual.

8. A(n) _____ can be used at a Wi-Fi hotspot to create a secure path over the Internet.

9. A(n) _____ can be added to a file or an e-mail message to verify the identity of the sender and guarantee the file or message has not been changed.

10. Match each computer crime to its description, and write the corresponding number in the blank to the left of the description.

a. _____ A person working for the Motor Vehicle Division deletes a friend's speeding ticket from a database.

b. _____ An individual does not like someone's comment on a message board and begins to send that individual harassing e-mail messages.

c. _____ An individual sells the same item to 10 individuals via an online auction site.

d. _____ A person accesses a computer belonging to the IRS without authorization.

1. Online auction fraud
2. Hacking
3. Data or program alteration
4. Cyberstalking

1. Write the appropriate letter in the blank to the left of each term to indicate whether it is related to unauthorized access (U) or computer sabotage (C).

a. _____ Time bomb   **c.** _____ Malware   **e.** _____ War driving

b. _____ DoS attack   **d.** _____ Wi-Fi piggybacking

2. Is the password *john1* a good password? Why or why not? If not, suggest a better password.

3. Supply the missing words to complete the following statements regarding public/private key pairs.

a. With an encrypted e-mail message, the recipient's _____ key is used to encrypt the message, and the recipient's _____ key is used to decrypt the message.

b. With a digital signature, the sender's _____ key is used to sign the document, and the sender's _____ key is used to validate the signature.

4. To secure files on your computer so they are unreadable to a hacker who might gain access to your computer, what type of encryption (public key or private key) would be the most appropriate? Explain.

5. List two precautions you can take to protect against someone hacking your social media accounts.

NET

1. The term *hacktivism* is sometimes used to refer to the act of hacking into a computer system for a politically or socially motivated purpose. While some view hacktivists no differently than they view other hackers, hacktivists contend that they break into systems in order to bring attention to political or social causes. Is hacktivism a valid method of bringing attention to specific causes? Why or why not? Should hacktivists be treated differently from other types of hackers when caught?

2. According to security experts, several worms released in past years contain more than just the virus code—they contain code to remove competing malware from the computers they infect and messages taunting other virus writers. The goal seems to be not only to gain control of an increasing number of infected machines—a type of "bot war" to build the biggest botnet—but also to one-up rivals. If this trend continues, do you think it will affect how hackers and other computer criminals will be viewed? Will they become cult heroes or be viewed as dangerous criminals? Will continuing to increase prosecution of these individuals help or hurt the situation?

PROJECTS

HOT TOPICS

1. **Wi-Fi Hotspot Safety** As mentioned in the chapter, it is possible to inadvertently connect to an evil twin instead of the legitimate Wi-Fi hotspot you intended to connect to and, even if you are connected to a legitimate hotspot, any data you send unsecured via the hotspot can be intercepted by a criminal. In either case, if a thief intercepts your credit card number, Web site passwords, or other sensitive data, it can be used for identity theft and other criminal activities.

   For this project, research these and any other possible risks you can think of related to using a Wi-Fi hotspot. For each risk, identify a possible precaution that can be taken to guard against that risk. If you have ever used a Wi-Fi hotspot, were you at risk? Knowing what you do now, would you take any different precautions the next time you use one? Is it possible to surf safely using a Wi-Fi hotspot? What about activity performed via your smartphone wireless provider—is that safe? At the conclusion of your research, prepare a one-page summary of your findings and opinions and submit it to your instructor.

SHORT ANSWER/ RESEARCH

2. **New Viruses** Unfortunately, new computer viruses and other types of malware are released all the time. In addition to malware targeted toward computers, there is also mobile malware targeted to smartphones, media tablets, and other Internet-enabled devices.

   For this project, identify a current virus or worm (most security companies, such as Symantec and McAfee, list the most recent security threats on their Web sites) and answer the following questions: When was it introduced? What does it do? How is it spread? Is it targeted to computers or mobile devices? How many devices have been affected so far? Is there an estimated cost associated with it? Is it still in existence? At the conclusion of your research, prepare a one-page summary of your findings and submit it to your instructor.

HANDS ON

3. **Virus Check** There are several Web sites that include a free virus check, as well as other types of diagnostic software.

   For this project, locate a free virus check (such as one available from Microsoft or from a company that makes antivirus software) and run the free virus check. NOTE: If you are on a school computer, only run online checks, not downloaded programs. If the check takes more than 10 minutes and there is an option to limit the check to a particular drive and folder, redo the check but scan only part of the hard drive (such as the Documents folder) to save time. After the virus scan is completed, print the page displaying the result. Did the program find any viruses or other security threats? At the conclusion of this task, submit your printout with any additional comments about your experience to your instructor.

4. **Teaching Computer Viruses** Some college computer classes include instruction on writing computer viruses. At one university, precautions for containing code created during this course include allowing only fourth-year students to take the course, not having a network connection in the classroom, and prohibiting the removal of storage media from the classroom. Do you think these precautions are sufficient? Should writing virus code be allowed as part of a computer degree curriculum? Some believe that students need to know how viruses work in order to be able to develop antivirus software; however, the antivirus industry disagrees, and most antivirus professionals were never virus writers. Is it ethical for colleges to teach computer virus writing? Is it ethical for students to take such a course? Will teaching illegal and unethical acts (such as writing virus code) in college classes help to legitimize the behavior in society? Would you feel comfortable taking such a course? Why or why not?

For this project, form an opinion about the ethical implications of writing virus code in college classes and be prepared to discuss your position (in class, via an online class discussion group, in a class chat room, or via a class blog, depending on your instructor's directions). You may also be asked to write a short paper expressing your opinion.

ETHICS IN ACTION

5. **Virus Hoaxes** In addition to the valid reports about new viruses found in the news and on antivirus software Web sites, reports of viruses that turn out to be hoaxes abound on the Internet. In addition to being an annoyance, virus hoaxes waste time and computing resources. In addition, they may eventually lead some users to routinely ignore all virus warning messages, leaving them vulnerable to a genuine, destructive virus.

For this project, visit at least two Web sites that identify virus hoaxes, such as the Symantec or McAfee Web sites and Snopes.com. Explore the sites to find information about recent virus hoaxes, as well as general guidelines for identifying virus hoaxes and other types of online hoaxes. Share your findings with the class in the form of a short presentation. The presentation should not exceed 10 minutes and should make use of one or more presentation aids, such as a whiteboard, handouts, or a computer-based slide presentation (your instructor may provide additional requirements). You may also be asked to submit a summary of the presentation to your instructor.

PRESENTATION/ DEMONSTRATION

NET

6. **Is Mobile Banking More Secure than Online Banking?** You may have used your smartphone to pay a bill or deposit a check. While becoming common today, it is still newer than traditional online banking performed via a computer and so does not have as long of a track record. While banks are continually upgrading their security systems in response to new threats and technologies, is the security of online and mobile banking equal? Some consider traditional online banking safer because it has been tested longer, is used with computers that may have better security software installed, and is performed via home computers that are not as likely to be lost or misplaced as mobile devices. Others view mobile banking as safer because individuals tend to have their phones with them at all times and so can be notified more quickly of security breaches, GPS information can be used to identify transactions that occur in a different physical location from the registered location of the phone (and therefore might be fraudulent), and mobile banking accounts are often associated with a single phone. Mobile banking can be performed via a Web app, mobile Web site, or text messaging. Is one method safer than the other? How do the risks associated with mobile banking compare with the risks associated wtih traditional online banking? Would you feel safer using one or the other? Why?

Pick a side on this issue, form an opinion and gather supporting evidence, and be prepared to discuss and defend your position in a classroom debate or in a 1–2 page paper, depending on your instructor's directions.

BALANCING ACT

expert insight on . . .
Networks and the Internet

Courtesy McAfee

An Intel Company

Greg Hampton is the
Vice President of Product
Management for the
Network Security team at
McAfee. Before joining
McAfee, Hampton served
as the Vice President of
Marketing at Clearswift
Corporation, an e-mail
and Web security
company based in the
UK. He was also a
founder and the CEO of
a Silicon Valley start up
for delivering network
management solutions.
Greg has a Bachelor
of Arts degree in
Economics and brings a
broad range of enterprise
software experience to
the company.

A conversation with GREG HAMPTON
Vice President, Product Management, McAfee

". . . protect your identity and your online reputation—it will keep you and your data safe and will improve your career prospects."

My Background . . .

I am the Vice President of Product Management for Network Security at McAfee. In product management, our role is to ensure that our product roadmap is forward looking, and to help connect users with engineers so that we can build outstanding products that meet user needs. I became involved with product management when I was a general manager for a high tech company overseeing its Canadian and Latin American operations and I was asked to oversee a newly acquired company. In the process, I was exposed to the role of product management and developed an interest in it. I have found my experiences in sales management and marketing roles at high tech companies directly applicable and useful to my current position. In addition, pursuing my Bachelor of Arts degree was invaluable. It helped me develop an interest in and the skills needed to be able to learn new ideas in new areas, which is essential for individuals who work in the world of high tech.

It's Important to Know . . .

How the Internet and other networks work. Because the Internet is so integrated into our society today, it is important for people to understand the basic functions of the Internet—how it connects devices and resources, how people access it, how data is stored, and what the cloud is—so that they may understand how best to use and secure this resource in both their personal and professional lives.

That it is essential to protect your identity. Online theft, identity theft, and other privacy and security risks impact what we call our "identity." Protecting identities is a unique area of security that is important because it touches each of us personally—as employees, as students, and as individuals. In the digital world, you are your digital identity. What is associated with your digital identity becomes associated with you—and that could impact your finances, your legal standing, and your career.

Passwords alone are not an adequate security control. Today, most of our digital identities are protected by passwords. Unfortunately, a simple username and password is easy to break. What's worse, many of us use the same username and password over and over again so once one account— say, an online e-mail account—is breached, all other accounts (such as your bank account) using that same combination are then directly accessible. To make matters worse, the password policies often implemented to help prevent this (such as using a unique strong password for every account, changing them every few months, and telling people not to save them anywhere) increases these habits. Implementing better controls, such as two-factor and biometric authentication (e.g. voice and facial recognition used with our LiveSafe cloud storage product), is both safer and easier to use!

How I Use this Technology . . .

Because my job involves collecting requirements for Internet Security software and appliances, I use this knowledge and these solutions daily in my professional life. But I also use them in my personal life. For example, I use antivirus protection for all of my devices and I use two-factor or strong authentication to protect my financial and personal e-mail accounts.

What the Future Holds . . .

Today in our connected society, our identity is our most valuable and our most vulnerable link. And our society will continue to become more connected. The Internet of Things (IoT) is moving beyond mobile devices and networked cars to wearable devices, household items, medical devices, and other items we use in our daily lives. In the near future, we will be connected in ways we're just beginning to imagine. As this happens, it will become increasingly important that we—as individuals, students, and a business community—continue to watch the trends around identity protection; how trust relationships are established between people, systems, data and applications; and the laws and governance for personal privacy.

Already, the most vulnerable link in our networks today is our identity, and it will become more vulnerable in the even more connected future. And, as the consumerization of IT increases the pressure to move business tools and applications to the cloud, businesses will be more challenged than ever to securely grant remote, mobile, and highly social business users and their identities easy access while not compromising their security—especially as the lines between the personal and professional continue to blur. To address these challenges, McAfee, Intel, and other companies are actively developing solutions like McAfee One Time Password and McAfee LiveSafe for businesses and consumers that use technologies like multi-factor authentication, which combines passwords with other methods like biometrics, smartphones, chips in our devices like Intel Identity Protection Technology (IPT), or other physical objects.

In the future, we can expect to see accelerated movement toward these solutions and technologies as we leave our weak and difficult-to-keep-track-of passwords behind.

> *" . . . a simple username and password is easy to break "*

My Advice to Students . . .

Protect yourself by implementing multi-factor authentication and strong passwords—today. And all of us, particularly students, should be careful of what we publish in social media. You can expose yourself to risk by sharing too much data about where you live, who you know, and what you are doing. If you share too much information, it can also impact your online reputation. Employers are increasing their scrutiny of social presence when considering job applicants and you don't want something you say or post online to hurt your job prospects in the future.

So, protect your identity and your online reputation—it will keep you and your data safe, and will improve your career prospects.

Discussion Question

Greg Hampton stresses the importance of protecting your digital identity. Think about the systems that contain personal data about you. How would you feel if those systems were breached and your information was stolen? Does your viewpoint change if the information was monetary (such as credit card information) versus private information (such as grades or health information)? What security precautions, if any, do you think should be imposed by laws? Are organizations that hold your personal data morally responsible for going beyond the minimum requirements? Be prepared to discuss your position (in class, via an online class discussion group, in a class chat room, or via a class blog, depending on your instructor's directions). You may also be asked to write a short paper expressing your opinion.

>For more information about McAfee, visit www.mcafee.com. For information about specific security issues and solutions, visit www.mcafee.com/identity and blogs.mcafee.com.

REFERENCES AND RESOURCES
GUIDE

INTRODUCTION

When working on a computer or taking a computer course, you often need to look up information related to computers, smartphones, and other devices. For instance, you may need to find out when the IBM PC was first invented, you may want tips about what to consider when buying a new device, or you may want to find out more about how numbering systems work. To help you with the tasks just mentioned and more, this References and Resources Guide brings together in one convenient location a collection of technology-related references and resources.

OUTLINE

COMPUTER HISTORY TIMELINE

The earliest recorded calculating device, the abacus, is believed to have been invented by the Babylonians sometime between 500 B.C. and 100 B.C. It and similar types of counting boards were used solely for counting.

Blaise Pascal invented the first mechanical calculator, called the Pascaline Arithmetic Machine. It had the capacity for eight digits and could add and subtract.

Dr. John V. Atanasoff and Clifford Berry designed and built ABC (for Atanasoff-Berry Computer), the world's first electronic, digital computer.

500 B.C.   1642   1937

500, 1642, 1804, 1944: Courtesy of IBM Archives; 1621: Courtesy of Mark Konshak, Curator, sliderulemuseum.com; 1937: Courtesy of Iowa State University

Precomputers and Early Computers

1621   1804   1944

French silk weaver Joseph-Marie Jacquard built a loom that read holes punched on a series of small sheets of hardwood to control the weave of the pattern. This automated machine introduced the use of punch cards and showed that they could be used to convey a series of instructions.

The Mark I, considered to be the first digital computer, was introduced by IBM. It was developed in cooperation with Harvard University, was more than 50 feet long, weighed almost five tons, and used electromechanical relays to solve addition problems in less than a second; multiplication and division took about 6 and 12 seconds, respectively.

The slide rule, a precursor to the electronic calculator, was invented. Used primarily to perform multiplication, division, square roots, and the calculation of logarithms, its widespread use continued until the 1970s.

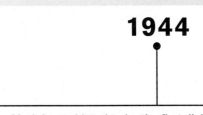

Precomputers and Early Computers (before approximately 1945)

Most precomputers and early computers were mechanical machines that worked with gears and levers. Electromechanical devices (using both electricity and gears and levers) were developed toward the end of this era.

First Generation (approximately 1946–1957)

Powered by vacuum tubes, these computers were faster than electromechanical machines, but they were large and bulky, generated excessive heat, and had to be physically wired and reset to run programs. Input was primarily on punch cards; output was on punch cards or paper. Machine and assembly languages were used to program these computers.

The UNIVAC 1, the first computer to be mass produced for general use, was introduced by Remington Rand. In 1952, it was used to analyze votes in the U.S. presidential election and correctly predicted that Dwight D. Eisenhower would be the victor only 45 minutes after the polls closed, though the results were not aired immediately because they weren't trusted.

The COBOL programming language was developed by a committee headed by Dr. Grace Hopper.

The first floppy disk (8 inches in diameter) was introduced.

UNIX was developed at AT&T's Bell Laboratories; Advanced Micro Devices (AMD) was formed; and ARPANET (the predecessor of today's Internet) was established.

IBM unbundled some of its hardware and software and began selling them separately, allowing other software companies to emerge.

1951   1960   1967   1969

First Generation   **Second Generation** **Third Generation**

1947   1957   1964   1968

The FORTRAN programming language was introduced.

Robert Noyce and Gordon Moore founded the Intel Corporation.

John Bardeen, Walter Brattain, and William Shockley invented the transistor, which had the same capabilities as a vacuum tube but was faster, broke less often, used less power, and created less heat. They won a Nobel Prize for their invention in 1956 and computers began to be built with transistors shortly afterwards.

The IBM System/360 computer was introduced. Unlike previous computers, System/360 contained a full line of compatible computers, making upgrading easier.

The first mouse was invented by Doug Engelbart.

Second Generation (approximately 1958–1963)

Second-generation computers used transistors instead of vacuum tubes. They allowed the computer to be physically smaller, more powerful, more reliable, and faster than before. Input was primarily on punch cards and magnetic tape; output was on punch cards and paper; and magnetic tape and disks were used for storage. High-level programming languages were used with these computers.

Third Generation (approximately 1964–1970)

The third generation of computers evolved when integrated circuits (IC)—computer chips—began being used instead of conventional transistors. Computers became even smaller and more reliable. Keyboards and monitors were introduced for input and output; magnetic disks were used for storage. The emergence of the operating system meant that operators no longer had to manually reset relays and wiring.

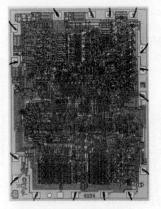

The first microprocessor, the Intel 4004, was designed by Ted Hoff. The single processor contained 2,250 transistors and could execute 60,000 operations per second.

Bill Gates and Paul Allen wrote a version of BASIC for the Altair, the first computer programming language designed for a personal computer. Bill Gates dropped out of Harvard to form Microsoft with Paul Allen.

Software Arts' Visi-Calc, the first electronic spreadsheet and business program for personal computers, was released. This program is seen as one of the reasons personal computers first became widely accepted in the business world.

IBM introduced the IBM PC. This DOS-based PC used a 4.77 MHz 8088 CPU with 64 KB of RAM and quickly became the standard for business personal computers.

1971

1975

1979

1981

Fourth Generation

1972

1976

1980

1982

The C programming language was developed by Dennis Ritchie at Bell Labs.

Sony Electronics introduced the 3.5-inch floppy disk and drive.

Intel introduced the 80286 CPU.

Seymour Cray, called the "father of supercomputing," founded Cray Research, which would go on to build some of the fastest computers in the world.

Steve Wozniak and Steve Jobs founded Apple computer and released the Apple I (a single-board computer), followed by the Apple II (a complete personal computer that became an instant success in 1977). They originally ran the company out of Jobs' parents' garage.

Seagate Technology announced the first Winchester 5.25-inch hard disk drive, revolutionizing computer storage.

IBM chose Microsoft to develop the operating system for its upcoming personal computer. That operating system was PC-DOS.

TIME magazine named the computer its "Machine of the Year" for 1982, emphasizing the importance of the computer in our society.

Fourth Generation (approximately 1971–present)

The fourth generation of computers began with large-scale integration (LSI), which resulted in chips that could contain thousands of transistors. Very large-scale integration (VLSI) resulted in the microprocessor and the resulting microcomputers. The keyboard and mouse are predominant input devices, though many other types of input devices are now available; monitors and printers provide output; and storage is obtained with magnetic disks, optical discs, and memory chips.

The first version of Microsoft Windows, a graphical environment, was released.

The first general-interest CD-ROM product (*Grolier's Electronic Encyclopedia*) was released, and computer and electronics companies worked together to develop a universal CD-ROM standard.

Linus Torvalds created Linux, which launched the open source revolution. The penguin logo/mascot soon followed.

The first Internet domain name was registered.

Tim Berners-Lee of CERN invented the World Wide Web.

Compaq Corporation released the first IBM-compatible personal computer that ran the same software as the IBM PC, marking the beginning of the huge PC-compatible industry.

Intel introduced the Intel386 CPU.

Intel introduced the Intel486 chip, the world's first million transistor CPU.

The number of Internet users worldwide surpassed 100 million.

1983   1985   1989   1994   1997

1984   1986   1993   1995

The Apple Macintosh debuted. It featured a simple, graphical user interface, used an 8 MHz, 32-bit Motorola 68000 CPU, and had a built-in 9-inch black-and-white screen.

Intel introduced the Pentium CPU.

Windows 95 was released and sold more than 1 million copies in 4 days.

NCSA released the Mosaic Web browser, developed by students at the University of Illinois. Mosaic was one of the first browsers to support graphics, and it was the first to support both Windows and Macintosh computers. Three million people were connected to the Internet.

Both eBay and Amazon.com were founded.

Apple's Steve Jobs founded Pixar.

Microsoft was listed on the New York Stock Exchange and began to sell shares to the public; Bill Gates became one of the world's youngest billionaires.

Sun Microsystems released Java, which is still a popular Web programming language.

Apple introduced the iPod personal music player.

Intel's first 64-bit CPU, the Itanium, was introduced.

Apple released the iMac, a modernized version of the Macintosh computer. Its futuristic design helped to make this computer immensely popular.

Microsoft shipped Windows 98.

Microsoft released its XP line of products, including Windows XP and Office XP.

The Internet and wireless networks enabled people to work and communicate with others while on the go.

Spyware became a major problem; some studies indicated that over 80% of computers had spyware installed.

New Internet-enabled gaming consoles, like the Wii console shown here, were released.

Use of the Internet for online shopping and entertainment continued to grow.

Broadband Internet access approached the norm and improvements to wireless networking (such as WiMAX) continued to be developed.

1998   2001   2004   2006

2000   2003   2005   2007

The first USB flash drives were released.

AMD released the 64-bit Opteron server CPU and the Athlon 64, the first 64-bit CPU designed for desktop computer use.

Microsoft shipped the Office 2003 editions of its Microsoft Office System.

Phishing and identity theft became household words.

Twitter was launched.

Microsoft released Windows Vista and Office 2007.

Intel introduced its Pentium 4 CPU chip. A popular advertising campaign, launched in 2001, featured the Blue Man Group.

Digital camera sales in the United States exceeded 14 million, surpassing film camera sales for the first time.

Intel and AMD both released their first dual-core CPUs.

Apple released the revolutionary iPhone.

Quad-core CPUs were released by both Intel and AMD.

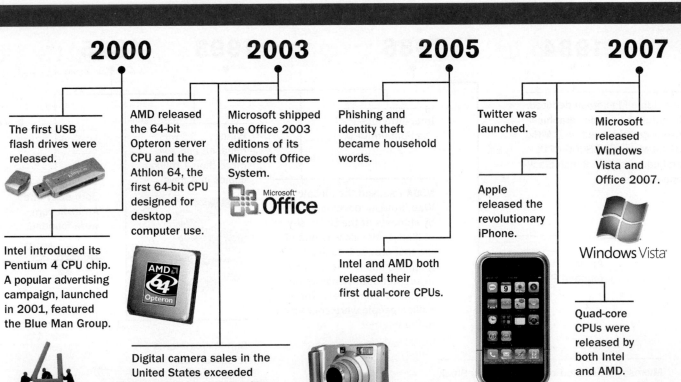

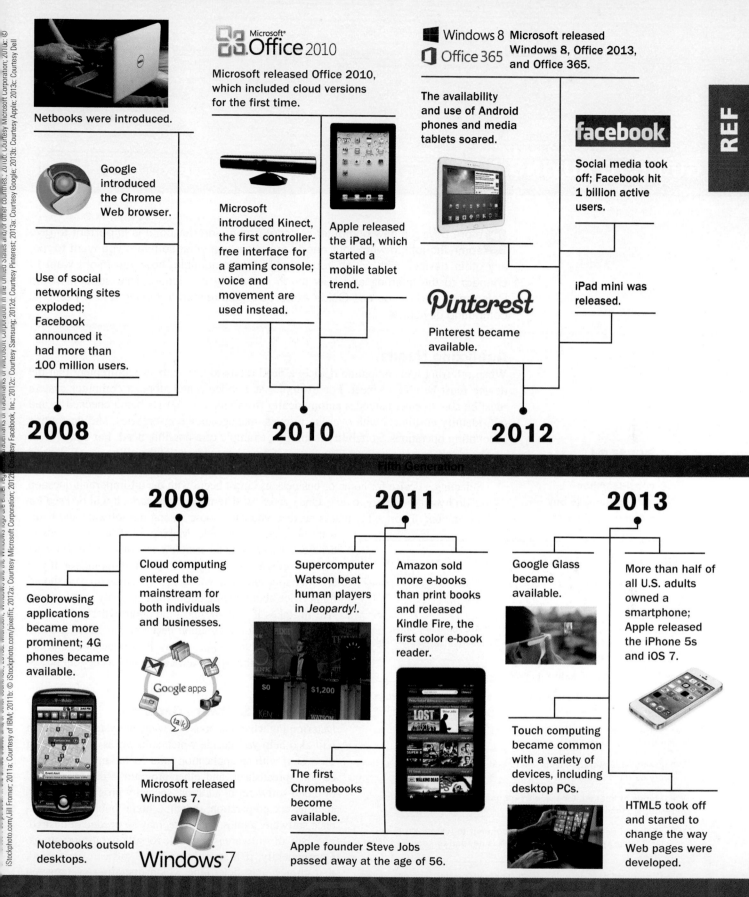

Netbooks were introduced.

Microsoft released Office 2010, which included cloud versions for the first time.

Microsoft released Windows 8, Office 2013, and Office 365.

REF

Google introduced the Chrome Web browser.

Microsoft introduced Kinect, the first controller-free interface for a gaming console; voice and movement are used instead.

Apple released the iPad, which started a mobile tablet trend.

The availability and use of Android phones and media tablets soared.

Social media took off; Facebook hit 1 billion active users.

facebook

Use of social networking sites exploded; Facebook announced it had more than 100 million users.

Pinterest became available.

iPad mini was released.

2008

2010

2012

Fifth Generation

2009

2011

2013

Geobrowsing applications became more prominent; 4G phones became available.

Cloud computing entered the mainstream for both individuals and businesses.

Google apps

Supercomputer Watson beat human players in *Jeopardy!*.

Amazon sold more e-books than print books and released Kindle Fire, the first color e-book reader.

Google Glass became available.

More than half of all U.S. adults owned a smartphone; Apple released the iPhone 5s and iOS 7.

Microsoft released Windows 7.

Windows 7

Notebooks outsold desktops.

The first Chromebooks become available.

Apple founder Steve Jobs passed away at the age of 56.

Touch computing became common with a variety of devices, including desktop PCs.

HTML5 took off and started to change the way Web pages were developed.

Fifth Generation (now and the future)
The fifth generation of computers is in its infancy stage. Today, they tend to be based on artificial intelligence and include voice and touch input. In the future, they are expected to be constructed differently, such as in the form of optical computers, tiny computers that utilize nanotechnology, and as general-purpose computers built into desks, home appliances, and other everyday devices.

Before buying a new computer or other computing device, it is important to give some thought to what your needs are, including what software you want to run, any other devices with which you need to be compatible, how you might want to connect to the Internet, and how much portability is needed. This section of the References and Resources Guide explores topics related to buying a new personal computing device. ■

Analyzing Needs

When referring to a computing device, a need refers to a functional requirement that the device must be able to meet. For example, at a video rental store, a computer system must be able to enter barcodes automatically from videos or DVDs being checked in and out, identify customers with overdue movies, manage movie inventories, and do routine accounting operations. Portability is another example of a possible need. For example, if you need to take your device with you as you travel or work out of the office, you will need a portable computer or a media tablet instead of a desktop computer.

Selecting a device for home or business use must begin with the all-important question "What do I want the device to do?" Once you have determined what tasks it will be used for and the amount of portability that is needed, you can choose among the software and hardware alternatives available. Making a list of your needs in the areas discussed in the next few sections can help you get a picture of what type of system you are shopping for. If you are not really sure what you want a system to do, you should think twice about buying one—you can easily make expensive mistakes if you are uncertain about what you want a system to do. Some common decision categories are discussed next; Figure R-1 provides a list of questions that can help you define the type of device that will meet your needs.

FIGURE R-1
Questions to consider when getting ready to buy a computing device.

POSSIBLE QUESTIONS

What tasks will I be using the device for (writing papers, accessing the Internet, watching TV, making phone and video calls, composing music, playing games, etc.)?

Do I have an operating system preference? Are there any other devices I need my documents and storage media to be compatible with?

How fast do I need the system to be?

Do I need portability? If so, do I need a powerful desktop replacement notebook or will a less-powerful notebook or a media tablet suffice?

What size screen do I need? Do I need to be able to connect to a second monitor or an HDTV set?

What removable storage media will I need to use (such as DVDs, flash memory cards, or USB flash drives)?

What types of Internet access will I be using (such as DSL, cable, satellite, or mobile wireless)?

What types of networks will I need to connect to (wired, Wi-Fi, cellular)? What type of network adapter is needed to connect to those networks?

What additional hardware do I need (scanner, printer, wireless router, digital camera, notebook stand, or tablet stand, for example)?

What brand(s) do I prefer? When do I need the device?

Do I want to pay extra for a better warranty (such as a longer time period, more comprehensive coverage, or on-site service)?

Application Software Decisions

Determining what functions you want the system to perform will also help you decide which software is needed. Most users start with an application suite containing a word processor, spreadsheet, and other programs—either installed or cloud software. In addition, specialty programs or apps, such as tax preparation, drawing, home publishing, reference software, games, and more, may be needed or desired.

Not all software is available for all operating systems. Consequently, if a specific piece of software is needed, that choice may determine which operating system you need to use. In addition, your operating system and application software decisions may already be made for you if your documents need to be compatible with those of another computer (such as other office computers or between a home and an office computer).

Platforms and Configuration Options

If your operating system has already been determined, that is a good start in deciding the overall platform you will be looking for—most users will choose between the PC-compatible and Apple Macintosh platforms. PC-compatible computers usually run either Windows or Linux; Apple computers almost always use Mac OS. Mobile devices typically run either Android or iOS.

Configuration decisions initially involve determining the size of the device desired (see Figure R-2). For nonportable systems, you have the choice between tower, desktop, or all-in-one configurations; in addition, the monitor size needs to be determined. Fully functioning personal computers can be notebook or tablet computers. For tablet computers, you need to decide if you will require keyboard use on a regular basis; if so, a hybrid notebook-tablet computer would be the best choice. If a powerful fully functioning computer is not required, you may decide to go with an even more portable option, such as a netbook or media tablet.

You should also consider any other specifications that are important to you, such as the size and type of internal storage (hard drive or flash memory media, for instance), types of other storage devices needed, amount of memory required, and so forth. As discussed in the next section, these decisions often require reconciling the features you want with the amount of money you are willing to spend.

Power vs. Budget Requirements

As part of the needs analysis, you should look closely at your need for a powerful system versus your budgetary constraints. Most users do not need a state-of-the-art system. Those who do should expect to pay more than the average user. A device that was top of the line six months or a year ago is usually reasonably priced and more than adequate for most users' needs. Individuals who want a device only for basic tasks, such as using the Internet and word processing, can likely get by with an inexpensive device designed for home use.

When determining your requirements, be sure to identify the features and functions that are absolutely essential for your primary computing tasks (such as a large hard drive and lots of memory for multimedia applications, a fast video card for gaming, a fast Internet connection, a TV tuner card for individuals who want to use the computer as a TV set, and so forth). After you have the minimum configuration determined, you can add optional or desirable components, as your budget allows.

Listing Alternatives

After you consider your needs and the questions mentioned in Figure R-1, you should have a pretty good idea of the hardware and software you will need. You will also know what purchasing options are available to you, depending on your time frame (while some retail stores have systems that can be purchased and brought home the same day, special orders or some systems purchased online will take longer). The next step is to get enough information from possible vendors to compare and contrast a few alternative systems that satisfy your stated needs. Most often, these vendors are local stores (such as computer stores, warehouse clubs, and electronic stores) and/or online stores (such as manufacturer Web sites and e-tailers). To compare prices and specifications for possible systems, find at least three systems that meet or exceed your needs by looking through newspaper advertisements, configuring systems online via manufacturer and e-tailer Web sites, or calling or visiting local stores. A comparison sheet listing your criteria and the systems you are considering, such as the one in Figure R-3, can help you summarize your options. Although it is sometimes very difficult to compare the prices of systems since they typically have somewhat different configurations and some components (such as CPUs) are difficult to compare, you can assign an approximate dollar value to each extra feature a system has (such as $50 for an included printer or a larger hard drive). Be sure to also include any sales tax and shipping charges when you compare the prices of each total system.

DESKTOPS

Courtesy Lenovo

NOTEBOOKS

Courtesy Apple

HYBRID NOTEBOOK-TABLETS

Courtesy Lenovo

MEDIA TABLETS

Courtesy of Samsung

FIGURE R-2
Configuration options.

COMPONENT	EXAMPLE OF DESIRED SPECIFICATIONS	SYSTEM #1 VENDOR:	SYSTEM #2 VENDOR:	SYSTEM #3 VENDOR:
Type of device	Notebook computer			
Operating system	Windows 8			
Manufacturer	Sony or Dell			
CPU	Intel quad core			
RAM	8 GB or higher			
Hard drive	2 TB or higher			
Removable storage	Flash memory card reader			
Optical drive	Blu-ray Disc drive			
Monitor	Widescreen 17"; touch screen			
Video card and video RAM	Prefer video card and HDMI			
Keyboard/mouse	Portable USB mouse with scroll wheel			
Sound card/speakers	No preference			
Modem	None			
Networking	Wi-Fi (802.11ac); Bluetooth			
Printer	Laser if get a good package deal			
Included software	Microsoft Office 365			
Warranty	3 years min.			
Other features	3 USB ports minimum			
Price				
Tax				
Shipping				
TOTAL COST				

FIGURE R-3
Comparing computing alternatives. A checklist such as this one can help to organize your desired criteria and evaluate possible systems.

If your budget is limited, you will have to balance the system you need with extra features you may want. But do not skimp on memory or hard drive space because sufficient memory can help your programs to run faster and with fewer problems and hard drive space is consumed quickly. Often for just a few extra dollars, you can get additional memory, a faster CPU, or a larger hard drive, which is significantly cheaper than trying to upgrade any of those features later. A good rule of thumb is to try to buy a little higher system than you think you need. On the other hand, do not buy a top-of-the-line system unless you fall into the power user category and really need it. Generally, the second or third system down from the top of the line is a very good system for a much more reasonable price. Some guidelines for minimum requirements for a new computer for most home users are as follows:

➤ A relatively fast multi-core CPU.

➤ 6 GB of RAM for desktop and notebook users.

➤ 500 GB or more hard drive space.

➤ Recordable or rewritable DVD or Blu-ray Disc drive.

➤ Network adapter or modem for the desired type(s) of Internet access.

➤ Sound card and speakers; built-in webcam and microphone.

➤ At least 2 USB ports.

➤ A built-in flash memory media reader.

A LOOK AT NUMBERING SYSTEMS

As discussed in Chapter 2 of this text, a numbering system is a way of representing numbers. People generally use the *decimal numbering system* explained in Chapter 2 and reviewed next; computers process data using the *binary numbering system*. Another numbering system related to computer use is the *hexadecimal numbering system*, which can be used to represent long strings of binary numbers in a manner more understandable to people than the binary numbering system. Following a discussion of these three numbering systems, we take a look at conversions between numbering systems and principles of computer arithmetic, and then close with a look at how to perform conversions using a scientific calculator. ■

The Decimal and Binary Numbering System

The *decimal* (*base 10*) numbering system uses 10 symbols—the digits 0, 1, 2, 3, 4, 5, 6, 7, 8, and 9—to represent all possible numbers and is the numbering system people use most often. The *binary* (*base 2*) numbering system is used extensively by computers to represent numbers and other characters. This system uses only two digits—0 and 1. As illustrated in Figure 2-3 in Chapter 2, the place values (columns) in the binary numbering system are different from those used in the decimal system.

FIGURE R-4
Hexadecimal characters and their decimal and binary equivalents.

The Hexadecimal Numbering System

Computers often output diagnostic and memory-management messages and identify network adapters and other hardware in *hexadecimal* (*hex*) notation. Hexadecimal notation is a shorthand method for representing the binary digits stored in a computer. Because large binary numbers—for example, 1101010001001110—can easily be misread by people, hexadecimal notation groups binary digits into units of four, which, in turn, are represented by other symbols.

The hexadecimal numbering system is also called the *base 16 numbering system* because it uses 16 different symbols. Since there are only 10 possible numeric digits, hexadecimal uses letters instead of numbers for the additional 6 symbols. The 16 hexadecimal symbols and their decimal and binary counterparts are shown in Figure R-4.

The hexadecimal numbering system has a special relationship to the 8-bit bytes of ASCII and EBCDIC that makes it ideal for displaying addresses and other data quickly. As you can see in Figure R-4, each hex character has a 4-bit binary counterpart, so any combination of 8 bits can be represented by exactly two hexadecimal characters. For example, the letter N (represented in ASCII by 01001110) has a hex representation of *4E* (see the Binary Equivalent column for the hexadecimal characters *4* and *E* in Figure R-4).

HEXADECIMAL CHARACTER	DECIMAL EQUIVALENT	BINARY EQUIVALENT
0	0	0000
1	1	0001
2	2	0010
3	3	0011
4	4	0100
5	5	0101
6	6	0110
7	7	0111
8	8	1000
9	9	1001
A	10	1010
B	11	1011
C	12	1100
D	13	1101
E	14	1110
F	15	1111

Converting Between Numbering Systems

In Figure 2-3 in Chapter 2, we illustrated how to convert from binary to decimal. Three other types of conversions computer professionals sometimes need to make are discussed next.

Hexadecimal to Decimal

As shown in Figure R-5, the process for converting a hexadecimal number to its decimal equivalent is similar to converting a binary number to its decimal equivalent, except the base number is 16 instead of 2. To determine the decimal equivalent of a hexadecimal number (such as 4F6A, as shown in Figure R-5), multiply the decimal equivalent of each individual hex character (determined by using the table in Figure R-4) by the appropriate power of 16 and then add the results to obtain the decimal equivalent of that hex number.

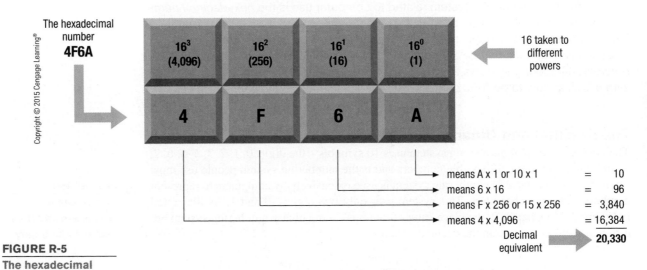

The hexadecimal number **4F6A**

16^3 (4,096) 16^2 (256) 16^1 (16) 16^0 (1)   16 taken to different powers

4   F   6   A

means A x 1 or 10 x 1	=	10
means 6 x 16	=	96
means F x 256 or 15 x 256	=	3,840
means 4 x 4,096	=	16,384
Decimal equivalent		**20,330**

FIGURE R-5

The hexadecimal (base 16) numbering system. Each digit in a hexadecimal number represents 16 taken to a different power.

Hexadecimal to Binary and Binary to Hexadecimal

To convert from hexadecimal to binary, we convert each hexadecimal digit separately to 4 binary digits (using the table in Figure R-4). For example, to convert F6A9 to binary, we get

F	6	A	9
1111	0110	1010	1001

or 1111011010101001 in binary representation. To convert from binary to hexadecimal, we go through the reverse process. If the number of digits in the binary number is not divisible by 4, we add leading zeros to the binary number to force an even division. For example, to convert the binary number 1101101010011 to hexadecimal, we get

0001	1011	0101	0011
1	B	5	3

or 1B53 in hexadecimal representation. Note that three leading zeros were added to change the initial 1 to 0001 before making the conversion.

Decimal to Binary and Decimal to Hexadecimal

To convert from decimal to either binary or hexadecimal, we can use the *remainder method*. To use the remainder method, the decimal number is divided by 2 (to convert to a binary number) or 16 (to convert to a hexadecimal number). The *remainder* of the division operation is recorded and the division process is repeated using the *quotient* as the next dividend, until the quotient becomes 0. At that point, the collective remainders (written backwards) represent the equivalent binary or hexadecimal number (see Figure R-6).

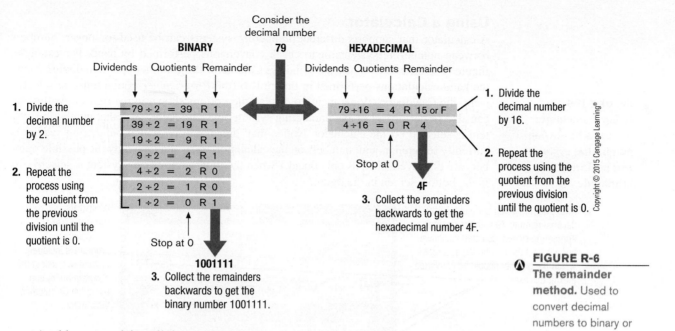

A **FIGURE R-6**
The remainder method. Used to convert decimal numbers to binary or hex format.

A table summarizing all the numbering system conversion procedures covered in this text is provided in Figure R-7.

FIGURE R-7
Summary of conversions.

	TO BASE		
FROM BASE	**2**	**10**	**16**
2		Starting at the rightmost digit, multiply binary digits by 2^0, 2^1, 2^2, etc., respectively, and then add products.	Starting at the rightmost digit, convert each group of four binary digits to a hex digit.
10	Divide repeatedly by 2 using each quotient as the next dividend until the quotient becomes 0, and then collect the remainders in reverse order.		Divide repeatedly by 16 using each quotient as the next dividend until the quotient becomes 0, and then collect the remainders in reverse order.
16	Convert each hex digit to four binary digits.	Starting at the rightmost digit, multiply hex digits by 16^0, 16^1, 16^2, etc., respectively, and then add products.	

FIGURE R-8
Adding and subtracting with the decimal, binary, and hexadecimal numbering systems.

Computer Arithmetic

To most people, decimal arithmetic is second nature. Addition and subtraction of binary and hexadecimal numbers is not much different from the process used with decimal numbers—just the number of symbols used in each system varies. For instance, the digits in each column are added or subtracted and you carry to and borrow from the column to the left as needed as you move from right to left. Instead of carrying or borrowing powers of 10, however—as you would in the decimal system—you carry or borrow powers of 2 (binary) or 16 (hexadecimal).

Figure R-8 provides an example of addition and subtraction with decimal, binary, and hexadecimal numbers.

	DECIMAL	BINARY	HEXADECIMAL
	1	1 1 1	1
	144	100101	8E
	+ 27	+ 10011	+ 2F
Addition	171	111000	BD
	3	0 0	7
	1̶4̶4	1̶00̶101	8̶E
	− 27	− 10011	− 2F
Subtraction	117	10010	5F

Using a Calculator

A calculator that supports different numbering systems can be used to convert numbers between numbering systems or to check conversions performed by hand. For example, Figure R-9 shows how to use the Windows Calculator Programmer option to double-check the hand calculations performed in Figure R-6 (the *Programmer* option must be selected using the Calculator's View menu to display the options shown in the figure). Arithmetic can also be performed in any numbering system on a calculator, once that numbering system is selected on the calculator. Notice that, depending on which numbering system is currently selected, not all numbers on the calculator are available—only the possible numbers are displayed, such as only 0 and 1 when the binary numbering system is selected, as in the bottom screen in the figure.

FIGURE R-9

Using a calculator to convert between numbering systems and perform arithmetic.

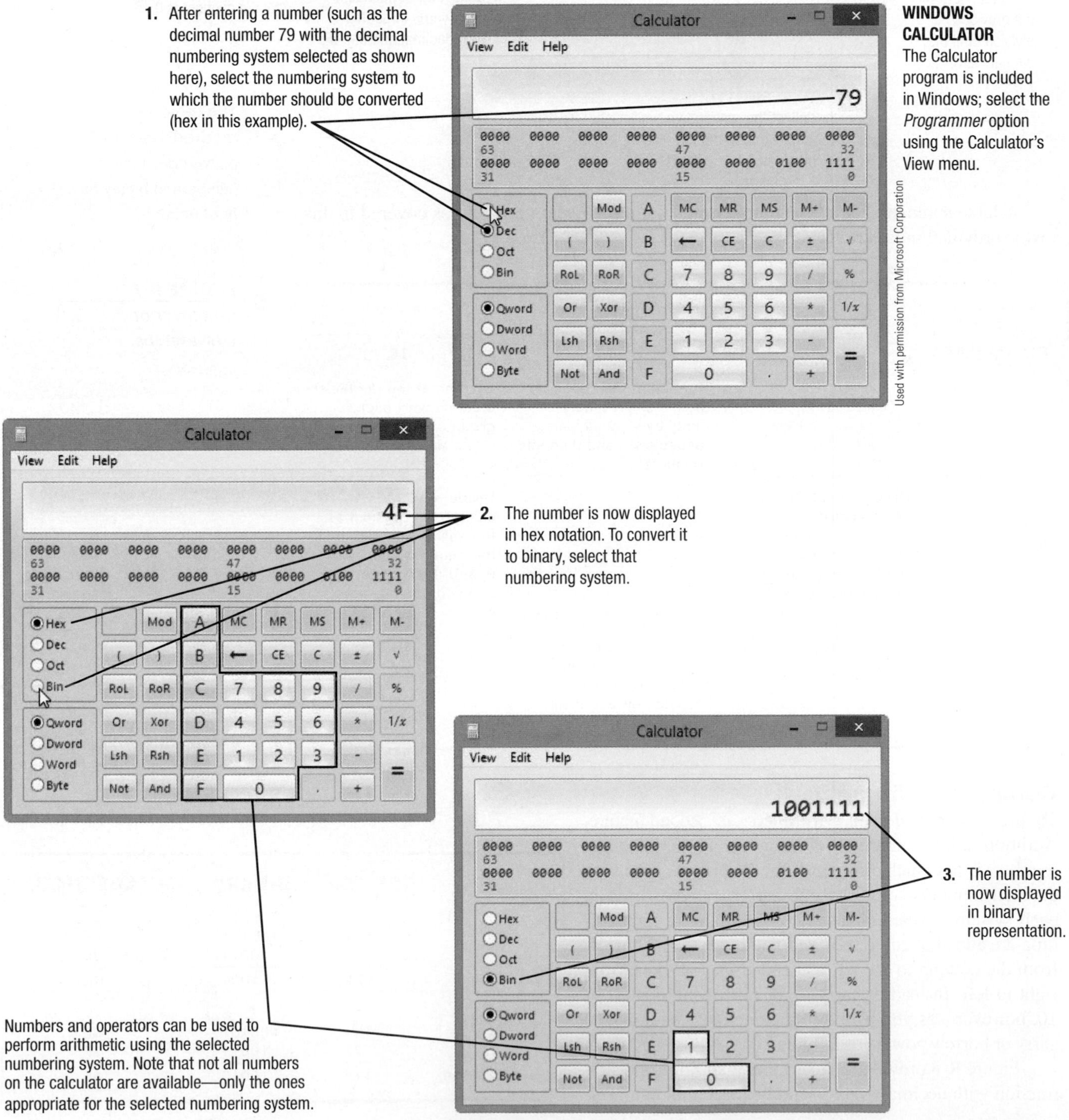

1. After entering a number (such as the decimal number 79 with the decimal numbering system selected as shown here), select the numbering system to which the number should be converted (hex in this example).

WINDOWS CALCULATOR
The Calculator program is included in Windows; select the *Programmer* option using the Calculator's View menu.

Used with permission from Microsoft Corporation

2. The number is now displayed in hex notation. To convert it to binary, select that numbering system.

3. The number is now displayed in binary representation.

Numbers and operators can be used to perform arithmetic using the selected numbering system. Note that not all numbers on the calculator are available—only the ones appropriate for the selected numbering system.

CODING CHARTS

As discussed in Chapter 2 of this text, coding systems for text-based data include ASCII, EBCDIC, and Unicode. ∎

ASCII and EBCDIC

Figure R-10 provides a chart listing the 8-digit ASCII and EBCDIC representations (in binary) for most of the symbols found on a typical keyboard.

FIGURE R-10
ASCII and EBCDIC binary codes for typical keyboard symbols.

SYMBOL	ASCII	EBCDIC	SYMBOL	ASCII	EBCDIC	SYMBOL	ASCII	EBCDIC
A	0100 0001	1100 0001	e	0110 0101	1000 0101	8	0011 1000	1111 1000
B	0100 0010	1100 0010	f	0110 0110	1000 0110	9	0011 1001	1111 1001
C	0100 0011	1100 0011	g	0110 0111	1000 0111	(	0010 1000	0100 1101
D	0100 0100	1100 0100	h	0110 1000	1000 1000	)	0010 1001	0101 1101
E	0100 0101	1100 0101	i	0110 1001	1000 1001	/	0010 1111	0110 0001
F	0100 0110	1100 0110	j	0110 1010	1001 0001	-	0010 1101	0110 0000
G	0100 0111	1100 0111	k	0110 1011	1001 0010	*	0010 1010	0101 1100
H	0100 1000	1100 1000	l	0110 1100	1001 0011	+	0010 1011	0100 1110
I	0100 1001	1100 1001	m	0110 1101	1001 0100	,	0010 1100	0110 1011
J	0100 1010	1101 0001	n	0110 1110	1001 0101	.	0010 1110	0100 1011
K	0100 1011	1101 0010	o	0110 1111	1001 0110	:	0011 1010	0111 1010
L	0100 1100	1101 0011	p	0111 0000	1001 0111	;	0011 1011	0101 1110
M	0100 1101	1101 0100	q	0111 0001	1001 1000	&	0010 0110	0101 0000
N	0100 1110	1101 0101	r	0111 0010	1001 1001	\	0101 1100	1110 0000
O	0100 1111	1101 0110	s	0111 0011	1010 0010	$	0010 0100	0101 1011
P	0101 0000	1101 0111	t	0111 0100	1010 0011	%	0010 0101	0110 1100
Q	0101 0001	1101 1000	u	0111 0101	1010 0100	=	0011 1101	0111 1110
R	0101 0010	1101 1001	v	0111 0110	1010 0101	>	0011 1110	0110 1110
S	0101 0011	1110 0010	w	0111 0111	1010 0110	<	0011 1100	0100 1100
T	0101 0100	1110 0011	x	0111 1000	1010 0111	!	0010 0001	0101 1010
U	0101 0101	1110 0100	y	0111 1001	1010 1000	|	0111 1100	0110 1010
V	0101 0110	1110 0101	z	0111 1010	1010 1001	?	0011 1111	0110 1111
W	0101 0111	1110 0110	0	0011 0000	1111 0000	@	0100 0000	0111 1100
X	0101 1000	1110 0111	1	0011 0001	1111 0001	_	0101 1111	0110 1101
Y	0101 1001	1110 1000	2	0011 0010	1111 0010	'	0110 0000	1011 1001
Z	0101 1010	1110 1001	3	0011 0011	1111 0011	{	0111 1011	1100 0000
a	0110 0001	1000 0001	4	0011 0100	1111 0100	}	0111 1101	1101 0000
b	0110 0010	1000 0010	5	0011 0101	1111 0101	~	0111 1110	1010 0001
c	0110 0011	1000 0011	6	0011 0110	1111 0110	[	0101 1011	0100 1010
d	0110 0100	1000 0100	7	0011 0111	1111 0111	]	0101 1101	0101 1010

A 0041	N 004E	a 0061	n 006E	0 0030	{ 007B	* 002A	■ 25A0	অ 0985
B 0042	O 004F	b 0062	o 006F	1 0031	| 007C	+ 002B	□ 25A1	গ 0997
C 0043	P 0050	c 0063	p 0070	2 0032	} 007D	, 002C	▲ 25B2	ৌ 09C7
D 0044	Q 0051	d 0064	q 0071	3 0033	~ 007E	- 002D	% 2105	৶ 09F6
E 0045	R 0052	e 0065	r 0072	4 0034	! 0021	. 002E	℞ 211E	݅ 0685
F 0046	S 0053	f 0066	s 0073	5 0035	" 0022	/ 002F	⅓ 2153	ڴ 06B4
G 0047	T 0054	g 0067	t 0074	6 0036	# 0023	£ 20A4	⅔ 2154	ڪ 06AA
H 0048	U 0055	h 0068	u 0075	7 0037	$ 0024	Σ 2211	♔ 2655	α 03B1
I 0049	V 0056	i 0069	v 0076	8 0038	% 0025	∅ 2205	☂ 2602	β 03B2
J 004A	W 0057	j 006A	w 0077	9 0039	& 0026	√ 221A	❐ 2750	Δ 0394
K 004B	X 0058	k 006B	x 0078	[005B	' 0027	∞ 221E	☀ 2742	φ 03A6
L 004C	Y 0059	l 006C	y 0079	\ 005C	(0028	≤ 2264	➲ 27B2	Ω 03A9
M 004D	Z 005A	m 006D	z 007A	] 005D	) 0029	≥ 2265	♥ 2665	Ϋ 03AB

⬥ **FIGURE R-11**
Selected Unicode codes.

⬥ **FIGURE R-12**
Using Unicode.

Unicode

Since consistent worldwide representation of symbols is increasingly needed today, use of Unicode is growing rapidly. Unicode can be used to represent every written language, as well as a variety of other symbols. Unicode codes are typically listed in hexadecimal notation—a sampling of Unicode is shown in Figure R-11.

The capability to display characters and other symbols using Unicode coding is incorporated into many programs. For instance, when the Symbol dialog box is opened using the INSERT tab in Microsoft Office Word, the Unicode representation (as well as the corresponding ASCII code in either decimal or hexadecimal representation) can be viewed (see Figure R-12). Some programs allow you to enter a Unicode symbol using its Unicode hexadecimal value. For instance, in Microsoft Office programs you can use the Alt+X command when the insertion point is just to the right of a Unicode hex value to convert that hex value into the corresponding symbol. For example, the keystrokes

2264Alt+X

result in the symbol corresponding to the Unicode code 2264 (the less than or equal sign ≤) being inserted into the document; entering 03A3 and then pressing Alt+X inserts the symbol shown in the Word screen in Figure R-12.

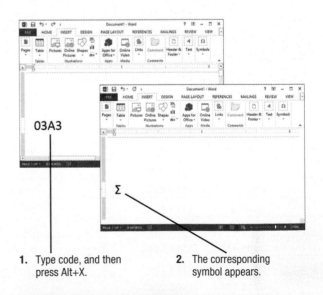

Unicode representation for Greek capital letter sigma Σ symbol.

1. Type code, and then press Alt+X.

2. The corresponding symbol appears.

03A3

Σ

UNICODE REPRESENTATION
The Symbol dialog box shown here lists the Unicode representation of each symbol as it is selected. If preferred, the ASCII representation can be displayed.

INSERTING SYMBOLS USING UNICODE
In Microsoft Office programs, typing the hexadecimal Unicode code for a symbol and then pressing Alt+X displays the corresponding symbol.

Chapter 1

1. T 2. F 3. F 4. F 5. T 6. Input 7. hybrid notebook-tablet 8. Virtualization 9. electronic mail or e-mail 10. a. 4 b. 2 c. 1 d. 3

Chapter 2

1. T 2. F 3. T 4. T 5. F 6. tera-scale computing 7. quad-core 8. port 9. multiprocessing 10. a. 6 b. 2 c. 4 d. 9 e. 7 f. 1 g. 8 h. 5 i. 3

Chapter 3

1. F 2. T 3. F 4. T 5. F 6. C 7. volatile 8. optical 9. smart card 10. flash memory

Chapter 4

1. F 2. T 3. T 4. T 5. F 6. handwriting recognition 7. scanner, optical scanner, flatbed scanner, or portable scanner 8. pixel 9. flat-panel or LCD; cathode-ray tube or CRT 10. a. 2 b. 5 c. 1 d. 4 e. 3

Chapter 5

1. T 2. F 3. T 4. F 5. F 6. Multitasking 7. iOS 8. file compression 9. back up 10. a. 3 b. 4 c. 2 d. 1

Chapter 6

1. T 2. T 3. F 4. F 5. F 6. open source 7. insertion point or cursor 8. function 9. table 10. a. 2 b. 3 c. 1

Chapter 7

1. F 2. T 3. F 4. T 5. F 6. bus 7. dual-mode 8. personal area network or PAN 9. virtual private network or VPN 10. a. 3 b. 4 c. 1 d. 5 e. 2

Chapter 8

1. F 2. F 3. T 4. T 5. F 6. Digital Subscriber Line or DSL 7. keyword; directory 8. social network or social networking site 9. online auction 10. a. 2 b. 4 c. 1 d. 3

Chapter 9

1. F 2. T 3. F 4. T 5. F 6. war driving 7. Biometric 8. virtual private network or VPN 9. digital signature 10. a. 3 b. 4 c. 1 d. 2

Chapter 10

1. F 2. T 3. F 4. T 5. T 6. Streaming 7. intended audience; objectives 8. Web site authoring 9. page layout 10. a. 1 b. 3 c. 2

Chapter 11

1. T 2. F 3. T 4. F 5. T 6. brokerage 7. NFC or Near Field Communications 8. banner ad 9. Search engine optimization or SEO 10. a. 1 b. 3 c. 2

Chapter 12

1. T 2. F 3. F 4. T 5. F 6. inference engine 7. systems analyst 8. tangible 9. prototype 10. a. 2 b. 3 c. 1

Chapter 13

1. F 2. T 3. T 4. F 5. F 6. variable 7. interpreter 8. logic 9. agile 10. a. 3 b. 2 c. 5 d. 4 e. 1

Chapter 14

1. T 2. T 3. F 4. F 5. T 6. field or column; record or row 7. integrity 8. direct 9. client-server 10. a. 2 b. 3 c. 1

Chapter 15

1. F 2. T 3. T 4. F 5. F 6. disaster recovery 7. digital counterfeiting 8. filter 9. opt out; opt in 10. a. 3 b. 5 c. 1 d. 2 e. 4

Chapter 16

1. F 2. T 3. T 4. F 5. F 6. copyright; trademark 7. plagiarism 8. cybersquatting 9. digital divide 10. a. 2 b. 4 c. 1 d. 3

INDEX